Medical Management of HIV Infection

2003 Edition

Medical Management of HIV Infection

2003 Edition

John G. Bartlett, M.D.
Professor of Medicine,
Chief, Division of Infectious Diseases,
Director, Johns Hopkins AIDS Service,
Department of Medicine,
Johns Hopkins University School of Medicine

Joel E. Gallant, M.D., M.P.H.
Associate Professor of Medicine,
Division of Infectious Diseases,
Associate Director, Johns Hopkins AIDS Service,
Department of Medicine,
Johns Hopkins University School of Medicine

Published by Johns Hopkins University,
Division of Infectious Diseases and AIDS Service
Baltimore, Maryland
United States of America

Some of the information contained in this book may cite the use of a particular drug in a dosage, for an indication, or in a manner other than recommended or FDA-approved. Therefore, the manufacturers' package inserts should be consulted for complete prescribing information.

Published by Johns Hopkins University, Division of Infectious Diseases and AIDS Service.

Library of Congress Catalog Card Number: 95-070888

ISBN: 0-9716241-1-9

Address of the publisher:
2003 MMHIV Infection
c/o JHU ID @ Lighthouse Point
2700 Lighthouse Point East, Ste. 220
Baltimore, MD 21224

Acknowledgements

We thank our colleagues for their consultation and content review:

Richard Ambinder, M.D., Ph.D., Department of Oncology-HIV-associated Malignancies.

Jean R. Anderson, M.D., Department of Gynecology and Obstetrics – Pregnancy and PAP Smears

Richard E. Chaisson, M.D., The Johns Hopkins Center for Tuberculosis Research – Mycobacterial Disease

Joseph Cofrancesco, Jr., M.D., Johns Hopkins AIDS Service – Wasting and Lipodystrophy

Douglas Jabs, M.D., Department of Ophthalmology – CMV Retinitis

Brooks Jackson, M.D., Department of Pathology – HIV Laboratory Testing

Ciro Martins, M.D., Department of Dermatology – Dermatology

Justin McArthur, M.B., B.S., M.P.H., Department of Neurology – Peripheral Neuropathy and CNS Section

Paul Pham, Pharm. D., Johns Hopkins AIDS Service – Pharmacology

Timothy Sterling, M.D., The Johns Hopkins Center for Tuberculosis Research – Mycobacterial Infections

Mark Sulkowski, M.D., The Johns Hopkins Hepatitis Center – Hepatitis B and C Detection and Management

Glenn Treisman, M.D., Ph.D. and Andrew F. Angelino, M.D., Department of Psychiatry – Mental Health

Business development: Sharon McAvinue

Project director: Mary Beth Hansen, M.A.

Project manager: Lisa Darrah, B.A.

Editorial assistant: Matthew Giuliano, B.A.

Review: Richard Dunning

Design: WorldComp, Sterling, Virginia

Typesetting: PR Graphics, Timonium, Maryland

Printed in the U.S.A. by PMR Printing, Sterling, Virginia

Note

This book is provided as a resource for physicians and other health care professionals in providing care and treatment to patients with HIV/AIDS. Every possible effort is made to ensure the accuracy and reliability of material presented in this book; however, recommendations for care and treatment change rapidly, and opinion can be controversial. Therefore, physicians and other healthcare professionals are encouraged to consult other sources and confirm the information contained within this book. The author, reviewers, and production staff will not be held liable for errors, omissions, or inaccuracies in information or for any perceived harm to users of this book. It is up to the individual physician or other health care professional to use his/her best medical judgment in determining appropriate patient care or treatment because no single reference or service can take the place of medical training, education, and experience.

Neither The Johns Hopkins University, The Johns Hopkins Health System Corporation, nor the authors and reviewers are responsible for deletions or inaccuracies in information or for claims of injury resulting from any such deletions or inaccuracies. Mention of specific drugs or products within this book does not constitute endorsement by the authors, The Johns Hopkins University Division of Infectious Diseases, or The Johns Hopkins University School of Medicine. With regard to specific drugs or products, physicians are advised to consult their normal resources before prescribing to their patients.

Additional sources of information include the websites of the Johns Hopkins University Division of Infectious Diseases:

The Johns Hopkins AIDS Service: **http://www.hopkins-aids.edu**

The Hopkins ABX-Guide: **http://www.hopkins-abxguide.org**

The Johns Hopkins Center for Tuberculosis Research: **http://www.hopkins-tb.org**

Foreword

The 2003 edition of *Medical Management of HIV Infection* reflects substantial changes in the treatment of patients with HIV infection and AIDS since the 2001-2002 edition was published. This edition was completed in December 2002, so new developments in treatment guidelines occurring after that time are not included. Updates are available on the Johns Hopkins AIDS Service website: **http://www.hopkins-aids.edu**

The 2001-2002 edition was distributed to approximately 60,000 readers in more than 60 countries and accessed by more than 15,000 additional readers online. The book is currently translated into Portuguese, Russian, and Chinese. Translations into Vietnamese is pending.

This edition includes 132 tables and more than 300 references to publications or presentations in 2002, reflecting the authors' efforts to keep abreast of new developments by attendance at major scientific conferences and by systematic review of 42 relevant journals. Recommendations presented here are largely based on federal guidelines: Antiretroviral therapy for adults, pregnancy management, opportunistic infection prophylaxis, management of occupational exposure, management of TB co-infection, management of HCV co-infection, and management of sexually transmitted diseases. The authors have provided recommendations based on available data and personal experience/opinion when no federal guidelines exist.

There have been some major changes in the 2003 edition compared with prior editions: There is more extensive referencing to more carefully documented sources, and there is also less referencing of conference abstracts because they are neither critically reviewed nor easily obtained. The major stylistic and content changes are in Chapters 5 and 7. Chapter 5 presents pathogens in alphabetical order with a text presentation that now includes diagnostic methods, treatment, and the expected outcome of treatment. Chapter 7 provides a systems review (by organ system) with a new format that includes outlines, tables, and algorithms.

As always, comments and suggestions are welcome.

Contents

1 | Natural History and Classification

Stages

The natural history of untreated HIV infection is divided into the following stages:

Viral transmission —2-3 wks→ Acute retroviral syndrome —2-3 wks→ Recovery + seroconversion —2-4 wks→ Asymptomatic chronic HIV infection —Avg. 8 yrs→ Symptomatic HIV infection/AIDS —Avg. 1.3 yrs→ Death

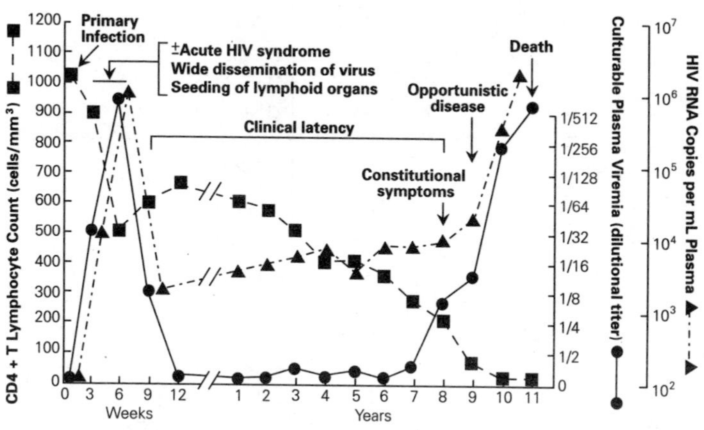

■ FIGURE 1-1: **Natural history of HIV infection in an average patient without antiretroviral therapy from the time of HIV transmission to death at 10-11 years.** The initial event is the acute retroviral syndrome, which is accompanied by a precipitous decline in CD4 cell counts (closed squares), high plasma viremia (closed circles), and high concentrations of HIV RNA in plasma (closed triangles). Clinical recovery is accompanied by a reduction in plasma viremia, reflecting development of cytotoxic T-cell (CTL) response. The CD4 cell count decreases are due to HIV-induced cell death (*J Exp Med* 2001;194:1277). The slope of the CD4 cell decline depends on the viral load; in one study the median rate of decline was 4%/year for each $\log_{10}$ HIV RNA/mL (*J Infect Dis* 2002;185:905). The slope increases in late stage disease. HIV RNA concentrations in plasma show an initial "burst" during acute infection and then decline to a "set point" as a result of seroconversion and development of an immune response. With continued infection, HIV RNA levels gradually increase (*J Infect Dis* 1999;180:1018). Late-stage disease is characterized by a CD4 count <200 cells/mm³ and the development of opportunistic infections, selected tumors, wasting, and neurologic complications. In an untreated patient, the median survival after the CD4 count has fallen to <200 cells/mm³ is 3.7 years; the median CD4 count at the time of the first AIDS-defining complication is 60-70 cells/mm³; the median survival after an AIDS-defining complication is 1.3 years. (Figure reprinted with permission from *Ann Intern Med* 1996;124:654).

■ TABLE 1-1: **Correlation of Complications With CD4 Cell Counts (see *Arch Intern Med* 1995;155:1537)**

CD4 Cell Count*	Infectious Complications	Noninfectious† Complications
>500/mm³	■ Acute retroviral syndrome ■ Candidal vaginitis	■ Persistent generalized lymphadenopathy (PGL) ■ Guillain-Barré syndrome ■ Myopathy ■ Aseptic meningitis
200-500/mm³	■ Pneumococcal and other bacterial pneumonia ■ Pulmonary tuberculosis ■ Herpes zoster ■ Oropharyngeal candidiasis (thrush) ■ Cryptosporidiosis, self-limited ■ Kaposi's sarcoma ■ Oral hairy leukoplakia	■ Cervical intraepithelial neoplasia ■ Cervical cancer ■ B-cell lymphoma ■ Anemia ■ Mononeuronal multiplex ■ Idiopathic thrombocytopenic purpura ■ Hodgkin's lymphoma ■ Lymphocytic interstitial pneumonitis
<200/mm³	■ *Pneumocystis carinii* pneumonia ■ Disseminated histoplasmosis and coccidioidomycosis ■ Miliary/extrapulmonary TB ■ Progressive multifocal leuko-encephalopathy (PML)	■ Wasting ■ Peripheral neuropathy ■ HIV-associated dementia ■ Cardiomyopathy ■ Vacuolar myelopathy ■ Progressive polyradiculopathy ■ Non-Hodgkin's lymphoma
<100/mm³	■ Disseminated herpes simplex ■ Toxoplasmosis ■ Cryptococcosis ■ Cryptosporidiosis, chronic ■ Microsporidiosis ■ Candidal esophagitis	
<50/mm³	■ Disseminated cytomegalovirus (CMV) ■ Disseminated *Mycobacterium avium* complex	■ Central nervous system (CNS) lymphoma

* Most complications occur with increasing frequency at lower CD4 cell counts.

† Some conditions listed as "non-infectious" are probably associated with transmissible microbes. Examples include lymphoma (Epstein-Barr virus [EBV]) and cervical cancer (human papillomavirus [HPV]).

■ TABLE 1-2: **Primary HIV Infection: Signs and Symptoms (Department of Health and Human Services [DHHS] Guidelines [*Ann Intern Med* 2002;137:381])**

Fever – 96%	Myalgias – 54%	Hepatosplenomegaly – 14%
Adenopathy – 74%	Diarrhea – 32%	Weight loss – 13%
Pharyngitis – 70%	Headache – 32%	Thrush – 12%
Rash* – 70%	Nausea & vomiting – 27%	Neurologic symptoms† – 12%

* Rash – erythematous maculopapular rash on face and trunk, sometimes extremities, including palms & soles. Some have mucocutaneous ulceration involving mouth, esophagus, or genitals.

† Aseptic meningitis, meningoencephalitis, peripheral neuropathy, facial palsy, Guillain-Barré syndrome, brachial neuritis, cognitive impairment, or psychosis.

Diagnosis: Primary HIV Infection

HIV RNA >10,000 c/mL + indeterminant or negative HIV serology or recent seroconversion (*Ann Intern Med* 2001;134:25).

■ TABLE 1-3: **AIDS Surveillance Case Definition for Adolescents and Adults: 1993**

	Clinical Categories		
	A	**B**	**C***
CD4 Cell Categories	**Asymptomatic, or PGL, or Acute HIV Infection**	**Symptomatic† (not A or C)**	**AIDS Indicator Condition (1987)**
>500/mm³ (≥29%)	A1	B1	C1
200 to 499/mm³ (14% to 28%)	A2	B2	C2
<200/mm³ (<14%)	A3	B3	C3

* All patients in categories A3, B3, and C1-3 are defined as having AIDS based on the presence of an AIDS-indicator condition (Table 1-4, p. 4) and/or a CD4 cell count <200/mm³.

† Symptomatic conditions not included in Category C that are: a) attributed to HIV infection or indicative of a defect in cell-mediated immunity or b) considered to have a clinical course or management that is complicated by HIV infection. Examples of B conditions include, but are not limited to, bacillary angiomatosis; thrush; vulvovaginal candidiasis that is persistent, frequent, or poorly responsive to therapy; cervical dysplasia (moderate or severe); cervical carcinoma *in situ*; constitutional symptoms such as fever (38.5°C) or diarrhea >1 month; oral hairy leukoplakia; herpes zoster involving two episodes or >1 dermatome; idiopathic thrombocytopenic purpura (ITP); listeriosis; pelvic inflammatory disease (PID) (especially if complicated by a tubo-ovarian abscess); and peripheral neuropathy.

■ TABLE 1-4: **Indicator Conditions in Case Definition of AIDS (Adults) – 1997***

Candidiasis of esophagus, trachea, bronchi, or lungs – 3,846 (16%)
Cervical cancer, invasive† ‡ – 144 (0.6%)
Coccidioidomycosis, extrapulmonary† – 74 (0.3%)
Cryptococcosis, extrapulmonary – 1,168 (5%)
Cryptosporidiosis with diarrhea >1 month – 314 (1.3%)
CMV of any organ other than liver, spleen, or lymph nodes; eye – 1,638 (7%)
Herpes simplex with mucocutaneous ulcer >1 month or bronchitis, pneumonitis, esophagitis – 1,250 (5%)
Histoplasmosis, extrapulmonary† – 208 (0.9%)
HIV-associated dementia†: Disabling cognitive and/or other dysfunction interfering with occupation or activities of daily living – 1,196 (5%)
HIV-associated wasting†: Involuntary weight loss >10% of baseline plus chronic diarrhea (≥2 loose stools/day ≥30 days) or chronic weakness and documented enigmatic fever ≥30 days – 4,212 (18%)
Isoporosis with diarrhea >1 month† – 22 (0.1%)
Kaposi's sarcoma in patient under 60 yrs (or over 60 yrs)† – 1,500 (7%)
Lymphoma, Burkitt's – 162 (0.7%), immunoblastic – 518 (2.3%), primary CNS – 170 (0.7%)
Mycobacterium avium, disseminated – 1,124 (5%)
Mycobacterium tuberculosis, pulmonary – 1,621 (7%), extrapulmonary – 491 (2%)
Pneumocystis carinii pneumonia – 9,145 (38%)
Pneumonia, recurrent-bacterial (≥2 episodes in 12 months)† ‡ – 1,347 (5%)
Progressive multifocal leukoencephalopathy – 213 (1%)
Salmonella septicemia (nontyphoid), recurrent† – 68 (0.3%)
Toxoplasmosis of internal organ – 1,073 (4%)
Wasting syndrome due to HIV (as defined above – HIV-associated wasting) (18%)

* Indicates frequency as the AIDS-indicator condition among 23,527 reported cases in adults for 1997. The AIDS diagnosis was based on CD4 count in an additional 36,643 or 61% of the 60,161 total cases. Numbers indicate sum of definitive and presumptive diagnosis for stated condition. The number in parentheses is the percentage of all patients reported with an AIDS-defining diagnosis; these do not total 100% because some had a dual diagnosis.

† Requires positive HIV serology.

‡ Added in the revised case definition, 1993.

2 | Laboratory Tests

Laboratory tests recommended for initial evaluation and follow-up of all patients are summarized in Tables 2-1, p. 12, and 2-8, pp. 28-29.

HIV Types and Subtypes

HIV infection is established by detecting antibodies to the virus, viral antigens, viral RNA/DNA, or by culture (*Lancet* 1996;348:176). The standard test is serology for antibody detection. There are two HIV types: HIV-1 and HIV-2, which show 40% to 60% amino acid homology. HIV-1 accounts for nearly all cases except a minority of strains that originate in West Africa. HIV-1 is divided into subtypes designated A to K (collectively referred to as "M subtypes") and O. Subtype O shows 55% to 70% homology with the M subtypes. A new group of viruses labeled "N" for "new" was reported in 1998 (*Nat Med* 1998;4:1032; *Science* 2000;287:607). Over 98% of HIV-1 infections in the United States are caused by subtype B; most non-B subtypes in the United States were acquired in other countries (*J Infect Dis* 2000;181:470); the relatively rare O and N subtypes are found primarily in West Africa.

HIV-1 Subtype Distribution (*J Acquir Immune Defic Syndr* 2002;29:184)

PREDOMINANT SUBTYPES

- **A:** W. Africa, E. Africa, Central Africa, East Europe, Mideast
- **B:** N. America, Europe, Mideast, E. Asia, Latin America
- **C:** S. Africa, S. Asia, Ethiopia
- **D:** E. Africa
- **E:** S.E. Asia

HIV-2

HIV-2 is another human retrovirus that causes immune deficiency due to depletion of CD4 cells. It is found primarily in West Africa.* Compared with HIV-1, HIV-2 is less transmissible (5- to 8-fold less efficient than HIV-1 in early-stage disease and rarely the cause of vertical transmission), is

* Endemic areas in West Africa – Benin, Burkina Faso, Cape Verde, Cote d'Ivoire, Gambia, Ghana, Guinea Guinea-Bissau, Liberia, Mali, Mauritania, Niger, Nigeria, São Tome, Senegal, Sierra Leone, and Togo; other African countries – Angola and Mozambique (*MMWR* 1992;4[RR-12]:1).

associated with a lower viral load, and is associated with a slower rate of both CD4 cell decline and clinical progression (*Lancet* 1994;344:1380; *AIDS* 1994;8 [suppl 1]:585; *J Infect Dis* 1999;180:1116; *J Acquir Immune Defic Syndr* 2000;24:257; *Arch Intern Med* 2000;160:3286; *J Infect Dis* 2002;185:905). HIV-2 shows reduced homology with HIV-1 compared with HIV-1 subtypes (*Nature* 1987;328:543), and 20% to 30% have negative antibody tests depending on which enzyme immunosorbent assay (EIA) is used. Western blots (WBs) for HIV-2 are neither well standardized nor FDA approved (*Ann Intern Med* 1993;118:211; *JAMA* 1992;267:2775). An HIV-2 EIA was licensed by the FDA in 1990 and became mandatory for screening blood donors in 1992. Some commercial labs now use combination EIA screening assays to detect HIV-1 and HIV-2 simultaneously, although this is not recommended by the CDC for routine testing (*MMWR* 1992;41[RR-12]:1). Viral load tests are not generally available for HIV-2 (*Arch Intern Med* 2000;160:3286). There were 78 persons diagnosed with HIV-2 infection in the United States between 1987 and January 1998; 52 were born in West Africa, and most of the rest had either traveled there, had a sexual partner from that region, or had incomplete data (*MMWR* 1995;44:603; *JAMA* 1992;267:2775). The CDC recommends that HIV-2 serology be included in serologic testing of 1) Natives of endemic areas,* 2) Needle-sharing and sex partners of persons from an endemic area,* 3) Sex partners or needle-sharing partners of persons with HIV-2 infection, 4) Persons who received transfusions or nonsterile injections in endemic areas,* and 5) Children of women with risk for HIV-2 infection. Contact CDC for HIV-2 serologic testing.

HIV Serology

Standard Test

The standard serologic test consists of a screening EIA followed by a confirmatory WB. EIA screening requires a "repeatedly reactive" test, which is the criterion for WB testing. WB detects antibodies to HIV-1 proteins, including core (p17, p24, p55), polymerase (p31, p51, p66), and envelope (gp41, gp120, gp160). WB testing should always be coupled with EIA screening due to a 2% rate of false positives. Results (*Am J Med* 2000;109:568) of WB are interpreted as follows:

- **Negative:** No bands.
- **Positive:** Reactivity to gp41 + gp120/160 or p24 + gp120/160.
- **Indeterminate:** Presence of any band pattern that does not meet criteria for positive results.

ACCURACY: Standard serologic assays (EIA and WB or immuno-

* Endemic areas in West Africa – Benin, Burkina Faso, Cape Verde, Cote d'Ivoire, Gambia, Ghana, Guinea Guinea-Bissau, Liberia, Mali, Mauritania, Niger, Nigeria, São Tome, Senegal, Sierra Leone, and Togo; other African countries – Angola and Mozambique (*MMWR* 1992;4[RR-12]:1).

fluorescent assay) show sensitivity and specificity rates of >98% (*JAMA* 1991;266:2861; *Am J Med* 2000;109:568). Positive tests should be confirmed with repeat tests or with corroborating clinical or laboratory data.

FALSE-NEGATIVE RESULTS: False-negative results are usually due to testing in the "window period." The rate of false negatives ranges from 0.3% in a high-prevalence population (*J Infect Dis* 1993;168:327) to <0.001% in low-prevalence populations (*N Engl J Med* 1991;325: 593). Causes of false-negative results include:

- **Window period:** The time delay from infection to positive EIA averages 14 to 22 days with newer test reagents (*Clin Infect Dis* 1997;25:101; *Am J Med* 2000;109:568). Some do not seroconvert for 3 to 4 weeks, but virtually all patients seroconvert within 6 months (*Am J Med* 2000;109:568).
- **Seroreversion:** Rare patients serorevert in late-stage disease (*JAMA* 1993;269:2786; *Ann Intern Med* 1988;108:785). Seroreversion has also been reported in patients who achieve prolonged immune reconstitution due to highly active antiretroviral therapy (HAART) (*N Engl J Med* 1999;340:1683).
- **"Atypical host response"** accounts for rare cases and is largely unexplained (*AIDS* 1995;9:95; *MMWR* 1996;45:181; *Clin Infect Dis* 1997;25:98).
- **Agammaglobulinemia**
- **Type N or O strains or HIV-2:** EIA screening tests may fail to detect the O subtype (*Lancet* 1994;343:1393; *Lancet* 1994;344:1333; *MMWR* 1996;45:561). This strain is rare; only two patients with strain O HIV infection were detected in the United States through July 2000 (*MMWR* 1996;45:561; *Emerg Infect Dis* 1996;2:209; *AIDS* 2002;18:269). The N group is another variant that causes false-negative EIA screening tests but may be positive by WB (*Nat Med* 1998;4:1032). There have been no recognized infections with the N strain in the United States through March 2000 (*J Infect Dis* 2000;181:470). Standard EIA screening tests are falsely negative in 20% to 30% of patients infected with HIV-2. Detection may require tests specifically for HIV-2. Risks for HIV-2 are summarized above (pp. 5-6).
- **Technical or clerical error**

FALSE-POSITIVE RESULTS: The frequency of false-positive HIV serology (both EIA and WB) was reported to range from 0.0004% to 0.0007% (*N Engl J Med* 1988;319:961; *Ann Intern Med* 1989;110:617). Changes in the interpretive criteria instituted since those reports were published have led to an even lower frequency (*JAMA* 1998;280:1080). Causes of false-positive results include:

- **Autoantibodies:** A single case was reported in which a false-positive serology was ascribed to autoantibodies in a patient with lupus erythematosus and end-stage renal disease (*N Engl J Med* 1993;328:1281). However, a subsequent report indicated that this patient did have HIV infection as verified by positive cultures (*N Engl J Med* 1994;331:881). Another patient with two positive tests and two indeterminate WB tests was found to be uninfected, with a negative HIV culture and PCR (*Clin Infect Dis* 1992;15:707).
- **HIV vaccines:** HIV vaccines are the most common cause of false-positive HIV serology. In an analysis of 266 healthy volunteers in HIV vaccine studies, 68% had positive EIA tests, and 0% to 44% had positive WB, depending on the antigen used in the vaccine (*Ann Intern Med* 1994;121:584).
- **Factitious HIV infection:** This refers to patients who report a history of a positive test that is erroneous, due to either misunderstanding or an intent to deceive (*Ann Intern Med* 1994;121:763). It is important to confirm anonymous tests and to repeat laboratory reports that cannot be obtained, using either repeat serology or viral load testing. [Note that 2% to 9% of viral load tests are falsely positive, usually with low viral titers (*Ann Intern Med* 1999;130:37)].
- **Technical or clerical error**

INDETERMINATE RESULTS: Indeterminate test results account for 4% to 20% of WB assays with positive bands for HIV-1 proteins. Causes of indeterminate results include:

- **Serologic tests in the process of seroconversion**; anti-p24 is usually the first antibody to appear.
- **Late-stage HIV infection**, usually with loss of core antibody.
- **Cross-reacting nonspecific antibodies**, as seen with collagen-vascular disease, autoimmune diseases, lymphoma, liver disease, injection drug use, multiple sclerosis, parity, or recent immunization.
- **Infection with O strain or HIV-2**
- **HIV vaccine recipients** (see above)
- **Technical or clerical error**

The most important factor in evaluating indeterminate results is risk assessment. Patients in low-risk categories with indeterminate tests are almost never infected with either HIV-1 or HIV-2; repeat testing often continues to show indeterminate results, and the cause of this pattern is infrequently established (*N Engl J Med* 1990;322:217). For this reason, such patients should be reassured that HIV infection is extremely unlikely, although follow-up serology at 3 months is recommended to provide absolute assurance. Patients with indeterminate tests who are in the process of seroconversion usually have positive WBs within 1 month. Repeat tests at 1, 2, and 6 months are generally advocated, along with appropriate precautions to prevent viral transmission in the interim (*J Gen Intern Med* 1992;7:640; *J Infect Dis* 1991;164:656; *Arch Intern Med* 2000; 160:2386; *J Acquir Immune Defic Syndr* 1998;17:376).

FREQUENCY OF TESTING: Periodic tests are recommended for patients who practice high-risk behavior. The frequency is arbitrary, but most suggest annual testing for high risk patients (*MMWR* 2002;51:736; *MMWR* 2002;57[RR-6]:7). Annual seroconversion rates are estimated as follows: general population – 0.02%, military recruits – 0.04%, MSM – 0.5% to 2% (higher among younger MSM), and injection drug users in areas with high seroprevalence – 0.7% to 6% (*Am J Epidemiol* 1991;134:1175; *J Acquir Immune Defic Syndr* 1993;6:1049; *Arch Intern Med* 1995;155:1305; *Am J Public Health* 1996;86:642; *Am J Public Health* 2000;90:352; *MMWR* 2001;50:440).

Alternative HIV Serologic Tests (Table 2-1, p. 12)

IFA: This is another method to detect HIV antibodies using patient serum reacted with HIV infected cells. A fluorochrome is used as the indicator method.

HOME KITS: *Home Access Express Test* (Home Access Health Corp., Hoffman Estates, Ill; 800-HIV-TEST) is the only available home kit. This test is sold in retail and online pharmacies for approximately $49.99 for routine mailing with results in 7 days or for $59.99 for *Federal Express* transport with results in 3 days. Blood is obtained by lancet, and a filter strip with blotted blood is mailed in a protected envelope using an anonymous code. Home Access' tests use a double EIA with a confirmatory IFA. Sensitivity and specificity approach 100%. Callers learn of a negative test through a prerecorded message, but the patient can access a representative to discuss results if desired. Callers with positive results receive counseling. In a study of 174,316 HIV home sample collection tests in 1996 to 1997, 0.9% were positive and 97% of users called for their results. Nearly 60% of all users and 49% of HIV-positive persons had never previously been tested (*JAMA* 1998;280:1699). Merits of this type of home testing are debated (*N Engl J Med* 1995;332:1296).

RAPID TESTS: There are two FDA-approved rapid tests: *OraQuick HIV-1 Antibody Test* (OraSure Technologies Inc.; Bethlehem, Pa; 800-672-7873) and *SUDS HIV-1 Test* (Murex Diagnostics; Norcross, Ga; 770-662-0660; marketed by Abbott Laboratories; North Chicago, Ill; 847-937-6100). *OraQuick* may be read by the provider at the site of care. Results are available within 20 minutes; sensitivity and specificity exceed 99% (*J Acquir Immune Defic Syndr* 1993;6:115; *Am J Emerg Med* 1991;9:416; *Ann Intern Med* 1996;125:471; *J Human Virol* 2001;4:

278; *Int J STD AIDS* 2002;13:171). The cost is $20 to $30 per test. This test is recommended for determining the serologic status of the source in health care worker exposures (*MMWR* 2001;50[RR-11]:1; *Infect Control Hosp Epidemiol* 2001;22:289); for pregnant women who present in labor and have not been tested (*J Hum Virol* 2001;4:278); for patients who are unlikely to return for test results, including patients seen in sexually transmitted disease clinics and emergency rooms (*MMWR* 1998;47:215); and for other settings requiring rapid decisions such as the administration of the smallpox vaccine. Other rapid tests are under review by the FDA including *Determine* (Abbott Labs; Chicago, Ill) and *Double Check* (Organies, Vavne, Israel) (*Ann Intern Med* 1999;131:4810; *J Clin Microbiol* 1999;37:3698; *ASM News* 2000; 66:451). A prior limitation to the use of these tests was the requirement for interpretation by a CLIA-certified lab technologist; causing a substantial delay and increased cost. This requirement was has now been waived. Negative tests are regarded as definitive; positive tests need confirmation by standard serology.

SALIVA TEST: *OraSure* (OraSure Technologies, Inc.; Bethlehem, Pa; 800-672-7873), is an FDA-approved device for collecting saliva and concentrating IgG for application of EIA tests for HIV antibody. The *OraSure* test system consists of a specimen collection device, the bioMérieux *Vironostika* HIV-1 antibody screen, and the WB confirmatory assay, at a cost of $24.15 per test. It is available for testing in public health departments, physicians' offices, community-based service organizations, and AIDS Service organizations. *OraSure* testing is also available by calling 800-Ora-Sure or 800-672-7873. The test may be anonymous or confidential. Results are available by phone or fax within 3 days. The test uses a specially treated pad that is placed between the lower cheek and gum for 2 minutes. The pad is then placed in a vial that is submitted to a lab. The amount of IgG obtained from saliva is far higher than in plasma and is well above the 0.5 mg/L level necessary for detection of HIV antibodies. Specimens saved from 3,570 subjects showed correct results compared with standard serology in 672 of 673 (99.9%) positives and 2,893 of 2,897 (99%) negatives (*JAMA* 1997;277:254). Potential advantages over standard serologic testing are the ease of collecting specimens, reduced cost, and better patient acceptance.

URINE TEST: *Calypte* HIV-1 Urine EIA (Calypte Biomedical Corp; Alameda, Calif; 877-225-9783) is an FDA-approved screening EIA. This test can be administered only by a physician, and positive results require confirmation by a standard serologic test. Reported sensitivity is 99% (88/89), specificity is 94% (49/52) (*Lancet* 1991;337:183; *Clin Chem* 1999;45:1602). The supplier has included a pretest counseling form, which should be read to and initialed by the patient prior to administration. The assay is sold as a 192-test kit at $816 or a 480-test kit at $1,920. The cost per test is $4.00.

VAGINAL SECRETIONS: HIV antibodies can be detected in vaginal secretions with IgG EIA (*Wellcozyme* HIV-1&2, Gracelisa Murex Diagnostics Ltd., Dartford, UK). This test is recommended by the CDC for victims of rape because HIV IgG antibodies are in semen (*MMWR* 1985;34:75S; *J Clin Microbiol* 1994;32:1249).

Viral Detection

Other methods to establish HIV infection include techniques to detect HIV antigen (p24 antigen), DNA (HIV-1 DNA PCR), or RNA (HIV-1 RNA by bDNA or RT-PCR (Table 2-1, p. 12). HIV-1 DNA PCR is the most sensitive and can detect 1 to 10 copies of HIV proviral DNA, but the reagents are not well standardized or FDA-approved. None of these tests is considered to be more accurate than routine serology, but some may be useful in patients with confusing serologic test results, when there is a need to clarify indeterminate test results for virologic monitoring in therapeutic trials, and for HIV detection when routine serologic tests are likely to be misleading, as in patients with agammaglobulinemia, acute retroviral infection, neonatal HIV infection, and patients in the window period following viral exposure. In most cases, confirmation of positive serology is accomplished simply by repeat serology. The sensitivity of tests for detection of HIV varies with the stage of disease and test technique but is usually reported at >99% for DNA-PCR, 90% to 95% for quantitative HIV-RNA, 95% to 100% for viral culture of peripheral blood mononuclear cells (PBMC), and 32% to 89% for p24 antigen detection (*J Clin Microbiol* 1993;31:2557; *N Engl J Med* 1989;321:1621; *J Acquir Immune Defic Syndr* 1990;3:1059; *J Infect Dis* 1994;170:553; *Ann Intern Med* 1996;124:803; *Ann Intern Med* 2001;134:25). None of these tests should replace serology to circumvent the informed consent process.

■ TABLE 2-1: **Tests for HIV-1**

Assay	Sensitivity	Comments
Routine serology	99.7%	Readily available and inexpensive. Sensitivity >99.7% and specificity >99.9% (*MMWR* 1990;39:380; *N Engl J Med* 1988;319:961; *JAMA* 1991;266:2861).
Rapid test *OraQuick HIV-1 Antibody Test* (OraSure Technologies Inc., Bethlehem, Pa) and *SUDS* (Murex Diagnostics, Norcross, Ga).	>99%	Results are available in 20 min. and may be read by the provider at the site of care. Specificity is >99%; some recommend that positive tests should be confirmed. Highly sensitive; negative tests do not usually require confirmation. Other rapid tests are available but are not FDA approved (*Int J STD AIDS* 1997;8:192; *Vox Sang* 1997;72:11; *J Hum Virol* 2001;4:278).
Salivary test (*OraSure* Test System)	99.9%	Salivary collection device to collect IgG for EIA and WB. Advantage is avoidance of phlebotomy. Sensitivity and specificity are comparable with standard serology (*JAMA* 1997;227:254).
Urine test (*Calypte HIV-1 Test*)	>99%	Used for EIA test only, so positive results must be verified by serology. Must be administered by a physician. Cost is low – about $4 per test.
PBMC culture	95% to 100%	Viral isolation by co-cultivation of patient's PBMC with phytohemagglutinin-stimulated donor PBMC with IL-2 over 28 days. Expensive and labor-intensive. May be qualitative or quantitative. Main use of qualitative technique is viral isolation for further analysis such as sequence analysis. Studies prior to availability of quantitative HIV RNA showed quantitative culture results correlated with stage: Mean titer was 2000/10^6 cells in patients with AIDS (*N Engl J Med* 1989;321:1621).
DNA PCR assay	>99%	Qualitative DNA PCR is used to detect cell-associated proviral DNA; primers are commercially available from Roche Laboratories. Sensitivity is >99%, and specificity is 98% (*Pediatr Infect Dis J* 2002;21:885). This is not considered sufficiently accurate for diagnosis without confirmation and is not FDA approved (*Ann Intern Med* 1996;124:803). Main use is for viral detection in the case of neonatal HIV at >4 months and disputed or indeterminate serologic tests.
HIV RNA PCR	95% to 98%	False-positive tests in 2% to 9%, usually at low titer (<10,000 c/mL). Sensitivity depends on viral load, threshold of assay, and status of antiretroviral therapy. Sensitivity approaches 100% with acute HIV infection; specificity is 97% but nearly 100% with viral load >10,000 c/mL.
p24 antigen	30% to 90%	Sometimes used as an alternative to HIV RNA test to detect acute HIV infection due to reduced cost. Specificity is 100%, but sensitivity is about 90% – less than quantitative HIV RNA tests (*Ann Intern Med* 2001;134:25).

Quantitative Plasma HIV RNA (Viral Load)

TECHNIQUES (see Table 2-2, p. 17)

- **HIV RNA PCR** (*Amplicor HIV-1 Monitor Test* versions 1.0 and 1.5, Roche; 800-526-1247). Version 1.5 detects non-B subtypes. Both the 1.0 and 1.5 versions are available in the "standard" assay and the "ultrasensitive" assay (*J Clin Microbiol* 1999;37:110).
- **Branched chain DNA or bDNA** (*Versant HIV-1 RNA 3.0 Assay*, Bayer; 800-434-2447 [formerly *Quantiplex* Chiron]). Version 2.0 is being phased out.
- **Nucleic acid sequence-based amplification** or *NucliSens* HIV-1 QT (bioMérieux), 800-682-2666.

REPRODUCIBILITY: Commercially available assays vary based on the lower level of detection and dynamic ranges, as shown in Table 2-2 (*J Clin Microbiol* 1996;34:3016; *J Med Virol* 1996;50:293; *J Clin Microbiol* 1996;34:1058; *J Clin Microbiol* 1998;36:3392). Two standard deviations (95% confidence limits) with this assay are 0.3 to 0.5 log_{10} (2- to 3-fold) (*J Infect Dis* 1997;175:247; *AIDS* 1999;13:2269). This means that the 95% confidence limit for a value of 10,000 c/mL ranges from 3,100 to 32,000 c/mL. Quantitative results with the *Amplicor* (Roche) assay version 1.5 were about one-half (0.3 log_{10} c/mL) lower compared with *Quantiplex* version 3.0, but the current bDNA assay (*Versant* 3.0) shows results that are comparable except at the low end of the linear range (<1,500 c/mL) (*J Clin Microbiol* 2000;38:2837; *J Clin Microbiol* 2000;38:1113). Comparative testing for the *NucliSens* (bioMérieux) assay is less extensive but appears comparable (*J Clin Microbiol* 2000;38:3882; *J Clin Microbiol* 2000;38:2837).

SUBTYPES: *Versant* 3.0 (Bayer) and *Amplicor* 1.5 (Roche) assays show reasonable accuracy, comparability, and reproducibility for subtypes A-G, although one comparative trial favored the bDNA (Bayer) assay (*J Acquir Immune Defic Syndr* 2002;29:330).

SEX DIFFERENCE: There appears to be a modest difference in viral load that averages 0.23 log_{10} c/mL (about 2-fold) lower in women compared with men according to a meta-analysis of 12 reports (*J Acquir Immune Defic Syndr* 2002;31:11). However, these differences are no longer present at CD4 counts <300 cells/mm^3 and are therefore unlikely to affect treatment decisions (*J Acquir Immune Defic Syndr* 2000;24:218; *J Infect Dis* 1999;180:666; *Clin Infect Dis* 2002;35:313; *Lancet* 1998;352:1510; *N Engl J Med* 2001;344:720).

COST: $100 to $150 per assay (Medicare reimbursement $111 to $130).

INDICATIONS: Quantitative HIV RNA is useful for diagnosing acute HIV infection, for predicting probability of transmission, predicting the rate of progression in chronically infected patients, and for therapeutic monitoring (*Ann Intern Med* 1995;122:573; *N Engl J Med* 1996;334: 426; *J Infect Dis* 1997;175:247; *J Infect Dis* 2002;185:905).

- **Acute HIV infection:** Plasma HIV RNA levels are commonly determined to detect the acute retroviral syndrome prior to seroconversion. Most studies show high levels of virus (10^5 to 10^6 c/mL). Note that 2% to 9% of persons without HIV infection have false-positive results, virtually always with low HIV RNA titers (<10,000 c/mL) (*Ann Intern Med* 1999;130:37; *J Clin Microbiol* 2000; 38:2837; *Ann Intern Med* 2001;134:25). The alternative is the HIV p24 antigen assay, which is less expensive ($20 vs $100) and highly specific but only 89% sensitive (*Ann Intern Med* 2001;134:25).
- **Prognosis:** Viral load correlates with the rate of CD4 decline (CD4 slope) and serves as an important prognostic indicator in early stage disease (*J Infect Dis* 2002;185:908). The most comprehensive study to assess the association between viral load and natural history is the analysis of stored sera from the Multicenter AIDS Cohort Study (MACS), which showed a strong association between "set point" and rate of progression that was independent of the baseline CD4 count (*Ann Intern Med* 1995;122:573; *Science* 1996;272:1167; *J Infect Dis* 1996;174:696; *J Infect Dis* 1996;174:704; *AIDS* 1999;13: 1305; *N Engl J Med* 2001;349,720).
- **Risk of opportunistic infection:** The viral load appears to predict opportunistic infections independently of CD4 count when counts are <200 cells/mm^3 (*JAMA* 1996;276:105; *AIDS* 1999;13:341; *AIDS* 1999;13:1035; *J Acquir Immune Defic Syndr* 2001;27:44). The only prospective study examining this association was ACTG 722, which showed that the failure to decrease viral load by ≥1 log_{10} c/mL in patients with a baseline CD4 count of <150 cells/mm^3 increased the risk of an opportunistic infection 15-fold (*J Acquir Immune Defic Syndr* 2002;30:154). A retrospective review of over 12,000 patients showed CD4 counts were the best method to predict progression defined as an AIDS-defining complication (*Lancet* 2002;360:119), but the viral load predicts the rate of CD4 decline (*J Infect Dis* 2002;185:908).
- **Probability of transmission:** The probability of HIV transmission with nearly any type of exposure is directly correlated with viral load (*N Engl J Med* 2000;342:921; *J Acquir Immune Defic Syndr* 1996;12:427; *J Acquir Immune Defic Syndr* 1998;17:42; *J Acquir Immune Defic Syndr* 1999;21:120; *J Infect Dis* 2002;185:428; *Lancet* 2001;357:1149; *AIDS* 2001;15:621; *Clin Infect Dis* 2002;34:391).
- **Therapeutic monitoring:** Following initiation of therapy, there is a rapid initial decline in HIV RNA level over 1 to 4 weeks (alpha slope), reflecting activity against free plasma HIV virions and HIV in acutely infected CD4 cells. This is followed by a second decline (beta slope) that is longer in duration (months) and more modest in degree (see

quantitation, below, under "Frequency and therapeutic monitoring"). The latter reflects activity against HIV infected macrophages and HIV released from other compartments, especially those trapped in follicular dendritic cells of lymph follicles. The maximum antiviral effect is expected by 4 to 6 months. Most authorities now believe that HIV RNA levels are the most important barometer of therapeutic response (*N Engl J Med* 1996;335:1091; *Ann Intern Med* 1996; 124:984; *J Infect Dis* 2002;185:178).

- **Unexpectedly low viral load:** Aberrant results should be repeated. The RT-PCR assay (Roche) version 1.0 uses primers designed primarily for detection of clade B strains of HIV, but version 1.5 RT-PCR (Roche), bDNA (Bayer), and the *NucliSens* (bioMérieux) assay all quantitate the M subtypes A-G. None is accurate for the non-M subtypes (N or O) or HIV-2 strains.
- **Reservoirs:** HIV resides in some anatomical sites that may be differently affected by antiretroviral drugs and may be the source of archived strains resistant to these drugs. The major sources are the latent CD4 cells; others are the CNS and genital tract (*AIDS* 2002;16:39; *J Clin Microbiol* 2000;38:1414).

RECOMMENDATIONS: Adapted from the International AIDS Society–USA (*JAMA* 2002;288:222) and DHHS Guidelines (*MMWR* 2002;51 [RR-7]:1; *Ann Intern Med* 2002;137:381).

- **Quality assurance:** Assays on individual patients should be obtained at times of clinical stability, at least 4 weeks after immunizations or intercurrent infections, and with use of the same lab and same technology over time.
- **Frequency and therapeutic monitoring:** Tests should be performed at baseline (x 2) followed by routine testing at 2- to 4-month intervals according to guidelines from DHHS and IAS-USA (*Clin Infect Dis* 2001;33:1060). With new therapy and changes in therapy, assays should be obtained at 1 to 4 weeks (alpha slope), at 12 to 16 weeks, and at 16 to 24 weeks. An expected response to therapy is a decrease of 0.75-1.0 $\log_{10}$ c/mL at 1 week (*Lancet* 2001;358:1760; *J Acquir Immune Defic Syndr* 2002;30:167), a decrease of 1.5-2 $\log_{10}$ to <5,000 c/mL at 4 weeks (*J Acquir Immune Defic Syndr* 2000;25:36; *AIDS* 1999;13:1873), <500 c/mL at 8 to 16 weeks (*Ann Intern Med* 2001;135:945; *J Acquir Immune Defic Syndr* 2000;24:433), and <50 c/mL at 16 to 24 weeks. The time to viral load nadir is dependent on pretreatment viral load as well as potency of the regimen, compliance, pharmacology, and resistance. Patients with high baseline viral loads take longer to achieve suppression. Failure to reduce viral load 1 $\log_{10}$ c/mL (90%) by 4 weeks suggests non-adherence, resistance, or inadequate drug exposure, and failure to reduce viral load 1 $\log_{10}$ c/mL at 8 weeks constitutes virologic failure by the IAS-USA guidelines (*JAMA* 2002;288:228). The target

of therapy is a viral load <50 c/mL, although some authorities claim this threshold to be unsupported by clinical trials (*Lancet* 1999;353:863; *JAMA* 2001;285:777). It should be noted that even with "no detectable virus" as defined by viral load <20-50 c/mL, there is still ongoing viral replication (*JAMA* 1999;282:1627; *Nat Med* 1999;5:512). Nevertheless, there is minimal viral evolution with this low-level viral replication, at least for resistance mutations (*JAMA* 2001;286:196).

- **Interpretation:** Changes of ≥50% (0.3 $\log_{10}$ c/mL) are considered significant.
- **Factors not measured by viral load tests:** Immune function, CD4 regenerative reserve, susceptibility to antivirals, infectivity, syncytial vs nonsyncytial inducing forms, and viral load in compartments other than blood (e.g., lymph nodes, CNS, genital secretions).
- **Factors that increase viral load**
  - Progressive disease
  - Failing antiretroviral therapy due to inadequate potency, inadequate drug levels, nonadherence, and resistance.
  - Active infections; active TB increases viral load 5- to 160-fold (*J Immunol* 1996;157:1271); pneumococcal pneumonia increases viral load 3- to 5-fold.
  - Immunizations such as influenza and *Pneumovax* (*Blood* 1995;86:1082; *N Engl J Med* 1996;335:817; *N Engl J Med* 1996;334:1222). Increases are modest and transient (2 to 4 weeks).
- **Falsely low viral loads:** 1) Non-B subtypes using the *Amplicor* (Roche) version 1.0, 2) HIV-2 infection, and 3) Dual HIV-1 and HIV-2 infection.
- **Relative merit of tests:** The *Versant* version 3.0 assay has good reproducibility for viral load levels of 75 to 500,000 c/mL. The linear range for *Amplicor* is 50 to 75,000 c/mL for the ultrasensitive test. It should not be used in patients expected to have higher viral loads (*J Clin Microbiol* 2000;38:2837). The *NucliSens* assay has a broad dynamic range (176 to 3,500,000 c/mL) and can be used for HIV quantification on blood or on various body fluids or tissue such as seminal fluid, CSF, breast milk, saliva, and vaginal fluid (*J Clin Microbiol* 2000;38:1414).

■ TABLE 2-2: **Comparison of Assay Methods for Viral Load**

	Roche	Bayer	bioMérieux
Contact	800-526-1247	800-434-2447	800-682-2666
Trade name	*Amplicor*	*Versant*	*NucliSens*
Technique	RT-PCR	bDNA	NASBA
Comparison of results	Results with the RT-PCR assay are similar to bDNA results using version 2.0 or 3.0.	Results with versions 2.0 or 3.0 are comparable with RT-PCR (*Amplicor*) assays.	Results appear comparable with RT-PCR and bDNA assays, but supporting data are less robust.
Advantages/ disadvantages	■ Fewer false-positives in patients without HIV infection compared with Bayer. ■ FDA-approved	■ Technician time demands are less. ■ Good dynamic range, but higher threshold for no detectable virus. ■ FDA-approved	■ May be used with tissue or body fluids such as genital secretions. ■ Greatest dynamic range. ■ FDA-approved
Dynamic range	■ Standard: (*Amplicor* 1.0 & 1.5) 400 to 750,000 c/mL ■ Ultrasensitive: (*Ultra-Direct* 1.0 & 1.5) 50 to 75,000 c/mL	bDNA Version 3.0: 75 to 500,000 c/mL	*NucliSens* HIV-1 QT: 176-3,500,000 c/mL depending on volume
Subtype amplified	■ Version 1.0: B only ■ Version 1.5: B to G	A to G	A to G
Specimen volume	■ *Amplicor*: 0.2 mL ■ Ultrasensitive: 0.5 mL	1 mL	10 µL to 2 mL
Tubes	EDTA (lavender top)	EDTA (lavender top)	EDTA, heparin, whole blood, any body fluid, PBMC, semen, tissue, etc.
Requirement	Separate plasma <6 hours and freeze prior to shipping at -20°C or -70°C.	Separate plasma <4 hours and freeze prior to shipping at -20°C or -70°C.	Separate serum or plasma <4 hours and freeze prior to shipping at -20°C or -70°C.

CD4 Cell Count

This is a standard test to stage the disease, formulate the differential diagnosis, explain signs or symptoms (Table 1-1, p. 2), and to make therapeutic decisions regarding antiviral treatment and prophylaxis for opportunistic pathogens. It is the most reliable indicator of prognosis (*Ann Intern Med* 1997;126:946; *Lancet* 2002;360:119). CD8 cell counts have not been found to predict outcome (*N Engl J Med*

1990;322:166); HIV-specific CD8 cells (CD38 cells) are important for controlling HIV levels but cannot be routinely measured (*Science* 1999;283:857; *J Acquir Immune Defic Syndr* 2002;29:346).

Technique

The standard method for determining CD4 count uses flow cytometers and hematology analyzers that are expensive and require fresh blood (<18 hours old). The cost of the test ranges from $50 to $150. An alternative system that uses EIA technology is the *TRAX* CD4 Test Kit (*J Acquir Immune Defic Syndr* 1995;10:522). This may be attractive in resource-limited areas, although most clinicians who do not have access to CD4 counts will probably use total T-lymphocyte counts (TLC) (*Scaling Up Antiretroviral Therapy in Resource Limited Settings*, WHO, 2002).

Normal Values

Normal values for most laboratories are a mean of 800 to 1050 cells/mm^3, with a range representing two standard deviations of approximately 500 to 1400 cells/mm^3 (*Ann Intern Med* 1993;119:55).

Frequency of Testing

Every 3 to 6 months in untreated patients and at 2 to 4 month intervals for antiretroviral monitoring (*Clin Infect Dis* 2001;33:1060; *JAMA* 2002;288:222; *Ann Intern Med* 2002;137:381). The test should be repeated when results are inconsistent with prior trends. Frequency will vary with individual circumstances. In the absence of therapy, the average rate of CD4 decline is 4% per year for each $\log_{10}$ HIV RNA c/mL (*J Infect Dis* 2002;185:905). With initial therapy or a change in therapy, the recommendation is that CD4 counts (and viral load) be measured at 4, 8 to 12, and 16 to 24 weeks (IAS-USA guidelines, *JAMA* 2002;288:228).

Factors that Influence CD4 Cell Counts

Factors that influence CD4 cell counts include analytical variation, seasonal and diurnal variations, some intercurrent illnesses, and corticosteroids. Substantial analytical variations, which account for the wide range in normal values (usually about 500 to 1400 cells/mm^3), reflect the fact that the CD4 cell count is the product of three variables: the white blood cell count, percent lymphocytes, and the percent CD4 cells (cells that bear the CD4 receptor). There are also seasonal changes (*Clin Exp Immunol* 1991;86:349) and diurnal changes, with the lowest levels at 12:30 PM and peak values at 8:30 PM (*J Acquir Immune Defic Syndr* 1990;3:144); these variations do not clearly correspond to the circadian rhythm of corticosteroids. Modest decreases in the CD4 cell count have been noted with some acute infections and with major surgery. Corticosteroid administration may have a profound effect, with decreases from 900 cells/mm^3 to less than 300 cells/mm^3 with acute administration; chronic administration has a less pronounced effect (*Clin Immunol Immunopathol* 1983;28:101). Acute changes are probably due to a redistribution of leukocytes between the peripheral circulation and the marrow, spleen, and lymph nodes (*Clin Exp Immunol* 1990;80:460). Co-infection with HTLV-1 may result in a deceptively high CD4 cell count despite immune suppression from HIV-1. Splenectomy may also cause deceptively high levels. The following have minimal effect on the CD4 cell count: gender, age in adults, risk category, psychological stress, physical stress, and pregnancy (*Ann Intern Med* 1993;119:55).

CD4 Count Percentage

The CD4 cell percentage is sometimes used in preference to the absolute number because this reduces the variation to a single measurement (*J Acquir Immune Defic Syndr* 1989;2:114). In the AIDS Clinical Trial Group (ACTG) laboratories, the within-subject coefficient of variation for percent CD4 was 18% compared with 25% for the CD4 count (*J Infect Dis* 1994;169:28). Corresponding CD4 cell counts are provided in the table below.

■ TABLE 2-3: **Approximate CD4/CD4% Equivalents**

CD4 Cell Count	% CD4
>500/mm^3	>29%
200 to 500/mm^3	14% to 28%
<200/mm^3	<14%

Response to HAART

The CD4 count typically increases ≥50 cells/mm^3 at 4 to 8 weeks after viral suppression with HAART and then increases an additional 50-100 cells/mm^3/year thereafter (*JAMA* 2002;288:222; *J Infect Dis* 2002;185:471; *AIDS* 2001;15:735). Despite good virological response, there may be an initial delay in CD4 response that cannot be explained (*JAMA* 2002;288:222). The CD4 response generally correlates with viral load suppression, but discordant results are common (*J Infect Dis* 2001;183:1328). The CD4 count usually declines rapidly, up to 100-150 cells/mm^3 in 3 to 4 months, when therapy is discontinued (*Clin Infect Dis* 2001;33:344; *Clin Infect Dis* 2001;32:1231). This decrease may be seen with or without antecedent viral suppression.

Total Lymphocyte Count (TLC)

The TLC is sometimes used as a surrogate for CD4 count in resource limited areas (*JAMA* 1993;269:622; *Am J Med Sci* 1992;304:79). TLC of <1200/mm^3 combined with clinical symptoms is recommended as a surrogate for a CD4 count of <200 cells/mm^3 as an indication for antiretroviral therapy in the DHHS guidelines (*Scaling Up Antiretroviral Therapy in Resource Limited Settings*, WHO, 2002).

Precautions

Precautions in the use and interpretation of CD4 cell counts include the need for both clinicians and patients to be aware of the fluctuations described above. Test results that represent "milestones" for therapeutic decisions should be repeated, especially if they show values that do not correlate well with prior trends. Prior studies show that the 95% confidence range for a true count of 200 cells/mm^3, for example, is 118-337 cells/mm^3 (*J Acquir Immune Defic Syndr* 1993;6:537). Deceptively high CD4 cell counts are noted in patients with concurrent human T-cell leukemia virus (HTLV)-1 infection and splenectomized patients. HTLV-1 is closely related to HTLV-2, and most serologic assays do not distinguish between the two, but only HTLV-1 causes deceptively high CD4 cell counts. Serologic studies in the United States show HTLV-1/2 infection rates of 7% to 12% in injection drug users and 2% to 10% in commercial sex workers (*N Engl J Med* 1990;326:375; *JAMA* 1990;263:60); 80% to 90% of these are HTLV-2 in both populations. High rates of concurrent HIV and HTLV-1 have been reported in Brazil (*JAMA* 1994;271:353) and Haiti (*J Clin Microbiol* 1995;33:1735). Analysis of patients with co-infection suggests that CD4 counts are 80% to 180% higher than in controls for comparable levels of immunosuppression (*JAMA* 1994;271:353).

The CD4 cell count may be used as a surrogate marker of HIV infection in patients for whom serologic results are delayed or not available. The median CD4 cell count at the time of an AIDS-defining diagnosis is 60 cells/mm^3, and <10% have an AIDS-defining diagnosis with a CD4 count >200 cells/mm^3 (*Am J Epidemiol* 1995;141:645). Thus, a patient with a CD4 cell count of 800/mm^3 with thrush, possible PCP, or cryptococcal meningitis is unlikely to have HIV infection as the underlying cause.

CD4 Repertoire

Progressive immunodeficiency in HIV infection is associated with both quantitative and qualitative changes in CD4 cells. The two major categories of CD4 cells are naïve cells and memory cells. In early life, all cells are naïve and express the isoform of CD45RA$^+$. Memory cells (CD45RA$^-$) represent the component of the T-cell repertoire that has been activated by exposure to antigens. These are the CD4 cells with specificity for most opportunistic infections, such as *P. carinii*, cytomegalovirus, and *Toxoplasma gondii.* It is the depletion of these cells that accounts for the inability to respond to recall antigens, a defect noted relatively early in the course of HIV infection. Studies of HIV infected patients show a preferential decline in naïve cells. With HAART, there is a three-phase component to the CD4 rebound. The initial increase is due primarily to redistribution of CD4 cells from lymphatic sites. The second phase is characterized by an influx of CD4 memory cells with reduced T-cell activation and improved response to recall antigens. In the third phase there is an increase in naïve cells following at least 12 weeks of HAART (*Nat Med* 1997;5:533; *Science* 1997;277:112). By 6 months the CD4 repertoire is diverse. The competence of these cells is evidenced by favorable control of selected chronic infections such as cryptosporidiosis, microsporidiosis, and molluscum contagiosum, the ability to discontinue maintenance therapy for disseminated MAC and CMV, and the ability to safely discontinue primary prophylaxis for PCP and MAC in responders. Nevertheless, some patients with immune reconstitution have deficits in CTL responses to specific antigens that may result in PCP or relapses in CMV retinitis despite CD4 counts >300 cells/mm^3 (*J Infect Dis* 2001;183:1285).

Idiopathic CD4 Lymphocytopenia (ICL)

Idiopathic CD4 lympoytopenia (ICL) is a syndrome characterized by a low CD4 cell count that is unexplained by HIV infection or other medical conditions. Case definition criteria include: 1) CD4 less than 300 cells/mm^3 or a CD4 percent less than 20% on two or more measurements; 2) lack of laboratory evidence of HIV infection; and 3) absence of alternative explanation for the CD4 cell lymphocytopenia including Sjogrens Syndrome, sarcoid, radiation, atopic dermatitis, collagen vascular disease, steroid therapy, or lymphoma. Transient, unexplained decreases in CD4 cells may occur in healthy persons (*Chest* 1994;105:1335; *Eur J Med* 1993;2:509; *Am J Med Sci* 1996;312:240). One study of 430 HIV negative TB patients showed 62 (14%) had ICL (*J Infect Dis* 2000;41:167). The CDC receives notice of about one ICL case/month (Dr. T.J. Spira, personal communication). Conclusions from the experience with patients having ICL are: 1) They lack risk factors for HIV infection; 2) There is no evidence of an infectious agent based on clustering or contact evaluations; 3) They have fewer OIs than AIDS patients for a given CD4 level; 4) The predominant OIs associated with ICL are cryptococcosis, molluscum, and histoplasmosis – infections with *P. carinii*, *Candida*, and HHV-8 [KS] are unusual; 5) Their CD4 counts tend to remain stable, and their prognosis is relatively good; 6) Recommended prophylaxis is TMP-SMX with persistent counts <200/mm^3; and 7) Treatment of ICL has included IL-2 and gamma interferon, but the experience is very limited (*Lancet* 1992;340:273; *N Engl J Med* 1993;328:373; *N Engl J Med* 1993;328:380; *N Engl J Med* 1993;328:386; *N Engl J Med* 1993;328: 393; *Clin Exp Immunol* 1999;116:322; *Clin Infect Dis* 2000:3:E20; *Clin Infect Dis* 2001;33:E125). Cases of this syndrome should be reported to local/state health departments rather than reported directly to the CDC as originally advocated.

Resistance Testing

The prevalence of ≥1 major resistance mutation in patients receiving antiretroviral therapy is about 50% (*Lancet* 2002;359:49; *Nature Med* 2001;7:1016). The frequency of ≥1 major resistance mutation in treatment-naïve, recently infected patients is 5% to 20% (*Nat Med* 2001;7:1016; *BMJ* 2001;322:1087; *AIDS* 2001;15:601; *JAMA* 2002;288:181; *N Engl J Med* 2002;347:385). These observations have made resistance testing an increasingly important component of HIV care, but many feel that both the technology and the interpretation still need substantial improvement. The limitations include the following: 1) Resistance assays measure only dominant species at the time the test is performed; resistant variants that comprise less than 20% of the total viral population in blood and species in "sequestered havens" (CNS, latent CD4 cells, genital tract, etc.) are not detected; 2) There must be a sufficient viral load to perform the test, usually ≥500 to 1,000 c/mL; 3) Genotypic assays are often difficult to interpret because multiple mutations are required for antiretroviral agents other than 3TC and non-nucleoside reverse transcriptase inhibitors (NNRTIs); 4) Phenotypic assays may be difficult to interpret due to the arbitrary thresholds used to define susceptibility, particularly for RTV-boosted regimens, and they are also less sensitive at detecting emerging resistance; 5) Clinical trials with resistance tests compared with "standard care" for selection of salvage regimens have shown variable results (*AIDS* 2002;16:579; *AIDS* 2002;16:209; *Antivir Ther* 2000; 5[suppl 3]:78; *AIDS* 2000;14:F83; *J Infect Dis* 2001;183:401). As a result of these limitations, the following conclusions can be drawn:

- **Resistance testing most reliably identifies drugs that should be avoided** but is less reliable at detecting the drugs that are most likely to be active.
- **Testing should be performed in the presence of the antiretroviral agents in question** because discontinuation of therapy often results in the proliferation of wild type virus, which outgrows resistant strains and renders them undetectable (*N Engl J Med* 2001;344:472). The time between discontinuation of HAART and the shift from resistant strains to wild type virus varies considerably, ranging from days to weeks for 3TC resistance, weeks to months for PI resistance, and months to years for some NNRTI and thymidine analog mutations. The usual recommendation is that resistance testing be performed while the patient is on therapy or within 2 to 3 weeks of stopping.
- **Interpretation of results in patients who have received prior antiretroviral agents is difficult**, and this may account for variations in clinical experience. Resistance to previously used drugs may be present even if resistance assays indicate susceptibility, so that prior drug history and outcome are important factors in regimen selection.

- **A viral load of 500 to 1,000 c/mL is usually required.**
- **Results are most accurate with failure of early regimens.**
- **There is no clear preference** for genotypic vs phenotypic analysis.

Indications for Resistance Testing

DHHS Guidelines (http://www.aidsinfo.nih.gov/guidelines; *Ann Intern Med* 2002;137:381) and IAS-USA Guidelines (http://www.iasusa.org; *JAMA* 2002;288:222; *JAMA* 2000;283:2417; *Top HIV Med* 2002;10 No2:11).

CHRONICALLY INFECTED PATIENT WITH VIROLOGIC FAILURE

(Recommended by virtually all guidelines – see Table 2-4)

Most guidelines make the following recommendation for resistance testing for chronically infected patients receiving ART who meet one of the following criteria:

- Failure to decrease viral load >0.5 to 0.7 $\log_{10}$ c/mL by 4 weeks.
- Failure to decrease viral load >1 $\log_{10}$ c/mL by 8 weeks.
- Viral load >1000 c/mL after 16 to 24 weeks.

■ TABLE 2-4: **Comparison of Recommendations for Resistance Testing (*J Acquir Immune Defic Syndr* 2001;26:551)**

Category	British HIV Assoc.	European Assoc.*	IAS-USA†	USA-DHHS‡
Acute HIV	Recommend	Recommend	Consider	Consider
Chronic HIV				
Rx naïve	Recommend	Consider	Consider	Defer
Virologic failure	Recommend	Recommend	Recommend	Recommend
Pregnancy	Recommend	Recommend	Recommend	Only for above indications

* *AIDS* 2001;15:309
† *JAMA* 2000;238:2417
‡ http://www.aidsinfo.nih.gov, August, 2002

EVALUATION: A meta-analysis of published reports and conference presentations through February 2001 compared virologic results at 3 to 6 months after using resistance testing vs clinician decision or standard of care (SOC) for salvage regimens (*HIV Clin Trials* 2002;3:1). For genotypic analysis, there was a modest but statistically significant benefit with genotypic testing. Results were significantly better with expert interpretation of the genotypic resistance assay. There was no significant benefit with phenotypic resistance testing compared with SOC (although the analyses were done prior to currently accepted thresholds to define resistance). Results for viral suppression at 6 months after regimen change based on genotypic analysis vs SOC were genotype 168/432 (39%) vs SOC 115/400 (29%).

Test Methods

There are two types of tests, genotypic and phenotypic assays. These are compared in Table 2-5, p. 25.

GENOTYPIC ASSAYS: Genotype analysis identifies mutations associated with phenotypic resistance. These assays vary considerably in terms of cost, number of mutations tested, and simplicity and accuracy of reporting. The methodology involves: 1) Amplication of the reverse transcriptase (RT), protease (Pr) gene, or both by RT PCR. 2) DNA sequencing of amplicons generated for the dominant species (mutations are limited to those present in >20% of plasma virions). 3) Reporting of mutations for each gene using a letter-number-letter standard, in which the first letter indicates the amino acid at the designated codon with wild type virus, the number is the codon, and the second letter indicates the amino acid substituted in the mutation (Table 2-6, p. 25). Thus, the RT mutation K103N indicates that asparagine (N) has substituted for lysine (K) on codon 103. This could be expressed as "103N" because the substituted amino acid may vary, and these differences may impact susceptibility. The table indicates the amino acids and corresponding letter codes used to describe mutations in genotype analyses. Updated information on resistance testing can be obtained at http://www.iasusa.org or http://hivdb.stanford.edu/pages/seqAnalysis.html.

PHENOTYPIC ASSAYS: Phenotype analysis measures the ability of HIV to replicate at different concentrations of tested drugs. It measures susceptibility to individual drugs, not combinations. The method involves insertion of the RT and protease genes from the patient's strain into a backbone laboratory clone by cloning or recombination. Replication is monitored at various drug concentrations and compared with a reference wild type virus. This assay is comparable with conventional *in vitro* tests of anti-microbial sensitivity, in which the microbe is grown in serial dilutions of antiviral agents. Results are reported as the IC_{50} for the test strain relative to that of a reference or wild type strain. The interpretation was previously based on a fixed ratio such as 4x to define resistance, meaning resistance is 4-fold greater than that of the reference strain. The newer method is to individualize by drug. For *Virco*, the fold changes that define resistance are zidovudine (AZT) – 4.0, lamivudine (3TC) – 4.5, didanosine (ddI) – 3.5, zalcitabine (ddC) – 3.5, stavudine (d4T) – 3.0, abacavir (ABC) – 3.0, nevirapine (NVP) – 8.0, delavirdine (DLV) – 10.0, efavirenz (EFV) – 6.0, indinavir (IDV) – 3.0, ritonavir (RTV) – 3.5, nelfinavir (NFV) – 4.0, saquinavir (SQV) – 2.5, amprenavir (APV) – 2.5 (*AIDS* 2001;15:1671). These PI thresholds do not account for drug levels that can be achieved with RTV boosting.

VIRTUAL PHENOTYPE: This is a prediction of the phenotype of the test strain based on genotypic analysis. The mutational pattern of the test strain is compared with results of phenotypic assay using strains showing similar mutations from a databank of >55,000 HIV isolates.

■ TABLE 2-5: **Comparison of Genotypic and Phenotypic Assays**

Advantages	Disadvantages
Genotypic Assays	
▪ Less expensive ($300 to $480/test). ▪ Short turn-around of 1 to 2 weeks. ▪ May detect presence of resistance mutations before they have resulted in phenotypic resistance.	▪ Detect resistance only in dominant species (>20%). ▪ Interpretation requires knowledge of mutational changes, i.e., expertise. ▪ Technician experience influences results. ▪ May show discrepancy with phenotype. ▪ Require viral load >1000 c/mL.
Phenotypic Assays	
▪ Interpretation more analogous to resistance testing of bacteria. ▪ Assesses total effect, including mutations, mutational interactions. ▪ Reproducibility is good. ▪ Advantage over genotype when there are multiple mutations.	▪ More expensive (usually $800 to $1000). ▪ Report takes 2 to 3 weeks. ▪ Thresholds to define susceptibility are arbitrary and do not account for boosted PI levels. ▪ Detects resistance only to single drug, not combinations. ▪ Detect resistance only in dominant species (>20%). ▪ Require viral load >500-1000 c/mL.

Cost: Medicare/Medicaid reimbursement per HCFA announcement January 8, 2001 – Genotype test $355.78 (code 87901); phenotype test $675.29 (code 8703), each additional drug $36.02 (code 8704).

■ TABLE 2-6: **Letter Designations for Amino Acids***

A	Alanine	**I**	Isoleucine	**R**	Arginine
C	Cytosine	**K**	Lysine	**S**	Serine
D	Aspartic acid	**L**	Leucine	**T**	Threonine
E	Glutamic acid	**M**	Methionine	**V**	Valine
F	Phenylalanine	**N**	Asparagine	**W**	Tryptophan
G	Glycine	**P**	Proline	**Y**	Tyrosine
H	Histidine	**Q**	Glutamine		

* Amino acids and corresponding single-letter codes used in describing genotypes.

■ TABLE 2-7: **Resistance Mutations Adapted From IAS-USA (*Top HIV Med* 2002:105:21). Updated at http://www.iasusa.org. Also see: http://hivdb.stanford.edu/pages/seqAnalysis.html.**

Drug	Codon Mutations*	Comment
Nucleosides and Nucleotides		
AZT	41, 67, 70, 210, 215, 219	Mutations are "TAMs"* – reduce susceptibility to AZT, d4T, ABC, ddI, ddC, TDF, 3TC.
3TC	184 (44, 118)	184 – high level 3TC resistance, increases activity of d4T, AZT, and TDF, reduces susceptibility to ddI, ddC, ABC.
ddC	65, 69, 74, 184	
ddI	65, 74	Presence of 74 or 65 alone or combined with TAMs is associated with resistance to ddI. Multiple TAMs also decrease ddI susceptibility.
d4T‡	41, 67, 70, 75, 210, 215, 219	The d4T-specific mutation at 75 is seen mostly *in vitro. In vitro* resistance depends on number of TAMs, which reduce susceptibility to all NRTIs.
ABC‡	41, 65, 67, 70, 74, 115, 184, 210, 215, 219	Resistance depends on number of TAMs ± M184V; 184 alone does not confer resistance. Presence of M184V plus ≥3-4 TAMs associated with ABC resistance. ABC selects for mutations that may confer cross-resistance to 3TC, ddI, and TDF.
TDF	65,69 insertion, ≥3 TAMS including 41L or 210W	Reduced activity with K65R and resistance with 69 insertion.
Multinucleoside resistance – A Q151M complex	151, 62, 75, 77, 116	Occurs with or without TAMs. Confers resistance to all NRTIs but not to tenofovir.
Multinucleoside resistance – B T69 insertion	69 (insertion), 41, 62, 67, 70, 210, 215, 219	Requires TAMs. Confers resistance to all NRTIs and TDF but not to DAPD.
Multinucleoside resistance – Multiple TAMs	41, 67, 70, 210, 215, 219	Confer resistance to all NRTI including TDF
NNRTIs		
NVP	100, 103, 106, 108, 181, 188C/L/H, 190	Y181C is favored mutation with NVP, unless combined with AZT, in which case K103N is favored.
DLV	103, 181, 236, 318	
EFV	100, 103, 108, 181, 188L, 190, 225	181C is not selected, but its presence contributes to low-level cross resistance. Resistance with 188L but not 188C or 188H.
Multi-NNRTI resistance	103, 188L	Either mutation substantially reduces activity of all NNRTIs.
Multi-NNRTI resistance accumulation	100, 106, 181, 190, 230	≥2 of these mutations substantially reduces activity of all NNRTIs

■ TABLE 2-7: **Resistance Mutations *(Continued)***

Drug	Major[†]	Minor[‡]	Comment
Protease Inhibitors (PIs)			
IDV	46, 82, 84	10, 20, 24, 32, 36, 54, 71, 73, 77, 90	At least 3 mutations required for resistance (>4x decrease in susceptibility).
NFV	30, 90	10, 36, 46, 71, 77, 82, 84, 88	D30N most common mutation: No PI cross-resistance. L90M occurs in some, leading to greater PI cross-resistance.
RTV	82, 84	10, 20, 32, 33, 36, 46, 54, 71, 77, 90	Cross resistance with IDV common.
SQV	48, 90	10, 54, 71, 73, 77, 82, 84	90 develops 1st, then 48; Codon 48 mutation unique, but L90M contributes to PI cross-resistance.
APV	50V, 84	10, 32, 46, 47, 54, 73, 90	I50V is associated with cross-resistance to LPV.
LPV/r	73	10, 20, 24, 32, 33, 46, 47, 50V, 53, 54, 63, 71, 73, 82, 84, 90	≥6 mutations cause reduced response; the number may be as low as 4. I50V (selected by APV) decreases LPV susceptibility.
Atazanavir	50L	32, 46, 54, 71, 82, 84, 88, 90	Selects for 50L and 71 when initial PI; in PI experienced patients selects for 54 and 84
Multi-PI resistance	46, 82, 84, 90	10, 54	≥4 or 5 usually cause multiple PI resistance.
Fusion Inhibitors			
Enfuvirtide (T20)			Resistance in the gp41 envelope gene at positions 36-45.

* The distinction between primary and secondary mutations has been eliminated for NRTIs NNRTIs by the International AIDS Society Expert Committee; this distinction has been retained for PIs, but with the terms "Major" or "Minor."

† **Major mutations** develop first or are associated with decreased drug binding or reduced viral activity; these effect phenotype resistance.

‡ **Minor mutations** appear later and, by themselves, do not significantly change phenotype resistance.

Screening Laboratory Tests

The usual screening battery advocated for patients with established HIV infection is summarized in Table 2-8, pp. 28-29 (*Clin Infect Dis* 1995;21[suppl 1]:S13).

Complete Blood Count

The CBC is important because anemia, leukopenia, lymphopenia and thrombocytopenia are found in 30% to 40% of patients (*J Acquir Immune Defic Syndr* 1994;7:1134; *J Acquir Immune Defic Syndr*

2001;28:221). Repeat at 3- to 6-month intervals, in part because this is a necessary component of monitoring the CD4 cell count. It should be repeated more frequently in patients with symptoms suggesting marrow suppression, in those receiving marrow-suppressing drugs such as AZT, and in those with marginal or low counts.

Serum Chemistry Panel

This panel is advocated in the initial evaluation of HIV infection due to high rates of hepatitis (*J Infect Dis* 2002;186:231) to help stage the disease, to obtain baseline values in patients who are likely to have multisystem disease, and/or to require multiple drugs with variable toxicity. Studies of HIV infected patients at baseline have shown that up to 75% have abnormal transaminases, 20% have severe abnormalities, and about half have elevated lactic dehydrogenase (LDH) levels (*J Acquir Immune Defic Syndr* 1994;7:1134).

■ TABLE 2-8: **Routine Laboratory Tests in Asymptomatic Patients**

Test	Cost*	Frequency and Comment
Serologic Tests		
CMV IgG	\$10 to \$15	Advocated for low-risk patients (not MSM or IDV); seroprevalence in U.S. adults is 50% to 60%, and for MSM and IV drug abuse patients it is $\geq$90%.
Hepatitis	\$20 to \$30 HAV	HAV: Screen for vaccine candidates with total HAV antibody.
	\$10 to \$15 HBV	HBV: Screen for vaccine candidates with anti-HBc or anti-HBs (screen for chronic hepatitis B with HBsAg at \$20 to \$25).
	\$25 HCV EIA	HCV: Screen with EIA; confirm positives with qualitative HCV RNA at \$150
	\$60 to \$80	Abnormal transaminase levels – "hepatitis screen": anti-HAV IgM, anti-HCV and HBsAg.
HIV (see p. 6)	\$30 to \$60	Repeat test for patients with positive test results and: 1) No confirmation available, 2) Denial of commonly accepted risk factors, 3) Test performed with techniques other than standard serology, 4) Asymptomatic, and 5) Other reason for concern such as undetectable viral load and normal CD4 cell count. Repeat test for indeterminate results at 3 to 6 months.
Syphilis – VDRL or RPR	\$5 to \$16	Repeat annually in sexually active patients.
Toxoplasmosis	\$12 to \$15	Screen all patients and repeat in seronegatives if CD4 cell count is $\leq 100/mm^3$ and patient does not take trimethoprim-sulfamethoxazole (TMP-SMX) for *P. carinii* prophylaxis and symptoms suggest toxoplasmosis encephalitis. Agglutination assays for IgG are preferred. IgM is not useful.

■ TABLE 2-8: **Routine Laboratory Tests in Asymptomatic Patients *(Continued)***

Test	Cost*	Frequency and Comment
Chemistry		
Chemistry panel	$10 to $15	Repeat annually or more frequently in patients with abnormal results and with administration of hepatotoxic or nephrotoxic drugs.
G6-PD	$14 to $20	Test: 1) Susceptible hosts: Primarily men (X-linked), with the following ancestry African-American, Italian, Sephardic Jew, Arab, and those from India and Southeast Asia; 2) Those receiving oxidant drugs, especially dapsone and primaquine; 3) Those with typical symptoms of G6-PD deficiency with testing following recovery (see p. 37). Some authorities recommend screening all patients.
Lipid profile and blood glucose (fasting)	$20 to $40	Therapeutic monitoring recommended for patients receiving antiretroviral regimens that include a PI or NNRTI; consider at baseline and at 3 to 6 months with subsequent measurements based on initial results and risks.
Hematology		
Complete blood count (CBC)	$6 to $8	Repeat at 3 to 6 months, more frequently for low values and with administration of marrow-toxic drugs.
CD4 cell count and %	$60 to $150	Repeat every 3 to 6 months and repeat for results that represent "milestones" for therapeutic decisions (antiretroviral therapy and prophylaxis for opportunistic pathogens), and with results that are inconsistent with prior trends. Routine testing when counts are <50 cells/mm^3 is of minimal use except for monitoring response to antiretroviral therapy.
Other		
Chest x-ray	$40 to $140	Indicated for symptoms and signs suggesting pulmonary disease or newly detected positive PPD.
PAP smear	$25 to $40	Repeat at 6 months and then annually if results are normal. Results reported as "inadequate" should be repeated. Refer to a gynecologist for results showing atypia or greater on the Bethesda scale (see pp. 33-33).
PPD skin test	$1	Repeat testing: Annual testing should be considered in previously PPD-negative patients who have risk for tuberculosis, and repeat testing should be considered if initial test was negative and the CD4 count has subsequently increased to >200 cells/mm^3 in response to HAART.
Urine NAAT for *N. gonorrhoeae* and *C. trachomatis*	$60 to $100	Advocated as marker of high risk behavior (and need for enhanced counseling) and for treatment + contact tracing. Repeat annually in sexually active patients. (NAAT=nucleic acid amplification test)

*Common charges are based on survey of five laboratories.

Syphilis Serology (*MMWR* 2002;51[RR-6]:19)

The usual screening with a nontreponemal test (VDRL or RPR) should be performed at baseline and annually thereafter due to high rates of co-infection (*MMWR* 2002;51[RR-6]:19). Up to 6% of patients with HIV infection have biologic false-positive (BFP) screening tests. Risk factors for biologic false-positive results include injection drug use, pregnancy, and HIV infection (*Clin Infect Dis* 1994;19:1040; *J Infect Dis* 1992;165:1124; *J Acquir Immune Defic Syndr* 1994;7:1134; *Am J Med* 1995;99:55). Nontreponemal tests are antibody titers that correlate with disease activity. Positive screening tests are confirmed with a fluorescent treponemal antibody adsorbed (FTa-ABS) or *T. pallidum* particle agglutination (TP-PA test). Many patients will have positive treponemal tests for life, but the VDRL or RPR usually becomes negative or persists at low titer. Some HIV infected patients have "atypical serology" with unusually high, unusually low, or fluctuating titers, but "for most HIV infected patients, serologic tests are accurate and reliable for the diagnosis of syphilis and for the response to therapy" (*MMWR* 2002;51[RR-6]:19). A lumbar puncture is recommended in the following cases: 1) For patients with neurological signs or symptoms (cognitive dysfunction, motor or sensory deficits, ophthalmic or auditory symptoms, cranial nerve palsies, or signs of meningitis); 2) For patients with therapeutic failures (defined as persistent signs or symptoms or a sustained 4-fold increase in titer with evaluation at 6 and 12 months); 3) Tertiary syphilis (aortitis, gumma or iritis); and 4) In all patients with late latent syphilis (>1 year) or latent syphilis of unknown duration (*MMWR* 2002;51[RR-6]:19). For primary and secondary syphilis in HIV infected patients, "some specialists" recommend CSF exam at 6 to 12 months post therapy, and CSF exam should be strongly considered if nontreponemal tests do not decrease 4-fold within 6 to 12 months (*MMWR* 2002;51[RR-6]:24). CSF interpretation may be confounded by HIV-associated abnormalities of CSF, including mononuclear pleocytosis and elevated protein. Relapse is common even with recommended therapy, so follow-up VDRL titers are advised at 3, 6, 9, 12, and 24 months for primary and secondary syphilis, and at 6, 12, 18, and 24 months after treatment of latent syphilis.

Urine Screen for *N. gonorrhoeae* and *C. trachomatis*

Infections with these two sexually transmitted pathogens are common in patients with HIV infection (*AIDS* 2000;14:297) and are often asymptomatic in both men and women (*STD* 2001;28:33). Screening for *N. gonorrhoeae* and *C. trachomatis* is commonly advocated in sexually active HIV infected patients at baseline and annually. The usual tests are the urine-based nucleic acid amplification tests (NAAT) for *C. trachomatis* and *N. gonorrhoeae*, which are non-invasive, relatively inexpensive, sensitive, and specific (*MMWR* 2002;51[RR-15]:10). The cost is about $80 to $100 for both tests in most clinical laboratories.

The purpose is to detect high-risk behavior that might not otherwise be apparent (for enhanced counseling), for contact tracing, and for treatment.

Chest X-Ray

The frequency of lung disease with HIV infection is high even in the HAART era (*Am Rev Respir Crit Care Med* 2001;164:21; *Chest* 2001;120:1888). A routine baseline chest x-ray is recommended by the CDC (*MMWR* 1986;35:448), both for detection of asymptomatic tuberculosis and as a baseline for patients who are at high risk for pulmonary disease. Nevertheless, in a longitudinal study of 1,065 patients at various stages of HIV infection, routine x-rays performed at 0, 3, 6, and 12 months (*Arch Intern Med* 1996;156:191) detected an abnormality in only 123 (2%) of 5,263 x-rays. None of the asymptomatic PPD negative patients had evidence of active tuberculosis, and only 1 of 82 with a positive PPD had an abnormality on x-ray. The authors concluded that routine chest x-rays in HIV infected patients with negative PPD skin tests are not warranted. DHHS Guidelines recommend an x-ray "when clinically indicated" (*MMWR* 1998;47[RR-1]:38).

PPD Skin Testing

The CDC recommends the Mantoux-method TST (Tuberculin Skin Test), using 5 TU of PPD, for HIV infected patients who have not had a prior positive test. TST should be repeated annually if initial test(s) were negative and if the patient belongs to population with a high risk of tuberculosis (eg, residents of prisons or jails, injection drug users, and homeless individuals). The PPD should also be repeated with immune reconstitution when the CD4 count increases to >200 cells/mm^3 (2002 USPHS/IDSA Guidelines for the Prevention of Opportunistic Infections (*MMWR* 2002;51[RR-6]). Induration of ≥5 mm at 48 to 72 hours constitutes a positive test. Anergy testing is not recommended.

PAP Smear

The CDC and the Agency for Health Care Policy and Research (AHCPR) recommend that a gynecological evaluation with pelvic exam and PAP smear be performed at baseline, repeated at 6 months and annually thereafter (*MMWR* 2002;517[RR-6]:59; *JAMA* 1994;271:1866; *MMWR* 1999;48[RR-10]:31), with management according to guidelines in Table 2-9, p. 33. More aggressive testing is recommended because of a several-fold increase in rates of squamous intraepithelial lesion (SIL) (33% to 45% HIV+ vs 7% to 14% HIV-) and a 1.7-fold increase in rates of cervical cancer in young women with HIV (*Arch Pediatr Adolesc Med* 2000;154:127; *Obstet Gynecol Clin N Am* 1996;23,861). Severity and frequency of cervical dysplasia increase with progressive immune compromise. There is a strong association between HIV infection and detectable and persistent HPV infection by HPV types associated with cervical cancer (16, 18, 31, 33, and 35); this association increases with progressive immunosuppression (*Clin Infect Dis* 1995;21[suppl 1]:S121; *N Engl J Med* 1997;337:1343; *J Infect Dis* 2001;184:682).

METHOD: The cervix is scraped circumflexually using an *Ayer* spatula or a curved brush; a sample from the posterior fornix or the "vaginal pool" may also be included. The endocervical sample is taken with a saline-moistened cotton-tipped applicator or straight ectocervical brush that is rolled on a slide and immediately fixed in ethyl ether plus 95% ethyl alcohol or 95% ethyl alcohol alone. The yield is 7-fold higher with the brush specimen. The following are important steps in obtaining an adequate sample:

- Collect PAP prior to bimanual exam.
- Avoid contaminating sample with lubricant.
- Obtain PAP before samples for STD testing.
- Carefully remove large amounts of vaginal discharge (if present) with large swab before obtaining PAP smear.
- Obtain ectocervical sample before endocervical sample.
- Defer PAP smear if patient is bleeding heavily (small amounts of blood will not interfere with cytologic sampling.)
- Apply collected material to slide uniformly, with no clumping. Fix rapidly to avoid air drying. If spray fixatives are used, the spray should be held at least 10 inches away from the slide to prevent disruption of cells by propellant.

When performing speculum examination, if an ulcerative or exophytic lesion suspicious for invasive cancer is noted, the patient should be referred for possible biopsy.

Newer methods of cytologic evaluation using liquid-based collection and thin-layer processing increase sensitivity, decrease frequency of inadequate smears, permit HPV testing, and provide better resolution of ASCUS.

Analysis for HPV-DNA: Screening of PAP smears for high-risk HPV DNA types (including 16, 18, 31, 33, and 35) was compared with standard thin layer PAPs for detecting intraepithelial neoplasia (CIN grade 3) or cancer (*JAMA* 2002;288:1749). Testing for these high-risk HPV types showed higher sensitivity (91% vs 61%) but less specificity (73% vs 82%).

■ TABLE 2-9: **Recommendations for Intervention Based on Results of PAP Smear (*MMWR* 2002;51[RR-6]:58; *JAMA* 1989;262:931; *JAMA* 2002;287:2114)**

Results	Management
Severe inflammation	Evaluate for infection; repeat PAP smear, preferably within 2 to 3 months.
Atypia, atypical squamous cells of undetermined significance (ASCUS) ■ ASC-US (undetermined significance) ■ ASC-H (cannot exclude HSIL). ASC-H is intermediate between ASC-US and HSIL	Consider HPV testing: If high risk type (16, 18, 31, 33, or 35) – colposcopy. Alternative without HPV testing is follow-up. Follow-up PAP without colposcopy every 4 to 6 months x 2 years until three are negative; if second report of ASCUS, perform colposcopy.
Low-grade squamous intraepithelial lesion (LSIL)	Colposcopy ± biopsy or follow with PAP smear every 4 to 6 months, as above, with colposcopy and biopsy if repeat smears are abnormal.*
High-grade squamous intraepithelial lesion (HSIL) (carcinoma *in situ*)	Referral for colposcopy ± biopsy.
Invasive carcinoma	Colposcopy with biopsy or conization; treat with surgery or radiation.

* Most gynecologists recommend evaluation with any abnormality due to the high prevalence of underlying SIL.

ANAL PAP SMEAR FOR SIL AND CARCINOMA IN MSM

Anal cancer is similar to cervical cancer in many ways, including the facts that both are caused by HPV infection, several HPV types appear to be oncogenic, low-grade lesions often progress to high-grade lesions, and PAP smear appears to be an effective screening method (*Am J Med* 2000;108:674). The prevalence of HPV in MSM is 60% to 75% (*J Infect Dis* 1998;177:361), and the frequency of anal carcinoma is about 80 times that of the general population. Some authorities recommend anal PAP smears in MSM at 3-year intervals, which is comparable with cervical PAP smear with regard to cost-effectiveness (*Am J Med* 2000;108:634). Anal PAP shows sensitivity similar to cervical PAP but less accurately indicates grade of abnormality. Therefore, abnormal anal PAPs should lead to referral for anoscopy and biopsy.

Hepatitis A Serology

HAV susceptibility is determined using the total HAV antibody (anti-HAV IgG). The usual purpose is to identify candidates for HAV vaccine, including susceptible persons with chronic HCV infection, injection drug users, MSM, persons with clotting disorders, persons with chronic liver disease, and travelers to HAV-endemic areas (*MMWR* 1996;45[RR-15]:1). Some authorities believe that all HIV infected persons who are susceptible should be vaccinated for HAV. Susceptibility is defined by negative serologic tests for anti-HAV. The prevalence of anti-HAV is 62% in injection drug users and 32% in MSM (*Clin Infect Dis* 1997;25:726; *MMWR* 1999;48:[RR-12]:1). To diagnose acute hepatitis the preferred test is anti-HAV IgM. The anti-HAV IgG becomes positive at 8 to 16 weeks.

Hepatitis B Serology

Unvaccinated HIV-infected patients with negative HBV serology should be vaccinated. Patients with HBsAg should be evaluated for HbeAg and HBV DNA level to determine HBV replicative status and need for HBV therapy. HIV and its treatment has a poorly defined impact on the natural history of HBV-associated hepatitis (*J Acquir Immune Defic Syndr* 2000;24:211; *JAMA* 2000;283:74). It is also a preventable disease. The 2002 USPHS/IDSA Guidelines for the Prevention of Opportunistic Infections recommend screening for hepatitis B core antibody (anti-HBc) (*MMWR* 2002;51[RR-6]:63) with HBV vaccination of those who are susceptible. Antibody screening is advocated for high-risk populations to avoid the expense of unnecessary vaccination. HBV seroprevalence is 35% to 80% for MSM, 60% to 80% for injection drug users, 60% to 80% for hemophiliacs, 5% to 20% for heterosexuals with multiple partners, and 3% to 14% for the general population. The CDC recommends post-vaccination serology with anti-HBs in patients with HIV infection at 1 to 2 months after the third dose of vaccine to confirm an antibody response (*MMWR* 1999;48:33). Response is defined as HBsAb levels ≥10 IU/mL (*MMWR* 2001;50[RR-1]). Patients who fail to respond should be considered for revaccination using the standard 3 dose regimen (*Ann Intern Med* 1982;97:362; *MMWR* 2002;51[RR-6]:64). HIV infected patients with abnormal transaminases should be tested for chronic viral hepatitis using a combination of HBV surface antigen (HBsAg) and hepatitis C antibody (anti-HCV). There are occasional false-negative serologic tests for anti-HBc or anti-HCV among patients with low CD4 cell counts.

HCV Testing

(Management of Chronic Hepatitis C. Agency for Healthcare Research and Quality, NIH Consensus Report, Evidence Report 60, issued 8/27/02; http://concensus.nih.gov/cons/116cdc_intro.htm)

The seroprevalence of HCV is 1.8% in the general population, 4% to 6% in MSM, and 70% to 90% in injection drug users and hemophiliacs. The 2001 USPH/IDSA OI Guidelines recommend that all HIV infected persons be tested for HCV infection using the EIA screening assay for anti-HCV antibodies. The third generation EIAs have a sensitivity and specificity of >99% in immunocompetent patients, but there may be false-negatives with severe immunosuppression as with CD4 count <100 cells/mm^3 (*J Acquir Immune Defic Syndr* 2002;31:

154). The qualitative HCV RNA assay could help with suspected false-negatives. For patients with a positive EIA screening test, the qualitative HCV RNA assay is commonly recommended for confirmation but may be unnecessary with liver disease plus increased risk. Qualitative HCV RNA assays have a threshold of detection of 50-100 IU/mL. Quantitative HCV assays (bDNA or RNA PCR) are viral load assays that are used to measure response to therapy. Genotype assay identifies 6 genotypes and >90 subtypes. Genotype 1 accounts for 70% of HCV infected persons in the United States and is associated with a poor response to therapy compared with genotypes 2 and 3. Patients co-infected with HCV and HIV should be: 1) Advised not to drink alcohol, 2) Vaccinated for hepatitis A, if susceptible, and 3) Monitored for hepatoxicity if on ART. Patients should be evaluated for treatment with pegylated interferon based on the following criteria: 1) Liver biopsy showing portal or bridging fibrosis and at least moderate inflammation and necrosis, 2) HCV RNA levels >50 IU/mL, 3) Patient acceptance, 4) Lack of contraindications to interferon, and 5) Stable HIV.

Available data indicate that HCV-HIV co-infection causes more rapid progression of HCV (*J Infect Dis* 1999;179:1254; *Science* 1999;285:26; *Clin Infect Dis* 2000;31:154; *Clin Infect Dis* 2001;33:1579; *J Acquir Immune Defic Syndr* 2001;27:426; *Clin Infect Dis* 2001;33:562; *Clin Infect Dis* 2001;33:240; *Clin Infect Dis* 2001;32:1207; *J Infect Dis* 2001;183:1112). The effect of HCV infection on HIV rate of progression is controversial, but the largest analyses show no important effect (*JAMA* 2002;288:199).

Note: The authors recommend evaluation of patients for HCV, but the full evaluation, with quantitative HCV, genotype analysis, and liver biopsy, is an unnecessary expense in patients who are not candidates for therapy.

HOME KIT: The FDA has approved a home test kit for HCV. The consumer obtains blood by a lancet, and the blood is placed on a filter strip and submitted by mail to a reading center. Results are available in 10 days. The cost is about $70 per test.

■ TABLE 2-10: **Tests for HCV**

Test	Cost	Comment
Anti-HCV EIA	\$25 to \$45	Includes EIA and RIBA; indicates past or present HCV infection. Sensitivity ≥97%. EIA lacks specificity in low-prevalence populations – supplemental assay required for confirmation. RIBA – of little utility in HIV infected patients.
RIBA	\$75	
HCV RNA (HCV RT-PCR)	\$160 to \$200	RT-PCR technology to detect HCV RNA; may have false-positives and negatives. Threshold for detection is 50 IU/mL.
Quantitative HCV PCR or bDNA	\$160 to \$225	Determines concentration using RT-PCR or bDNA technology. Less sensitive than qualitative RT-PCR. Threshold of detection is 500 IU/mL; most patients with chronic HCV infection have 10^5 to 10^7 c/mL. HCV RNA level should be monitored during therapy. Magnitude of HCV RNA level may predict response to therapy but does not predict disease prognosis. It has largely supplanted qualitative HCV RNA tests due to adequate sensitivity and comparable cost.
Genotype	\$200 to \$250	6 genotypes – genotype 1 predominates in United States (70%) and shows poorest response to therapy.

Toxoplasmosis Serology

Toxoplasma serology (anti-*Toxoplasma* IgG) is recommended to assist in the differential diagnosis of complications involving the CNS, to identify candidates for toxoplasmosis prophylaxis (*Ann Intern Med* 1992;117:163), and to counsel patients on preventive measures if seronegative. The preferred method is an agglutination assay for IgG; IgM assays are not useful, and the Sabin-Feldman dye test is less accurate than the agglutination assay. Toxoplasmosis seroprevalence among adults in the United States is 10% to 30%, and the seroconversion rate is up to 1%/year. The sensitivity of the test is 95% to 97%. Most infections in AIDS patients represent relapse of latent infection, which is noted in 20% to 47% with CD4 counts <100 cells/mm^3, positive toxoplasmosis serology, and no prophylaxis (*Clin Infect Dis* 1992;15:211; *Clin Infect Dis* 2002;34:103).

A negative *Toxoplasma* serology should be repeated after the CD4 cell count is ≤100 cells/mm^3 if the patient does not take atovaquone or TMP-SMX phophylaxis for PCP (2002 USPHS/IDSA Guidelines for the Prevention of Opportunistic Infections, *MMWR* 2002;51:[RR-6]) or if the diagnosis toxoplasmosis encephalitis is being considered when prior tests were negative.

CMV Serology

This is advocated by the USPHS/IDSA Guidelines for HIV infected persons who have low risk for CMV infection, specifically those who are not MSM or injection drug users (*MMWR* 2002;51[RR-8]:17). This information has the following possible applications: 1) Identification of seronegative patients for counseling on CMV prevention (although the message is not different from the "safe sex message" for preventing HIV transmission); 2) Assessment of the likelihood of CMV disease in late-stage HIV infection; 3) Identification of seronegative individuals who should receive CMV-antibody-negative blood or leukocyte-reduced blood products for nonemergent transfusions (*JAMA* 2001;285:1592). Seroprevalence for adults in the United States is about 50%; in MSM and injection drug users it is >90% (*J Infect Dis* 1985;152:243; *Am J Med* 1987;82:593). It should be noted there are multiple methods to detect CMV, including pp65 antigen assays, CMV DNA PCR assays, NASBA early antigen assays, and culture of blood and urinary tests using culture and urinary CMV DNA PCR. None of these has proven consistently effective in predicting CMV disease (*J Clin Microbiol* 2000;38:563).

Glucose-6-Phosphate Dehydrogenase Levels (G6-PD)

G6-PD deficiency is a genetic disease that predisposes to hemolytic anemia following exposure to oxidant drugs commonly used in patients with HIV infection. Over 150 G6-PD variants are inherited on the X chromosome, but the most frequent are Gd^{A-}, which is found in 10% of black men and in 1% to 2% of black women, and Gd^{med}, found predominantly in men from the Mediterranean area (Italians, Greeks, Sephardic Jews, Arabs), India, and Southeast Asia. With most defects, the hemolysis is mild and self-limited because only the older red cells are involved, and the bone marrow can compensate even with continued administration of the implicated drug. The important exception is Gd^{med}, which may cause life-threatening hemolysis. The limited hemolysis in patients with Gd^{A-} may be significant in patients with HIV infection, who often have anemia from other causes. The severity of anemia also depends on the concentration of the drug in red cells and the oxidant potential of the inducing agent: The most likely offending agents are dapsone and primaquine. Sulfonamides cause hemolysis less commonly. G6-PD deficiency may be partial, in which case the contraindication for oxidant drugs is relative. Options for screening include: 1) Obtaining the test at baseline in all patients; 2) Restricting testing to those most likely to have a defect; and 3) Reserving testing for the occasional case of hemolytic anemia following exposure to typical inducing agents. Typical findings with this hemolysis include elevated bilirubin, elevated LDH, decreased haptoglobin, methemoglobinemia, reticulocytosis, and a peripheral smear showing the characteristic "bite cells." During hemolysis, G6-

PD levels are usually normal because the susceptible red cells are destroyed; testing must consequently be delayed until about 30 days after discontinuation of the offending agent. Some laboratories report results as units/g Hgb, with fewer than three indicating severe deficiency, in men and homozygous women; other labs report qualitative results.

Adverse Drug Reaction Monitoring

Adverse drug reactions attributed to antiretroviral agents include diabetes mellitus, blood lipid changes associated with risks for coronary artery disease and stroke, lactic acidosis/steatosis attributed to nucleoside analogs, and hepatic toxicity (see pp. 91-92 and Table 4-13, p. 63).

3 Disease Prevention: Prophylactic Antimicrobial Agents and Vaccines

Recommendations of the 2002 USPHS/IDSA Guidelines for the Prevention of Opportunistic Infections in Persons Infected with Human Immunodeficiency Virus (*MMWR* 2002;51[RR-8]:1)

■ TABLE 3-1: **Categories Reflecting Strength and Quality of Evidence**

Rating System for Strength of Recommendation and Quality of Evidence Supporting the Recommendation	
Category	**Definition**
Categories Reflecting the Strength of Each Recommendation	
A	Both strong evidence for efficacy and substantial clinical benefit support recommendation for use. Should always be offered.
B	Moderate evidence for efficacy, or strong evidence for efficacy, but only limited clinical benefit, supports recommendation for use. Should generally be offered.
C	Evidence for efficacy is insufficient to support a recommendation for or against use, or evidence for efficacy may not outweigh adverse consequences (eg, toxicity, drug interactions, or cost of the chemoprophylaxis or alternative approaches). Optional.
D	Moderate evidence for lack of efficacy or for adverse outcome supports a recommendation against use. Should generally not be offered.
E	Good evidence for lack of efficacy or for adverse outcome supports a recommendation against use. Should never be offered.
Categories Reflecting Quality of Evidence Supporting the Recommendation	
I	Evidence from at least one properly randomized, controlled trial
II	Evidence from at least one well-designed clinical trial without randomization, from cohort or case-controlled analytic studies (preferably from more than one center), or from multiple time-series studies or dramatic results from uncontrolled experiments.
III	Evidence from opinions of respected authorities based on clinical experience, descriptive studies, or reports of expert committees.

Strongly Recommended as Standard of Care

Pneumocystis carinii (P. jiroveci)

RISK: CD4 count <200 cells/mm³, prior PCP or HIV-associated thrush, or unexplained fever x 2 weeks (AII)

PREFERRED REGIMEN: TMP-SMX 1 DS/day or 1 SS/day (AI)

ALTERNATIVE REGIMENS

- TMP-SMX 1 DS 3x/week (BI)
- Dapsone 100 mg/day or 50 mg PO bid (BI)
- Dapsone 50 mg/day plus pyrimethamine 50 mg/week plus leukovorin 25 mg/week (BI)
- Dapsone 200 mg/week plus pyrimethamine 75 mg/week plus leukovorin 25 mg/week (BI)
- Aerosolized pentamidine 300 mg/month by *Respirgard II* nebulizer using 6 mL diluent delivered at 6L/min from a 50 psi compressed air source until reservoir is dry (usually 45 min), with or without albuterol (2 whiffs) to reduce cough and bronchospasm (BI)
- Atovaquone 1500 mg PO qd with meals (*N Engl J Med* 1998;339: 1889) (BI)

COMMENTS: The risk of PCP without prophylaxis is 60% to 70% per year in those with prior PCP and 40% to 50% per year for those with a CD4 count <100 cells/mm³. The mortality for patients hospitalized with PCP is 15% to 20%. PCP prophylaxis reduces the risk of PCP 9-fold, and patients who get PCP despite prophylaxis have a low mortality rate (*Am J Respir Crit Care Med* 1997;155:60). The major reasons for PCP prophylaxis failure are CD4 count <50 cells/mm³ and non-compliance (*JAMA* 1995;273:1197; *Arch Intern Med* 1996;156: 177). TMP-SMX has established efficacy for reducing the incidence of bacterial infections and toxoplasmosis. This drug is active against *Nocardia*, *Legionella*, most *Salmonella*, most methicillin-sensitive *S. aureus*, many gram-negative bacilli, most *H. influenzae*, and about 70% of *S. pneumoniae*. No other PCP prophylaxis regimen has this spectrum of activity. Adverse reactions sufficiently severe to require discontinuation of the drug are noted in 25% to 50% with TMP-SMX, 25% to 40% with dapsone, and 2% to 4% with aerosolized pentamidine (*N Engl J Med* 1995:332:693). Patients who have a non-life-threatening reaction to TMP-SMX should continue this drug if it can be tolerated. Those who have had such a reaction in the past should be rechallenged, possibly using desensitization (see pp. 318-319). Gradual initiation of TMP-SMX prophylaxis reduces the rate of rash and/or fever by about 50% (*J Acquir Immune Defic Syndr* 2000;24:337) (see pp. 316-317 for regimen). This suggests that most reactions are not allergic or IgE mediated. Patients given dapsone should be tested for G6-PD deficiency if at risk. Data are inadequate to establish the efficacy and safety of parenteral pentamidine (4 mg/kg/month), or clindamycin-primaquine. Fansidar is rarely used due to possible severe hypersensitivity reactions.

IMMUNE RECONSTITUTION: Patients who have increases in CD4 count to >200 cells/mm³ x ≥3 months may safely discontinue primary PCP prophylaxis (AI) (*N Engl J Med* 1999;340:1301; *Lancet* 1999;353:1293; *Lancet* 1999;353:201; *J Infect Dis* 2000;181:1635) and secondary prophylaxis (BII) (*N Engl J Med* 2001;344:159; *N Engl J Med* 2001;344:168). Prophylaxis should be restarted when the CD4 count falls to <200 cells/mm³ (AIII). A meta-analysis of 14 controlled trials involving discontinuation of PCP prophylaxis found (*Clin Infect Dis* 2001;33:1901) no difference in risk for PCP between those who continued prophylaxis and those who discontinued for a CD4 count >200 cells/mm³. The rates were 19.1 vs 18.2 PCP episodes per 100 patient-years for primary prophylaxis and 43.5 vs 41.9 PCP cases per 1000 patient-years for secondary prophylaxis. The rate of adverse reactions was 34.5 vs 8.6 cases per 1000 patient-years favoring discontinuation.

CONTACT: Some authorities recommend avoidance of "high-intensity exposure," meaning that a patient with PCP should not room with a vulnerable patient (*N Engl J Med* 2000;342:1416; *Am J Respir Crit Care Med* 2000;162:167). Recent reports do not support this recommendation (*JAMA* 2001;286:2450).

M. tuberculosis

RISK (*MMWR* 1998;47:[RR-20]): Positive PPD (≥5 mm induration) without prior prophylaxis or treatment (AI), recent TB contact (AII), or history of inadequately treated TB that healed (AII) (*MMWR* 2000;49[RR-6]). The rate of active TB in those with a positive PPD is magnified 7- to 80-fold by HIV co-infection (*Lancet* 2000;356:470; *MMWR* 2000;49[RR-6]). It also appears that active TB accelerates the rate of HIV progression (*J Acquir Immune Defic Syndr* 1998;19:361; *BMJ* 1995;311:1468). HIV-positive persons who are close contacts of active TB cases should be evaluated to exclude active disease and should receive treatment for latent TB infection regardless of PPD results.

PREFERRED REGIMEN FOR COMPLIANT PATIENT LIKELY TO COMPLETE 9-MONTH COURSE (*MMWR* 2000;49[RR-6]; *MMWR* 2001;50:773)

- INH 300 mg + pyridoxine 50 mg PO qd x 9 months (AII); or
- NH 900 mg + pyridoxine 100 mg PO 2x/week x 9 months (BII).

PREFERRED REGIMEN FOR PATIENT UNLIKELY TO COMPLETE 9-MONTH INH COURSE WITHOUT CONCURRENT PI OR NNRTI

- Rifampin 600 mg qd + PZA 15-20 mg/kg qd x 2 months (AI) (see monitoring advocated for the PZA + rifampin/rifabutin regimens, p. 42)

- **Alternative regimen:** Rifampin 600 mg/day x 4 months (BII). There is no experience in HIV infected patients, and there is concern for rifampin resistance.

PREFERRED REGIMEN FOR PATIENT UNLIKELY TO COMPLETE 9-MONTH INH COURSE WITH CONCURRENT PI OR NNRTI

- Rifabutin (see rifabutin dose below) + PZA 15-20 mg/kg qd x 2 months (AI) (see monitoring advocated for the PZA + rifampin/ rifabutin regimens, p. 43)
- Rifampin in standard dose may be used with EFV-based HAART or SQV/RTV (400/400 or 1000/100 mg bid)-based HAART. Rifabutin in place of Rifampin (CIII) using the dose adjustments below.

  Dose regimens for rifabutin and the concurrent PI or NNRTI:*
  - APV 1200 mg bid; rifabutin 150 mg/day or 300 mg 3x/week
  - EFV standard; rifabutin 450-600 mg/day 2-3x/week
  - IDV 1000 mg q8h; rifabutin 150 mg/day or 300 mg 3x/week
  - NFV 1000 mg tid or 1250 mg bid; rifabutin 150 mg/day or 300 mg 3x/week
  - RTV standard dose; rifabutin 150 mg 2-3x/week 8
  - RTV + SQV 400/400 mg bid; rifabutin 150 mg 3x/week
  - LPV/r standard dose; rifabutin 150 mg 3x/week
  - NVP 200 mg bid; rifabutin 300 mg/day

*Note: Rifabutin should not be combined with DLV, and dose schedules are not available for SQV (*Fortovase*). Rifampin or rifabutin should be combined with PZA 20 mg/kg/day with >60 doses x 2 months or up to 3 months with interruptions (BIII).

CONTACT WITH INH-RESISTANT STRAIN: Rifampin plus PZA x 2 months (above doses) (AI). Alternative: Rifampin/PZA (above doses x 2 months) (BIII); rifabutin 300 mg/day PO x 4 months (CIII). See rifamycin adjustments summarized above if patient is receiving a PI or NNRTI.

CONTACT WITH STRAIN RESISTANT TO INH AND A RIFAMYCIN: Use two agents with anticipated activity – ethambutol (EMB)/PZA or levofloxacin/PZA. Levofloxacin dose – 500 mg bid (*Arch Chest Dis* 2002;57:39); moxifloxacin also has good activity (*Antimicrob Agents Chemother* 1999;43:85).

PREGNANCY: INH regimens

MONITORING (Rifampin/rifabutin + PZA short-course recipients): Recipients of PZA + rifampin/rifabutin: There have been 40 cases of severe hepatotoxicity, including 7 deaths reported with the PZA + rifampin 2-month regimen (*MMWR* 2001;50:733; *MMWR* 2002;51:998; *Am Rev Respir Crit Care Med* 2001;164:1319). None of these patients was known to have HIV infection or concurrent active viral hepatitis; 3 had prior INH-associated hepatotoxicity. This regimen is still preferred for HIV infected patients who are considered unlikely to complete the 9-month INH regimen, providing there is no prior INH associated hepatotoxicity. The rationale is based in part on the high risk of active TB with HIV co-infection and good tolerability of this regimen in HIV infected persons. Monitoring should include patient visits at 0, 2, 4, 6, and 8 weeks with bilirubin + ALT measurements at 0, 2, 4, and 6 weeks. Prophylaxis should be discontinued with ALT elevations of 5x ULN in asymptomatic patients and with any elevation of ALT when accompanied by hepatitis symptoms (*MMWR* 2002;51:998). Cases of severe liver injury with this regimen should be reported to the CDC: 404-639-8116.

MONITORING (Recipients of INH): Clinical monitoring at monthly intervals. Bilirubin ALT, AST, and CBC measurements at baseline, 3 months, and prn. Patient should report any symptoms of hepatitis – jaundice, dark urine, nausea, vomiting, abdominal pain, and/or fever >3 days. INH should be discontinued with ALT elevation to >5x ULN without symptoms or ALT >3x ULN with symptoms.

Toxoplasma gondii

RISK: CD4 count <100 cells/mm³ plus positive IgG serology for *T. gondii*

PREFERRED: TMP-SMX 1 DS/day (AII)

ALTERNATIVES

- TMP-SMX 1 SS/day (BIII)
- Dapsone 50 mg/day PO + pyrimethamine 50 mg/week + leukovorin 25 mg/week (BI)
- Dapsone 200 mg/week PO + pyrimethamine 75 mg/week PO + leukovorin 25 mg/week PO
- Atovaquone 1500 mg/day ± pyrimethamine 25 mg/day + leukovorin 10 mg/day (CIII)

IMMUNE RECONSTITUTION: Studies confirm the safety of discontinuing primary and secondary prophylaxis for toxoplasmosis (*Lancet* 2000;355:2217; *J Infect Dis* 2000;181:1635; *AIDS* 1999;13:1647; *AIDS* 2000;14:383; *Ann Intern Med* 2002;137:239).

- **Primary prophylaxis:** Discontinue prophylaxis with CD4 count >200 cells/mm³ for >3 months (AI); restart when CD4 count is <100-200 cells/mm³ (AIII).
- **Maintenance therapy:** Discontinue prophylaxis with CD4 count >200 cells/mm³ for ≥6 months providing initial therapy has been completed and the patient is asymptomatic for toxoplasmosis (CIII); restart prophylaxis when CD4 count is <200 cells/mm³ (AIII).

M. avium complex

RISK: CD4 count <50 cells/mm³. Note: Physician compliance with MAC prophylaxis recommendations is only about 50%, compared with 80% for PCP prophylaxis (*N Engl J Med* 2000;342:1416).

PREFERRED: Clarithromycin 500 mg PO bid (AI) or azithromycin 1200 mg PO weekly (AI).

ALTERNATIVE: Rifabutin 300 mg/day PO (BI) or azithromycin 1200 mg/week plus rifabutin 300 mg/day (CI) (see rifabutin dose adjustment for use with PIs or NNRTIs, p. 42). Use caution when rifabutin is combined with clarithromycin due to drug interactions resulting in reduced levels of clarithomycin (*J Infect Dis* 2000;181:1289).

IMMUNE RECONSTITUTION: It is safe to discontinue primary and secondary MAC prophylaxis with immune reconstitution (CII) (*N Engl J Med* 1998;338:853; *N Engl J Med* 2000;342:1085; *Ann Intern Med* 2000;133:493; *J Infect Dis* 1998;178:1446).

- **Primary prophylaxis:** Discontinue prophylaxis with CD4 count >100 cells/mm³ for >3 months (AI); restart when CD4 count is <100 cells/mm³ (AIII).
- **Maintenance therapy:** Discontinue when CD4 cell count is >100 cells/mm³ for >6 months, 12 months of therapy have been completed, and the patient is asymptomatic for MAC (CIII). Restart when CD4 count is <100 cells/mm³ (AIII).

Varicella

RISK (PRIMARY INFECTION): Significant exposure to chickenpox or shingles in individuals who are either seronegative for VZV or have no history of primary or secondary VZV.

PREFERRED: VZIG 5 vials (6.25 mL) IM within 96 hours of exposure, preferably within 48 hours (AIII).

ALTERNATIVE: Prophylactic acyclovir was included in the 1995 USPHS/IDSA Guidelines, but was deleted from the 1999 version due to lack of supporting clinical evidence of efficacy.

Generally Recommended as Standard of Care

S. pneumoniae

RISK: All patients with HIV infection. Risk for invasive pneumococcal infection is 50- to 100-fold greater than in the general population (*Ann Intern Med* 2000;132:182; *J Infect Dis* 1996;173:857; *J Acquir Immune Defic Syndr* 2001;27:35; *AM J Respir Crit Care Med* 2000;162:2063).

PREFERRED: *Pneumovax* 0.5 mL IM x 1 (CD4 count >200 cells/mm³ – BII; CD4 count <200 cells/mm³ – CIII).

REVACCINATE: When CD4 count increases to >200 cells/mm³ if initial immunization was given with CD4 count <200 cells/mm³ (CIII) (*MMWR* 1999;[RR-10]:16). Revaccination is recommended at 3- to 5-year intervals (*N Engl J Med* 2000;342:1416), but see "Note" below.

ALTERNATIVE: The 7 valent protein-conjugated pneumococcal vaccine approved by the FDA in March 2000 is recommended only for children, but studies in adults are ongoing because this may be a superior immunogen in immunosuppressed patients.

NOTE: Studies of pneumococcal vaccine in HIV infected persons have shown variable results. A CDC report indicated 49% efficacy (*Arch Intern Med* 2000;160:2633). Others show poor efficacy in immunosuppressed hosts (*N Engl J Med* 1986;315:1318; *JAMA* 1993;270: 1826), and a study in Uganda showed increased rates of pneumococcal disease in vaccine recipients (*Lancet* 2000;355:2106). Some authorities think this result may be idiosyncratic to the location of the study. Based on the controversial data regarding efficacy, the OI Guidelines Panel has deleted *Pneumovax* as a recommended performance indicator (*Clin Infect Dis* 2000;30:51). A review of available data found no evidence of efficacy in the target population (*BMJ* 2002;325:292).

Hepatitis B

RISK: Negative anti-HBc or anti-HBs screening test.

PREFERRED: *Recombivax HB* 10 ug IM x 3 (BII) or *Engerix-B* 20 μg IM x 3 (BII).

Influenza

RISK: All patients annually.

PREFERRED: Influenza vaccine 0.5 mL IM each year, preferably October to November (BIII).

ALTERNATIVE: The OI Panel recommends amantadine 100 mg PO bid (CIII) or rimantadine 100 mg PO bid (CIII). Zanamivir (*Relenza*, 10 mg inhaled/day) and oseltamivir (*Tamiflu*, 75 mg/day) are also active for prophylaxis for both influenza A and B but are far more expensive. Oseltamivir, rimantadine, and amantadine are FDA-approved for prophylaxis. The AWP price/month for standard doses is $31/month for amantadine, $174/month for rimantadine, and $266/month for oseltamivir (*Med Letter* 2002;44:75).

Hepatitis A

RISK: 1) MSM, 2) illegal drug users (injection and non-injection), and 3) persons with chronic liver disease, including chronic HBV and HCV (*MMWR* 2002;51[RR-6]:61). Susceptibility is defined by negative anti-HAV which is present in 33% of American adults. Consider for all susceptible patients as defined by negative HAV serology (total anti-HAV antibody).

PREFERRED: HAV vaccine 0.5 mL IM x 2 separated by 6 months (BIII).

Not Recommended for Most Patients; Consider for Selected Patients

Cryptococcosis

RISK: CD4 count <50 cells/mm^3.

PREFERRED: Fluconazole 100-200 mg/day PO (CI).

ALTERNATIVE: Itraconazole 200 mg/day PO (CIII).

IMMUNE RECONSTITUTION: Discontinue secondary prophylaxis when CD4 count is >100-200 cells/mm^3 for $\geq$6 months, initial therapy completed, and asymptomatic for cryptococcosis (CIII); restart secondary prophylaxis when CD4 count is <100-200 cells/mm^3 (AIII). The largest study of the safety of discontinuing secondary prophylaxis with immune reconstitution showed no relapses in 39 patients followed an average of 2 years (*Ann Intern Med* 2002;137:239).

Histoplasmosis

RISK: CD4 count <100 cells/mm^3 plus residence in endemic area.

PREFERRED: Itraconazole 200 mg/day PO (CI).

IMMUNE RECONSTITUTION: No criteria for discontinuing secondary prophylaxis.

Coccidioidomycosis

RISK: CD4 count <200 cells/mm^3 (*J Infect Dis* 2000;181:1428). The frequency in the endemic area is about 4% per year in AIDS patients, 0.2% per year for HIV without AIDS, and 0.015% per year in the general population (*J Infect Dis* 2000;181:1428).

PREFERRED: Fluconazole 400 mg/day PO or itraconazole 200 mg bid PO (secondary prophylaxis).

IMMUNE RECONSTITUTION: No criteria for discontinuing secondary prophylaxis.

Cytomegalovirus (CMV)

RISK: CD4 count <50 cells/mm^3 plus positive CMV serology.

PREFERRED: Oral ganciclovir 1 g PO tid (CI).

IMMUNE RECONSTITUTION: It is safe to discontinue maintenance therapy when the CD4 count is >100-150 cells/mm^3 for >3 to 6 months providing there is no evidence of active disease, and there will be regular ophthalmic exams (BII). Secondary prophylaxis should be restarted when the CD4 count is <100-150 cells/mm^3 (AIII) (*J Infect Dis* 1998;177:1182; *J Infect Dis* 1998;177;1080; *Ophthalmology* 1998;105:1259; *JAMA* 1999;282:1633; *AIDS* 1999;13:647; *AIDS* 2001; 15:23; *JAMA* 2000;283;653). Nevertheless, there are isolated cases of relapses even with CD4 counts >400 cells/mm^3. These changes appear to be due to pathogen-specific immune defense (*N Engl J Med* 2000;342:1416; *J Infect Dis* 2001;18:1285). The largest study showed two relapses following discontinuation of secondary prophylaxis in 162 patients (*Ann Intern Med* 2002;137:239).

4 | Antiretroviral Therapy

Recommendations for Therapy

Based on the recommendations of the DHHS/Kaiser Family Foundation as of December 2002: DHHS Panel on Clinical Practices for Treatment of HIV Infection Guidelines for Use of Antiretroviral Agents in HIV Infected Adults and Adolescents (*MMWR* 2002;51[RR-7]; *Ann Intern Med* 2002;137:381; updated version: http://www.aidsinfo.nih.gov and International AIDS Society-USA (*JAMA* 2002;288:222). In general, recommendations given here reflect these guidelines except in areas not covered, areas that needed updating, and authors' opinion (which are noted). WHO guidelines intended for resource-limited areas are also provided (*Scaling Up Antiretroviral Therapy in Resource Limited Settings*, WHO, 2002).

Goals of Therapy

CLINICAL GOALS: Prolongation of life and improvement in quality of life.

VIROLOGIC GOALS: Greatest possible reduction in viral load (preferably to <20-50 c/mL) for as long as possible to

- Halt disease progression.
- Prevent or delay resistance.

Note that CD4 response is often good with partial viral suppression, and opportunistic infections are uncommon with viral loads <5000 c/mL (*J Infect Dis* 2000;181:946; *J Acquir Immune Defic Syndr* 2002;30:154). However, partially suppressive regimens are less durable and lead to the emergence of drug-resistant virus.

IMMUNOLOGIC GOALS: Immune reconstitution that is both quantitative (CD4 cell count in normal range) and qualitative (pathogen-specific immune response).

THERAPEUTIC GOALS: Rational sequencing of drugs in a fashion that achieves clinical, virologic, and immunologic goals while

- Maintaining therapeutic options.
- Minimizing side effects and drug toxicity.
- Maximizing adherence.

EPIDEMIOLOGIC GOALS: Reduce HIV transmission

Indications for Therapy (see Tables 4-3 and 4-4)

Recommendations are based on CD4 cell count, symptoms, and viral load. It is assumed that the patient is ready and willing to start therapy and understands the critical importance of adherence.

The CD4 count is the most important indicator for initiating treatment according to guidelines, and all agree that treatment is indicated for all patients with a CD4 count <200 cells/mm³. Whether to initiate therapy in the CD4 stratum between 200-350 cells/mm³ is more controversial. Some studies show no clear benefit with initiation at this stage (*JAMA* 2001;286:2560; *JAMA* 2001;286:2568), and others demonstrate only modest benefit, which must be interpreted in the context of the risk: benefit ratio (*Lancet* 2002;360:119). The role of the viral load is controversial: Prior studies in untreated patients indicated that viral load predicts progression independent of the CD4 count. The rate of progression to an AIDS-defining complication within three years was 5% in patients with a CD4 count of 200-350 cells/mm³ and a viral load <20,000 c/mL but was 40% in patients with a CD4 count >350 cells/mm³ and a viral load >55,000 c/mL (see Table 4-1, p. 51). Nevertheless, a meta-analysis assessing response to HAART in 13 cohorts found that the most important predictor of progression was the CD4 cell count at baseline (*Lancet* 2002;360:119). The data on baseline CD4 count and viral load are summarized in Table 4-1 and 4-2; two sets of guidelines based on these and other observations are summarized in Table 4-3 (DHHS), and Table 4-4 (IAS-USA).

■ TABLE 4-1: **Probability of Developing an AIDS-Defining OI Within 3 Years in the Absence of ART, Based on Baseline CD4 Count and Viral Load. Data from Multicenter AIDS Cohort Study (MACS) (*Ann Intern Med* 1997;126:946; updated June, 2002 per A. Munoz)**

VL (RT-PCR)* c/mL	% AIDS-Defining Complication			
CD4 <200 cells/mm³	**N**	**3 yrs.**	**6 yrs.**	**9 yrs.**
7,000-20,000	7	14	29	64
20,000-55,000	20	50	75	90
>55,000	70	84	98	100
CD4 201-350 cells/mm³	**N**	**3 yrs.**	**6 yrs.**	**9 yrs.**
1,500-7,000	27	0	20	37
7,000-20,000	44	7	44	66
20,000-55,000	53	36	72	85
>55,000	104	64	89	93
CD4 >350 cells/mm³	**N**	**3 yrs.**	**6 yrs.**	**9 yrs.**
<1,500	119	2	6	13
1,500-7,000	227	2	16	30
7,000-20,000	342	7	30	54
20,000-55,000	323	15	51	74
>55,000	262	40	72	85

* Plasma HIV RNA levels in c/mL using RT-PCR.

■ TABLE 4-2: **Prognosis in HAART Recipients: Meta-analysis of 12 Cohort Studies With 12,574 Adult Patients (*Lancet* 2002;360:119)**

Baseline (Pretreatment)	Probability of AIDS or Death*
CD4 Cell Count	
<50/mm³	420/1917 (22%)
50-99/mm³	195/1219 (16%)
100-199/mm³	215/2088 (10%)
200-349/mm³	144/3217 (4%)
>350/mm³	120/4133 (3%)
Viral Load	
<1000 c/mL	41/998 (4%)
1,000-9,999 c/mL	80/1333 (6%)
10,000-99,999 c/mL	272/4702 (6%)
>100,000 c/mL	701/5541 (13%)

*AIDS = AIDS defining event. Median follow-up – 2.3 years.

When to Start Antiretroviral Therapy

DHHS GUIDELINES: These recommendations are more conservative than prior DHHS guidelines based on the following observations:

- HIV cannot be cured with currently available antiretroviral agents.
- Therapeutic trials have not been performed that determine efficacy of antiretroviral therapy in patients with CD4 counts >200 cells/mm³.
- Retrospective analyses of several large cohorts indicate that a CD4 threshold of 200-350 cells/mm³ is a rational threshold because all experts agree with the 200 cells/mm³ threshold (*JAMA* 2001; 286:2560; *JAMA* 2001;286:2568), and some studies support the 350 cells/mm³ threshold (*AIDS* 2001;15:983; *JAMA* 2000;284:3128; *Arch Intern Med* 2000;160:1323; *Lancet* 2002;360:119).
- Antiretroviral therapy is associated with substantial toxicity and adherence problems (*Lancet* 2000;355:2147; *Ann Intern Med* 2000;132:306).
- These recommendations generally define a group at about 15% risk for an AIDS-defining diagnosis within 3 years, except for those with a CD4 count of 200-350 cells/mm³ and a viral load <20,000 c/mL, who have a lower risk.

■ TABLE 4-3: **Indications to Initiate Antiretroviral Therapy – DHHS Guidelines, August 2002 (http://www.aidsinfo.nih.gov)**

Clinical Category	CD4 Cell Count	Plasma HIV RNA	Recommendation
Symptomatic (AIDS or severe symptoms)	Any value	Any value	Treat
Asymptomatic AIDS	<200 cells/mm³	Any value	Treat
Asymptomatic	200 to 350 cells/mm³	Any value	Treatment should usually be offered; controversy exists for patients with viral load <20,000 c/mL due to low probability of AIDS-defining diagnosis within 3 years.
Asymptomatic	>350 cells/mm³	>55,000 c/mL (bDNA or RT-PCR)	Some experts would trea because viral load above this threshold predicts a 3-year risk of AIDS of ≥30% despite high baseline CD4 cell count. Some would defer therapy and monitor CD4 cell count more frequently.

WHO GUIDELINES (http://www.who.int/hiv/topics/arv/ISBN9241545674.pdf)

Indications for initiating antiretroviral therapy are divided into two categories, depending on whether CD4 cell counts are available or not. The total lymphocyte count (TLC) can be used as a substitute for the CD4 count, although it is considered "less useful in asymptomatic patients." The threshold for initiation of therapy using the CD4 count is 200 cells/mm³. When the TLC is used, treatment is recommended at a TLC of 1000-1200 cells/mm³ in a symptomatic patient.

- **CD4 count available**
  - WHO stage IV* (AIDS-defining diagnosis)
  - WHO stage I-III* plus CD4 <200 cells/mm³
- **CD4 count not available**
  - WHO stage IV*
  - WHO stage II* or III* plus TLC <1000-1200 cells/mm³ (includes thrush and recurrent invasive bacterial infections; does not include asymptomatic patient regardless of TLC).

*Clinical stages

- Clinical stage I: Asymptomatic or PGL, and/or normal activity
- Clinical stage II: Weight loss <10%, minor mucocutaneous conditions, zoster <5 years, recurrent URIs, and/or symptomatic plus normal activity
- Clinical stage III: Weight loss >10%, unexplained diarrhea >1 month, unexplained fever >1 month, thrush, oral hairy leukoplakia, pulmonary TB in past year, or severe bacterial infection, and/or bed-ridden <50% of days in the past month
- Clinical stage IV: CDC-defined AIDS and/or bed-ridden >50% of days in the past month

IAS-USA GUIDELINES

■ TABLE 4-4: **When to Start Antiretroviral Therapy: IAS-USA Guidelines (*JAMA* 2000;288:222)**

Status	Recommendations
Symptomatic HIV	Treatment recommended
Asymptomatic with CD4 <200 cells/mm³	Treatment recommended
Asymptomatic with CD4 >200 cells/mm³	Treatment individualized based on: ■ CD4 count (some use 350 cells/mm³) ■ CD4 rate of decline >100/mm³/year ■ HIV viral load >50,000 – 100,000 c/mL ■ Risk of toxicity and drug-drug interactions

The Initial Regimen

REGIMEN SELECTION: Preferred regimens for initial therapy are summarized according to guidelines for DHHS (Table 4-5), IAS-USA (Table 4-6), WHO (Table 4-7), and the authors' choice (Table 4-8). Recommendations for special patient populations are provided as follows: Pregnancy: p. 96, Tuberculosis: p. 146, Methadone recipients Table 4-8, p. 55. Resource-limited settings (WHO Guidelines, Table 4-7 p. 55).

■ TABLE 4-5: **Initial Regimen: DHHS Guidelines (February, 2003)**

One from column A and one from column B in the preferred category		
	Column A	**Column B**
Preferred	EFV IDV NFV RTV/SQV RTV/IDV LPV/r	d4T/3TC AZT/ddI AZT/3TC d4T/ddI* ddI/3TC
Alternative	ABC APV DLV NVP RTV SQV *(Fortovase)* NFV/SQV *(Fortovase)*	AZT/ddC
No recommendation (insufficient data)	Hydroxyurea RTV/APV RTV/NFV	3TC/ABC† 3TC/TDF†
Not recommended	SQV *(Invirase)*	ddC/ddI ddC/d4T ddC/3TC AZT/d4T

* The combination ddI/d4T should be avoided in pregnant women due to the risks for lactic acidosis and hepatotoxicity.

† Recent data support use as a preferred combination (authors).

■ TABLE 4-6: **Initial Regimen: IAS-USA (*JAMA* 2002;288:222)**

Preferred:
■ 2 nucleosides + 1 PI ± low dose RTV ■ 2 nucleosides + 1 NNRTI ■ 3 nucleosides
Under some circumstances:
■ 1 PI (± low dose RTV) + NNRTI ± 1-2 NRTI

■ TABLE 4-7: **Initial Regimen for Resource Poor Settings: WHO Guidelines (April, 2002)**

NNRTI (PI sparing)	Triple NRTI Regimen (PI + NNRTI sparing)	PI Regimen (NNRTI sparing)
■ Pregnancy or potential for pregnancy: AZT + 3TC* + NVP ■ No pregnancy issues: AZT + 3TC* + either NVP or EFV	AZT + 3TC + ABC	AZT + 3TC* + ■ IDV/RTV 800/100 mg bid ■ LPV/r 400/100 mg bid ■ SQV/RTV 1000/100 mg bid ■ NFV 1250 mg bid

* Other appropriate dual nucleosides are d4T/3TC, d4T/ddI + AZT/ddI.

Preferred	■ NNRTI-based HAART: EFV plus AZT/3TC, d4T/3TC, or TDF/3TC ■ PI-based HAART: LPV/r plus AZT/3TC, d4T/3TC, or TDF/3TC ■ NRTI-based HAART: AZT/3TC/ABC or AZT/3TC/ABC/TDF
Alternatives	■ NNRTI-based HAART: NVP plus 2 NRTIs ■ PI-based HAART: IDV/RTV (800/100 bid or 400/400 bid) plus 2 NRTIs*, APV/RTV (1200/200 qd or 600/200 bid) plus 2 NRTIs*, SQV/RTV (*Fortovase* or *Invirase*) 1000/100 bid or 400/400 bid† plus 2 NRTIs*, NFV plus 2 NRTIs*
Special settings	■ Baseline viral load: >100,000 c/mL: EFV or LPV/r-based HAART ■ Pregnancy: Include AZT if tolerated, avoid EFV and ddI/d4T ■ Pregnancy potential: Avoid EFV ■ Methadone: Avoid EFV and NVP or increase methadone dose; may need increase in ddI dose ■ Tuberculosis (latent): Use INH, avoid rifampin – pyrazinamide regimen unless EFV or NRTI-based HAART ■ Tuberculosis treatment (active): EFV, SQV/RTV, or NRTI-based HAART ■ Once daily therapy: TDF/3TC/EFV or ddI/3TC/EFV; also consider ABC or NVP, although neither is FDA-approved for once daily dosing ■ NRTI-sparing: SQV/RTV, IDV/EFV ± SQV, LPV/r/EFV, LPV/r/SQV
Generally avoided	■ ddC ■ d4T/ddI, d4T/AZT ■ *Invirase* without RTV ■ DLV ■ Hydroxyurea

* Nucleoside pairs: AZT/3TC, TDF/3TC, ABC/3TC, d4T/3TC, ddI/3TC. May also consider use of AZT/3TC/ABC in combination with fourth agent, especially in patients with high viral loads.

† *Invirase*/RTV 1000/100 bid is preferred.

■ TABLE 4-9: **Advantages and Disadvantages of Antiretroviral Agents and Combinations**

Agents	Advantages	Disadvantages
2 NRTIs + 1 PI		
Amprenavir	■ Minimal food effect ■ Preserves NNRTI options	■ Less extensive experience ■ High pill burden ■ Large capsule size ■ High incidence of rash ■ Nausea ■ Cross-resistance with LPV/r (I50V) ■ PI class toxicity
Indinavir	■ Long term experience documenting sustained benefit ■ Clinical outcome data ■ Preserves NNRTI options	■ Food restrictions ■ Fluid requirement ■ q8h dosing ■ Nephrolithiasis ■ Skin/hair effects ■ Decreased efficacy with viral load >100,000 c/mL ■ PI cross-resistance ■ PI class toxicity
Nelfinavir	■ Generally well tolerated ■ Extensive experience ■ No PI cross-resistance with D30N ■ Extensive experience establishing safety in pregnancy ■ Preserves NNRTI options	■ Diarrhea ■ High pill burden (until 625 mg form available) ■ Possible reduced potency compared with other PIs ■ Decreased efficacy with viral load >100,000 c/mL ■ Food effect (absorption improved with high fat meal) ■ PI cross-resistance with L90M ■ PI class toxicity
Saquinavir (*Fortovase*)	■ Preserves NNRTI options	■ High pill burden ■ Poor GI tolerability ■ Food effect ■ PI cross-resistance ■ PI class toxicity
Ritonavir	■ No food effect ■ Preserves NNRTI options	■ Extensive drug interactions ■ Poor GI tolerability ■ High pill burden ■ ↑ hyperlipidemia ■ ↑ hepatotoxicity ■ PI cross-resistance ■ PI class toxicity

■ TABLE 4-9: **Advantages and Disadvantages of Antiretroviral Agents and Combinations *(Continued)***

Agents	Advantages	Disadvantages
2 NRTIs + RTV-boosted PI		
Saquinavir	■ Extensive experience ■ May use with rifampin ■ No food effect ■ qd regimen available (not FDA-approved) ■ Preserves NNRTI options	■ High pill burden ■ GI side effects (decreased with *Invirase* form) ■ PI class toxicity
Nelfinavir	■ Preserves NNRTI options	■ Minimal pharmacologic advantage ■ Limited data ■ Increased GI side effects ■ PI class toxicity
Amprenavir	■ qd regimen available (FDA-approved) ■ No food effect ■ Preserves NNRTI options	■ Large capsule size ■ Rash ■ Nausea ■ PI class toxicity
Indinavir	■ No food effect ■ bid regimen ■ Preserves NNRTI options	■ 400/400 dose: Poor GI tolerability ■ 800/100 dose: ↑ nephrolithiasis ■ Fluid requirements ■ PI class toxicity
Lopinavir	■ Co-formulation ■ High potency documented ■ Equal potency with viral load >100,000 c/mL ■ No PI resistance with initial failure ■ Preserves NNRTI options	■ Nausea, diarrhea ■ Food effect ■ PI class toxicity
2 NRTI + NNRTI		
Efavirenz	■ High potency documented ■ Equal potency with viral load >100,000 c/mL ■ qd dosing ■ One capsule per day ■ No food effect ■ Preserves PI options	■ Neuropsychiatric toxicity ■ Rash ■ Contraindicated in pregnancy and with pregnancy potential ■ Single mutation confers class resistance ■ Methadone interaction ■ Reduces PI levels
Nevirapine	■ Generally well tolerated in pregnancy. ■ Low pill burden ■ Preserves PI options ■ qd dosing possible (not FDA-approved)	■ Hepatotoxicity including lethal hepatic necrosis ■ High rate of rash including life-threatening hypersensitivity ■ Single mutation confers class resistance ■ Methadone interaction

continued on next page

■ TABLE 4-9: **Advantages and Disadvantages of Antiretroviral Agents and Combinations *(Continued)***

Agents	Advantages	Disadvantages
	■ Minimal lipid changes	■ Reduces PI levels ■ May be less potent than EFV ■ May be less potent with high baseline viral loads
Delavirdine	■ Increases PI levels ■ Preserves PI options	■ Minimal efficacy data ■ tid dosing ■ Rash ■ Single mutation confers class resistance
3 NRTIs		
AZT/3TC/ABC	■ Extensive experience ■ Low pill burden ■ Preserves PI and NNRTI options ■ Co-formulated	■ Reduced potency with viral loads >100,000 c/mL ■ ABC hypersensitivity reactions ■ AZT effects (see AZT/3TC) 2 NRTIs
2 NRTIs (as component of HAART regimen)		
AZT/3TC	■ Extensive experience ■ Low pill burden ■ Co-formulated ■ No food effect ■ M184V (3TC) slows AZT resistance	■ Side effects (AZT) ■ Anemia and neutropenia (AZT) ■ TAMs and NRTI cross-resistance with prolonged failure
TDF/3TC	■ qd regimen ■ Both effective against HBV ■ Well tolerated ■ Low pill burden ■ Avoids TAMs ■ Low potential for mitochondrial toxicity	■ Food effect ■ Contraindicated in renal failure ■ No long-term data ■ No data on resistance after failure – risk of ABC and ddI cross resistance
ddI/d4T	■ Extensive experience ■ Low pill burden ■ qd regimen available (not FDA-approved)	■ Contraindicated in pregnancy ■ Relatively high rate of lactic acidosis, peripheral neuropathy, pancreatitis, and lipoatrophy ■ Food effect ■ May increase risk of TAMs and multi-nucleoside resistance mutations ■ Hyperlipidemia (d4T) ■ Ascending motor paralysis (d4T)
AZT/ddI	■ Extensive experience ■ Low pill burden	■ Side effects ■ Anemia and neutropenia (AZT) ■ May increase risk of TAMs and multi-nucleoside resistance mutations

■ TABLE 4-9: **Advantages and Disadvantages of Antiretroviral Agents and Combinations *(Continued)***

Agents	Advantages	Disadvantages
		■ Complex dosing (AZT tolerability improved with food, ddl taken on empty stomach)
ddl/3TC	■ qd regimen ■ Low pill burden ■ Avoid TAMs	■ Minimal data ■ Pancreatitis ■ Neuropathy (ddl) ■ Food effect ■ No data on resistance after failure – risk of K65R with ABC and TDF cross-resistance
d4T/3TC	■ Good short-term tolerability ■ Low food effect ■ Low pill burden ■ M184V (3TC) slows d4T resistance	■ Lactic acidosis ■ Ascending motor paralysis, neuropathy, lipoatrophy, and hyperlipidemia (d4T) ■ TAMs and cross-resistance with prolonged failure
ABC/3TC	■ No food effect ■ qd regimen (not FDA-approved) ■ Low pill burden ■ Well tolerated ■ Avoids TAMs	■ Limited data ■ ABC hypersensitivity reaction ■ No data on resistance after failure – risk of TDF and ddl cross-resistance

■ TABLE 4-10: **Once Daily Drugs**

Class	FDA-approved	Probably Effective Based on Pharmacology
NRTI	■ ddl 400 mg ■ TDF 300 mg ■ 3TC 300 mg ■ d4T XR 100 mg	ABC 600 mg
NNRTI	EFV 600 mg	NVP 400 mg
PI	APV/RTV 1200/200 mg	■ SQV/RTV (*Invirase* or *Fortovase*) 1600/100 mg ■ LPV/r 800/200 mg ■ IDV/RTV 1200/400 mg

Factors That Influence Probability of Prolonged Viral Suppression

ADHERENCE: Obvious but critical, as shown in a study that demonstrated a strong correlation between virologic response and adherence (*Ann Intern Med* 2000;133:21). Most important was the demonstrated need for >95% adherence to achieve viral suppression in 80%. The virologic failure rate with <95% adherence was >50%

(Table 4-11). Multiple other studies have shown similar results (*AIDS* 2001;15:2109; *Clin Infect Dis* 2001;33:386; *AIDS* 2000;14:357; *Clin Infect Dis* 2002;34:115; *J Gen Intern Med* 2002;17:377).

■ TABLE 4-11: **Correlation Between Adherence and Virologic Response to HAART (*Ann Intern Med* 2000;133:21)**

Adherence to HAART*	Viral Load <400 c/mL at 6 Months
>95% adherence	78%
90 to 95% adherence	45%
80 to 90% adherence	33%
70 to 80% adherence	29%
<70% adherence	18%

* Number of doses prescribed/number taken

BASELINE VIRAL LOAD: Most studies demonstrate a direct correlation between baseline viral load and probability of achieving viral suppression to <50 c/mL or <500 c/mL (*AIDS* 1999;13:187; *Clin Infect Dis* 1999;29:75; *Arch Intern Med* 2000;160:1323; *AIDS* 2001;15:1793; *JAMA* 2001;286:2560). Exceptions are EFV or LPV/r plus 2 NRTIs, which demonstrated equal efficacy in patients with baseline viral loads >100,000 c/mL compared with those with lower viral loads (*N Eng J Med* 1999;341:1865; *N Engl J Med* 2002;346:2039). The baseline viral load also predicts time required to reach undetectable virus.

PRIOR EXPOSURE TO ANTIRETROVIRAL AGENTS: Multiple studies demonstrate a reverse correlation between response and the extent of prior antiretroviral therapy with regard to number of agents, number of classes, and duration of treatment. In the Swiss Cohort study (*Lancet* 1999;353:863), for example, the probability of achieving a viral load <500 c/mL with HAART therapy was 91% in treatment-naïve patients compared with 75% in treatment-experienced patients. Among patients who achieved undetectable virus, the probability of maintaining a viral load <500 c/mL at 2 years was 80% for treatment-naïve patients compared with 62% for treatment-experienced patients. The conclusion of many authorities is that the initial regimen is the most important regimen because it is associated with the greatest probability of achieving prolonged viral suppression (*J Acquir Immune Defic Syndr* 2000;24:115).

VIRAL LOAD NADIR: Multiple studies demonstrate that the viral load nadir predicts the durability of response and, in fact, may be the single most important predictor of a durable response (*AIDS* 2002;16:1521; *JAMA* 1998;279:930; *Lancet* 2001;358:1760; *J Acquir Immune Defic Syndr* 2002;30:167; *AIDS* 1998;12:F9).

RAPIDITY OF VIRAL LOAD RESPONSE: The trajectory of the viral load response predicts the nadir plasma HIV RNA level and consequently the durability of HIV response. To achieve an optimal and durable virologic response, treatment-naïve patients treated with HAART should respond as follows:

- Decrease 0.7-1.0 $\log_{10}$ c/mL at 1 week (*Lancet* 2001;358:1760; *J Acquir Immune Defic Syndr* 2002;30:167)
- Decrease 1.5-2.0 $\log_{10}$ c/mL to <5,000 c/mL at 4 weeks (*AIDS* 1999;13:1873; *J Acquir Immune Defic Syndr* 2000;25:36)
- Decrease to <500 c/mL at 8 to 16 weeks and <50 c/mL at 16 to 24 weeks (*Ann Intern Med* 2001;135:954; *J Acquir Immune Defic Syndr* 2000;24:433)

Failure to achieve these goals suggests lack of antiretroviral potency, non-adherence, resistance or inadequate drug levels due to drug interactions, poor absorption, etc.

CHOICE OF REGIMEN: Preferred regimens based on antiviral efficacy may be defined by clinical trial data showing a viral load <50 c/mL at ≥24 weeks for >40% of participants by intent-to-treat analysis. It should also be noted that there is substantial variation in efficacy among the preferred regimens, and some appear to be more potent in patients with high baseline viral loads and/or low CD4 cell counts than others. Regimens satisfying these objectives are summarized in Tables 4-5, 4-6, 4-7, and 4-8. These guidelines from three sources (DHHS, IAS-USA, WHO) make the assumption that specific combinations of 3-4 drug regimens are the same providing a recommended nucleoside pair is combined with the preferred NNRTI, PI, or RTV-boosted PI. ACTG 384 showed that EFV combined with AZT/3TC was superior to EFV/ddI/d4T, but NFV/AZT/3TC was comparable with NFV/ddI/d4T. This suggests that specific combinations may be important (14th International AIDS Conference, Barcelona, 7/02, Abstract LB20).

FACTORS THAT PREDICT CLINICAL PROGRESSION (AIDS-DEFINING DIAGNOSIS OR DEATH) AFTER INITIATING HAART: Based on EuroSIDA data (*J Infect Dis* 2002;185:178) and meta-analysis of 13 cohort studies (*Lancet* 2002;360:119;Table 4-2). The following predict progression after initiation of HAART:

- Baseline viral load >100,000 c/mL (see Table 4-2, p. 51)
- Age >50 years (*Lancet* 2002;360:119)
- Injection drug use – only HIV risk category with increased risk of progression or death (*Lancet* 2002;360:119)
- Hemoglobin <14 g% (males) or <12 g% (female) (*J Infect Dis* 2002;185:178)

■ TABLE 4-12: **Monitoring Therapy (DHHS Guidelines and/or IAS-USA Guidelines) at Initiation of HAART or With Change in Regimen**

Test	When	Comment
Viral Load	**Baseline**	
After starting or changing therapy	4 weeks, 8 to 12 weeks, 16 to 24 weeks (IAS-USA)* 2 to 8 weeks (DHHS)*	■ Expect 1 log decrease within 4 weeks; if not, suspect resistance, poor adherence, or inadequate drug exposure. ■ Expect continued viral suppression with goal of <50 c/mL at 16 to 24 weeks.
Chronic therapy	Every 8 to 12 weeks (IAS-USA)* Every 3 to 4 months (DHHS)*	■ Confirm suppression to <50 c/mL then monitor viral load every 8 to 12 weeks. ■ Occasional "blips" to 50-200 c/mL do not predict failure and should not be grounds for changing therapy unless they persist.
CD4 Count	**Baseline**	
After starting or changing therapy	4 weeks, 8 to 12 weeks, 16 to 24 weeks	■ Expect increase by ≥50 cells/mm³ at 4 to 8 weeks (with some unexplained exceptions despite good viral suppression).
Chronic therapy	Every 8 to 12 weeks	■ Expect additional increase of 50-100 cells/mm³/year. ■ Discordant results for CD4 count and viral load in 20%.

* Refers to 2002 guidelines from IAS-USA and/or DHHS.

■ TABLE 4-13: **Monitoring for Adverse Reactions**

Adverse Reactions		
Toxicity	**Routine Tests**	**Comment**
Lactic acidosis	None	■ Serum lactate only with symptoms. Must obtain with strict methods for quality assurance. ■ See pp. 84-85
Hyperlipidemia	Fasting total, LDL, HDL, cholesterol and triglycerides at baseline + every 3 to 6 months	■ Treat according to Framingham risks and National Cholesterol Education Program (NCEP) guidelines ■ Associated with PIs especially RTV (dose dependent). ■ Consider switch to non-PI-based regimen. ■ See pp. 87-91
Insulin Resistance	FBS at baseline + every 3 to 6 months (IAS-USA) FBS at baseline + every 3 to 4 months x I year (DHHS)	■ Associated with PIs. ■ Glucose tolerance test at baseline is not indicated. ■ Treat hyperglycemia, preferably with insulin sensitizing agents, or switch to non-PI-containing regimen. ■ See pp. 85-86
Fat accumulation and lipoatrophy	No screening test	■ Monitoring: CT, MRI, DXA + US – research tools only. ■ Best monitoring: Waist or waist/hip and breast measurement. ■ No established treatment, but some support for drug switches (PI- to non-PI-based regimens for fat accumulation, NRTI switches for lipoatrophy). ■ See pp. 82-84
Hepatitis	■ Regular monitoring of transaminases (all regimens) ■ NVP: Monitor more closely for hepatotoxicity (see comments)	■ NVP: IAS-USA: Baseline, at 2 weeks, then 2 weeks post dose increase. ■ NVP: DHHS: Baseline, every two weeks x 2, then every month x 11 months, then every 1 to 3 months. ■ See pp. 91-92

When to Modify Therapy

DEFINING TREATMENT FAILURE

- Treatment failure is defined by the IAS-USA as failure to achieve a viral load of <50 c/mL or any sustained return of viral load to >400 c/mL (*JAMA* 2002;288:222).
- The goal of therapy is to reduce HIV RNA to as low a level as possible for as long as possible, preferably using antiretroviral regimens that preserve future options, are relatively free of side effects, and are tailored to individual patient needs for adherence.
- Analysis of virologic results from many studies indicates that the post-treatment viral load reduction at 1 to 4 weeks is the best predictor of subsequent virologic suppression, and the viral goal is the best predictor of the durability of virologic response (see p. xx). The goal is a decrease in viral load by ≥1 $\log_{10}$ c/mL (90%) within four weeks and viral load <20-50 c/mL by 16 to 24 weeks. Studies show that <5% of all AIDS-defining complications occur in patients with a viral load of <5,000 c/mL, suggesting that thresholds that define virologic failure and clinical failure may be different (*AIDS* 1999;13:1035; *AIDS* 1999;13:341; *J Acquir Immune Defic Syndr* 2001;27:44; *J Acquir Immune Defic Syndr* 2002;30:154). However, the assumption is that virologic failure will eventually lead to clinical and immunologic failure. Unfortunately, clinical studies show that only 15% to 30% of patients in most urban clinics achieve a sustained level of <20 to 50 c/mL (*Ann Intern Med* 1999;131:18; *AIDS* 1999;13:F35), and the HIV Cost and Services Utilization Study Consortium (HCSUS) study suggests that only about 28% of persons in the United States who are receiving HIV care have a viral load <500 c/mL (*J Acquir Immune Defic Syndr* 2000;25:115). Based on these observations, most authorities consider a reduction to <20 to 50 c/mL to be the ultimate goal of therapy but acknowledge that this may be unrealistic in many patients. More importantly, the attempt to achieve unrealistic virologic responses may severely limit future therapeutic options due to the evolution of resistance.

CD4 RESPONSE: The CD4 response is generally a mirror image of the HIV RNA decay curve, with increases that average 50-60 cells/mm^3 in the first 4 months with subsequent increases at a rate of 3-6 cells/mm^3/month or 50-100 cells/mm^3/year with good viral suppression (*J Infect Dis* 2002;185:471; *Ann Intern Med* 2001;135:954; *AIDS* 2001;15:1793; *AIDS* 2001;15:983). However, 20% to 30% of patients have discordant results, either with a decrease in viral load, without an appropriate CD4 response, or with a CD4 increase despite a poor virologic response (*J Infect Dis* 2001;183:1328; *JAMA* 2001;285:777). Therapeutic decisions are usually made based on viral load data.

CAUSE OF VIROLOGIC FAILURE: Inadequate virologic response is ascribed to: 1) Lack of adherence; 2) Reduced potency of the regimen;

3) Pharmacologic failure due to reduced drug delivery to the site of infection (due to malabsorption, protein binding, or drug interactions); and 4) Resistance. In general, most of the failure in the first 24 weeks of treatment using recommended HAART regimens in treatment-naïve patients is due to lack of adherence or inadequate potency, and most late failures that follow good virologic response are due to resistance.

GUIDELINES FOR CHANGING ANTIRETROVIRAL REGIMEN

(Modified from DHHS Guidelines, 2002 and IAS-USA Guidelines, 2002)

- **Guidance for changes based on intolerance**
  - Changes based on ADRs or intolerance can be made with single agent substitution, provided the patient has an appropriate virologic response to the original regimen.
- **Guidance for changes based on virologic failure**
  - Resistance testing: Changes due to virologic failure are often based on resistance test results and history of prior exposure. Resistance tests are valid indicators of resistance only to drugs being taken at the time the test is performed or within a few weeks of discontinuation. Resistance may be anticipated for drugs given previously during sustained periods of virologic failure. Expertise is critical when selecting regimens based on the drug exposure history and the interpretation of resistance tests (see Table 2-7, p. 26 and below).
  - Intensification refers to the addition of a drug to a regimen with suboptimal virologic response. Common intensification tactics are the addition of ABC or TDF or adding RTV for pharmacologic boosting of PI-based regimens.
  - Multiple failures: Patients with virologic failures and limited options due to multiple resistance mutations may do best with continuation of a regimen that provides only partial viral suppression. Multiple studies demonstrate that even patients with complete virologic failure derive clinical benefit, presumably due to altered HIV fitness (supported by reduced replicative capacity compared with wild type strain *in vitro*) or partial viral suppression (*Lancet* 1998;351:723; *Lancet* 1999;353:363; *N Engl J Med* 2001;344:472). The drawback to this approach is the accumulation of additional resistance mutations that may affect response to other available drugs or agents in development.

GUIDANCE FOR REGIMEN CHANGES DUE TO CLASS-RELATED TOXICITY

- **Hyperlipidemia** caused by protease inhibitors may improve with a switch to an NNRTI (especially NVP) or a third NRTI.
- **Insulin resistance and hyperglycemia** generally improve with a switch from a PI to another class of agents.

- **Fat accumulation** caused by protease inhibitors sometimes improves with a switch to another class of agents, although the data are conflicting.
- **Lipoatrophy**, which appears to be caused by NRTIs or by the interaction of NRTIs with PIs, was thought to be irreversible. However, preliminary data from several switch studies suggest that there may be some reversal with NRTI switches (d4T or AZT to ABC in one study, d4T to AZT or ABC in another). It has been suggested, based on their effects on mitochondrial DNA, that ddC and d4T are the NRTIs most likely to cause lipoatrophy, followed by AZT and ddI, followed by ABC, 3TC, and TDF.
- **Hyperlactatemia and lactic acidosis** may also be caused by NRTI-induced mitochondrial toxicity. Patients with severe lactic acidosis generally require temporary discontinuation of all antiretroviral agents, but those with less severe hyperlactatemia may respond with an NRTI switch, as discussed above.
- **Hepatotoxicity** can occur with all three classes of agents. Among the PIs, RTV is the drug most likely to increase transaminases, and NVP appears to cause more hepatotoxicity (including fulminant hepatic necrosis) than EFV or DLV. When hepatotoxicity is observed in patients taking NRTIs, especially d4T, the clinician should consider the possibility of lactic acidosis with hepatic steatosis.
- **Enhanced bleeding in patients with hemophilia** has been attributed to PIs, but supporting data are sparse.
- **Osteopenia** (with potential for osteoporosis) and osteonecrosis (with potential for avascular necrosis) have been observed in patients on HAART, but the causal relationship has not been established. These processes may be caused by long-standing HIV infection rather than HAART.

GUIDANCE FOR ADHERENCE ISSUES

- **Establish readiness** prior to initiating HAART.
- **Address common problems:** Knowledge and understanding of issues; deal with adverse reactions, food issues, pill burden, and dosing frequency.
- **Use facilitators:** Multidisciplinary teams (nurses, pharmacists, peers, etc), friends/relatives/partners, CBOs
- **Use adherence aids:** Pill boxes, pictures, calendars. alarms, pagers
- **Documentation:** Pharmacy records, questionnaire results, blood levels, partner

OPTIONS FOR SWITCHING THERAPY: Options may be limited by cross-resistance or toxicity. The best decisions are made based on resistance test results combined with treatment history. Initial results from trials in which rescue regimens were selected by genotypic resistance test results compared with "standard of care" show three major benefits of resistance testing: 1) Virologic outcome at 12 to 24 weeks appears to be modestly superior, although a meta-analysis of published reports through February 2001 showed a substantial difference only with expert interpretation of genotypic testing (*HIV Clin Trials* 2002;3:1); 2) The number of drugs changed is reduced (*J Infect Dis* 2001;183:401; *Lancet* 1999;353:2185; *AIDS* 1999;13:1861); and 3) Testing appears to be cost-effective (*Ann Intern Med* 2001;134:440). Interpretation of results is now improving. Resistance testing to facilitate drug selection after therapeutic failure is now considered standard of care (*JAMA* 2002;288:222). Data are lacking to recommend a specific method of testing: Genotypic, phenotypic, genotypic plus phenotypic, or *Virtual Phenotype* (*JAMA* 2002;288:222). Empiric changes should be avoided, although some generalizations can be made about cross-resistance and sequencing:

- **PI failure**
  - Dual PIs, usually SQV/RTV, IDV/RTV, APV/RTV, or LPV/r are sometimes effective after failure of salvage PIs.
  - PI salvage after failure of PI-containing regimens is most likely to be successful if the viral load is relatively low when the switch is made.
  - IDV and RTV demonstrate nearly complete cross-resistance, so the main reason to combine them is to increase IDV levels.
  - Some data suggest that PIs are more likely to be effective following NFV therapy than after failure of other PIs because of the lack of PI cross-resistance associated with the D30N mutation. However, NFV therapy can also result in the emergence of the L90M mutation, which is associated with PI cross-resistance.
  - APV and LPV/r may be more active against HIV resistant to other PIs.
  - Patients failing therapy with APV, especially when boosted with RTV, typically develop the I50V mutation, which is associated with decreased susceptibility to LPV.
  - Initial failure of a PI-based regimen is often associated with minimal or no PI resistance. Therefore, many of these PI sequencing issues are not relevant if changes are made early.
- **NNRTI failure**
  - Patients failing NNRTI-containing regimens are presumed to have class-wide cross-resistance unless indicated otherwise by resistance test results. The most common cause of NNRTI resistance is the K103N mutation, which causes high-level resistance to DLV, NVP, and EFV.

- Some less common NNRTI mutations may confer resistance to some but not all NNRTIs. For example, the Y181C mutation is associated with high level NVP resistance but less EFV resistance. However, clinical data on NNRTI sequencing are lacking.

- **NRTI failure**
  - TAMs (41L, 67N, 70R, 210W, 215Y/F, 219Q) are selected for by AZT and d4T and cause resistance to all NRTIs, including TDF.
  - The M184V mutation selected for by 3TC causes high-level resistance to 3TC and low-level resistance to ddI and ddC. It can increase susceptibility of either wild type or resistant virus to AZT, d4T, and TDF.
  - Cross-resistance to ddI, ABC, and TDF can result from the following NRTI mutations: 65R, 74V, and 115L.
  - ABC resistance is likely with M184V and three to four TAMs.
  - TDF resistance is likely with three or more TAMs that include either 41L, 210W, or both.
  - The Q151M multi-nucleoside resistance complex causes resistance to all NRTIs.
  - The T69 insertion mutation, which always occurs in the presence of TAMs, causes resistance to all NRTIs and TDF.

Triple-class regimens: The risks associated with the triple-class regimens are exposure to all classes with the potential for multi-class resistance if the regimen fails; the lack of information about the pharmacology of some drug combinations; and sparse clinical trial data. Nevertheless, these may represent the most effective regimens in patients who fail standard 2-class regimens.

MULTIPLE FAILURES: With multiple courses of treatment and resistance to multiple agents, it becomes increasingly difficult to provide antiretroviral regimens that fully suppress viral replication. Toxicity and non-adherence may also limit options. In these cases, there is often clinical benefit with antiretroviral therapy despite virologic failure (*J Infect Dis* 2000;181:946). The presumed mechanism is reduced "fitness" or replicative capacity relative to wild-type virus, which is demonstrable with clinical trials *in vivo* and with replicative capacity assays *in vitro* (*J Virol* 2001;75:6410; *Nat Med* 2001;7:712). The goal of therapy in the face of virologic failure without fully suppressive options is prevention of HIV-related complications and preservation or increase in CD4 count (*JAMA* 2002;288:222).

Antiretroviral Agents

Antiretroviral Agents Approved by the FDA

■ TABLE 4-14: **Antiretroviral Drugs Approved by the FDA for HIV**

Generic Name (Abbreviation)	Brand Name	Manufacturer	FDA Approval Date
Zidovudine (AZT, ZDV)	*Retrovir*	GlaxoSmithKline	March 1987
Didanosine (ddI)	*Videx*	Bristol Myers-Squibb	October 1991
Zalcitabine (ddC)	*Hivid*	Hoffman-La Roche	June 1992
Stavudine (d4T)	*Zerit*	Bristol Myers-Squibb	June 1994
Lamivudine (3TC)	*Epivir*	GlaxoSmithKline	November 1995
Saquinavir (SQVhgc)	*Invirase*	Hoffman-La Roche	December 1995
Ritonavir (RTV)	*Norvir*	Abbott Laboratories	March 1996
Indinavir (IDV)	*Crixivan*	Merck & Co., Inc.	March 1996
Nevirapine (NVP)	*Viramune*	Boehringer Ingelheim	June 1996
Nelfinavir (NFV)	*Viracept*	Agouron Pharmaceuticals	March 1997
Delavirdine (DLV)	*Rescriptor*	Pharmacia	April 1997
Zidovudine/Lamivudine (AZT/3TC)	*Combivir*	GlaxoSmithKline	September 1997
Saquinavir (SQVsgc)	*Fortovase*	Hoffman-La Roche	November 1997
Efavirenz (EFV)	*Sustiva*	DuPont Pharmaceuticals	September 1998
Abacavir (ABC)	*Ziagen*	GlaxoSmithKline	February 1999
Amprenavir (APV)	*Agenerase*	GlaxoSmithKline	April 1999
Lopinavir/Ritonavir (LPV/r)	*Kaletra*	Abbott	September 2000
Zidovudine/lamivudine/ abacavir (AZT/3TC/ABC)	*Trizivir*	GlaxoSmithKline	November 2000
Tenofovir DF (TDF)	*Viread*	Gilead Sciences	October 2001

■ TABLE 4-15: **Nucleoside Analogs**

	AZT, ZDV	ddI	ddC	d4T	3TC	ABC	TDF
Trade name	*Retrovir*	*Videx* and *Videx EC*	*Hivid*	*Zerit*	*Epivir*	*Ziagen*	*Viread*
How supplied	■ 100 mg caps and 300 mg tabs ■ 300 mg + 3TC 150 mg as *Combivir* caps ■ 300 mg + 3TC 150 mg + ABC 300 mg as *Trizivir* tabs ■ 10 mg/mL IV solution	■ 125, 200, 250, and 400 mg enteric coated cap (*Videx EC*) ■ 25, 50, 100, and 150 mg buffered tabs ■ 100 167, and 250 mg powder packets ■ 200 mg buffered tabs for 1-2x daily dosing ■ Pediatric powder with 4 g/240 mL	■ 0.375 and 0.75 mg tabs	■ 15, 20, 30, and 40 mg caps ■ 1 mg/mL oral sol'n ■ *Zerit XR* 100, 75 mg caps	■ 150, 300 mg tabs ■ 150 mg with AZT 300 mg as *Combivir* caps ■ 10 mg/mL oral solution ■ 150 mg with AZT 300 mg and ABC 300 mg as *Trizivir* tabs	■ 300 mg tabs ■ ABC 300 mg + AZT 300 mg + 3TC 150 mg as *Trizivir* tabs	■ 300 mg tabs
Dosing recommendations	■ 300 mg bid (or with 3TC as *Combivir* 1 tab bid or with 3TC + ABC as *Trizivir* 1 tab bid)	■ Tablets or oral solution* ■ >60kg: 400 mg cap (*Videx EC*) qd 200 mg bid or 400 mg qd (tabs) or 250 mg bid or 500 mg qd (powder) ■ <60 kg: *Videx EC* 250 mg qd or 250 mg qd or 125 mg bid (tabs) or 167 mg bid or 250 mg qd (powder)	■ 0.75 mg tid	■ >60kg: 40 mg bid or *Zerit XR* 100 mg qd ■ <60kg: 30 mg bid or *Zerit XR* 75 mg qd	■ 150 mg bid, 300 mg qd, or with AZT as *Combivir* (1 tab bid) or with AZT + ABC as *Trizivir* (1 tab bid) ■ <50 kg: 2 mg/kg bid	■ 300 mg bid or with AZT + 3TC as *Trizivir* (1 tab bid)	■ 300 mg qd
Oral bioavailability	■ 60%	■ 30% to 40%	■ 85%	■ 86%	■ 86%	■ 83%	■ 25% to 39%
Food effect	■ None; may be better tolerated with food	■ Levels ↓55% ■ *Videx EC* – take 1 hour before and 2 hours after meal ■ *Videx* – Take 1/2 hour before and 2 hours after meal	■ None	■ None	■ None	■ None ■ Alcohol ↑ ABC levels 41%	■ Levels ↑ ■ Take with meal, especially fat

	AZT, ZDV	ddI	ddC	d4T	3TC	ABC	TDF
Serum half-life	■ 1.1 hour	■ 1.6 hours	■ 1.2 hour	■ 1.0 hour	■ 3 to 6 hours	■ 1.5 hours	■ 17 hours
Intracellular half-life	■ 3 hours	■ 25 to 40 hours	■ 3 hours	■ 3.5 hours	■ 12 hours	■ >12 hours	■ 10 to 50 hours
CNS penetration (% serum levels)	■ 60%	■ 20%	■ 20%	■ 30 to 40%	■ 10%	■ 30%	■ ?
Elimination	■ Metabolized to AZT Glucuronide (GAZT) ■ Renal excretion of GAZT	■ Renal excretion 50%	■ Renal excretion 70%	■ Renal excretion 50%	■ Renal excretion unchanged	■ Metabolized ■ Renal excretion of metabolites 82%	■ Renal
Major toxicity Class toxicity†	■ Bone marrow suppression: Anemia and/or neutropenia ■ Subjective complaints: GI intolerance, headache, insomnia, asthenia	■ Pancreatitis ■ Peripheral neuropathy ■ GI intolerance – nausea, diarrhea. ■ *Videx EC* has fewer GI side effects ■ Avoid combination with d4T in pregnancy‡	■ Peripheral neuropathy ■ Stomatitis	■ Peripheral neuropathy ■ Avoid combination with ddI in pregnancy‡	■ Minimal toxicity	■ Hypersensitivity (2% to 5%), with fever, nausea, vomiting, anorexia, cough, dyspnea, malaise, morbilliform rash. ■ Re-challenge may be life-threatening	■ Minimal toxicity ■ Occasional GI intolerance, lactic acidosis (presumed, but not reported)
Drug interactions	■ Ribavirin may inhibit AZT phosphorylation; avoid combination if possible ■ Antagonism with d4T	■ Methadone ↓ ddI levels 41%; consider ddI dose increase ■ Tenofovir increases ddI AUC 44%. Use 250 mg qd.	■ None	■ Methadone ↓ d4T levels 27%. No dose adjustment. ■ Antagonism with AZT	■ None	■ None	■ Increase ddI AUC 44% ■ May increase serum levels of cidofovir, valacyclovir, ganciclovir

* For adults, ddI pediatric oral solution can be mixed by the pharmacist with liquid antacids. See package insert for instructions.

† Lactic acidosis with hepatic steatosis is an infrequent but potentially life-threatening toxicity.

‡ The combination of d4T + ddI should be avoided in pregnancy due to risk of lactic acidosis (see p. 84).

Non-Nucleoside Reverse Transcriptase Inhibitors (NNRTIs)

■ TABLE 4-16: **Non-Nucleoside Reverse Transcriptase Inhibitors**

	NVP	DLV	EFV
Trade Name	*Viramune*	*Rescriptor*	*Sustiva*
Form	▪ 200 mg tabs ▪ 50 mg/5 mL oral solution	▪ 100 mg and 200 mg tabs	▪ 50, 100, 200 mg caps ▪ 600 mg tabs
Dosing recommendations	▪ 200 mg PO qd x 14 days, then 200 mg PO bid	▪ 400 mg PO tid	▪ 600 mg PO qd hs
Oral bioavailability	▪ >90%	▪ 85%	▪ 42%
Food effect	▪ No effect	▪ No effect	▪ Absorption increased 50% with high-fat meal; avoid after high-fat meal ▪ Take on an empty stomach, especially tablets, to minimize side effects
Serum half-life	▪ 25 to 30 hours	▪ 5.8 hours	▪ 40 to 55 hours
Elimination	▪ Metabolized by cytochrome P450 (CYP3A4 inducer); ▪ 80% excreted in urine (glucuronidase metabolites, <5% unchanged), 10% in feces	▪ Metabolized by cytochrome P450 (CYP3A4 inducer); ▪ 51% excreted in urine (<5% unchanged), 44% in feces	▪ Metabolized by cytochrome P450 enzymes (CYP3A4 mixed inhibitor/inducer); ▪ 14% to 34% excreted in urine (<1% unchanged), 16% to 61% in feces
Major toxicity Class toxicity	▪ Rash (15% to 30%); discontinuation required in 7%; rare cases of Stevens-Johnson syndrome ▪ Hepatitis with hepatic necrosis. Must monitor LFTs	▪ Rash (10% to 15%); discontinuation required in 4% ▪ Increased transaminase levels. ▪ Headache	▪ CNS: Dizziness, "disconnectedness," somnolence, insomnia, abnormal dreams, confusion, amnesia, agitation, hallucinations, poor concentration – 40% to 50%, usually resolves within 2 to 3 weeks (take in evening) ▪ Discontinuation of EFV for CNS toxicity in 2.6% ▪ Rash (5% to 10%); discontinuation required in 1% to 7%; rare reports of Stevens-Johnson syndrome ▪ Teratogenic in cynomolgus monkeys; avoid in pregnancy, and women should use adequate contraception methods. ▪ False-positive drug screening test for cannabinoids – marijuana ▪ Hepatitis

■ TABLE 4-17: **Protease Inhibitors**

	IDV	RTV	SQV		NFV	APV	LPV/r
	Crixivan	*Norvir*	*Invirase*	*Fortovase*	*Viracept*	*Agenerase*	*Kaletra*
Supplier	Merck	Abbott	Roche	Roche	Agouron/Pfizer	GlaxoSmithKline	Abbott
Form	■ 200, 333, 400 mg caps	■ 100 mg caps ■ 600 mg/7.5 mL PO sol'n	■ 200 mg caps (hard-gel caps)	■ 200 mg caps (soft-gel caps)	■ 250 mg caps ■ 50 mg/g oral powder	■ 50, 150 mg caps ■ 15 mg/mL oral sol'n	■ 133 mg LPV + 33 mg RTV caps ■ 80 mg LPV + 20 mg RTV/mL oral solution
Usual unboosted dose (most PIs are boosted with RTV, see Table 4-20, p. 80)	■ 800 mg q8h ■ Separate buffered ddI dose by 1 hour	■ 600 mg bid* ■ Separate buffered ddI dose by 2 hrs	■ Should not be prescribed without RTV boosting (see Table 4-20, p. 80)	■ 1200 mg tid	■ 1250 mg bid or 750 mg tid	■ 1200 mg bid (caps) ■ 1400 mg bid (oral solution)	■ 400/100 mg (3 caps or 5 mL) bid
Food effect	■ Levels ↓ 77% ■ Take 1 hr before or 2 hrs after meals ■ May take with low-fat snack or skim milk ■ No food effect when taken with RTV	■ Levels ↑ 15% ■ Take with food if possible to improve tolerability	■ No food effect when taken with RTV	■ Levels ↑ 6x ■ Take with large meal unless taken with RTV	■ Levels ↑ 2x to 3x ■ Take with meal or snack; high fat meal preferred	■ High-fat meal ↓ AUC 20% ■ Can be taken with or without food, but high-fat meal should be avoided.	■ Fat ↑ AUC 50% to 80% ■ Take with food

continued on next page

■ TABLE 4-17: **Protease Inhibitors *(Continued)***

	IDV	RTV	SQV		NFV	APV	LPV/r
	Crixivan	*Norvir*	*Invirase*	*Fortovase*	*Viracept*	*Agenerase*	*Kaletra*
Bioavailability	■ 65% (on empty stomach)	■ Not determined	■ 4%	■ Not determined (estimated to be 13x higher than *Invirase*)	■ 20% to 80%	■ Not determined ■ 15% lower with oral solution	■ Not determined
Storage	■ Room temp	■ Room temp or refrigerate if stored >30 days	■ Room temp	■ Room temp or refrigerate	■ Room temp	■ Room temp	■ Room temp: stable x 2 months ■ Refrigerate until date on label
Serum half-life	■ 1.5 to 2 hours	■ 3 to 5 hours	■ 1 to 2 hours	■ 1 to 2 hours	■ 3.5 to 5 hours	■ 7 to 10 hours	■ 5 to 6 hours
CNS penetration	■ Moderate	■ Poor	■ Poor	■ Poor	■ Moderate	■ Moderate	■ Not known
Elimination	■ Biliary metabolism cytochrome P450, CYP3A4 inhibitor	■ Biliary metabolism cytochrome P450, CYP3A4>2D6; most potent 3A4 inhibitor	■ Biliary metabolism cytochrome P450, CYP3A4 inhibitor	■ Biliary metabolism cytochrome P450, CYP3A4 inhibitor	■ Biliary metabolism cytochrome P450, CYP3A4 inhibitor	■ Biliary metabolism cytochrome P450, CYP3A4 inhibitor (similar to IDV and NFV)	■ Biliary metabolism cytochrome P450, CYP3A4 inhibitor

	IDV	RTV	SQV		NFV	APV	LPV/r
	Crixivan	*Norvir*	*Invirase*	*Fortovase*	*Viracept*	*Agenerase*	*Kaletra*
Side effects	■ GI intolerance (10% to 15%) ■ Nephrolithiasis or nephrotoxicity (10% to 20%) take >1.5 L/day; ■ Miscellaneous: Headache, blurred vision, thrombocytopenia, hepatitis, asthenia, dizziness, rash, metallic taste, ITP, alopecia, dry skin, chapped lips, paronychia ■ Lab: Increase indirect bilirubinemia (inconsequential) ■ See Class Adverse Drug Reactions, p. 82	■ GI intolerance (20% to 40%): Nausea, vomiting, diarrhea ■ Circumoral and extremities (10%) ■ Taste perversion (10%) ■ Lab: Increased transaminase levels, increased CPK and uric acid levels ■ Miscellaneous: Asthenia, hepatitis, alcohol content of oral solution contains EtOH, possible disulfiram reaction ■ See Class Adverse Drug Reactions, p. 82	■ GI intolerance (10% to 20%) ■ Miscellaneous: Headache, increased transaminase levels ■ See Class Adverse Drug Reactions, p. 82	■ GI intolerance (20% to 30%) ■ Miscellaneous: Headache, increased transaminase levels, hypoglycemia in diabetics ■ See Class Adverse Drug Reactions, p. 82	■ Diarrhea (10% to 30%) ■ Increased transaminase levels ■ See Class Adverse Drug Reactions, p. 82	■ GI intolerance (10% to 30%): Nausea, vomiting, diarrhea ■ Rash (20% to 25%): Usually at 1 to 10 weeks, Stevens-Johnson syndrome (1%) ■ Paresthesias (10% to 30%): Perioral or peripheral ■ Increased transaminase function tests ■ See Class Adverse Drug Reactions, p. 82	■ GI intolerance: Nausea, vomiting, diarrhea ■ Asthenia ■ Hepatitis ■ Oral solution is 42% EtOH – possible disulfiram reaction ■ See Class Adverse Drug Reactions, p. 82

* Dose escalation for boosted RTV: days 1 and 2: 300 mg bid; days 3 to 5: 400 mg bid; days 6 to 13: 500 mg bid; day 14: 600 mg bid.

Drug Interactions

■ TABLE 4-18: **Drugs That Should Not Be Used With Protease Inhibitors or NNRTIs***

Drug Category†	IDV	RTV	SQV	NFV	APV	LPV/r	DLV	EFV
Cardiac	None	Amiodarone, encainide, flecainide, propafenone, quinidine	None	None	None	Flecainide, propafenone	None	None
Lipid-lowering agents	Simvastatin, lovastatin	Simvastatin, lovastatin	Simvastatin, lovastatin	Simvastatin, lovastatin	Simvastatin, lovastatin	Simvastatin, lovastatin	Simvastatin, lovastatin	None
Antimycobacterial	Rifampin	None	Rifampin	Rifampin	Rifampin	Rifampin	Rifampin, rifabutin	None
Ca^{++} channel blocker	None	Bepridil	None	None	Bepridil	None	None	None
Antihistamine	Astemizole, terfenadine	Astemizole, terfenadine	Astemizole, terfenadine	Astemizole, terfenadine	Astemizole, terfenadine	Astemizole, terfenadine	Astemizole, terfenadine	Astemizole, terfenadine
GI	Cisapride	Cisapride	Cisapride	Cisapride	Cisapride	Cisapride	Cisapride, H_2 blockers, proton pump inhibitors	Cisapride
Neuroleptic	None	Pimozide	None	None	None	Pimozide	None	None
Psychotropic	Midazolam, triazolam	Midazolam, triazolam	Midazolam, triazolam	Midazolam, triazolam	Midazolam, triazolam	Midazolam, triazolam	Midazolam, triazolam	Midazolam, triazolam
Ergot alkaloid (vasoconstrictor)	Dihydroergotamine, ergotamine (various forms)	Dihydroergotamine, ergotamine (various forms)	Dihydroergotamine, ergotamine (various forms)	Dihydroergotamine, ergotamine (various forms)	Dihydroergotamine, ergotamine (various forms)	Dihydroergotamine, ergotamine (various forms)	Dihydroergotamine, ergotamine (various forms)	Dihydroergotamine, ergotamine (various forms)
Herbs	St. John's wort	St. John's wort	St. John's wort	St. John's wort	St. John's wort	St. John's wort	St. John's wort	St. John's wort

* NVP: See p. 267. Note: NVP – none except antimycobacterial agents where data are insufficient.

† Alternatives: Rifabutin (MAC) – clarithromycin, ethambutol, azithromycin. Antihistamine – loratadine, fexofenadine, cetirizine. Psychotropic – temazepam, lorazepam. Lipid-lowering – atorvastatin, pravastatin.

■ TABLE 4-19: **Drug Interactions Requiring Dose Modifications or Cautious Use**

Drugs Affected	IDV	RTV	SQV*
Antifungals			
Ketoconazole	■ Levels: IDV ↑68% ■ Dose: IDV 600 mg tid	■ Ketoconazole ↑3x ■ Use with caution; do not exceed 200 mg/d	■ Levels: SQV ↑30% ■ Dose: Standard
Antimycobacterials			
Rifampin	■ IDV ↓89% ■ Contraindicated	■ RTV ↓35% ■ May increase hepatotoxicity (?)	■ SQV ↓84% ■ Contraindicated unless using RTV + SQV, then rifampin 600 mg qd or 2-3x/week
Rifabutin	■ IDV ↓32% ■ Rifabutin ↑2x ■ ↓ Rifabutin to 150 mg qd or 300 mg 2-3x/ week IDV 1,000 mg tid	■ Rifabutin ↑4x ■ ↓ Rifabutin to 150 mg qod or dose 3x week ■ RTV standard dose	■ SQV ↓40% ■ SQV + RTV rifabutin 150 mg 3x/week ■ SQV alone: No dose change
Clarithromycin	■ Clarithromycin ↑53% ■ No dose adjustment	■ Clarithromycin ↑77% ■ Dose adjust for renal insufficiency	■ Clarithromycin ↑45% ■ SQV ↑177% ■ No dose adjustment except in renal failure ■ With RTV/SQV: Clarithromycin 150 mg 3x/week
Oral contraceptives	■ Norethindrone ↑26% ■ Ethinylestradiol ↑24% ■ No dose adjustment	■ Ethinyl estradiol ↓40% ■ Use alternative method	■ No data
Lipid lowering agents (see Table 4-22, p. 89)	■ Avoid simvastatin and lovastatin	■ Avoid simvastatin and lovastatin	■ Avoid simvastatin and lovastatin
Anticonvulsants Phenobarbital Phenytoin Carbamazepine	■ Carbamazepine ↓IDV levels substantially. ■ Use alternative ART or RTV + IDV ■ Consider valproic acid	■ Unknown ■ Use with caution ■ Monitor anticonvulsant levels ■ Consider valproic acid	■ Unknown, but may ↓SQV levels substantially ■ Monitor anticonvulsant levels ■ Consider valproic acid
Methadone (see p. 261)	■ No change in methadone levels	■ Methadone ↓37% ■ Slight ↓ in active R isomer	■ No data ■ Slight ↓ in active R isomer
Miscellaneous	■ Grapefruit juice ↓IDV levels by 26% ■ Sildenafil: Do not exceed 25 mg/48 hours	■ Desipramine ↑145% ■ Reduce dose theophylline ↓47%, monitor theophylline levels ■ Many possible interactions (see product insert) ■ Sildenafil: Do not exceed 25 mg/48 hours	■ Grapefruit juice ↑SQV levels ■ Dexamethasone ↓SQV levels ■ Sildenafil: Do not exceed 25 mg/48 hours

* Some drug interaction studies were conducted with *Invirase*. Results may not necessarily apply to use with *Fortovase*.

■ TABLE 4-19: **Drug Interactions Requiring Dose Modifications or Cautious Use *(Continued)***

Drugs Affected	NFV	APV	LPV/r
Antifungals			
Ketoconazole	■ No dose adjustment necessary	■ Ketoconazole ↑44% APV ↑31% ■ Combination under investigation	■ Ketoconazole ↑3x ■ LPV ↑13% ■ Do not exceed 200 mg/d
Antimycobacterials			
Rifampin	■ NFV ↓82% ■ Contraindicated	■ APV ↓82% ■ Contraindicated	■ LPV ↓75%, ■ Avoid
Rifabutin	■ NFV ↓32% ■ Rifabutin ↑2x ■ ↓ Rifabutin to 150 mg qd or 300 mg 2-3x/week ■ NFV ↑ to 1000 mg tid	■ APV ↓15% ■ Rifabutin ↑193% ■ ↓ Rifabutin to 150 mg qd ■ APV dose standard	■ LPV ↓17% ■ Rifabutin: ↑3x, ↓ Rifabutin dose to 150 mg qod ■ LPV/r standard
Clarithromycin	■ No data	■ APV ↑18% ■ No dose adjustement necessary	■ No data
Oral contraceptives	■ Norethindrone ↓18% ■ Ethinylestradiol ↓47% ■ Use alternative method	■ Not studied ■ Use alternative method	■ Ethinylestradiol ↓42% ■ Use alternative method
Lipid lowering agents (see Table 4-22, p. 89)	■ Atorvastatin AUC ↑74%; use with caution ■ Avoid simvastatin and lovastatin	■ Avoid simvastatin and lovastatin	■ Atorvastatin AUC ↑5.8x; use with caution ■ Pravastatin AUC ↑33%; no dose change ■ Avoid simvastatin and lovastatin
Anticonvulsants Phenobarbital Phenytoin Carbamazepine	■ Unknown, but may ↓ NFV levels substantially ■ Monitor anticonvulsant levels ■ Consider valproic acid	■ Unknown, but may ↓ APV levels substantially ■ Monitor anticonvulsant levels ■ Consider valproic acid	■ Unknown ■ Monitor anticonvulsant levels ■ Consider valproic acid
Methadone (see p. 256)	■ NFV decreases methadone significantly but no change in active R isomer. ■ Monitor; may need to ↑ metadone dose	■ No data ■ Methadone levels ↓35% ■ No change in active R isomer	■ Methadone ↓53% ■ Monitor; may need to ↑ methadone dose
Miscellaneous	■ Sildenafil: Do not exceed 25 mg/48 hours	■ ABC: APV ↑30% ■ Sildenafil: Do not exceed 25 mg/48 hours	■ Sildenafil: Do not exceed 25 mg/48 hours

■ TABLE 4-19: **Drug Interactions Requiring Dose Modifications or Cautious Use *(Continued)***

Drugs Affected	NVP	DLV	EFV
Antifungals			
Ketoconazole	■ Ketoconazole ↓63% ■ NVP ↑15% to 30% ■ Not recommended	■ Not studied	■ Not studied
Antimycobacterials			
Rifampin	■ NVP ↓37% ■ Not recommended	■ DLV ↓96% ■ Contraindicated	■ EFV ↓25% ■ No dose adjustment
Rifabutin	■ NVP ↓16% ■ No dose change	■ DLV ↓80% ■ Rifabutin ↑100% ■ Not recommended	■ EFV unchanged ■ Rifabutin ↓35% ■ Dose ↑ Rifabutin to 450 mg/day or 600 mg 2 to 3x/week ■ EFV dose: Standard
Clarithromycin	■ NVP ↑26% ■ Clarithromycin ↓30% ■ Dose: Standard	■ Clarithromycin ↑100% ■ DLV ↑44% ■ Dose: Adjust for renal failure	■ Clarithromycin ↓39% but 14-OH metabolite ↑34% ■ High rate of rash. ■ Alternative recommended
Oral contraceptives	■ Ethinylestradiol ↓20% ■ Use alternative method	■ No data	■ Ethinylestradiol ↑37% ■ Use alternative method of birth control
Lipid lowering agents (see Table 4-22, p. 89)	■ No data	■ Avoid simvastatin and lovastatin	■ No data
Anticonvulsants Phenobarbital Phenytoin Carbamazepine	■ Unknown ■ Monitor anticonvulsant level	■ Unknown, but may ↓ DLV levels substantially ■ Monitor anticonvulsant levels	■ Unknown ■ Use with caution ■ Monitor anticonvulsant levels
Methadone (see p. 261)	■ NVP unchanged ■ Methadone ↓60% ■ Titrate methadone dose	■ Methadone ↓ ■ Titrate methadone dose	■ Methadone levels ↓52% ■ Titrate methadone dose
Miscellaneous		■ May ↑ levels of dapsone, warfarin, and quinidine ■ Sildenafil: Do not exceed 25 mg/48 hours	■ Monitor warfarin when used concomitantly

■ TABLE 4-20: **Drug Interactions: PIs and NNRTIs Effect of Drug on Levels (AUCs)/Dose**

Drug Affected	RTV	SQV	NFV	APV	LPV/r	NVP	DLV	EFV
IDV	■ IDV ↑2 to 5x ■ Dose: IDV 400 mg bid + RTV 400 mg bid, or IDV 800 mg bid + RTV 100-200 mg bid	■ IDV no effect ■ SQV ↑4-7x† ■ Dose: Insufficient data	■ IDV ↑50% NFV ↑80% ■ Dose: Limited data for IDV 1200 mg bid + NFV 1250 mg bid	■ IDV ↓38% AUC ■ APV ↑33% ■ Dose: Standard APV and IDV	■ IDV ↑ ■ Dose: IDV 600 mg bid + LPV/r standard	■ IDV ↓28% ■ NVP no effect ■ Dose: IDV 1,000 mg q8h; standard NVP	■ IDV ↑40%; ■ DLV no effect ■ Dose: IDV 600 mg q8h; standard DLV	■ Levels: IDV ↓31% ■ Dose: IDV 1000 mg q8h; EFV 600 mg hs or IDV 800 mg/RTV 200 mg bid/EFV 600 mg hs
RTV	–	■ RTV no effect ■ SQV ↑20x*† ■ Dose: SQV (*Invirase* or *Fortovase*) + RTV 400/400 mg bid; or 1000/100 mg bid or 1600/100 mg qd	■ RTV no effect ■ NFV ↑1.5x ■ Dose: RTV 400 mg bid + NFV 500 to 750 mg bid	■ APV ↑ AUC 2.5x ■ RTV no change ■ Dose: APV 600 mg bid + RTV 100 mg bid or APV 1,200 mg qd + RTV 200 mg qd	■ Co-formulated	■ RTV ↓11% ■ NVP no effect ■ Dose: Standard for both drugs	■ RTV ↑70% ■ DLV no effect ■ Dose: Limited data	■ Levels: RTV ↑18% EFV ↑21% ■ Dose: RTV 600 mg bid (500 mg bid for intolerance); EFV 600 mg hs
SQV	–	–	■ SQV ↑3 to 5x ■ NFV ↑20%† ■ Dose: NFV 1250 mg bid + FTV 1200 mg bid (PK data) or NFV 750 mg tid + SQV 800-1200 mg tid (clinical data)	■ APV ↓ AUC 32% ■ SQV† ↓19% ■ Dose: SQV 800 mg tid, APV 800 mg tid (limited data)‡	■ SQV ↑ AUC ■ Dose: *Fortovase* or *Invirase* 1000 mg bid + LPV/r standard	■ SQV ↓25% ■ NVP no effect ■ Dose: NVP standard ■ FTV standard (not recommended without RTV)	■ SQV ↑5x† ■ DLV no effect ■ Dose: *Fortovase* 800 mg tid, standard DLV (monitor transaminase levels)	■ Levels: SQV ↓62% EFV ↓12% ■ Co-administration not recommended without RTV

Drug Affected	RTV	SQV	NFV	APV	LPV/r	NVP	DLV	EFV
NFV	–	–	–	■ NFV ↑15% APV ↑1.5x ■ Dose: NFV 750 mg tid, APV 800 mg tid (insufficient data)‡	■ No data	■ NFV ↑10% ■ NVP no effect ■ Dose: Standard for both drugs	■ NFV ↑2x ■ DLV ↓50% ■ Dose: NFV 750 mg tid + DLV 400 mg tid (limited data; monitor for neutropenic complications)‡	■ Levels: NFV ↑20% ■ Dose: Standard for both drugs
APV	–	–	–	–	■ APV ↑ or ↓ ■ LPV ↓ or unchanged ■ Dose: APV 750 mg bid + LPV/r standard or 533/133 (4 caps) bid	■ No data	■ DLV↓ 60% ■ APV ↓125% ■ Not recommended	■ APV ↓36% ■ Dose: APV 1200 mg tid as single PI or APV 1200 mg bid + RTV 200 mg bid + EFV 600 mg qd
LPV/r	–	–	–	–	–	■ LPV ↓55% ■ Dose: LPV/r 533/133 mg (4 caps) bid + NVP standard (limited data)	■ No data	■ Levels: LPV ↓40%; EFV no change ■ Dose: LPV/r 533/133 mg (4 caps) bid + EFV 600 mg hs

* Conducted with *Invirase*

† Combinations with RTV may use either *Fortovase* or *Invirase* formulations. Many authorities now prefer *Invirase* due to better GI tolerance.

‡ Added by authors (not included in DHHS Guidelines, December 2002)

Class Adverse Drug Reactions (ADRs) to Antiretroviral Agents

(DHHS Guidelines (*MMWR* 2002;51[RR-7]) with additions by authors)

A number of class-related toxicities have been recognized and attributed to antiretroviral agents since their approval. Some of these toxicities are potentially serious and may limit patients' ability or willingness to remain on therapy. Causal relationships are well defined in some cases and controversial or elusive in others. DHHS and ISA-USA recommendations for monitoring are summarized in Table 4-12, p. 62.

Lipodystrophy

In the early years of the HAART era, so-called "fat-redistribution" or lipodystrophy was attributed to the use of protease inhibitors. Patients with this "syndrome" presented with a combination of peripheral loss of subcutaneous fat ("lipoatrophy") and fat accumulation within the abdominal cavity ("Crix-belly" or "protease paunch"), the upper back (dorsocervical fat pad or "buffalo hump"), the breasts (gynecomastia), and in subcutaneous tissue (peripheral lipomatosis). Many such patients also had hyperlipidemia and/or hyperglycemia, which was included in some definitions of lipodystrophy.

It now appears that these two morphologic complications of therapy may not be part of the same syndrome. Fat accumulation has been more closely linked to use of protease inhibitors, but it is now clear that nucleoside analogs play a role in the development of lipoatrophy.

The most significant association is with d4T or d4T/ddI, although AZT may also cause fat loss (*Sex Trans Infect* 2001;77:158).

INCIDENCE: Lipodystrophy is reported in 20% to 80% of patients receiving antiretroviral therapy, a wide range reflecting a heterogeneous population and the lack of a standard case definition (*AIDS* 1999;13:1287; *AIDS* 1999;13:2493; *Lancet* 2000;356:1423; *Clin Infect Dis* 2002;34:248). The incidence based on perceived changes in body fat sufficiently severe to be detected by the patient and physician in patients receiving 2 NRTIs plus a PI was 17%, with a median follow-up of 18 months (*Lancet* 2001;357:592). The frequency of abdominal fat accumulation was 9.2/100 pt-yrs, and 7.7/100 pt-yrs for lipoatrophy. Other cohort studies of 580 to 2258 patients show lipodystrophy rates of 38% (*Clin Infect Dis* 2000;31:1482), 50% (*AIDS* 2002;15:231), and 33% (*Antiviral Therapy* 2000;5:558).

ANTIRETROVIRAL AGENTS: Data from several sources suggest that

- Fat accumulation is primarily associated with PI use (*AIDS* 2001;15:231; *AIDS* 1999;13:2493) but may be seen in the absence of PI exposure. The changes may occur without hyperlipidemia (*J Acquir Immun Defic Syndr* 2000;23:351; *Arch Intern Med* 2000;150:2050).

- Lipoatrophy is more closely linked with NRTIs, especially d4T or d4T/ddI (*AIDS* 2000;14;F25; *AIDS* 1999;13:1659), although some data are conflicting (*Lancet* 2001;15:231; *Antiviral Therapy* 2000;5: S55). The presumed mechanism is inhibition of DNA polymerase gamma resulting in depletion of mitochondrial DNA (*N Engl J Med* 2002;346:81).

EVALUATION (*Lancet* 2000;356:1412; *Lancet* 2001;357:592; *AIDS* 1999; 13:2493)

- Patient perception
- Physical examination, serial photography
- Waist-hip ratio (>0.85 for women, >0.95 for men)
- Dual energy x-ray absorptiometry (DEXA)
- Ultrasound
- Computed tomography
- MRI

TREATMENT

- **Low fat diet and aerobic exercise** can be partly effective in treating fat accumulation (*AIDS* 1999;13:231), although they may exacerbate lipoatrophy.
- **Testosterone replacement therapy (in hypogonadal men) or anabolic steroids (eugonadal men)** may be beneficial in cases of fat accumulation. In combination with resistance exercise, it may increase muscle mass, which may help to compensate for lipoatrophy involving limbs. Lost fat will not be restored, however.
- **Growth hormone** (6 mg/kg/day) may reduce fat accumulation (*Ann Intern Med* 1996;125:873; *AIDS* 1999;13:2099; *J Clin Endocrinol Metab* 1997;82:727), but the benefits disappear after treatment is stopped (*J Acquir Immune Defic Syndr* 2002;35:249). Disadvantages include high price and side effects, including hyperglycemia, further loss of subcutaneous fat, and the need for maintenance treatment. Current studies are exploring the utility of lower doses of growth hormone (*J Acquir Immune Defic Syndr* 2002;30:379).
- **Metformin** (500 mg bid) improves insulin sensitivity and results in weight loss and decreased intra-abdominal fat in patients with fat accumulation and insulin resistance (*JAMA* 2000;284:472). It also improves some markers of cardiovascular risk (*J Clin Endocrinol Metab* 2002;87:4611).
- **Restorative surgery**, for fat accumulation, includes removal of lipomas, breast/fat tissue or dorso-cervical fat pad by either surgery or liposuction. A number of implants and injections are being investigated for facial fat atrophy. Injections of fat or collagen are associated with rapid resorption, and the changes are short-lived.

Permanent implants, such as silicone and "semi-permanent" polylactic acid injections, which are biodegradable but leave a more durable change in the underlying tissue, are undergoing FDA "device" approval. All implants run the risk of skin granuloma formation and scarring, require multiple treatments, and should only be considered by an expert, certified dermatologist or surgeon using pure compound.

- **Regimen changes** with a switch from PIs to an NNRTI or ABC are sometimes partially successful in reversing fat accumulation, although data are conflicting (Table 4-25, p. 92) (*J Infect Dis* 2001;184:914; *J Infect Dis* 2001;27:229; *Clin Infect Dis* 2000;31:1266). More recent data suggest that switches from d4T to ABC or AZT or from d4T or AZT to ABC may lead to subtle improvements in lipoatrophy, although these data are very preliminary (9th CROI, Seattle 2002, Abstract 700; 9th CROI, Seattle 2002, Abstract 701; 9th CROI, Seattle 2002, Abstract 32).

Lactic Acidosis/Hepatic Steatosis

Hyperlactatemia is defined as a venous lactate level >2 mM. It can be asymptomatic or can be associated with overt, sometimes fatal lactic acidosis. It appears to be a complication of NRTI therapy, and although it was originally described as a rare but potentially fatal complication of AZT therapy in the early 1990s, it is now seen primarily as a complication of d4T therapy. Initial reports focused on critically ill patients, with a mortality rate of 55% (*Clin Infect Dis* 2002;34:838). Mild asymptomatic elevations of lactic acid are now seen more frequently, and treatment strategies are evolving. The presumed mechanism is nucleoside analog-mediated inhibition of DNA polymerase gamma, leading to depletion of mitochondrial DNA (*N Engl J Med* 2002;346:811; *Nat Med* 1995;1:417; *J Clin Invest* 1995;96:126).

DIAGNOSIS: Patients with elevated lactates may be asymptomatic, critically ill, or may have non-specific symptoms, such as fatigue, myalgia, nausea, vomiting, diarrhea, abdominal distention, weight loss, or dyspnea (*Ann Intern Med* 2000;133:192; *Clin Infect Dis* 2002;34:838). Diagnosis is established with an elevated lactic acid level, which requires the use of a pre-chilled fluoride-oxalate tube and blood sampling without a tourniquet, with blood delivered rapidly to the lab on ice for processing within 4 hours. The patient should not exercise for 24 hours prior to sampling and should be well hydrated. In general, lactic acid levels correlate with prognosis: 0-2 mM is normal; 5-10 mM is associated with a 7% mortality; 10-15 mM with a >30% mortality, and >15 mM with a >60% mortality (*Clin Infect Dis* 2002;34:838). Surrogate markers include elevated CPK, LDH, amylase or AST, increased anion gap (Na - [Cl + CO_2] >16), CT scan, ultrasound, or biopsy of liver showing hepatic steatosis.

TREATMENT: Routine screening with lactic acid levels in asymptomatic patients is not recommended. Lactic acid levels <5 mM may not require treatment or modification of therapy in the absence of symptoms. Symptomatic patients usually have levels >5 mM and typically require discontinuation of NRTIs. In some cases, a switch from d4T, ddI, or AZT to ABC, 3TC, or TDF may be reasonable, provided the patient is not seriously ill and can be carefully observed. Lactic acid levels >10 mM, if properly obtained, should be viewed as a medical emergency because of the high mortality. Seriously ill patients require supportive care, which may include intravenous hydration, mechanical ventilation, and/or dialysis. Recovery may be protracted. The half-life of mitochondrial DNA ranges from 4.5 to 8 weeks, and the time required for clinical recovery is 4 to 28 weeks (*AIDS* 2000;14:F25); *N Engl J Med* 2002;346:811). Anecdotal case reports show possible benefit of thiamine, riboflavin, L-carnitine, vitamin C, and antioxidants (*Clin Infect Dis* 2002;34:838). The experience with riboflavin (50 mg/day) appears to be the most extensive and favorable.

FREQUENCY: The frequency of lactic acidosis depends on the definition, duration of NRTI exposure, specific agents used, and demographics of the population studied. Lactic acidemia without symptoms or with mild symptoms is noted in 8% to 20% of patients. This does not predict serious lactic acidosis, however, and may not require treatment. Most reports show a rate of symptomatic hyperlactatemia of 0.5-1/100 patient-years of NRTI exposure (*AIDS* 2001;15:717; *Clin Infect Dis* 2001;33:1931; *AIDS* 2000;14:2723; *Lancet* 2000;356:1423). Based in part on *in vitro* assays of mitochondrial toxicity and in part on clinical observations and cross-sectional studies, d4T appears to be the NRTI most likely to cause lactic acidosis, followed by AZT and ddI, followed by ABC and 3TC. Lactic acidosis due to tenofovir has not been reported. The risk of hyperlactatemia also depends on the number of NRTIs. The combination of d4T/ddI appears to be the most frequently implicated dual NRTI (*Clin Infect Dis* 2002;34:838; *N Engl J Med* 2002;346;811; *Clin Infect Dis* 2000;31:162; *Clin Infect Dis* 2001;33:2072; *AIDS* 2001;15:717). Duration of treatment is inconsistently correlated (*Clin Infect Dis* 2002;34:558). Early reports suggested that obese women were at greater risk, but this association is now in question. However, pregnant women do appear to be at higher risk, and three deaths have been reported among pregnant women taking ddI/d4T.

Insulin Resistance

Insulin resistance is noted in 30% to 90% of patients treated with protease inhibitors, and overt diabetes occurs in 1% to 11%, with a mean of approximately 7% at 5 years (*AIDS* 1999;13:F63; *Lancet* 1999;353:2093; *Arch Intern Med* 2000;160:2050). The changes in insulin sensitivity and blood glucose are usually apparent within 2 to 3 months and can be detected with glucose tolerance tests (*Lancet* 1999;353:2093). The role of PIs has been clearly established (*AIDS* 2001;15:11; *J Acquir Immun Defic Syndr* 2000;23:35), but it is not clear that all PIs are equally implicated.

SCREENING

- Random blood glucose, fasting blood glucose, and HgA1c measurements are insensitive methods to measure insulin resistance, due to compensatory increases in insulin. PI-treated patients with normal fasting blood glucose levels may have severe insulin resistance demonstrated by glucose clamp techniques (*AIDS* 2000;25:312).
- There are no standardized methods for evaluating insulin resistance. The 2002 DHHS and IAS-USA guidelines recommend fasting blood glucose levels at baseline and at 3 to 6 month intervals in PI-treated patients, with more measurements based on initial results and diabetes risk. More aggressive testing may include fasting insulin levels, C-peptide, and oral glucose tolerance testing for those with borderline fasting glucose levels (110-126 mg/dL).

RISK: The practical application of insulin resistance is its role as a risk for atherosclerosis (*N Engl J Med* 1996;334:952; *Am J Med* 1997;103:152) and dyslipidemia with elevated triglycerides and low HDL levels. The relationship of insulin resistance to lipodystrophy is unclear, but it may play a role in fat accumulation (*Diabetes* 1994;43:1271; *J Clin Invest* 1995;95:2045; *Lancet* 1998;351:1881; *Blood* 2000;95:3191). Risk assessment should include risk factors for diabetes and atherosclerosis, including family history, smoking, hypertension, obesity, and dyslipidemia.

TREATMENT: Standard treatment of type II diabetes is diet and exercise. The daily diet should consist of 50% to 60% carbohydrates, 10% to 20% protein, and <30% fat, with <100 mg cholesterol per day and <10% of total calories from saturated fat. When drug therapy is necessary, the two major classes of agents are insulin secretagogues (sulfonylureas) and insulin-sensitizing agents (metformin and thiazolidinediones). Metformin or a glitazone have the potential advantage of improving insulin resistance and decreasing visceral fat accumulation (*AIDS* 1999;13:100; *JAMA* 2000;284:472), with a possible reduction in cardiovascular risk. A potential though theoretical disadvantage is an increased risk of lactic acidosis. An alternative strategy is to change the HAART regimen to a non-PI-based regimen (*AIDS* 1999;13:805; *J Acquir Immun Defic Syndr* 2001;27:229; *Clin Infect Dis* 2000;31:1266). Such switches are acceptable in patients with no anticipated resistance to the drugs in the new regimen, and appear to be successful about 50% of the time (Table 4-25, p. 92).

Hyperlipidemia

Changes in blood lipids have emerged as an important complication of HAART, with the obvious concern being the potential for premature atherosclerosis and coronary artery disease. Studies in the pre-HAART era showed that HIV progression was associated with elevated triglyceride levels and decreased cholesterol levels (*Am J Med* 1991;90:154). With PI-based HAART there is usually an increase in triglycerides and cholesterol. Triglyceride levels may increase to over 1000 mg/dL, levels associated with an increased risk of both pancreatitis and atherosclerosis. Total and LDL cholesterol levels increase an average of 30 mg/dL (*J Acquir Immun Def Syndr* 2000;23:35; *Arch Intern Med* 2000;160:2050; *J Aquir Immun Defic Syndr* 2000;23:261; *Lancet* 1998;352:1031; *AIDS* 1998;12:F51; *Circulation* 1999;100:700). All PIs appear to have this effect, with the possible exception of the investigational PI, atazanavir; however, the most profound changes are seen with ritonavir and are dose dependent (*J Aquir Immun Defic Syndr* 2000;23:261; *N Engl J Med* 1995;333:1528). These changes are usually apparent within 2 to 3 months of initiating PI therapy.

RISK: An increased risk of cardiovascular disease associated with HAART has not been clearly established but is inferred based on anecdotal reports (*Lancet* 1998;351:1328; *Lancet* 1998;351:1959; *AIDS* 1998;12:F51). The large cohort study by Kaiser California showed no increase in coronary events for patients receiving PIs compared with untreated HIV infected persons (*J Acquir Immune Defic Syndr* 2002;30:471), but the obvious concern is the follow-up period was only four years. The possible risk of atherogenesis caused by dyslipidemia is compounded by insulin resistance (see "Insulin Resistance"), visceral fat accumulation (see "Lipodystrophy"), and possibly by chronic inflammation. Risk assessment needs to include a review of other cardiovascular risk factors as defined by the National Cholesterol Education Program (NCEP) (*JAMA* 2001;285:2486). These include a history of atherosclerosis (stroke, coronary artery disease, etc.), smoking, hypertension (>140/90 or need for antihypertensives), HDL cholesterol <40 mg/dL, or family history (first degree relative with coronary artery disease in male <55 years or female <65 years) and increased age (male >45 years or female >55 years) (see Table 4-21, p. 89).

TREATMENT

- Treatment decisions are based on assessment of need for PI-based therapy and risk assessment including cardiovascular disease fasting lipid profile.
- Hyperlipidemia with increases in LDL cholesterol and triglycerides are most clearly associated with PI-based HAART and especially with ritonavir-containing regimens. Efavirenz and possibly nevirapine are associated with increases in total and HDL cholesterol; it is

unclear whether the increased HDL cholesterol levels are protective. One option for initial treatment of patients at high risk is preferential use of non-PI-based HAART. For those already on PI-based regimens who are experiencing hyperlipidemia, switching to a non-PI-based regimen may result in improvement in the lipid profile. Reports involving switches to regimens consisting of 2 NRTIs plus efavirenz, nevirapine, or abacavir typically show partial or complete reversal of PI-associated hyperlipidemia and insulin resistance (*J Acquir Immun Defic Syndr* 2001;27:229; *Clin Infect Dis* 2000;31:1266) (see Table 4-25, p. 92). Viral suppression in these studies has generally been maintained, although virologic failure has been observed among patients with pre-existing NRTI resistance who switched to triple-NRTI regimens.

- Treatment of dyslipidemia is based on the NCEP guidelines (see Table 4-21, p. 89). Note that many statins cannot be used with PIs and NNRTIs, and others require close monitoring.
- **ACTG** (*Clin Infect Dis* 2000;31:1216), **NCEP** (*JAMA* 2001;285:2486) **and IAS-USA** (*JAMA* 2002;288:222) **recommendations**
  - Baseline: Baseline risk assessment and lipid profile, including cholesterol, LDL + HDL cholesterol, and triglycerides after fasting at least 8 (preferably 12) hours. Fasting is necessary for accurate measurement of triglycerides and the calculation of LDL cholesterol but has minimal effect on total cholesterol. LDL cholesterol measurements are unreliable with triglyceride levels >400 mg/dL.
  - Monitoring: The lipid profile should be repeated at 3 to 4 months, and then with a frequency depending on the 3- to 4-month values and risk assessment (at least once per year).
  - Therapeutic life changes: Diet, exercise, and weight loss for obesity should be recommended for triglycerides >400 mg/dL, cholesterol >240 mg/dL, and HDL <35 mg/dL.
  - Triglyceride levels >1000 mg/dL (ACTG) or >500 mg/dL (NCEP): Therapeutic life changes + drug therapy, usually gemfibrozil 600 mg bid or fenofibrate 54-160 mg qd.

■ TABLE 4-21: **CHD Risks, LDL, Goals, and Treatment Indications From the NCEP**

Risk	LDL Goal†	Drug Therapy
Coronary artery disease or other form of atherosclerosis, diabetes, or multiple risk factors	<100 mg/dL	10 yr risk >20% LDL >130 100-130: Optional
Multiple risks with ≥2 of the following: smoking, HBP, HDL <40, hereditary factors	<130 mg/dL	10 yr risk 10% to 20%* >130 10 yr risk <10%* >160
Risk factors 0-1	<160	>190 160-190: Optional

* Risk determined by multiple factors including age, cholesterol, HDL, and systolic BP.

† Major interventions: Therapeutic life style changes: diet, exercise, and weight reduction. Diet: Reduced saturated fat (<7% calories), reduced cholesterol (<200 mg/d), increased fiber (20-30 g/day), LDL lowering plant stanols/sterols (2 g/day), protein 15% calories, carbohydrates 50% to 60% total calories – predominantly complex carbohydrates. Drugs (see Table 4-22).

■ TABLE 4-22: **Lipid Lowering Agents (*JAMA* 2001;285:2486)**

Agent	Effect	Interaction With PIs + NNRTIs and Contraindications
Statins*	■ LDL ↓18% to 66% ■ HDL ↑5% to 15% ■ TG ↓7% to 30%	■ Preferred class for ↑ LDL cholesterol ■ Atorvastatin 10 mg/d or pravastatin 20 mg/d ■ Fluvastatin + cerivastatin – possible alternatives butminimal data ■ Lovastatin and simvastatin – avoid ■ Avoid class with liver disease
Bile acid sequestrants	■ LDL ↓16% to 30% ■ HDL ↑3% to 5% ■ TG no change	■ Avoid due to uncertain interactions with PIs + NNRTIs
Fibric acid*	■ LDL ↓6% to 30% ■ HDL ↑10% to 20% ■ TG ↓20% to 50%	■ Used for ↑ LDL cholesterol + ↑ triglycerides ■ Gemfibrozil and fenofibrate ■ Avoid with renal or liver failure
Nicotinic acid (niacin)	■ LDL ↓6% to 25% ■ HDL ↑15% to 35% ■ TG ↓20% to 50%	■ Used for ↑ triglyceride and ↑ LDL cholestrol ■ Can cause insulin resistance ■ Insulin resistance is a relative contraindication to nicotinic acid.

* Combination of a statin with a fibrate requires close monitoring.

■ TABLE 4-23: **Concurrent Use of Statins and PIs**

Agent	Metabolism	PI/NNRTI Interactions
Lovastatin, simvastatin	■ CYP3A4 (*Nephron* 1993;65:410; *South Med J* 1998;91:202; *AIDS* 2002;16:569)	■ Avoid PIs, avoid DLV ■ No data on EFV and NVP: Recommend avoiding concurrent use
Fluvastatin	■ CYP2C9 (*Int J Clin Pharmacol Ther* 1995;33:246)	■ Interaction with NFV ■ Concurrent use with IDV, SQV, RTV, APV, LPV/r, EFV, or NVP not studied
Cerivastatin	■ Limited data	■ Concurrent use with IDV, SQV, RTV, APV, NFV, LPV/r, EFV, or NVP not studied
Atorvastatin	■ CYP3A4 (*AIDS* 2002;16:569)	■ Concurrent use okay with IDV, SQV, RTV, APV ■ Levels of atorvastatin ↑6x with LPV/r ■ Atorvastatin AUC is increased 79% by RTV/SQV sgc and 5.8-fold by LPV/r. Use higher doses with caution
Pravastatin*	■ No cytochrome P450 interactions (*Clin Pharmacol Ther* 1998;63:332; *AIDS* 2002;16:567)	■ Concurrent use IDV, SQV, RTV, APV, LPV/r okay ■ Pravastatin AUC is increased 33% by LPV/r (but AUC was decreased 50% with RTV/SQV)

* Preferred by ACTG committee for concurrent use with PIs and NNRTIs (*Clin Infect Dis* 2000;31:1216).

HYPERTRIGLYCERIDEMIA: Normal fasting triglycerides levels are <200 mg/dL. Elevated levels are 200-500 mg/dL. Very high levels are >500 mg/dL. Very high levels should be treated aggressively to prevent atherosclerosis and pancreatitis. Treatment options include:

- Very low fat diet (<15% of calories)
- Weight reduction
- Physical activity, including aerobic exercise
- Fibrates and/or niacin
- Statins (atorvastatin may have a greater effect on triglycerides than other statins)

■ TABLE 4-24: **Treatment of Hyperlipidemia (*Clin Infect Dis* 2000;31:1216)**

Lipid Problem	Preferred	Alternative	Comment
Isolated high LDL	Statin	Niacin*	Start low doses and titrate upwards. With PIs, watch for myopathy.
High cholesterol and triglycerides	Statin or fibrate	Start one and add other	Combination may increase risk of myopathy.
Isolated high triglycerides	Fibrate	Statin	Combination may increase risk of myopathy.

* Added by authors.

Hepatotoxicity

All antiretroviral agents have been implicated as potential causes of hepatotoxicity. Lactic acidosis with hepatic steatosis can occur with nucleoside analogs, especially d4T, ddI, and AZT. PIs, especially RTV, can cause hepatotoxicity, and hepatitis also occurs with NNRTIs, especially NVP (*J Infect Dis* 1998;177:1533; *AIDS* 1998;12:1722; *Lancet* 1997;349:924).

Hepatotoxicity has also been seen in patients treated with antiretroviral agents in the presence of HCV- or HBV-associated liver disease. It is often not clear whether this reflects an adverse reaction to the antiretroviral agent or an expression of immune reconstitution with enhanced cytolytic activity against the hepatitis virus (*AIDS* 1998;122:116; *AIDS* 1998;12:2289; *Clin Infect Dis* 1998;27:1255). Despite these reports, in a large prospective review of patients with HIV/HCV co-infection, there was only a modest increase in hepatotoxicity compared with those without chronic HCV, and no irreversible hepatotoxic effects were observed (*JAMA* 2000;283:74). Chronic hepatitis with a positive HBsAg usually responds to 3TC but may flare when this drug is discontinued for any reason, and HBV often becomes resistant to 3TC during therapy. Tenofovir is active against HBV including 3TC-resistant strains and should be considered in HIV/HBV co-infected patients.

Of the currently available antiretroviral drugs, the most hepatotoxic appears to be NVP, followed by full-dose RTV (*JAMA* 2000;283;74). NVP hepatotoxicity may take two forms. The early form occurs during the first 12 weeks of treatment, appears to be more common in women and patients with high CD4 counts, often has clinical features of a hypersensitivity reaction, and may cause hepatic necrosis. The second form occurs later in the course and is clinically similar to other forms of drug-induced hepatotoxicity. Neither RTV nor NVP appears to be more hepatotoxic in patients with chronic hepatitis, so that antiretroviral therapy should not be avoided, and specific agents are not contraindicated in co-infected patients. Nevertheless, liver enzymes should be carefully monitored during therapy. Early monitoring of transaminase levels is recommended for all patients receiving NVP, regardless of whether they have underlying liver disease (see Table 4-13, p. 63). Dose reduction for AZT, all PIs, and all NNRTIs should be considered in patients with overt liver failure.

Increased Bleeding in Patients With Hemophilia

Increased spontaneous bleeding episodes in patients with hemophilia A and B have been observed with the use of PIs. Most of the reported episodes involved joints and soft tissues. However, more serious bleeding episodes, including intracranial and GI bleeding, have also been reported. The bleeding episodes occurred a median of 22 days after initiation of PI therapy. Some patients received additional coagulation factor while continuing PI therapy (*Hemophilia* 2000; 6:487).

Osteopenia/Osteoporosis and Osteonecrosis/Avascular Necrosis

Osteonecrosis and avascular necrosis is another possible late complication that may be due to HAART. There have been 67 reported cases of osteonecrosis in HIV infected patients (*Clin Infect Dis* 2000;31:1488; *Ann Intern Med* 2002;137:17). Reported prevalence based on routine MRI scans is 1.3% to 4.4%. The most common site is the femoral head; many patients have other risk factors, including alcohol abuse, hyperlipidemia, lipid lowering agents, testosterone therapy, corticosteroid use, and hypercoagulability. Bone density studies using dual energy x-ray absorptiometry (DEXA) scanning show that osteopenia and osteoporosis are relatively common, although there is no clear association with specific agents, drug classes, or lipodystrophy (*AIDS* 2000;14:F63). X-rays are not sensitive for detecting avascular necrosis. Screening of asymptomatic patients is not recommended. CT scan or MRI should be considered in patients with symptoms and risk.

■ TABLE 4-25: **Switch Studies (see *Topics in HIV Medicine* 2002;10:47)***

Switch From PI to	Number of Studies	Number of Patients	Blood Lipids		Insulin Resistance	Body Change	
			Trig. ↓	Chol. ↓		Accum.	Atrophy
NVP	10	984	10/10 ↓†	5/10 ↓†	4/6 ↓	3/7 ↓	—
EFV	15	910	7/15 ↓	3/15 ↓	4/9 ↓	3/11 ↓	—
ABC	7	640	4/5 ↓	4/6 ↓	1/2 ↓	—	4/7 ↓

* Summary of studies addressing switch therapy due to hyperlipidemia, insulin resistance, or fat redistribution. Results indicate the number of studies that showed the designated change at 24 to 52 weeks; denominator refers only to the studies that reported the designated variable.

† Number of studies showing the indicated change/number of studies examining this variable.

■ TABLE 4-26: **Dosing of ART Agents in Renal and Hepatic Failure**

Drug Name	Usual Adult Dose	Dosing for GFR >50 mL/min	Dosing for GFR 10-50 mL/min	Dosing for GFR <10 mL/min	Dosing in Hemodialysis	Dosing in Peritoneal Dialysis	Hepatic Failure
AZT	■ 300 mg bid	■ 300 mg bid	■ Usual dose †	■ 300 mg qd	■ 300 mg qd	■ 300 mg qd	■ 200 mg bid
ddI	■ Weight >60 kg dose: 400 mg qd or 200 mg bid ■ Weight <60 kg dose: 250 mg qd or 125 mg bid	■ Usual dose	■ 50% of usual dose	■ 25% of usual dose	■ 25% of usual dose* ■ Give post dialysis*	■ 25% of usual dose	■ Consider empiric dose reduction§
d4T	■ Weight >60 kg dose: 40 mg bid ■ Weight <60 kg dose: 30 mg bid	■ Usual dose	■ Weight >60 kg dose: 20 mg every 12 to 24 hours ■ Weight <60 kg dose: 15 mg every 12 to 24 hours	■ Weight >60 kg dose: 20 mg every 24 hours ■ Weight <60 kg dose: 15 mg every 24 hours	■ Weight >60 kg dose: 20 mg every 24 hours ■ Weight <60 kg dose: 15 mg every 24 hours ■ Give post dialysis*	■ Weight >60 kg dose: 20 mg every 24 hours ■ Weight <60 kg dose: 15 mg every 24 hours	■ No data: Usual dose
ddC	■ 0.75 mg tid	■ 0.75 mg tid	■ 0.75 mg tid	■ 0.75 mg bid	■ No data	■ No data	■ Usual dose
TDF	■ 300 mg qd	■ Usual dose	■ CrCl 30-50 mL/min: 300 mg every 2 days ■ CrCl 10-29: 300 mg every 3-4 days	■ 300 mg every 7 days ■ 300 mg following completion of 12 hours of dialysis (usually every 7 days)	■ 300 mg every 7 days ■ Give post dialysis*	■ No data: Avoid	■ Avoid
3TC	■ 150 mg bid	■ 150 mg bid	■ 150 mg qd	■ 150 mg, then 50 mg qd or 150 mg qod or 300 mg every 72-96 hours.	■ 150 mg, then 25-50 mg qd	■ 50 mg qd	■ No data: Usual dose

■ TABLE 4-26: **Dosing of ART Agents in Renal and Hepatic Failure** ***(Continued)***

Drug Name	Usual Adult Dose	Dosing for GFR >50 mL/min	Dosing for GFR 10-50 mL/min	Dosing for GFR <10 mL/min	Dosing in Hemodialysis	Dosing in Peritoneal Dialysis	Hepatic Failure
ABC	■ 300 mg bid	■ Usual dose	■ Usual dose	■ Usual dose	■ Usual dose	■ Usual dose	■ No data: Usual dose
EFV	■ 600 mg qd	■ Usual dose likely†	■ Usual dose	■ Usual dose likely‡	■ Usual dose (not removed)	■ Usual dose (not removed)	■ Consider empiric dose reduction§
NVP	■ 200 mg qd x 14 days then 200 mg bid	■ Usual dose†	■ Usual dose	■ Usual dose	■ Usual dose	■ Usual dose	■ Consider empiric dose reduction§
DLV	■ 400 mg tid	■ Usual dose	■ Usual dose likely†	■ Usual dose likely‡	■ Usual dose likely‡	■ Unlikely to be removed in dialysis due to high protein binding‡	■ Consider empiric dose reduction§
NFV	■ 750 mg tid or 1250 mg bid	■ Usual dose	■ Usual dose	■ Usual dose	■ Usual dose ■ Must give post dialysis	■ Usual dose	■ Consider empiric dose reduction§
IDV	■ 800 mg tid‖	■ Usual dose	■ Usual dose	■ Usual dose	■ Usual dose	■ No data: Usual dose likely‡	■ 600 mg every 8 hours§
RTV	■ 600 mg bid	■ Usual dose	■ Usual dose	■ Usual dose	■ Usual dose ■ Must give post dialysis	■ No data: Usual dose likely‡	■ Consider empiric dose reduction§
SQV	■ *Invirase*: 1000 mg bid, 400 mg bid, or 1600 mg qd (plus RTV)‖ ■ *Fortovase*: 1200 mg tid	■ Usual dose	■ Usual dose	■ Usual dose	■ Usual dose	■ No data: Usual dose likely‡	■ Consider empiric dose reduction§

Drug Name	Usual Adult Dose	Dosing for GFR >50 mL/min	Dosing for GFR 10-50 mL/min	Dosing for GFR <10 mL/min	Dosing in Hemodialysis	Dosing in Peritoneal Dialysis	Hepatic Failure
APV	■ 1200 mg bid[II]	■ Usual dose	■ Usual dose likely[‡]	■ Usual dose likely[‡]	■ No data: Usual dose likely[‡]	■ No data: Usual dose likely[‡]	■ Impairment moderate: 450 mg bid ■ Increase to standard size
LPV/r	■ 400/100 mg bid	■ Usual dose	■ Usual dose likely	■ Usual dose likely	■ Usual dose	■ No data: Usual dose likely[‡]	?

* Administer post dialysis on dialysis days. Hemodialysis removes significant amounts of ddI (*Clin Pharm Ther* 1996;60:535); d4T (*Antimicrob Agents Chemother* 2000;44:2149); ddC; 3TC; TDF; and NFV (*AIDS* 2000;14:89). Hemodialysis removes little or none of the following: AZT (*J Acquir Immune Defic Syndr* 1992;5:242); ABC; EFV (*AIDS* 2000;14:618); NVP (*Nephro Dial Transplant* 2001;16:192); IDV (*Nephro Dial Transplant* 2000;15:1102); RTV (*Nephron* 2001;87:186); SQV (*Nephron* 2001;87:186); and LPV/r (*AIDS* 2001;15:662).

† There are sparse data for most antiretroviral agents for dose adjustments based on removal with peritoneal dialysis. Removal is anticipated or established with d4T, and ddC, which should be dosed post dialysis. TDF is not recommended with peritoneal dialysis. Others are not removed or are not expected to be removed.

‡ Prediction based on pharmacokinetic principles. Drugs likely to be removed have a VD <0.7 L/kg, protein binding <80%, and size <1500 daltons.

§ Indicates extensive hepatic metabolism.

II Dose modified when combined with second PI – see Table 4-20, p. 80

Recommendations For Antiretroviral Therapy In Pregnancy

(Based on Revised DHHS Guidelines of December 2002; http://www.aidsinfo.nih.gov)

Principles (*N Engl J Med* 2002;346:1879)

- Pregnancy has no clear effect on HIV progression.
- Data from developing countries show increased rates of preterm delivery, low birth weight, and stillbirth. This has not been observed in industrialized countries.
- Probability of perinatal transmission is directly related to viral load at the time of delivery. Other risks include substance abuse, rupture of membranes, HCV coinfection, and preterm gestation.
- The probability of perinatal transmission with no treatment is 20% to 28%, with AZT monotherapy is 8% to 11%, with HAART is 1% to 2%.
- HAART is recommended for treatment of HIV in the pregnant woman based on guidelines that apply to the general population; HAART is recommended to prevent perinatal transmission in any woman with a viral load >1000 c/mL. With viral load <1000 c/mL (without treatment) consider AZT monotherapy.
- Avoid hydroxyurea, EFV, and d4T + ddI. When possible, include AZT (but not AZT + d4T). Preferred regimens in WHO guidelines: 2 NRTIs + either ABC, NVP, or NFV.
- Elective caesarean section reduces risk of perinatal transmission and should be offered at 38 weeks to pregnant women with viral loads likely to be >1,000 c/mL at delivery. There is no evidence of benefit after onset of labor, after rupture of membranes, or with viral load <1000 c/mL.

Antiretroviral Drugs for Preventing Perinatal Transmission

The largest report of the U.S. experience is the Women and Infants Transmission Study (WITS) Group, which was designed to examine the natural history of HIV in pregnant women and their infants in five cities (*J Acquir Immune Defic Syndr* 2002;29:484). Table 4-27, p. 97 summarizes the results for perinatal transmission for 1542 patients from 1990 to 2000:

■ TABLE 4-27: **Antiretroviral Treatment and Perinatal Transmission (*J Acquir Immune Defic Syndr* 2002;29:484)**

Category	No.	HIV Transmission (95% confidence interval)
Untreated	396	20.0% (16.1% to 23.9%)
AZT monotherapy	710	10.4% (8.2% to 12.6%)
Dual Therapy, non-HAART	186	3.8% (1.1% to 6.5%)
HAART	250	1.2% (0% to 2.5%)

HIV Testing and Counseling

HIV TESTING: Standard serologic test with counseling is recommended for all pregnant women. Testing should be repeated at 28 weeks. The rapid (*SUDS* or *OraQuick*) test is recommended for previously untested women presenting in labor.

COUNSELING (*MMWR* 2001;50[RR-19]:1): Minimum information to be conveyed includes the following:

- HIV is the virus that causes AIDS and is spread by sex and drugs.
- Women may be infected and not know it.
- There are effective interventions that protect the infant and reduce morbidity and mortality in adults.
- HIV serology is recommended for all pregnant women.
- Services are available to help pregnant women prevent HIV transmission.
- Women who refuse the test will receive the usual care for themselves and their infants.

LEGAL ISSUES (UNITED STATES): Testing and counseling pregnant women has been endorsed by most professional societies and implemented by most states, but with substantial variations in strategy. No states mandate testing pregnant women without informed consent, and only two (New York and Connecticut) require testing newborns. An Institute of Medicine report recommends universal HIV testing of pregnant women with patient notification of results as a component of prenatal care. This is under consideration.

Factors that Reduce Perinatal Transmission

For women who do not breastfeed, intrauterine transmission accounts for 25% to 40% and delivery accounts for 60% to 75% (*MMWR* 2001;50[RR-19]:63). It should be noted that all three components of the AZT regimen (pre-natal, perinatal, and post-natal) have merit.

VIRAL LOAD: There is a direct correlation between maternal viral load and probability of perinatal transmission. A large study showed that the rate of perinatal transmission with viral load >100,000 c/mL was 41%; with 1,000 to 10,000 m/L it was 17%; and with <1,000 c/mL it was 0% (*N Engl J Med* 1999;13:407; *J Infect Dis* 2001;183:206; *J Acquir Immune Defic Syndr* 2002;29:484). Despite these findings, it should be emphasized that there is no viral load that can be regarded as safe because other factors also play a role (*AIDS* 1999;13:1377; *AIDS* 1999;13:407; *J Infect Dis* 1999;179:590). In an analysis of seven prospective studies, there were 44 cases of HIV in babies born to 1,202 women with viral loads <1,000 c/mL (*J Infect Dis* 2001;183:539).

AZT: This drug should be included when possible to prevent perinatal transmission because it has the largest experience for safety and efficacy. This includes significant reduction in perinatal transmission that is independent of viral load (*N Engl J Med* 1996;335:1621; *Lancet* 1999;354:156) and independent of AZT resistance (*J Infect Dis* 1998;177:557), although the latter point is somewhat controversial (*AIDS* 2000;14:263). Analysis of ACTG 076 showed that AZT significantly reduces perinatal transmission even when the baseline viral load is <1,000 c/mL (*J Infect Dis* 2001;183:539). This provides the rationale for AZT monotherapy in untreated pregnant women with a baseline viral load <1,000 c/mL.

■ TABLE 4-28: **Rates of Perinatal Transmission With AZT**

Study Format	Rx	Transmission Rate: C-section	Transmission Rate: Other Modes	Odds Ratio
Observational (*AIDS* 2000;14:263)	■ No AZT ■ AZT	■ 58/559 (10.4%) ■ 4/96 (2%)	■ 1021/5385 (19%) ■ 92/1255 (7.3%)	■ 0.49 ■ 0.26
Randomized trial (*Clin Infect Dis* 2001;33:3)	■ No AZT ■ AZT	■ 2/51 (4%) ■ 1/119 (1%)	■ 16/82 (20%) ■ 5/117 (4%)	■ 0.2 ■ 0.2

NVP: NVP is the best studied and best tolerated "third drug" (WHO guidelines). It has established merit in preventing perinatal transmission in multiple studies, most performed in resource limited areas with a single maternal dose and one infant dose. HIVNET 012 was a randomized trial conducted in Africa comparing NVP (200 mg by mouth given to the mother during labor and a single 2 mg/kg dose given within 72 hours to the infant) vs AZT (600 mg at onset of labor followed by 300 mg every 3 hours until delivery to mother and 4 mg/kg/day x 7 days to the infant). Transmission was significantly lower in the NVP arm (13.1% vs 21.5%). However, analysis of participants given NVP at 6 to 8 weeks postpartum showed NVP resistance mutations in 11 of 70, including the K103N mutation in 10 (*AIDS*

2000;14:F111). These mutations are not associated with increased perinatal transmission. The mutations were no longer detectable in 4 of 7 at 13 to 18 months; it is assumed that the mutant virus remains archived indefinitely, although this is not currently known.

CESAREAN SECTION: C-section has established efficacy in reducing perinatal transmission when maternal viral load exceeds 1,000 c/mL. A meta-analysis of 15 studies with 8,533 mother-infant pairs showed a 2-fold reduction in perinatal transmission in women given AZT vs no antiretroviral and a 4-fold reduction when AZT was combined with cesarean section (Table 4-28, p. 98). A study of the European Mode of Delivery Collaboration randomly assigned patients to vaginal delivery vs C-section. The C-section group had a perinatal transmission rate of 3/170 (1.8%) compared with 21/200 (10.5%) in the vaginal delivery group. However, C-section appears to confer little or no benefit in pregnant women who are treated with HAART and have good virologic control (*BMJ* 2001;322:511). This decision is based in part on the risk:benefit ratio. There may be an increased risk associated with C-section in women with low CD4 cell counts (*AIDS* 1995;9:913; *JAMA* 1999;281:1946; *Lancet* 1999;354:1612; *Obstet Gynecol* 1999;94:942; *Obstet Gynecol* 1998;92:945; *Obstet Gynecol* 1998;92:507). Recent studies show that the risk is slight (*Am J Obstet Gynecol* 2002;186:784; *J Acquir Immune Defic Syndr* 2001;26:236; *Am J Obstet Gynecol* 2001;184:1108). The current DHHS recommendations are for C-section to be offered to women with a viral load >1,000 c/mL in late pregnancy. This should be performed at 38 weeks instead of the standard 39 weeks, but the earlier time entails a small risk of fetal respiratory distress that must be balanced against the risk of premature rupture of membranes or labor. C-section performed at the time of labor or in a patient with ruptured membranes incurs an increased risk of infectious complications and no benefit for reducing perinatal transmission. Other risks for adverse outcome(s) are non-elective C-section, malnutrition, obesity, smoking, genital infection, low socioeconomic status, prolonged labor, and membrane rupture. The major complications noted in these patients are wound infections, pneumonia, and endometritis. In the largest U.S. study (WITS), there were 2 deaths among 207 HIV infected women who underwent C-section, both had PCP (*J Acquir Immune Defic Syndr* 2001;26:218).

BREASTFEEDING: The risk of HIV transmission with breastfeeding is 16% (*J Infect Dis* 1996;174:722; *JAMA* 2000;283:1167; *Lancet* 1992;340:385; *JAMA* 2000;283:1175). The risk appears to be greatest in the first 4 to 6 months (*JAMA* 1999;282:744). Other risk factors include mastitis, cracked nipples, infant with thrush, primary HIV infection during pregnancy, and prolonged breastfeeding. Breast-feeding is consequently discouraged for HIV infected women in the developed world; the issue is more complex in the developing world (*JAMA* 2000;238:1167). It is estimated, for example, that 1.7 million babies develop HIV each year due to breastfeeding but that 1.5 million babies would die each year if not breastfed (*BMJ* 2001;322:511).

SAFETY OF ANTIRETROVIRAL THERAPY: To date the data support the safety of antiretroviral agents in pregnancy except for ddI + d4T, EFV, and hydroxyurea (*J Acquir Immune Defic Syndr* 2000;25:306; *MMWR* 2002;51[RR-7]:1; *N Engl J Med* 2002;346:1879). The combination of ddI + d4T should be avoided or used cautiously due to reports of three maternal deaths ascribed to lactic acidosis and/or hepatotoxicity. EFV should be avoided in the first trimester due to teratogenic effects when given to primates, which included neural tube defects in 3 of 20 monkeys. A single case reported twice concerns an infant with a neural tube defect, a meningocele, born to a woman who received EFV during conception and early pregnancy (*Arch Intern Med* 2002;162:355; *AIDS* 2002;16:299). NVP appears safe but has been studied most extensively when given at delivery (*J Acquir Immune Defic Syndr* 1999;354:795). Tenofovir given in high doses to gravid monkeys caused a reduction in body length and reduction in insulin-like growth factor (*J Acquir Immune Defic Syndr* 2002;29:207). Implications for humans are unclear. Hydroxyurea is unsafe in pregnancy and carries a class D FDA rating. A report from France suggested mitochondrial toxicity with neurologic sequelae in 8 of 1754 infants exposed to AZT alone or AZT/3TC *in utero* (*Lancet* 1999; 354:1084). Evaluation of 16,000 infants exposed to AZT *in utero* has not confirmed the report and showed no evidence of immunologic, cardiac, oncogenic, or neurologic consequences (*N Eng J Med* 2000;3:805). The conclusion is that AZT exposure *in utero* causes mitochondrial toxicity in ≤0.3% (*N Engl J Med* 2002;346:1879). Rodent studies show an increase in vaginal tumors but only at 30 times the size-adjusted dose in humans (*J Nat Cancer Inst* 1997;89:1602). There are no supporting data in humans (*J Acquir Immune Defic Syndr* 1999;20:43). Liquid amprenavir contains large quantities of propylene glycol and should be avoided in pregnancy.

PHARMACOLOGY: All NRTIs and NVP cross the placenta; PIs cross poorly. Passage of antiretrovirals into breast milk is assumed; it is established for AZT, 3TC, and NVP. Serum concentrations of PIs appear lower in pregnancy, but antiretroviral effects appear adequate and toxic effects appear to be the same as for non-pregnant women (*N Engl J Med* 2002;346:1879).

WHEN TO INITIATE THERAPY DURING PREGNANCY: The safety of antiretroviral agents during the first trimester is sometimes questioned because this is the time of fetal organ formation. There are no data to support or refute these concerns. Some experts recommend a delay in starting antiretroviral agents or suspending treatment during the first trimester. This is a risk-benefit decision.

TOLERABILITY OF ANTIRETROVIRAL AGENTS: Pregnant women may experience unusual difficulty in tolerating antiretroviral regimens due to nausea and vomiting, especially during the first trimester. All antiretroviral drugs should be discontinued during periods of intolerance, and an attempt should be made to identify the best-tolerated regimen with established potency. Glucose intolerance is common during pregnancy and is also a complication of PI-based HAART; this indicates the need for careful glucose monitoring.

RESISTANCE: The frequency of AZT resistance in pregnant women in the U.S. is about 25% for any AZT resistance mutation and 10% for high level resistance (*AIDS* 2000;14:263; *J Infect Dis* 2001;184:1120). It is possible that resistance reduces perinatal transmission due to reduced fitness (*AIDS* 2000;143:263; *J Infect Dis* 1999;179:705). Dual nucleoside therapy with AZT + 3TC is associated with high rates of M184V mutations in pregnant women (*JAMA* 2001;285:2083); this dual nucleoside combination without a third agent is not generally recommended, but might be considered in women with a very low viral load treated only to prevent perinatal transmission (*MMWR* 2002;51[RR-7]:20). Single-dose NVP has been associated with high rates of K103N mutations, but their significance is unclear (*AIDS* 2000;14:F111). The prevalence of high-level resistance to NNRTIs and PI in treatment-naïve patients is low (*J Infect Dis* 2000;182:330; *JAMA* 1999;282:1142; *JAMA* 1999;282:1135). The International AIDS Society-USA and Euro Guidelines Group for HIV Resistance recommend routine resistance testing for all pregnant women (*JAMA* 2000;283:2417; *AIDS* 2001;15:309). The DHHS HIV Guidelines Panel and DH Watts (*N Engl J Med* 2002;346:1879) recommend testing only for the same indications used for non-pregnant patients. The rationale for the latter recommendation is the lack of data showing improved maternal outcome or reduced risk of transmission with routine resistance testing in pregnancy.

ISSUES FOR DEVELOPING COUNTRIES (*Lancet* 2002;359:992): The rate of perinatal transmission without intervention is 19% to 36% (*AIDS* 2001;15:379). The prevalence of HIV in pregnant women in some locations is as high as 25%. Antiretroviral drugs, including AZT, NVP, and combination regimens, have established merit in preventing perinatal transmission and are cost-effective (*BMJ* 1999;318:1650), including AZT and NVP or combination regimens. These regimens include short course AZT, short-course AZT + 3TC, and single-dose nevirapine regimens (*JAMA* 1999;281:151; *N Engl J Med* 1999; 340:1042; *Lancet* 1999;354:795; *N Engl J Med* 2000;343:982). Antiretrovirals are now frequently available without charge, so the cost is primarily for voluntary testing and counseling. The ability to implement counseling and testing services is variable, but an alternative strategy for clinics with less capacity and with high HIV-prevalence is consideration of universal nevirapine.

WHO GUIDELINES FOR RESOURCE POOR SETTINGS FOR HIV INFECTED WOMEN WHO ARE PREGNANT OR POTENTIALLY PREGNANT

- Two NRTIs plus
  - Nevirapine
  - Abacavir
  - Nelfinavir
  - PI with low dose RTV boosting
- IDV/RTV 800/100 mg bid
- LPV/r 400/100 mg bid
- SQV/RTV 1000/100 mg bid

ACTG 076 Protocol (*MMWR* 2002;51[RR-7]:1)

ANTEPARTUM: AZT 300 mg bid or 200 mg tid from week 14 to delivery

INTRAPARTUM: AZT IV 2 mg/kg 1st hour, then 1 mg/kg/hour until delivery

POSTPARTUM: AZT syrup, 2 mg/kg q6h (or 1.5 mg/kg q6h IV) x 6 weeks for the infant

HIV Infected Women Without Prior Therapy

PRESENTS IN EARLY PREGNANCY (<36 weeks)

- **Viral load >1,000 c/mL:** HAART regardless of CD4 cell count with:
  - Inclusion of AZT if possible according to ACTG 076.
  - Possible delay until 10 to 12 weeks gestation.
  - Avoid EFV (teratogenic), hydroxyurea (teratogenic), d4T + ddI (lactic acidosis), d4T + AZT (pharmacologic antagonism), and liquid amprenavir (propylene glycol).
  - Viral load <1,000 c/mL and CD4 count >350 cells/mm^3: AZT monotherapy according to the 076 protocol, including a delay until 10 to 12 weeks gestation. (Some authorities discuss and offer HAART.)
- Monitor viral load, CD4 cell count, and resistance tests as recommended for nonpregnant patients.
- At 36 weeks, inform patient of risks and benefits of C-section; encourage C-section at 38 to 39 weeks if viral load >1,000 c/mL.

PRESENTS IN LATE PREGNANCY (≥36 weeks)

- Initiate standard antiretroviral regimen including 076 protocol with AZT with avoidance of hydroxyurea, liquid amprenavir, AZT + d4T, and d4T + ddI; encourage C-section at 38 weeks if viral load is >1,000 c/mL.

PRESENTS IN LABOR (Options are in no particular order of priority)

- NVP 200 mg at onset of labor
  - Infant receives single dose of 2 mg/kg at 48-72 hours
- AZT 600 mg PO at onset of labor, then 300 mg PO q3h until delivery plus 3TC 150 mg PO at onset of labor and 150 mg q12h until delivery
  - Infant: AZT 4 mg/kg PO q12h plus 3TC 2 mg/kg q12h x 7 days
- AZT 2 mg/kg IV, then 1 mg/kg/hour IV until delivery
  - Infant: AZT 2 mg/kg PO q6h x 6 weeks (076 protocol)
- NVP 200 mg PO plus AZT PO at onset of labor + AZT 2 mg/kg IV bolus then 1 mg/kg/hour IV infusion until delivery
  - Infant: NVP single 2 mg/kg PO at 48 hours to 72 hours + AZT 2 mg/kg PO q6h x 6 weeks

PRESENTS POST DELIVERY

- Initiate 6-week AZT protocol for infant
- Evaluate infant for HIV infection when feasible
- Evaluate mother for indications for antiretroviral therapy

Treated Patients

PRESENTS IN EARLY PREGNANCY (36 weeks)

- Continue antiretroviral therapy with standard monitoring with three differences:
  - Include AZT if tolerated and appropriate from a virologic standpoint
  - Avoid hydroxyurea, and avoid d4T + ddI, EFV, and liquid APV
  - Consider discontinuation of all antiretroviral agents during first trimester based on CD4 count, viral load, tolerability, and patient concerns.

PRESENTS IN LATE PREGNANCY (≥36 Weeks)

- Continue antiretroviral therapy, including all agents except those that are contraindicated in late pregnancy; avoid HAART interruption during delivery
- Inform patient of risks and benefits of C-section
- Encourage C-section at 38 to 39 weeks if viral load >1,000 c/mL

CESAREAN SECTION

- If elective, it should be performed at 38 weeks. C-section at 38 weeks carries a small but significant risk of infant respiratory distress requiring mechanical ventilation (*Acta Paediatr* 1999;88: 1244). This risk must be balanced with the risk of labor or premature rupture of membranes between 38 to 39 weeks. IV AZT should begin 3 hours before surgery; all other antiretrovirals should continue without interruption. Give antibiotic prophylaxis for C-section.

- If C-section is planned, but patient presents in labor: Initiate 076 protocol, intrapartum component.
  - Rapid progression of labor: Vaginal delivery.
  - Long labor anticipated: Consider loading dose of AZT or oxytocin to expedite delivery.
- Patient presents with recent onset of labor or rupture of membranes: Consider C-section depending on viral load and length of labor (no data).

MONITORING DURING PREGNANCY: CD4 counts, viral load, and resistance tests should be performed according to standards for non-pregnant patients.

ANTIRETROVIRAL PREGNANCY REGISTRY: Cases of prenatal exposure should be reported to the Antiretroviral Pregnancy Registry. This registry collects observational data; patients are anonymous, and the Registry obtains birth outcome data. The Registry can be contacted at:

Antiretroviral Pregnancy Registry
115 N. Third St., Suite 306,
Wilmington, NC 28401
TEL: 800-258-4263
FAX: 800-800-1052

■ TABLE 4-29: **Safety of Antiretroviral Agents in Pregnancy (Adapted from *Guidelines for Use of Antiretroviral Drugs in Pregnant HIV-1 Infected Women for Maternal Health and Interventions to Reduce Perinatal HIV-1 Transmission in the U.S.* [*MMWR* 2002;51(RR-7):1])**

Antiretroviral Drug	FDA Category*	Placental Passage Newborn:Maternal Drug Ratio	Long-term Animal Carcinogenicity Studies	Rodent Teratogen
AZT	C	Yes (human) [0.85]	Positive (rodent, vaginal tumors)	Positive (near lethal dose)
ddC	C	Yes (rhesus) [0.3-0.50]	Positive (rodent, thymic lymphomas)	Positive (hydrocephalus at high dose)
ddI	B	Yes (human) [0.5]	Negative (no tumors, lifetime rodent study)	Negative
d4T	C	Yes (rhesus) [0.76]	Not completed	Negative (but sternal bone calcium decreases)
3TC	C	Yes (human) [~1.0]	Negative (no tumors, lifetime rodent study)	Negative
ABC	C	Yes (rats)	Not completed	Positive (anasarca and skeletal malformations at 1,000 mg/kg, 35 x human exposure, during organogenesis)
TDF	B	Yes (rats and monkeys)	Not completed	Negative
SQV	B	Minimal (human)	Not completed	Negative
IDV	C	Minimal (human)	Not completed	Negative (but extra ribs in rats)
RTV	B	Minimal (human)	Positive (rodent liver adenomas and carcinomas in male mice)	Negative (but cryptorchidism in rats at maternally toxic doses)
NFV	B	Minimal (human)	Not completed	Negative
APV	C	Unknown	Not completed	Positive (thymic elongation; incomplete ossification of bones; low body weight)
NVP	C	Yes (human) [~1.0]	Not completed	Negative
DLV	C	Unknown	Not completed	Ventricular septal defect
EFV	C	Yes (cynomolgus monkeys, rats, rabbits) [~1.0]	Not completed	Anencephaly; anophthalmia; microphthalmia (cynomolgus monkeys)
LPV/r	C	Unknown	Not completed	Negative (but delayed ossification and increase in skeletal variations in rats at maternally toxic doses)

* See p. 163 for pregnancy categories.

Postexposure Prophylaxis (PEP)

Occupational Exposure

RISK OF TRANSMISSION

- A total of 23 studies of needle sticks among health care workers demonstrate HIV transmission in 20 of 6,135 (0.33%) exposed to an HIV infected source (*Ann Intern Med* 1990;113:740). With mucosal surface exposure, there was one transmission in 1,143 exposures (0.09%), and there were no transmissions in 2,712 skin exposures. As of June 2000, there were a total of 56 healthcare workers in the United States who had occupationally acquired HIV infection as indicated by seroconversion in the context of an exposure to an HIV infected source. There are an additional 132 healthcare workers who had possible occupationally acquired HIV; these latter healthcare workers did not have documented seroconversion in the context of an exposure. Occupations of the 56 confirmed cases: Nurses (23), laboratory technicians (20), and physicians (6). All transmissions involved blood or bloody body fluid except for three involving laboratory workers exposed to HIV viral cultures. Exposures were percutaneous in 48, mucocutaneous in 5, and both in 2 cases. To date, there are no confirmed seroconversions in surgeons and no seroconversions with exposures to a suture needle.
- A retrospective case-control study of needle-stick injuries from an HIV-infected source by the CDC included 33 cases who seroconverted and 739 controls (*MMWR* 1996;45:468; *N Engl J Med* 1997;337:1485). The risks for seroconversion included: 1) deep injury; 2) visible blood on the device; 3) needle placement in a vein or artery; and 4) a source with late-stage HIV infection (presumably reflecting high viral load). There was also evidence that AZT prophylaxis was associated with a 79% reduction in transmission rates. On the basis of this experience, revised preliminary guidelines recommending more aggressive antiretroviral therapy were published in June 1996 (*MMWR* 1996;45:468), updated in 1997 (*Am J Med* 1997;102:117), and then updated again in 2001 (*MMWR* 2001;50[RR-11]).

■ TABLE 4-30: **Risk of Viral Transmission With Sharps Injury From Infected Source**

Source	Risk
HBV (unvaccinated):	
Source HBeAg+	37% to 62%
Source HBeAg-	23% to 37%
HCV	1.8%
HIV	0.3%

DATA SUPPORTING POSTEXPOSURE PROPHYLAXIS IN THE U.S.

Results of PEP Registry (*Infect Control Hosp Epidemiol* 2000;21:780)

- **Period reviewed:** October 1996 to December 1998
- **Number of injuries reviewed:** 492
- **HIV status of source known to be positive:** 258 (60%)
- **Type of exposure:** Percutaneous 85%; mucocutaneous 10%
- **Fluid:** Blood – 71%; bloody fluid – 13%; HIV culture – 2.3%
- **Time to initiate PEP antiretroviral therapy:** 1.8 hours (median)
- **Treatment:** Three drugs – 59%, two drugs – 36%, four drugs – 4%
- **Side effects:** Any – 76%, nausea – 57%, fatigue – 38%, headache – 18%, vomiting – 16%, diarrhea – 14%; side effects with AZT + 3TC regimen – 63%; side effects with AZT/3TC/IDV – 83%
- **Proportion who discontinued or modified treatment due to side effects:** 54%
- **HIV transmission:** None, but none would be expected given the historic rate of 0.3% for needlestick injuries without prophylaxis.

PEP RECOMMENDATIONS AND CHOICE OF REGIMEN: Recommendations are based on the type of exposure, HIV status of the source, or, if the status is unknown, the risk status of the source.

MANAGEMENT RESOURCES (PHS Statement on the Management of Occupational Exposures to HIV and Recommendations for Postexposure Prophylaxis [*MMWR* 2001;50(RR-1)])

- National Clinician's Postexposure Prophylaxis Hotline (HRSA, AETC, CDC) (available at all times): 888-448-4911 or http://www.ucsf.edu/hivcntr
- Needlestick (UCLA): http://www.needlestick.mednet.ucla.edu
- Hepatitis hotline: 888-443-7232 or http://www.cdc.gov/hepatitis
- CDC Reporting (occupationally acquired HIV and PEP failure): 800-893-0485
- FDA: Unusual or severe toxicity of antiretrovirals: 800-332-1088 or http://www.fda.gov/medwatch
- HIV/AIDS Treatment Information: http://www.aidsinfo.nih.gov

■ TABLE 4-31: **HIV Postexposure Prophylaxis for Percutaneous Injuries**

Exposure	Status of Source		
	Source HIV+ and Low Risk*	Source HIV + and High Risk*	HIV Status of Source is Unknown
Not severe: Solid needle, superficial	2 drug PEP†	3 drug PEP†	Usually none; consider 2 drug PEP‡
Severe: Large bore, deep injury, visible blood in device, needle in patient artery/vein	3 drug PEP†	3 drug PEP†	Usually none; consider 2 drug PEP‡

* Low risk: Asymptomatic HIV or viral load <1,500 c/mL. High risk: Symptomatic HIV, AIDS, acute seroconversion, and high viral load.

† Concern for drug resistance: Initiate prophylaxis without delay and consult an expert.

‡ Consider 2 drug PEP if source is high risk for HIV or exposure is from an unknown source with HIV infection likely.

■ TABLE 4-32: **HIV Post Exposure Prophylaxis for Mucous Membranes and Non-Intact Skin Exposures***

Exposure	Status of Source		
	Source HIV+ and Low Risk†	Source HIV + and High Risk†	HIV Status of Source is Unknown
Small volume (drops)	Consider 2 drug PEP	2 drug PEP	Usually no PEP; consider 2 drug PEP‡
Large volume (major blood splash)	2 drug PEP	3 drug PEP	Usually no PEP; consider 2 drug PEP‡

* Non-intact skin: Dermatitis, abrasion, wound

† Low risk: Asymptomatic or viral load <1500 c/mL; high risk: Acute seroconversion or high viral load

‡ Consider if source has HIV risk factors or exposure from unknown source where HIV infected source is likely.

RECOMMENDED REGIMENS: 2 DRUG COMBINATIONS

- AZT + 3TC
- 3TC + d4T
- d4T + ddI
- TDF + 3TC – not included in PHS guidelines because TDF was not available at the time this document was published. It is attractive due to good tolerability and effectiveness in preventing HIV transmission in primates.

3 DRUG COMBINATIONS

- 2 nucleosides (above list) + indinavir, nelfinavir, efavirenz, abacavir, ritonavir, *Fortovase*, amprenavir, delavirdine, or lopinavir/ritonavir.
- Decisions should be made based in part on information about the source, including antiretroviral therapy, response to therapy, viral load, and any data on HIV resistance testing. Decisions should not delay initiation of PEP, and modifications can be made after treatment has started.

TESTING IN THE SOURCE PATIENT: If there is no recent positive or negative serology, a rapid test is preferred (such as *SUDS* or *OraQuick*). Since results should be available in 20 minutes, they are highly reliable for excluding HIV infection and are cost effective (*Infect Control Hosp Epidemiol* 2001;22:289). Standard serologic tests may take 3 to 7 days, but a negative EIA screening assay is usually available in 24 to 48 hours and is adequate for the decision to discontinue PEP. Some states permit testing the source of a health care worker exposure without informed consent; about half require informed consent. If the source has had an illness compatible with acute HIV syndrome, testing should include plasma HIV RNA levels.

MONITORING AND COUNSELING THE HEALTHCARE WORKER

- **Testing the healthcare worker:** HIV serology should be performed at the time of injury, and repeated at 6 weeks, 3 months, and 6 months. There have been three health care workers who seroconverted at >6 months postexposure. This represents about 4% of confirmed seroconversions in healthcare workers (*Am J Med* 1997;102:117). Most healthcare workers who seroconverted had symptomatic acute HIV syndrome, usually 2 to 6 weeks postexposure.
- **Caution:** The health care worker should be advised to practice safe sex or abstain until serology is negative at 6 months postexposure. The greatest risk is the first 6 to 12 weeks.
- **Time:** PEP should be initiated as quickly as possible, preferably within 1 to 2 hours of exposure and up to 36 hours postexposure. The median time from exposure to treatment in 432 health care workers with HIV exposure from October 1996 to December 1998 was 1.8 hours (*Infect Control Hosp Epidemiol* 2000;21:780).

TOLERABILITY AND TOXICITY

- **Side effects:** For health care workers who receive PEP, about 74% experience side effects, primarily nausea (58%), fatigue (37%), headache (16%), vomiting (16%), or diarrhea (14%). About 53% discontinue treatment before completion of the 4-week course due to multiple factors including side effects of drugs (*Infect Control Hosp Epidemiol* 2000;21:780). A similar experience with PEP was reported from France, where ADRs occurred in 85%, most commonly with GI intolerance (*Clin Infect Dis* 2001; 32:1494)

- **Pregnancy:** There is evidence of carcinogenicity ascribed to AZT using 12 to 15x the standard dose in rodents. The relevance of this experience to patients is unknown. Extensive experience with 20,000 infants exposed to AZT *in utero* failed to reveal any clear evidence of toxicity. With regard to other agents, EFV and the combination of ddI + d4T should be avoided in pregnancy. Counseling health care workers with childbearing capacity should include a discussion of these risks and the limited data regarding safety of any antiretroviral agents, especially during the first trimester, and the limited studies of PIs in pregnant women. CDC guidelines state that pregnancy should not preclude PEP (*MMWR* 1998;47:1).
- **Breastfeeding:** Consider temporary discontinuation of breastfeeding during antiretroviral therapy.
- **Confidentiality:** This is considered critical.
- **Agent selection**
  - AZT is advocated because it has been used extensively and is the only antiretroviral agent that has established merit for preventing transmission in healthcare workers. Safety in this setting appears well established, and efficacy appears to be about 80%. AZT use in pregnancy suggests efficacy even when the implicated source strain shows genotypic resistance to AZT, although efficacy is reduced (*J Infect Dis* 1998;177:557). Other agents in the standard PEP regimen are suggested based on enhanced antiretroviral potency and toxicity profile. AZT is usually combined with 3TC. The main problem with AZT is poor tolerability with headache, fatigue, and GI side effects. Alternative dual combinations that show better tolerability are TDF/3TC and d4T/3TC.
  - For higher risk exposures the CDC recommends "triple therapy" with IDV or NFV because these were favored PIs when the recommendations were written. Other options now often preferred are LPV/r or other RTV-boosted PI regimens. NVP should be avoided due to reports of 12 cases of hepatotoxicity and 14 cases of severe skin rashes when used for PEP (*MMWR* 2001;49:1153). EFV may be problematic due to the CNS side effects that commonly occur during the first 2 to 3 weeks of treatment. Teratogenicity of EFV is also a concern in female health care workers with childbearing potential.
  - Anticipated or established resistance of the source strain in the face of virologic failure should also influence this decision.
- **Resistance testing:** Some advocate testing resistance of the source strain to facilitate drug selection in the exposed health care worker. The obvious problem is the time required for test results

and the importance of rapid institution of prophylaxis. Most authorities recommend that decisions be based on the drug history and viral load of the source. In a review of 52 patients who were the source of occupational exposures, 39% had major mutations conferring resistance (7th CROI, San Francisco, Calif., February 2000, Abstract 469).

- **Postexposure registry:** The registry was closed effective June 30, 1999 (*MMWR* 1999;48:194).

HEALTHCARE WORKER TO PATIENT TRANSMISSION

- **Healthcare worker to patient transmission:** This became a topical issue in 1990 with the case of Dr. Acer, a Florida dentist, who was identified as the source of HIV infection for six dental patients (*Ann Intern Med* 1992;116:798; *Ann Intern Med* 1994;121:886). The source of the virus was established by genetic sequencing (*J Virol* 1998;72:4537), but the mechanism of transmission was never established. This disclosure led to a series of "look backs," in which serologic tests were performed on over 22,000 patients who received care from 59 health providers with known HIV infection. No transmissions were identified (*Ann Intern Med* 1995;122:653). Since this time, there has been one additional case, an orthopedic surgeon in France who may have transmitted HIV infection to a patient during a total hip replacement in 1992 (*Ann Intern Med* 1999;130:1).
- **Management**
  - The incident with the Florida dentist raised great concern about this issue and led to a federal law in 1991 requiring states to establish guidelines for HIV-positive HCWs. Most states adopted CDC recommendations that required persons who perform "exposure prone invasive procedures" (surgery in a blind body cavity) to: 1) Advise the patient of the HCW's serostatus and 2) Obtain written informed consent from the patient. This applies to surgeons, nurses, and other members of the operating team.
  - A review by Julie Gerberding of the CDC did not mention these recommendations regarding management of HIV infected health care workers (*Ann Intern Med* 1999;130:64) but did emphasize the following: Patients who have exposures analogous to what would be defined as a potentially high-risk occupational exposure in a health care worker should be managed by standard guidelines with respect to counseling, serologic testing, and antiretroviral therapy. This means that a patient exposed to blood from an HIV infected surgeon, such as an accidental needle injury resulting in contamination of the surgical field with the surgeon's blood, needs counseling regarding the exposure and the option of antiretroviral treatment. One issue that is often overlooked is that anonymity is an ethical and legal requirement for the health care workers interacting with HIV infected patients, but there are no

such restrictions on the patient who is notified about a health care worker with HIV. Disclosure of a surgeon's serologic status may end his/her career.

OCCUPATIONAL EXPOSURE TO HEPATITIS B VIRUS (HBV)

- **HBV postexposure prophylaxis:** Recommendations are based on the vaccine status of the healthcare worker, evidence of serologic response, (anti-HBs levels >10 mIU/mL), and the source.

■ TABLE 4-33: **HBV Postexposure Prophylaxis**

Vaccination Status of Healthcare Worker	Features of Source: HBsAg Positive	Features of Source: Source Unknown
Unvaccinated	HBIG* + vaccine series (3 doses)	HBV vaccine (3 doses)
Vaccinated		
Responder†	No Rx	No Rx
Non responder	HBIG x 1 + vaccine series or HBIG x 2‡	Rx as source positive if high risk
Antibody status	Test for anti-HBs unknown ■ Anti-HBs >10 mIU/mL – no Rx ■ Anti-HBs <10 mIU/mL – HBIG x 1 + vaccine booster	

* HBIG = Hepatitis B Immune Globulin; dose is 0.06 mL/kg IM. Should be given as soon as possible and within 7 days.

† Responder defined by antibody to HBsAg of >10 mIU/mL.

‡ HBIG + the vaccine series is preferred for non-responders who did not complete the 3 dose series; HBIG x 2 doses is preferred if there were 2 vaccine series and no response.

OCCUPATIONAL EXPOSURE TO HEPATITIS C VIRUS (HCV)

- **HCV postexposure prophylaxis**
  - Risk: 1.8% with sharps injury from HCV infected source.
  - Source testing: Anti-HCV; confirm positives as with RIBA.
  - Health care worker: Anti-HCV and ALT at baseline and at 4 to 6 months.
  - HCV RNA may be tested at 4 to 6 weeks to detect acute HCV prior to seroconversion. Persons with documented acute HCV infection should be considered for anti-HCV therapy (*N Engl J Med* 2001;345:1452 and NIH HCV concensus guidelines – see p. 355).
  - Positive anti-HCV tests should be confirmed as with qualitative HCV RNA tests.
  - No prophylaxis with IG or with antiviral agents (interferon + ribavirin) is recommended.

Non-Occupational HIV Exposure (Sexual Contact or Needle Sharing)

RISK OF TRANSMISSION

■ TABLE 4-34: **Risk of HIV Transmission With Single Exposure From an HIV Infected Source**

Exposure	Risk/10,000 Exposures*
Needle sharing	67
Percutaneous (occupational exposure)	30
Receptive anal intercourse	10 to 30
Receptive vaginal intercourse	8 to 20
Insertive vaginal sex	3 to 9
Insertive anal sex	3

* (*Am J Med* 1999;106:324; *Ann Intern Med* 1996;125:497; *J Acquir Immune Defic Syndr* 1992;5:1116; *N Engl J Med* 1997;336:1072)

■ TABLE 4-35: **Risk of HIV Transmission in 415 Untreated Discordant Couples (*N Engl J Med* 2000;342:921)**

Viral Load	Transmissions/100 Person-years
<400 c/mL	0
400-3,500 c/mL	4.8
3,500-50,000 c/mL	14.0
>50,000 c/mL	23.0

CDC RECOMMENDATIONS (*MMWR* 1998;47[RR-17])

- **Conclusion:** The PHS is unable to recommend for or against prophylaxis after non-occupational exposure due to the lack of data.
- **If prophylaxis is attempted, the healthcare provider must**
  - Inform the patient about the lack of data.
  - Make judicious use of antiretroviral agents (no specific regimen is recommended).
  - Address the importance of risk reduction.
  - Restrict use of PEP to high-risk exposures: unprotected receptive and or vaginal intercourse with a known HIV-infected source.

- **Cost:** $800 (estimate for 28-day course of antiretroviral agents)
- **Current practice guidelines:** British Columbia Centre for Excellence in HIV/AIDS: "A Guideline for Accidental Exposure to HIV," which recommends antiretroviral agents for rape victims. The Center provides a "starter kit" with a 5-day supply of AZT and 3TC to emergency rooms.
- **Registry, U.S.:** The CDC has established a new Non-occupational HIV Postexposure Prophylaxis Registry that includes 6 forms and 17 pages. All information can be provided by telephone 877-448-1737, on the internet (http://www.hivpepregistry.org), or by hard copy. Write to Non-occupational HIV PEP Registry, John Snow Inc., 44 Farnsworth St., Boston, MA 02210-1211; fax 877-448-7737. The provider incentive is a $10 gift certificate to a national chain.

RECOMMENDATIONS OF SAN FRANCISCO DEPARTMENT OF PUBLIC HEALTH AND UCSF (*Ann Intern Med* 1998;128:306; *Am J Med* 1999;106:323)

- **Recommendations for PEP**
  - High risk: Unprotected receptive or insertive vaginal or anal intercourse, or unprotected receptive fellatio with ejaculation *and*
  - Patient's partner is known to have HIV infection or to be in a high-risk category (MSM, injection drug user, sex worker, etc.) *and*
  - Exposure is an isolated event and patient has made a commitment to safer sex in the future *and*
  - The exposure occurred ≤72 hours of presentation for care.
- **Treatment regimens x 4 weeks**
  - Standard: Combivir (AZT 300 mg bid/3TC 150 mg bid)
  - Alternative: d4T (40 mg bid) + ddI (400 mg qd)
  - Protease inhibitor: Consider adding nelfinavir (1250 mg bid with meals) or IDV (800 mg tid on empty stomach) or IDV + RTV or LPV/r (400/100 mg bid) if source has viral load >50,000 c/mL, advanced HIV disease, or source has been treated with one or both NRTIs
- **Testing of exposed patient (pregnancy test if appropriate):** HIV, HCV, HBV, gonorrhea, syphilis, *Chlamydia trachomatis*; baseline tests for PEP (CBC, liver function tests, renal function tests).
- **Cost**
  - Estimated at $500 for the two-NRTI regimen and $1,100 to $1,200 for the PI-containing regimen.
  - Medical care and laboratory testing add about $500 for a total of $1,000 to $1,700.

- **Initial experience** (*J Infect Dis* 2001;183:707)
  - Number treated: 397
  - Number given AZT + 3TC 351/397 (86%); number who completed treatment 309/357 (78%)
  - Adverse reactions: Nausea 52%, fatigue 44%, headache 24%, diarrhea 13%, anorexia 12%, lab abnormalities – none
  - Median time from exposure to treatment: 33 hours
  - Numbers of seroconversion: 0. However, conclusions about efficacy are not possible given that 57% of sources had unknown serostatus, many of the rest were receiving antiretroviral therapy that might reduce transmission, and the Rakai study indicated an average of 560 sexual exposures per transmission among untreated discordant couples.

5 | Management of Infections
(Pathogens are listed alphabetically)

Aspergillus sp. (Aspergillosis)

Invasive Pulmonary or Disseminated Infection

DIAGNOSIS: Definite = positive histology + positive culture or positive culture from a normally sterile site. Probable = two positive cultures of sputum or one positive bronchoscopy + appropriate host (AIDS, prednisone, ANC <500) (National Mycosis Study Group, *Clin Infect Dis* 2001;33:1824). Halo sign on CT scan is highly suggestive (*Lancet* 2000;355:423).

TREATMENT

- **Preferred regimen:** (invasive disease) Voriconazole, 6 mg/kg IV q12h x 2, then 4 mg/kg IV q12h ≥1 week, then 200 mg bid (*N Engl J Med* 2002;347:408).
- **Alternative regimens**
  - Amphotericin B 0.7-1.4 mg/kg/day or lipid formulation of amphotericin: *Amphotec, Abelcet,* or *AmBisome.* Doses up to 7.5 mg/kg have been used (*Antimicrob Agents Chemother* 2001;45:3487).
  - Itraconazole 200 mg PO tid x 3 days, then 400 mg/day as caps with meal ± acidic drink or 200-400 mg/day solution on empty stomach.
  - Surgery for localized disease.
  - Caspofungin 70 mg IV day 1, then 50 mg IV qd (*Lancet* 2002; 359:1135).
- **Comments**
  - Randomized trial in 277 patients with invasive *Aspergillus* showed voriconazole was significantly better than amphotericin (1-1.5 mg/kg/day) in rates of response and survival (*N Engl J Med* 2002;347:408).
  - Promising azoles include posaconazole + ravuconazole (*Clin Microbiol Rev* 1999;12:40).
  - There is no evidence that combination therapy is more effective (*Lancet* 2002;359:1135).
  - *In vitro* sensitivity tests have not been standardized for *Aspergillus* (*J Antimicrob Chemother* 2001;47:333).

- Predisposing factors: Corticosteroids: Reduce dose or discontinue if possible; neutropenia: G-CSF and avoid 5-FC + AZT, avoid marijuana.

RESPONSE: Prognosis with invasive pulmonary disease is poor without immune reconstitution (*Clin Infect Dis* 1992;14:141; *Clin Microbiol Rev* 1999;12:310). Recent report of 277 patients without HIV infection showed good response in 52% given voriconazole and 20% given amphotericin B (*N Engl J Med* 2002;347:408). Median survival in review of 110 cases in patients with AIDS was 3 months (*Clin Infect Dis* 2000;31:1253). A review of 33 reported cases of CNS aspergillosis in AIDS patients showed all were fatal; amphotericin was uniformly unsuccessful (*Medicine* 2000;79:269).

Bartonella henselae and *quintana*

Bacillary Angiomatosis and Peliosis Hepatitis

DIAGNOSIS: Clinical illness compatible with *Bartonella* associated syndrome plus detection of organisms using tissue specimens for culture (fresh blood or chocolate agar, requires 7 days) and/or stain (Warthin-Starry, Dieterle), and/or serology (EIA or radioimmunoprecipitans).

TREATMENT

- **Preferred regimen (oral, skin involvement):** Erythromycin 500 mg PO qid x >3 months
- **Alternative:** Doxycycline 100 mg PO bid, azithromycin 0.5-1 g/day PO, or doxycycline + rifampin 300 mg IV or PO bid x >3 months
- **IV therapy (bone, parenchymal tissue, endocarditis, or neurologic syndrome):** Erythromycin, doxycycline, or azithromycin (± rifampin or rifabutin)
- **Comments**
  - Prevention: Macrolide for MAC prophylaxis is protective.
  - Duration: May require life-long therapy.
  - *In vitro* sensitivity does not predict response. Lesions develop in presence of TMP-SMX, betalactams, fluoroquinolones.

RESPONSE: The role of antibiotic therapy is often unclear, but it is usually recommended for the immunosuppressed host and for parenchymal involvement or bacteremia. Treatment rapidly reduces microbial load. Clinical response is slow and relapse is common.

Candida spp.

Esophagitis

DIAGNOSIS: Empiric treatment with thrush, odynophagia + CD4 <100 cells/mm^3; endoscopy recommended with atypical presentation or failure to respond to empiric treatment.

TREATMENT: INITIAL INFECTION

- **Preferred regimen:** Fluconazole 200 mg/day PO; up to 800 mg/day x 2 to 3 weeks.
- **Alternative regimens**
  - Itraconazole 200 mg PO as caps with meal ± acidic drink or 200 mg/day oral solution on empty stomach.
  - Voriconazole 200 mg PO bid.
  - Amphotericin B IV 0.3-0.6 mg/kg/day x 10 to 14 days.
  - Caspofungin IV 70 mg day 1, then 50 mg/day.
- **Comments**
  - Fluconazole is clinically superior to ketoconazole for initial therapy.
  - Caspofungin was superior to amphotericin (0.5 mg/kg/day) in two comparative trials (*Antimicrob Agents Chemother* 2002;46:451; *Clin Infect Dis* 2001;33:1529).
  - Voriconazole 200 mg/day is equivalent to fluconazole (*Clin Infect Dis* 2001;33:1447).
  - Relapse rate is 84% within 1 year in absence of maintenance therapy.
  - Resistance: See oropharyngeal candidiasis, below.

RESPONSE: Most patients respond in 5 days. For refractory cases: 1) Change therapy – increase fluconazole dose, alternative azole (voriconazole or itraconazole), or IV treatment (caspofungin, amphotericin or fluconazole) or 2) Endoscopy to establish dx ± *Candida* culture for *in vitro* sensitivity tests. Many patients relapse after therapy and require maintenance or immune reconstitution.

MAINTENANCE

- **Preferred regimen:** Fluconazole 100-200 mg/day PO.
- **Alternative regimen:** Itraconazole 200 mg/day PO as caps (with food ± acidic drink) or 100-200 mg/day oral solution on empty stomach.
- **Comment:** Consider maintenance therapy in all patients with recurrent esophagitis, although this increases the possibility of resistance (*J Infect Dis* 1996;173:219). Best treatment is immune reconstitution (*J Infect Dis* 1998;27:1291; *AIDS* 2000;14:23).

Oropharyngeal candidiasis

Thrush

DIAGNOSIS: Typical white pseudo-membranous plaques with risk factor: CD4 <250 cells/mm³, antibiotics, chronic steroids, etc. Culture for *in vitro* sensitivity test in refractory cases.

TREATMENT: INITIAL INFECTION

- **Preferred regimen:** Clotrimazole oral troches 10 mg 5x/day *(HIV Clin Trials* 2000;1:47) until lesions resolve.
- **Alternative regimens**
  - Nystatin 500,000 units gargled 4-5x day.
  - Fluconazole 100 mg/day PO.
  - Itraconazole 100 mg/day oral suspension swished and swallowed, empty stomach.
  - Amphotericin B oral suspension 1-5 mL qid swish and swallow. No longer available commercially but can be prepared by pharmacist with 100 mg/mL.
  - Amphotericin B IV 0.3-0.5 mg/kg/day.
- **Comments**
  - Treat until symptoms resolve (usually 10 to 14 days).
  - Tolerance: Nystatin has a bitter taste, many GI side effects, must be taken 4 to 5x daily and is significantly less effective than fluconazole for rates of response and relapse. Clotrimazole is easier to take and more effective (*HIV Clin Trials* 2000;1:47).
  - Fluconazole is superior to ketoconazole in terms of efficacy, with fewer drug interactions, and more predictable absorption.
  - Liquid itraconazole is comparable with fluconazole in efficacy but is less predictably absorbed and has important drug interactions (*HIV Clin Trials* 2000;1:47; *Am J Med* 1998;104:33).
  - *In vitro* azole resistance is most common with prolonged prior azole exposure and late-stage HIV infection with CD4 count <50 cells/mm³ (*Clin Infect Dis* 2000;30:749). Definition of *in vitro* resistance is often arbitrary (*Lancet* 2002;359:1135). Molecular typing shows a single strain of *C. albicans* that becomes progressively more resistant (*Eur J Clin Microbiol Infect Dis* 1997;16:601). Some report high rates of non-*albicans* species. Their role in causing thrush is often unclear (*Lancet* 2002;359:1135; *HIV Clin Trials* 2000;1:47) but sometimes indisputable (*Clin Rev Microbiol* 2000;26:59). Some report high rates of response (48/50) to fluconazole despite *in vitro* resistance (*J Infect Dis* 1996;174:821).

RESPONSE: Most respond within 5 days; for failure with topical agents use oral fluconazole; for failure of fluconazole: 1) Use empiric treatment or 2) Culture to determine *in vitro* sensitivity. Options are higher dose fluconazole (400-800 mg/day), liquid itraconazole, oral amphotericin, voriconazole, or IV treatment (amphotericin, fluconazole, caspofungin). Relapses within 3 months after treatment are common and require intermittent therapy, maintenance therapy, or immune reconstitution.

MAINTENANCE (Optional or As Needed)

- **Preferred Regimens:** Clotrimazole (above dose), nystatin (above dose).
- **Alternative Regimens**
  - Fluconazole 100 mg/day PO or 200 mg 3x week.
  - Itraconazole 200 mg/day as caps with meals ± acidic drink or 100-200 mg/day solution on empty stomach.
  - Ketoconazole 200 mg/day PO.
- **Comments**
  - Immune reconstitution is highly effective (*AIDS* 2000;14:979).
  - Advantage of fluconazole for maintenance treatment: Prevention of deep fungal infection, cryptococcosis, and *Candida* esophagitis with CD4 count <100/mm^3 (*N Engl J Med* 1995;332:700) and reduction in frequency of thrush relapses.
  - Problems with use of continuous or intermittent fluconazole include azole resistance, drug interactions, and cost. Risks for azole resistant *Candida* infections are prolonged azole exposure, use of TMP/SMX prophylaxis for PCP, and low CD4 cell count (*J Infect Dis* 1996;173:219). Most authorities try to avoid continued use of fluconazole except where necessary, such as in cases of cryptococcal meningitis (*Clin Infect Dis* 2000;30:749) or severe recurrent esophagitis and (*J Infect Dis* 1998;27:1291).

Vaginitis (*MMWR* 2002;51[RR-6]:45)

DIAGNOSIS: Typical symptoms are pruritus + discharge, examination shows erythema + white discharge + 10% KOH prep or gram stain showing yeast or pseudohyphae. Most cases are in immunocompetent women.

TREATMENT

- **Preferred Regimens: Intravaginal**
  - Butoconazole 2% cream 5 g/day x 3 days* or clotrimazole 1% cream 5 g/day x 7 to 14 days* 100 mg vaginal tab/day x 7 to 14 days, 100 mg vaginal tab bid x 3 days, 500 mg vaginal tab x 1.

- Miconazole 2% cream 5 g/day x 7 days* 100 mg vaginal supp/day x 7 days*, 200 mg supp/day x 3 days.*
- Tioconazole 6.5% ointment 5 g x 1*, 0.4% cream 5 g/day x 7 days, 0.8% cream 5 g/day x 3 days 80 mg supp/day x 3 days.
- Fluconazole 150 mg PO x 1.

* Available over-the-counter

- **Alternative regimen:** Ketoconazole 200 mg/day PO or bid x 5 to 7 days or 200 mg PO bid x 3 days.
- **Comments**
  - Treatment is identical for women with and without HIV infection.
  - Clotrimazole, tioconazole and miconazole are available over the counter. Self administration advised only if prior diagnosis and typical symptoms.
  - Azole resistant strains of *Candida* are rare causes of vaginitis.
  - Creams and suppositories may weaken condoms and diaphragms.
  - Severe disease: Topical azole x 7 to 14 days or oral fluconazole 150 mg PO x 2 separated by 72 hours.
  - Pregnancy: Topical azole only.

RESPONSE: Symptoms resolve and cultures are negative by completion of treatment in 80% to 90%. For severe cases (extensive erythema, edema, excoriations) use topical azole 7 to 14 days or fluconazole 150 mg PO repeated at 72 hours. With recurrent disease (defined as ≥4 episodes/year) culture to detect non-*albicans* sp., especially *C. glabrata* and azole resistant *C. albicans* and treat as above for severe cases.

MAINTENANCE (with ≥4 episodes/year): Clotrimazole 500 mg supply every week, or fluconazole 100-150 mg PO every week or ketoconazole 200 mg PO every week or itraconazole 400 mg every month or 100 mg every week, all x 6 months.

Coccidioides immitis

Coccidioidomycosis

DIAGNOSIS: Culture from any source, spherules on stain are diagnostic; CF serology titer >1:16 suggests extrapulmonary disease; CF in CSF is diagnostic of meningitis.

INITIAL TREATMENT

- **Preferred regimen**
  - Acute pulmonary or disseminated: Amphotericin B 0.5-1 mg/kg/day IV ± fluconazole x 7 to 10 days.
  - Lipid amphotericin formulations (limited data).

- Mild disease: Fluconazole 400-800 mg/day PO or itraconazole 200-400 mg/day PO.
- Meningitis: Fluconazole 400-800 mg/day PO (preferred) or itraconazole 200-400 mg PO bid.

- **Comments**
  - Therapeutic trial of fluconazole 400 mg/day vs itraconazole 200 mg bid in 198 patients with non-meningeal coccidiodomycosis showed no significant difference, but a trend favoring itraconazole (*Ann Intern Med* 2000;133:676). No studies show any azole to be superior to another.
  - Fluconazole preferred for meningitis (*Ann Intern Med* 1993;119:28).
  - Intrathecal amphotericin B should be added for coccidioidomycosis meningitis that fails to respond to fluconazole.
  - Focal lesions often require debridement or drainage.
  - Extrapulmonary: Treat ≥1 year and 2 to 6 months past clinical improvement.

RESPONSE: Response is slow over weeks, and relapses are common. Options for non-response are increase fluconazole dose, alternative azole, amphotericin, and/or surgical debridement or drainage.

MAINTENANCE

- **Preferred regimen:** Fluconazole 400 mg/day or itraconazole 200 mg PO bid.
- **Comments:** Fluconazole is preferred due to better absorption and fewer drug interactions (*Antimicrobial Agents Chemother* 1995;39:1907).

PROPHYLAXIS: Indication: Serologic screening is sometimes suggested for those living in endemic areas; if positive, consider treatment with itraconazole or fluconazole, 400 mg/day (*Clin Infect Dis* 1995;20:1281). In a retrospective review, AIDS increased the risk 300-fold, and azole prophylaxis was effective (*J Infect Dis* 2000;181:1428).

- **Preferred regimen:** Prophylaxis is not generally recommended. If used, the preferred regimen is fluconazole or itraconazole 400 mg/day.
- **Comment:** Immune reconstitution: No criteria have been recommended for stopping prophylaxis (CDC/IDSA Guidelines, http://www.aidsinfo.nih.gov; accessed January, 2003).

Cryptococcus neoformans

Cryptococcal Meningitis

DIAGNOSIS (NIAID Mycosis Study Group Recommendations, *Clin Infect*

Dis 2000;30:710): Serum antigen (screening) – 95% sensitive. CSF analysis: Cryptococcal antigen >95%, culture positive >95%, India ink positive 60% to 80%. CSF usually shows increased protein (50-150 mg/dL) and mononuclear pleocytosis (5-100 mg/dL) (*N Engl J Med* 1992;329:83; *N Engl J Med* 1997;337:15). Cryptococcal meningitis may be asymptomatic.

INITIAL TREATMENT

- **Preferred regimen:** Amphotericin B 0.7 mg/kg/day IV + 5-FC PO 100 mg/kg/day x 14 days ("induction phase"), then fluconazole 400 mg/day x 8 weeks or until CSF is sterile ("consolidation phase"), then maintenance therapy, fluconazole 200 mg/day ("suppressive phase"). See comments regarding management of elevated intracranial pressure.
- **Elevated intracranial pressure:** Focal neurologic signs or obtundation – CNS imaging before LP to define lesions that contraindicate LP.
  - Opening pressure (OP): <250 mm H_2O: Medical management
  - OP >250 mm H_2O: CSF drainage until pressure is <200 or 50% of OP; repeat LP daily until stable.
  - Elevated pressure persists: Lumbar drain or ventricular-peritoneal shunt.
- **Alternative regimens**
  - Amphotericin B 0.7-1.0 mg/kg/day IV (without 5-FC) x 14 days, then fluconazole 400 mg/day x 8 to 10 weeks.
  - Fluconazole 400-800 mg/day PO + 5-FC 100 mg/kg/day PO x 6 to 10 wks.
  - *AmBisome* 4 mg/kg/day IV x 14 days, then fluconazole 400 mg/day x 8 to 10 weeks. *Abelcet* (5 mg/kg) showed clinical response equivalent to amphotericin B but slower CSF sterilization in a small trial (*Clin Infect Dis* 1996;22:315).
- **Comments**
  - LP if new symptoms or new clinical findings. LP at 2 weeks for persistent symptoms.
  - Management of increased intracranial pressure is critical (*Clin Infect Dis* 2000;30:47).
  - Refractory cases, consider intrathecal amphotericin (*Am J Med* 1986;81:24).
  - Amphotericin B + flucytosine is superior to amphotericin B alone in preventing relapse but does not improve immediate outcome *(N Engl J Med* 1997;337:15; *Ann Intern Med* 1990;113:183). There may be no need for flucytosine in patients with anticipated response to HAART.

- ▫ Fluconazole + flucytosine is effective but toxic, possibly due to higher 5-FC doses used (*Clin Infect Dis* 1994;19:741; *Clin Infect Dis* 1998;26:1362).
- ▫ Lipid amphotericin: Data are limited except for *AmBisome* at 4 mg/kg/day (*AIDS* 1997;11:1463).
- ▫ Amphotericin B + flucytosine will sterilize CSF at 2 weeks in 60% to 90% (*N Engl J Med* 1987;317:334).
- ▫ Resistance: Amphotericin B resistance is rare or hard to demonstrate (*Antimicrob Agents Chemother* 1993;37:1383; *Clin Microbiol Rev* 2001;14:643; *Antimicrob Agents Chemother* 1999;43:1463). Resistance develops rapidly with flucytosine monotherapy (*Lancet* 2002;359:1135). Fluconazole resistance is rare (*Antimicrob Agents Chemother* 1999;43:1856; *Antimicrob Agents Chemother* 2001;45:420).

RESPONSE: The major early concern is elevated intracranial pressure, which can lead to cranial nerve deficits or herniation. Management of elevated intracranial pressure with lumbar drainage is critical *(Clin Infect Dis* 2000;30:47). CSF cultures are usually negative at 2 weeks. Serum antigen titers are not useful in following course (*HIV Clin Trials* 2000;1:1). Relapse is unusual with immune reconstitution or with adherence with maintenance fluconazole. *In vitro* sensitivity testing is not standardized, and azole resistance is not well defined.

MAINTENANCE

- **Preferred regimen:** Fluconazole 200 mg/day PO.
- **Alternative regimens**
  - ▫ Amphotericin B 1.0 mg/kg/week or twice weekly.
  - ▫ Fluconazole: May increase maintenance dose to 400 mg/day.
  - ▫ Itraconazole 200 mg bid PO as caps with meal + acidic drink or 100-200 mg PO bid solution on empty stomach.
- **Comments**
  - ▫ Fluconazole maintenance (200 mg/day) is superior to amphotericin B maintenance (*N Engl J Med* 1992;326:793) and superior to itraconazole at a dosage of 200 mg/day PO (*Clin Infect Dis* 1999; 28:291).
  - ▫ Immune reconstitution: Discontinue treatment (secondary prophylaxis) when CD4 cell count is >100-200/mm^3 for >6 months, initial therapy is completed, and patient is asymptomatic (CDC/IDSA Guidelines, http://www.aidsinfo.nih.gov; accessed January, 2003).
  - ▫ Primary prophylaxis is not recommended.

Pulmonary, Disseminated, or Antigenemia

DIAGNOSIS: Positive cultures of blood, urine, and/or respiratory secretions virtually always indicate cryptococcal disease and mandates test to exclude meningitis. Serum antigenemia suggests cryptococcosis especially with titer >1:8; this test should be confirmed with positive culture.

TREATMENT

- **Preferred regimen:** Fluconazole 200-400 mg/day PO indefinitely unless immune reconstitution is achieved.
- **Alternative regimen:** Itraconazole 200 mg PO bid as caps with meal + acidic drink or 200 mg bid oral suspension on empty stomach indefinitely unless immune reconstitution is achieved.
- **Comments**
  - Goal of treatment is to prevent meningitis.
  - Refractory lung and bone lesions may require surgery.
  - Non-meningeal sites include lungs, skin, joints, eye, adrenal gland, GI tract, liver, pancreas, prostate, and urinary tract.
  - Antigenemia: Obtain chest x-ray, LP, urine and blood culture. If no focus identified and antigenemia at >1:8 confirmed, treat with fluconazole (*Clin Infect Dis* 1996;23:827).

MAINTENANCE (Need for maintenance therapy with non-meningeal cryptococcosis is not established.)

- **Preferred regimen:** Fluconazole 200 mg/day PO.
- **Alternative regimens:** Itraconazole 200 mg/day as caps with meal + acidic drink or 100-200 mg/day oral suspension on empty stomach or amphotericin B 0.6-1 mg/kg IV weekly or twice/week.

Cryptosporidium parvum

Cryptosporidiosis (See *Clin Microbiol Rev* 1999;12:554; *Clin Infect Dis* 2001;32:331; *N Engl J Med* 2002;346:1723)

DIAGNOSIS: Stool assays with acid fast stain, IFA or EIA are sensitive, specific, and nearly equal in diagnostic utility (*N Engl J Med* 2002;346:1723). Patterns of disease with AIDS: 1) asymptomatic carriage (4%); 2) self-limited diarrhea <2 months (29%); 3) chronic diarrhea >2 months (60%); 4) fulminant diarrhea with >2 k/day (8%) (*N Engl J Med* 2002;346:1723). The chronic and fulminant form are seen almost exclusively with CD4 counts <100 cells/mm^3.

TREATMENT

- **Preferred regimens**
  - HAART with immune reconstitution is the only treatment that controls persistent cryptosporidiosis.
  - Most commonly used antimicrobial: Paromomycin 500 mg PO tid or 1000 mg PO bid with food x 14 to 28 days, then 500 mg PO bid.
  - Symptomatic treatment: Fluids (sports rehydration beverages such as *Gatorade*, bouillon, oral rehydration; see comments below), nutritional supplements and anti-diarrheal agents: *Lomotil*, loperamide, paregoric, bismuth subsalicylate (*Pepto-Bismol*), and deodorized tincture of opium.
- **Alternative regimens** (None work well)
  - Nitazoxanide (Unimed Pharmaceuticals, Buffalo Grove, Ill.) 500 mg PO bid.
  - Paromomycin 1 g bid + azithromycin 600 mg qd x 4 weeks, then paromomycin alone x 8 weeks.
  - Octreotide (*Sandostatin*) 50-500 µg tid SQ or IV at 50 µg/hour.
  - Azithromycin 1200 mg PO x 2 first day, then 1200 mg/day x 27 days, then 600 mg/day.
  - Atovaquone 750 mg PO suspension bid with meal.
- **Comments**
  - Antimicrobials: Over 95 drugs have been tried, and none is consistently successful. (*N Engl J Med* 2002;346:1723; *J Infect Dis* 2001;184:103; *Clin Infect Dis* 2000;31:1084; *Lancet* 2002;360:1375). This includes paromomycin, azithromycin, and nitazoxanide.
  - Oral rehydration (severe diarrhea): NaCl 3.5 g (3/4 tsp), $NaHCO_3$ 2.5 g (1 tsp baking soda), KCl 1.5 g (1 cup orange juice or bananas) in 1 liter water. Packets of pre-mixed salts available from Cera Products (888-237-2598) and Jianas Brothers (816-421-2880).
  - Clarithromycin or rifabutin prophylaxis for MAC prophylaxis may reduce risk of cryptosporidiosis (*JAMA* 1998;279:384).

RESPONSE: Cryptosporidiosis in patients with CD4 count >100 cells/mm^3 usually resolves spontaneously after 2 to 8 weeks, as it does with immunocompetent hosts. For AIDS patients with fulminant or chronic, persistent cryptosporidiosis, the goal is immune reconstitution – even modest elevations in CD4 count may result in resolution of symptoms and pathogen elimination (*J Acquir Immune Defic Syndr* 1998;12:35; *J Acquir Immune Defic Syndr* 2000;25:124).

Cytomegalovirus (CMV)

CMV Retinitis

DIAGNOSIS: Typical findings on funduscopic exam by an ophthalmologist are diagnostic. Blood cultures and antigen assays are not helpful *(J Clin Microbiol* 2000;323:563), but blood cultures may be useful for *in vitro* sensitivity tests in reference labs for patients with relapses.

INITIAL TREATMENT

- **Preferred regimens**
  - Vision threatening lesion or immune reconstitution unlikely: Intraocular ganciclovir implant (*Vitrasert*) every 6 months + valganciclovir 900 mg PO bid with food. (Induction dose of valganciclovir is not needed.)
  - Immune reconstitution expected: Intraocular ganciclovir implant + oral valganciclovir (above doses) or systemic therapy only with IV ganciclovir, IV foscarnet, or valganciclovir PO (doses below).
  - Foscarnet 60 mg/kg IV q8h or 90 mg/kg IV q12h x 14 to 21 days then 90-120 mg/kg IV q12h.
  - Ganciclovir 5 mg/kg IV bid x 14 to 21 days then 5 mg/kg/day IV.
  - Valganciclovir 900 mg PO bid x 21 days, then 900 mg/day.
- **Alternative regimen:** Cidofovir IV 5 mg/kg/week x 2, then 5 mg/kg q 2 weeks + probenecid, 2 g PO 3 hours before each dose, 1 g PO at 2 and 8 hours post dose or fomivirsen, 330 mg by intravitreal injection day 1 and 15, then monthly.
- **Comments**
  - Intraocular ganciclovir implant requires replacement every 6 to 8 months in absence of immune reconstitution.
  - Randomized controlled clinical trials have shown that IV ganciclovir and IV foscarnet are equivalent for controlling CMV retinitis. Oral ganciclovir is less effective than IV ganciclovir for maintenance, but oral valganciclovir appears to be similar to IV ganciclovir. The ganciclovir intraocular implant is superior to IV ganciclovir. One small study suggested that IV cidofovir is similar to the implant plus oral ganciclovir for controlling retinitis.
  - Valganciclovir is a prodrug of ganciclovir and provides serum levels comparable with IV ganciclovir in standard doses (*N Engl J Med* 2002;346:1119).
  - Foscarnet requires an infusion pump, long infusion time, and saline hydration.
  - *Vitrasert* (intraocular ganciclovir release device) was superior to IV ganciclovir in time to relapse (220 days vs 71 days), but there is increased risk of involvement of the other eye and increased risk

of extraocular CMV disease without concomitant systemic anti-CMV therapy (*N Engl J Med* 1997;337:83). The same concern applies to fomivirsen injections. Any local therapy should be accompanied by systemic anti-CMV therapy such as valganciclovir.

PROGRESSION OR RELAPSE

- **Preferred regimens**
  - Intraocular ganciclovir implant (if not used previously) plus systemic treatment with ganciclovir, foscarnet, cidofovir or valganciclovir, with drug selection based on anticipated or measured CMV resistance.
  - Induction dose of the same agent (ganciclovir 10 mg/kg/day, foscarnet 180-240 mg/kg/day, or valganciclovir 900 mg bid) or switch to an alternative drug (induction doses).
- **Alternative regimens**
  - Combination treatment with ganciclovir/foscarnet in maintenance doses (*J Infect Dis* 1993;168:444; *Am J Ophthalmol* 1994;117:776; *Arch Ophthalmol* 1996;114:23).
  - Cidofovir 5 mg/kg (as above).
  - Fomivirsen, 330 mg by intravitreal injection day 1 and 15, then monthly.
- **Comments**
  - Early relapse (<3 months) is usually not due to drug resistant CMV; late relapse (>6 months) usually is.
  - Resistance rates are similar for ganciclovir, foscarnet, and cidofovir, but there is little cross resistance. For ganciclovir it is <10% at 3 months and 25% to 30% at 9 months (*J Infect Dis* 1998;177:770; *Antimicrob Agents Chemother* 1998;42:2240; *J Infect Dis* 1991;163:716; *J Infect Dis* 2001;183:333; *Am J Ophthalmol* 2001;132:700).
  - Retinitis in the contralateral eye or relapse in the treated eye while receiving systemic therapy is a clinical clue to resistance (*Am J Ophthalmol* 2001;132:700; *J Infect Dis* 1998;177:770).
  - Monitoring CMV viral load may predict resistance (*AIDS* 1998;12:615). Sequencing the CMV gene for UL 97 mutations also predicts resistance (*J Clin Infect* 1995;95:257).
  - Time to relapse varies with definition, use of retinal photographs, and treatments summarized above. Subsequent relapses occur more rapidly.
  - ACTG 228 compared IV ganciclovir, foscarnet, or both for relapses. There was no difference between re-induction with the same drug compared with switching to the alternative drug. The longest time to progression was with combination treatment (4.8 months vs 1.6 to 2.1 months) (*Arch Ophthalmol* 1996;114:23).

RESPONSE: Goals of therapy are to prevent further vision loss with anti-CMV drugs and to control disease control with immune reconstitution using HAART. Vision loss prior to therapy is typically irreversible. Evaluation of response is by ophthalmological examination. Most patients stabilize, but most eventually relapse unless there is immune recovery. Early relapse (<3 months) is usually not associated with ganciclovir resistance; relapse at >6 months usually is. Relapse after immune recovery is ascribed to lack of CMV specific CD4 cell response (*J Infect Dis* 2001;183:1285).

MAINTENANCE

- **Preferred regimens**
  - Valganciclovir 900 mg/day PO.
  - Intraocular ganciclovir implant every 6 months + oral valganciclovir 900 mg/day.
- **Alternative regimens**
  - Foscarnet 90-120 mg/kg/day IV.
  - Ganciclovir 5-6 mg/kg/day IV 5 to 7 days/week or 1000 mg PO tid.
  - Cidofovir 5 mg/kg IV every other week.
- **Immune reconstitution:** Discontinue maintenance therapy when the CD4 cell count is >100-150/mm^3 for ≥6 months, there is no evidence of active disease, and there will be regular ophthalmologic exams. Restart prophylaxis when CD4 count is <50-100 cells/mm^3. Relapses occur when the CD4 count decreases to <50 cells/mm^3 (*AIDS* 2000;14:173). Safety of these recommendations has been shown (*AIDS* 2001;15:23), but rare patients have relapses with CD4 counts >100 cells/mm^3 x 3 months due to lack of CMV-specific immunity (*J Infect Dis* 2001;183:1285).

IMMUNE RECOVERY VITRITIS

- **Preferred regimen:** Systemic or periocular corticosteroids.
- **Comments**
  - Posterior segment inflammation in patients with inactive CMV retinitis and immune recovery is associated with HAART (*Arch Ophthalmol* 1998;116:169), and may be complicated by cystoid macular edema, epiretinal membranes, and papillitis.
  - Incidence is highly variable, from 0.11/person-years to 0.86/person-years (*Am J Ophthalmol* 2000;129:634; *J Infect Dis* 1999;179:697). Lower rate may be due to better CMV suppression before HAART started.
  - Must exclude other causes of uveitis, including syphilis, toxoplasmosis, lymphoma, and drug reactions (e.g., rifabutin) (*Am J Ophthalmol* 1998;125:292).

- Other expressions of CMV activation include colitis, pancreatitis, and submandibular adenopathy.

CMV Extraocular Disease – Gastrointestinal (Usually esophagitis or colitis)

DIAGNOSIS: Requires demonstration of typical inclusion on biopsy or positive culture of biopsy material.

TREATMENT

- **Preferred regimens**
  - Valganciclovir 900 mg PO bid with food x 2 to 3 weeks.
  - Ganciclovir 5 mg/kg IV bid x 2 to 3 weeks.
  - Foscarnet 60 mg/kg q8h or 90 mg/kg IV q12h x 2 to 3 weeks.
  - Indication for maintenance therapy: Relapse on or after therapy.
- **Alternative regimen:** Failure: Ganciclovir/foscarnet.
- **Comments**
  - All patients with symptomatic CMV esophagitis should be treated; indications to treat CMV colitis are less clear due to poor response.
  - Ganciclovir and foscarnet are equally effective for CMV colitis (*Am J Gastroenterol* 1993;88:542).
  - Valganciclovir provides ganciclovir serum levels comparable with IV ganciclovir and is generally preferred in patients who can swallow.
  - Patients should have ophthalmoscopic screening.

RESPONSE: CMV esophagitis usually responds within 1 to 2 weeks with decrease in fever and odynophagia. Patients with colitis respond poorly – abdominal pain and diarrhea may not improve or may improve only modestly; viral shedding is markedly reduced.

CMV Neurological Disease

DIAGNOSIS: PCR for CMV in CSF: Sensitivity >80%, specificity 90% (CSF cultures usually negative). Brain biopsy with histopathology or culture is diagnostic. With encephalitis CSF shows mononuclear pleocytosis; with radiculomyelopathy CSF shows PMNs.

TREATMENT

- **Preferred regimen**
  - Ganciclovir 5 mg/kg IV bid x 3 to 6 weeks + foscarnet 90 mg/kg IV bid x 3 to 6 weeks, then maintenance with ganciclovir/valganciclovir + foscarnet.
  - Immune reconstitution is most important.

- **Alternative regimen:** Ganciclovir 5 mg/kg IV bid x 3 to 6 weeks, then maintenance with ganciclovir IV or valganciclovir PO.
- **Comments**
  - Ganciclovir + foscarnet is probably optimal, but tolerability is poor, and response is limited. In one report of 36 patients treated with this combination, the median survival was 3 months (*AIDS* 2000;14:517). This combination is associated with poor quality of life (*J Infect Dis* 1993;167:1184). The most important factor is immune reconstitution with HAART.
  - Cidofovir: There is minimal experience with neurologic disease.
  - Treatment does not significantly prolong survival, and irreversible damage is often present when treatment is started (*Neurology* 1996;46:444; *Clin Infect Dis* 2002;34:103).

RESPONSE

- CMV encephalitis: A trial of ganciclovir + foscarnet for CMV encephalitis showed a median survival of 94 days vs 42 days in historic controls (*AIDS* 2000;14:517).
- CMV polyradiculopathy: Improvement occurs within 2 to 3 weeks (*Neurology* 1993;43:493).
- Induction therapy may need to be continued for several months in severe cases (*Clin J Infect Dis* 1993;17:32). Maintenance therapy is life-long. It is unclear if valganciclovir is adequate for induction.

CMV Pneumonitis

DIAGNOSIS: Minimum diagnostic criteria include all of the following (*Clin Infect Dis* 1996;23:76):

- Pulmonary infiltrates.
- Detection of CMV with culture, antigen, or nucleic studies of pulmonary secretions.
- Characteristic intracellular inclusions in lung tissue or BAL macrophages.
- Absence of another pulmonary pathogen.

TREATMENT: Ganciclovir 5 mg/kg IV bid > 21 days, foscarnet 60 mg/kg q8h or 90 mg/kg IV q12h >21 days, or valganciclovir 900 mg PO bid x 21 days.

- **Comments**
  - Response to ganciclovir is >60% (*Clin Infect Dis* 1996;23:76).
  - Indications are unclear for long term maintenance therapy.

Entamoeba histolytica (*Clin Infect Dis* 2001;32:331)

DIAGNOSIS: Stool always shows blood with invasive disease; fecal leukocytes are usually not present. O&P examination x 3 has 85% to 95% sensitivity. Antigen assay with monoclonal antibody distinguishes pathogenic *E. histolytica* from *E. dispar* which in non-pathogenic, more common, and looks the same on smear (*J Clin Microbiol* 1993;31:2845).

TREATMENT

- **Preferred regimens:** Metronidazole 750 mg PO or IV tid x 5 to 10 days, plus diiodohydroxyquin 650 mg tid x 20 days or metronidazole plus paromomycin 500 mg tid x 7 days.
- **Alternative regimen:** Paromomycin 500 mg PO tid x 7 days.
- **Comments:** Pathogen distinction: *E. histolytica* is responsible for amebiasis – dysentery and liver abscesses. *E. dispar* accounts for over 90% of stool isolations; most laboratories do not use the serologic or stool EIA tests that distinguish between the two (*Clin Infect Dis* 2000;30:959; *Clin Infect Dis* 2000;30:955). Only *E. histolytica* causes disease and requires therapy.

RESPONSE: Cure rate with metronidazole x 10 days is 90%; second agent is given to assure elimination of intraluminal encysted organism.

Haemophilus influenzae

TREATMENT

- **Preferred regimen:** Cefuroxime.
- **Alternative regimens**
  - TMP-SMX.
  - Cephalosporins, 2nd and 3rd generation.
  - Fluoroquinolones.
- **Comments**
  - Standard therapy is usually adequate (*Clin Infect Dis* 2000;30:461).
  - *H. influenzae* vaccine is not recommended for adults because most infections involve non-encapsulated strains that are not covered by the vaccine.

Hepatitis viruses – see p. 355

Herpes Simplex (*MMWR* 2002;51[RR-6]:13)

DIAGNOSIS: Culture is the preferred method for mucocutaneous lesions; yield decreases rapidly with healing. Other tests are less available, less sensitive, or less specific: DFA, serology, Tzanck prep + PCR (*MMWR* 2002;51[RR-6]:13). HSV PCR in CSF + MRI is preferred method to detect HSV encephalitis.

TREATMENT

- **Preferred regimen**
  - Herpes labialis: Penciclovir topical q2h until healed. With HIV infection, often manage with systemic agent – valacyclovir, famciclovir, or acyclovir.
  - Genital, initial: Acyclovir 400 mg PO tid x 7 to 10 days or famciclovir 200 mg PO tid x 7 to 10 days or valacyclovir 1 g PO bid x 7 to 10 days.
  - Genital, recurrent (HIV): Acyclovir 400 mg PO tid x 5 to 10 days, famciclovir 500 mg bid x 5 to 10 days, or valacyclovir 1 g PO bid x 5 to 10 days.
  - Genital, severe: Acyclovir 5-10 mg/kg IV q8h initially.
  - Acyclovir resistant HSV: Foscarnet 40 mg/kg q8h until resolution or topical cidofovir gel 1% applied once daily x 5 days (must be compounded by pharmacy).
  - Genital, pregnancy: Herpetic lesions at onset of labor is indication for Cesarean section to prevent neonatal herpes. Safety of acyclovir, famciclovir, and valacyclovir is not clearly established; some advocate acyclovir for pregnancy with first episode, or severe recurrent HSV.
  - Severe disease with pneumonitis, esophagitis, disseminated infection, or hepatitis: Acyclovir 5-10 mg/kg IV q8h for 2 to 7 days or until improvement, then PO to complete 10 days.
  - Encephalitis: Acyclovir 10 mg/kg IV q8h x 14 to 21 days.

RESPONSE: Early treatment shortens duration of mucocutaneous lesions, reduces systemic symptoms, and reduces viral shedding (*Arch Int Med* 1996;156:1729); it does not change probability of recurrence (*Med Letter* 1995;37:117). With refractory disease plus HIV infection: Suspect acyclovir resistance (*N Engl J Med* 1991;325:551). Acyclovir resistant strains are resistant to famciclovir, valacyclovir and (usually) ganciclovir. Treatment options are topical cidofovir or IV foscarnet (*J Infect Dis* 1997;17:862, *N Engl J Med* 1993;327:968) or topical trifluridine (*Viroptic* 1%) (*J Acquir Immune Defic Syndr* 1996;12:147).

SUPPRESSION

- **Indication:** ≥6 recurrences/year; alternative is to treat each episode.

- **Suppressive regimens:** Acyclovir 400 mg bid, famciclovir 250 mg bid, or valacyclovir 0.5 or 1 g qd.
- **Comments**
  - Acyclovir, famciclovir and valacyclovir are clinically equivalent (*Sex Trans Dis* 1997;24:481; *J Infect Dis* 1998;178:603; *JAMA* 2001;144:818; *Br J Dermatol* 2001;144:188).
  - Patient information services recommended by CDC: 800-227-8922, http://www.ashastd.org.
  - Allergy to acyclovir is rare but will contraindicate famciclovir and valacyclovir. Desensitization has been described (*Ann Allergy* 1993;70:386).
  - Acyclovir registry for exposure in first trimester of pregnancy does not indicate risk (*Am J Obstet Gynecol* 2000;182:159).
  - Suppression in late pregnancy may reduce risk of need for Caesarean section and is advocated by some (*Br J Obstet Gynecol* 1998;105:275).

Herpes Zoster

Dermatomal

DIAGNOSIS: Dermatomal vesicles are virtually diagnostic. Culture or DFA stain of vesicular lesion is diagnostic. Tzanck prep supportive but only 60% sensitive. PCR is experimental and most useful with CSF; patients with dermatomal zoster often have positive CSF PCR for VZV without evidence of encephalitis.

TREATMENT

- **Preferred regimens**
  - Antiviral agents.
  - Famciclovir 500 mg PO tid or valacyclovir 1 g PO tid x >7 to 10 days.
  - Severe cutaneous or visceral: Acyclovir IV 30 mg/kg/day.
  - Suspected resistance: Foscarnet IV 40 mg/kg q8h or 60 mg/kg q12h.
  - Pain control: Gabapentin, tricyclics, carbamazepine, lidocaine patch, narcotics (effective and underutilized).
- **Comments**
  - Some authorities recommend corticosteroids to prevent post-herpetic neuralgia (*Ann Intern Med* 1996;125:376). Prednisone 60 mg/d x 7 days, 30 mg/d for days 8 to 14, 15 mg/d for days 15 to 21.
  - Postherpetic neuralgia is uncommon in persons <55 years, including AIDS patients.
  - Foscarnet preferred for acyclovir-resistant cases (*N Engl J Med* 1993;308:1448).

- Comparative trial of acyclovir vs valacyclovir showed slight advantage of valacyclovir (*Antimicrob Agents Chemother* 1995;39:1546).
- Treatment can be started as long as new lesions are forming.

- **Disseminated, ophthalmic nerve involvement, or visceral**
  - **Preferred regimen:** Acyclovir 30-36 mg/kg/day IV at least 7 days.
  - **Alternative regimen:** Foscarnet 40 IV mg/kg q8h or 60 mg/kg q12h.
  - **Comment:** Role of maintenance therapy unclear.
- **Acyclovir-resistant strains**
  - **Preferred regimen:** Foscarnet IV 40 mg/kg q8h or 60 mg/kg q12h (*J Acquir Immune Defic Syndr* 1993;7:254; *Ann Intern Med* 1991;115:9).
  - **Alternative regimens:** Cidofovir IV or topical trifluridine.
- **Retinal necrosis**: Preferred: CD4 <100 cells/mm^3: Ganciclovir + foscarnet; CD4 >100 cells/mm^3: Acyclovir IV
- **Chickenpox**
  - Preferred: Acyclovir 10 mg/kg IV q8h or 800 mg PO qid
  - Alternative: Valacyclovir 1 g q8h or famciclovir 500 mg

RESPONSE: Antiviral therapy of zoster reduces the duration of lesions, reduces the number of new lesions, and reduces systemic complaints, but the benefits are modest and largely limited to those receiving therapy within 24 hours of onset (*N Engl J Med* 1991;325:1539). For most patients the main concern is pain, and for older patients it is post-herpetic neuralgia.

PREVENTION

- **Preferred regimen:** Varicella zoster immune globulin (VZIG) 5 vials (6.25 mL) within 96 hours of exposure.
- **Alternative regimen:** Acyclovir 800 mg PO 5x/day x 3 weeks. Note: Acyclovir has been removed from the 1999 USPHS/IDSA guidelines for prophylaxis due to lack of documented efficacy.
- **Indication:** Exposure to chickenpox or shingles plus no history of either and, if available, negative VZV serology. Preventive treatment must be initiated within 96 hours of exposure and preferably within 48 hours.

Histoplasma capsulatum

Histoplasmosis, Disseminated

DIAGNOSIS: Culture is diagnostic. The yield in AIDS patients with bronchoscopy (with lung involvement) is 90%, blood or marrow (with disseminated disease) is 50%, and CSF (with meningitis) is 25% to

60% (*Medicine* 1990;69:361). Many now rely on assays of *H. capsulatum* polysaccharide in blood and urine for diagnosis and to document response to therapy. In disseminated disease, the urine test shows 90% sensitivity, and the blood shows 85% sensitivity; other body fluids can also be tested (*Ann Intern Med* 1991;115:936). This test is available from Dr. Joe Wheat at 866-MIRAVISA, 317-856-2681, or http://www.miravistalabs.com.

INITIAL TREATMENT

- **Preferred regimens**
  - Acute infection: Amphotericin B IV 0.7 mg/kg/day, 3 to 10 days.
  - *AmBisome* IV 3-5 mg/kg/day, 3 to 10 days.
  - Continuation phase: Itraconazole 200 mg PO tid x 3 days, then 200 mg PO bid x 12 weeks.
  - Mild to moderate illness: Itraconazole, above doses.
- **Alternative regimen:** Fluconazole 800 mg/day.
- **Comments**
  - Itraconazole may be used for initial treatment of mild to moderate histoplasmosis without CNS involvement, or it may be used for maintenance after induction with amphotericin B (*Am J Med* 1995; 98:336).
  - Fluconazole is inferior to itraconazole *in vitro* and in a controlled clinical trial (*Clin Infect Dis* 2001;33:1910). This study showed a correlation between *in vitro* resistance and clinical response; fluconazole resistant strains were sensitive *in vitro* to itraconazole.
  - A therapeutic trial of amphotericin B vs *AmBisome* in AIDS patients showed more rapid defervescence and fewer adverse reactions in the *AmBisome* group (*Antimicrob Agents Chemother* 2001;45:2354). The AWP is $800/day as compared with $12/day for amphotericin B.
  - Itraconazole levels: Some recommend measurement of serum levels to assure levels of >1 μg/mL after >5 days of itraconazole (San Antonio Lab, 210-567-4131). Inadequate levels: Make sure caps are given with meal ± acidic drink, avoid drugs that neutralize gastric acid or interact with itraconazole (PIs and NNRTIs), or use liquid formulation without food.
  - Fluconazole is less active than itraconazole; use only if itraconazole is not tolerated (*Am J Med* 1997;103(3):223-32).

RESPONSE: Most patients show subjective and objective response within 1 week. The rate of clinical response with *AmBisome* or itraconazole is similar (86% vs 85%); conversion to negative blood cultures at 2 weeks was 85% (*AmBisome*) and 53% (itraconazole) (*Antimicrob Agents Chemother* 2001;45:2354). Antigen assays usually show decreased titers after 2 to 4 weeks; blood and urine assays are obtained at 3 to 6 month intervals during maintenance therapy to detect relapse. Clinical failure correlates with *in vitro* sensitivity test results, especially with fluconazole, which is far less active than itraconazole (*Clin Infect Dis* 2001;33:1910).

MAINTENANCE

- **Preferred regimen:** Itraconazole 200 mg/day PO.
- **Alternative regimens:** Amphotericin B 1.0 mg/kg 1x/week or fluconazole 800 mg/day PO.
- **Comment:** Immune reconstitution: No criteria recommended for stopping (CDC/IDSA Guidelines, *MMWR* 2002;51[RR-8]:16). Some recommend discontinuing antifungal therapy if CD4 >150 cells/mm^3, itraconazole treatment >1 year, and serum and urine antigen <4 units/mL.

PROPHYLAXIS

- **Indication:** Consider in endemic area with CD4 count <100 cells/mm^3, especially if at high risk due to occupation (work with soil) or hyperendemic rate (>10 cases/100 pt-yrs) (*Clin Infect Dis* 1999; 28:1049).
- **Preferred regimen:** Not generally recommended.
- **Alternative regimens:** Itraconazole 200 mg/day PO or fluconazole 200 mg/day PO.

Isospora belli

Isosporiasis

DIAGNOSIS: Detection of oocysts in stool with acid fast stain is specific and reasonably sensitive, but several stool specimens may be required.

TREATMENT

- **Acute Infection**
  - Preferred regimen: TMP-SMX PO bid (2 DS PO bid or 1 DS tid) x 2 to 4 weeks.
  - Alternative regimen: Pyrimethamine 50-75 mg/day PO + leucovorin acid 5-10 mg/day x 1 month.
- **Comment:** Immunocompetent patients usually have self limited diarrhea lasting 2 to 3 weeks. AIDS patients may have severe or persistent diarrhea and are usually treated. Duration of therapy is not well defined. Case report of refractory infection that responded to pyrimethamine plus sulfadiazine (*Diagn Microbiol Infect Dis*

1996;26:87).

RESPONSE: AIDS patients usually respond to TMP-SMX within several days (*N Engl J Med* 1986;315:87; *N Engl J Med* 1989;320:1024). Stool examination may show continued shedding after clinical response.

SUPPRESSIVE THERAPY

- **Preferred regimen:** TMP-SMX 1-2 DS/day or 3x/week.
- **Alternative regimens**
  - Pyrimethamine 25 mg + sulfadoxine 500 mg/week PO (1 *Fansidar*/week).
  - Pyrimethamine 25 mg + folinic acid 5 mg/day.
- **Duration:** Some advocate treatment indefinitely unless there is immune recovery.

JC Virus

Progressive Multifocal Leukoencephalopathy (PML)

DIAGNOSIS: Definitive diagnosis – brain biopsy positive DFA stain for JC virus and typical inclusions in oligodendrocytes; suspect with CD4 <100 cells/mm^3, neurological disease and no fever, no headache, no enhancement (MRI) and no changes in CSF. PCR for JCV has a sensitivity of 80%, specificity of 90%. A subset have higher CD4 counts (*Clin Infect Dis* 2002;34:103).

TREATMENT

- **Preferred regimen:** HAART
- **Alternative regimen:** Interferon alpha (3 MU/day) or cidofovir plus HAART
- **Comments**
  - Positive PCR in CSF plus typical clinical and MRI findings constitute presumptive PML. If PCR is negative, consider brain biopsy depending on probability of a treatable alternative diagnosis.
  - Prognosis: Median survival after PML diagnosis is 2 to 4 months (*J Acquir Immune Defic Syndr* 1992;5:1030; *N Engl J Med* 1998; 338:1345; *Clin Infect Dis* 2002;34:103).
  - HAART: In the largest series (n=57), neurologic improvement was seen in 26%, and there was eradication of JCV DNA in CSF in 57%. New PML lesions developed in nine patients after response to HAART (*J Infect Dis* 2000;182:1077). Others have shown variable clinical and virologic responses to HAART (*AIDS* 1999;13: 1881; *Clin Infect Dis* 1999;28:1152; *Clin Infect Dis* 2000;30:95).
  - Treatment trials: Possible response to cidofovir (*AIDS* 2002;16: 1791; *J Neurovirol* 2001;7:364; *J Neurovirol* 2001;7:374) and alpha

interferon (*J Neurovir* 1998;4:324). Failed treatments in clinical trials include amantadine, adenosine arabinoside, foscarnet and ganciclovir, cytosine arabinoside and intrathecal cytosine arabinoside (*N Engl J Med* 1998;338:1345; *AIDS* 2000;14:517).

RESPONSE: Progressive neurologic disease with no good treatment; even immune reconstitution is of questionable benefit but should be attempted.

Microsporidia

Microsporidiosis (*Clin Infect Dis* 2001;32:331)

DIAGNOSIS: Electron microscopy of intestinal biopsies is the gold standard, but this is impractical. The practical alternatives are the trichrome stain and the calcoflour stains, which can be performed on stool and show sensitivity and specificity of about 100% and 80%, respectively (*J Clin Microbiol* 1998;36:2279). These tests must be specifically requested.

TREATMENT

- **Preferred regimens**
  - *E. bieneusi*: Fumagillin 60 mg/day x 14 days (this dose is associated with high rates of neutropenia and thrombocytopenia).
  - Symptomatic treatment with nutritional supplements and antidiarrheal agents (*Lomotil*, *loperamide*, paregoric, etc.).
  - *E. intestinalis*: Albendazole 400 mg PO bid x >3 weeks.
  - Ocular: Fumidil B 3mg/mL saline (fumagillin 70 mg/mL) eye drops, forever.
- **Alternative regimens**
  - Metronidazole 500 mg PO tid (*E. intestinalis*).
  - Thalidomide 100 mg/day (*AIDS* 1995;9:658).
  - Nitazoxanide 500 mg PO bid (experimental).
- **Comments**
  - Fumagillin proved effective in a controlled trial for microsporidiosis due to *E. bieneusi* (*N Engl J Med* 2002;346:1963).
  - Albendazole efficacy: Established only for infections involving *E. intestinalis*, which causes 10% to 20% of cases.
  - Anecdotal success: Reported with itraconazole, fluconazole, nitazoxanide, nitrofurantoin, atovaquone, and metronidazole (*Infect Dis Clin N Amer* 1994;8:483).
  - Immune reconstitution: Best therapy, especially for the 80% to 90% of cases involving *E. bieneusi* (*Lancet* 1998;351:256; *AIDS*

1998;12:35; *J Clin Microbiol* 1999;37:421; *J Acquir Immune Defic Syndr* 2000;25:124).

- Extraintestinal: *E. bellum* – sinusitis and disseminated disease; *E. cuniculi* – CNS, conjunctiva, renal, lungs; *T. hominis* – myositis; *Braciola* – myositis.

RESPONSE: With fumagillin treatment of *E. bieneusi* there is response by week 4 as indicated by elimination of loperamide use and elimination of detectable Microsporidia in stool (*N Engl J Med* 2002;346:1963).

Mycobacterium avium Complex

Disseminated MAC

DIAGNOSIS

- Disseminated disease: Positive culture of non-pulmonary, normally sterile site; blood cultures are 90% to 95% sensitive but usually require 7 to 14 days. Rarely requires biopsy of liver, bone marrow, or lymph nodes. Sputum and stool are insensitive and non-specific culture sources (*J Infect Dis* 1994;168:1045; *J Infect Dis* 1994;169:289).
- Pulmonary MAC: Infiltrate on x-ray and culture with ≥2+ growth and ≥1 positive AFB stain (*Am J Respir Crit Care Med* 1997;155:2041).

TREATMENT

- **Preferred regimens**
  - Clarithromycin 500 mg bid PO + ethambutol 15 mg/kg/day PO.
  - Azithromycin 500-600 mg/day + ethambutol 15 mg/kg/day PO.
  - Severe symptoms: Two drugs (above) + ciprofloxacin 500-750 mg PO bid or levofloxacin 500-750 mg qd PO or rifabutin 300 mg/day PO or amikacin IV 10-15 mg/kg/day.
- **Comments**
  - With severe disease use 3-drug combination, but the best third drug is unclear (*Clin Microbiol Rev* 1993;176:126; *Clin Infect Dis* 1993;17:7; *Clin Infect Dis* 1994;18:S237).
  - Failure: ≥2 new drugs; benefit of continuing clarithromycin or azithromycin if resistant *in vitro* is not known.
  - Clarithromycin drug interactions: Clarithromycin levels are increased with concurrent IDV (50%), RTV (75%), and SQV (177%); NFV, APV, and NVP have minimal effect on clarithromycin levels. LPV has not been studied. Clarithromycin plus EFV should be given with caution due to high rate of rash reactions (see Table 4-19, p. 79). Clarithromycin levels are decreased with concurrent rifabutin (*N Engl J Med* 1996;335:428).

- Rifabutin dose: 300-600 mg/day, but should not exceed 300 mg/day if given with clarithromycin or fluconazole. Note interactions with PIs and NNRTIs (see p. 289).
- *In vitro* susceptibility: Useful only for macrolides in patients with prior macrolide exposure (*N Engl J Med* 1996;335:392; *Clin Infect Dis* 1998;27:1369; *J Infect Dis* 2000;181:1289).
- Clarithromycin vs azithromycin: In a comparative trial for MAC bacteremia, clarithromycin was superior in time to negative blood cultures (*Clin Infect Dis* 1998;27:1278; see also *Antimicrob Agents Chemother* 1999;43:2869). Nevertheless, another large trial using azithromycin 600 mg/day vs clarithromycin 500 mg bid, each combined with EMB, showed comparable results (*Clin Infect Dis* 2000;31:1254).
- 3-drug combination: Comparison of clarithromycin/EMB vs clarithromycin/EMB/rifabutin showed no clinical benefit to 3-drug regimen but a decreased rate of clarithromycin resistance (*Clin Infect Dis* 1999;28:1080).
- ASA or NSAID often effective for symptom relief.
- Clarithromycin dose: >1000 mg/day was associated with increased mortality (*Ann Intern Med* 1994;121:905).
- Immune reconstitution: Discontinue maintenance therapy when CD4 count >100 cells/mm^3 x 6 months + ≥12 months treatment and asymptomatic.

RESPONSE: Response is slow, and prognosis is poor without immune reconstitution. Clinical improvement is usually noted at 2 to 4 weeks. Clinical trials in pre-HAART era showed that standard therapy resulted in negative blood cultures in 50% at 12 weeks, 30% had relapses after sterile blood cultures, and the all-cause mortality at 24 weeks was 60% (*Clin Infect Dis* 2000;31:1245; *Clin Infect Dis* 1998;27:1278).

MAC Immune Recovery Lymphadenitis

DIAGNOSIS: Clinical features are characterized by high fever, leukocytosis, and lymphadenopathy often involving the periaortic and mesenteric nodes. Biopsy shows granulomatous lymphadenitis with AFB in large numbers. Occurs within 1 to 3 months of HAART with robust CD4 response (*Lancet* 1998;351:252; *J Acquir Immune Defic Syndr* 1999;20:122; *Ann Intern Med* 2000;133:447). Less common presentations include osteomyelitis, bursitis, adrenal insufficiency, and skin nodules (*Ann Intern Med* 2000;133:447).

TREATMENT

- **Preferred regimen:** Clarithromycin 500 mg bid + EMB 15 mg/kg/day ± rifabutin 300 mg/day PO.

- **Alternative regimen**
  - Azithromycin + EMB + rifabutin.
  - Corticosteroids with rapid taper for severe symptoms or draining sinuses.
  - Surgical drainage may be indicated.

PROPHYLAXIS: See p. 44.

Mycobacterium chelonae

TREATMENT

- **Preferred regimen:** Clarithromycin 500 mg bid x >6 months.
- **Alternative regimen:** Variable activity: Cefoxitin, amikacin, doxycycline, imipenem, tobramycin, erythromycin.
- **Comment:** *In vitro* susceptibility test results needed. Clinical: Skin and soft tissue, bone and joint.

Mycobacterium fortuitum

TREATMENT

- **Preferred regimen:** Amikacin 400 mg q12h + cefoxitin 12 g/day x 2 to 4 weeks, then oral agents based on *in vitro* tests – clarithromycin 1 g/day, doxycycline 200 mg/day, SMX 1 g tid, ciprofloxacin 500 mg bid.
- **Comments**
  - Duration: >3 months for cutaneous lesions and >6 months for bone lesions in non-HIV infected patients.
  - Clinical: Skin and soft tissue, bone, CNS, disseminated.

Mycobacterium genavense

TREATMENT

- **Preferred regimen:** Clarithromycin/EMB/rifampin.
- **Alternative regimen:** Other possible agents: Ciprofloxacin, amikacin, and PZA.
- **Comments**
  - Clarithromycin-containing regimens are most effective (*AIDS* 1993;7:1357).
  - Clinical: Similar to *M. avium* (*AIDS* 1995;9:659).

Mycobacterium gordonae

TREATMENT

- **Preferred regimen:** INH/rifampin/clofazimine or clarithromycin.
- **Alternative regimen:** SM may be useful.

- **Comments:** Validity: Most isolates are contaminants (*Dermatology* 1993;187:301; *AIDS* 1992;6:1217; *Antimicrob Agents Chemother* 1992;36:1987).

Mycobacterium haemophilum

TREATMENT

- **Preferred regimen:** INH/rifampin/EMB.
- **Alternative regimen:** Clarithromycin, doxycycline, ciprofloxacin, and amikacin are active *in vitro.*
- **Comment:** Clinical: Skin and disseminated disease (*Ann Intern Med* 1994;120:118). Experience is limited (*Eur J Clin Microbiol Infect Dis* 1993;12:114).

Mycobacterium kansasii

(*Am J Respir Crit Care Med* 1997;156:S1)

TREATMENT

- **Preferred Regimen:** INH 300 mg/day PO + rifampin 600 mg/day PO + EMB 25 mg/kg/day x 2 months, then 15 mg/kg/day x 18 months (total) to life long therapy ± SM 1 g IM 2x/week x 3 months.
- **Alternative Regimen:** Also consider ciprofloxacin 750 mg PO bid and clarithromycin 500 mg PO bid.
- **Comments**
  - Experience in HIV infected patients is limited (*J Acquir Immune Defic Syndr* 1991;4:516; *Ann Intern Med* 1991;114:861).
  - *In vitro* sensitivity data is needed.
  - Duration is arbitrary – many treat HIV infected patients for life.
  - Most strains are resistant to INH, but it is usually included in the regimen with little supporting data. All are resistant to PZA.
  - Immune reconstitution: Reports of cervical and mediastinal adenopathy, osteomyelitis and arthritis due to *M. kansasii* during the first 3 months of HAART.

Mycobacterium malmoense

TREATMENT

- **Preferred regimen:** Clarithromycin or azithromycin, rifabutin, ethambutol, and ciprofloxacin.
- **Comment:** Clinical: Cavitary pulmonary, CNS (*Clin Infect Dis* 1993; 16:540; *J Clin Microbiol* 1996;34:731).

Mycobacterium scrofulaceum

TREATMENT

- **Preferred regimen:** Surgical excision.
- **Alternative regimen:** Clarithromycin, azithromycin, rifabutin ± streptomycin, cycloserine + sulfonamides.
- **Comments:** Cervical adenitis.

Mycobacterium Tuberculosis (TB)

DIAGNOSIS: The standard test for pulmonary TB is AM expectorated sputa x 3 days for AFB smear and culture. Induced sputa and bronchoscopy are used if there is no sputum production. Sensitivity of AFB smear is about 50%, is similar for patients with and without AIDS, and is not better with induced sputum or bronchoscopy specimens compared with expectorated sputum (*Chest* 1992;101:1211; *Chest* 1992;102:1040; *Am J Respir Crit Care Med* 2000;162:2238). Specificity of the smear depends on prevalence of MAC (*J Clin Microbiol* 1998;36:1046), but most positive AFB smears of respiratory specimens in patients with AIDS indicate TB even in areas where MAC is common (*Clin Infect Dis* 1998;19:334). Nucleic acid amplification (Gen-Probe *Amplified MTD Test*; Roche *Amplicor MTB Test*) is more sensitive than AFB smear (80% vs 50%), is specific for *M. tuberculosis*, is 95% sensitive in AFB-smear positive cases, and hastens mycobacterial identification with culture and smear, but the tests are expensive ($50-100/assay). Current recommendation is that they be used with positive AFB smear or negative AFB smear and high level of suspicion (*Am J Respir Crit Care Med* 2001;164:2020; *MMWR* 2000;49:593). With miliary TB, sputum cultures are positive in only 25%, but multiple other specimens are AFB smear or culture positive, including blood in 50% to 60%. PPD skin tests have high rates of false-negative results that correlate inversely with CD4 count – up to 65% false-negatives in AIDS patients with active TB (*J Infect Dis* 1992;166:194). Positive cultures for *M. tuberculosis* approach 100% for sensitivity and 97% for specificity (*Clin Infect Dis* 2001;31:1390).

■ TABLE 5-1: **TB Treatment Regimens**

Rifampin-based Therapy (no current use of PIs or NNRTIs)		
Induction	**Maintenance**	**Comments**
INH/rifampin/PZA/EMB daily x 8 weeks (preferred if CD4 count <100 cells/mm³)	INH/rifampin daily or 2-3x/week x 18 weeks*	■ With CD4 count <100 cells/mm³ daily or 3x/week therapy is recommended for maintenance phase. Rifampin-containing regimens preclude concurrent PIs or NNRTIs except with EFV, RTV, and RTV + SQV ■ Assess HIV at 3-month intervals to determine need for ART ■ A 2-week wash-out period is required between the last rifampin dose and initiation of PI or NNRTIs
INH/rifampin/PZA/EMB daily x 2 weeks, then 2-3x/week x 6 weeks	INH/rifampin 2-3x/week x 18 weeks*	
INH/rifampin/PZA/EMB 3x/week x 8 weeks	INH/rifampin 3x/week x 18 weeks*	
Rifabutin-based Therapy (concurrent PI or NNRTI)		
Induction	**Maintenance**	**Comments**
INH/rifabutin/PZA/EMB daily x 8 weeks	INH/rifabutin daily or 2-3x/week x 18 weeks*	■ Monitor for rifabutin toxicity-arthralgias, uveitis, leukopenia ■ Dose modifications of rifabutin and PIs/NNRTI when given concurrently, see below ■ CD4 <100/mm³ maintenance phase should be daily or 3x/week
INH/rifabutin/PZA/EMB daily x 2 weeks, then 3x/week x 6 weeks*	INH/rifabutin daily or 2-3x/week x 18 weeks*	

* Rifamycins given as DOT at 1 to 2x/week resulted in rifamycin resistance in patients with CD4 count <100 cells/mm³. Rifampin or rifabutin should be given ≥3x/week in patients with a CD4 count <100 cells/mm³ (*MMWR* 2002;51:214).

TREATMENT: Treatment should be continued 7 months (9 months total) if sputum culture at 2 months is positive (***Am J Respir Crit Care Med*** **2003;167:603;** ***MMWR*** **2000;49:185; http://www.cdc.gov/nchstpl/tb/pubs/mmwr/rr4720.pdf)**

- **Initiation of HIV treatment:** Do not initiate treatment of both TB and HIV simultaneously due to overlapping drug toxicities, drug interactions, adherence requirements, and possible paradoxical reactions (immune reconstitution). Always treat active TB first. WHO guidelines (4/02): With CD4 <50 cells/mm³, initiate HIV treatment as soon as TB drugs are tolerated; with CD4 50-200 cells/mm³, delay initiating HIV treatment for 8 weeks. Patients already receiving HAART should continue with appropriate adjustments for drug interactions.
- **Paradoxical worsening:** May occur due to immune reconstitution.

- Characterized by worsening of symptoms and x-ray changes, with high fever, adenopathy, expanding CNS lesions, large effusions. Rule out other causes, especially TB treatment failure and lymphoma.
- Severe reaction: Prednisone 1 mg/kg/day x 1 to 2 weeks, then taper. Continue TB and HIV therapy.
- Mild to moderate reaction: Treat symptomatically and continue TB and HIV therapy.

■ TABLE 5-2: **Drug Doses With Daily Therapy and DOT**

	Daily Dose	DOT Dose 2x to 3x per Week*
INH	5 mg/kg (300 mg)†	15 mg/kg (900 mg)†
Rifampin‡	10 mg/kg (600 mg)†	10 mg/kg (600 mg)†
SM	15 mg/kg (1 g)†	25-30 mg/kg (1.5 g)†
PZA (kg)	20-25 mg/kg/day (2.0 g)†	■ 2x/week: 45-50 mg/kg (4.0 g)† ■ 3x/week: 30-35 mg/kg (3.0 g)†
EMB (kg)	15-20 mg/kg/day (1.6 g)†	■ 2x/week: 35-45 mg/kg (4.0 g)† ■ 3x/week: 25-30 mg/kg (2.4 g)†

* Intermittent therapy with CD4 count <100 cells/mm³ should be 3x/week.

† Maximum dose

‡ Rifampin may be used with EFV, RTV, or RTV + SQV when there are no other PIs or NNRTIs. See below for rifabutin regimens.

■ TABLE 5-3: **Dose Adjustments for PI/NNRTIs When Used With Rifabutin**

PI or NNRTI	Rifabutin
IDV 1000 mg q8h	150 mg/day or 300 mg 2x to 3x/week*
NFV 1000 mg tid or 1250 mg bid	150 mg/day or 300 mg 2x to 3x/week*
APV 1200 mg bid	150 mg/day or 300 mg 2x to 3x/week*
EFV 600 mg qd	450 mg/day or 600 mg 2x to 3x/week*
RTV standard	150 mg 2x to 3x/week
NVP 200 mg bid	300 mg/day
RTV, standard	150 mg 2x to 3x/week*
RTV/SQV 400/400 mg bid	150 mg 2x to 3x/week*
LPV/r 400/100 mg bid	150 mg qod
Fortovase, DLV	Inadequate data

* Intermittent treatment of active TB should be >3x/week with CD4 <100 cells/mm³.

- **Options for antiretroviral therapy**
  - Regimen that does not contain a PI or NNRTI or a rifampin containing regimen with EFV, 600-800 mg/day or SQV/RTV, 400/400 mg bid or 1000/100 mg bid (*Invirase* preferred).
  - Rifabutin-based treatment with dose adjustments (*MMWR* 2000;49:185). See dose adjustments (Table 5-3, p. 147).
- **Principles of TB therapy** (*N Engl J Med* 2001;345:189)
  - DOT is always preferred.
  - Extrapulmonary TB is treated like pulmonary TB; exceptions are miliary TB and bone/joint TB and meningeal TB – 9 to 12 months.
  - INH resistance: Treat with rifampin, PZA + EMB x 6 months.
  - Rifampin resistance: Treat with INH + PZA x 18 months or INH, EMB + streptomycin x 9 months.
  - Pregnancy: INH, rifampin + EMB; add PZA if resistance likely.

MONITORING

- **Baseline:** LFTs (ALT/AST, bilirubin) if pre-exisiting liver disease, EMB – visual acuity and color discrimination.
- **Clinical monitoring:** Clinical assessment monthly. Warn of symptoms of hepatitis to discontinue therapy and obtain medical care – nausea, vomiting, dark urine, malaise, fever >3 days.
- **Laboratory monitoring:** LFTs monthly with symptoms of hepatitis. Sputum smear and culture should be done ≤ monthly until negative. Some recommend chest x-ray at 2 months and at the termination of therapy.
- **Hepatotoxicity:** If ALT/AST ≥5x ULN, discontinue INH, rifampin + PZA, and give an alternative such as EMB, streptomycin + quinolone. When LFTs normal – reintroduce primary drugs one at a time (*Ann Intern Med* 1993;119:400).

RESPONSE: Response to therapy is similar to that in patients without HIV except: 1) Drug interactions with anti-TB + HIV drugs and 2) paradoxical reactions with immune reconstitution. Most patients become afebrile within 7 to 14 days; persistence of fever beyond this time suggests resistance or another cause of fever (*Clin Infect Dis* 1992;102:797). Sputum culture becomes negative ≤2 months in 85% (*N Engl J Med* 2001;345:189). Persistence of positive cultures at ≥2 months suggests non-compliance or drug resistance. Immune reconstitution may cause the paradoxical reaction noted above; this needs to be distinguished from therapeutic failure.

TREATMENT OF LATENT TB

- **Indications:** PPD>5 mm induration, high-risk exposure, or prior positive PPD without treatment. Must rule out active disease.
- **Preferred regimens**
  - INH 300 mg/day PO + pyridoxine 50 mg/day PO x 9 months.
  - INH 900 mg 2x/week + pyridoxine 50 mg 2x/week x 9 months (DOT).
  - PZA 20 mg/kg/day plus rifabutin in place of rifampin to permit concurrent PI or NNRTI (see Table 5-3, p. 147 for doses) x 2 months.
- **Comments**
  - Rifampin-containing regimens have drug interactions with PIs and NNRTIs; the preferred regimens are INH or short-course prophylaxis with PZA plus rifampin or rifabutin using dose adjustments shown in Table 5-3, p. 147.
  - Rifampin/PZA previously favored because it is as effective as INH for 9 months, and probability of completing the two month course is better (*JAMA* 2000;283:1445). However, there have been subsequent reports of severe hepatotoxicity, including 6 deaths attributed to this regimen, although none of these patients had concurrent HIV infection (*MMWR* 2001;50;773). Due to high risk of active TB, this regimen is recommended for HIV infected patients who are not expected to complete the 9-month INH regimen, but these patients should be seen every 2 weeks and have CBC and LFTs (bilirubin and transaminase levels) monitored at baseline, 2, 4, and 6 weeks.

TREATMENT OF INH RESISTANT STRAIN: Rifampin 600 mg/day PO + PZA 20 mg/kg x 2 months or rifabutin 150-450 mg/day (see Table 5-3, p. 147) + PZA x 2 months. The choice of rifampin or rifabutin depends on current HAART.

TREATMENT OF MULTIPLY RESISTANT STRAIN: Fluoroquinolone + PZA or EMB + PZA (Base decision on susceptibility tests and consultation with public health officials).

Mycobacterium xenopi

TREATMENT

- **Preferred regimen:** Rifampin, EMB, and SM
- **Comments:** Clinical: Pulmonary nodules (*Clin Infect Dis* 1997;25: 206)

Nocardia asteroides

DIAGNOSIS: Recovery of *Nocardia* sp. + compatible clinical syndrome. Warn laboratory to perform modified AFB stain and use appropriate media. Growth requires 3 to 5 days.

TREATMENT

- **Preferred regimens:** Sulfadiazine or trisulfapyridine 3-12 g/day PO or IV to maintain 2 hour post-dose sulfa level at 100-150 mg/L x ≥6 months or TMP-SMX 5-15 mg/kg/day TMP PO or IV.
- **Alternative regimens**
  - Minocycline 100 mg PO bid x ≥6 months.
  - Other suggested regimens: Imipenem/amikacin; sulfonamide/ amikacin or minocycline; ceftriaxone/amikacin.
- **Comments**
  - Sulfonamides preferred; TMP is inactive against *Nocardia*, but TMP-SMX is often used due to the convenience of formulation.
  - May desensitize if hypersensitive to sulfa (see TMP-SMX, p. 316).
  - Dose of sulfonamides or TMP-SMX determined by severity of illness; pulmonary or skin – low dose; CNS, severe or disseminated disease – high dose.
  - Parenteral therapy is usually given 3 to 6 weeks, then oral therapy.
  - Sulfa therapy – monitor sulfa level (for therapeutic level); monitor renal function (for crystalluria and azotemia) and force fluids.

RESPONSE: Most show clinical response in 5 days. Causes of failure: 1) Resistance, 2) Overwhelming infection, or 3) Need for drainage. May need imipenem + amikacin (*Clin Infect Dis* 1996;22:891).

Penicillium marneffei

Penicilliosis

DIAGNOSIS: Exposure to endemic area and evidence of pathogen in culture, smear, or histopathology; most frequent in smear of skin, lesion, node biopsy, or marrow (*Lancet* 1994;344:110). Smears show 2 x 3-6 um yeast (*J Med Mycol* 1993;4:195).

INITIAL TREATMENT (*N Engl J Med* 1993;339:1739)

- **Preferred regimens**
  - Severe: Amphotericin B 0.7-1.0 mg/kg/day until clinically improved (usually 1 to 2 weeks), then itraconazole 200 mg PO bid.
  - Mild to moderately severe: Itraconazole 200 mg PO bid.
- **Maintenance:** Itraconazole 200 mg/day for lifetime.

- **Comments**
  - Clinical Features: Fever ± pneumonitis, adenopathy, skin, and mucosal lesions (papules, nodules, or pustules).
  - Location: Endemic in Thailand, Hong Kong, China, Vietnam, and Indonesia (*Emerg Infect Dis* 1996;2:109; *Lancet* 1994;344:110).
  - *In vitro* sensitivity tests: Good activity with amphotericin B, ketoconazole, miconazole, and 5-FC (*J Mycol Med* 1995;5:21; *Antimicrob Agents Chemother* 1993;37:2407).
  - Itraconazole is superior to fluconazole (*Antimicrob Agents Chemother* 1993;37:2407).

RESPONSE: Response rate of 93% reported for amphotericin/ itraconazole regimen recommended (*Clin Infect Dis* 1998;26:1107).

Progressive Multifocal Leukoencephalopathy (PML), see JC Virus, p. 139

*Pneumocystis carinii (P. jiroveci)**

Pneumonia (PCP)

DIAGNOSIS: X-ray is negative in 10% to 20% (*J Acquir Immune Defic Syndr* 1994;7:39); high resolution CT scan usually shows "ground glass appearance" in x-ray negative cases (*Am J Roentgen* 1997;169:967). For microbial detection, standard specimens are: 1) induced sputum with sensitivity of 60% to 95% in published reports (*N Engl J Med* 1988;318:589; *JAMA* 2001;286:2450); 2) bronchoscopy with sensitivity of 95%.

* *P. carinii* has been renamed *P. jiroveci* but the eponym PCP is retained (*Emerg Infect Dis* 2002;8:891).

TREATMENT

- **Preferred regimens**
  - Trimethoprim 15 mg/kg/day + sulfamethoxazole 75 mg/kg/day PO or IV x 21 days in 3 to 4 divided doses (typical oral dose is 2 DS tid). May treat for only 14 days if mild disease and rapid response.
  - Hypoxemia: Patients with moderately severe or severe disease (PO_2 <70mm Hg or A-a gradient >35 mm Hg) should receive corticosteroids (prednisone 40 mg PO bid x 5 days, then 40 mg qd x 5 days, then 20 mg/day to completion of treatment). IV methylprednisolone can be given as 75% of prednisone dose. Efficacy of corticosteroids for hypoxemia is established (*N Engl J Med* 1990;323:1451; *N Engl J Med* 1990;323:1500). Side effects include CNS toxicity, thrush, cryptococcosis, *H. simplex* infection, tuberculosis, and other OIs (*J Acquir Immune Defic Syndr* 1995;8:345).

- **Alternative regimens**
  - TMP 15 mg/kg/day PO + dapsone 100 mg/day PO x 21 days (*Ann Intern Med* 1996;124:792; *N Engl J Med* 1990;320:323:776).
  - Pentamidine 3-4 mg/kg/day IV infused over ≥60 min x 21 days; usually reserved for severe cases (*Ann Intern Med* 1986;105:37; *Ann Intern Med* 1990;113:203; *Ann Intern Med* 1994;121:174).
  - Clindamycin 600-900 mg IV q6h-q8h or 300-450 mg PO q6h + primaquine* 15-30 mg/day base PO x 21 days (*Clin Infect Dis* 1994;18:905; *Clin Infect Dis* 1998;27:524; *Arch Intern Med* 2001;161:1529).
  - Atovaquone 750 mg suspension PO bid with meal x 21 days (*N Engl J Med* 1993;328:1521; *Ann Int Med* 1994;121:154).
  - Trimetrexate 45 mg/m²/day IV plus leucovorin 20 mg/m² PO or IV q6h; leucovorin for 3 days longer than trimetrexate (*J Infect Dis* 1994;170:165).
- **Comments**
  - Some recommend TMP dose of 20 mg/kg/day (TMP). The lower dose appears to be as effective and better tolerated (*N Engl J Med* 1993;328:1521; *Ann Intern Med* 1996;124:792).
  - In a comparative trial (ACTG 108), TMP-SMX, TMP-dapsone and clindamycin-primaquine were equally effective for mild-moderate PCP (*Ann Intern Med* 1996;124:792).
  - Resistance of *P. carinii* to sulfonamides: Mutations on the dihydropteroate synthase gene have been noted and appear to correlate with sulfonamide exposure (*J Infect Dis* 2000;182:1192; *J Infect Dis* 1999;180:1969; *J Infect Dis* 2000;182:551), but there does not appear to be an association with treatment failure (*J Infect Dis* 2000;182:551; *JAMA* 2001;286:2450).
  - Intolerance to TMP-SMX has been noted in 25% to 50%, primarily rash (30% to 55%), fever (30% to 40%), leukopenia (30% to 40%), azotemia (1% to 5%), hepatitis (20%), thrombocytopenia (15%), and hypokalemia (TMP) (*J Infect Dis* 1995;171:1295; *Lancet* 1991; 338:431). Most can be "treated through" using antihistamines for rashes, antipyretics for fever, and antiemetics for nausea.
  - Opinions vary regarding initiation of HAART during treatment of PCP. Some report better short term survival (*J Infect Dis* 2001;183:1409); others report paradoxical worsening.
  - Geographic clustering of cases suggests person-to-person spread (*Am J Respir Crit Care Med* 2000;162:1617; *Am J Respir Crit Care Med* 2000;162:1622; *N Engl J Med* 2000;19:1416). However, isolation from other vulnerable patients is not generally advocated.
- **Prophylaxis:** See p. 40

RESPONSE: Response to therapy is slow – usually 5 to 7 days. Preferred therapy (TMP-SMX) should not be changed based on an assumption of clinical failure until ≥5 days. Drug toxicity is common and may be mistaken for therapeutic non-response (*Ann Intern Med* 1996;124:972). Some patients do not respond to any therapy; the mortality rate of PCP with hospitalized patients given standard regimens is 15% to 20%. One meta-analysis suggested primaquine-clindamycin is the most effective salvage regimen (*Arch Int Med* 2001;161:1529).

Pseudomonas aeruginosa

DIAGNOSIS: Clinically compatible case + recovery from a normally sterile source. Caution is necessary with interpretation of *P. aeruginosa* in contaminated respiratory tract specimens (sputum, bronchoscopy, etc.), especially if prior antibiotics or recovered in low numbers.

TREATMENT

- **Preferred regimen:** Aminoglycoside + antipseudomonal beta-lactam (ceftazidime, cefoperazone, cefepime, ticarcillin, imipenem, piperacillin).
- **Alternative regimen:** Monotherapy with antipseudomonas beta-lactam, (ceftazidime, cefepime, piperacillin), carbapenem (imipenem, meropenem), ciprofloxacin, aminoglycoside.
- **Comments**
  - Antibiotic selection requires *in vitro* susceptibility data.
  - Risks: Reverse risk factors when feasible – neutropenia, corticosteroids, CD4 <50 cells/mm^3.

Rhodococcus equi

DIAGNOSIS: Compatible clinical illness + CD4 <100 cells/mm^3 + recovery from respiratory tract or blood; 80% of AIDS patients with this infection have bacteremia (*Clin Infect Dis* 2002;34:1379).

TREATMENT

- **Preferred regimen:** Vancomycin 2 g/day IV or imipenem 2 g/day IV, usually combined with rifampin 600 mg/day PO or ciprofloxacin 750 mg PO bid or erythromycin PO or IV x ≥2 weeks, then oral treatment for 6 months.
- **Comments**
  - Sensitivity test guides therapy: Generally sensitive to fluoroquinolones, vancomycin, aminoglycosides; imipenem, erythromycin, and rifampin resistant *in vitro* to penicillins and cephalosporins (*Clin Infect Dis* 2002;34:1379).

  - Other drugs sometimes used based on *in vitro* sensitivity testing are tetracyclines, clindamycin, and TMP-SMX.
  - Duration of therapy is arbitrary, but relapses are common; most use prolonged oral maintenance therapy with macrolide or fluoroquinolone. Resistance to these agents may develop.
  - Immune reconstitution with HAART may be critical for cure.

RESPONSE: Prognosis prior to HAART era was poor (*Medicine* 1994;73:119). The prognosis with antibacterial agents plus immune reconstitution is good; the disease is chronic or fatal in 30% to 40% without HAART or with no response to HAART.

Salmonella spp.

DIAGNOSIS: Recovery of *Salmonella* from virtually any site; most commonly stool and blood.

TREATMENT (*Clin Infect Dis* 2001;32:331)

- **Preferred regimen:** Ciprofloxacin 500 mg PO bid x >2 weeks
- **Alternative regimen:** TMP 5-10 mg/kg/day/SMX IV or 1 DS bid x >2 weeks or ceftriaxone 1-2 g/day IV ≥2 weeks.
- **Comments**
  - Relapse is common. Eradication of *Salmonella* carrier state has been demonstrated only with ciprofloxacin.
  - AZT is active against most *Salmonella* strains and may be effective prophylaxis (*J Infect Dis* 1999;179:1553).
  - Drug selection requires *in vitro* susceptibility data, especially for ampicillin. TMP-SMX preferred if sensitive. Ciprofloxacin resistance is reported (*N Engl J Med* 2001;344:1572) but is rare.
  - Maintenance: Some authorities recommend ciprofloxacin 500 mg PO bid x several months or TMP-SMX 5 mg/kg/day, TMP (1 DS PO bid). Need for maintenance therapy, specific regimens, and duration are not well defined.

Staphylococcus aureus

DIAGNOSIS: Compatible clinical illness + recovery of *S. aureus* from normally sterile site.

TREATMENT

- **Preferred regimens**
  - Methicillin-sensitive *S. aureus* (MSSA): Antistaphylococcal penicillin (nafcillin, oxacillin) ± gentamicin 1 mg/kg IV q8h or rifampin 300 mg PO bid.

- Methicillin-sensitive *S. aureus* (MSSA): Cephalexin 500 mg qid, dicloxacillin 500 mg qid, clindamycin 300 mg tid, or fluoroquinolone.
- Methicillin-resistant *S. aureus* (MRSA): Vancomycin 1 g IV q12h ± gentamicin or rifampin (above doses).

- **Alternative regimens**
  - MSSA: Cephalosporin: first generation ± gentamicin or rifampin.
  - MRSA: Linezolid IV or PO 600 mg bid. Many community-acquired MRSA are sensitive to clindamycin, macrolides, and fluoroquinolones.
- **Comments**
  - Fluoroquinolones: Use of quinolone requires *in vitro* sensitivity results. Resistance is 10% for MSSA and 90% for nosocomial MRSA. Prevalence of MRSA in community-acquired infections varies by geography but is commonly reported at 5% to 10%; many of these strains are resistant to methicillin + cephalosporins, but sensitive to clindamycin, macrolides, and fluoroquinolones (*Nature* 2002;417:477; *Lancet* 2002;359:1819; *JAMA* 2000;286:1201).
  - Tricuspid valve endocarditis: nafcillin + gentamicin (MSSA) x 2 weeks (*Ann Intern Med* 1988;109:619), but abbreviated courses are generally not advocated for HIV infected persons.
  - For tricuspid valve endocarditis due to MSSA, nafcillin/oxacillin is preferred to vancomycin (*Clin Infect Dis* 2001;33:120).

RESPONSE: Most patients with *S. aureus* tricuspid valve endocarditis have negative blood cultures by day 3, and the cure rate is 90% (*N Engl J Med* 2001;345:1318).

Streptococcus pneumoniae

DIAGNOSIS: Compatible clinical illness + recovery of *S. pneumoniae* from a normally sterile site; presumptive pneumococcal pneumonia – acute pneumonia with infiltrate and gram stain or culture evidence of *S. pneumoniae*.

TREATMENT

- **Preferred regimens:** Penicillin, amoxicillin, cefotaxime, ceftriaxone (see Comments), or fluoroquinolone: Levofloxacin, moxifloxacin, or gatifloxacin.
- **Alternative regimens:** Macrolide, vancomycin.
- **Comments**
  - *In vitro* susceptibility: Susceptibility of *S. pneumoniae* based on CDC surveillance report with 3475 strains from invasive infections in the United States in 1998: Penicillin resistance – 14%,

macrolides – 11%, clindamycin – 3%, doxycycline – 6%, fluoroquinolones – 0.2% (*N Engl J Med* 2000;343:1917).

- Penicillin resistant strains: Strains highly resistant to penicillin should be treated with vancomycin, linezolid, or newer quinolones (levofloxacin, gatifloxacin, or moxifloxacin). TMP-SMX is now considered inadequate for empiric use due to high rates of resistance. Fluoroquinolone resistance is at a low rate (<2%) but increasing (*N Engl J Med* 2002;346:747; *Emerg Infect Dis* 2002;8:594).

RESPONSE: Most patients respond well with clearance of bacteremia in 24 to 48 hours and clinical improvement in 1 to 3 days. Patients with pneumococcal pneumonia may transition from IV to oral antibiotics when they are clinically better, vital signs and blood gases are improved, and they can take pills.

Toxoplasma gondii

Toxoplasmic encephalitis

DIAGNOSIS: Typical features are CD4 <100 cells/mm^3 (80%), ≥2 ring enhancing lesions or MRI, fever, focal neurologic defect, and positive anti-*T. gondii* IgG (>90%). CSF *T. gondii* PCR is 50% sensitive and >96% specific. Most respond to therapy with clinical + MRI improvement ≤2 weeks (*Clin Infect Dis* 2001;34:103).

TREATMENT: ACUTE INFECTION (3 to 6 weeks)

- **Preferred regimen:** Pyrimethamine 200 mg loading dose, then 50-75 mg/day PO + leucovorin 10-20 mg/day PO + sulfadiazine 1000-1500 mg PO q6h x 3 to 6 weeks (*Clin Infect Dis* 1996;22:268).
- **Alternative regimens**
  - Pyrimethamine + leucovorin (see preferred regimen) + clindamycin IV 600 mg q6h for 3 to 6 weeks.
  - Pyrimethamine + leucovorin (see preferred regimen) + one of the following: Azithromycin 900-1200 mg/day PO (*AIDS* 2001;15:583), clarithromycin 500 mg PO bid (*Antimicrob Agents Chemother* 1991;35:2049), atovaquone 1500 mg PO bid with food (*Clin Infect Dis* 2002;34:1243), minocycline PO or IV 150-200 mg bid, doxycycline.
  - TMP-SMX, 5 mg/kg TMP + 25 mg/kg SMX PO or IV bid (*Antimicrob Agents Chemother* 1998;42:1346).
  - Atovaquone 1500 mg PO bid with food + sulfadiazine 1000-1500 mg PO q6h or atovaquone (prior dose) + pyrimethamine 200 mg x 1, then 75 mg/day + leucovorin 10-20 mg/day (*Clin Infect Dis,* 2002;34:1243).
  - 5 fluoro-uracil 1.5 mg/kg/day PO + clindamycin PO or IV 1.8-2.4 g bid (*AIDS* 1993;7:143)

- Minocycline PO or IV 150-200 mg bid + clarithromycin 500 mg PO bid or sulfadiazine 1000-1500 mg PO q6h.
- Doxycycline PO or IV 300-400 mg/day + clarithromycin 500 mg PO bid or sulfadiazine 1000-1500 mg PO q6h.

- **Comments**
  - Pyrimethamine + sulfadiazine is preferred; pyrimethamine + clindamycin is less effective but better tolerated (*Clin Infect Dis* 1996;22:268). All other regimens listed have been less well studied.
  - Clinical improvement expected within 1 week and improvement by CT scan or MRI within 2 weeks. Failure to respond and/or uncertain diagnosis is usually an indication for stereotactic brain biopsy, which yields a definitive diagnosis in 98% of cases (*Clin Infect Dis* 2000;30:49).
  - Use corticosteroids only if significant edema/mass effect (dexamethasone PO or IV 4 mg q6h). Avoid anticonvulsants unless seizures are prolonged or recurrent.
  - Leucovorin dose can be increased to ≥50 mg/day to reduce pyrimethamine toxicity.
  - Atovaquone regimens: May wish to confirm level ≥18 mcg/mL due to variable absorption.

MAINTENANCE

- **Preferred regimen:** Pyrimethamine 50-75 mg/day PO + leucovorin 10-20 mg/day + sulfadiazine 1000-1500 mg PO q6h.
- **Alternative regimen:** Pyrimethamine 25-75 mg/day PO + leucovorin 10-25 mg qd + clindamycin 300-450 mg PO q6h-q8h.
- **Comments**
  - Regimens with established efficacy: Pyrimethamine plus sulfadiazine or clindamycin.
  - PCP prophylaxis: Pyrimethamine-sulfadiazine, TMP-SMX, and atovaquone + pyrimethamine provide effective PCP prophylaxis, pyrimethamine-clindamycin does not.

IMMUNE RECONSTITUTION: Discontinue maintenance therapy when CD4 count >200 cells/mm^3 x 6 months, initial therapy completed + asymptomatic.

PROPHYLAXIS: See p. 43

RESPONSE: Clinical response expected in 1 week in 60% to 80% and MRI response expected in 2 weeks. Failure to achieve these goals should prompt consideration of alternative diagnosis, especially primary CNS lymphoma, tuberculous, or brain abscess.

Treponema pallidum

Syphilis (*MMWR* 2002;51[RR-6])

DIAGNOSIS: Early syphilis – darkfield and DFA test of exudate. Late syphilis (secondary + tertiary) – non-treponemal test (VDRL or RPR) + treponemal test (FTA-ABS). Non-treponemal test titers correlate with disease activity.

TREATMENT

- **Preferred regimens**
  - Primary, secondary, and early latent syphilis (<1 year): Benzathine penicillin G 2.4 mil units IM weekly x 1 (see Comments).
  - Late latent syphilis (>1 year or unknown): Benzathine penicillin G 2.4 mil units IM weekly x 3.
  - Neurosyphilis: Aqueous penicillin G, 18-24 mil units/day IV x 10 to 14 days (3-4 mil units q4h).
- **Alternative regimens**
  - No alternative to penicillin has established merit with HIV co-infection, although ceftriaxone appears equivalent in preliminary trials (*Clin Infect Dis* 2000;30:540). Non-pregnant patients with non-neurosyphilis may be treated with doxycycline 100 mg bid x 14 days for primary and secondary syphilis and doxycycline 100 mg bid x 28 days for late latent syphilis. There must be careful follow-up. The alternative for these patients is penicillin skin test and, if positive, desensitization.
  - Penicillin allergy and neurosyphilis or pregnancy: Skin testing is recommended with a history of penicillin related anaphylaxis or asthma or other conditions suggesting a risk for anaphylaxis. Minor determinants are sometimes not available, so the sensitivity of testing is only 90% to 97%. The test includes a screening 15 minute epicutaneous test using *Pre-Pen* (Taylor Pharmacal Company), positive results are a wheal of >4 mm at 15 minutes. A negative histamine control test negates the validity of a negative epicutaneous test. Patients with a positive histamine and negative epicutaneous test then have intradermal tests with *Pre-Pen* ± minor determinants using duplicate injections of the reagents and the diluent controls.

    Desensitization can be done orally or parenterally; oral is usually preferred (see Table 5-4, p. 160). Desensitization: 1 unit IV, then double dose at 15-minute intervals or increase dose 10-fold at 20- to 30-minute intervals.
- **Comments**
  - Follow-up primary and secondary cases clinically and serologically at 3, 6, 9, 12, and 24 months; for latent cases, follow-up serologically at 6, 12, 18, and 24 months.

- In a therapeutic trial of benzathine penicillin G 2.4 mil units for primary or secondary syphilis, HIV infected patients responded less well serologically, but clinical failures were rare (*N Engl J Med* 1997;337: 307).
- Patients with latent syphilis of uncertain duration are considered to have late latent syphilis.
- LP is recommended with neurologic symptoms, treatment failure, and late latent syphilis.
- An ACTG trial showed that ceftriaxone (2 g IV once daily x 10 days) was equivalent to penicillin G (4 mil units IV q4h x 10 days for neurosyphilis), but these results were considered inconclusive due to a small sample size (30 patients) and baseline differences in the patients in the two groups (*Clin Infect Dis* 2000;30:540).
- Compared with syphilis without HIV infection, there is slightly greater risk of false-negative serology and greater risk of neurologic disease.
- Local health departments are frequently able to provide previous RPR titers for patients with a history of syphilis.

■ TABLE 5-4: **Penicillin Allergy Skin Test and Desensitization (*MMWR* 2002;51[RR-6]:28)**

Penicillin Skin Test:

- Reagents: Benzylpenicilloyd poly-L-lysine (*Pre-Pen*) + minor determinant if available. If minor determinants is not available, use *Pre-Pen* only.
- Positive control for epicutaneous test is commercial histamine (1 mg/mL).
- Negative control is diluent, usually saline.
- Sequence: Epicutaneous test → Positive (wheal >4 mm at 15 min) = penicillin allergy; negative histamine control + negative prick test = unreliable; positive histamine test + negative prick test = do intradermal test.
- Epicutaneous (prick) test: Drops on forearm pierced with #26 needle without blood wheal >4 mm at 15 min is positive.
- Intradermal test: 0.02 mL intradermal injection forearm with #26 or #27 needle; at 15 min a wheal >2 mm larger than negative controls and the initial wheal = positive

Desensitization:

- Indication: Positive skin test.
- Route: Oral or IV; oral is safer and easier.
- Site: Hospital setting.
- Time: Requires 4 hours.
- Schedule: Administer every 15 minutes using the following amount in 30 mL aliquots for oral administration.

Dose	Units/mL	mL	Units	Dose	Units/mL	mL	Units
1	1,000	.10	100	**8**	10,000	1.20	12,000
2	1,000	.20	200	**9**	10,000	2.40	24,000
3	1,000	.04	400	**10**	10,000	4.80	48,000
4	1,000	.80	800	**11**	80,000	1.00	80,000
5	1,000	1.60	1,600	**12**	80,000	2.00	160,000
6	1,000	3.20	3,200	**13**	80,000	4.00	320,000
7	1,000	6.40	6,400	**14**	80,000	8.00	640,000

6 | Drug Information

DRUG PROFILES are listed alphabetically by generic drug names (except for *Trizivir*).

TRADE NAME and pharmaceutical company source are provided unless there are multiple providers. Trade names are for United States brands.

COST is based on average wholesale price (AWP) according to Price Alert, First DataBank, San Bruno, California, March 15, 2002. Prices are generally given for generic products when generics are available.

PHARMACOLOGY, SIDE EFFECTS, AND DRUG INTERACTIONS: Data are from Drug Information 2002, American Hospital Formulary Service, Bethesda, MD; *PDR* 2002.

CREATININE CLEARANCE

- **Males:** Weight (kg) x (140-age in years)/72x serum creatinine (mg/dL)
- **Females:** Determination for males x 0.85
- **Obese patients:** Use lean body weight.
- **Formula assumes stable renal function.** Assume creatinine clearance (CrCl) of 5-8 mL/min for patients with anuria or oliguria.
- **Pregnancy and volume expansion:** GFR may be increased in third trimester of pregnancy and with massive parenteral fluids.

PATIENT ASSISTANCE PROGRAMS: Most pharmaceutical companies that provide this service require all of the following:

- Income eligibility criteria such as an annual income <$12,000 for an individual or <$15,000 for a family.
- Non-availability of prescription drug payment from public or private third party sources.
- A prescription and a letter of verification.

Note: Most will provide a 3-month supply subject to re-review at that time (see http://www.needymeds.com).

CLASSIFICATION OF CONTROLLED SUBSTANCES

Category	Interpretation
I	**High potential for abuse and no current accepted medical use.** Examples are heroin and LSD.
II	**High potential for abuse.** Use may lead to severe physical or psychological dependence. Examples are opioids, amphetamines, short-acting barbiturates, and preparations containing codeine. Prescriptions must be written in ink or typewritten and signed by the practitioner. Verbal prescriptions must be confirmed in writing within 72 hours and may be given only in a genuine emergency. No renewals are permitted.
III	**Some potential for abuse.** Use may lead to low-to-moderate physical dependence or high psychological dependence. Examples are barbiturates and preparations containing small quantities of codeine. Prescriptions may be oral or written. Up to five renewals are permitted within 6 months.
IV	**Low potential for abuse.** Examples include chloral hydrate, phenobarbital, and benzodiazepines. Use may lead to limited physical or psychological dependence. Prescriptions may be oral or written. Up to five renewals are permitted within 6 months.
V	**Subject to state and local regulation.** Abuse potential is low; a prescription may not be required. Examples are antitussive and antidiarrheal medications containing limited quantities of opioids.

CLASSIFICATION FOR DRUG USE IN PREGNANCY BASED ON FDA CATEGORIES: Ratings range from "A" for drugs that have been tested for teratogenicity under controlled conditions without showing evidence of damage to the fetus to "D" and "X" for drugs that are definitely teratogenic. The "D" rating is generally reserved for drugs with no safer alternatives. The "X" rating means there is absolutely no reason to risk using the drug in pregnancy.

Category	Interpretation
A	**Controlled studies show no risk.** Adequate, well-controlled studies in pregnant women have failed to demonstrate risk to the fetus.
B	**No evidence of risk in humans.** Either animal findings show risk, but human findings do not, or, if no adequate human studies have been performed, animal findings are negative.
C	**Risk cannot be ruled out.** Human studies are lacking, and animal studies are either positive for fetal risk, or lacking as well. However, potential benefits may justify the potential risk.
D	**Positive evidence of risk.** Investigational or postmarketing data show risk to the fetus. Nevertheless, potential benefits may outweigh the potential risk.
E	**Contraindicated in pregnancy.** Studies in animals or humans, or investigational or postmarketing reports, have shown fetal risk that clearly outweighs any possible benefit to the patient.

PREGNANCY REGISTRY FOR ANTIRETROVIRAL DRUGS: This is a joint project sponsored by staff from pharmaceutical companies with an advisory panel with representatives from the CDC, NIH obstetrical practitioners, and pediatricians. The registry allows anonymity of patients and birth outcome follow-up is obtained by registry staff. Healthcare professionals should report prenatal exposures to antiretroviral agents to: Antiretroviral Pregnancy Registry, 155 N. Third Street, Suite 306, Wilmington, NC 28401; 800-258-4263; fax 800-800-1052.

ABACAVIR (ABC)

TRADE NAME: *Ziagen* (GlaxoSmithKline)

FORMS AND PRICES: 300 mg tabs at $7.08 or $5,171/year; oral suspension with 10 mg/mL; available as *Trizivir* tabs with AZT (300 mg), 3TC (150 mg), and ABC (300 mg) for bid administration at $18.50/tab.

CLASS: Nucleoside analog

INDICATIONS AND DOSE: See Table 4-15, p. 70. 300 mg tab PO bid (no food restrictions); *Trizivir* – 1 tab bid (no food restrictions). Pharmacokinetics support qd dosing (600 mg qd).

CLINICAL TRIALS: With monotherapy, ABC reduced viral load 1.5-2.0 logs – significantly more than other nucleosides.

- **CNA 3014** compared the AZT/3TC (*Combivir*) plus either abacavir or indinavir, in a randomized, multicenter open-label trial (1st IAS Conference, Buenos Aires, 2001, Abstract 63). A total of 342 patients were enrolled. By intent-to-treat analysis, 66% of ABC recipients had viral loads <400 c/mL compared with 50% of the IDV group (p<0.002). By as-treated analysis, results were 85% and 83%, respectively. When analysis was confined to patients with baseline viral loads >100,000 c/mL, proportions of ABC and IDV recipients with viral loads <400 c/mL were 60% and 51%, respectively, by intent-to-treat analysis, and 70% and 79% by as-treated analysis. Among patients with baseline viral loads >100,000 c/mL, viral load was <50 c/mL in 48% vs 46% by intent-to-treat analysis, and 59% vs 73% using an as-treated analysis. Adherence was significantly better among ABC recipients in this open-label trial.
- **CNA 3003** was the first major comparative trial (AZT/3TC/ABC vs AZT/3TC) in 173 treatment-naïve patients with CD4 count >100 cells/mm^3. At 24 weeks, 70% of those in the three-drug arm had viral load <400 c/mL, and the average increase in CD4 count was 86 cells/mm^3. This was significantly better than results in the AZT/3TC arm. The response at 48 weeks was sustained; however, a subset analysis of participants with baseline viral loads of >100,000 c/mL demonstrated that only 33% achieved undetectable virus (6th CROI, Chicago, Illinois, 1999, Abstract 16).
- **CNA 3005** compared the triple NRTI regimen AZT/3TC/ABC with IDV/AZT/3TC in 562 treatment-naïve patients. At 48 weeks, 51% in both groups had achieved viral load <400 c/mL by intent-to-treat analysis. Only 31% receiving the ABC regimen with a baseline viral load >100,000 c/mL had reduction in viral load to <400 c/mL, compared with 45% in the IDV arm. There was comparable immune restoration in the two groups with median CD4 count increases of about 100 cells/mm^3 at 48 weeks. Genotypic resistance analysis of HIV strains from 43 virologic failures on AZT/3TC/ABC at 96 weeks

showed that the major NRTI resistance mutation was M184V in 35% (*JAMA* 2001;285:1155).

- **TARGET** was a single arm trial in which AZT/3TC/ABC was given to 81 patients with viral loads <50,000 c/mL and CD4 counts >50 cells/mm³ who had previously received one or two NRTIs. The proportion with viral load <400 c/mL increased from 34% to 82% with no difference based on prior exposure to AZT or 3TC (*J Infect Dis* 2001;183:571).
- **Expanded access and 3002:** Other studies of nucleoside-experienced patients were disappointing. In the expanded access program, which included 13,000 patients who failed standard therapy with two nucleosides plus a PI and had CD4 counts <100 cells/mm³ and viral loads >30,000 c/mL, only 31% experienced a reduction in viral load of ≥0.5 $\log_{10}$ with the addition of ABC (*Clin Infect Dis* 2002;34:535). In study 3002, patients receiving any prior regimen with viral load 500-50,000 c/mL had their regimens "intensified" with ABC. At 8 weeks, 39% of ABC recipients had viral load <400 c/mL. There was no difference between those with or without prior 3TC experience or the M184V mutation.
- **CNA 2006** was a non-randomized study of ABC/APV in treatment-naïve patients with CD4 counts >400 cells/mm³. By intent-to-treat analysis at 72 weeks, 68% had viral load <50 c/mL and 40% had viral load <5 c/mL. The mean CD4 count increase was 239 cells/mm³ (7th CROI, San Francisco, California, 2000, Abstract 336).
- **CNA 2007** involved the use of ABC/APV/EFV as a salvage regimen for patients with viral load >500 c/mL despite receiving PI-containing regimens for >20 weeks. At 16 weeks, 26% achieved viral load <400 c/mL by intent-to-treat analysis. The best results were seen in patients with low viral load at entry and in patients naïve to NNRTIs.
- **The Swiss Cohort Study** examined 163 patients who responded to PI-containing regimens, with viral load <50 c/mL for ≥6 months, and were then randomized to continue the PI regimen or switch to a triple NRTI regimen with AZT/3TC/ABC. Virologic failure at 48 weeks was more common in the ABC group (15% vs 6%) and was ascribed to NRTI resistance in archived strains due to prior AZT monotherapy or dual NRTI therapy. The ABC recipients had a prompt and impressive decrease in cholesterol (median of 35 mg/dL) and triglycerides (median decreased 43 mg/dL) (*J Infect Dis* 2002;185:1251).
- Other studies have examined ABC in combination with PIs or NNRTIs with good results (*J Acquir Immune Defic Syndr* 2001; 26:332).
- **Summary:** ABC is a potent NRTI, although experience with combination treatment using antiretroviral drugs other than AZT/3TC is limited. The "triple nuke" regimen is an appropriate option for initial therapy in selected patients, with the advantages of preserved options, probable reduction in lipodystrophy, and convenient dosing

regimen. Disadvantages include the potential for the ABC hypersensitivity reaction and possible reduced potency in patients with baseline viral loads >100,000 c/mL. It is possible that potency could be improved with the addition of tenofovir DF, although this four-drug combination has not been studied. ABC does not appear to be effective as a component of salvage therapy in patients with extensive NRTI experience. Some authorities advocate the addition of ABC to any regimen containing AZT and 3TC because this increases potency with minimal risk of increased resistance. Others advocate reserving ABC for intensification in patients with low-level virologic failure. The combination of ABC and 3TC as a dual NRTI component of HAART is attractive due to good tolerability, low potential for mitochondrial toxicity, and no thymidine analog mutations after failure; the disadvantage is paucity of experience. The CLASS study (XIV International AIDS Conference, Barcelona, 2002, Abstract 1189) used ABC/3TC as a backbone for all three arms of a HAART trial with good results, especially in the EFV arm.

***IN VITRO* ACTIVITY:** The IC_{50} vs HIV-1 is 0.07-1.0 μM. There is synergy when ABC is combined with APV, NVP, and AZT; activity is additive when ABC is combined with ddI, 3TC, d4T, and ddC.

RESISTANCE: ABC selects for the following mutations on the RT gene: 65, 74, 115, and 184. The 184 mutation leads to complete cross-resistance to 3TC, but by itself does not significantly decrease ABC susceptibility. Mutations at codons 65 and 74 lead to cross-resistance to ddI and ddC. Each of these mutations results in a 2- to 4-fold decrease in susceptibility to ABC. Significant resistance requires multiple mutations, usually in addition to the 184 mutation. Clinical trials indicate that the presence of the M184V mutations plus at least three thymidine analog mutations (TAMs) predicts ABC failure.

PHARMACOLOGY

- **Bioavailability:** 83%; alcohol increases ABC levels by 41%.
- **T½:** 1.5 hours (serum); intracellular T½: >12 hours. CSF levels: 27% to 33% of serum levels.
- **Elimination:** 81% metabolized by alcohol dehydrogenase and glucuronyl transferase with renal excretion of metabolites; 16% recovered in stool, and 1% unchanged in urine. Metabolism does not involve the cytochrome P450 pathway.
- **Dose modification in renal failure:** None (*Nephron* 2000;87:186)

SIDE EFFECTS

- **Hypersensitivity reaction** *(Clin Infect Dis* 2002;34:1137): This serious side effect is noted in 3% to 9% (average 3.7%) of patients. Clinical features include fever (usually 39°C to 40°C), skin rash (maculopapular or urticarial), fatigue, malaise, GI symptoms (nausea, vomiting, diarrhea, abdominal pain), arthralgias, cough, and/or dyspnea. The rash occurs in 70%. Laboratory changes may include increased CPK, elevated liver function tests, and lymphopenia. Over 93% occur within the first 6 weeks of therapy, and the median time of onset is 9 days (*Clin Infect Dis* 2002;34:1137; *Clin Infect Dis* 2002;34:535; *Lancet* 2000;356:1423). Susceptibility to this drug appears to be genetic and has been associated with the HLA-DR7 and HLA-DQ3 haplotypes. This 57-1 ancestral haplotype was found in 78% of Caucasians from western Australia with typical ABC hypersensitivity reactions and 3% of controls in one report (*Lancet* 2002;359:727). HLA typing is available in many laboratories; the cost is $500 to $800/test; the results are most predictive with Caucasians, and detection may reduce the rate of reactions substantially (9% to 2%), but does not eliminate the risk (*Lancet* 2002;359:722). Re-challenge may cause an anaphylactic-like reaction in 20% with hypotension, bronchoconstriction, and/or renal failure (*AIDS* 1999:13:999). Treatment is supportive with IV fluids, dialysis, etc. Steroids and antihistamines are not usually effective. Re-challenge has been associated with death in at least three patients. A comparison of symptoms of ABC hypersensitivity in 15 patients and influenza in 30 patients found that flu is less likely to cause GI symptoms, but there was considerable overlap (8th CROI, Chicago, Illinois, February 2001, Abstract 622). Hypersensitivity reactions should be reported to the Abacavir Hypersensitivity Registry at 800-270-0425. For more information call 800-334-0089. Patients should be warned to consult their provider immediately if they note skin rash plus fever, typical GI symptoms, cough, dyspnea, or constitutional symptoms, especially during the first month of therapy. A warning sheet is available from pharmacists. An obvious concern is that common intercurrent illnesses or other drug reactions may be erroneously attributed to this reaction, preventing the subsequent use of the drug. A possible solution in unclear cases is continued administration under observation because patients experiencing true ABC hypersensitivity will experience worsening symptoms with each dose.

- **Other side effects** include nausea, vomiting, malaise, headache, diarrhea, or anorexia.
- **Patients may develop lactic acidosis** with or without hepatic steatosis, although this is thought to be less common than with other NRTIs.

DRUG INTERACTIONS: Alcohol increases ABC levels by 41%; ABC has no effect on alcohol levels (*Antimicrob Agents Chemother* 2000;283:1811).

PREGNANCY: Category C. Rodent teratogen test showed skeletal malformations and anasarca at 35x the comparable human dose. Placental passage positive in rats.

ACYCLOVIR (also includes famciclovir and valacyclovir)

TRADE NAME: *Zovirax, Valtrex* (valacyclovir) (GlaxoSmithKline), *Famvir* (famciclovir) (Novartis), or generic

FORMS AND PRICES

- **Acyclovir:** Caps: 200 mg at $1.06. Tabs: 400 mg at $1.90, 800 mg at $3.69. Suspension: 200 mg/5 cc at $122/480 mL. IV vials: 500 mg at $47.50. 5% ointment: 3 g at $25.25, 15 g at $78.01 (utility limited)
- **Famciclovir:** 125 mg tabs at $3.37
- **Valacyclovir:** Tabs: 500 mg at $4.02, 1000 mg at $6.43

CLASS: Synthetic nucleoside analogs derived from guanine

PATIENT ASSISTANCE PROGRAM: 800-722-9294 (acyclovir and valacyclovir)

INDICATIONS AND DOSES: For oral therapy, valacyclovir and famciclovir are generally preferred for the immunosuppressed host (*Lancet* 2001;353:1513). Acyclovir is also available in an IV formulation in this class. The following acyclovir doses are based on recommendations primarily for immunocompetent patients (*N Engl J Med* 1999;340: 1255; *N Engl J Med* 2002;347:340; *Lancet* 2001;357:1513; *MMWR* 2002;51[RR-6]:14; *Lancet* 2001;357:1513). For doses of valacyclovir and famciclovir, see Table 6-1, p. 169.

- **HSV herpes labialis:** Topical penciclovir cream is an alternative to acyclovir in mild cases (*Arch Derm* 2001;37:1153). Patients with severe disease and/or advanced HIV should be treated according to guidelines for genital and progressive mucocutaneous HSV.
- **HSV genital and perirectal** (see Table 6-1, p. 169):
  - Progressive mucocutaneous: 5-10 mg/kg IV q8h x 7 to 14 days
  - Prophylaxis: 400 mg PO bid (this is the standard dose in immunocompetent patients); 400 mg PO 3-5x/day may be required for AIDS patients. Prophylaxis is contraindicated in pregnancy.
  - Acyclovir-resistant: Doses up to 800 mg 5x/day PO or 10 mg/kg IV q8h or by constant infusion or foscarnet, 40 mg/kg IV q8h. Note: There is a good correlation between *in vitro* activity and *in vivo* response. Probability of failure with acyclovir-resistant strains using standard dose of acyclovir is 95% (*Antimicrob Agents Chemother* 1994;38:1246).
  - Encephalitis: 10-15 mg/kg IV q8h x 14 to 21 days.
- **VZV treatment:** Should be started within 4 days or while new lesions are still forming (*N Engl J Med* 2002;347:340).
  - Primary (chickenpox): 800 mg PO 5x/day x 7 to 10 days
  - Dermatomal zoster (shingles): 10 mg/kg IV q8h x 7 days or 800 mg PO 5x/day x 7 days. Famciclovir or valacyclovir are preferred

for oral therapy of shingles due to easier adherence, better efficacy, or improved drug levels (see Table 6-1, p. 169).

- Disseminated zoster: 10 mg/kg IV q8h x 7 days; with pneumonia, consider corticosteroids (*Int J Infect Dis* 2002;6:6; *J Chemother* 2002;14:220).
- Note: Varicella vaccine is a live virus vaccine and is contra-indicated in persons with HIV.

■ TABLE 6-1: **Comparison of Drugs for Infections Caused by Herpes Simplex and Varicella Zoster** (see *N Engl J Med* 1999;340:1255; *Lancet* 2001;357:1513; *MMWR* 2002;51[RR-2]; *N Eng J Med* 2002;347:340)

	Duration	Acyclovir	Valacyclovir	Famciclovir	Other
HERPES SIMPLEX					
Genital					
First episode	7 to 10 days	400 mg tid	1 g bid	250 mg tid	—
Recurrent	5 days	400 mg bid	500 mg bid	125 or 250 mg bid	—
Suppression	Years	400 mg bid	500 mg or 1 g qd	125-250 mg bid	—
Severe disease	≥5 days	5-10 mg/kg/ day q8h IV	1 g tid	—	—
Immuno-suppressed	Not significant	Not recommended	500 mg bid	250 mg bid	—
Perirectal	7 to 10 days	800 mg tid	—	—	—
Oral HSV					
Treatment	5 days	200 mg 5x/day	2 gm q12h x 2 doses	—	Penciclovir topical
Prophylaxis	—	400 mg bid	—	—	—
Mucocutaneous progressive	10 days	400 mg 5x/day; 5 mg/kg q8h IV	1 g tid	—	—
Acyclovir-resistant	—	—	—	—	Cidofovir,* foscarnet,* topical trifluridine*
Encephalitis	14 to 21 days	10-15 mg/kg IV q8h	—	—	—
VARICELLA ZOSTER					
Dermatomal	7 days	800 mg 5x/day; 10 mg/kg q8h IV	1 g tid	500 mg tid	—
Disseminated	7 days	10 mg/kg q8h IV	—	—	—
Acyclovir-resistant	—	—	—	—	Foscarnet

* HSV resistant or refractory to treatment with acyclovir may be treated with topical or intravenous cidofovir (*J Infect Dis* 1997;176:892; *Antimicrob Agents Chemother* 1995;39:2120; *Clin Infect Dis* 1994;18:570), topical trifluridine (*J Acquir Immune Defic Syndr* 1996;12:147), or foscarnet (*N Engl J Med* 1991;325:551; *N Eng J Med* 2002;347:340).

- **EBV, Oral hairy leukoplakia:** 800 mg PO 5x/day x 2 to 3 weeks, then 1.2-2.0 g/day. (Most cases are not treated, and those that are usually relapse after treatment. In addition to acyclovir, ganciclovir and valganciclovir are also effective.)

■ TABLE 6-2: **Activity of Antivirals Against Herpesviruses**

	HSV	VZV	EBV	CMV	HHV 6-8
Acyclovir	++	+	+	—	—
Famciclovir	++	+	+	—	—
Valacyclovir	++	+	+	—	—
Ganciclovir	++	+	++	++	+
Foscarnet	+	+	++	+	+
Cidofovir	+	+	++	+	++

PHARMACOLOGY

- **Bioavailability:** 15% to 20% with oral administration
- **T½:** 2.5 to 3.3 hours, CSF levels: 50% serum levels
- **Elimination:** Renal

■ TABLE 6-3: **Acyclovir Dose Modification in Renal Failure**

Usual Dose	Creatinine Clearance	Adjusted Dose
200 mg 5x/day	>10 mL/min	200 mg 5x/day
	≤10 mL/min	200 mg q12h
800 mg 5x/day	>50 mL/min	800 mg 5x/day
	10-50 mL/min	800 mg q8h
	<10 mL/min	800 mg q12h
5-10 mg/kg IV q8h	>50 mL/min	5-10 mg/kg IV q8h
	10-50 mL/min	5-10 mg/kg q12h-q24h
	<10 mL/min	5-10 mg/kg q24h

- **Famciclovir:** CrCl 10-50 mL/min ½ usual dose; CrCl <10 mL/min ¼ standard dose
- **Valacyclovir:** CrCl 10-50 mL/min ½ usual dose; CrCl <10 mL/min 500 mg qd

SIDE EFFECTS (infrequent and rarely severe)

- Irritation at infusion site, rash, nausea and vomiting, diarrhea, renal toxicity (especially with rapid IV infusion, prior renal disease, and concurrent nephrotoxic drugs), dizziness, abnormal liver function tests, itching, and headache
- Rare complications include CNS toxicity with encephalopathy, disorientation, seizures, hallucinations, anemia, neutropenia, thrombocytopenia, and hypotension

DRUG INTERACTIONS

- Increased meperidine and theophylline levels
- Probenecid prolongs half-life of acyclovir.

PREGNANCY: Category C. Not teratogenic, but potential to cause chromosomal damage at high doses. The CDC Registry shows no increased incidence of fetal abnormalities among 601 women for whom pregnancy outcome data were available (*MMWR* 1993;42:806). The CDC Registry contact number is 800-258-4263. The CDC recommends use of acyclovir during pregnancy only for life-threatening disease.

AGENERASE – see Amprenavir (p. 176)

ALBENDAZOLE

TRADE NAME: *Albenza* (GlaxoSmithKline)

FORM AND PRICE: 200 mg tablets at $1.38

INDICATION AND DOSE: Microsporidiosis; 400 mg PO bid x ≥3 weeks

CLINICAL TRIALS: Albendazole (400 mg bid x 3 weeks) is highly effective with microsporidiosis involving *Encephalitozoon (Septata) intestinalis* but is not effective for *Enterocytozoon bieneusi. E. bieneusi* accounts for about 80% of cases of microsporidiosis in AIDS patients. These species can be distinguished by EM or PCR.

PHARMACOLOGY

- **Bioavailability:** Low, but absorption is increased 5-fold if taken with a fatty meal vs administration in a fasting state. Should be taken with fatty meal.
- **T½:** 8 hours
- **Elimination:** Metabolized in liver to albendazole sulfoxide, then excreted by enterohepatic circulation
- **Dose modification in renal failure:** None

SIDE EFFECTS: Adverse reactions are rare and include reversible hepatotoxicity, GI intolerance (abdominal pain, diarrhea, nausea, vomiting), reversible hair loss, hypersensitivity reactions (rash, pruritus, fever), reversible neutropenia, and CNS toxicity (dizziness, headache). Some recommend monitoring and liver function tests every 2 weeks.

PREGNANCY: Category C. Albendazole is teratogenic and embryotoxic in rodents at doses of 30 mg/kg. Not recommended for use in pregnancy.

ALPRAZOLAM

TRADE NAME: *Xanax* (Pharmacia) or generic

FORMS AND PRICES (generic): Tabs: 0.25 mg at $0.60, 0.5 mg at $0.80, 1 mg at $0.94, 2 mg at $1.69

CLASS: Benzodiazepine, controlled substance category IV

INDICATIONS AND DOSES

- **Anxiety:** 0.25-0.5 mg tid; increase if necessary at intervals of 3 to 4 days to maximum of 4 mg/day.
- **Dose reduction or withdrawal:** Decrease by ≥0.5 mg every 3 days; some suggest decrease by 0.25 mg at 3 to 7 intervals.

PHARMACOLOGY

- **Bioavailability:** >90%
- **T½:** 11 hours, prolonged with obesity and hepatic dysfunction
- **Elimination:** Metabolized and renally excreted

SIDE EFFECTS: See Benzodiazepines (Table 6-8, p. 186). Seizures, delirium, and withdrawal symptoms with rapid dose reduction or abrupt discontinuation. Possible amnesia during drug action. Withdrawal symptoms at 18 hours to 3 days after abrupt discontinuation. Seizures usually occur at 24 to 72 hours after abrupt withdrawal.

DRUG INTERACTIONS: Additive CNS depression with other CNS depressants including alcohol. Disulfiram and cimetidine prolong the half-life of alprazolam. Levels of aprazolam are increased by some PIs, but concurrent use is not contraindicated.

RELATIVE CONTRAINDICATIONS: History of serious mental illness, drug abuse, alcoholism, open-angle glaucoma, seizure disorder, severe liver disease.

PREGNANCY: Category D. Fetal harm – contraindicated. Possible role in cleft lip and heart abnormalities.

AMPHOTERICIN B

TRADE NAME: Parenteral form, generic (oral form is no longer available from commercial sources but can be prepared by a pharmacy).

FORMS AND PRICE: 50 mg vials at $11.64/vial

CLASS: Amphoteric polyene macrolide with activity against nearly all pathogenic and opportunistic fungi.

INDICATION: Sharply reduced in past year due to concerns about nephrotoxicity and availability of alternatives: Voriconazole, caspofungin, and lipid amphotericin formulations. The indication for IV amphotericin B is for patients who have normal renal function, will receive short courses (≤2 weeks), and have conditions that cannot be easily treated with azoles.

ADMINISTRATION – ORAL: Oral suspension for thrush is no longer available commercially, but it can be prepared by a pharmacist to a strength of 100 mg/mL of amphotericin B. Dose: 1-5 mL qid; use calibrated dropper to place directly on tongue, then swish as long as possible, then swallow.

ADMINISTRATION – IV: Slow infusion; first dose is 1 mg in 50 mL 5% dextrose given over 30 minutes with monitoring of vital signs every 30 minutes x 4 hours. Alternatively, less serious infections may be treated with double doses on alternative days. The daily dose should never exceed 1.5 mg/kg, and monitoring should include CBC, serum creatinine, and serum electrolytes. Infusions should be given over ≥4 hours (*BMJ* 2000;332:579). There is no reason to protect infusions from sunlight.

■ TABLE 6-4: **Systemic (Intravenous) Amphotericin B (*Clin Infect Dis* 2000;30:652)**

Condition	Daily Dose	Total Dose	Comment
Aspergillus	0.5-1.5 mg/kg	30-40 mg/kg	■ Voriconazole is preferred for invasive asperillosis.
Candida Stomatitis Esophagitis Line sepsis Disseminated	 0.2-0.3 mg/kg 0.5-1.0 mg/kg 0.3-0.5 mg/kg 0.3-0.8 mg/kg	 200-500 mg 2 to 3 weeks 200-500 mg 20-40 mg/kg	■ Reserved for refractory cases 0.8-1.0 mg/kg for severe cases. ■ Fluconazole is preferred for systemic treatment of most *Candida* infections. ■ Voriconazole and caspofungin are the preferred agents for many fluconazole-resistant *Candida* infections (*J Antimic Chem* 2000:46:323).
Coccidioidomycosis Non-meningeal diffuse or disseminated	0.5-1.0 mg/kg	Variable	■ Meningeal disease: Fluconazole. ■ Lipid amphotericin B: Experience is limited. ■ Maintenance: With fluconazole, itraconazole, ketoconazole, or amphotericin B 1 mg/kg weekly.
Cryptococcosis	0.7 mg/kg	2 weeks	■ Maintenance with fluconazole, itraconazole, or amphotericin B 0.6-1 mg/kg once or twice weekly.
Histoplasmosis	0.7 mg/kg	3 to 10 days	■ IV amphotericin until clinical response ■ Alternative is lipid amphotericin B 3 mg/kg/day. ■ Maintenance with itraconazole or amphotericin B 1 mg/kg weekly.
Penicilliosis (severely ill)	0.7 mg/kg	1 to 2 weeks	

PHARMACOLOGY

- **Bioavailability:** There is no significant absorption with oral administration – serum levels of 0.05 μg/mL with 400-600 mg/day PO; CSF levels – 3% of serum concentrations.
- **T½:** 24 hours with IV administration, detected in blood and urine up to 4 weeks after discontinuation.
- **Elimination:** Serum levels in urine; metabolic pathways are unknown.
- **Dose adjustment in renal failure:** None

SIDE EFFECTS: Oral form: Rash, GI intolerance, and allergic reactions. Toxicity with IV form is dose-related and less severe with slow administration.

- Chills, usually 1 to 3 hours post infusion and lasting for up to 4 hours post infusion. Reduce with hydrocortisone (10-50 mg added to infusion, but only if necessary due to immunosuppression); alternatives that are now often preferred are meperidine, ibuprofen, or napofam prior to infusion.
- Hypotension, nausea, vomiting, usually 1 to 3 hours post infusion; may be reduced with compazine.
- Nephrotoxicity in up to 80% ± nephrocalcinosis, potassium wasting, renal tubular acidosis. Reduce with gradual increase in dose, adequate hydration, avoidance of concurrent nephrotoxic drugs, and possibly sodium loading. Discontinue or reduce dose with BUN >40 mg/dL and creatinine >3 mg/dL. Lipid amphotericin preparations are less nephrotoxic and could be substituted.
- Hypokalemia, hypomagnesemia, and hypocalcemia corrected with supplemental K^+, Mg^{++}, and Ca^{++}.
- Normocytic normochromic anemia with average decrease of 9% in hematocrit
- Phlebitis and pain at infusion sites – add 1200-1600 units of heparin to infusate.

DRUG INTERACTIONS: Increased nephrotoxicity with concurrent use of nephrotoxic drugs – aminoglycosides, cisplatin, cyclosporine, methoxyflurane, vancomycin; increased hypokalemia with corticosteroids and diuretics. Potential for digoxin toxicity secondary to hypokalemia.

PREGNANCY: Category B. Harmless in experimental animal studies, but no data for humans.

Alternative Preparations

LIPID PREPARATIONS OF AMPHOTERICIN B INCLUDE

- ***Abelcet* (The Liposome Co.):** Amphotericin B complexed with 2 phospholipids – DMPC and DMPG

- ***Amphotec* (InterMune):** Amphotericin B colloidal dispersion with cholesterol sulfate
- ***AmBisome* (Gilead Sciences):** Liposomal amphotericin B is a true liposomal delivery system

ADVANTAGES: Compared with amphotericin B in D5W, the newer formulations are advocated primarily to reduce nephrotoxicity and infusion-related reactions (*N Engl J Med* 1999;340:764). Other potential advantages are increased daily dose and high concentrations in reticulo-endothelial tissue (lungs, liver, spleen). Costs (AWP) are about $500 to $1,400/day compared with amphotericin B at $37/day (*Clin Infect Dis* 2000;30:653). A common dispute regarding cost is the purchase price vs total cost of care based on studies showing that the morbidity and mortality due to amphotericin B-associated renal failure justifies the high cost of the lipid formulations (*Clin Infect Dis* 2001; 32:686). This argument does not apply when amphotericin B is given empirically as, for example, for antibiotic-refractory fever in the neutropenic host (*J Clin Oncol* 2000;18:2476).

■ TABLE 6-5: **Comparison of Amphotericin B Preparations**

	Amphotericin B	*Abelcet*	*Amphotec*	*AmBisome*
	50 mg Vial	**100 mg Vial**	**50+100 mg Vials**	**50 mg Vials**
Cost/dose*	$37	$825	$336-$560	$824-$1,374
Usual dose	1.0 mg/kg/day	5 mg/kg/day	3-6 mg/kg/day	3-5 mg/kg/day
Infusion rate (infusion duration)	0.2-0.4 mg/kg/hour (2 to 5 hours)	2.5 mg/kg/hour (2 hours)	1 mg/kg/hour (3 to 4 hours)	1.5-2.5 (2 hours)
ADRs†				
Chills	55%	15% to 20%	50% to 70%	18%
Fever >1°C	40%	10% to 20%	10% to 20%	7%
Creatinine rise ≥2x baseline	30% to 50%	15% to 20%	10% to 25%	19%

* Prices = AWP for 1 day's treatment of a 70 kg patient.

† Frequencies of ADRs cannot be accurately compared because results are not from comparative trials except for those with *AmBisome* vs amphotericin B (*N Engl J Med* 1999;340:764) and *Amphotec* vs amphotericin B (*Clin Infect Dis* 2002;35:359).

SUMMARY OF FUNGAL INFECTION SYMPOSIUM (ICAAC 2002, San Diego, CA, Symposium 69)

- **Indications for amphotericin B:** Short-course therapy in patients with CrCl >50 mL/min.
- **Renal toxicity:** Amphotericin B > *Amphotec* > *Abelcet* > *AmBisome.*
- **Infusion reactions:** Amphotericin B = *Amphotec* > *Abelcet* > *AmBisome.*
- **Cost:** Amphotericin B ≪ *Amphotec* < *Abelcet* < *AmBisome.*

- **Dose:** Usual for lipid formulations is 5 mg/kg/day.
- **Preferred:** *Candida* – fluconazole; fluconazole-resistant *Candida* – voriconazole or caspofungin; molds – caspofungin
- **Sensitivity tests:** Usually not necessary or reliable. Most reliable if performed in a research laboratory.

CONCLUSIONS REGARDING FORMULATIONS OF AMPHOTERICIN B

- The lipid complex preparations permit delivery of high doses with less nephrotoxicity. They would be preferred over conventional amphotericin B for virtually all systemic mycoses if the prices were comparable.
- Many authorities conclude that *AmBisome*, *Abelcet*, and *Amphotec* are comparable with each other in efficacy; *Amphotec* is associated with increased rates of ADRs compared with *AmBisome* (*Clin Infect Dis* 2000;31:1155).
- Use in hospitalized patients may be regulated due to high cost. Indications are controversial. The IDSA guidelines (*Clin Infect Dis* 2000;30:653) suggest the following criteria for use:
  - Serious, life-threatening infections with molds (*Aspergillus, Mucor,* or *Fusaria*).
  - Pre-existing renal failure with baseline serum creatinine >2.0-2.5 mg/mL.
  - Increased serum creatinine to >2.0-2.5 mg/mL with amphotericin B infusions despite volume expansion.
  - Intolerable infusion-related toxicity.
  - Disease progression after ≥500 mg amphotericin B.
- Drug distribution does not appear to be problematic. *Abelcet* and *AmBisome* are comparable with amphotericin B for the treatment of cryptococcal meningitis based on CSF fungal clearance.
- Doses: For empiric therapy, the usual dose is amphotericin B 0.6 mg/kg/day and for lipid preparations is 3 mg/kg/day. For serious infections such as aspergillosis, the recommendation is amphotericin B 1.0-1.4 mg/kg/day and for all lipid preparations is 5 mg/kg/day.

AMPRENAVIR (APV)

TRADE NAME: *Agenerase* (GlaxoSmithKline)

FORMS AND PRICE: 50 mg and 150 mg soft-gel capsules at $1.53 per 150 mg cap ($8,954/year for standard dose); 15 mg/mL oral solution

PATIENT ASSISTANCE PROGRAM: 800-722-9294

RECOMMENDED DOSES: 1200 mg bid (eight 150 mg caps bid), given with or without food, but concurrent high-fat meal should be avoided. Note that doses of solution and tablet form are not interchangeable.

The standard regimen for the oral solution is 1400 mg bid. With adolescents 13 to 16 years and weigh <50 kg, the doses are 20 mg/kg q12h to maximum of 2400 mg/day (caps) or 2800 mg/day (oral solution). The standard doses of APV/RTV are 1200/200 mg qd or 600/100 mg bid. The 1200/200 mg qd regimen is the only PI regimen that is FDA approved for once daily dosing.

CLINICAL TRIALS: Monotherapy with the currently recommended dose resulted in a median decrease in plasma HIV RNA levels of 1.95 $\log_{10}$ c/mL.

- **In PROAB 3001** APV was combined with AZT/3TC vs AZT/3TC alone in 332 treatment-naïve patients. At 48 weeks, viral load was <400 c/mL in 41% in the APV arm vs 3% in the dual NRTI arm, but the study was marred by the high drop-out rate in both arms (39th ICAAC, San Francisco, California, 1999, Abstract 509).
- Bart and colleagues studied APV/ABC in 41 treatment-naïve patients (6th CROI, Chicago, Illinois, 1999, Abstract 626). By intent-to-treat analysis and as-treated analysis, the proportion with RNA <50 c/mL was 58% and 78%, respectively, at 60 weeks. This was accompanied by a mean CD4 increase of 265 cells/mm^3 including 130/mm^3 naïve cells and 84/mm^3 memory cells.
- **PROAB 3006** was a randomized multicenter study comparing APV (1200 mg bid) + 2 NRTIs vs IDV (800 mg q8h) + 2 NRTIs in 504 patients. Criteria for inclusion were lack of prior treatment with PIs and HIV RNA levels >400 c/mL. Interim intent-to-treat analysis at 24 weeks showed that 43% of patients achieved HIV RNA levels <400 c/mL in the APV group compared with 53% in the IDV group; this 10% difference was ascribed mostly to drug discontinuation due to adverse reaction: 16% for APV vs 8% for IDV.
- **APV 20001** was a trial in which patients treated with APV/ABC/3TC were continued on APV 1200 mg bid or switched to APV 600 mg bid + RTV 100 mg bid or APV 1200 mg qd + RTV 200 mg qd; all three arms continued ABC/3TC. At 12 weeks, all 15 patients given daily dosing with APV/RTV had viral load <400 c/mL (8th CROI, Chicago, Illinois, 2001, Abstract 332). Another study with APV/RTV 600/100 mg bid showed good virologic control and good tolerance of this regimen (8th CROI, Chicago, Illinois, 2001, Abstract 405).
- **ACTG 398** (7th CROI, San Francisco, California, 2000, Abstract LB7) was a salvage protocol in PI-experienced patients who were treated with APV/ABC/EFV/adefovir plus either IDV, NFV, or SQV. Among 481 patients, only 34% had a viral load <200 c/mL at 24 weeks, indicating poor utility of APV for patients with extensive prior PI experience.
- **QUEST** was a multicenter study of therapy of primary HIV infection using AZT/3TC/ABC/APV. Among 98 patients followed to ≥28 weeks, the viral load decreased from a median of 5.2 $\log_{10}$ c/mL at baseline to <50 c/mL in 87% and <5 c/mL in 58%; the mean CD4 cell count

increase was 249/mm³ (7th CROI, San Francisco, California, 2000, Abstract 552).

- **The CLASS study** compared efavirenz, APV/RTV (1200 mg/200 mg qd), and d4T, each combined with an NRTI backbone of ABC plus 3TC in treatment-naïve patients with CD4 >50 cells/mm³ and viral load >5,000 c/mL (XIV International AIDS Conference, Barcelona 2002, Abstract 1189). Patients were allowed within-class substitutions if necessary (e.g., due to toxicity). In a preliminary analysis at 48 weeks, the proportion of patients achieving a viral load <50 c/mL was 93%, 73%, and 73% among those receiving EFV, APV/RTV, and d4T, respectively, by intent-to-treat; missing data=failure analysis (p=0.047 favoring EFV). Among those with baseline viral load >100,000 c/mL, 77% of the efavirenz group achieved viral load <50 c/mL, compared with 53% of the protease inhibitor group and 55% of the triple nucleoside group. Abacavir hypersensitivity occurred in 6% of patients.
- **Salvage therapy** with APV/ABC/EFV (1200 mg bid/300 mg bid/600 mg qd) demonstrated limited efficacy, possibly due to reduced APV (AUC ↓ 24%) resulting from combination with EFV without RTV (*Clin Infect Dis* 2000;30:313).

RESISTANCE: At least two mutations, at codons 46, 47 and/or 50, are required to increase phenotypic resistance 10-fold. The I50V mutation was originally thought to cause no cross-resistance with other PIs, but it now appears to cause reduced susceptibility to LPV. Mutations at codons 10, 54, 84, and 90 foster cross-resistance to other PIs. Low trough levels of APV are associated with the I54L/M mutation, and the I50V mutation is associated with the highest levels of APV resistance (8th CROI, Chicago, Illinois, 2001, Abstract 465). Phenotypic testing shows that 37% of HIV strains resistant to all other PIs are susceptible to APV, but it is not known whether this translates into clinical benefit in salvage regimens (7th CROI, San Francisco, California, 2000, Abstract 726).

PHARMACOLOGY

- **Bioavailability:** Estimated at 89%; high-fat meal decreases AUC 21% – can be taken with or without meal, but avoid a high-fat meal.
- **T½:** 7.1 to 10.6 hours
- **Elimination:** Hepatic metabolism – most found in stool; 14% in urine. CYP3A4 inhibition is RTV>IDV=NFV=APV>SQV.
- **Renal disease:** Standard dose. There are no data for dialysis to guide dosing.
- **Hepatic disease:** AUC increases 2.5x with liver disease, 4.5x with severe cirrhosis; dose recommendation is based on pharmacokinetic data 450 mg bid with liver disease and 300 mg bid with severe cirrhosis (39th ICAAC, San Francisco, California, 1999, Abstract 326).

SIDE EFFECTS: The major side effects in clinical trials were GI intolerance (nausea – 5%, diarrhea – 14%, vomiting – 5%), rash – 11% (APV is a sulfonamide), headache – 6%, and oral paresthesias – 28%. APV may cause hepatotoxicity. Among patients in phase III trials who discontinued APV temporarily or permanently for side effects, the reason was nausea in 3%, rash in 6%, and paresthesias in 0.6%. Therapeutic trials show high rates of drop-out for adverse reactions, primarily nausea, vomiting, and rash. Class side effects: Diabetes, fat redistribution, blood lipid changes, and increased bleeding in hemophilia.

The oral solution of APV contains 55% propylene glycol, compared with 5% for the capsules. The oral solution is contraindicated in patients with renal failure, hepatic failure, in pregnant women, or in patients receiving disulfiram or metronidazole. Patients treated with the oral solution should be monitored for adverse effects of propylene glycol, which include seizures, stupor, tachycardia, hyperosmolarity, lactic acidosis, renal failure, and hemolysis. Patients taking the oral solution should change to the capsule form when able to do so, and they should avoid alcoholic beverages when taking the oral solution.

■ TABLE 6-6: **APV Interactions With Other PIs and NNRTIs**

Drug	Concurrent Drug AUC	AUC APV	Dose
IDV	↓38%	↑33%	IDV 800 mg tid + APV 800 mg tid
NFV	↑15%	↑1.5x	NFV 750 mg tid + APV 800 mg tid
SQV soft-gel capsule (*Fortovase*)*	↓19%	↓32%	800 mg tid + APV 800 mg tid (limited data)
EFV	↑15%	↓24%	EFV 600 mg qhs + APV 1200 mg tid *or* APV 1200 mg bid + RTV 200 mg bid + EFV 600 mg hs
RTV*	No change	↑2.5x	RTV 100 mg bid + APV 600 mg bid or RTV 200 mg qd + APV 1200 mg qd* *or* RTV 200 mg bid + APV 1200 mg bid + EFV 600 mg hs
LPV/r	No change or ↓	Increased or decreased	APV 750 mg bid + LPV/r 400/100 mg bid or 533/133 bid (several studies show ↓ LPV levels with APV so that higher LPV/r doses may be necessary)
NVP	No data	No data	No data
DLV	↓60%	↑25%	Not recommended

* Pharmacokinetic studies show that RTV increases APV peak and trough levels by 238% and 1325%, respectively, supporting feasibility of once-daily dosing (*Antimicrob Agents Chemother* 2001;45:3663; *Clin Infect Dis* 2000;30:313), which is now FDA-approved.

DRUG INTERACTIONS

- **The following drugs are contraindicated for concurrent use:** Astemizole, bepridil, cisapride, dihydroergotamine, ergotamine, midazolam, terfenadine, triazolam, rifampin, simvastatin, lovastatin, and St. John's wort.
- **The following drugs should be given concurrently with caution:** Phenobarbital, phenytoin, carbamazepine, and oral contraceptives. Ethinyl estradiol/norethindrone decrease APV levels; alternative birth control methods should be used. Methadone levels decrease 35% and APV levels are decreased. Consider alternative antiretroviral agent; if used together, monitor for methadone withdrawal.
- **PIs:** See Table 6-6, p. 179
- **Other drug interactions:** Rifampin decreases APV AUC by 82% and should not be used concurrently. Rifabutin decreases APV AUC by 15% and APV increases rifabutin AUC by 193%; use standard APV dose and rifabutin at 150 mg qd or 300 mg 2-3x/week. Clarithromycin increases APV AUC by 18%; use standard doses of both drugs. Ketoconazole increases APV AUC by 32% and ketoconazole AUC increases 44%; recommendations for concurrent use are not available. APV increases sildenafil AUC by 2-11x; do not exceed 25 mg/48 hours. APV contains large amounts of vitamin E: 1,744 units/day with 2400 mg/day; patients taking vitamin E supplements could develop a bleeding diathesis.

PREGNANCY: Category C. Rat teratogen test shows incomplete ossification, thymic elongation, and low birth weight. Placental passage is unknown.

ANADROL – see Oxymetholone (p. 274)

ANCOBON – see Flucytosine (p. 223)

ANDROGEL – see Testosterone (p. 308)

ATIVAN – see Lorazepam (p. 259)

ATORVASTATIN

TRADE NAME: *Lipitor* (Pfizer)

FORMS AND PRICES: Tabs: 10 mg at $2.31, 20 mg at $3.37, 40 mg at $3.60, and 80 mg at $3.60

CLASS: Statin (HMG-CoA reductase inhibitor)

INDICATIONS AND DOSES: Elevated total and LDL cholesterol and/or triglycerides. Usual initiation regimen is 10 mg/day with increases at 2 to 4 week intervals to maintenance doses of 10-80 mg/day in one daily dose. Take in evening with or without food.

MONITORING: Blood lipids at <4 week intervals until desired results are achieved, then periodically. Obtain transaminase levels at baseline, at 12 weeks, and then at 6 month intervals. Patients should be warned to report muscle pain, tenderness, or weakness promptly, especially if accompanied by fever or malaise. Obtain CPK for suspected myopathy.

PRECAUTIONS: Atorvastatin (and other statins) are contraindicated with pregnancy, breastfeeding, concurrent conditions that predispose to renal failure (e.g., sepsis, hypotension), and active hepatic disease. Alcoholism is a relative contraindication.

PHARMACOLOGY

- **Bioavailability:** 14%
- **T½:** 14 hours
- **Elimination:** Fecal (biliary and unabsorbed) – 98%; renal – <2%
- **Renal failure:** No dose adjustment
- **Hepatic failure:** Levels of atorvastatin are markedly elevated.

SIDE EFFECTS

- **Musculoskeletal:** Myopathy with elevated CPK plus muscle pain, weakness or tenderness ± fever and malaise. Rhabdomyolysis with renal failure reported.
- **Hepatic:** Elevated transaminases in 1% to 2%; discontinue if ALT and/or AST shows unexplained increase >3x upper limit of normal (ULN) x 2.
- **Miscellaneous:** Diarrhea, constipation, nausea, heartburn, stomach pain, dizziness, headache, skin rash, impotence (rare), insomnia

DRUG INTERACTIONS

- **PIs:** Concurrent use is considered safe with IDV, SQV, RTV, and APV. Levels of atorvastatin are increased 6x with LPV/r and are increased 74% with NFV; use with caution and avoid dose >10-20 mg/day.
- **Grapefruit juice** increases atorvastatin levels up to 24%; avoid large amounts before or after administration.

- **Erythromycin:** Atorvastatin levels increased by 40%.
- **Antacids:** Atorvastatin levels decreased by 35%.
- **Other interactions with increased risk of myopathy:** Azoles (ketoconazole, itraconazole), cyclosporine, fibric acid derivatives, niacin
- **Niacin and gemfibrozil:** Increased risk of myopathy; rhabdomyolysis reported only with lovastatin + niacin, but could occur with other statins.

PREGNANCY: Category X

ATOVAQUONE

TRADE NAME: *Mepron* (GlaxoSmithKline)

FORM AND PRICE: 750 mg/5 mL bottle: $738/210 mL bottle (21 day supply)

PATIENT ASSISTANCE PROGRAM: 800-722-9294

INDICATIONS AND DOSE: PCP: Oral treatment of mild to moderate PCP (A-a O_2 gradient <45 mm Hg and P_AO_2 >60 mm Hg) and PCP prophylaxis in patients who are intolerant of TMP-SMX and dapsone; toxoplasmosis treatment (third line) and prophylaxis (third line).

- **PCP treatment:** 750 mg (5 mL) twice daily with meals x 21 days
- **PCP prophylaxis:** 1500 mg qd or 750 mg bid with meals
- **Toxoplasmosis treatment:** 1500 mg PO bid with meals combined with pyrimethamine 200 mg x 1, then 75 mg/day or sulfadiazine 1.5 g qid (*Clin Infect Dis* 2002; 34:1243).

PHARMACOLOGY

- **Bioavailability:** Absorption of suspension averages 47% in fed state (with meals) vs 23% with the tablet form. Concurrent administration of fatty food increases absorption by 2-fold. There is significant individual variation in absorption. Administration with fatty food needs emphasis.
- **T½:** 2.2 to 2.9 days
- **Elimination:** Enterohepatic circulation with fecal elimination; <1% in urine
- **CSF/plasma ratio:** <1%
- **Effect of hepatic or renal disease:** No data

SIDE EFFECTS: Rash (20%), GI intolerance (20%), diarrhea (20%); possibly related – headache, fever, insomnia; life-threatening side effects: None; number requiring discontinuation due to side effects: 7% to 9% (rash – 4%).

DRUG INTERACTIONS: Rifampin reduces atovaquone levels by 50%; rifabutin probably has a similar effect. Avoid combination or increase dose of atovaquone (*MMWR* 1999;48[RR-10]:47). Lopinavir has potential for induction of metabolism of atovaquone requiring dose increase.

PREGNANCY: Category C. Not teratogenic in animals; no studies in humans.

AVENTYL – see Nortriptyline (p. 272)

AZITHROMYCIN

TRADE NAME: *Zithromax* (Pfizer)

FORMS AND PRICES: Tabs: 250 mg tab at $7.16; 600 mg at $17.23; 1 g packet at $22.30. *Z-Pak* with 6 tabs (500 mg, then 250 mg/day x 4 days) at $43.09; *Tri-Pak* with 3 tabs (500 mg x 3 days) for exacerbations of bronchitis; IV formulation as 500 mg vial at $26.73

PATIENT ASSISTANCE PROGRAM: 800-207-8990

CLASS: Macrolide

INDICATIONS AND DOSES: see Table 6-7, p. 184

ACTIVITY: *S. pneumoniae* (about 15% to 20% of *S. pneumoniae* strains are resistant to azithromycin and other macrolides), streptococci (not *Enterococcus*), erythromycin-sensitive *S. aureus, H. influenzae, Legionella* (but not FDA approved for Legionnaires' disease), *C. pneumoniae, M. pneumoniae, C. trachomatis, M. avium*, and *T. gondii*. There is concern about increasing rates of macrolide resistance by *S. pneumoniae* in the United States (*J Infect Dis* 2000;182:1417; *Antimicrob Agents Chemother* 2002;46:265; *Antimicrob Agents Chemother* 2001;45:2147), and several cases of breakthrough pneumococcal bacteremia have been reported (*Clin Infect Dis* 2000;31:1008). Azithromycin appears to reduce risk of *P. carinii* pneumonia beyond that achieved with standard PCP prophylaxis (*Lancet* 1999;354:891). For MAC bacteremia, one study showed that azithromycin 600 mg/day was equivalent to clarithromycin 500 mg/day (*Clin Infect Dis* 2000;31:1245). The VA trial showed clarithromycin to be superior (*Clin Infect Dis* 31;1245). For syphilis, preliminary studies in patients without HIV infection showed that azithromycin (2 g PO x 1) was equivalent to benzathine penicillin (2.4 mil units IM x 1) for treatment of early syphilis (*Sex Transm Dis* 2002;29:486).

■ TABLE 6-7: **Azithromycin Regimens by Condition**

Indication	Dose†
M. avium prophylaxis*	1.2 g (two 600 mg tabs) as 1 dose/week (or 1 g powder packet)
M. avium treatment*	600 mg qd + EMB ± rifabutin (*Clin Infect Dis* 2000;31:1245)
Pneumonia*	500 mg IV qd x ≥2 days (hospitalized patients), then 500 mg PO qd x 7 to 10 days
Sinusitis	500 mg x 1, then 250 mg PO/day x 4 (6 tabs)
*C. trachomatis** (nongonococcal urethritis or cervicitis)	1 g or 1.2 g (two 600 mg tablets) PO x 1
Gonococcal urethritis or cervicitis	2 g PO
Toxoplasmosis	900 mg PO x 2 on day 1, then 1200 mg/day as single dose x 6 weeks, then 600 mg/day (patients <50 kg receive half dose) (efficacy not established)
Cryptosporidiosis	600 mg/day + paromomycin 1 g bid x 4 weeks then paromomycin alone (*J Infect Dis* 1998;178:900)

* FDA-approved indications.

† Caps must be taken ≥1 hour before or >2 hours after a meal; food facilitates absorption and tolerance of tabs and powder.

PHARMACOLOGY

- **Bioavailability:** Absorption is ~30% to 40%. The 250 mg caps should be taken 1 hour before or 2 hours after meals; the 600 mg tabs and the 1 g powder packet may be taken without regard to food, but food improves tolerability. (Note: Food reduces absorption of capsules and promotes absorption of the tablet form.)
- **T½:** 68 hours; detectable levels in urine at 7 to 14 days; with the 1200 mg weekly dose, the azithromycin levels in peripheral leukocytes remain above 32 µg/mL for 60 hours.
- **Distribution:** High tissue levels; low CSF levels (<0.01 µg/mL)
- **Excretion:** Primarily biliary; 6% in urine
- **Dose modification in renal or hepatic failure:** Use with caution.

SIDE EFFECTS: GI intolerance (nausea, vomiting, pain); diarrhea – 14%. With 1200 mg dose weekly, major side effects are diarrhea, abdominal pain, and/or nausea in 10% to 15%; reversible dose-dependent hearing loss is reported in 5% at mean day of onset at 96 days and mean exposure of 59,000 mg (package insert). Frequency of discontinuation in AIDS patients receiving high doses – 6%, primarily GI intolerance and reversible ototoxicity – 2%; rare – erythema multiforme, increased transaminases.

CONTRAINDICATIONS: Hypersensitivity to erythromycin

DRUG INTERACTIONS: Al- and Mg-containing antacids and food reduce absorption of caps. Azithromycin increases levels of theophylline and coumadin. Concurrent use with antiretroviral agents, rifampin, and rifabutin is safe. Concurrent use with pimozide may cause fatal arrythmias and must be avoided.

PREGNANCY: Category B (safe in animal studies; no data in humans)

AZT – see Zidovudine (p. 327)

BACTRIM – see Trimethoprim-Sulfamethoxazole (p. 316)

BENZODIAZEPINES

Benzodiazepines are commonly used for anxiety and insomnia. They are also commonly misused and abused, with some studies showing that up to 25% of AIDS patients take these drugs. The decision to use these drugs requires careful consideration of side effects along with a discussion of the following issues with the patient:

- **Dependency:** Larger than usual doses or prolonged daily use of therapeutic doses.
- **Abuse potential:** Most common in those with abuse of alcohol and other psychiatric drugs.
- **Tolerance:** Primarily to sedation and ataxia; minimal to antianxiety effects.
- **Withdrawal symptoms:** Related to duration of use, dose, rate of tapering, and drug half-life. Features include: 1) Recurrence of pretreatment symptoms developing over days or weeks; 2) Rebound with symptoms that are similar to but more severe than pretreatment symptoms occurring within hours or days (self-limited); and 3) The benzodiazepine withdrawal syndrome with autonomic symptoms, disturbances in equilibrium, sensory disturbances, etc.
- **Daytime sedation, dizziness, incoordination, ataxia, and hang-over:** Use small doses initially and gradually increase. Patient must be warned that activities requiring mental alertness, judgment, and coordination require special caution; concomitant use with alcohol or other sedating drugs is hazardous. Patients often experience amnesia for events during the drug's time of action.
- **Drug interactions:** Sedative effects are antagonized by caffeine and theophylline. Erythromycin, clarithromycin, fluoroquinolones, PIs (IDV, NFV, SQV, RTV), cimetidine, omeprazole, and INH may reduce hepatic metabolism and prolong half-life. Rifampin and oral contraceptives increase hepatic clearance and reduce half-life.
- **Miscellaneous side effects:** Blurred vision, diplopia, confusion, memory disturbance, amnesia, fatigue, incontinence, constipation, hypotension, disinhibition, bizarre behavior

- **Antiretroviral agents:** Concurrent use of triazolam and midazolam with PIs and DLV is contraindicated.

SELECTION OF AGENT AND REGIMEN: Drug selection is based largely on indication and pharmacokinetic properties (see Table 6-8, p. 186). Drugs with rapid onset are desired when temporary relief of anxiety is needed. The smallest dose for the shortest time is recommended, and patients need frequent re-evaluation for continued use. Long-term use should be avoided, especially in patients with a history of abuse of alcohol or other sedative-hypnotic drugs. Dose adjustments are usually required to achieve the desired effect with acceptable side effects. Long-term use (more than several weeks) may require an extended tapering schedule over 6 to 8 weeks (20% to 30% dose reduction weekly) adjusted by symptoms and sometimes facilitated by antidepressants or hypnotics.

■ TABLE 6-8: **Comparison of Benzodiazepines**

Agent	Trade Name	Anxiety	Insomnia	Tmax (hrs)	Mean Half-life (hrs)	Dose Forms	Regimens
Chlordiazepoxide	*Librium*	+	–	0.5-4.0	10	5, 10, 25 mg tabs	15-100 mg/day hs or 3 to 4 doses
Clorazepate	*Tranxene*	+	–	1-2	73	3.75, 7.5, 15, 11.25, 22.5 mg tabs	15-60 mg/day hs or 2 to 4 doses
Diazepam	*Valium*	+	+	1.5-2.0	73	2, 4, 5, 10 mg tabs	15-60 mg/day hs or 2 to 4 doses
Flurazepam	*Dalmane*	–	+	0.5-2.0	74	15, 30 mg caps	4-40 mg/day, 2 to 4 doses
Quazepam	*Doral*	–	+	2	74	7.5, 15 mg tabs	30 mg hs
Alprazolam	*Xanax*	+	–	1-2	11	0.25, 0.5, 1, 2 mg tabs	0.75-1.5 mg/day in 3 divided doses
Lorazepam	*Ativan*	+	+	2	14	0.5, 1, 2 mg tabs	0.25-0.5 mg tid up to 4 mg/day
Oxazepam	*Serax*	+	+	1-4	7	10, 15, 30 mg caps	2-6 mg/day in 2 to 3 doses
Temazepam	*Restoril*	–	+	1.0-1.5	13	15, 30 mg caps	30-120 mg/day in 3 to 4 doses
Triazolam*	*Halcion*	–	+	1-2	3	0.125, 0.25 mg tabs	0.25 mg hs

* Concurrent use with PIs or DLV is contraindicated.

BIAXIN – see Clarithromycin (p. 192)

BUPROPION

TRADE NAME: *Wellbutrin*, *Wellbutrin SR*, and *Zyban* (GlaxoSmithKline)

FORMS AND PRICES: Tabs: 75 mg at $0.90, 100 mg at $1.20, 150 mg sustained-release at $1.70

CLASS: Atypical antidepressant

INDICATIONS AND DOSES: Depression: 150 mg qd x 4 days then 150 mg bid (SR formulation); antidepressant effect may require 4 weeks. *Zyban* for smoking cessation. Dose same as SR formulation x 7 to 12 weeks.

PHARMACOLOGY

- **Bioavailability:** 5% to 20%
- **T½:** 8 to 24 hours
- **Elimination:** Extensive hepatic metabolism to ≥6 metabolites including two with antidepressant activity; metabolites excreted in urine.
- **Dose modification in renal or hepatic failure:** Not known, but dose reduction may be required.

SIDE EFFECTS: Seizures, which are dose dependent and minimized by gradual increase in dose; dose not to exceed 450 mg/day, maximum singie dose of 150 mg. Use with caution in seizure-prone patients and with concurrent use of alcohol and other antidepressants.

OTHER SIDE EFFECTS: Agitation, insomnia, restlessness; GI – anorexia, nausea, vomiting; weight loss – noted in up to 25%; rare cases of psychosis, paranoia, depersonalization

BUSPAR – see Buspirone (below)

BUSPIRONE

TRADE NAME: *BuSpar* (Bristol-Myers Squibb)

FORMS AND PRICES: Tabs: 5 mg tab at $0.79, 10 mg tab at $1.37, 15 mg tab at $2.35, 30 mg tab at $4.25

CLASS: Nonbenzodiazepine-nonbarbiturate antianxiety agent; not a controlled substance

INDICATIONS AND DOSES: Anxiety: 5 mg PO tid; increase by 5 mg/day every 2 to 4 days. Usual effective dose is 15-30 mg/day in 2 to 3 divided doses. Onset of response requires 1 week, and full effect requires 4 weeks. Total daily dose should not exceed 60 mg/day.

PHARMACOLOGY

- **Bioavailability:** >90% absorbed when taken with food.
- **T½:** 2.5 hours
- **Elimination:** Rapid hepatic metabolism to partially active metabolites; <0.1% of parent compound excreted in urine
- **Dose adjustment in renal disease:** Dose reduction of 25% to 50% in patients with anuria
- **Hepatic disease:** May decrease clearance and must use with caution.

SIDE EFFECTS: Sleep disturbance, nervousness, headache, nausea, diarrhea, paresthesias, depression, increased or decreased libido, dizziness, and excitement. Compared with benzodiazepines, dependency liability of buspirone is nil, it does not potentiate CNS depressants including alcohol, it is usually well tolerated by elderly, and there is no hypnotic effect, no muscle relaxant effect, less fatigue, less confusion, and less decreased libido but nearly comparable efficacy for anxiety. Nevertheless, the CNS effects are somewhat unpredictable, and there is substantial individual variation; patients should be warned that buspirone may impair ability to perform activities requiring mental alertness and physical coordination such as driving.

PREGNANCY: Category B

CHLORAL HYDRATE

TRADE NAME: *Aquachloral Supprettes* suppositories (Polymedica), *Somnote* (Breckenridge Pharmaceutical), or generic

FORMS AND PRICES: Caps: 325 mg, 500 mg at $0.17, and 650 mg; 500 mg at $0.17/cap. Suppositories at $0.19/325 mg. Syrup with 250 and 500 mg, 5 mL syrup at $0.32/500 mg

CLASS: Nonbenzodiazepine-nonbarbiturate hypnotic; controlled substance category IV

INDICATIONS AND DOSES

- **Insomnia:** 500 mg to 1 g PO hs; usually produces sleep within 30 minutes, which lasts 4 to 8 hours.
- **Sedation:** 250 mg PO tid
- **Note:** Tolerance develops within 5 weeks.

PHARMACOLOGY

- **Bioavailability:** >90%
- **T½:** Hepatic metabolism to achieve metabolite (trichloroethanol) with a half-life of 4.0 to 9.5 hours
- **Elimination:** Renal excretion of trichloroethanol
- **Hepatic or renal disease:** Contraindicated

SIDE EFFECTS: Gastric intolerance; dependence and tolerance with long-term use

DRUG INTERACTIONS: Potentiates action of oral anticoagulants

PREGNANCY: Category C

CIDOFOVIR

TRADE NAME: *Vistide* (Gilead Sciences)

FORM AND PRICE: 375 mg in 5 mL vial at $846

PATIENT ASSISTANCE PROGRAM AND REIMBURSEMENT HOTLINE: 800-226-2056

ACTIVITY: Active *in vitro* against CMV, VZV, EBV, HHV-6, and HHV-8; less active against HSV (*Exp Med Biol* 1996;394:105). CMV strains resistant to ganciclovir are usually sensitive to cidofovir; cidofovir-resistant strains are usually resistant to ganciclovir and sensitive to foscarnet. HSV resistant to acyclovir is often sensitive to cidofovir.

INDICATIONS AND DOSE: CMV retinitis; efficacy in other forms of CMV disease has not been established but is expected (*Arch Intern Med* 1998;158:957).

- **Induction dose:** 5 mg/kg IV over 1 hour* weekly x 2
- **Maintenance dose:** 5 mg/kg IV over 1 hour every 2 weeks*

* Probenecid, 2 g given 3 hours prior to cidofovir and 1 g given at 2 and 8 hours after infusion (total of 4 g). Patients must receive >1 L 0.95 N (normal) saline infused over 1 to 2 hours immediately before cidofovir infusion.

CLINICAL TRIALS: A Studies of the Ocular Complications of AIDS (SOCA) trial comparing cidofovir vs deferred treatment of patients with CMV retinitis demonstrated a median time to progression of 120 days in the treated group compared with 22 days in the deferred group (*Ann Intern Med* 1997;126:257). Dose-limiting nephrotoxicity was noted in 24%, and dose-limiting toxicity to probenecid was noted in 7%. Another SOCA study showed that cidofovir was comparable with the ganciclovir implant plus oral ganciclovir in a small number of patients (n=61) with CMV retinitis. Studies of cidofovir for PML have shown modest benefit for those who also responded to HAART (*AIDS* 2002;16:1791).

NOTES ON ADMINISTRATION

- Cidofovir is diluted in 100 mL 0.9% saline.
- Renal failure: Cidofovir is contraindicated in patients with preexisting renal failure (serum creatinine >1.5 mg/dL, creatinine clearance ≤55 mL/min or urine protein >100 mg/dL or 2+ proteinuria).
- Co-administration of nephrotoxic drugs is contraindicated, including non-steroidal anti-inflammatory agents, amphotericin B,

aminoglycosides, and IV pentamidine; there should be a 7-day "washout" following use of these drugs.

- Dose adjustment for renal failure during cidofovir treatment:
  - Serum creatinine increase 0.3-0.4 mg/dL: Reduce dose to 3 mg/kg.
  - Serum creatinine increase ≥0.5 mg/dL or ≥3 + proteinuria: Discontinue therapy.
- Gastrointestinal tolerance of probenecid may be improved with ingestion of food or an antiemetic prior to administration. Antihistamines or acetaminophen may be used for probenecid hypersensitivity reactions.
- Cases of nephrotoxicity should be reported to Gilead Sciences, Inc. 800-GILEAD-5, or to the FDA's Medwatch 800-FDA-1088.

PHARMACOLOGY

- **Bioavailability:** Requires IV administration; probenecid increases AUC by 40% to 60%, presumably by blocking tubular secretion. CSF levels are undetectable.
- **T½:** The elimination half-life of the active intracellular metabolite is 17 to 65 hours permitting long intervals between doses.
- **Excretion:** 70% to 85% excreted in urine.

SIDE EFFECTS: The major side effect is dose-dependent nephrotoxicity. Proteinuria is an early indicator. IV saline and probenecid must be used to reduce nephrotoxicity. Monitor renal function with serum creatinine and urine protein within 48 hours prior to each dose. About 25% will develop ≥2 + proteinuria or a serum creatinine >2-3 mg/dL, and these changes are reversible if treatment is discontinued (*Ann Intern Med* 1997;126:257,264). Cases of nephrotoxicity should be reported to 800-GILEAD-5.

OTHER SIDE EFFECTS: Neutropenia in about 15% (monitor neutrophil count) and metabolic acidosis with Fanconi's syndrome and decreased serum bicarbonate indicating renal tubule damage. Probenecid causes side effects in about 50% of patients including fever, chills, headache, rash, or nausea, usually after 3 to 4 treatments. Side effects usually resolve within 12 hours. Dose-limiting side effect is usually GI intolerance. Side effects may be reduced with antiemetics, antipyretics, antihistamines, or by eating before taking probenecid (*Ann Intern Med* 1997;126:257).

DRUG INTERACTIONS: Avoid concurrent nephrotoxic drugs including aminoglycosides, amphotericin B, foscarnet, IV pentamidine and NSAIDs. Patients receiving these drugs should have a ≥7 day "washout" prior to treatment with cidofovir. Probenecid prolongs the half-life of acetaminophen, acyclovir, aminosalicylic acid, barbiturates, beta-lactam antibiotics, benzodiazepines, bumetadine, clofibrate, methotrexate, famotidine, furosemide, NSAIDs, theophylline, and AZT.

PREGNANCY: Category C. Use only if potential benefit justifies the risk.

CIPRO – see Ciprofloxacin (below)

CIPROFLOXACIN –

(see "Fluoroquinolones," see Table 6-19, p. 224, for comparisons)

TRADE NAME: *Cipro* (Bayer)

FORMS AND PRICES: Tabs: 250 mg at $4.40, 500 mg at $5.16, 750 mg at $5.16. Vials for IV use: 200 mg at $15.60 and 400 mg at $30.00.

PATIENT ASSISTANT PROGRAM: 800-998-9180

CLASS: Fluoroquinolone

INDICATIONS AND DOSES

- **Respiratory infections:** 500-700 mg PO bid x 7 to 14 days
- **Gonorrhea:** 500 mg x 1
- ***M. avium*:** 500-750 mg PO bid
- **Tuberculosis:** 500-750 mg PO bid
- **Salmonellosis:** 500-750 mg PO bid x 2 to 4 weeks
- **UTI:** 250-500 mg PO bid x 3 to 7 days
- **Traveler's diarrhea:** 500 mg PO bid x 3 days

ACTIVITY: Active against most strains of *Enterobacteriaceae, P. aeruginosa, H. influenzae, Legionella, C. pneumoniae, M. pneumoniae, M. tuberculosis, M. avium*, most bacterial enteric pathogens other than *C. jejuni* and *C. difficile*. Somewhat less active against *S. pneumoniae* than levofloxacin, gatifloxacin, and moxifloxacin; the clinical significance of this difference is debated when using full doses of ciprofloxacin (750 mg PO bid), and some authorities now feel levofloxacin should also be used in full dose (750 mg/day) for pneumococcal infections. There is increasing and substantial resistance by *S. aureus* (primarily MRSA) (*Clin Infect Dis* 2000;32:S114), *P. aeruginosa* (*Clin Infect Dis* 2000;32:S146), and *C. jejuni* (*Clin Infect Dis* 2001;32:1201). There is escalating concern about fluoroquinolone-resistant *S. pneumoniae,* especially in some geographic areas (*Emerg Infect Dis* 2002;8:594), although overall rates of resistance in the United States remained at <1% through 2000 (*Antimicrob Agents Chemother* 2002;46:680; *Antimicrob Agents Chemother* 2002;46:265).

PHARMACOLOGY

- **Bioavailability:** 60% to 70%
- **T½:** 3.3 hours
- **Excretion:** Metabolized and excreted (parent compound and metabolites) in urine

- **Dose reduction in renal failure:** CrCl>50 mL/min – 250-750 mg q12h; CrCl 10-50 mL/min – 250-500 mg q12h; CrCl<10 mL/min – 250-500 mg q18h

SIDE EFFECTS: Usually well tolerated; most common include:

- **GI intolerance** with nausea – 1.2%; diarrhea – 1.2%
- **CNS toxicity:** Malaise, drowsiness, insomnia, headache, dizziness, agitation, psychosis (rare), seizures (rare), hallucinations (rare)
- **Tendon rupture:** About 70 cases reported involving fluoroquinolones; the incidence in a review of 46,776 courses was 0.1% with increased age and steroids as confounding risks (*Brit Med J* 2002;324:1306).
- **Torsades de pointes:** Rates/10 million are: Moxifloxacin – 0, ciprofloxacin – 0.3, levofloxacin – 5.4, gatifloxacin – 27 (*Pharmacother* 2001;21:1468).
- ***Candida* vaginitis**
- **Fluoroquinolones are contraindicated in persons <18 years** due to concern for arthropathy, which has been seen in beagle dogs, but application to human disease is debated, and the FDA is reviewing application for pediatric use (*Pediatr Infect Dis J* 2002; 21:345; *Pediatr Infect Dis J* 2002;21:525). Some fluoroquinolones may cause false positive urine screening tests for opiates (*JAMA* 2001;286:3115).

DRUG INTERACTIONS: Increased levels of theophylline and caffeine; reduced absorption with cations (Al, Mg, Ca) in antacids, sucralfate, buffered ddI; gastric achlorhydria does not influence absorption.

PREGNANCY: Category C. Arthropathy in immature animals with erosions in joint cartilages; relevance to patients is not known, but fluoroquinolones are not FDA-approved for use in pregnancy or in children <18 years.

CLARITHROMYCIN

TRADE NAME: *Biaxin* (Abbott Laboratories)

FORMS AND PRICES: Tabs: 250 mg at $4.13, 500 mg at $4.13, 500 mg XL at $4.55 (for qd dosing). Suspension: 250 mg/5 mL at $71.61 per 100 mL.

PATIENT ASSISTANCE PROGRAM: 800-659-9050

CLASS: Macrolide

■ TABLE 6-9: **Clarithromycin Indications and Doses**

Indication	Dose Regimen*
Pharyngitis, sinusitis, otitis, pneumonitis, skin and soft tissue infection†	250-500 mg PO bid or 1 g 2XL tabs qd
M. avium prophylaxis†	500 mg PO bid (*MMWR* 1995;44[RR-8]:1)
M. avium treatment† (plus EMB ± ciprofloxacin)	500 mg PO bid
Toxoplasmosis (plus pyrimethamine)	500 mg PO bid

* Doses of ≥2 g/day are associated with excessive mortality (*Clin Infect Dis* 1999;29:125).

† FDA-approved for this indication.

CLINICAL TRIALS: Clarithromycin is highly effective in the treatment and prevention of MAC disease (*N Engl J Med* 1996;335:385; *Clin Infect Dis* 1998;27:1278). Clarithromycin was superior to azithromycin in the treatment of MAC bacteremia in terms of median time to negative blood cultures 4.4 weeks vs >16 weeks (*Clin Infect Dis* 1998;27:1278). However, this point is debated and may be a dose issue (*Clin Infect Dis* 2000;31:1254). There is no evidence that it is superior to azithromycin for MAC prophylaxis. Clarithromycin should be given with caution with rifabutin due to decreased levels of clarithromycin (*N Engl J Med* 1996;335:428). This is the presumed explanation for the lack of superior outcome with rifabutin plus clarithromycin vs clarithromycin alone (*J Infect Dis* 2000;181:1289).

ACTIVITY: *S. pneumoniae* (15% to 20% of strains and 40% of penicillin-resistant strains are resistant in most areas of the United States), erythromycin-sensitive *S. aureus, S. pyogenes, M. catarrhalis, H. influenzae, M. pneumoniae, C. pneumoniae, Legionella, M. avium, T. gondii, C. trachomatis,* and *U. urealyticum.* Activity against *H. influenzae* is often debated, although a metabolite shows better *in vitro* activity than the parent compound, and the FDA has approved clarithromycin for pneumonia caused by *H. influenzae.* There is concern about increasing rates of macrolide resistance by *S. pneumoniae* (*J Infect Dis* 2000;182:1417; *Antimicrob Agents Chemother* 2001;45:2147; *Antimicrob Agents Chemother* 2002;46:265), and breakthrough pneumococcal bacteremia has been reported (*Clin Infect Dis* 2000;31:1008).

PHARMACOLOGY

- **Bioavailability:** 50% to 55%
- **T½:** 4 to 7 hours
- **Elimination:** Rapid first-pass hepatic metabolism plus renal clearance to 14 – hydroxyclarithromycin
- **Dose modification in renal failure:** CrCl <30 mL/min half usual dose or double interval.

SIDE EFFECTS: GI intolerance – 4% (vs 17% with erythromycin); transaminase elevation – 1%, headache – 2%, PMC – rare.

DRUG INTERACTIONS: Clarithromycin increases levels of rifabutin 56%, and levels of clarithromycin are decreased 50%. Clarithromycin should not be combined with rifampin, carbamazepine (*Tegretol*), cisapride (*Propulsid*), pimozide (*Orap*), and *Seldane*; increased levels of *Seldane*, pimozide, and *Propulsid* may cause fatal arrhythmias. (Azithromycin has no substantial interaction with these drugs.) NVP induces clarithromycin metabolism to reduce AUC 35% (but increases OH metabolite) – monitor closely (*MMWR* 1999;48[RR-10]:47). Reduce dose of clarithromycin by 50% when combined with RTV or LPV/r in patients with a creatinine clearance <60 mL/min, and reduce by 75% for <30 mL/min (*MMWR* 1999;48[RR-10]:47). Clarithromycin increases theophylline (AUC 17%), digoxin levels, and warfarin levels – monitor for toxicity of concurrent drug.

■ TABLE 6-10: **Clarithromycin Interactions With PIs and NNRTIs**

Agent	Clarithromycin	PI/NNRTI	Regimen
IDV	↑53%	↑29%	Standard
RTV	↑77%	↑12%	Reduce clarithromycin dose by 50% if CrCl 30-60 mL/min, and by 75% if CrCl <30 mL/min
SQV	↑45%	↑177%	Standard
NFV	No data	No data	No data
APV	No change	↑18%	Standard
LPV/r	No data	—	Reduce clarithromycin dose by 50% if CrCl 30-60 mL/min, and by 75% if CrCl <30 mL/min
NVP	↓16% to 35%	↑26%	Standard; monitor for efficacy
EFV	↓39%	—	Avoid
DLV	↑44%	↑100%	Dose reduction for renal failure

PREGNANCY: Category C. Teratogenic in animal studies and no adequate studies in humans.

CLINDAMYCIN

TRADE NAME: *Cleocin* (Pharmacia) or generic

FORMS AND PRICES

- **Clindamycin HCl caps:** 75 mg at $1.15, 150 mg at $1.19, 300 mg at $4.56
- **Clindamycin PO_4 with 150 mg/mL in 2, 4, and 6 mL vials:** 600 mg/mL vial at $13.84

PATIENT ASSISTANT PROGRAM: 800-242-7014

INDICATIONS AND DOSES

- **PCP:** Clindamycin 600-900 mg q6h-q8h IV or 300-450 mg q6h PO/primaquine 15 mg (base)
- **Toxoplasmosis:** Clindamycin 600 mg IV q6h or 300-450 mg PO q6h/pyrimethamine 100-200 loading dose, then 50-100 mg/day PO/leucovorin, 10-25 mg day
- **Other infections:** 600-900 mg q8h IV or 150-300 mg PO q6h-q8h

ACTIVITY: Most gram-positive cocci are susceptible except *Enterococcus* and some *Staphylococci*. Nosoconmial MRSA are usually resistant. Most anaerobic bacteria are susceptible.

PHARMACOLOGY

- **Bioavailability:** 90%
- **T½:** 2 to 3 hours
- **CNS penetration:** Poor
- **Elimination:** Metabolized; 10% in urine
- **Dose modification in renal failure:** None

SIDE EFFECTS: GI – diarrhea in 10% to 30%. Six percent of patients develop *C. difficile*-associated diarrhea; most respond well to discontinuation of the implicated antibiotic ± metronidazole (250 mg qid or 500 mg tid x 10 days). Other GI side effects include nausea, vomiting, and anorexia. Rash – generalized morbilliform is most common; less common is urticaria, pruritus, Stevens-Johnson syndrome.

DRUG INTERACTIONS: Loperamide or diphenoxylate HCl with citropine sulfate (*Lomotil*) increases risk of diarrhea and *C. difficile*-associated colitis.

PREGNANCY: Category B

CLOFAZIMINE

TRADE NAME: *Lamprene* (Novartis)

This drug is no longer used for *M. avium* infections because it does not improve outcome and is associated with high rates of side effects and increased mortality (*N Engl J Med* 1996;335:377).

CLOTRIMAZOLE

TRADE NAMES: *Lotrimin* (Schering-Plough), *Mycelex* (Bayer), *Gyne-Lotrimin* (Schering-Plough), *FemCare* (Schering), or generic

FORMS AND PRICES

- Troche 10 mg at $0.82

- Topical cream (1%) 15 g at $16.21; 30 g at $27.53
- Topical solution/lotion (1%) 10 mL at $14.29; 30 mL at $31.06
- Vaginal cream (1%) 1 g at $1.29; 45 g at $7.20
- Vaginal tablets 100 mg at $1.71 (x 7 days)=$7.45
- Vaginal tablets 500 mg at $13.88 (single dose)

CLASS: Imidazole (related to miconazole)

INDICATIONS AND DOSES

- **Thrush:** 10 mg troche 5x/day; must be dissolved in the mouth. Clotrimazole troches are only slightly less effective than fluconazole for thrush but are often preferred to avoid azole-resistance (*HIV Clin Trials* 2000;1:47). The problem is the need for 5 doses/day, although lower doses are often successful.
- **Dermatophytic infections and cutaneous candidiasis:** Topical application of 1% cream, lotion, or solution to affected area bid x 2 to 8 weeks; if no improvement, reevaluate diagnosis.
- **Candidal vaginitis:** Intravaginal 100 mg tab bid x 3 days (preferred); alternatives: 100 mg tabs qd x 7; 500 mg tab x 1. Vaginal cream: One applicator (about 5 g) intravaginally at hs x 7 to 14 days.

ACTIVITY: Active against *Candida* species and dermatophytes.

PHARMACOLOGY

- **Bioavailability:** Lozenge (troche) dissolves in 15 to 30 minutes; administration at 3-hour intervals maintains constant salivary concentrations above MIC of most *Candida* strains. Topical application of 500 mg tab intravaginally achieves local therapeutic levels for 48 to 72 hours. Small amounts of drug are absorbed with oral, vaginal, or skin applications.

SIDE EFFECTS: Topical to skin (rare) – erythema, blistering, pruritus, pain, peeling, urticaria; topical to vagina (rare) – rash, pruritus, dyspareunia, dysuria, burning, erythema; lozenges – elevated AST (up to 15% – monitor LFTs); nausea and vomiting (5%)

PREGNANCY: Category C. Avoid during first trimester.

CRIXIVAN – see Indinavir (p. 238)

CYTOVENE – see Ganciclovir (p. 229)

DALMANE – see Benzodiazepines (p. 185)

DAPSONE

TRADE NAME: Generic

FORMS AND PRICES: Tabs: 25 mg at $0.19, 100 mg at $0.20

- **Comparison prices for PCP prophylaxis:**
  - Dapsone (100 mg/day)=$6.00/month
  - TMP-SMX (1 DS/day)=$5.40/month
  - Aerosolized pentamidine=$138/month (plus administration costs)

CLASS: Synthetic sulfone with mechanism of action similar to sulfonamides–inhibition of folic acid synthesis by inhibition of dihydropteroate synthetase.

■ TABLE 6-11: **Dapsone Indications and Dose Regimens**

Indication	Dose Regimen
PCP prophylaxis	100 mg PO qd
PCP treatment	100 mg PO qd (plus trimethoprim 15 mg/kg/day PO) x 3 weeks
PCP + Toxoplasmosis prophylaxis	50 mg PO qd (plus pyrimethamine 50 mg/week plus folinic acid 25 mg/week) or dapsone 200 mg (+ pyrimethamine 75 mg + leucovorin 25 mg) once weekly

EFFICACY: A review of 40 published studies found dapsone (100 mg/day) to be slightly less effective than TMP-SMX for PCP, prophylaxis, but comparable with aerosolized pentamidine and highly cost-effective (*Clin Infect Dis* 1998;27:191). For PCP treatment, dapsone/trimethoprim is as effective as TMP-SMX for patients with mild or moderately severe disease (*Ann Intern Med* 1996;124:792).

PHARMACOLOGY

- **Bioavailability:** Nearly completely absorbed except with gastric achlorhydria (dapsone is insoluble at neutral pH).
- **T½:** 10 to 56 hours, average – 28 hours
- **Elimination:** Hepatic concentration, enterohepatic circulation, maintains tissue levels 3 weeks after treatment is discontinued.
- **Dose modification in renal failure:** None

SIDE EFFECTS

- **Most common in AIDS patients:** Rash, pruritus, hepatitis, anemia, and/or neutropenia in 20% to 40% receiving dapsone prophylaxis for PCP at a dose of 100 mg/day.
- **Most serious reaction:** Dose-dependent hemolytic anemia, with or without G6-PD deficiency, and methemoglobinemia; rare cases of

agranulocytosis and aplastic anemia. Suggested monitoring includes screening for G6-PD deficiency prior to treatment, especially in high-risk patients, including African-American men and men of Mediterranean extraction. G6-PD deficiency is not a contraindication to dapsone in the case of the African variant but enhances need for monitoring; dapsone should not be used with the Mediterranean variant of G6-PD deficiency. Hemolysis and Heinz body formation are exaggerated in patients with a G6-PD deficiency, methemoglobin reductase deficiency, or hemoglobin M. Asymptomatic methemoglobinemia independent of G6-PD deficiency has been found in up to two thirds of patients receiving 100 mg dapsone/day plus trimethoprim (*N Engl J Med* 1990;373:776). Acute methemoglobinemia is uncommon, but the usual features are dyspnea, fatigue, cyanosis, deceptively high pulse oximetry, and chocolate-colored blood (*J Acquir Immune Defic Syndr* 1996;12:477). Methemoglobinemia levels are related to the dose and duration of dapsone; TMP increases dapsone levels, so TMP may precipitate methemoglobinemia. Methemoglobin levels are usually <25%, which is generally tolerated except in patients with lung disease. Patients with glutathione or G6-PD deficiency are at increased risk. The usual laboratory findings are increased indirect bilirubin, haptoglobin <25 mg/dL, elevated LDH, and a smear showing spherocytes and fragmented RBCs. For G6-PD deficiency elevation, see p. 37. Treatment consists of oxygen supplementation, packed cell transfusions for anemia, and discontinuation of the implicated drug. This is usually adequate if the methemoglobin level is <30%. Activated charcoal (20 mg qid) may be given to reduce dapsone levels. Treatment for severe cases in the absence of G6-PD deficiency is IV methylene blue (1-2 mg/kg by slow IV infusion). In less emergent situations methylene blue may be given orally (3-5 mg/kg q4h-q6h); methylene blue should not be given with G6-PD deficiency because methylene blue reduction requires G6-PD; hemodialysis also enhances elimination.

- **GI intolerance:** Common; may reduce by taking with meals.
- **Infrequent ADRs:** Headache, dizziness, peripheral neuropathy. Rare side effect is "sulfone syndrome" after 1 to 4 weeks of treatment, consisting of fever, malaise, exfoliative dermatitis, hepatic necrosis, lymphadenopathy, and anemia with methemoglobinemia (*Arch Dermatol* 1981;117:38).

DRUG INTERACTIONS: Decreased dapsone absorption – buffered ddI, H_2 blockers, antacids, omeprazole, and other proton pump inhibitors; decreased levels of dapsone – rifampin and rifabutin; trimethoprim – increases levels of both drugs; coumadin – increased hypoprothrombinemia; pyrimethamine – increased marrow toxicity (monitor CBC); probenecid – increases dapsone levels; primaquine – hemolysis due to G6-PD deficiency.

RELATIVE CONTRAINDICATIONS: G6-PD deficiency – monitor hematocrit and methemoglobin levels if anemia develops.

PREGNANCY: Category C. No data in animals; limited experience in pregnant patients with Hansen's disease shows no toxicity. Hemolytic anemia with passage in breast milk reported (*Clin Infect Dis* 1995;21[suppl 1]:S24).

DARAPRIM – see Pyrimethamine (p. 285)

DAUNORUBICIN CITRATE LIPOSOME INJECTION

TRADE NAME: *DaunoXome* (Gilead Sciences)

NOTE: Liposomal doxorubicin (*Doxil*), 20 mg/m^2 every 2 weeks, is equally as effective.

FORM AND PRICE: Vials containing equivalent of 50 mg daunorubicin at $421.25/50 mg vial

CLASS: Daunorubicin encapsulated within lipid vesicles or liposomes

INDICATIONS AND DOSES (FDA labeling): First-line cytotoxic therapy for advanced HIV-associated Kaposi's sarcoma (KS). Usual indications in trials are symptomatic visceral KS, >25 skin lesions, "B" symptoms, or lymphedema. Administer IV over 60 minutes in dose of 40 mg/m^2; repeat every 2 weeks. CBC should be obtained before each infusion and therapy withheld if absolute leukocyte count is <750/mL. Treatment is continued until there is evidence of tumor progression with new visceral lesions, progressive visceral disease, >10 new cutaneous lesions, or 25% increase in the number of lesions compared with baseline.

CLINICAL TRIALS: Controlled trials comparing liposomal doxorubicin (*Doxil*) or liposomal daunorubicin vs chemotherapy show better response and less toxicity with *Doxil* and *DaunoXome*, which are considered equivalent (*J Clin Oncol* 1996;14:2353; *J Clin Oncol* 1998;16:2445; *J Clin Oncol* 1998;16:683).

PHARMACOLOGY: Mechanism of selectively targeting tumor cells is unknown. Once at the tumor, daunorubicin is released over time.

SIDE EFFECTS

- **Granulocytopenia** is the most common toxicity requiring monitoring of the CBC.
- **Cardiotoxicity** is the most serious side effect. It is most common in patients who have previously received anthracyclines or who have preexisting heart disease. Common features of cardiomyopathy are decreased left ventricular ejection fraction (LVEF) and usual clinical

features of congestive heart failure. Cardiac function (history and physical examination) should be evaluated before each infusion, and LVEF should be monitored when the total dose is 320 mg/m², 480 mg/m², and every 160 mg/m² thereafter.

- **The triad of back pain, flushing, and chest tightness** is reported in 14%; this usually occurs in the first 5 minutes of treatment, resolves with discontinuation of the infusion, and does not recur with resumption of infusion at a slower rate.
- Care should be exercised to avoid drug extravasation, which can cause tissue necrosis.

DRUG INTERACTIONS: None established

PREGNANCY: Category D. Studies in rats showed severe maternal toxicity, embryolethality, fetal malformations, and embryotoxicity.

ddC – see Zalcitabine (p. 325)

ddI – see Didanosine (p. 202)

DELAVIRDINE (DLV)

TRADE NAME: *Rescriptor* (Pfizer)

FORMS AND PRICES: Tabs: 100 mg ($0.87), 200 mg ($1.76) or $3,844/year

PATIENT ASSISTANCE PROGRAM: 888-777-6637

CLASS: NNRTI

INDICATIONS AND DOSE: See Chapter 4. 400 mg PO tid. Take without regard to meals, but separate dosing of buffered form of ddI and antacids by 1 hour. The 100 mg tabs should be dispersed in ≥3 oz water to produce a slurry. The 200 mg tab should be taken intact.

CLINICAL TRIALS

- **Study 0021** demonstrated a modest benefit for DLV + AZT vs AZT alone with regard to viral load.
- **Study 0071** demonstrated equivalence between DLV + ddI vs ddI monotherapy with regard to CD4 response and viral load. In ACTG 261, the following three regimens were equivalent in terms of viral load and CD4 cell count: DLV/AZT, DLV/ddI, and AZT/ddI. In an as-treated analysis of protocol 0021-2 at 52 weeks, 70% of patients receiving DLV/AZT/3TC had viral loads <400/mL accompanied by CD4 cell count increases of 49-135/mm³. The viral load results were significantly superior to those achieved with AZT/3TC or DLV/AZT.

- **Protocol 0063:** DLV + IDV (400-600 mg bid) + AZT produced increased IDV peak levels compared with IDV 800 mg tid and viral load response at 24 weeks that was comparable with results with IDV, AZT, and 3TC.
- **In Protocol 0073**, a limited clinical trial comparing DLV (600 mg bid) + NFV (1250 mg bid) + ddI ± d4T, a good virologic response was seen at 40 weeks. DLV appears to resensitize HIV to AZT.
- **Protocol 0081** was a pilot study of DLV/AZT/3TC/SQV soft-gel capsules (*Fortovase*) in varying doses of DLV (600 mg bid or 400 mg tid) and SQV (1400 mg bid or 1000-1200 mg tid). Pharmacokinetic and virologic studies favored DLV 600 mg/SQV 1400 mg bid; at 24 weeks viral load was <400 c/mL in 83% of 24 patients receiving this combination (8th CROI, Chicago, Illinois, February 2001, Abstract 331).

RESISTANCE: Monotherapy results in 50- to 500-fold reduction in susceptibility in most patients within 8 weeks. The major mutation changes associated with resistance are at codons 103, 181, and 236, which confer cross-resistance to efavirenz and nevirapine. NNRTIs are not active against HIV-2.

PHARMACOLOGY

- **Bioavailability:** Absorption is 85%; there are no food restrictions. Food reduces absorption by 20%. Antacids, buffered ddI, and gastric achlorhydria decrease absorption.
- **Distribution:** CSF: Plasma ratio=0.02
- **T½:** 5.8 hours
- **Elimination:** Primarily metabolized by hepatic cytochrome P450 (CYP3A4) enzymes. DLV inhibits cytochrome P450 CYP3A4, indicating it inhibits its own metabolism as well as that of IDV, NFV, RTV, and SQV. Excretion is in urine (50%) and stool (44%). The standard dose is recommended in renal failure.
- **Dose reduction in renal or hepatic failure:** None; consider empiric dose reduction with severe liver disease.

SIDE EFFECTS: Rash noted in about 18%; 4% require drug discontinuation. Rash is diffuse, maculopapular, red, and predominantly on upper body and proximal arms. Erythema multiforme and Stevens-Johnson syndrome have been reported. Duration of rash averages 2 weeks and usually does not require dose reduction or discontinuation (after interrupted treatment). Rash accompanied by fever, mucous membrane involvement, swelling, or arthralgias should prompt discontinuation of treatment. Hepatotoxicity – less frequent and severe than with NVP. Other side effects include headache.

DRUG INTERACTIONS: Inhibits cytochrome P450 enzymes. The following drugs should not be used concurrently: Terfenadine

(*Seldane*), rifampin, rifabutin, simvastatin, lovastatin, ergot derivatives, astemizole, cisapride, midazolam, triazolam, simvastatin, lovastatin, H_2 blockers, and proton pump inhibitors. Other drugs that either probably or definitely have increased half-life when given with DLV: Clarithromycin, dapsone, quinidine, sildenafil; the dose of sildenafil should not exceed 25 mg/48 hours. Ethinyl estradiol levels decrease 20%; use alternative or additional method of birth control. Ketoconazole levels increase 50%. There are no data on interactions with methadone. Drugs that decrease levels of DLV: Carbamazepine, phenobarbital, phenytoin, rifabutin and rifampin. Absorption of DLV is decreased with antacids, buffered ddI (administer ≥1 hour apart), H_2 blockers, and proton pump inhibitors.

■ TABLE 6-12: **DLV Combined With PIs**

Drug	AUC	Regimen
IDV	IDV ↑>40% DLV no change	IDV 600 mg q8h DLV 400 mg tid
RTV	RTV ↑70% DLV no change	No data
SQV (*Fortovase*)	SQV ↑5x DLV no change	*Fortovase* 800 mg tid DLV 400 mg tid (monitor transaminase levels)
NFV	NFV ↑2x DLV ↓50%	NFV 1250 mg bid DLV 600 mg bid (limited data)
APV	APV ↑125% DLV ↓60%	Not recommended
LPV/r	LPV ↑8% to 134% DLV no change	Limited data

PREGNANCY: Category C. Ventricular septal defects in rodent teratogenicity assay; placental passage studies show a newborn:maternal drug ratio of 0.15.

d4T – see Stavudine (p. 303)

DESYREL – see Trazodone (p. 313)

DIDANOSINE (ddI)

TRADE NAMES: *Videx* and *Videx EC* (Bristol-Myers Squibb)

FORMS AND PRICES

- ***Videx EC* (delayed release enteric coated) caps:** 125 mg, 200 mg at $4.76, 250 mg at $5.97, 400 mg at $9.53. Take >1 hour before and >2 hours after a meal. *Videx EC* is preferred (*J Acquir Immune Defic Syndr* 2001;28:150) due to improved palatability, once-daily dosing, avoidance of buffer-related drug interactions, and buffer-related side effects, especially diarrhea.

- **Chewable buffered tabs:** 25 mg, 50 mg, 100 mg tab at $2.18, 150 mg tab, 200 mg tab at $4.37. Tabs are chewed or mixed with water.
- **Buffered powder packets:** 100 mg, 167 mg, 250 mg at $4.93
- **Pediatric powder for oral solution:** 4 oz bottle containing 2 g ddl or 8 oz bottle containing 4 g ddl.
- Buffered formulation should be taken >½ hour before or >2 hours after a meal.

FINANCIAL ASSISTANCE: 800-272-4878

CLASS: Nucleoside analog

■ TABLE 6-13: **ddl Dose Regimen**

Dose	Tabs*	Buffered Powder
Wt ≥60 kg	*Videx EC*: 400 mg PO qd Buffered tabs: 200 mg PO bid or 400 mg PO qd	250 mg PO bid
Wt <60 kg	*Videx EC*: 250 mg PO qd Buffered tabs: 125 mg PO bid or 250 mg PO qd	167 mg PO bid

* *Videx EC* is the preferred formulation due to improved tolerability and pharmacokinetics. All ddl formulations should be taken on an empty stomach.

RESISTANCE: L74V and K65R are the most important resistance mutations. The K65R mutation causes cross-resistance with abacavir and tenofovir DF.

CLINICAL TRIALS: ddl has been included in numerous trials in combination with 3TC, d4T, and AZT. ACTG 384 is one of the few studies that defined a significant difference between NRTI combinations in HAART. This trial compared AZT/3TC vs ddl/d4T, each in combination with NFV or EFV. Results with 980 participants at 160 weeks showed superior virologic outcomes with EFV/AZT/3TC compared with EFV/ddl/d4T or to either NRTI combination with NFV. Treatment – limiting toxicity, especially peripheral neuropathy, was significantly greater in ddl/d4T recipients (XIV International AIDS Conference, Barcelona, July 2002, Abstract LB20a). ddl is also being studied as a component of once-daily regimens. In the French Montana Study, 40 antiretroviral-naïve patients took a once-daily combination of ddl, EFV, and emtricitabine (FTC) (*J Infect Dis* 2000;182:599). At 24 weeks, 93% had viral load <50 c/mL.

PHARMACOLOGY

- **Bioavailability:** Tablet – 40%; powder – 30%; food decreases bioavailability by 55%. Take all formulations on an empty stomach.
- **T½:** 1.5 hours
- **Intracellular T½:** 25 to 40 hours

- **CNS penetration:** CSF levels are 20% of serum levels (CSF: plasma ratio=0.16-0.19).
- **Elimination:** Renal excretion: 40% unchanged in urine. Renal failure: Table 6-14, below.

■ TABLE 6-14: **Dosing of ddI in Renal Failure**

		Creatine Clearance (mL/min)			
Formulation	**Body Weight**	**>50**	**30-49**	**10-29**	**<10**
Videx EC	≥60 kg	400 mg qd	200 mg qd	125 mg qd	125 mg qd
	<60 kg	250 mg qd	125 mg qd	125 mg qd	Use alternate formulation
Buffered tablets	≥60 kg	400 mg qd or 200 mg bid	200 mg qd or 100 mg bid	150 mg qd	100 mg qd
	<60 kg	250 mg qd or 125 mg bid	150 mg qd or 75 mg bid	100 mg qd	75 mg qd
Buffered powder	≥60 kg	250 mg bid	100 mg bid	167 mg qd	100 mg qd
	<60 kg	167 mg bid	100 mg bid	100 mg qd	100 mg qd

All doses should be taken on an empty stomach.

CAUTION: FDA warning for ddI + ribavirin based on 23 cases of pancreatitis and/or lactic acidosis; use with caution. Tenofovir increases levels of ddI; consider dose reduction to 250 mg/day. The combination of d4T + ddI is contraindicated in pregnant women.

SIDE EFFECTS

- **Pancreatitis:** Reported in 1% to 9% and is fatal in 6% of those with pancreatitis (*J Infect Dis* 1997;175:255). The frequency of pancreatitis is dose-related. The drug should be discontinued if there is clinical evidence of pancreatitis. In November 1999, Bristol-Myers Squibb issued a warning about pancreatitis as a result of four deaths ascribed to this complication in an ACTG trial. Analysis of these cases and those reported to the FDA MedWatch showed that most cases were associated with ddI/d4T with or without hydroxyurea. Risk factors for ddI-associated pancreatitis include renal failure, alcohol abuse, morbid obesity, history of pancreatitis, hypertriglyceridemia, cholelithiasis, endoscopic retrograde cholangio-pancreatography (ERCP), and concurrent use of d4T, hydroxyurea, allopurinol, or pentamidine.
- **Peripheral neuropathy** with pain, numbness, and/or paresthesias in extremities. Frequency is 5% to 12%; it is increased significantly when ddI is given with d4T, hydroxyurea, or both (*AIDS* 2000;14:273). Onset usually occurs at 2 to 6 months of ddI therapy and may be persistent and debilitating if ddI is continued despite symptoms.
- **GI intolerance** with buffered tablets and powder are common. For that reason, *Videx EC* is the preferred formulation because it causes

fewer GI side effects. If the buffered ddI preparation is used, an alternative is to use ddI pediatric powder reconstituted with 200 mL water and mixed with 200 mL *Mylanta DS* or *Maalox* extra strength with anti-gas suspension in patient's choice of flavor. The final concentration is 10 mg/mL, and the usual dose is 25 mL.

- **Hepatitis** with increased transaminase levels
- **Miscellaneous:** Rash, marrow suppression, hyperuricemia, hypokalemia, hypocalcemia, hypomagnesemia, optic neuritis, and retinal changes
- **Sodium load in buffered formulations:** 11.5 mEq/tab and 60 mEq/powder packet. Mg^{++} load: 8.6 mEq/tab (may be problematic in renal failure).
- **Class adverse effect:** Lactic acidosis and severe hepatomegaly with hepatic steatosis. This complication should be considered in patients with fatigue, abdominal pain, nausea, vomiting, and dyspnea. Laboratory studies show elevated serum lactate (>2 mmol/L), CPK, ALT, and/or LDH and low bicarbonate. CT scan or liver biopsy may show steatosis. This is a life-threatening reaction, and NRTIs should be stopped if the serum lactate level is >2 mmol/L with typical symptoms; most cases are associated with lactate levels >5 mmol/L. The most frequent cause is ddI/d4T. This combination should be avoided in pregnancy due to high rates of lactate acidosis, including at least two fatal cases. Didanosine can presumably cause lipoatrophy, which is believed to be mediated by mitochondrial toxicity.

DRUG INTERACTIONS

- **Tenofovir:** Concurrent TDF and ddI results in a 40% to 60% increase in the ddI AUC. This occurs whether given with food or in a fasting state, whether administered simultaneously or separately, and whether ddI is given in buffered or EC formulation. Based on available data, it seems reasonable to use a reduced dose of ddI (*Videx EC* 250 mg qd if ≥60 kg) when coadministering with TDF.
- **Buffered formulation:** Drugs that require gastric acidity for absorption, including dapsone, IDV, RTV, DLV, ketoconazole, tetracyclines, and fluoroquinolones, should be given 1 to 2 hours before or after ddI if the buffered formulation is used. (This limitation does not apply to NFV, APV, SQV, EFV, or NVP, and it does not apply when using *Videx EC*).
- **Drugs that cause pancreatitis** (EMB or pentamidine) should be avoided.
- **Alcohol:** The package insert states that patients taking ddI should avoid alcohol because it may increase the risk of pancreatitis or liver damage. However, there is no evidence that moderate alcohol consumption increases the risk of ddI-induced pancreatitis or hepatotoxicity.

- **Drugs that cause peripheral neuropathy** should be used with caution or avoided: EMB, INH, vincristine, gold, disulfiram, or cisplatin. Concurrent use of d4T and/or hydroxyurea potentiates the risk of peripheral neuropathy and pancreatitis. Co-administration of ddI and ddC is contraindicated due to anticipated high rates of peripheral neuropathy and pancreatitis.
- **Methadone** reduces AUC of ddI by 41% with the buffered tablet form; the liquid, powder, and enteric coated forms were not studied and may show better bioavailability. ddI has no effect on methadone levels (*J Acquir Immune Defic Syndr* 2000;24:241). Consider ddI dose increase or convert to enteric coated formulation when using ddI in a patient taking methadone.
- **Allopurinol** increases ddI concentrations. Avoid co-administration.
- **Oral Ganciclovir** increases ddI AUC by 100% when administered 2 hours after ddI or concurrently. Monitor for ddI toxicity and consider dose reduction.
- **Ribavirin** potentiates ddI activity and toxicity by increasing intracellular triphosphate levels of didanosine. Avoid coadministration or use cautiously.

PREGNANCY: Category B. No lifetime harm in rodent teratogen and carcinogenicity studies; placental passage in humans shows newborn:maternal drug ratio of 0.5; no controlled studies have been performed in humans. The combination of ddI and d4T should be avoided in pregnancy due to excessive rates of lactic acidosis and hepatic steatosis. Three deaths in pregnant women have been reported.

DIFLUCAN – see Fluconazole (p. 220)

DOXYCYCLINE

TRADE NAMES: *Vibramycin* (Pfizer), *Doryx* (Warner Chilcott), or generic

FORMS AND PRICES: 50 mg cap, 100 mg tab at $0.56. IV form 100 mg at $18.89

CLASS: Tetracycline

INDICATIONS AND DOSE: 100 mg PO bid

- ***C. trachomatis:*** 100 mg PO bid x 7 days. Common respiratory tract infections (sinusitis, otitis, bronchitis) – 100 mg PO bid x 7 to 14 days
- **Bacillary angiomatosis:** 100 mg PO bid x 6 weeks

PHARMACOLOGY

- **Bioavailability:** 93%. Complexes with polyvalent cations (Ca^{++}, Mg^{++}, Fe^{++}, Al^{+++}, etc.), so milk, mineral preparations, cathartics, and antacids with metal salts should not be given concurrently.
- **T½:** 18 hours
- **Elimination:** Excreted in stool as chelated inactive agent independent of renal and hepatic function.
- **Dose modification with renal or hepatic failure:** None

SIDE EFFECTS: GI intolerance (10% and dose-related, reduced with food), diarrhea; deposited in developing teeth – contraindicated from mid-pregnancy to term and in children <8 years of age (Committee on Drugs, American Academy of Pediatrics); photosensitivity (exaggerated sunburn); *Candida* vaginitis; "black tongue;" rash.

DRUG INTERACTIONS: Chelation with cations to reduce oral absorption; half-life of doxycycline decreased by carbamazepine (*Tegretol*), cimetidine, phenytoin, barbiturates; may interfere with oral contraceptives; potentiates oral hypoglycemics, digoxin, and lithium.

PREGNANCY: Category D. Use in pregnant women and infants may cause retardation of skeletal development and bone growth; tetracyclines localizes in dentin and enamel of developing teeth to cause enamel hypoplasia and yellow-brown discoloration. Tetracyclines should be avoided in pregnant women and children <8 years unless benefits outweigh these risks.

DRONABINOL

TRADE NAME: *Marinol* (Unimed Pharmaceuticals)

FORMS AND PRICES: Gel-caps: 2.5 mg at $4.16, 5 mg at $8.68, 10 mg at $15.90

CLASS: Psychoactive component of marijuana

INDICATION AND DOSE: For anorexia associated with weight loss (also used in higher doses as antiemetic in cancer patients). Long-term therapy with dronabinol has led to significant improvement in appetite but minimal weight gain. When weight gain is achieved, it is primarily due to an increase in body fat (*J Pain Symptom Manage* 1997;14:7; *AIDS* 1992;6:127).

- 2.5 mg bid (before lunch and before dinner)
- CNS symptoms (dose-related mood high, confusion, dizziness, somnolence) usually resolve in 1 to 3 days with continued use. If these symptoms are severe or persist, reduce dose to 2.5 mg before dinner and/or administer at hs.

- If tolerated and additional therapeutic effect desired, increase dose to 5 mg bid.
- 10 mg bid is occasionally required, especially for control of nausea.

PHARMACOLOGY

- **Bioavailability:** 90% to 95%
- **T½:** 25 to 36 hours
- **Elimination:** First-pass hepatic metabolism and biliary excretion; 10% to 15% in urine.
- **Biologic effects post dose**
  - Onset of action: 0.5 to 1.0 hour, peak 24 hours
  - Duration of psychoactive effect: 4 to 6 hours; appetite effect: ≥24 hours

SIDE EFFECTS (dose-related)

- 3% to 10%: CNS with "high" euphoria, somnolence, dizziness, paranoia, GI intolerance
- Others: Depersonalization, confusion, visual difficulties, central sympathomimetic effects, hypotension, palpitations, vasodilation, tachycardia, and asthenia

DRUG INTERACTIONS: Sympathomimetic agents (amphetamines, cocaine) – increased hypertension and tachycardia; anticholinergic drugs (atropine, scopolamine), amitriptyline, amoxapine, and other tricyclic antidepressants – tachycardia, drowsiness.

WARNINGS: Dronabinol is a psychoactive component of *Cannabis sativa* (marijuana).

- **Schedule II (CII):** Potential for abuse. Use with caution in patients with psychiatric illness (mania, depression, schizophrenia), with cardiac disorder (hypotension), and in elderly patients. Caution should also be exercised in patients concurrently receiving sedatives and/or hypnotics and in patients with history of or current substance abuse.
- **Warn patient of the following:**
  - CNS depression with concurrent use of alcohol, benzodiazepines, barbiturates.
  - Avoid driving, operating machinery, etc. until safety and tolerance is established.
  - Mood and behavior changes.

PREGNANCY: Category C

EFAVIRENZ (EFV)

TRADE NAME: *Sustiva* (Bristol-Myers Squibb), *Stocrin* (Merck)

FORM AND PRICES: 50 mg, 100 mg, 200 mg capsules at $4.79. 600 mg tablet at $15 ($5,475/year)

PATIENT ASSISTANCE PROGRAM: 800-272-4878

CLASS: NNRTI

INDICATIONS AND DOSE: See Chapter 4. 600 mg/day, usually in combination with two nucleosides, taken in the evening to reduce the CNS side effects that are common in the first 2 to 3 weeks. Patients should be warned of these side effects and of the possibility of rash. When changing from a PI-containing regimen to EFV, may consider overlapping the PI and EFV by 1 week because this is the time required to reach therapeutic levels. A high fat/caloric meal increases peak concentration of the 600 mg tablet form by 79% and the 600 mg capsule form by 39%; take on an empty stomach during early therapy. May be taken with food if tolerated after CNS side effects have resolved.

CLINICAL TRIALS

- **Combination with PIs:** The combination most extensively studied is EFV (600 mg qd) + IDV (1000 mg q8h). In trial DMP-003, 74% had <50 c/mL at 48 weeks; in trial DMP-024, 53% had <50 c/mL at 24 weeks. These results are inferior to those achieved with EFV + two NRTIs; therefore, NRTIs should be included when possible. Many authorities are reluctant to use this combination in treatment-naïve patients due to the potential problem of resistance to both PIs and NNRTIs. Other NRTI-sparing regimens that are sometimes used are EFV/APV/RTV and EFV/LPV/r.
- **DuPont 006** included 1266 participants with CD4 cell counts >50/mm³ and viral loads >10,000 c/mL who had not received NNRTIs, PIs, or 3TC. Participants were randomized to receive EFV/AZT/3TC, EFV/IDV, or IDV/AZT/3TC. By intent-to-treat analysis at 48 weeks, 64% of those given EFV + two NRTIs had viral load <50 c/mL compared with 43% given IDV + two NRTIs and 47% given IDV/EFV (p<0.01) (*N Engl J Med* 1999;341:1865). The mean increase in CD4 cell counts was 180-201/mm³ in these three groups. Subset analysis showed that EFV was as effective in patients with a baseline viral load >100,000 c/mL as in those with viral load <100,000 c/mL. The 144 week follow-up of this study showed virologic rebound in 8%, 7%, and 3.5% of patients on the AZT/3TC/EFV arm at years 1, 2, and 3, respectively (8th CROI, Chicago, Illinois, 2001, Abstract 325).
- **DuPont 020** included 327 NRTI-experienced patients with a CD4 cell count >50/mm³, viral load >10,000 c/mL, and no prior treatment with NNRTIs or PIs. Participants were randomized to receive EFV/IDV + one to two NRTIs vs IDV + one to two NRTIs. At 24 weeks, 60% in the EFV arm had an undetectable viral load (<400 c/mL) compared with 50% in the IDV arm without EFV. The superior response with EFV was statistically significant (*J Infect Dis* 2001;183:392).

- **EuroSIDA:** In analysis of a heterogeneous group of patients, virologic failure occurred in 48% of 1202 EFV recipients compared with 65% of 730 NVP recipients (8th CROI, Chicago, Illinois, 2001, Abstract 324).
- **ACTG 364** enrolled 195 patients who failed treatment with NRTIs but were naïve to PIs and NNRTIs. Participants received one to two NRTIs + NFV, EFV, or NFV/EFV. Results at 40 to 48 weeks showed viral load <50 c/mL in 22%, 44%, and 67%, respectively. The superior results with EFV vs NFV were statistically significant (*N Engl J Med* 2001;345:398).
- **ACTG 384** was a 6-arm trial with 980 treatment-naïve patients in which EFV and NFV were compared, each in combination with either ddI/d4T or AZT/3TC. In addition, the combination of both EFV and NFV was also evaluated, combined with both of the two dual-NRTI backbone combinations. Efficacy was superior for EFV/3TC/AZT compared with EFV/ddI/d4T and the NFV combinations. The four-drug, three-class regimens were superior to the NFV-based regimens and to EFV/ddI/d4T but not to EFV/AZT/3TC. (XIV International AIDS Conference, Barcelona, 2002, Abstract LB20a; XIV International AIDS Conference, Barcelona, 2002, Abstract LB20b).
- **GS 903** (Gilead) was a randomized, placebo-controlled trial comparing tenofovir DF vs d4T in combination with 3TC and efavirenz in naïve patients (XIV International AIDS Conference, Barcelona 2002, Abstract LB17). In an intention-to-treat (missing=failure) analysis after 48 weeks of follow-up, 82% of the patients in the tenofovir arm (n=299) had a viral load <50 c/mL, compared with 81% of the patients in the d4T arm (n=301)(p=NS). There were no differences in efficacy by baseline viral load. The drop-out rate was low, and rates of adverse events and drug discontinuation were similar in both arms, although random cholesterol and triglycerides were significantly higher in d4T-treated patients (p<0.001), and there was a suggestion of increased peripheral neuropathy in the d4T arm as well.
- **The CLASS study** compared efavirenz, APV/RTV (1200 mg/200 mg qd), or d4T combined with an NRTI backbone of abacavir plus 3TC in treatment-naïve patients with CD4 >50 cells/mm³ and viral load >5,000 c/mL (XIV International AIDS Conference, Barcelona 2002, Abstract 1189). Patients were allowed within-class substitutions if necessary (e.g., due to toxicity). In a preliminary analysis at 48 weeks, the proportion of patients achieving a viral load <50 c/mL was 93%, 73%, and 73% among those receiving EFV, APV/RTV, and d4T, respectively, by intention-to-treat, missing=failure analysis (p=0.047 favoring EFV). Among those with baseline viral load >100,000 c/mL, 77% of the efavirenz group achieved viral load <50 c/mL, compared with 53% of the protease inhibitor group and 55% of the triple nucleoside group. Abacavir hypersensitivity occurred in 6% of patients.

- **M98-957** was a salvage trial involving 57 patients who failed more than two PI-containing regimens (40th ICAAC, Toronto, Canada, September 2000, Abstract 697). Participants received LPV/r in two doses, each in combination with EFV. Results by ITT at 48 weeks showed viral load <400 c/mL in 71% who received high-dose LPV/r (533/133 mg bid) vs 59% in the group that received 400/100 mg bid.
- **DMP 049** was a study of patients who were responding well to PI-containing HAART regimens with viral load <20 c/mL and were randomized to continue the PI-based regimen or switch to EFV (8th CROI, Chicago, Illinois, 2001, Abstract 20). At 48 weeks, the frequency of viral load <50 c/mL was 97% in the EFV arm and 85% in the PI continuation arm.
- EFV is a favored agent in patients who have failed PI-containing regimens and do not have prior NNRTI exposures or the K103N mutation. EFV/IDV proved superior to IDV alone in patients who had extensive prior NRTI exposure but had not received PIs or NNRTIs (*J Infect Dis* 2001;183:392). EFV is also favored as a substitute for the PI component of HAART in patients who have good virologic response, but who experience PI-related toxicity, such as fat accumulation, hyperlipidemia, or hyperglycemia. These studies show that virologic control is maintained, and metabolic parameters often improve, but the effect on fat accumulation is less clear (*J Acquir Immune Defic Syndr* 2001;27:459).
- An uncontrolled, retrospective review of the Swiss cohort compared EFV-based regimens with PI-based regimens. EFV-based regimens proved superior in terms of virologic response (*AIDS* 2001;15:1793). A retrospective review of 545 patients at Johns Hopkins Hospital also showed EFV-based HAART to be superior to SQV/RTV-based HAART (*AIDS* 2001;15:1679).
- **EFV vs NVP:** A randomized trial of EFV vs NVP, each combined with ddI/d4T in 67 treatment-naïve patients with viral loads <100,000 c/mL, showed comparable results for virologic outcome (*HIV Clin Trials* 2002;3:186). However, retrospective analysis of three large cohorts with >1000 patients have shown significantly better virologic outcomes in patients treated with EFV-based HAART compared with NVP-based HAART (*AIDS* 2001;15:238; *AIDS* 2002;16:53; *HIV Clin Trials* 2002;3:296).
- **"Switch Studies":** There are multiple studies that address the issue of lipodystrophy complicating PI-based HAART to determine the effect of changing to EFV-based HAART vs continuation of the original regimen. A review of 14 such studies with 910 patients (*Topics HIV Med* 2002;10:47) showed virologic failure in only about 6. Effects on triglycerides and cholesterol were variable, and fat redistribution was rarely changed (see Table 4-25, p. 92).

RESISTANCE: The K103N mutation causes high-level resistance to EFV as well as NVP and DLV. Due to this relatively frequent one-step mutation that reduces susceptibility 10-fold, patients must be counseled about the importance of adherence. Other mutations associated with reduced susceptibility are at RT codons 100, 108, 181, 225, and 188, but only 188L. The Y181C/I mutation is not selected by EFV, but this mutation contributes to low-level EFV resistance; clinical significance is not known. Genotypic resistance testing of early EFV virologic failures failed to show characteristic resistance mutations in 11/32 patients; these failures did not appear to be related to nonadherence and are unexplained (7th CROI, San Francisco, California, 2000, Abstract 752). NNRTIs are not active against HIV-2.

PHARMACOLOGY

- **Oral bioavailability:** 40% to 45% with or without food; high-fat meals increase absorption by 50% and should be avoided. Serum levels are highly variable for reasons that are unclear (*AIDS* 2001;15:71).
- **T½:** 40 to 55 hours
- **Distribution:** Highly protein-bound (>99%); CSF levels are 0.25% to 1.2% plasma levels, which is above the IC_{95} for wild-type HIV (*J Infect Dis* 1999;180:862).
- **Elimination:** Metabolized by cytochrome P450 (CYP3A4); 14% to 34% excreted in the urine as glucuronide metabolites and 16% to 61% in stool.
- **Dose modification with renal or hepatic disease:** No dose modification (*AIDS* 2000;14:618; *AIDS* 2000;14:1062).

SIDE EFFECTS

- **Rash:** Approximately 15% to 27% develop a rash, which is usually morbilliform and does not require discontinuation of the drug. More serious rash reactions that require discontinuation are blistering and desquamating rashes, noted in about 1% to 2% of patients, and Stevens-Johnson syndrome, which has been reported in 1 of 2,200 recipients of EFV. The median time of onset of the rash is 11 days, and the duration with continued treatment is 14 days. The frequency with which the rash requires discontinuation of EFV is 1.7% compared with 7% given NVP and 4.3% given DLV.
- **CNS** side effects have been noted in up to 52% of patients but are sufficiently severe to require discontinuation in only 2% to 5%. Symptoms are noted on day 1 and usually resolve after 2 to 4 weeks. They include confusion, abnormal thinking, impaired concentration, depersonalization, abnormal dreams, and dizziness. Other side effects include somnolence, insomnia, amnesia, hallucinations, and euphoria. Patients need to be warned of these side effects before starting therapy and should also be told that symptoms improve with continued dosing and rarely persist longer than 2 to 4 weeks. It is recommended that the drug be given in the evening during the initial weeks of treatment. This reduces side effects but does not eliminate

them because of the long half-life of EFV. There is a potential additive effect with alcohol or other psychoactive drugs. Patients need to be cautioned to avoid driving or other potentially dangerous activities if they experience these symptoms.

- **Hyperlipidemia** with increased cholesterol, including an increase in high-density cholesterol levels, has been noted.
- **False-positive urine cannabinoid (marijuana) test:** This occurs with the screening test only, and only with the Microgenic's *CEDIA DAU* Multilevel THC assay.
- **Increased aminotransferase levels:** Levels >5 x ULN in 2% to 8% (*Hepatology* 2002;35:182). Frequency is increased with hepatitis C or with concurrent hepatotoxic drugs. Hepatotoxicity is less frequent and less severe than seen with NVP.

DRUG INTERACTIONS: EFV both induces and inhibits the cytochrome P450 CYP3A4 enzymes, exerting a variable effect on concentrations of concurrently administered drugs that utilize this pathway.

CONTRAINDICATED DRUGS FOR CONCURRENT USE: Astemizole, terfenadine, midazolam, triazolam, cisapride, and ergot alkaloids

OTHER DRUGS WITH SIGNIFICANT INTERACTIONS: Rifabutin, rifampin, ethinyl estradiol, anticonvulsants, and warfarin. EFV may reduce concentrations of phenobarbital, phenytoin, and carbamazepine; monitor levels of anticonvulsant. Rifampin decreases EFV levels by 25%; rifampin levels are unchanged: Use standard doses. Rifabutin has no effect on EFV levels, but EFV reduces levels of rifabutin by 35%; with concurrent use, the recommended dose of rifabutin is 450-600 mg/day or 600 mg 3x/week plus the standard EFV dose (*MMWR* 2002;51[RR-7]:48). Concurrent use with ethinyl estradiol increases levels of the contraceptive by 37%; implications are unclear, but a second form of contraception is recommended. EFV reduces methadone levels by 52%; titrate methadone levels to avoid opiate withdrawal. There are no data on interactions between EFV and the lipid-lowering agents simvastatin and lovastatin, although atorvastatin, pravastatin, or fluvastatin may be preferred. Monitor warfarin carefully when used with EFV. There is a 46% incidence of rash reactions when combining EFV and clarithromycin, and levels of clarithromycin are decreased 39%. Interactions and dose recommendations for EFV in combination with PIs are listed in Table 6-15, p. 214.

■ TABLE 6-15: **PI Interactions and Dose Recommendations**

PI	PI AUC	EFV AUC	Recommendation
IDV	↓31%	No change	IDV 1000 mg q8h + EFV 600 mg qhs or IDV 800 mg bid + RTV 200 mg bid + EFV 600 mg qd
RTV	↑18%	↑21%	RTV 500-600 mg bid + EFV 600 mg qhs
NFV	↑20%	No change	NFV 1250 mg bid + EFV 600 mg qhs
SQV	↓62%	↓12%	Not recommended when SQV is used as single PI
APV	↓36%	No change	APV 1200 mg tid as single PI *or* APV 1200 mg bid + RTV 200 mg bid + EFV 600 mg qhs
SQV/RTV	No change	No change	Standard doses
LPV/r	↓40%	No change	LPV/r 533/133 mg (4 caps) bid + EFV 600 mg qhs

COMBINATION OF 2 PIs/EFV

- EFV 600 mg qd/SQV 400 mg bid/RTV 400 mg bid
- EFV 600 mg qd/APV 1200 mg bid/RTV 200 mg bid
- EFV/RTV/IDV combination is under study. Consider EFV 600 mg qd + IDV 800 mg bid + RTV 200 mg bid.
- EFV/APV/LPV/r under study with EFV 600 mg qd + APV 750 mg bid + LPV/r 4 caps bid.

PREGNANCY: Category C. This drug caused birth defects (anencephaly, anophthalmia, and microphthalmia) in 3 of 20 gravid cynomolgus monkeys. Other antiretroviral drugs have not been studied for safety in nonhuman primates, and the FDA has assigned FDA pregnancy category C, which is the same as with AZT, d4T, 3TC, ABC, IDV, APV, NVP, and DLV. The current recommendation is to avoid EFV during the first trimester of pregnancy, to warn potentially pregnant women of this complication, and to ensure adequate contraceptive protection. There has been a single case of myelomeningocele in a newborn child born to a woman who was taking EFV during conception and early pregnancy (*Arch Intern Med* 2002;162:355; *AIDS* 2002;16:299).

ENFUVIRTIDE – see *Fuzeon* (p. 428)

EPIVIR – see Lamivudine (3TC) (p. 252)

EPOGEN – see Erythropoietin (see below)

ERYTHROPOIETIN (EPO)

TRADE NAME: *Procrit* (Ortho Biotech)

FORMS AND PRICES: Vials with 2000, 3000, 4000, 10,000, 20,000, and 40,000 units. Standard dose of 40,000 U/week costs $445 per week. FDA-approved dose of 10,000 U 3x/week costs $334 per week.

PATIENT ASSISTANCE PROGRAM: 800-553-3851

PRODUCT INFORMATION: Recombinant human erythropoietin (rHU EPO) is a hormone produced by recombinant DNA technology. It has the same amino acid sequence and biologic effects as endogenous erythropoietin, which is produced primarily by the kidneys in response to hypoxia and anemia. Both forms act by stimulating the proliferation of red blood cells from progenitor cells found in the bone marrow.

INDICATIONS: Serum erythropoietin level <500 milliunits/mL plus anemia ascribed to HIV infection, or to medications, including AZT in doses >600 mg/day (*Ann Intern Med* 1992;117:739; *J Acquir Immune Defic Syndr* 1992;5:847).

DOSE RECOMMENDATIONS: Although the FDA-approved dose for initial therapy is 10,000 U 3 times per week, the standard starting dose used in clinical practice is 40,000 U weekly, and trials investigating every other week dosing are in progress. Onset of action is within 1 to 2 weeks, reticulocytosis is noted at 7 to 10 days, increases in hematocrit are noted in 2 to 6 weeks, and desired hematocrit is usually attained in 8 to 12 weeks. Response is dependent on the degree of initial anemia, baseline EPO level, dose, and available iron stores. Transferrin saturation should be ≥20%; serum ferritin should be ≥100 ng/mL. If levels are suboptimal, supplement with iron. (Some experts advocate routine iron supplementation in all patients taking EPO.) If after 4 weeks of therapy the Hb rise is <1 g/dL, dose may be increased to 60,000 U SQ weekly. After an additional 4 weeks, if Hb does not increase by at least 1 g/dL from baseline value, discontinue EPO therapy. After achieving the desired response (i.e., increased Hb/Hct level or reduction in transfusion requirements), titrate the dose for maintenance. If Hb >13 g/dL or Hct >40%, decrease EPO by 10,000 U/week. When Hb is >15 g/dL, discontinue EPO, or reduce dose by 10,000 U/week. With failure to respond or suboptimal response, consider iron deficiency, occult blood loss, folic acid or B12 deficiency, or hemolysis.

EFFICACY: A United States trial using EPO was initiated in July 1989, with 1,943 evaluable patients. Participants had serum EPO levels of <500 U/L and hematocrits <30%; 75% were receiving AZT at entry or at some point during the study period. The initial dose was 4,000 U SQ 6 days/week; mean weekly doses ranged from 22,700-32,500 U/week (340-490 U/kg/week). Response to treatment, defined as an increase in baseline hematocrit by 6 percentage points (i.e., 30% to 36%) with no transfusions within 28 days, was achieved in 44%. Transfusion requirements decreased from 40% of participants in 6 weeks pretreatment to 18% at weeks 18 to 24. The average hematocrit among participants was 28% at entry and 35% at 1 year. To determine whether the effects of EPO therapy would be comparable for patients not receiving AZT, Balfour and colleagues performed a retrospective analysis of a subgroup of patients who were AZT-naïve or received AZT previously but not at the time of the study. Response to treatment was similar for all groups and was independent of AZT administration (*Int J Antimicrob Agent* 1997;8:189). One report showed that anemia was a risk factor for death. This risk was decreased with EPO (*Clin Infect Dis* 1999;29:44).

PHARMACOLOGY

- **Bioavailability:** EPO is a 165-amino acid glycoprotein that is not absorbed with oral administration. IV or SQ administration is required; SQ is preferred.
- **T½:** 4 to 16 hours
- **Elimination:** Poorly understood but minimally affected by renal failure.
- **Dose adjustment in renal or hepatic failure:** None

SIDE EFFECTS: Generally well tolerated; adverse side effects reported in clinical trials are consistent with progression of HIV infection. Headache and arthralgias are most common; less common are flu-like symptoms, GI intolerance, diarrhea, edema, and fatigue. Hypertension is an uncommon complication that has been noted more frequently in patients with renal failure. EPO is contraindicated in patients with hypertension that is uncontrolled. The most common reactions noted in the therapeutic trial with 1,943 AIDS patients were rash, medication site reaction, nausea, hypertension, and seizures; relationship to EPO was often unclear.

PREGNANCY: Category C. Teratogenic in animals; no studies in humans.

ETHAMBUTOL (EMB)

TRADE NAME: Generic

FORM AND PRICE: 400 mg tabs at $1.99/tab

PATIENT ASSISTANT PROGRAM: 800-859-8586

INDICATIONS AND DOSE: Active tuberculosis or infections with *M. avium* complex or *M. kansasii*

■ TABLE 6-16: **Ethambutol Dosing for Tuberculosis**

Dosing Interval	Regimen
Daily dose	15-20 mg/kg/day (1.6 g max)
2x/week	35-50 mg/kg (4.0 g max)
3x/week	25-30 mg/kg (2.4 g max)

Note: For *M. Avium*: 15 mg/kg/day

PHARMACOLOGY

- **Bioavailability:** 77%
- **T½:** 3.1 hours
- **Elimination:** Renal
- **Dose modification in renal failure:** CrCl >50 mL/min – 15-25 mg/kg q24h; CrCl 10-50 mL/min – 15-25 mg/kg q24h-q36h; CrCl <10 mL/min – 15-25 mg/kg q48h

SIDE EFFECTS: Dose-related ocular toxicity (decreased acuity, restricted fields, scotomata, and loss of color discrimination) with 25 mg/kg dose (0.8%), hypersensitivity (0.1%); peripheral neuropathy (rare); GI intolerance

WARNINGS: Patients to receive EMB in doses of 25 mg/kg should undergo a baseline screening for visual acuity and red-green color perception; this examination should be repeated at monthly intervals during treatment (*MMWR* 1998;47[RR-20]:31).

DRUG INTERACTIONS: Al^{++} containing antacids may decrease absorption.

PREGNANCY: Category C. Teratogenic in animals; no reported adverse effects in women; "use with caution."

FAMCICLOVIR – see Acyclovir (p. 168)

FENOFIBRATE

TRADE NAME: *Tricor* (Abbott Laboratories)

FORMS AND PRICES: 54 mg tab at $0.86 and 160 mg tab at $2.58

CLASS: Fibrate

INDICATIONS AND DOSES: Hypertriglyceridemia, especially levels of >500-700 mg/dL, then increase if necessary at 4 to 8 week intervals; maximum dose – 160 mg/day. Take as a single daily dose with meal.

MONITORING: Triglyceride levels – discontinue use if response is inadequate after 2 months at 160 mg/day. Warn patients to report symptoms of myositis and obtain CPK if muscle tenderness, pain, or weakness; monitor AST + ALT – discontinue if there is otherwise unexplained increase to ≥3x ULN.

PRECAUTIONS: Avoid or use with caution with gallbladder disease, hepatic disease, renal failure with CrCl <50 mL/min.

PHARMACOLOGY

- **Bioavailability:** Good, improved 35% with food.
- **T½:** 20 hours

- **Elimination:** Renal – 60%; fecal – 25%
- **Renal failure:** 54 mg/day; increase with caution due to risk of myopathy, and monitor CPK.

SIDE EFFECTS

- **Hepatic:** Dose-related hepatotoxicity with increased transaminase levels to >3x ULN in 6% receiving doses of 134-201 mg/day; most had return to normal levels with drug discontinuation or with continued treatment.
- **Influenza-like syndrome**
- **Rash, pruritus, and/or urticaria** in 1% to 3%
- **Myositis:** Warn patient regarding symptoms of muscle pain, tenderness, and/or weakness, especially with fever or malaise. Get CPK and discontinue if significantly typical symptoms occur.
- **Rare:** Pancreatitis, agranulocytosis, cholecystitis, eczema, thrombocytopenia.

DRUG INTERACTIONS

- **Oral anticoagulants:** Potentiates warfarin activity.
- **Cholestyramine and colestipol:** These drugs bind fenofibrate – take fenofibrate >1 hour before or 4 to 6 hours after bile acid binding agent.
- **Statins:** Increased risk of rhabdomyolysis with renal failure.

PREGNANCY: Category C

FENTANYL

TRADE NAME: *Duragesic* (Janssen), *Fentanyl Oralet* (Abbott Laboratories)

FORMS AND PRICES

- Injection-fentanyl citrate, 50 μg/mL at $21
- Buccal (transmucosal) lozenge – 200, 300, 400 μg up to 4/day
- Transdermal
  - 25 μg/hour (2.5 mg/cm²) *Duragesic* 25: $12.80
  - 50 μg/hour (5 mg/cm²) *Duragesic* 50: $21.20
  - 75 μg/hour (7.5 mg/cm²) *Duragesic* 75: $33.80
  - 100 μg/hour (40 mg/cm²) *Duragesic* 100: $42.60

CLASS: Opiate; Schedule II controlled substance

INDICATIONS: Chronic pain requiring opiate analgesia

DOSING RECOMMENDATIONS

- Dose depends on desired therapeutic effect, patient weight, and most importantly, existing opiate tolerance. The initial dose in opiate-naïve patients is a system delivering 25 μg/hour.
- Cachectic patients should not receive a higher initial dose unless they have been receiving the equivalent of 135 mg of oral morphine. Most patients are maintained with patch applications at 72-hour intervals. Adequacy of analgesia should be evaluated at 72 hours. The dose should be increased to maintain the 72-hour interval if possible, but application every 48 hours is another option. Supplemental opiates may be required with initial use to control pain and to determine optimal fentanyl dose. The suggested conversion ratio is 90 mg of oral morphine/24 hours to each 25 μg/hour labeled delivery. To convert patients who currently receive opiate therapy, the following daily doses are considered equivalent to 30-60 mg of oral morphine sulfate: Morphine sulfate, 10 mg IM; codeine 200 mg PO, heroin 5 mg IM or 60 mg PO, meperidine 75 mg IM, methadone 20 mg PO, and oxycodone 15 mg IM or 30 mg PO. The equivalent doses of fentanyl patches are listed in Table 6-17 below:

■ TABLE 6-17: **Equivalence of Fentanyl Patches and Oral Morphine Sulfate**

Oral MS/day	Fentanyl (μg/hour)	Oral MS/day	Fentanyl (μg/hour)
45-134 mg	25	495-584 mg	150
135-224 mg	50	675-764 mg	200
225-314 mg	75	855-994 mg	250
315-404 mg	100	1035-1124 mg	300

APPLICATION INSTRUCTIONS: The protective liner-cover should be peeled just prior to use. Application is to a dry, non-irritated, flat surface of the upper torso by firm pressure for 30 seconds. Hair should be clipped, not shaven, and the skin cleansed with water (not soaps or alcohol that could irritate skin) prior to application. Avoid external heat to the site because absorption is temperature-dependent. Rotate sites with sequential use. After removal, the used system should be folded so the adhesive side adheres to itself and flushed in the toilet.

NOTE: Buccal (transmucosal) form should be used only with monitoring in the hospital (OR, ICU, EW) due to life-threatening respiratory depression. Use in AIDS is primarily restricted to management of chronic pain in late-stage disease using the transdermal form. This drug should not be used for the management of acute pain.

PHARMACOLOGY: Transdermal fentanyl systems deliver an average of 25 μg/hour/10 cm^2 at a constant rate. Serum levels increase slowly, plateau at 12 to 24 hours, and then remain constant for up to 72 hours.

The labeling indicates the amount of fentanyl delivered per hour. Peak serum levels for the different systems are the following: Fentanyl – 25: 0.3-1.2 ng/mL, 50: 0.6-1.8 ng/mL, 75: 1.1-2.6 ng/mL, and 100: 1.9-3.8 ng/mL. After discontinuation, serum levels decline with a mean half-life of 17 hours. Absorption depends on skin temperature and theoretically increases by one third when the body temperature is 40° C. In acute pain models, the 100 µg/hour form provided analgesia equivalent to 60 mg of morphine IM.

SIDE EFFECTS

- **Respiratory depression** with hypoventilation. This occurs throughout the therapeutic range of fentanyl concentration but increases at concentrations >2 ng/mL in opiate-naïve patients and in patients with pulmonary disease.
- **CNS depression** is seen with concentrations >3 ng/mL in opiate-naïve patients. At levels of 10-20 ng/mL there is anesthesia and profound respiratory depression.
- **Tolerance** occurs with extended courses, but there is considerable individual variation.
- **Local effects** include erythema, papules, pruritus, and edema at the site of application.
- **Drug interactions** include increased fentanyl levels with PIs given concurrently.

PREGNANCY: Category C

FILGRASTIM – see G-CSF (p. 232)

FLAGYL – see Metronidazole (p. 262)

FLUCONAZOLE

TRADE NAME: *Diflucan* (Pfizer)

FORMS AND PRICE: Tabs: 50 mg at $5.31, 100 mg at $8.07, 150 mg at $12.88, 200 mg at $12.23. IV vials: 200 mg at $85.50, 400 mg at $133.14

PATIENT ASSISTANCE PROGRAM: 800-207-8990

CLASS: Triazole related to other imidazoles – ketoconazole, clotrimazole, miconazole; triazoles (fluconazole and itraconazole) have three nitrogens in the azole ring.

DOSE: See Table 6-18, p. 222

RESISTANCE: The major concern with long-term use of fluconazole is azole-resistant *Candida* sp. Resistance correlates with azole exposure and CD4 count <50 cells/mm³ (*J Infect Dis* 1996;173:219). All oral azoles predispose to resistance. Some cases involve evolution of resistance by *C. albicans*, and others reflect substitution with non-*albicans* species such as *C. glabrata* or *C. krusei* (*Antimicrob Agents Chemother* 2002;46:1723). Resistance is uncommon when fluconazole is used to treat vaginitis (*Clin Infect Dis* 2001;33:1069). Fluconazole-resistant strains of *Candida* can often be treated with caspofungin or voriconazole (*Antimicrob Agents Chemother* 2002;46:1723).

PHARMACOLOGY

- **Bioavailability:** >90%
- **CSF levels:** 50% to 94% serum levels
- **T½:** 30 hours
- **Elimination:** Renal, 60% to 80% of administered dose excreted unchanged in the urine
- **Dose modification in renal failure:** CrCl >50 mL/min – usual dose; 10-50 mL/min – half dose; CrCl <10 mL/min – quarter dose

SIDE EFFECTS: GI intolerance (1.5% to 8%, usually does not require discontinuation); rash (5%); transient increases in hepatic enzymes (5%), increases of ALT or AST to >8x upper limit of normal requires discontinuation (1%); dizziness, hypokalemia, and headache (2%). Reversible alopecia in 10% to 20% receiving ≥400 mg/day at median time of 3 months after starting treatment (*Ann Intern Med* 1995;123:354).

DRUG INTERACTIONS: Inhibits cytochrome P450 hepatic enzymes to cause increased levels of atovaquone, benzodiazepines, clarithromycin, opiate analgesics, warfarin, SQV, phenytoin, oral hypoglycemics, rifabutin, and cyclosoporine; cisapride (*Propulsid*) may cause life-threatening arrhythmias. Fluconazole levels are reduced with rifampin and rifabutin; fluconazole increases levels of rifabutin with increased risk of uveitis. Can be used with PIs and NNRTIs without dose adjustments (unlike ketoconazole).

■ TABLE 6-18: **Dose Recommendations for Fluconazole** (*Clin Infect Dis* 2000;30:652)

Indications	Dose Regimen	Comment
CANDIDA		
Thrush		
Acute	50-100 mg/day PO x 14 days	Response rate 80% to 100%, usually within 5 days. Maintenance therapy often required in late-stage disease without immune reconstitution. Up to 400 mg/day for refractory cases (*AIDS Clin Trials* 2000;1:47). However, chronic azole exposure increases risk of fluconazole resistance (*Clin Infect Dis* 2000;30:749).
Prevention	100-200 mg PO qd	
Esophagitis		
Acute	200 mg/day PO x 2 to 3 weeks	Superior to ketoconazole. (*Ann Intern Med* 1992;117:655). Relapse rate is >80% within 1 year in absence of maintenance therapy.
Prevention (maintenance)	100-200 mg PO qd	
Vaginitis	150 mg x 1 Multiple recurrences: Fluconazole 150 mg weekly	Response rate 90% to 100% in absence of HIV infection.
CRYPTOCOCCOSIS		
Non-meningeal, acute	200-400 mg/day PO	Fluconazole is recommended by the IDSA as the preferred treatment + flucytosine (100-150 mg/kg/day) for cryptococcal pneumonia (*Clin Infect Dis* 2000;3:710).
Meningitis		
Acute	400-800 mg/day PO x 10 to 12 weeks, followed by consolidation	Acute treatment with amphotericin B x 2 weeks is usually preferred (*Clin Infect Dis* 2000;30:710). Alternative in patients with mild-to-moderate disease is fluconazole 400-800 mg/day x 10 to 12 weeks ± flucytosine (100-150 mg/kg/day x 6 weeks).
Consolidation	400 mg PO qd x 8 weeks, followed by maintenance	
Maintenance	200 mg PO qd	
COCCIDIOIDOMYCOSIS		
Meningitis	400-800 mg IV or PO	Preferred for meningeal form.
Non-meningeal		
Acute	400-800 mg PO qd	Amphotericin B usually preferred.
Maintenance	200-400 mg PO qd	Itraconazole considered to be equally effective.
HISTOPLASMOSIS		
Treatment	800 mg/day	Amphotericin B and itraconazole preferred.

PREGNANCY: Category C. Animal studies show reduced maternal weight gain and embryolethality with dose >20x comparable doses in humans; no studies in humans.

FLUCYTOSINE (5-FC)

TRADE NAME: *Ancobon* (ICN Pharmaceuticals) or generic

FORMS AND PRICES: Caps: 250 mg at $4.04, 500 mg at $8.03

CLASS: Structurally related to fluorouracil

INDICATIONS AND DOSE: Used with amphotericin B or fluconazole to treat serious cryptococcosis. IDSA guidelines (*Clin Infect Dis* 2000;30: 710) recommend treating cryptococcal meningitis with amphotericin B + flucytosine 100 mg/kg/day in 4 doses for ≥2 weeks based on several studies showing benefit of this treatment (reduced rate of relapse and more rapid sterilization of CSF) compared with amphotericin B alone (*N Engl J Med* 1997;337:15; *N Engl J Med* 1992;326:83; *Ann Intern Med* 1990;113:183; *J Infect Dis* 1992;165:960; *Clin Infect Dis* 1999;28:291). The combination of fluconazole + flucytosine is also effective, but toxicity may limit use of 5-FC (*Clin Infect Dis* 1994;19:741; *J Infect Dis* 1992;165:960). Flucytosine may also be combined with fluconazole for treatment of nonmeningeal cryptococcosis (*Clin Infect Dis* 2000;30:710).

- **Dose:** 25.0-37.5 mg/kg PO q6h (100-150 mg/kg/day), usually 100 mg/kg/day in 4 doses

PHARMACOLOGY

- **Bioavailability:** >80%
- **T½:** 2.4 to 4.8 hours
- **Elimination:** 63% to 84% unchanged in urine
- **CNS penetration:** 80% serum levels
- **Dose modification in renal failure:** CrCl >50 mL/min – 25.0-37.6 mg/kg q6h; 10-50 mL/min – 25-37 mg/kg q12h-q24h; <10 mL/min – not recommended.
- **Therapeutic monitoring:** Measure serum concentration 2 hours post oral dose with goal of peak level of 50-100 mcg/mL.

SIDE EFFECTS: Dose-related leukopenia and thrombocytopenia, especially with levels >100 mcg/mL and concurrent use of other marrow-suppressing agents, and in patients with renal insufficiency, which can occur secondary to concurrent amphotericin B therapy; GI intolerance; rash; hepatitis; peripheral neuropathy.

PREGNANCY: Category C. Teratogenic in animals; no studies in human patients. Contraindicated in pregnancy unless benefits outweigh potential risks.

FLUOROQUINOLONES

■ TABLE 6-19: **Fluoroquinolone Summary**

	Ciprofloxacin *Cipro*	Levofloxacin *Levaquin*	Gatifloxacin *Tequin*	Moxifloxacin *Avelox*
Oral form IV form	+ +	+ +	+ +	+ +
Price (AWP) oral formulation	$5.15/500 mg	$8.88/500 mg	$8.18/400 mg	$9.40/400 mg
T½	3.3 hours	6.3 hours	8 hours	12 hours
T½ renal failure	8 hours	35 hours	16 hours	12 hours
Oral bioavailability	65%	99%	96%	90%
Activity *in vitro** *P. aeruginosa* *S. pneumoniae* Mycobacteria Anaerobes	 ++(60% to 80%) + ++ —	 + ++ ++ +	 + ++ ++ ++	 + ++ ++ ++
Regimens (oral)	250-750 mg bid	500-750 mg qd	400 mg qd	400 mg qd

*All fluoroquinolones are active against most *Enterobacteriaceae,* enteric bacterial pathogens (except *C. jejuni* and *C. difficile*), methicillin-sensitive *S. aureus, Neisseria* sp., and pulmonary pathogens including *S. pneumoniae, H. influenzae, C. pneumoniae, Legionella,* and *M. pneumoniae.* Major advantages of newer fluoroquinolones are once-daily dosing, good tolerance, and activity against *S. pneumoniae,* including >98% of penicillin-resistant strains (*Antimicrob Agents Chemother* 2002;46:265). Class side effects include prolongation of QT interval when given to persons predisposed primarily by concurrent medications, tendon rupture, and CNS toxicity including seizures. All are contraindicated in persons <18 years and in pregnant women. Divalent and trivalent cations reduce absorption – avoid concurrent antacids with Mg^{++} or Al^{++}, sucralfate, Fe^{++}, Zn^{++}, and ddI. The major concern is abuse and resistance, with particular concern for *P. aeruginosa, S. pneumoniae, Staph aureus, C. jejuni,* and *Salmonella.*

FLUOXETINE

TRADE NAME: *Prozac* (Eli Lilly) or generic

FORMS AND PRICES: Caps: 10 mg at $2.60, 20 mg at $2.67, 40 mg at $5.33. Solution 20 mg/5 mL at $4.91/20 mg.

CLASS: Selective Serotonin Reuptake Inhibitors (SSRI) antidepressant. Other drugs in this class include *Paxil* and *Zoloft.*

INDICATIONS AND DOSE

- **Major depression:** 10-40 mg/day usually given once daily in the morning. Onset of response requires 2 to 6 weeks. Doses of 5-10 mg/day may be adequate in debilitated patients.
- **Obsessive compulsive disorder:** 20-80 mg/day

PHARMACOLOGY

- **Bioavailability:** 60% to 80%

- **T½:** 7 to 9 days for norfluoxetine (active metabolite)
- **Elimination:** Metabolized by liver to norfluoxetine; fluoxetine eliminated in urine.
- **Dose modification in renal failure:** None
- **Dose modification in cirrhosis:** Half-life prolonged – reduce dose

SIDE EFFECTS: Toxicity may not be apparent for 2 to 6 weeks. GI intolerance (anorexia, weight loss, nausea) – 20%; anxiety, agitation, insomnia, sexual dysfunction – 20%; less common – headache, tremor, drowsiness, dry mouth, sweating, diarrhea, acute dystonia, akathisia (sensation of motor restlessness).

NOTE: Case reports have suggested an association with suicidal preoccupation; reanalysis of data showed no significant difference compared with treatment with other antidepressants or placebo (*J Clin Psychopharmacol* 1991;11:166), and the FDA concluded there was no unreasonable or unexpected risk.

DRUG INTERACTIONS

- **MAO inhibitors:** Avoid initiation of treatment with fluoxetine until ≥14 days after discontinuing MAO inhibitor; avoid starting MAO inhibitor until ≥5 weeks after discontinuing fluoxetine (risk is "serotonergic syndrome").
- **Inhibits cytochrome P450:** Increased levels of tricyclic agents (desipramine, nortriptyline, etc.), phenytoin, digoxin, coumadin, terfenadine (ventricular arrhythmias), SQV, astemizole, theophylline, haloperidol, carbamazepine.
- **Ritonavir:** Serotonin syndrome has been reported (*AIDS* 2001; 15:1281).

PREGNANCY: Category C

FLURAZEPAM – see Benzodiazepines (p. 185)

FOMIVIRSEN

TRADE NAME: *Vitravene* (Isis Pharmaceuticals)

FORM AND PRICE: .05 mL intravitreal injection at $880/dose ($1,760 first month, then $880/month)

CLASS: Antisense phosphorothioate oligonucleotide. This is a 21 nucleotide with a sequence that is complementary to mRNA transcribed from the major immediate-early transcriptional unit of CMV (*Antimicrob Agents Chemother* 1998;42:971; *Antimicrob Agents Chemother* 1996;40:2004).

INDICATION AND DOSE: CMV retinitis. 330 mcg (0.05 mL) intravitreal injection day 1 and day 15, then once monthly.

ACTIVITY: Potent activity against CMV including strains resistant to ganciclovir, foscarnet, and cidofovir (*Antimicrob Agents Chemother* 1998;42:971). Activity is 30-fold greater than ganciclovir (*Antiviral Res* 1995;28:101; *Antimicrob Agents Chemother* 1993;37:1945).

EFFICACY: Median time to response is 7 to 10 days, and median time to progression is 90 to 110 days. This drug provides treatment for the treated eye; it does not treat systemic CMV or the contralateral eye.

PHARMACOLOGY

- **T½ in vitreous humor:** 60 to 80 hours
- **Elimination:** Metabolism by exonuclease

SIDE EFFECTS

- Ocular inflammation (uveitis) with iritis and vitritis in 25%. Usually responds to topical corticosteroids.
- Increased intraocular pressure that is usually transient but should be monitored. Monitor light perception and optic nerve head perfusion after injection; monitor intraocular pressure. Suspend treatment if there is unacceptable inflammation. Systemic levels are nil.

PREGNANCY: Category C

FORTOVASE – see Saquinavir (p. 298)

FOSCARNET

TRADE NAME: *Foscavir* (AstraZeneca)

FORMS AND PRICES: Vials: 6000 mg at $76.58 and 12,000 mg with 24 mg/mL

- Induction: $146/day for 70 kg patient (Ganciclovir – $52/day)
- Maintenance: $73/day (Ganciclovir – $26/day)

PATIENT ASSISTANCE PROGRAM: 800-488-3247

INDICATIONS AND DOSING

■ TABLE 6-20: **Dose Recommendations for Foscarnet**

Indication	Dose Regimen
CMV retinitis	Induction: 60 mg/kg IV q8h or 90 mg/kg IV q12h x 14 days Maintenance: 90-120 mg/kg IV qd*
CMV (other)	60 mg/kg IV q8h or 90 mg/kg IV q12h x 14 to 21 days, indications for maintenance treatment are unclear
Acyclovir-resistant HSV	40 mg/kg IV q8h or 60 mg/kg q12h x 3 weeks
Acyclovir-resistant VZV	40 mg/kg IV q8h or 60 mg/kg q12h x 3 weeks

* Survival and time to relapse may be significantly prolonged with maintenance dose of 120 mg/day vs 90 mg/day (*J Infect Dis* 1993;168:444).

ACTIVITY: Active against herpesviruses including CMV, HSV-1, HSV-2, EBV (oral hairy leukoplakia), VZV, HHV-6, HHV-8 (KS-related herpes virus), most ganciclovir-resistant CMV, and most acyclovir-resistant HSV and VZV. Also active against HIV *in vitro* and *in vivo*. The frequency of CMV resistance *in vitro* is 20% to 30% after 6 to 12 months of foscarnet treatment (*J Infect Dis* 1998;177:770). Studies of patients with CMV retinitis showed a mean decrease of 0.5 log HIV RNA/mL during foscarnet therapy (*J Infect Dis* 1995;172:225). The major clinical experience is with CMV retinitis, which revealed that clinical effectiveness is equivalent to that of ganciclovir (*N Engl J Med* 1992;326:213; *Ophthalmology* 1994;101:1250). In two trials, foscarnet was associated with increased survival compared with ganciclovir (*N Engl J Med* 1992;326:213; *Am J Med* 1993;94:175) but had more treatment-limiting side effects. Many question the relevance of these data in the era of HAART. *In vitro* activity vs HHV-8 is good, but results with foscarnet treatment of KS are variable; if KS is a true neoplasm, this treatment is of doubtful significance once malignant transformation has occurred (*Science* 1998;282:1837).

ADMINISTRATION: Controlled IV infusion using ≤24 mg/mL (undiluted) by central venous catheter or <12 mg/mL (diluted in 5% dextrose or saline) via a peripheral line. No other drug is to be given concurrently via the same catheter. Induction dose of 60 mg/kg is given over ≥1 hour via infusion pump with adequate hydration. Maintenance treatment with 90-120 mg/kg is given over ≥2 hours by infusion pump with adequate hydration. Many use 90 mg/kg/day for initial maintenance and 120 mg/kg/day for maintenance after re-induction for a relapse.

PHARMACOLOGY

- **Bioavailability:** 5% to 8% absorption with oral administration, but poorly tolerated
- **T½:** 3 hours

- **CSF levels:** 15% to 70% plasma levels
- **Elimination:** Renal exclusively

■ TABLE 6-21: **Foscarnet Dose Adjustment In Renal Failure**

CrCl (mL/min/kg)	60 mg/kg Dose	90 mg/kg Dose	120 mg/kg Dose
>1.4	60	90	120
1.3	49	78	104
1.1	42	75	100
0.9	35	71	94
0.7	28	63	84
0.5	21	57	76

SIDE EFFECTS

- **Dose-related renal impairment:** 37% treated for CMV retinitis have serum creatinine increase to ≥2 mg/dL; most common in second week of induction and usually reversible with recovery of renal function within 1 week of discontinuation. Monitor creatinine 2 to 3x/week with induction and every 1 to 2 weeks during maintenance. Modify dose for creatinine clearance changes. Foscarnet should be stopped for creatinine clearance <0.4 mL/min/kg.
- **Changes in serum electrolytes** including hypocalcemia (15%), hypophosphatemia (8%), hypomagnesemia (15%), and hypokalemia (16%). Patients should be warned to report symptoms of hypocalcemia: Perioral paresthesias, extremity paresthesias, and numbness. Monitor serum calcium, magnesium, potassium, phosphate, and creatinine, usually ≥2x/week during induction and 1x/week during maintenance. If paresthesias develop with normal electrolytes, measure ionized calcium at start and end of infusion.
- **Seizures** (10%) related to renal failure and hypocalcemia
- **Penile ulcers**
- **Miscellaneous:** Nausea, vomiting, headache, rash, fever, hepatitis, marrow suppression

DRUG INTERACTIONS: Concurrent administration with IV pentamidine may cause severe hypocalcemia. Avoid concurrent use of potentially nephrotoxic drugs such as amphotericin B, aminoglycosides, and pentamidine. Possible increase in seizures with imipenem.

PREGNANCY: Category C. No adequate studies in animals or humans.

FOSCAVIR – see Foscarnet (p. 226)

FUNGIZONE – see Amphotericin B (p. 172)

FUZEON – see Enfuvirtide (p. 428)

GANCICLOVIR

TRADE NAME (IV AND ORAL FORMS): *Cytovene,* IV (Roche), *Vitrasert,* ganciclovir ocular implant (Bausch & Lomb); *Valcyte,* valganciclovir (Roche)

FORMS AND PRICES: IV: 500 mg vial at $37.10. Tab (valganciclovir): 450 mg at $28.78. Implant: 900 mg/day=$21,009/year

Valganciclovir is the preferred oral formulation because it provides blood levels of ganciclovir comparable with those achieved with recommended doses of IV ganciclovir (*N Engl J Med* 2002;346:1119). Oral ganciclovir should no longer be used, and IV ganciclovir is reserved primarily for seriously ill patients and those who are unable to take oral meds.

PATIENT ASSISTANCE PROGRAM: 800-282-7780

CLASS: Synthetic purine nucleoside analog of guanine

ACTIVITY: Active against herpes viruses including CMV, HSV-1, HSV-2, EBV, VZV, HHV-6, and HHV-8 (KS). About 10% of patients given ganciclovir ≥3 months for CMV will excrete resistant strains that are sensitive to foscarnet (*J Infect Dis* 1991;163:716; *J Infect Dis* 1991;163:1348). The frequency of ganciclovir resistance at 9 months in patients receiving maintenance IV ganciclovir therapy for CMV retinitis is 26% (*J Infect Dis* 1998;177:770). Ganciclovir is active *in vitro* against HHV-8, but the clinical experience with ganciclovir treatment of KS is variable; if KS is a true neoplasm, it may be necessary to treat HHV-8-seropositive patients prior to malignant transformation (*Science* 1998;282:1837).

INDICATIONS AND DOSE REGIMEN

- **CMV Retinitis:** A controlled trial of 141 patients randomized to receive IV ganciclovir (5 mg/kg/day x 3 weeks followed by 5 mg/kg) vs oral valganciclovir (900 mg bid x 3 weeks followed by 900 mg/day) showed comparable outcomes in terms of response rates (77% vs 72% at 4 weeks) and median time to progression (125 vs 160 days) (*N Engl J Med* 2002;346:1119). Oral valganciclovir is now the standard for ganciclovir treatment. Multiple trials show that IV ganciclovir, IV foscarnet, IV cidofovir, oral valganciclovir, and the ganciclovir implant are all effective, although time to relapse is longest with the implant (*N Engl J Med* 1997;337:83; *N Engl J Med* 1999;340:1063). Many authorities now prefer the sustained-release ganciclovir implant (*Vitrasert*), usually in combination with valganciclovir to prevent systemic CMV disease and contralateral retinitis (*N Engl J Med* 1997;337:83;337:105; *Am J Ophthalmol* 1999;127:329). Current guidelines for initial management of CMV retinitis reflect this preference and are modified based on the probability of rapid vision loss and anticipated benefit from HAART as summarized in Table 7-15, pp. 382-383. For early relapse, the options include reinduction of the same drug or combination treatment (*Ophthalmology* 1994;101:1250; *Arch Ophthalmol* 1996;114:23). Switching drugs for early relapse is usually not more effective than reinduction with the same drug (*Ophthalmology* 1994;101:1250). However, ganciclovir resistance rates increase to 26% by 9 months, so a foscarnet substitution is then more likely to be effective in late relapses. The intraocular ganciclovir device needs to be replaced every 6 to 8 months.

Discontinuation of maintenance therapy can be considered when there is immune reconstitution with a CD4 count >150 cells/mm^3 for 3 to 6 months (*JAMA* 1999;282:1633). The specific CDC/IDSA recommendation is to make this decision in consultation with an ophthalmologist based on magnitude and duration of the CD4 response, anatomic location of the lesion, vision in the other eye, and feasibility of ophthalmologic monitoring.

- **Other Forms of Disseminated CMV:** HAART therapy is the preferred method to manage CMV esophagitis and colitis. Severe cases should be treated with oral valganciclovir, IV ganciclovir or IV foscarnet for 14 to 21 days depending on ability to tolerate oral medications and neutropenia. Maintenance therapy may be given or delayed until there is a relapse. With CMV encephalitis, ganciclovir is often combined with foscarnet, but the prognosis is still poor, and the quality of life with these drugs is also poor (*AIDS* 2000;14:517; *Clin Infect Dis* 2002;34:101). Recommendations for suspending maintenance therapy with immune reconstitution are unclear, but most will follow the guidelines for CMV retinitis using a CD4 threshold of 100-150 cells/mm^3 x ≥3 months (*AIDS* 2001;15:F1). Failures ascribed to lack of CMV-specific CD4 responses with recurrent CMV retinitis have been reported (*J Infect Dis* 2001;183:1285).

PHARMACOLOGY

- **Bioavailability:** Valganciclovir – 60% with food vs 6% to 9% for oral ganciclovir. The valganciclovir formulation is rapidly hydrolyzed to ganciclovir after absorption.
- **Serum level:** Mean peak concentration with IV induction doses is 11.5 µg/mL (MIC_{50} of CMV is 0.1-2.75 µg/mL).

■ TABLE 6-22: **Mean AUC With Valganciclovir Compared With IV Ganciclovir in Standard Doses (*N Engl J Med* 2002;346:1119)**

	AUC (µg/hr/mL)	
	Valganciclovirir	IV Ganciclovir
Induction	32.8	28.6
Maintenance	34.9	30.7

- **CSF Concentrations:** 24% to 70% of plasma levels; intravitreal concentrations: 10% to 15% of plasma levels – 0.96 µg/mL *(J Infect Dis* 1993;168:1506).
- **T½:** 2.5 to 3.6 hours with IV administration; 3 to 7 hours with oral administration. Intracellular T½ – 18 hours.
- **Elimination:** IV form: 90% to 99% excreted unchanged in urine. Oral form: 86% in stool and 5% recovered in urine.

■ TABLE 6-23: **Ganciclovir and Valganciclovir Dose Modification in Renal Failure (Induction Dose)**

Creatinine Clearance (CrCl)			
Ganciclovir (IV Form)		**Valganciclovir* (Oral Form)**	
>80 mL/min	5 mg/kg q12h	>60 mL/min	900 mg bid
50-79 mL/min	2.5 mg/kg q12h	59 mL/min	900 mg qd
25-49 mL/min	2.5 mg/kg q24h	25-39 mL/min	900 mg qod
10-24 mL/min	1.25 mg/kg q24h	10-24 mL/min	900 mg/week
<10 mL/min	1.25 mg/kg tiw		

*Use ½ of these doses for maintenance.

SIDE EFFECTS, IV FORM

- **Neutropenia** with ANC <500/mm³ (25% to 40%) requires discontinuation of drug in 20%. Alternative is administration of G-CSF. Discontinuation or reduced dose will result in increased ANC in 3 to 7 days. Monitor CBC 2 to 3x/week and discontinue if ANC <500/mm³ or platelet count <25,000/mm³.
- **Thrombocytopenia** in 2% to 8%
- **CNS toxicity** in 10% to 15% with headaches, seizures, confusion, coma
- **Hepatotoxicity** in 2% to 3%
- **GI intolerance** 2%
- **Note:** Neutropenia (ANC <500/dL) or thrombocytopenia (<25,000/dL) are contraindications to initial use.

SIDE EFFECTS, ORAL FORM: Of 212 patients with CMV retinitis followed for a median of 272 days, 10% showed neutropenia with ANC <500/mm³, hemoglobin <8 g/mL in 12%, diarrhea in 35%, nausea in 23%, and fever in 18% (*J Acquir Immune Defic Syndr* 2002;30:392). This is similar to the side effects with oral or IV ganciclovir.

DRUG INTERACTIONS: AZT increases the risk of neutropenia, and concomitant use is not recommended. Other marrow-toxic drugs include interferon, sulfadiazine, hydroxyurea, and TMP-SMX. Oral and IV ganciclovir increase AUC of ddI by 100% – monitor for adverse effect of ddI (*MMWR* 1999;48[RR-10]:48). Probenecid increases ganciclovir levels by 50%. Additive or synergistic activity with foscarnet *in vitro* against

CMV and HSV. Use with caution with drugs that inhibit replication or rapidly dividing cells – dapsone, pentamidine, pyrimethamine, flucytosine, cytotoxic antineoplastic drugs (vincristine, vinblastine, doxorubicin), amphotericin B, TMP-SMX, and nucleoside analogs.

PREGNANCY: Category C. Teratogenic in animals in concentrations comparable to those achieved in humans; should be avoided unless need justifies the risk.

G-CSF (Filgrastim)

TRADE NAME: *Neupogen* (Amgen)

FORMS AND PRICE: 300 µg in 1 mL vial at $165.30 and 480 µg in 1.6 mL vial

REIMBURSEMENT ASSISTANCE/APPEAL: 800-272-9376

NOTE: 300 µg vial and 480 µg vial are the only forms available. Pharmacists commonly instruct patients to discard unused portion; the cost-effective alternative is to retain the unused portion in refrigerated syringes for later use. For example, a 75 µg dose=1 immediate dose and 3 syringes with subsequent doses.

PATIENT INSTRUCTIONS: Subcutaneous injections are usually self administered into the abdomen or upper thighs or in the back of upper arms if injected by someone else. Injection sites should be rotated. The drug should be stored in a refrigerator at 36°F to 46°F.

PRODUCT INFORMATION: A 20-kilodalton glycoprotein produced by recombinant technique that stimulates granulocyte precursors.

INDICATIONS: Neutropenia with ANC <500-750/mm^3 ascribed to 1) AZT (*Blood* 1991;77:2109), 2) Other drugs such as ganciclovir, foscarnet, ribavirin, flucytosine, amphotericin, pyrimethamine, TMP-SMX, hydroxyurea, and interferon, 3) Cancer chemotherapy (lymphoma or KS), or 4) HIV infection *per se*. Indications are arbitrary. Some authorities conclude that AIDS patients may tolerate low ANC levels better than cancer patients do in terms of infectious complications (*Arch Intern Med* 1995;155:1965; *Infect Control Hosp Epidemiol* 1991;12:429), and G-CSF is "not routinely indicated" for neutropenic patients with HIV infection, according to the guidelines of USPHS/IDSA (*MMWR* 1999;48[RR-10];*Clin Infect Dis* 2000;30[suppl 1]:S29). Nevertheless, the incidence of bacterial infections appears to be increased 2- to 3-fold in patients with an ANC <500/mL (*Lancet* 1989;2:91; *Arch Intern Med* 1995;155:1965), and most HIV infected patients respond. A therapeutic trial in 258 HIV infected patients with ANC of 750-1000/mm^3 showed G-CSF recipients had 31% fewer bacterial infections, 54% fewer severe bacterial infections and 45% fewer hospital days for these infections (*AIDS* 1998;12:65). A review of the 719 G-CSF recipients with neutropenia ascribed to ganciclovir treatment of CMV retinitis in three multicenter trials showed that G-CSF use reduced the incidence of neutropenia associated bacteremia and death, but this benefit was not statistically significant when adjusted for confounding variables (*AIDS* 2002;16:757).

- **GM-CSF (sargramostim):** May also be used for neutropenia in AIDS patients and is available as leukine (*Immunex*). There has been concern that stimulation of the monocyte/macrophage cells would enhance HIV replication, but this does not appear to be a problem with monitoring HIV RNA PCR (*AIDS Res Hum Retroviruses* 1996;12:1151). Another possible application is the use of GM-CSF to restore allostimulatory function of accessory cells (*HIV Clin Trials* 2002;3:219). Dosing recommendations and indications are 250 μg/m² IV over 2 hours qd. Note: Round off to nearest vial size of 250 or 500 mcg to reduce wastage.

DOSE: Initial dose is 5-10 μg/kg/day subcutaneously (lean body weight) usually 5 μg/kg/day. For practical purposes, the dose can be a convenient approximation of the calculated dose using a volume of 1 cc (300 μg), 0.5 cc (150 μg), 0.25 cc (75 μg) or 0.2 cc (60 μg). This may be increased by 1 μg/kg/day after 5 to 7 days up to 10 mcg/kg/day or decreased 50%/week and given either daily or every other day. Monitor CBC 2x/week and keep ANC >1,000 to 2,000/mL (*N Engl J Med* 1987;317:593). If unresponsive after 7 days at 10 μg/kg/day, treatment should be discontinued. Usual maintenance dose is 150-300 μg given 3 to 7x/week.

PHARMACOLOGY

- **Absorption:** Not absorbed with oral administration. G-CSF must be given IV or SQ; SQ is usually preferred.
- **T½:** 3.5 hours (SQ injection)
- **Elimination:** Renal

SIDE EFFECTS: Medullary bone pain is the only important side effect, noted in 10% to 20%, and usually controlled with acetaminophen.

RARE SIDE EFFECTS: Mild dysuria, reversible abnormal liver function tests, increased uric acid, and increased LDH.

DRUG INTERACTIONS: Should not be given within 24 hours of cancer chemotherapy.

PREGNANCY: Category C. Caused abortion and embryolethality in animals at 2-10x dose in humans; no studies in humans.

GEMFIBROZIL

TRADE NAME: *Lopid* (Pfizer) or generic

FORM AND PRICE: 600 mg tab at $1.24/tab

CLASS: Antihyperlipidemic; fibric acid derivative (like clofibrate)

INDICATIONS AND DOSE: Elevated serum triglycerides; may increase LDL cholesterol and cholesterol levels. 600 mg bid PO >30 minutes before meal.

MONITORING: Blood lipids, especially fasting triglycerides and LDL cholesterol; if marked increases in LDL cholesterol, discontinue gemfibrozil and expect return of LDL cholesterol to pretreatment levels in 6 to 8 weeks. Gemfibrozil should be discontinued if there is no decrease in triglyceride or cholesterol level at 3 months. Obtain liver function tests and CBC at baseline, at 3 to 6 months, and then yearly. Discontinue gemfibrozil if otherwise unexplained abnormal liver function tests.

PHARMACOLOGY

- **Bioavailability:** 97%
- **T½:** 1.3 hour
- **Elimination:** renal – 70%, fecal – 6%
  - Hepatic failure: Reduce dosage
  - Renal failure: Reduce dosage

PRECAUTIONS: Contraindicated with gallbladder disease, primary biliary cirrhosis, and severe renal failure.

SIDE EFFECTS

- **Blood lipids:** May increase LDL cholesterol and cholesterol by a mechanism that is poorly understood.
- **Gallbladder:** Gemfibrozil is similar to clofibrate and may cause gallstones and cholecystitis ascribed to increased biliary excretion of cholesterol.
- **Miscellaneous:** GI intolerance, decreased hematocrit, and/or WBC

DRUG INTERACTIONS

- **Gemfibrozil and "statins"** have resulted in rhabdomyolysis and renal failure; possible increased risk of myositis when used with other statins; monitor closely for evidence of myositis with concurrent use.
- **Oral anticoagulants:** May potentiate activity of warfarin.

PREGNANCY: Category C

GROWTH HORMONE, HUMAN (Somatropin)

TRADE NAME: *Serostim* (Serono)

FORMS AND PRICES: Vials of 4 mg (about 12 IU), 5 mg (about 15 IU), and 6 mg (about 18 IU) at $42/mg. The average cost is $252/day or $21,000 for a 12-week course.

PATIENT ASSISTANCE PROGRAM: 888-628-6673 for compassionate use and for support above the cap of $36,000/calendar year for each qualified patient.

CLASS: Human growth hormone produced by recombinant DNA technology.

INDICATIONS AND DOSES: Treatment of AIDS-associated wasting or cachexia (FDA labeling). Administer SQ at bedtime in the following doses:

- >55 kg – 6 mg SQ daily
- 45-55 kg – 5 mg SQ daily
- 35-45 kg – 4 mg SQ daily
- <35 kg – 0.1 mg/kg SQ daily
- Assess at 2 weeks

CLINICAL TRIALS: Benefits of growth hormone in AIDS patients include increased body weight, lean body mass, and body fitness (*Am J Managed Care* 2000;6:1003).

- In a therapeutic trial in 178 AIDS patients with wasting, those receiving 12 weeks of somatropin treatment had a mean 3.0 kg increase in body weight and a mean 1.6 kg increase in lean body mass compared with placebo recipients. The growth hormone recipients also had a 13% increase in median treadmill work output. There was no significant survival benefit (*Ann Intern Med* 1996;125:873).
- Another trial in 60 patients with wasting showed similar results (*Ann Intern Med* 1996;125:865). Drug cost was over $1000/week, raising questions about cost-effectiveness (*Ann Intern Med* 1996;125:932). One option to reduce cost is to limit use to 2 weeks during periods of OIs to reduce OI-associated weight loss (*AIDS* 1999;13:1195) or to use a lower dose, 1.4 mg/day (*Ann Intern Med* 1996;125:865).
- The most definitive study of growth hormone for fat redistribution was an observational trial of 30 patients with HAART-associated visceral fat accumulation. They were given growth hormone 6 mg/day x 6 months, followed by a wash-out period, and then an optional maintenance course of 4 mg qod. Results showed an average 42% reduction in visceral fat with the 6 mg/day dose, but visceral fat rebounded when therapy was discontinued. The effect on blood lipids was variable, 4 patients developed diabetes, and

many patients had joint pains and poor quality of life (*J Acquir Immune Defic Syndr* 2002;30:379).

PHARMACOLOGY

- **Bioavailability with SQ injection:** 70% to 90%
- **T½:** 3.9 to 4.3 hours
- **Elimination:** Metabolized primarily in renal cells; also metabolized in the liver.
- **Dose in liver or renal failure:** Decreased clearance but clinical significance and specific guidelines for dose modification are unknown.

SIDE EFFECTS: Growth hormone may cause dose-related fluid and sodium retention with edema (primarily in extremities), arthralgias, myalgias, and hypertension. The most common side effects are musculoskeletal discomfort (20% to 50%) and increased tissue turgor with swelling of hands and feet (25%); both usually subside with continued treatment. Fat atrophy and insulin resistance are noted above. Other side effects include flu-like symptoms, rigors, back pain, malaise, carpal tunnel syndrome, chest pain, nausea, and diarrhea. Side effects may be reduced by reduction in daily dose or by reduction in the number of doses per week.

DRUG INTERACTIONS: Not studied

PREGNANCY: Category B

HALCION –
see Triazolam (p. 314) and Benzodiazepines (p. 185)

HUMATIN – see Paromomycin (p. 276)

HYDROXYUREA (HU)

TRADE NAME: *Hydrea*, *Droxia* (Bristol-Myers Squibb), or generic

FORM AND PRICE: *Hydrea* caps: 500 mg at $1.27. *Droxia* caps: 200, 300, and 400 mg.

CLASS: HU is used primarily for sickle cell disease and is not FDA-approved for treatment of HIV. HU inhibits cellular ribonucleotide reductase, resulting in decreased intracellular deoxynucleoside triphosphates that are required for DNA synthesis (*AIDS* 1999;13:1433). This makes ddI a more potent inhibitor of HIV and *in vitro* studies show synergistic activity when HU is combined with ddI against HIV in resting lymphocytes (*Proc Natl Acad Sci USA* 1994;91:11017). Synergy was not demonstrated with concentrations that can be achieved clinically using hydroxyurea with AZT and ddC.

The cytostatic property causes blunting of the CD4 response. The combination of HU with ddI ± d4T appears to magnify nucleoside-associated mitochondrial toxicity.

DOSE: Optimum dose is not known. Usual dose is 500 mg bid or 1000 mg qd (with ddI ± additional agents).

CLINICAL TRIALS

- Some studies have shown that the addition of HU to a ddI-containing regimen improves virologic outcome and reduces viral load by an additional 0.2-0.6 $\log_{10}$ c/mL (*J Acquir Immune Defic Syndr* 1995;10:36; *HIV Clin Trials* 2000;1:1; *J Infect Dis* 1997;175:801), but these results are inconsistent. The CD4 count is usually not significantly increased due to the cytotoxic effect of HU, and ddI-associated complications are more frequent (*J Acquir Immune Defic Syndr* 2002;29:368).
- Some authorities continue to recommend HU in combination with ddI-containing regimens for primary HIV infection, intensification, salvage regimens, and clinical settings in which high CNS levels of antiretroviral agents are felt to be necessary. Conclusions about efficacy are limited by the lack of well-controlled trials or consistency in results of trials. More importantly, there is increasing concern about toxicity.
- **ACTG 5025** was discontinued prematurely after three deaths ascribed to pancreatitis were observed in the ddI/d4T/IDV/HU arm (7th CROI, San Francisco, California, 2000, Abstract 456), and the FDA reported a possible increase in hepatotoxicity with HU (8th CROI, Chicago, Illinois, 2001, Abstract 617).

PHARMACOLOGY

- **Bioavailability:** Well absorbed
- **T½:** 2 to 3 hours
- **Penetration:** Highly diffusible with good CNS penetration (*Science* 1994;266:801)
- **Elimination:** Half is degraded by the liver and excreted as respiratory CO_2 and in the urine as urea.

SIDE EFFECTS

- Dose-dependent bone marrow suppression with leukopenia, anemia, and thrombocytopenia in 5% to 7% (*AIDS* 1999;13:1433). Leukopenia is most common and usually occurs first. Recovery from marrow depression is usually rapid with discontinuation of treatment. In sickle cell anemia patients receiving 25-35 mg/kg/day for painful crises, 10% had myelosuppression, and these patients had marrow recovery within 2 weeks following drug discontinuation. CBC should be monitored during therapy at regular intervals.

- Other side effects include GI intolerance, which may be severe, including stomatitis, nausea, vomiting, anorexia, altered taste, diarrhea, and constipation. Mild reversible dermatologic side effects are common and include a maculopapular rash, facial erythema, hyperpigmentation, oral ulceration, desquamation of the face and hands, and partial alopecia (*J Am Acad Dermatol* 1997;36:178). Chronic leg ulcers may complicate therapy that exceeds 3 years (*Ann Intern Med* 1998;29:128).
- HU appears to potentiate ddI toxicity, with increased rates of ddI-associated peripheral neuropathy (*AIDS* 2000;14:273) and pancreatitis and hepatotoxicity (*AIDS* 2000;14:273; 8th CROI, Chicago, Illinois, 2001, Abstracts 617 and 620).
- Rare side effects include dysuria, neurologic complications (drowsiness, disorientation, hallucinations, convulsions), hyperuricemia, renal failure, fever, chills, and alopecia.

PREGNANCY: Category D

INDINAVIR (IDV)

TRADE NAME: *Crixivan* (Merck)

FORMS AND PRICE: Caps: 200 mg, 333 mg, and 400 mg at $2.91; 6/day=$6,375/year.

PATIENT ASSISTANCE PROGRAM: 800-850-3430

CLASS: PI

INDICATIONS AND DOSE: IDV is indicated for the treatment of HIV infection in adults when antiretroviral therapy is warranted. 800 mg q8h in fasting state (1 hour before or 2 hours after a meal), or with a light, nonfat meal, such as dry toast with jelly, juice, coffee (with skim milk and sugar) or corn flakes with skim milk. Patients should drink ≥48 oz fluids daily; 6-8 oz glasses of fluids/day, preferably water, to prevent IDV-associated renal calculi. Administration should be at 8-hour intervals; bid dosing is appropriate only when combined with RTV, NFV, or LPV/r.

CLINICAL TRIALS

- The mean decrease in viral load was 1.0-1.5 $\log_{10}$ c/mL in patients given IDV alone and >2 $\log_{10}$ c/mL with IDV + AZT/3TC or IDV + ddI + 3TC (ACTG 320 and Merck trial 035). CD4 cell counts in these two trials increased an average of 80-150/mm^3. In the IDV + AZT/3TC trial (Merck trial 035), viral load was <400 c/mL in 80% of the participants at 2 years (*N Engl J Med* 1997;337:734). A viral load <500 c/mL at 8 weeks in ACTG 320 predicted long-term benefit (*Ann Intern Med* 2001;135:954). An observational study of 1342 recipients of an IDVbased HAART regimen showed 54% had a viral load <400 c/mL at 1 year (*AIDS* 2001;15:999).

- **Merck trial 035** has continued as an open-label protocol; at 3 years, 20 of 31 patients (65%) had viral loads <50 c/mL by as-treated analysis (*Ann Intern Med* 2000;133:35). In ACTG 320, IDV + AZT/3TC was significantly better than AZT/3TC in terms of survival, rate of HIV-related complications, CD4 response, reduction in viral load, and quality of life among 1,156 participants with CD4 cell counts <200/mm^3 and prior AZT experience; the proportion that achieved viral load <500 c/mL at 24 weeks was 90% (*N Engl J Med* 1997;337:725).
- **Merck 060/ICC 004** is a trial of IDV/AZT/3TC in 199 treatment-naïve patients with CD4 cell counts >500/mm^3. At 48 weeks, 79% had viral load <50 c/mL by intent-to-treat analysis; the mean increase in CD4 cell count was 160/mm^3. Eight percent had nephrolithiasis (7th CROI, San Francisco, California, 2000, Abstract 511). AVANTI-2 was also a trial with IDV + AZT/3TC in treatment-naïve patients. At 52 weeks viral load was <20/mL in 41% by ITT analysis (*AIDS* 2000;14:367).
- Indinavir combined with NVP has been reported as a successful "rescue regimen" in 59% of patients who failed amprenavir-based HAART in ACTG 373 (*J Infect Dis* 2001;183:715). IDV may also be combined with EFV for "rescue" (*J Infect Dis* 2001;183:392).
- Comparative trials of IDV + AZT/3TC vs AZT/3TC/ABC in 562 patients showed equivalence with viral load <400 c/mL at 48 weeks in 51% in both groups. Similar results were noted in IDV recipients with a baseline viral load >100,000 c/mL (*JAMA* 2001;285:1155).
- Trials combining IDV with RTV have demonstrated favorable pharmacokinetics with marked increases in IDV trough levels permitting bid dosing (6th CROI, Chicago, Illinois, 1999, Abstracts 362, 363, 364, 631, and 677). The optimal dose regimen is not known. The regimen of 400 mg bid of both drugs is associated with trough IDV levels that are 3- to 4-fold higher and with lower peak levels, which would be expected to reduce the risk of nephrolithiasis. However, the dose of 400 mg bid of RTV is often poorly tolerated and may be complicated by higher blood lipids (*J Acquir Immune Defic Syndr* 2001;26:218). The alternative is to use IDV 800 mg bid + RTV 100-200 mg bid; this is better tolerated but is associated with higher peak levels of IDV and higher rates of nephrotoxicity. One study using the 800/100 mg bid regimen showed a good virologic response, but 23% had nephrolithiasis by week 24 (*HIV Clin Trials* 2000;1:13). Results from a trial involving RTV intensification in patients with detectable virus in IDV-containing regimens demonstrated increased IDV trough levels; 38% of patients achieved a viral load <50 c/mL at 48 weeks (8th CROI, Chicago, Illinois, 2001, Abstract 337). Trials are ongoing using

once-daily therapy with 3TC, d4T, and IDV 1200 mg + RTV 200 mg (8th CROI, Chicago, Illinois, 2001, Abstract 336).

RESISTANCE: Mutations at codons 10, 20, 24, 32, 36, 46, 54, 71, 73, 77, 82, 84, and 90 correlate with reduced *in vitro* activity (*Antimicrob Agents Chemother* 1998;42:2775). Substitutions at codons 46, 82, and 84 are major mutations that predict resistance but are not necessarily the first mutations. In general, at least three mutations are necessary to produce phenotypic resistance. Overlap with RTV is extensive, so that strains resistant to one are usually resistant to both. (The rationale for the RTV-IDV combination is pharmacologic enhancement with improved IDV trough levels that permit twice-daily administration.) The overlap with other PIs is less extensive, but multiple mutations generally imply class resistance (*Nature* 1995;374:569).

PHARMACOLOGY

- **Bioavailability:** Absorption is 65% in fasting state or with only a light, nonfat meal. Full meal decreases IDV levels 77%; give 1 hour before or 2 hours after meal, with light meal or with RTV. Food has minimal effect on IDV when it is coadministered with RTV.
- **T½:** 1.5 to 2.0 hours (serum)
- **C_{max}:** Peak >200 nm; 8 hours post dose – 80 nm (95% inhibition *in vitro* at 25-100 nm). Peak levels correlate with nephrotoxicity and trough levels correlate with efficacy. There appear to be substantial variations in IDV levels when used alone (*Antimicrob Agents Chemother* 2001;45:236) or when boosted with RTV (*J Acquir Immune Defic Syndr* 2002;29:374). This suggests a possible role for therapeutic drug monitoring, although results are highly variable (*Antimicrob Agents Chemother* 2001;45:236; 8th CROI, Chicago, Illinois, 2001, Abstracts 730 and 734). Penetration into CSF is moderate (CSF: serum=0.06-0.16) but is superior to that of other PIs and adequate to inhibit IDV-sensitive strains (*Antimicrob Agents Chemother* 2000;44:2173). The levels achieved are above the IC_{95} for most HIV isolates (*AIDS* 1999;13:1227). CSF trough levels of IDV are increased >5-fold when IDV is combined with RTV (7th CROI, San Francisco, California, 2000, Abstract 312).
- **Elimination:** Metabolized via hepatic glucoronidation and cytochrome P450 (CYP3A4)-dependent pathways. Urine shows 5% to 12% unchanged drug and glucuronide and oxidative metabolites.
- **Dose in renal failure:** Standard dose. This also applies to hemodialysis and peritoneal dialysis (*Nephrol Dial Transplant* 2000;15:1102).

SIDE EFFECTS

- **Asymptomatic increase in indirect bilirubin** to ≥2.5 mg/dL without an increase in transaminases noted in 10% to 15% of patients.

- **Mucocutaneous:** Paronychia and ingrown toenails, dry skin, mouth, eyes – common.
- **Class adverse effects:** Insulin-resistant hyperglycemia, fat redistribution, hyperlipidemia (increased triglyceride, cholesterol, LDL levels), and possible increased bleeding with hemophilia
- **Nephrolithiasis ± hematuria** in 10% to 28%, depending on duration of treatment, age, and fluid prophylaxis (*J Urol* 2000;164:1895). The frequency in the ATHENA cohort with 1219 IDV recipients was 8.3/100 patient-years; risk factors included low weight, low mean body mass, regimens with >1000 mg IDV, and warm climate (*Arch Intern Med* 2002;162:1493). Factors that do not appear to influence risk are CD4 cell count and urine pH. Patients should drink 48 oz of fluid daily to maintain urine output at ≥150 mL/hour during the 3 hours after ingestion; stones are crystals of IDV ± calcium (*Ann Intern Med* 1997;349:1294). Nephrolithiasis usually reflects peak plasma concentrations >10 µg/mL (*AIDS* 1999;13:473). This is most likely with IDV in standard doses or ritonavir-boosted IDV regimens, with the 800/100 mg bid IDV/RTV regimen (*J Acquir Immune Defic Syndr* 2002;29:374). Most patients with stones who resume IDV therapy achieve virologic control with a reduced dose (600 mg tid) (*AIDS* 1999;13:473).
- **Nephrotoxicity:** IDV crystals are found with urinalysis in up to 60% of IDV recipients. Nephrolithiasis with renal colic, flank pain, hematuria, and/or renal insufficiency is reported at 8/100 patient-years (*Arch Intern Med* 2002;162:1493). This rate is related to dose, body mass, state of hydration, and peak plasma levels. Interstitial nephritis with pyuria and renal insufficiency is reported in about 2% of IDV recipients (*Clin Infect Dis* 2002;34:1033).
- **Alopecia:** All hair bearing areas (*N Engl J Med* 1999;341:618)
- **GI intolerance** with nausea
- **Less common:** Increased transaminase levels, headache, nausea, vomiting, epigastric distress, diarrhea, metallic taste, fatigue, insomnia, blurred vision, dizziness, rash, and thrombocytopenia. Rare cases of fulminant hepatic failure and death. Fulminant hepatitis has been associated with steatosis and an eosinophilic infiltrate, suggesting a drug-related injury (*Lancet* 1997;349:924). Gynecomastia has been reported (*Clin Infect Dis* 1998;27:1539).
- Class adverse reactions include fat accumulation, insulin resistance, and hyperlipidemia (*AIDS* 2001;15:11).

DRUG INTERACTIONS

- **Nucleosides:** No effect; use standard doses.

■ TABLE 6-24: **Recommendations for IDV in Combination With Other PIs or With NNRTIs**

Agent	AUC	Concurrent Use Regimen
RTV*	IDV ↑2-5x	RTV 400 mg bid + IDV 400 mg bid or RTV 100 mg bid + IDV 800 mg bid or RTV 200 mg bid + IDV 800 mg bid
SQV	SQV ↑4-7x; IDV No effect	No data; possible *in vitro* antagonism (*J Infect Dis* 1997;176:265)
NFV	NFV ↑80%; IDV ↑50%	IDV 1200 mg bid + NFV 1250 mg bid (limited data)
NVP	NVP no effect; IDV ↓28%	IDV 1000 mg q8h + NVP standard
DLV	DLV no effect; IDV ↑40%	DLV 400 mg tid + IDV 600 mg q8h
EFV	EFV no effect; IDV ↓31%	EFV 600 mg qhs + IDV 1000 mg q8h IDV/RTV 800/200 mg bid + EFV 600 mg qhs
APV	APV ↑33%; IDV ↓38%	APV 800 mg tid + IDV 800 mg tid
LPV/r	LPV no change; IDV ↑3x	IDV 600 or 666 mg bid + LPV/r 400/100 mg bid

* It is possible that IDV/RTV could be given once daily (IDV/RTV 1200/400), but data are limited (7th CROI, San Francisco, California, 2000, Abstract 512). Note that the 400/400 mg bid regimen is often associated with GI intolerance and the 800/100-200 mg regimen is associated with increased rates of nephrotoxicity (*J Acquir Immune Defic Syndr* 2002;29:374).

- **Antimycobacterial agents:** Rifampin – concurrent use is contraindicated. Rifabutin – IDV levels decreased 32% and rifabutin levels increased 2x – reduce rifabutin dose to 150 mg/day or 300 mg 2 to 3x/week and increase IDV dose to 1000 mg tid.
- **Contraindicated for concurrent use:** Rifampin, astemizole, terfenadine, cisapride, midazolam, triazolam, ergotamines, simvastatin, lovastatin, and St. John's wort
- **ddI:** Use *Videx EC* formulation or separate doses by ≥2 hours.
- **Other interactions**
  - Ketoconazole and itraconazole increase IDV levels 70%; decrease IDV dose to 600 mg q8h.
  - Clarithromycin levels increase 53% – no dose change.
  - Grapefruit juice reduces IDV levels 26%.
  - Norethindrone levels increase 26% and ethinylestradiol levels increase 24% – no dose change.
  - Carbamazepine decreases IDV levels; consider alternative.
  - Co-administration of IDV and sildenafil (*Viagra*) increases the AUC for sildenafil 340% (*AIDS* 1999;13:F10). The maximum recommended dose is 25 mg/48 hours.
  - There is no change in levels of methadone.
  - St. John's wort reduces IDV AUC by 57% (*Lancet* 2000;355:547).

PREGNANCY: Category C. Negative rodent teratogenic assays; placental passage studies show high newborn:maternal drug levels in rats, low ratio in rabbits. Some authorities are concerned about the elevated indirect bilirubin and nephrolithiasis in the event that these complications may occur in the fetus.

INTERFERON – see also Pegylated Interferon (p. 276)

TRADE NAME: *Roferon* (Roche), *Intron* (Schering-Plough), *Infergen* (InterMune)

NOTE: Interferon use has been largely supplanted by pegylated interferon due to easier administration and superior outcome for treatment of HCV genotype 1. The drug is included here because some ADAP and other plans will not pay for the pegylated form due to high cost.

FORMS AND PRICES

- Interferon alfa-2a (*Roferon*): Vials of 3, 6, 9, 18, and 36 million units at $11.63/million units.
- Interferon alfa-2b (*Intron*): Vials of 3, 5, 10, 18, 25, and 50 million units at $11.89/million units.
- *Rebetron Combination Therapy Pac* consists of ribavirin for oral administration (200 mg caps) and *Intron* for parenteral administration in patients with hepatitis C infection in the following combinations and cost:

Ribavirin (200 mg caps)	*Intron* (3 million unit vials)	AWP
84	6	$720
70	6	$651
42	6	$534

PATIENT ASSISTANCE PROGRAMS: *Intron*: 800-521-7157; *Roferon*: 800-443-6676; cap program (983 million units ≤ year)

CLASS: Interferon-alfa is a family of highly homogeneous species-specific proteins of human origin (using donor cells, cultured human cell lines, or recombinant techniques with human genes) possessing complex antiviral, antineoplastic, and immunomodulating activities. The alfa-2a and alfa-2b refer to similar subtypes prepared by recombinant techniques.

INDICATIONS AND DOSES (Interferon alfa-2b)

- **Hepatitis C:** This interferon formulation has become antiquated with the approval of pegylated interferon, which has a more convenient dosing schedule (once vs 3x/week) and better efficacy (*Lancet* 2001;358:958). However, the cost differential is large:

$18,000/48 weeks for interferon + ribavirin vs $26,000/48 weeks for peginterferon + ribavirin. Efficacy was comparable for genotypes 2 and 3 compared to genotype 1 with low viral load in the pivotal study of *Peg-Intron* + ribavirin (*Lancet* 2001;358:958), but in the pivotal study of *Pegasys* + ribavirin, the pegylated formulation was superior to interferon alfa-2b + ribavirin regardless of genotype (*N Engl J Med* 2002;347:975). The usual interferon dose is 3 million units IM or SQ 3x/week x 12 to 18 months (*N Engl J Med* 1995;332:1457). Results are superior when interferon is given with ribavirin (*Lancet* 1998;351:83). See ribavirin for dosing instructions, p. 287. The 2002 guidelines from the NIH HCV Consensus Conference are available at: http://consensus.nih.gov/cons/116/116cdc_intro.htm.

- **Hepatitis B:** 5 million units IM or SQ daily or 10 million units 3x/week x 4 months. (Alternative and preferred drugs are lamivudine, adefovir, and tenofovir; peginterferon should work as well as interferon but has not been formally evaluated nor FDA-approved for HBV.)
- **Kaposi's Sarcoma*:** 30 to 36 million units IM or SQ (3 to 7x/week) until KS lesions resolve; toxicity or rapid progression of KS (average 7 months) precludes further treatment.

* Best response rates (40% to 50%) in patients with CD4 cell counts >200/mm³ and no "B symptoms"; response is dose-related.

ACTIVITY: Broad-spectrum antiviral agent with *in vitro* activity against HIV, HPV, HBV, HCV, HSV-1 and 2, CMV, and VZV

PHARMACOLOGY

- **Bioavailability:** Protein with 165 amino acids and molecular weight of 18,000-20,000; absorption after oral administration is nil; bioavailability with SQ or IM administration is 80%.
- **T½:** 2.0 to 5.1 hours
- **CSF level:** None detected
- **Elimination:** Metabolized by kidney

SIDE EFFECTS: All patients have side effects, especially with doses ≥18 million units. Most side effects diminish in frequency and severity with continued administration. Side effects include:

- **Flu-like syndrome** (50% to 98%): Fever, chills, fatigue, headache, and arthralgias, usually within 6 hours of administration, lasting 2 to 12 hours (reduced with NSAIDs)
- **GI intolerance** (20% to 65%): Anorexia, nausea, vomiting, diarrhea, metallic taste, and abdominal pain
- **Neuropsychiatric toxicity** with irritability, depression, or confusion (20% to 50%)
- **Marrow suppression** with neutropenia, anemia, or thrombocytopenia

- **Hepatotoxicity** (10% to 50%) with increased transaminase levels
- **Dyspnea and cough**
- **Rash ± alopecia** (25%)
- **Proteinuria** (15% to 20%)

DRUG INTERACTIONS: AZT – increased hematologic toxicity; increased levels of theophylline, barbiturates

PREGNANCY: Category C. Abortifacient in animals with doses 20 to 500x doses in humans. No data for humans. Use in pregnancy only when need justifies the risk.

INTRON – see Interferon (above)

INVIRASE – see Saquinavir (p. 298)

ISONIAZID (INH)

TRADE NAMES: *Nydrazid, Laniazid, Teebaconin*, or generic; combination with rifampin: *Rifamate* and *Rifater* (Aventis)

FORMS AND PRICES: 50, 100, and 300 mg tabs. *Hydrazid* IV – Injections 100 mg/mL 10 mL vial $20.26; INH liquid – $1.25 per 300 mg; *Rifater* – $1.90/tab

COMBINATIONS: Caps with rifampin: 150 mg INH + 300 mg rifampin (*Rifamate*) and tabs with 50 mg INH + 120 mg rifampin and 300 mg PZA (*Rifater*)

INDICATIONS AND DOSES: Prophylaxis and treatment of tuberculosis

■ TABLE 6-25: **INH Dosing Regimens**

	Daily	DOT	Pyridoxine (Vitamin B6)
Prophylaxis x 9 months	300 mg	900 mg 2x/week	50 mg/day or 100 mg 2x/week
Treatment	300 mg	900 mg 2 to 3x/week	50 mg/day or 100 mg 2x/week

- Treatment of active TB with *Rifamate*: 2 caps/day
- Treatment of active TB with *Rifater*: <65 kg – 1 tab/10 kg/day; >65 kg – 6 tabs/day

COMPLIANCE: Compliance concerns have resulted in a preference for DOT in all patients treated for active tuberculosis and is sometimes available for treatment of latent TB with HIV-coinfection. Many studies in the coinfected population show poor adherence that is improved with DOT, a monetary incentive (*Arch Intern Med* 2000;160:697), or treatment with the 8 week rifampin-PZA regimen despite the risk of severe liver injury (*Am J Respir Crit Care Med* 2001;164:1319).

PHARMACOLOGY

- **Bioavailability:** 90%
- **T½:** 1 to 4 hours; 1 hour in rapid acetylators
- **Elimination:** Metabolized and eliminated in urine. Rate of acetylation is genetically determined. Slow inactivation reflects deficiency of hepatic enzyme N-acetyltransferase and is found in about 50% of whites and African-Americans. Rate of acetylation does not affect efficacy of standard daily or DOT regimens.
- **Dose modification in renal failure:** Half dose with creatinine clearance <10 mL/min in slow acetylators.

SIDE EFFECTS

- **Hepatitis** risk varies by age (*Med Clin North Amer* 1988;72:661). The incidence in young, healthy adults is 0.3%; this increases to 2.6% in those who drink alcohol daily, have chronic liver disease, or are elderly. Another report demonstrated hepatotoxicity rates (defined as an ALT >5 ULN) of 0.15% in 11,141 patients treated for latent TB was 1% in those receiving multiple antituberculosis drugs for active TB (*JAMA* 1999;281:1014). INH should be stopped if transaminase levels increase to >5 times upper limit of normal.
- **Peripheral Neuropathy** due to increased excretion of pyridoxine, which is dose-related and rare with usual doses; it is prevented by concurrent pyridoxine (10-50 mg/day), which is recommended for diabetics, alcoholics, pregnant patients, AIDS patients, and malnourished patients.
- **Miscellaneous Reactions:** Rash, fever, adenopathy, GI intolerance. Rare reactions: Psychosis, arthralgias, optic neuropathy, marrow suppression.

DRUG INTERACTIONS

- Increased effects of warfarin, benzodiazepines, carbamazepine, cycloserine, ethionamide, phenytoin, theophylline
- INH absorption decreased with Al^{++} containing antacids
- Hepatitis: Increased frequency with excessive alcohol
- Ketoconazole: Decrease ketoconazole levels
- Food: Decreases absorption
- Tyramine (cheese, wine, some fish): Rare patients develop palpitations, sweating, urticaria, headache, and vomiting

PREGNANCY: Category C. Embryocidal in animals; not teratogenic. Large retrospective studies have shown no pattern of congenital abnormalities; small studies suggest possible CNS toxicity (*Clin Infect*

Dis 1995;21[suppl 1]:S24). American Thoracic Society recommendation is that pregnant women with positive PPD plus HIV infection should receive INH; begin after first trimester if possible.

ITRACONAZOLE

TRADE NAME: *Sporanox* (Janssen)

FORMS AND PRICES: 100 mg caps at $7.75; 150 mL oral solution with 10 mg/mL at $122.29; 200 mg vials for injection at $184.87

- Cost of treating histoplasmosis: $30/day for 200 mg cap bid
- Cost of treating thrush: $8.13/day for 100 mg solution/day

PATIENT ASSISTANCE PROGRAM: 800-652-6227

CLASS: Triazole (like fluconazole) with three nitrogens in the azole ring; other imidazoles have two nitrogens.

ACTIVITY AND PERSPECTIVE: *In vitro* activity against *H. capsulatum, B. dermatitidis, Aspergillus, Cryptococcus, Candida* sp. Strains of *Candida* that are resistant to fluconazole are often sensitive to itraconazole (*Antimicrob Agents Chemother* 1994;38:1530). Compared with fluconazole, itraconazole appears to be equivalent for non-meningeal coccidioidomycosis (*Ann Intern Med* 2000;133:676), superior for penicilliosis (*Am J Med* 1997;103:223), inferior for cryptococcosis (*Clin Infect Dis* 1999;28:291), and equivalent for most candidiasis (*HIV Clin Trials* 2000;1:47). Major concerns are somewhat erratic absorption, multiple drug interactions, and recently described cardiotoxicity (*FDA Health Advisory*, 5/09/02).

■ TABLE 6-26: **Itraconazole Dose Regimens** (*Clin Infect Dis* 2000;30:652)

Usual Doses

- **Loading dose:** 200 mg tid for serious infections
- **Capsules:** 100-200 mg PO qd or bid *with food* (200-400 mg/day)
- **Oral liquid formulation:** 100 mg PO qd or bid *on empty stomach* (100-200 mg/day)
- **IV:** 200 mg IV bid x 4 (loading), then 200 mg IV qd

Treatment by Pathogens

Pathogen	Dose (oral)	Comment
Aspergillosis	200-400 mg/day (caps)	Voriconazole preferred
Blastomycosis	200 mg qd or bid (caps)	
Candida ■ Thrush ■ Esophagitis ■ Vaginal	■ 200 mg/day (liquid) swish & swallow (S&S) ■ 200 mg/day (liquid) S&S ■ 200 mg/day x 3 days or 200 mg bid x 1	■ As effective as fluconazole, but absorption more erratic and there are more drug interactions (*HIV Clin Trials* 2000;1:47) ■ For fluconazole resistant *Candida*, options include itraconazole (PO or IV), voriconazole (PO or IV), caspofungin (IV), or amphotericin (IV). Voriconazole is the most predictably active triazole.
Coccidioidomycosis	200-400 mg bid (caps)	Non-meningeal form
Cryptococcosis	200 mg qd (caps)	For patients with meningeal form who cannot tolerate fluconazole and for non-meningeal cryptococcosis
Dermatophytes	200 mg qd (caps)	■ *Tinea corporis* and *T. cruris*: 15 days ■ *T. pedis, T. manum*: 30 days ■ *T. capitis*: 4 to 8 weeks
Histoplasmosis	■ Acute: 400 mg IV/day ■ Continuation: 200 mg PO tid x 3 days then 200 mg bid ■ Maintenance: 200 mg PO bid	Preferred azole
Onychomycosis ■ Fingernails ■ Toenails	200 mg/day (caps) ■ 1 week/month x 2 mos. ■ 1 week/month x 4 mos.	Warn patients of and monitor for cardiotoxicity and hepatotoxicity.
Penicilliosis	■ Acute: 200 mg PO bid ■ Maintenance: 200 mg PO/day	Preferred azole
Sporotrichosis	200 mg bid	

PHARMACOLOGY

- **Bioavailability:** Caps require gastric acid for absorption; average is 55% and improved when taken with food. Acidic drinks such as colas and orange juice may increase absorption in patients with gastric achlorhydria (*Antimicrob Agents Chemother* 1995;39:1671). Follow serum levels to ensure absorption. The usual therapeutic level anticipated with a standard dose is >2 μg/mL and <10 μg/mL. The liquid formulation is better absorbed and should be taken on an empty stomach. The supplier recommends a dose adjustment of one half of that recommended for capsules. Some consider the liquid formulation to be preferred for all oral itraconazole therapy. However, nearly all studies were performed using the capsule formulation, and bioavailability studies have shown substantial variation. Based on these concerns, some authorities prefer the liquid formulation only for thrush, where its topical effect may improve efficacy, for patients with known achlorhydria, and patients with inadequate serum levels.
- **Reference laboratories for serum levels:**
  - Dr. Michael Rinaldi, Dept. of Pathology, University of Texas Health Science Center, 7703 Floyd Curl Drive, San Antonio, TX 78284-7750; telephone 210-567-4131. Cost is $59.
  - Specimen should be serum or plasma. Volume >0.5 mL (2-4 mL preferred) sent in frozen state. Specimen can be obtained about 2 hours post dosing, after ≥5 days of treatment to assure steady state has been reached. Results are available in 3 days. Goal is level of ≥1 μg/mL.
- **T½:** 64 hours
- **Elimination:** Metabolized by liver by cytochrome P450 to metabolites including hydroxyitraconazole, which is active *in vitro* against many fungi. Renal excretion is 0.03% of parent drug and 40% of administered dose as metabolites.
- **Dose modification with renal failure:** None
- **Dose modification with liver disease:** No data. Manufacturer suggests monitoring serum levels.

SIDE EFFECTS: The most important side effects are the negative inotropic effect and hepatitis. These have prompted a "black box" FDA warning urging caution, especially when using itraconazole for trivial infections such as onychomycosis. The negative inotropic effect was noted in animal toxicity studies and in clinical trials combined with 58 cases of CHF reported to the FDA "Drug Watch," which is an anecdotal series of cases reported to the FDA and reported by that agency through May, 2001. Elevation of hepatic enzymes is seen in 4%, but clinically significant hepatitis is rare (*Lancet* 1992;340:251). Hepatic enzymes should be monitored in patients with prior hepatic disease, and patients should be warned to report symptoms of hepatitis. Most common side effects are GI intolerance (3% to 10%) and rash (1% to 9%, most common in immunosuppressed patients). Infrequent dose-related toxicities include hypokalemia, hypertension, and edema. Ventricular fibrillation due to hypokalemia has been reported (*J Infect Dis* 1993;26:348).

DRUG INTERACTIONS: Impaired absorption with H_2 blockers, omeprazole (and other proton pump inhibitors), antacids, or sucralfate. Increases levels of IDV (IDV dose decreased to 600 mg tid) and SQV; no dose adjustment for *Invirase* or NFV. Should not be given concurrently with terfenadine (*Seldane*), cisapride, astemizole, triazolam (*Halcion*), lovastatin (*Mevacor*), simvastatin (*Zocor*), rifampin, rifabutin, phenytoin, or phenobarbital. Itraconazole increases levels of loratadine (*Claritin*), cyclosporine, oral hypoglycemics, calcium channel blockers, and digoxin. Decreased itraconazole levels with administration of rifampin, rifabutin, phenobarbitol, carbamazepine, buffered ddl, isoniazid, and phenytoin.

PREGNANCY: Category C. Teratogenic to rats, no studies in humans.

KALETRA – see Lopinavir/Ritonavir (p. 255)

KETOCONAZOLE

TRADE NAME: *Nizoral* (Janssen)

FORMS AND PRICES: Tabs: 200 mg at $3.12; 2% cream: 15 g at $19.19, 30 g at $32.29, and 60 g; 2% shampoo: 120 mL at $23.72

PATIENT ASSISTANCE PROGRAM: 800-652-6227

CLASS: Azole antifungal agent

INDICATIONS AND DOSES

- **Thrush:** 200 mg PO 1 to 2x/day
- ***Candida* esophagitis:** 200-400 mg PO bid. Note: Fluconazole (200 mg/day) is superior, but initial treatment with ketoconazole may be cost-effective (*Ann Intern Med* 1992;117:655).
- ***Candida* vaginitis:** 200-400 mg/day PO x 7 days or 400 mg/day x 3 days

PHARMACOLOGY

- **Bioavailability:** 75% with gastric acid; decreased bioavailability with hypochlorhydria, which is common in AIDS patients.
- **Administration with hypochlorhydria:** Best alternative is to use an azole that does not require gastric acid, such as fluconazole. Alternatives are concurrent administration of 580 mg glutamic acid hydrochloride or 240 mL acidic drinks such as colas, ginger ale, or orange juice (*Antimicrob Agents Chemother* 1995;39:1671).

- **T½:** 6 to 10 hours
- **Elimination:** Metabolized by liver, but half-life is not prolonged with hepatic failure.
- **Dose modification in renal failure:** None

SIDE EFFECTS: Gastrointestinal intolerance; temporary increase in transaminase levels (2% to 5%); dose-related decrease in steroid and testosterone synthesis with impotence, gynecomastia, oligospermia, reduced libido, menstrual abnormalities (usually with doses ≥600 mg/day for prolonged periods); headache, dizziness, asthenia; rash; abrupt hepatitis with hepatic failure (1:15,000); rare cases of hepatic necrosis; marrow suppression (rare); hypothyroidism (genetically determined); hallucinations (rare).

DRUG INTERACTIONS

- **Important interactions:** Increase in gastric pH impairs ketoconazole absorption: Antacids, H_2 blockers, proton pump inhibitors, and buffered formulations of ddI should be taken ≥2 hours apart, use alternative antifungal agent, (*MMWR* 1999;48[RR-10]:47) or ddI EC. INH decreases ketoconazole effect; rifampin – decreased activity of both drugs; generic – terfenadine (*Seldane*) and cisapride – ventricular arrhythmias (avoid concurrent use).
- **PI and NNRTIs:**

■ TABLE 6-27: **Ketoconazole Interactions With Antiretroviral Agents**

Agent	PI/NNRTI	Ketoconazole	Dose
IDV	↑68%	—	IDV 600 mg q 8 hour
RTV	—	↑3x	Ketoconazole dose ≤200 mg/day
SQV	↑30%	—	Standard doses
NFV	—	—	Standard doses
APV	↑31%	↑44%	Dose implications unclear
LPV/r	↑13%	↑3x	Ketoconazole dose ≥200 mg/day
NVP	↑15% to 30%	↓63%	Not recommended
EFV	—	↓amount?	Dose implications unclear

- **Other:** Alcohol – possible disulfiram-like reaction; oral anticoagulants – increased hypoprothrombinemia; corticosteroids – increased levels of methylprednisolone; cyclosporine – increased cyclosporine activity; phenytoin – altered metabolism of both drugs; theophylline – increased theophylline levels.

PREGNANCY: Category C. Embryotoxic and teratogenic in experimental animals with large doses; no studies in humans; use with caution.

LAMIVUDINE (3TC)

TRADE NAME: *Epivir* (GlaxoSmithKline)

FORMS AND PRICES: 300 mg tables at $10.53/tab, 150 mg tablets at $5.27/tab; yearly price for tablets $3,845. Oral solution 10 mg/mL, bottles of 240 mL at $84.28 each. Available in combination with AZT as *Combivir* (150 mg 3TC + 300 mg AZT) for bid administration at $11.42/tab. Available as *Trizivir* (150 mg 3TC, 300 mg AZT, and 300 mg ABC) for bid administration at $18.50/tab or $234.50/week. **For hepatitis B:** 100 mg tab at $5.27 and oral solution 5 mg/mL at $63.20.

PATIENT ASSISTANCE: 800-722-9294

CLASS: Nucleoside analog

INDICATIONS AND DOSES

- 300 mg qd or 150 mg PO bid; <50 kg, 2 mg/kg bid or 4 mg/kg qd. Take without regard to meals.
- HIV Indications, see Chapter 4 (3TC is included in virtually all initial HAART regimens).
- **Hepatitis B:** 3TC is a potent inhibitor of HBV replication (*N Engl J Med* 1995;333:1657). Several studies have verified activity with loss of HBV DNA (*Ann Intern Med* 1996;125:705: *Lancet* 1995;345:396), elimination of HBeAg (*N Engl J Med* 1998;339:61), improved ALT levels (*J Infect Dis* 1999;180:607), and improved histology (*N Engl J Med* 1998;339:61). Mutations on the YMDD gene confer lamivudine resistance at a rate of 20% to 25% per year, leading to HBV virologic failure and, in some cases, a hepatitis flare (*J Clin Virol* 2002;24:173; *Lancet* 1997;349:20; *Clin Infect Dis* 1999;28:1032). Such flares may result from lamivudine discontinuation or lamivudine resistance. Tenofovir DF and adefovir are active against lamivudine-resistant HBV (*Hepatology* 2002;36:507). Although not studied, tenofovir plus lamivudine may presumably be used to treat HBV and HIV to avoid the evolution of HBV resistance.
- **HBV/HIV coinfection:** 100 mg/day x 52 weeks, but patients who are co-infected with HBV and HIV should receive the standard HIV dose of 150 mg bid or 300 mg qd.

CLINICAL TRIALS: There is extensive experience with 3TC combined with AZT, d4T, and ddI, generally confirming antiviral potency, excellent long, and short-term tolerance, and early acquisition of the M184V resistance mutation with inadequate viral suppression. More recently used NRTI pairings include 3TC/TDF and 3TC/ABC, which are well tolerated and potentially useful for once daily dosing.

- **ACTG 384** showed that AZT/3TC/EFV was superior to ddI/d4T/EFV in virologic suppression, but it was not superior when AZT/3TC was combined with NFV. AZT/3TC showed significantly better long-term tolerability due primarily to high rates of peripheral neuropathy in the ddI/d4T group (XIV International AIDS Conference, Barcelona, July 2002, Abstract LB20a).

- **Gilead 903** compared 3TC/TDF vs 3TC/d4T, each in combination with EFV, for initial therapy. Results at 48 weeks were similar, with 81% to 82% achieving viral load <50 c/mL in both groups (XIV International AIDS Conference, Barcelona, July 2002, Abstract L17).

RESISTANCE: Monotherapy with 3TC or non-suppressive therapy with 3TC-containing regimens result in the rapid selection of the M184V mutation, which confers high-grade resistance to 3TC. This drug should always be given as part of a suppressive HAART regimen. Strains with the M184V mutation have enhanced susceptibility to AZT, d4T, and tenofovir DF and decreased susceptibility to ABC when combined with TAMs. There is minimal loss of ABC susceptibility with the M184V mutation. The Q151M complex and the T69 insertion mutation are associated with 3TC resistance as well as with broad multinucleoside resistance.

EFFICACY: Four comparative trials with 3TC/AZT vs monotherapy revealed that the combination was superior based on surrogate marker endpoints. At 24 weeks, the mean CD4 increase was 20-75 cells/mm³ (*N Engl J Med* 1995;333:1662). The presumed explanation for the superior results with AZT/3TC in AZT-experienced patients is partially ascribed to delay or reversal of resistance to AZT *(Science* 1995;269:696). Lamivudine is well tolerated, potent, and easily administered (two tabs qd or one tab bid). It should always be combined with another NRTI. Co-formulation with AZT (*Combivir*) and AZT/ABC (*Trizivir*) has the advantage of low pill burden. The combination of AZT/3TC also appears to be substantially more effective than AZT alone in preventing perinatal transmission (*Lancet* 2002;359:1178).

PHARMACOLOGY

- **Bioavailability:** 86%
- **T½:** 3 to 6 hours; Intracellular T½: 12 hours
- **CNS penetration:** 13% (CSF: Plasma ratio=0.11). These levels exceed the IC_{50} and have been shown to clear HIV RNA from CSF (*Lancet* 1998;351:1547).
- **Elimination:** Renal excretion accounts for 71% of administered dose.

■ TABLE 6-28: **3TC Dose Adjustments With Renal Failure**

CrCl	Dose HIV	Dose HBV
>50 mL/min	300 mg qd or 150 mg bid	100 mg/day
10-49 mL/min	150 mg qd	100 mg, then 50 mg/day
<10 mL/min	150 mg, then 25-30 mg qd	35 mg, then 15 mg/day
Hemodialysis	150 mg, then 50 mg qd post dialysis	100 mg, then 25 mg post dialysis

SIDE EFFECTS: Experience with more than 25,000 patients given 3TC through the expanded access program showed minimal toxicity. Infrequent complications include headache, nausea, diarrhea, abdominal pain, and insomnia. Comparison of side effects in 251 patients given 3TC/AZT and 230 patients given AZT alone in four trials (A3001, A3002, B3001, and B3002) indicated no clinical or laboratory complications uniquely associated with 3TC. Pancreatitis has been noted in some pediatric patients given 3TC. The most common side effects in patients given 3TC plus AZT are headache (35%), nausea (18%), neuropathy (12%), neutropenia (7%), and anemia (3%). Most of these are ascribed to AZT.

- **Class side effect:** Lactic acidosis and steatosis; less common than with d4T (*Clin Infect Dis* 2002;34:838).
- **Hepatitis B:** In HIV infected patients with HBV co-infection, discontinuation of 3TC may cause hepatic deterioration with increases in HBV DNA levels and increases in ALT levels.

DRUG INTERACTIONS: TMP-SMX (1 DS daily) increases levels of 3TC; however, no dose adjustment is necessary due to the safety profile of 3TC.

PREGNANCY: Category C. Negative carcinogenicity and teratogenicity studies in rodents; placental passage studies in humans show newborn:maternal drug ratio of 1.0. Studies in pregnant women show that lamivudine is well tolerated and has pharmacokinetic properties similar to those of nonpregnant women (*MMWR* 1998;47[RR-2]:6). Use in pregnancy is extensive; safety is well established, and when combined with AZT, efficacy in preventing perinatal transmission is also well established (*Lancet* 2002;359:1178).

LAMPRENE – see Clofazimine (p. 195)

LEUCOVORIN (Folinic Acid)

TRADE NAME: Generic

FORMS AND PRICES

- Oral tabs: 5, 10, 15, and 25 mg tabs; 5 mg tab – $2.85
- Parenteral: 50, 100, and 350 mg; 3 mg/mL; 100 mg – $36.69

CLASS: Calcium salt of folinic acid

INDICATIONS: Antidote for folic acid antagonists

NOTE: Protozoa are unable to utilize leucovorin because they require p-aminobenzoic acid as a cofactor. It does not interfere with antimicrobial activity of trimethoprim. Usual use in HIV infected patients is to prevent hematologic toxicity of pyrimethamine and trimetrexate. Therapy is usually oral but should be parenteral if there is vomiting, NPO status, or the dose is >25 mg.

- **Toxoplasmosis treatment:** Pyrimethamine 50-75 mg/day + leucovorin 10-20 mg/day x 6 weeks; maintenance pyrimethamine 25-50 mg/day + leucovorin 10-25 mg/day
- **Toxoplasmosis prophylaxis:** Pyrimethamine/leucovorin, 25 mg every week (with dapsone + pyrimethamine)

PHARMACOLOGY: Normal folate levels are 0.005-0.015 μg/mL, levels <0.005 indicate folate deficiency, and levels <0.002 cause megaloblastic anemia. Oral doses of 15 mg/day result in mean level of 0.268 μg/mL.

SIDE EFFECTS: Nontoxic in therapeutic doses. Rare hypersensitivity reactions.

PREGNANCY: Category C

LOPINAVIR/RITONAVIR (LPV/r)

TRADE NAME: *Kaletra* (Abbott Laboratories)

FORMS AND PRICE: Capsules containing LPV 133 mg + RTV 33 mg at $3.90 ($23.44/day, standard dose; $8,555.60). Oral solution containing 80 mg LPV + 20 mg RTV/mL at $351.75/160 mL bottle.

PATIENT ASSISTANCE: 800-659-9050

CLASS: PI

DOSE: Three capsules (each containing LPV 133 mg/RTV 33 mg) bid with food (400/100 mg bid). Once daily therapy (800/200 mg qd) is under study. Trough levels with once-daily dosing are therapeutic but lower and more variable. May be less active, especially against PI-resistant strains.

ACTIVITY: LPV is approximately 10 times more potent than RTV against wild-type HIV. The protein binding-adjusted IC_{50} value for wild-type virus is 0.07 μg/mL. With bid dosing, the trough levels of LPV on average exceed the IC_{50} by >75-fold. Lopinavir combined with other PIs showed an additive effect *in vitro* with IDV and APV and synergy with SQV (*Antimicrob Agents Chemother* 2002;46:2249).

CLINICAL TRIALS

- **Trial M97-720** was a dose-finding phase II trial with LPV/r + d4T and 3TC in 100 treatment-naïve patients with viral load >5,000 c/mL. At 48 weeks, 82% given 400/100 mg bid had viral load <400 c/mL, and 78% had viral load <50 c/mL by ITT analysis (*AIDS* 2001;15:F1). At year 4, 70% still had <50 c/mL (42nd ICAAC, San Diego, California, Abstract H-165); the mean increase in CD4 cells from baseline was 440/mm³. Among 6 patients with sustained viral load rebound to >400 c/mL, no protease inhibitor resistance mutations have been observed.
- **Trial M98-863** was a phase III trial that compared LPV/r and NFV, each combined with d4T and 3TC in 653 treatment-naïve patients (*N Engl J Med* 2002;346:2039). By ITT analysis at 48 weeks, viral load was <400 c/mL in 75% of LPV/r recipients compared with 63% of NFV recipients (p=0.001) and <50 c/mL in 67% vs 52%, respectively (p<0.001). Both regimens were well tolerated. Among failures, PI resistance mutations were noted in 25 of 76 in the NFV arm and 0 of 37 in the LPV/r arm.
- **Trial M98-957** was a salvage trial involving 57 patients who had failed at least two PI-containing regimens. The trial compared two doses of LPV/r (533/133 mg bid and 400/100 mg bid), each combined with EFV. At 72 weeks, viral load was <400 and <50 c/mL in 88% and 81% of patients, respectively (as-treated analysis). By ITT analysis, viral loads were <400 and <50 c/mL in 67% and 61%, respectively. Response was correlated with the number of PI mutations to LPV at baseline, with viral load <400 c/mL in 91% of those with 0 to 5 mutations, 71% with 6 to 7 mutations, and 33% wit 8 to 10 mutations (*Antiviral Ther* 2002;7:165).
- **Trial M97-765** was a phase II study in 70 NNRTI-naïve patients with a viral load of 10^3-10^5 c/mL (median viral load 10,000 c/mL and median CD4 349/mm³) on their PI regimen. Patients received LPV/r + NVP and 2 NRTIs. At 48 weeks, 60% had viral load <50 c/mL by ITT analysis (*J Virol* 2001;75:7462).
- **Salvage:** In an open trial (expanded access) with 76 patients who failed alternative PI-based HAART, 63% had viral load <500 c/mL at 6 months (*HIV Clin Trials* 2002;3:304).

RESISTANCE: Major resistance mutations have not been defined. Treatment-naïve patients treated with LPV/r rarely acquire HIV resistance by genotypic or phenotypic testing; resistance usually results from multiple PI resistance mutations reflecting prior PI-containing regimens at codons 10, 20, 24, 32, 33, 46, 47, 50, 53, 54, 63, 71, 73, 82, 84, and 90. Clinical trial data demonstrate reduced response rates with ≥4 mutations (8th CROI, Chicago, Illinois, 2001, Abstract 525). The I50V mutation selected by amprenavir causes significant loss of susceptibility to LPV. Consider phenotypic testing to facilitate interpretation.

PHARMACOLOGY

- **Bioavailability:** LPV absorption ~80% bioavailability with food and 48% on an empty stomach. The addition of RTV results in a significant increase in LPV concentrations, AUC, and T½ due to inhibition of the cytochrome P450 CYP3A4 isoenzymes, which are the major excretory route for LPV. LPV has minimal effect on RTV pharmacokinetics; the C_{max} for RTV when given in the LPV/r formulation is approximately 0.6 µg/mL, compared with 11 µg/mL with standard doses of RTV (600 mg bid). The mean steady-state LPV plasma concentrations are 15- to 20-fold higher than those without RTV. Because RTV activity *in vitro* is 10-fold lower than that of LPV, RTV functions primarily as a pharmacologic enhancer and not as an antiretroviral agent *per se*.
- **T½:** 5 to 6 hours
- **Excretion:** Metabolized primarily by cytochrome P450 CYP3A4 isoenzymes. LPV/r inhibits CYP3A4 isoenzymes, but the effect is less than that of therapeutic doses of RTV, and similar to that of IDV. Less than 3% excreted unchanged in urine.
- **Renal failure:** No data are available, but usual dose is recommended. LPV/r is not removed with hemodialysis (*AIDS* 2001;15:662).

SIDE EFFECTS: The drug is generally well tolerated, with 2% discontinuing therapy due to adverse drug reactions in phase II and III clinical trials through 48 weeks. The most common adverse reactions were gastrointestinal, with diarrhea of at least moderate severity in 15% to 25%. Laboratory abnormalities through 72 weeks included transaminase increases (to >5x normal) in 10% to 12%.

- **Class adverse reactions:** Insulin resistance, fat accumulation, and hyperlipidemia. Clinical trials show triglyceride increases (to >750 mg/dL) in 12% to 22%, and cholesterol increases (to >300 mg/dL) in 14% to 22% of treatment-naïve patients receiving LPV/r. Trial M98-863 comparing LPV/r with NFV in 653 patients showed comparable mean increases in cholesterol (about 50 mg/dL) and a mean triglyceride increase of about 100 mg/dL for LPV/r vs 25 mg/dL for NFV.

DRUG INTERACTIONS: The major effect is due to the inhibition of CYP3A4 isoenzymes to prolong the half-life of drugs metabolized by the route. The inhibition is less than that seen with therapeutic doses of RTV.

- **Drugs contraindicated for concurrent use:** Astemizole, terfenadine, flecainide, propafenone, rifampin, simvastatin, lovastatin, midazolam, triazolam, cisapride, pimozide, ergot derivatives, and St. John's wort
- **Drugs that require a modified dose**
  - Rifabutin: C_{min} increased 3-fold; reduce rifabutin dose to 150 mg qod with standard LPV dose.
  - Methadone: AUC decreased by 53%; monitor for withdrawal.
  - Atorvastatin: AUC increased by 6x; use with caution or use alternative, such as pravastatin.
  - Pravastatin: Levels increased 33%; no dose adjustment.
  - Ketoconazole: Levels increased by 3x; do not exceed ketoconazole 200 mg/day.
  - Oral contraceptives: Ethinyl estradiol AUC decreased by 42%; use additional or alternative methods.
  - Sildenafil level increase anticipated; do not exceed 25 mg/48 hours.
  - Anticonvulsants: Anticipate large decrease in LPV level, and monitor anticonvulsant level.
  - Atovaquone: Levels of atovaquone may be decreased requiring dose adjustment.

■ TABLE 6-29: **Lopinavir Adjustments for Concurrent Use With Other Antiretroviral Agents**

Drug	Effect on Coadministered Drug	Effect on LPV	Dose Recommendation
APV	↑ or ↓	No change or ↓	APV 750 mg bid + LPV/r 400/100 mg bid or 533/133 mg bid
EFV	No change	C_{min} ↓39%	EFV 600 mg hs + LPV/r 533/133 mg bid
IDV	↑ C_{min} 3x	No change	IDV 600 mg bid + LPV/r 400/100 mg bid
NVP	No change	↓ C_{min} 55%	NVP standard + LPV/r 533/133 mg bid (limited data)
SQV	↑ C_{min} 3.6x		SQV (*Invirase* or *Fortovase*) 800 mg bid + LPV/r 400/100 mg bid*
NFV	No data	No data	No data
DLV	No change	↑8% to 134%	Limited data

* Shows synergy *in vitro* (*Antimicrob Agents Chemother* 2002;46:2249).

PREGNANCY: Category C. Placental passage shown in rats (newborn: maternal ratio=0.08) Animal carcinogenicity studies incomplete. Rodent teratogenic studies negative (but delayed skeletal ossification and skeletal variations in rats at maternally toxic doses).

LORAZEPAM

TRADE NAME: *Ativan* (Wyeth) or generic

FORMS AND PRICES: Tabs: 0.5 mg at $0.90, 1 mg at $1.17, 2 mg at $1.71. Vials: 2 mg, 4 mg, 20 mg, 40 mg

CLASS: Benzodiazepine, controlled substance category IV (see p. 185)

INDICATIONS AND DOSE REGIMENS

- Anxiety: 1-2 mg 2 to 3x/day; increase to usual dose of 2-6 mg/day in 2 to 3 divided doses
- IV administration: 2 mg
- Insomnia plus anxiety: 2-4 mg hs

PHARMACOLOGY

- **Bioavailability:** >90%
- **T½:** 10 to 25 hours
- **Elimination:** Renal excretion of inactive glucuronide metabolite. Not recommended with severe hepatic and/or renal disease.

SIDE EFFECTS: See Benzodiazepines (p. 185). Additive CNS depression with other CNS depressants including alcohol. Warn patient of prolonged sedation and decreased recall for ≥8 hours. Injected lorazepam may reduce physical coordination 24 to 48 hours.

PREGNANCY: Category D. Fetal harm: Contraindicated.

LOTRIMIN – see Clotrimazole (p. 195)

MARINOL – see Dronabinol (p. 207)

MEGACE – see Megestrol acetate (below)

MEGESTROL ACETATE

TRADE NAME: *Megace* (Bristol-Myers Squibb) or generic

FORMS AND PRICE: Tabs: 20 mg at $0.67, 40 mg at $1.15. Oral suspension: 40 mg/mL at $155/240 mL or $0.65/40 mg.

PATIENT ASSISTANCE: 800-272-4878

CLASS: Synthetic progestin related to progesterone

INDICATIONS: Appetite stimulant to promote weight gain in patients with HIV infection or neoplastic disease; a concern is that most weight gain is fat.

USUAL REGIMEN

- **Oral suspension:** 400 mg/day (20 mL in one daily dose), up to 800 mg/day.
- **Tablets:** 80 mg PO qid; up to 800 mg/day (suspension usually preferred).

EFFICACY: Average weight gain in uncontrolled study – 0.5 kg/week with average total weight gain of 4 kg (*Ann Intern Med* 1994;121:393; *Ann Intern Med* 1994;121:400). However, there was <2.25 kg weight gain in 35% despite doses of 800 mg/day for 12 weeks, and most of the gain is fat. Most authorities recommend use in combination with anabolic steroids, resistance exercises, or both (*N Engl J Med* 1999;340:1740).

PHARMACOLOGY

- **Bioavailability:** >90%
- **T½:** 30 hours
- **Elimination:** 60% to 80% excreted in urine

SIDE EFFECTS

- **Most serious** are hypogonadism (which may exacerbate wasting), diabetes, and adrenal insufficiency.
- **Most common** are diarrhea, impotence, rash, flatulence, asthenia, hyperglycemia (5%), and pain.
- **Less common or rare** include carpal tunnel syndrome, thrombosis, nausea, vomiting, edema, vaginal bleeding, and alopecia; high dose (480 mg to 1600 mg/day) – hyperpnea, chest pressure, mild increase in blood pressure, dyspnea, congestive heart failure.
- A review of FDA reports of adverse drug reactions with megestrol showed 5 cases of Cushing syndrome, 12 new-onset diabetes cases, and 17 cases of possible adrenal insufficiency (*Arch Intern Med* 1997;157:1651).

DRUG INTERACTIONS: No information

PREGNANCY: Category D. Progestational drugs are associated with genital abnormalities in male and female fetuses exposed during first 4 months of pregnancy.

MEPRON – see Atovaquone (p. 182)

METHADONE

TRADE NAME: *Dolophine* (Roxane) or generic

FORMS AND PRICES: Tabs: 5 mg at $0.08, 10 mg at $0.14. Usual yearly cost of medication for methadone maintenance averages $180.

CLASS: Opiate schedule II. The FDA restricts physician prescribing for methadone maintenance to those licensed to provide this service and those attached to methadone maintenance programs. Licensed physicians can prescribe methadone for pain control.

INDICATIONS AND DOSES

- **Detoxification** for substantial opiate abstinence symptoms: Initial dose is based on opiate tolerance, usually 15-20 mg; additional doses may be necessary. Daily dose at 40 mg usually stabilizes patient; when stable 2 to 3 days, decrease dose 20% per day. Must complete detoxification in <180 days or considered maintenance.
- **Maintenance** as oral substitute for heroin or other morphine-like drugs: Initial dose 15-30 mg depending on extent of prior use, up to 40 mg/day. Subsequent doses depend on response. Usual maintenance dose is 40-100 mg/day, but higher doses are sometimes required. Most states limit the maximum daily dose to 80 mg to 120 mg/day.
- **Note:** During first 3 months, and for all patients receiving >100 mg/day, observation is required 6 days/week. With good compliance and rehabilitation, clinic attendance may be reduced for observed ingestion 3 days/week with maximum 2-day supply for home administration. After 2 years, clinic visits may be reduced to 2x/week with 3-day drug supplies. After 3 years, visits may be reduced to weekly with a 6-day supply.
- **Pain control:** 2.5-10.0 mg PO, SQ or IM q3h-q4h or 5-20 mg PO q6h-q8h for severe chronic pain in terminally ill patients.

PHARMACOLOGY

- **Bioavailability:** >90% absorbed
- **T½:** 25 hours. Duration of action with repeated administration is 24 to 48 hours.
- **Elimination:** Metabolized by liver via CYP450 2B6>2C19>3A4. Parent compound excreted in urine with increased rate in acidic urine; metabolites excreted in urine and gut.

SIDE EFFECTS

- **Acute toxicity:** CNS depression (stupor or coma), respiratory depression, flaccid muscles, cold skin, bradycardia, hypotension

- **Treatment:** Respiratory support ± gastric lavage (even hours after ingestion due to pylorospasm) ± naloxone (but respiratory depression may last longer than with naloxone, and naloxone may precipitate acute withdrawal syndrome).
- **Chronic toxicity:** Tolerance/physical dependence with abstinence syndrome following withdrawal – onset at 3 to 4 days after last dose of weakness, anxiety, anorexia, insomnia, abdominal pain, headache, sweating, and hot-cold flashes.
- **Treatment:** Detoxification.

■ TABLE 6-30: **Drug Interactions With Methadone**

Drug	Effect on Methadone	Effect on Coadministered Drug	Comment
ABC	↓ levels	↓ Peak	Dose adjustment?
APV	↓35%	↓	Consider alternative antiretroviral
ddI	None	↓40% to 60%	May require ↑ ddI dose
d4T	None	↓27%	No dose adjustment
DLV	↑	?	Dose adjustment?
EFV	↓52%	?	Need ↑ methadone dose
Fluconazole	↑30%	–	No dose adjustment
IDV	None	–	No dose adjustment
LPV/r	↓53%	?	No dose adjustment
NFV	↓	–	No dose adjustment
NVP	↓53%	–	Need ↑ methadone dose
Rifampin	↓↓	–	Need ↑ methadone dose
Rifabutin	–	–	No dose adjustment
RTV	↓37%	–	No dose adjustment
AZT	None	AUC ↑40%	No AZT dose adjustment
Phenytoin	↓↓	–	May need ↑ methadone dose
SQV	↓	–	No dose adjustment

PREGNANCY: Category C. Avoid during first 3 months and use sparingly, in small doses, during last 6 months.

METRONIDAZOLE

TRADE NAME: *Flagyl* (Pharmacia & Upjohn); *Femazole, Metizol, MetroGel* (Galderma), *Metryl, Neo-Tric, Novonidazole, Protostat,* or generic

FORMS AND PRICES: Tabs: 250 mg at $0.19, 500 mg at $0.33. IV vials: $24.40/500 mg. Vaginal gel at $35.16/70 g.

CLASS: Synthetic nitroimidazole derivative

INDICATIONS AND DOSE REGIMENS

- **Gingivitis:** 250 mg PO tid or 500 mg PO bid
- **Intra-abdominal sepsis:** 1.5-2.0 g/day PO or IV in 2 to 4 doses
- **Amebiasis:** 750 mg PO tid x 5 to 10 days
- **Bacterial vaginosis:** 2 g x 1 or 500 mg PO bid x 7 days
- **Trichomoniasis:** 2 g x 1 or 250 mg PO tid x 7 days
- ***C. difficile* colitis:** 500 mg PO bid or 250 mg PO tid x 10 to 14 days
- **Giardiasis:** 250 mg PO tid x 5 to 10 days

ACTIVITY: Active against virtually all anaerobes (*Antimicrob Agents Chemother* 2001;45:1238), and selected enteric pathogens (*E. histolytica, Giardia*). Drug of choice for most anaerobic infections, gingivitis, *C. difficile* associated diarrhea, amebiasis, giardiasis, and bacterial vaginosis. Mixed anaerobic infections need a companion antibiotic if aerobes are considered important because metronidazole is active against only anaerobes.

PHARMACOLOGY

- **Bioavailability:** >90%
- **Note:** Metronidazole is virtually completely absorbed with oral administration and should be given IV only if patient can take nothing by mouth.
- **T½:** 10.2 hours; serum level after 500 mg dose: 10-30 µg/mL
- **Elimination:** Hepatic metabolism; metabolites excreted in urine
- **Dose adjustment in renal failure:** None
- **Liver failure:** Half-life prolonged; consider reduced daily dose in severe liver disease

SIDE EFFECTS: Most common are GI intolerance and unpleasant taste. Less common are glossitis, furry tongue, headache, ataxia, urticaria, dark urine. Rare – seizures. Prolonged use may cause reversible peripheral neuropathy; disulfiram (*Antabuse*)-type reaction with alcohol.

DRUG INTERACTIONS: Increases levels of coumadin and lithium. Mild disulfiram-like reactions noted with alcohol (flushing, headache, nausea, vomiting, cramps, sweating). This is infrequent and unpredictable. Patients should be warned, and manufacturer recommends that alcohol be avoided. Concurrent use with disulfiram may cause psychoses or confusion; disulfiram should be stopped 2 weeks prior to use of metronidazole.

PREGNANCY: Category B. Fetotoxicity in animals. Contraindicated in first trimester, although 206 exposures during the first trimester showed no increase in birth defects. Use during the last 6 months is not advised unless essential. For trichomoniasis, CDC recommends

2 g x 1 after first trimester. Alternative agents are available for most other conditions.

MYCELEX – see Clotrimazole (p. 195)

MYCOBUTIN – see Rifabutin (p. 288)

MYCOSTATIN – see Nystatin (p. 273)

NEBUPENT – see Pentamidine (p. 280)

NELFINAVIR (NFV)

TRADE NAME: *Viracept* (Agouron Pharmaceuticals, a Pfizer company)

FORMS AND PRICES: Tabs: 250 mg at $2.52 ($159/week for 750 mg tid or $233/week for 1250 mg bid). 625 mg tab is expected in early 2003. Oral powder 50 mg/mL at $66.48/144 g.

PATIENT ASSISTANCE: 800-777-6637

CLASS: PI

INDICATIONS AND DOSES: See Chapter 4. 1250 bid or 750 mg tid with meal or snack (fatty meal preferred).

CLINICAL TRIALS

- **Pre-registration trials** showed the drug was well tolerated, with 4% of 696 patients discontinuing treatment due to side effects. The major side effect was diarrhea in 10% to 30%, which was sufficiently severe to require discontinuation of NFV in 1.6%.
- **Trial 511** included 297 treatment-naïve participants randomized to receive "triple therapy" (NFV + 3TC/AZT) vs 3TC/AZT. At 52 weeks, the proportion with HIV RNA <500/mL was 75%, and the median increase in CD4 cells was 220/mm^3 (*AIDS* 2001;15:1971).
- **The COMBINE study** compared NFV vs NVP, each with AZT/3TC in 142 treatment-naïve patients. Results at 36 weeks demonstrated a superior virologic response in NVP recipients with 67% achieving viral load <20 c/mL compared with 44% in the NFV group (8th CROI, Chicago, Illinois, 2001, Abstract 327). Adherence was significantly lower in the NFV arm, which may account for the difference.

- **ACTG 384** was a six-arm trial examining two nucleoside combinations plus EFV, NFV, or both in 980 treatment-naïve patients. At 160 weeks, EFV + 3TC/AZT was significantly more effective than NFV + 3TC/AZT. Results with ddI/d4T combined with either NFV or EFV were similar and inferior to EFV + 3TC/AZT (XIV International AIDS Conference, Barcelona, July 2002, Abstract LB20a).
- **Combinations of NFV with other PIs** are not extensively studied or used because there are few favorable drug interactions. The NFV/SQV combination has been more extensively studied but requires a large number of pills. NFV has minimal drug interactions with NVP and EFV, permitting standard doses in "triple regimens" for salvage or for initial treatment of patients with poor prognosis.
- **ACTG 364** evaluated 195 patients with extensive NRTI exposure given one to two new NRTIs plus NFV, EFV, or both. At 48 weeks, the proportions with viral load <50 c/mL were: NFV – 22%, EFV – 44%, NFV/EFV – 67%.
- **Abbott M98-863** was a comparative trial of LPV/r vs NFV in 653 treatment-naïve patients. Results at 48 weeks showed significantly fewer virologic failures at 50 c/mL (67% vs 52%) in LPV/r recipients, although compliance with the NFV tid regimen might have contributed to decreased response (*New Engl J Med* 2002;346:2039).
- **NFV + RTV** was studied in 20 treatment-naïve patients using RTV 400 mg bid and NFV at 500 vs 750 mg bid. At 48 weeks, viral load <20 c/mL was achieved in 4 of 12 patients completing 48 weeks (*J Acquir Immune Defic Syndr* 2000;25:322).

RESISTANCE: The primary mutation conferring NFV resistance is the D30N mutation, which is associated with phenotypic resistance to NFV but not to other protease inhibitors (*Antimicrob Agents Chemother* 1998;42:2775). However, the L90M mutation can also occur and, unlike D30N, it confers cross-resistance to other PIs. Other less important or secondary mutations are those at codons 10, 36, 46, 71, 77, 82, 84, and 88. Some authorities believe cross-resistance is less problematic with NFV, thus making rescue treatment with other PIs more likely to succeed.

PHARMACOLOGY

- **Bioavailability:** Absorption with meals is 20% to 80%. Food increases absorption 2- to 3-fold. Fatty meal improves absorption.
- **T½:** 3.5 to 5.0 hours
- **CNS penetration:** No detectable levels in CSF (*J Acquir Immune Defic Syndr* 1999;20:39)
- **Excretion:** Primarily by cytochrome P450 CYP3A4. Inhibits CYP3A4. Only 1% to 2% is found in urine; up to 90% is found in stool, primarily as a hydroxylated metabolite designated M8, which

is as active as nelfinavir against HIV (*Antimicrob Agents Chemother* 2001;45:1086).

- **Storage:** Room temperature
- **Dose modification in renal or hepatic failure:** None in renal failure with hemodialysis; NFV is removed so that post dialysis dosing is important (*AIDS* 2000;14:89). The drug is not removed by peritoneal dialysis (*J Antimicrob Chemother* 2000;45:709). With severe liver disease, consider therapeutic drug monitoring. It appears that autoinduction of NFV metabolism is blunted in severe liver disease, and there is also a reduction in the M8 active metabolite. Standard doses may yield high or low levels.

SIDE EFFECTS: About 10% to 30% of 1,500 recipients have reported diarrhea or loose stools. This is a secretory diarrhea, characterized by low osmolarity and high sodium, possibly due to chloride secretion (7th CROI, San Francisco, California, 2000, Abstract 62). Management strategies include use of several over-the-counter, inexpensive ($4 to $10/month) remedies, including oat bran (1500 mg bid), psyllium (1 tsp qd or bid), loperamide (4 mg, then 2 mg every loose stool up to 16/day), or calcium 500 mg bid. Some respond to pancreatic enzymes (1 to 2 tabs with meals) at a cost of $30-$111/month (*Clin Infect Dis* 2000;30:908). Class adverse effects: Lipodystrophy, increased levels of triglycerides and/or cholesterol, hyperglycemia with insulin resistance and type 2 diabetes, osteoporosis, and possible increased bleeding with hemophilia.

DRUGS THAT SHOULD NOT BE GIVEN CONCURRENTLY: Simvastatin, lovastatin, rifampin, astemizole, terfenadine, cisapride, midazolam, triazolam, ergot derivatives, and St. John's wort

DRUGS THAT REQUIRE DOSE MODIFICATIONS

- Oral contraceptives: Levels of ethinyl estradiol decreased by 47%; use alternative or additional birth control method.
- Phenobarbital, phenytoin, and carbamazepine may decrease NFV levels substantially; monitor anticonvulsant levels.
- Sildenafil AUC increased 2- to 11-fold; do not exceed 25 mg/48 hours.
- Rifabutin levels are increased 2-fold, and NFV levels are decreased by 32%; increase NFV dose to 1000 mg tid and decrease rifabutin dose to 150 mg/day or 300 mg 2 to 3x/week.
- NFV reduces levels of methadone 30% to 50%, but in most cases no dose change is required (7th CROI, San Francisco, California, 2000, Abstract 87).
- Atorvastatin levels increase 74%; use with caution.
- No effect: Ketoconazole
- No data: Clarithromycin

- Anticonvulsants (phenobarbital, phenytoin and carbamazepine) may increase NFV levels substantially; monitor anticonvulsant levels.

■ TABLE 6-31: **Combinations With PIs and NNRTIs**

Drug	AUC	Regimen
IDV	IDV ↑50% NFV ↑80%	IDV 1200 mg bid + NFV 1250 mg bid (limited data)
RTV	RTV No change NFV ↑1.5x	RTV 400 mg bid + NFV 500-750 mg bid (limited data)
SQV	SQV ↑3 to 5x (*Fortovase*) NFV ↑20%	SQV (*Fortovase*) 800 mg tid or 1200 bid + NFV 1250 bid or 750 mg tid
APV	APV ↑1.5x NFV ↑15%	NFV 750 mg tid or 1250 mg bid + APV 800 mg tid or 1200 mg bid (limited data)
NVP	NVP no change NFV ↑10%	Standard doses both drugs
EFV	NFV ↑20% EFV no change	Standard doses both drugs
DLV	DLV ↓50% NFV ↑2x	NFV 1250 mg bid + DLV 600 mg (limited data)
LPV/r	No data	No data

PREGNANCY: Category A. Animal teratogenic studies – negative; long-term animal carcinogenicity studies – not completed; placental passage – not known. Experience to establish safety in pregnancy is extensive.

NEUPOGEN – see G-CSF (p. 232)

NEVIRAPINE (NVP)

TRADE NAME: *Viramune* (Boehringer Ingelheim)

FORMS AND PRICE: Tabs: 200 mg at $5.60 ($70.56/week). Suspension: 50 mg/5 mL.

PATIENT ASSISTANCE: 800-556-8317

CLASS: NNRTI

INDICATIONS AND DOSING: 200 mg PO qd x 2 weeks, then 200 mg PO bid. Patients experiencing a rash during the lead-in should not increase the dose until the rash has resolved. Patients with treatment interruption >7 days should restart at 200 mg daily. Liver function tests should be monitored during NVP therapy, especially during the first 4 to 6 weeks when the rate of hepatotoxicity is high. The pharmacokinetic properties of NVP support once-daily dosing, e.g., 400 mg PO qd (*AIDS* 2000;14:F77). However, a higher peak (above 6 ng/mL) was associated with increased risk of hepatotoxicity (*AIDS* 2002;16:290).

CLINICAL TRIALS

- **The INCAS trial** examined NVP combined with AZT and ddI in treatment-naïve patients. At 52 weeks, 52% had viral loads <400 c/mL (*J Acquir Immune Defic Syndr* 2000;15:433; *J Acquir Immune Defic Syndr* 1999;22:260).
- **The Atlantic Trial** was a multicenter trial involving 235 patients randomized to receive ddI/d4T + either NVP, IDV, or 3TC. At 48 weeks, 55% to 59% in all three groups had <400 c/mL by intent-to-treat analysis. The low viral load at entry (median 15,000 c/mL) limits the conclusions that can be drawn about relative antiviral activity, but lipid profiles were better with NVP than with IDV (*AIDS* 2001;15:2407).
- **The COMBINE study** compared NVP and NFV, each in combination with AZT/3TC in 142 treatment-naïve patients with a median baseline viral load of 4.8 $\log_{10}$ c/mL. At 36 weeks, viral load was <20 c/mL in 67% of NVP recipients compared with 44% in the NFV group by intent-to-treat analysis (8th CROI, Chicago, Illinois, 2001, Abstract 327). Adherence was significantly lower in the NFV arm, which may account for the difference.
- **NVP plus NFV** has been used as a salvage regimen (with full doses of each) with 52% achieving viral load <200 c/mL (*J Acquir Immune Defic Syndr* 2001;27:124). NVP has also been combined with IDV as a salvage regimen following failure of AMP-based HAART, with 59% achieving viral load <500 c/mL at 48 weeks (*J Infect Dis* 2001;183:715).
- **Switching therapy** from a PI-containing regimen to NVP due to lipodystrophy is associated with good virologic control and rapid improvement in blood lipid changes and insulin resistance but minimal change in lipodystrophy (*AIDS* 1999;13:805; *J Acquir Immune Defic Syndr* 2001;27:229). The ATHENA study was a review of 125 patients who switched to NVP-based HAART compared with 321 who continued PI-based HAART. All participants had achieved viral load <500 c/mL on PI based HAART. Treatment failure due to toxicity requiring a regimen change (36%) or virologic failure (6%) was greater in the PI continuation group (*J Infect Dis* 2002;185:1261).
- **In an observational study from EuroSIDA** involving a heterogeneous group of patients, including many with extensive prior therapy, virologic failure at 48 weeks occurred in 48% of 878 EFV recipients compared with 65% of 1325 NVP recipients ($p<0.0001$) (*AIDS* 2001;15:2385).

- **A meta-analysis of published reports** of NVP vs EFV-based HAART for treatment-naïve patients showed that these two regimens were equally effective in virologic outcome *(HIV Clin Trials* 2001;2:113). Retrospective analysis of three large cohorts of >1000 patients each has shown EFV to be superior to NVP for virologic suppression (*AIDS* 2001;15:2385; *AIDS* 2002;16:53; *HIV Clin Trials* 2002;3:296). A prospective head-to-head comparison trial (2NN) is in progress.
- **High baseline viral load:** An analysis of six reports with 416 NVP recipients showed the rate of viral load <500 c/mL with baseline viral loads of above and below 100,000 c/mL was 83% and 89%, respectively *(HIV Clin Trials* 2001;2:317).

RESISTANCE: Monotherapy is associated with rapid and high-level resistance, with primary RT mutations at codons 101, 103, and 181, which increase the IC_{90} by >100-fold (*J Acquir Immune Defic Syndr* 1995;8:141; *J Infect Dis* 2000;181:904). There is cross-resistance with DLV; cross-resistance with EFV is more variable, and *in vitro* it is usually seen with K103N, which causes cross-resistance to all currently available NNRTIs. There is evidence that administration of NVP with AZT may predispose to emergence of the K103N mutation. There is no cross-resistance with nucleoside analogs or PIs. When NVP is given alone or combined with AZT, there is >100-fold reduction in sensitivity to NVP within 8 weeks. NNRTIs are not active against HIV-2.

PHARMACOLOGY

- **Bioavailability:** 93%; not altered by food, fasting, ddI, or antacids
- **T½:** 25 to 30 hours
- **CNS penetration:** CSF levels are <45% peak serum levels (CSF: plasma ratio=0.45)
- **Metabolism:** Metabolized by cytochrome P450 (CYP3A4) to hydroxylated metabolites that are excreted primarily in the urine, which accounts for 80% of the oral dose. NVP autoinduces hepatic cytochrome P450 enzymes of the CYP3A4 type, reducing its own plasma half-life over 2 to 4 weeks from 45 hours to 25 hours (*J Infect Dis* 1995;171:537).
- **Dose modification with renal or hepatic failure:** NVP is extensively metabolized by the liver, and NVP metabolites are largely eliminated by the kidney with <5% unchanged in the urine. Usual doses are recommended (*Nephro Dial Transplant* 2001;16:192).

SIDE EFFECTS

- **Major toxicities:** Life-threatening cutaneous reactions and hepatotoxicity usually during the initial 8 weeks. Patients should be warned to report symptoms of a hypersensitivity reaction promptly (e.g., fever, rash, arthralgias, or myalgias). ALT and AST should be monitored, especially during the first 8 weeks of treatment. Criteria to suspend therapy and safety of rechallenge are unclear.

- **Most common toxicity:** Rash, which is seen in about 17%; the usual rash is maculopapular and erythematous with or without pruritus and is located on the trunk, face, and extremities. Many patients with rashes required hospitalization, and 7% of all patients required discontinuation of the drug, compared with 4.3% given DLV and 1.7% given EFV (package insert, PDR). NNRTIs should be discontinued for severe rash or rash accompanied by fever, blisters, mucous membrane involvement, conjunctivitis, edema, arthralgias, or malaise. Stevens-Johnson syndrome has been reported, and three deaths ascribed to rash have been reported with NVP (*Lancet* 1998;351:567).
- **Hepatotoxicity** that usually occurs in the first 8 weeks appears to be a hypersensitivity reaction and may be accompanied by drug rash, eosinophilia, and systemic symptoms (DRESS syndrome). This is more common in women and in individuals with higher CD4 counts and may be severe or fatal. The CDC issued a warning against using NVP for PEP based on reports of two healthcare workers with severe hepatitis, including one who required a liver transplant (*Lancet* 2001;357:687; *MMWR* 2001;49:1153). Some NVP recipients develop hepatotoxicity later in the course of treatment, a form of hepatitis that is more benign and similar to hepatitis seen with other anti-HIV drugs. FTC 302 was a therapeutic trial with NVP in which 64 of 385 recipients (17%) developed grade 3 to 4 hepatotoxicity; 49 (77%) occurred in the first 4 weeks of therapy (8th CROI, Chicago, Illinois, 2001, Abstract 18). Of these 64 cases, 36% had GI complaints, 31% had rashes, and only about 6% had chronic HBV or HCV. Prior reports indicate that 8% to 18% of NVP recipients develop hepatotoxicity (*J Acquir Immune Defic Syndr* 2002;29:340).

DRUG INTERACTIONS: NVP, like rifampin, induces CYP3A4 families of the cytochrome P450 mechanism. Maximum induction takes place 2 to 4 weeks after initiating therapy. The effect is modest compared to other NNRTIs and PIs in terms of drug interactions.

- **Drugs that are contraindicated or not recommended for concurrent use:** Rifampin, ketoconazole, and St. John's wort.

■ TABLE 6-32: **Dose Recommendations for NVP + PI Combinations**

PI	PI Level	NVP Level	Regimen Recommended
IDV	↓28%	No change	IDV 1000 mg q8h (NVP standard)
RTV	↓11%	No change	Standard doses
SQV	↓25%	No change	Not recommended
NFV	↑10%	No change	Standard doses
APV	?	?	No data
LPV/r	LPV ↓55%	No change	LPV/r 533/133 mg (4 caps) bid (NVP standard)

DRUGS THAT REQUIRE DOSE MODIFICATION WITH CONCURRENT USE

- NVP decreases AUC for ethinyl estradiol by about 30% *(J Acquir Immune Defic Syndr* 2002;29:471); alternative or additional methods of birth control should be used.
- NVP reduces clarithromycin AUC by 30% but increases levels of the 14-OH metabolite, which has antibacterial activity that compensates for this reduction, so no dose adjustment is necessary.
- Ketoconazole levels decreased 63% and NVP increases 15% to 30%; not recommended.
- Rifabutin levels are decreased by 16%; no dose alteration.
- Phenobarbital, phenytoin, carbamazepine: No data
- NVP reduces AUC of methadone by about 50%. Opiate withdrawal is a concern, and methadone dose increases are variable but average 15% to 25% (*Clin Infect Dis* 2001;33:1595).
- Other drugs that commonly require careful monitoring when given with PIs or other NNRTIs do not have substantial drug interactions with NVP including statins, rifabutin, and clarithromycin.

PREGNANCY: Category C. Negative rodent teratogenicity assays; placental passage in humans shows a newborn:maternal ratio of 1.0. Pharmacokinetic studies show the elimination half-life of NVP is longer in pregnant women, with a mean of 66 hours compared with 45 hours in non-pregnant women.

- In a study carried out in Uganda, a single intrapartum dose of NVP (200 mg PO at onset of labor) and a single dose given to the infant (2 mg/kg within 72 hours of birth) was superior to intrapartum AZT (600 mg at onset of labor, then 300 mg q3h until delivery) and AZT to the infant (4 mg/kg/day x 7 days). Perinatal transmission occurred in 13.1% of the NVP recipients vs 21.5% of the AZT recipients (*Lancet* 1999;354:795).
- The DHHS guidelines include NVP as an option for prevention of perinatal transmission for HIV infected women who present at term with no prior therapy. A single oral dose of 200 mg is given at the

onset of labor, and a single dose (2 mg/kg) is given to the infant at 48 to 72 hours (http://www.aidsinfo.org).

- WHO guidelines include NVP as a preferred regimen for HIV infected women who are pregnant or women for whom effective contraception cannot be assured in resource-limited areas (*Scaling Up Antiretroviral Therapy*, WHO, April 2002).

NIZORAL – see Ketoconazole (p. 250)

NORTRIPTYLINE – see also Tricyclic Antidepressants (p. 314)

TRADE NAMES: *Aventyl* (Eli Lilly), *Pamelor* (Mallinckrodt), or generic

FORMS AND PRICES: Caps: 10 mg at $0.41, 25 mg at $0.82, 50 mg at $1.52, 75 mg at $2.23. Oral suspension: 10 mg/5 mL, 480 mL at $45.68.

CLASS: Tricyclic antidepressant

INDICATIONS AND DOSE REGIMENS

- **Depression:** 25 mg hs initially; increase by 25 mg every 3 days until 75 mg, then wait 5 days, and obtain level with expectation of 100-150 ng/dL.
- **Neuropathic pain:** 10-25 mg hs; increase dose over 2 to 3 weeks to maximum of 75 mg hs. Draw serum levels if higher doses used.

PHARMACOLOGY

- **Bioavailability:** >90%
- **T½:** 13 to 79 hours, mean – 31 hours
- **Elimination:** Metabolized and excreted renally

SIDE EFFECTS: Anticholinergic effects (dry mouth, dizziness, blurred vision, constipation, urinary hesitancy), orthostatic hypotension (less compared with other tricyclics), sedation, sexual dysfunction (decreased libido), and weight gain.

DRUG INTERACTIONS: The following drugs should not be given concurrently: Adrenergic neuronal blocking agents, clonidine, other alpha-2 agonists, excessive alcohol, fenfluramine, cimetidine, MAO inhibitors, and any drugs that increase nortriptyline levels (cimetidine, quinidine, fluconazole).

PREGNANCY: Category D. Animal studies are inconclusive, and experience in pregnant women is inadequate. Avoid during first trimester, and when possible limit use in the last two trimesters.

NORVIR – see Ritonavir (p. 293)

NYSTATIN

TRADE NAMES: *Mycostatin* (Bristol-Myers Squibb) or generic

FORMS AND PRICES (generic)

- **Lozenges:** 200,000 units at $1.03/lozenge
- **Cream:** 100,000 U/g, 15 g at $2.64; 30 g at $5.00
- **Ointment:** 100,000 U/g, 15 g at $2.64; 30 g at $5.00
- **Suspension:** 100,000 U/mL, 60 mL at $6.25; 480 mL at $82.63
- **Oral tabs:** 500,000 units at $0.64/tab
- **Vaginal tabs:** 100,000 units at $0.47/tab

PATIENT ASSISTANCE PROGRAM (Bristol-Myers Squibb): 800-272-4878

CLASS: Polyene macrolide similar to amphotericin B

ACTIVITY: Active against *C. albicans* at 3 µg/mL and other *Candida* species at higher concentrations.

INDICATIONS AND DOSES

- **Thrush:** 5 mL suspension to be gargled 4x/day x 14 days. Disadvantages: *Nystatin* has a bitter taste, causes GI side effects, must be given 4x/day, and does not work as well as clotrimazole troches or oral fluconazole (*HIV Clin Trials* 2000;1:47).
- **Vaginitis:** 100,000 unit tab intravaginally 1-2x/day x 14 days

PHARMACOLOGY

- **Bioavailability:** Poorly absorbed and undetectable in blood following oral administration
- Therapeutic levels persist in saliva for 2 hours after oral dissolution of two lozenges.

SIDE EFFECTS: Infrequent, dose-related GI intolerance (transient nausea, vomiting, diarrhea)

OXANDROLONE

TRADE NAME: *Oxandrin* (BTG)

FORMS AND PRICE: 2.5 mg tab at $3.75 ($7.50 – $32.00/day) and 10 mg tab at $17.50

PATIENT ASSISTANCE PROGRAM: 866-692-6374

CLASS: Anabolic steroid

INDICATION AND DOSES: Wasting. Prior studies showed a modest weight gain after 16 weeks with a dose of 15 mg/day (*AIDS* 1996;10:1657; *AIDS* 1996;10:745; *Br J Nutr* 1996;75:129). 2.5 mg 2 to 4x/day, up to 20 mg/day in 2 to 4 doses depending on response.

TRIALS: In a placebo-controlled trial using oxandrolone at a dose of 15 mg/day, drug recipients had significant increases in weight, appetite, and physical activity (*AIDS* 1996;10:1657). Body impedance analysis with recipients of 20 mg/day show significant increases in lean body mass.

PHARMACOLOGY: Bioavailability is 97%

SIDE EFFECTS: Virilizing complications primarily in women, including deep voice, hirsutism, acne, clitoral enlargement, and menstrual irregularity. Some virilizing changes may be irreversible, even with prompt discontinuation. Men may experience increased acne and increased frequency of erections. Hepatic toxicity with cholestatic hepatitis; discontinue drug if jaundice occurs or abnormal liver function tests are obtained. Drug-induced jaundice is reversible. Peliosis hepatis (blood-filled cysts) has been reported and may result in life-threatening hepatic failure or intra-abdominal hemorrhage (reversible with drug discontinuation). Miscellaneous: Nausea, vomiting, changes in skin color, ankle swelling, depression, insomnia, and changes in libido.

DRUG INTERACTIONS: Increase activity of oral anticoagulants and oral hypoglycemic agents

PREGNANCY: Category X. Teratogenic

OXYMETHOLONE

TRADE NAME: *Anadrol-50* (Unimed Pharmaceuticals)

FORM AND PRICE: 50 mg tab at $14.88

CLASS: Anabolic steroid

INDICATIONS AND DOSES: Wasting. 1-5 mg/kg/day

MONITOR: LFTs, x-ray for bone density every 6 months, blood lipids, CBC

PHARMACOLOGY

- **Bioavailability:** (?)
- **T½:** 1 to 2 days (?)
- **Elimination:** Metabolized in liver; 20% to 25% excreted in urine

SIDE EFFECTS: Peliosis hepatis (blood-filled cysts in liver ± spleen with mildly abnormal LFTs), but may also cause cholestatic jaundice, overt liver failure, hepatic necrosis (rare), liver cancer (rare), or intra-abdominal hemorrhage. Decreased HDL with increased risk of cardiovascular disease. Virilization in women. GI: Nausea, vomiting, diarrhea. Osteoporosis, decreased TSH and T4, increased pro-time and blood glucose.

DRUG INTERACTION: *Coumadin* – increase prothrombin time

CONTRAINDICATIONS: Breast cancer, severe liver disease, nephrosis, prostate cancer

PREGNANCY: Category X. Animal studies show embryo toxicity, fetotoxicity, infertility, and masculinization.

PAMELOR – see Nortriptyline (p. 272)

PANCRELIPASE

TRADE NAME: *Pancrease* and *Pancrease MT* (Ortho-McNeil), *Viokase*, *Ultrase* and *Ultrase MT* (Scandipharm), or generic

FORMS AND PRICE: *Ultrase MT 6* capsules (6000 units lipase), *Ultrase MT 12* (12,000 units lipase), *Ultrase MT 18* (18,000 units lipase), *Ultrase MT 20* (20,000 units lipase) – $0.30/*MT 6* capsule and $1.56/*MT 20* capsule. *Pancrease MT 10* (10,000 units lipase).

CLASS: Enteric coated microspheres of porcine pancreatic enzymes – lipase, amylase, and protease

INDICATIONS AND DOSE: Indicated for pancreatic insufficiency (FDA labeling). 1 to 3 capsules with meals, up to 8 capsules for severe disease. Caps should be swallowed and not chewed.

EFFICACY IN HIV INFECTED PATIENTS: Limited data suggest benefit for some HIV infected patients with chronic diarrhea or with NFV-induced diarrhea. This treatment is suggested only after there is failure to respond to fiber supplements, antiperistaltic agents, and dietary modification. *Ultrase* has been most extensively studied in HIV infected patients and is relatively well tolerated, although other, less expensive preparations may also be effective.

PHARMACOLOGY: Irrelevant – not absorbed

SIDE EFFECTS: Gastrointestinal intolerance – abdominal pain (5%), diarrhea (4%)

DRUG INTERACTIONS: H_2 blockers and proton pump inhibitors decrease destruction of pancrelipase and may increase activity.

PREGNANCY: Category C

PAROMOMYCIN

TRADE NAME: *Humatin* (Monarch Pharmaceuticals and Caraco), or generic

FORM AND PRICE: 250 mg cap at $3.03 ($504/21 day course)

CLASS: Aminoglycoside (for oral use)

INDICATIONS AND DOSE: Cryptosporidiosis. 1 g PO bid or 500 mg PO qid

EFFICACY: The drug is active *in vitro* against cryptosporidia and in animal models but only at levels far higher than those achieved in humans. There are anecdotal reports of clinical response but controlled trials show marginal benefit and no cures (*Clin Infect Dis* 1992;15:726; *Am J Med* 1996;100:370). An uncontrolled trial showed good results with paromomycin 1 g bid + azithromycin 600 mg qd x 4 weeks, then paromomycin 1 g bid (alone) x 8 weeks (*J Infect Dis* 1998;178:900). At present, there is a consensus that there is no effective chemotherapy for cryptosporidiosis except immune reconstitution with HAART. Even modest increases in CD4 counts are effective (*N Engl J Med* 2002;346:1723).

PHARMACOLOGY

- **Bioavailability:** Not absorbed; most of oral dose is excreted unchanged in stool; lesions of the GI tract may facilitate absorption and serum levels may increase in presence of renal failure.

SIDE EFFECTS: GI intolerance (anorexia, nausea, vomiting, epigastric pain), steatorrhea, and malabsorption; rare complications include rash, headache; vertigo with absorption and serum levels. There could be ototoxicity and nephrotoxicity with systemic absorption as with other aminoglycosides.

PREGNANCY: Category C

PEGYLATED INTERFERON

TRADE NAMES: Peginterferon alfa-2a – *Pegasys* (Roche); peginterferon alfa-2b – *Peg-Intron* (Schering-Plough)

FORMS

- Peginterferon alfa-2a (*Pegasys*) is supplied as a solution ready for injection, which requires refrigeration and is available at a fixed dose of 180 µg per 1 mL solution.
- Peginterferon alfa-2b (*Peg-Intron*) is supplied as lyophilized powder to be reconstituted with 0.7 mL saline; several strengths are available based upon body weight shown in Table 6-33.

■ TABLE 6-33: **Pegylated Interferon Alfa-2b (*Peg-Intron*) Forms, Dose, and Price**

Body Weight	Peginterferon Alfa-2b Vial Strength	Amount to Administer	Volume (mL) to Administer	Cost/Package
<40 kg	50 µg per 0.5 mL	50 µg	0.5 mL	—
40-50 kg 51-60 kg	80 µg per 0.5 mL	64 µg 80 µg	0.4 mL 0.5 mL	$344.95
61-75 kg 75-85 kg	120 µg per 0.5 mL	96 µg 120 µg	0.4 mL 0.5 mL	$362.21
>85 kg	150 µg per 0.5 mL	150 µg	0.5 mL	$380.58

* Each package also contains 1.0 mL diluent, two syringes (1 for dilution and 1 for injection), and alcohol swabs. Store at 25°C.

PRICE (AWP): *Pegasys* – $17,460/year and *Peg-Intron* – $17,892/year. AWP costs for 70 kg patient treated for 48 weeks: Peginterferon + ribavirin – approximately $30,216 to $40,152

PATIENT ASSISTANCE PROGRAM: 877-734-2797 (*Pegasys*) and 800-521-7157 (*Peg-Intron*)

PRODUCT: Recombinant alfa-interferon conjugated with polyethylene glycol (PEG), which decreases the clearance rate of interferon and results in sustained concentrations permitting less frequent dosing. The side effect profile and efficacy of pegylated and non-pegylated interferons appear to be similar.

INDICATIONS AND DOSE: FDA indications: Treatment of compensated chronic hepatitis C not previously treated with interferon alpha. HIV-HCV co-infected patients are candidates for anti-HCV therapy if they are considered at high risk for cirrhosis based on a liver biopsy showing bridging fibrosis and inflammation plus HCV RNA levels >50 IU/mL (*Hepatology* 2002;36[suppl 1]:S161; Evidence Report #60, AHRO Pub No. 02-E030, July 2002). HCV patients with or without HIV are not considered candidates for this treatment if there is active substance abuse, decompensated liver disease, severe, active psychiatric disease or refusal (*Ann Intern Med* 2002;136:288).

- **Dose**
  - Peginterferon alfa-2a: 180 µg SQ every week + ribavirin 1000-1200 mg/day x 48 weeks for HCV genotype 1 and peginterferon alfa-2a: 180 µg SQ every week + 800 mg/day x 24 weeks for HCV genotype 2 or 3
  - Peginterferon alfa-2b: 1.5 µg/kg SQ every week (see Table 6-33) + ribavirin 800 mg/day (*Lancet* 2001;358:958) or weight-based ribavirin at 1000-1200 mg/day
  - Renal failure: Consider reduction to half dose with CrCl <50 mL/min (*N Engl J Med* 2002;347:975).

■ TABLE 6-34: **Guidelines for Treatment of HCV With Peginterferon + Ribavirin**

Duration Genotype	HCV Qualitative Test at Baseline and 12 Weeks*	Total Duration
1	<2 log ↓ and HCV RNA detectable: Discontinue treatment	48 weeks
2 or 3	Week 12 testing not indicated since >95% of patients achieve >2 $\log_{10}$ ↓	24-48 weeks†

* Probability of HCV eradication in persons with ≤2 $\log_{10}$ c/mL decrease at 12 weeks is 2% (*Hepatology* 2002 Nov;36:S145-51).

† HCV genotype 2 and 3 infection: SVR with 24 weeks is comparable to 48 weeks (European Association for the Study of the Liver, Madrid, Spain, 2002, Abstract 356)

AFTER RECONSTITUTION: Use immediately or store for up to 24 hours at 2°C to 8°C (36°F to 46°F). Discard unused portion.

MONITORING

- **Clinical response:** HCV RNA at 12 weeks (see Table 6-34). Persons with detectable HCV RNA at 12 weeks who demonstrates >2 $\log_{10}$ ↓ should be re-tested at 24 weeks of therapy. If HCV RNA is detectable after 24 weeks, considered discontinuation. Sustained virologic response is defined as undetectable HCV RNA at 24 weeks post therapy.
- **Toxicity:** CBC, Comprehensive Metabolic Panel at baseline, at 2 weeks, then every 6 weeks. TSH at baseline and then every 12 weeks
- **Patients with cardiac disease:** EKG at baseline and prn.
- **Women of childbearing potential:** Urine pregnancy testing every 4 to 6 weeks.

CLINICAL TRIALS: Meta-analysis of clinical trials indicates that the overall probability of achieving sustained virologic suppression with standard interferon ± ribavirin (no detectable HCV at 6 months post therapy) is 30% to 50%; with genotype 1, it is 20% to 30%, and for non-genotype 1, it is 40% to 80% (*Lancet* 2001;358:958; *N Engl J Med* 2000;343:1673). Poor prognostic indicators are cirrhosis, male gender, genotype 1, and prior interferon failure. More recent data with peginterferon alfa-2a (180 µg/week) or peginterferon alfa-2b (1.5 µg/kg/week) plus ribavirin in varying doses showed sustained virologic response in 42% to 46% with genotype 1 and 67% to 78% with genotype 2/3; (*Lancet* 2001; 358:958, *N Engl J Med* 2002;347:975). Peginterferon alfa-2a or alfa-2b + ribavirin is the treatment of choice (NIH Consensus).

PHARMACOLOGY

- **Bioavailability:** Increases with duration of therapy – mean trough with 1 µg/kg SQ at week 4=94 pg/mL, at week 48=320 pg/mL. C_{max} mean is 554 pg/mL at 15 to 44 hours and sustained up to 48 to 72 hours. Compared to non-pegylated interferon, peginterferon C_{max} is about 10x greater and AUC is 50x greater.
- **T½:** 22 to 60 hours (compared with 8 hours for non-pegylated interferon).

- **Elimination:** Renal 30% (7x lower clearance than non-pegylated interferon).

SIDE EFFECTS: Similar to those of interferon; about 10% in clinical trials discontinue therapy due to adverse reactions.

- **Neuropsychiatric:** Depression, suicidal or homicidal ideation, and relapse of substance abuse. Should be used with extreme caution in patients with history of psychiatric disorders. Warn patient and monitor. Depression reported in 21% to 29%. Suicides reported. Active depression with suicidal ideation is a contraindication.
- **Marrow suppression:** PMN counts decrease in 70%, <500/mm^3 in 1%, platelet counts decrease in 20%, <20,000/mm^3 in 1%. Recommendation:

■ TABLE 6-35: **Marrow Toxicity – Criteria for Dose Reduction/Discontinuation**

Laboratory Measurement	Criteria for Dose Reduction to 0.5 µg/mL	Criteria for Discontinue
PMN*	<750/mm^3	<500/mm^3
Platelet count	<50,000/mm^3	<25,000/mm^3

* Leukopenia generally responds to G-CSF, which may be preferred to avoid dose reduction.

- **Flu-like symptoms:** Most common; about 50% will have fever, headache, chills, and myalgias/arthralgias. May decrease with continued treatment. May be treated with NSAIDS or acetaminophen; with liver disease acetaminophen dose should be <2 g/day.
- **Thyroid:** Thyroiditis with hyperthyroidism or hypothyroidism. TSH levels should be measured at baseline and during therapy every 12 weeks.
- **Retinopathy:** Obtain baseline retinal evaluation in patients with diabetes, hypertension or other ocular abnormality.
- **Injection site reaction:** Inflammation, pruritus, pain (mild) in 47%
- **GI complaints:** Nausea, anorexia, diarrhea, and/or abdominal pain in 15% to 30%
- **Skin/hair:** Alopecia (20%), pruritus (10%), and/or rash (6%)
- **Miscellaneous:** Hyperglycemia, cardiac arrhythmias, elevated hepatic transaminase levels 2 to 5x, colitis, pancreatitis, autoimmune disorders, hypersensitivity reactions

DRUG INTERACTIONS: None (note: clinically important interactions with ribavirin, see p. 286)

PREGNANCY: Category C. Abortifacient potential in primates. Ribavirin is a potent teratogen and must be avoided in pregnancy and used with caution in women of childbearing potential and their male sexual partners. Breastfeeding: No data.

PENTAM – see Pentamidine (p. 280)

PENTAMIDINE

TRADE NAME: *Pentam* for IV use; *NebuPent* for inhalation (American Pharmaceutical Partners)

FORMS AND PRICE: 300 mg vial at $138

- Cost of PCP prophylaxis: $138/month, aerosolized
- Cost of PCP treatment: $2,900/month
- Alternatives for prophylaxis: TMP-SMX (1 DS/day): $5.40/month, dapsone $6.00/month

PATIENT ASSISTANCE PROGRAM: IV and aerosolized pentamidine 888-391-6300

CLASS: Aromatic diamidine-derivative antiprotozoal agent that is structurally related to stilbamidine

INDICATIONS AND DOSES

- ***P. carinii* pneumonia:** 3-4 mg/kg IV x 21 days. The approved dose is 4 mg/kg, but some clinicians prefer 3 mg/kg. TMP-SMX is preferred (*Ann Intern Med* 1986;105:37; *AIDS* 1992;6:301).
- ***P. carinii* prophylaxis:** 300 mg/month delivered by a *Respirgard II* nebulizer using 300 mg dose diluted in 6 mL sterile water delivered at 6 L/min from a 50 psi compressed air source until the reservoir is dry. TMP-SMX preferred due to superior efficacy in preventing PCP, efficacy in preventing other infections, reduced cost, and greater convenience (*N Engl J Med* 1995;332:693). Aerosolized pentamidine should not be used for PCP treatment (*Ann Intern Med* 1990;113:203).

PHARMACOLOGY

- **Bioavailability:** Not absorbed orally. With aerosol, 5% reaches alveolar spaces via *Respirgard II* nebulizer. Blood levels with monthly aerosol delivery are below detectable limits.
- **T½:** Parenteral – 6 hours
- **Elimination:** Primarily nonrenal but may accumulate in renal failure
- **Dose modification of parenteral form with renal failure:** CrCl >50 mL/min – 4 mg/kg q24h; 10-50 mL/min – 4 mg/kg q24h-q36h; <10 mL/min – 4 mg/kg q48h.

SIDE EFFECTS

- **Aerosolized pentamidine:** Risk of transmitting TB to patients and healthcare workers. Cough and wheezing – 30% (prevented with pretreatment with beta-2 agonist), sufficiently severe to require discontinuation of treatment in 5% (*N Engl J Med* 1990;323:769). Other reactions include laryngitis, chest pain, and dyspnea. The role of aerosolized pentamidine in promoting extrapulmonary *P. carinii* infection and pneumothorax is unclear.

- **Systemic pentamidine:** In a review of 106 courses of IV pentamidine, 76 (72%) had adverse reactions; these were sufficiently severe to require drug discontinuation in 31 (18%) (*Clin Infect Dis* 1997;24:854). The most common causes of drug discontinuation were nephrotoxicity and hypoglycemia. Nephrotoxicity is noted in 25% to 50%. It is usually characterized by a gradual increase in creatinine in the second week of treatment but may cause acute renal failure. Risk is increased with dehydration and concurrent use of nephrotoxic drugs. Hypotension is unusual (6%) but may cause death, most often with rapid infusions; drug should be infused over ≥60 minutes. Hypoglycemia with blood glucose 25 mg/dL in 5% to 10%, usually after 5 to 7 days of treatment and sometimes several days after treatment is stopped. Hypoglycemia may last days or weeks and is treated with IV glucose ± oral diazoxide. Hyperglycemia (2% to 9%) and insulin-dependent diabetes mellitus may occur with or without prior hypoglycemia. Leukopenia and thrombocytopenia are noted in 2% to 13%. GI intolerance with nausea, vomiting, abdominal pain, anorexia, and/or bad taste is common. Local reactions include sterile abscesses at IM injection sites (no longer advocated) and pain, erythema, tenderness, and induration (chemical phlebitis) at IV infusion sites. Other reactions include hepatitis, hypocalcemia (sometimes severe), increased amylase, hypomagnesemia, fever, rash, urticaria, toxic epidermal necrolysis (TEN), confusion, dizziness (without hypotension), anaphylaxis, arrhythmias including Torsade de pointes.

MONITORING

- **Aerosolized pentamidine:** This is considered safe for the patient but poses risk of TB to healthcare workers and other patients. Patient should be evaluated for TB (PPD, x-ray, sputum examination). Suspected or confirmed TB should be treated prior to aerosol treatments. Adequate air exchanges with exhaust to outside and appropriate use of particulate air filters are required. Some suggest pregnant HCWs should avoid environmental exposure to pentamidine until risks to fetus are better defined.
- **Parenteral administration:** Adverse effects are common and may be lethal. Due to the risk of hypotension, the drug should be given in supine position, the patient should be hydrated, pentamidine should be delivered over ≥60 minutes, and BP should be monitored during treatment and afterward until stable. Regular laboratory monitoring (daily or every other day) should include creatinine, potassium, calcium, and glucose; other tests for periodic monitoring include CBC, LFTs, and calcium.

DRUG INTERACTIONS: Avoid concurrent use of parenteral pentamidine with nephrotoxic drugs, including aminoglycosides, amphotericin B, and foscarnet and cidofovir. Amphotericin B – severe hypocalcemia.

PREGNANCY: Category C. Aerosolized pentamidine is considered safe because systemic absorption is limited (*Clin Infect Dis* 1995;21[suppl 1]:S24).

PRAVASTATIN

TRADE NAME: *Pravachol* (Bristol-Myers Squibb)

FORMS AND PRICES: Tabs: 10 mg at $2.78, 20 mg at $2.78, 40 mg at $4.34

CLASS: Statin (HMG-CoA reductase inhibitor)

INDICATIONS AND DOSES: Elevated total cholesterol, LDL cholesterol, and/or triglycerides and to increase HDL cholesterol. Initial dose is 40 mg once daily. If desired cholesterol levels are not achieved with 40 mg daily, 80 mg once daily is recommended. A starting does of 10 mg daily is recommended in patients with a history of significant hepatic or renal dysfunction. Can be administered as a single dose at any time of the day.

MONITORING: Blood lipids at 4-week intervals until desired results are achieved, then periodically. It is recommended that liver function tests be performed prior to the initiation of therapy, prior to the elevation of the dose, and when otherwise clinically indicated. Patients should be warned to report muscle pain, tenderness, or weakness promptly, especially if accompanied by fever or malaise; obtain CPK for suspected myopathy.

PRECAUTIONS: Pravastatin (and other statins) are contraindicated with pregnancy, breastfeeding, concurrent conditions that predispose to renal failure (sepsis, hypotension, etc.) and active hepatic disease. Alcoholism is a relative contraindication.

PHARMACOLOGY

- **Bioavailability:** 14%
- **T½:** 1.3 to 2.7 hours
- **Elimination:** Fecal (biliary and unabsorbed drug) – 70%; renal – 20%

SIDE EFFECTS

- **Musculoskeletal:** Myopathy with elevated CPK plus muscle tenderness, weakness, or pain + fever or malaise. Rhabdomyolysis with renal failure has been reported.
- **Hepatic:** Elevated transaminase levels in 1% to 2%; discontinue if otherwise unexplained elevations of ALT and/or AST are >3x ULN.
- **Miscellaneous:** Diarrhea, constipation, nausea, heartburn, stomach pain, dizziness, headache, skin rash (eczematous plaques), insomnia, and impotence (rare)

DRUG INTERACTIONS: PIs: Concurrent use considered safe with IDV, SQV, RTV, APV, and LPV/r. NNRTIs are thought to be safe for concurrent use. Possible interactions with spironolactone, cimetidine, and ketoconazole that reduce cholesterol levels and may effect adrenal and sex hormone production with concurrent use. Itraconazole increases pravastatin AUC and C_{max} 1.7x and 2.5x, respectively. Cholestyramine and colestipol decrease pravastatin AUC 40%. Niacin and gemfibrozil – increased risk of myopathy. Rare cases of rhabdomyolysis with acute renal failure secondary to myoglobinuria have been reported with pravastatin and other drugs in this class.

PREGNANCY: Category X

PRIMAQUINE

TRADE NAME: Generic

FORM AND PRICE: 15 mg base tabs (26 mg primaquine phosphate) at $0.90

CLASS: Antimalarial

INDICATIONS AND DOSES: *P. carinii* pneumonia: Primaquine 15-30 mg (base)/day + clindamycin 600-900 mg q6-8h IV or 300-450 mg PO q6-8h. **Note:** The published experience and recommendation is for "mild to moderately severe" PCP (*Ann Intern Med* 1996;124:792; *Clin Infect Dis* 1994;18:905; *Clin Infect Dis* 1998;27:524). A meta-analysis of published reports of PCP patients who failed initial treatment showed the clindamycin-primaquine regimen was superior to all others with responses in 42 of 48 (87%) (*Arch Intern Med* 2001;161:1529).

PHARMACOLOGY

- **Bioavailability:** Well absorbed
- **T½:** 4 to 10 hours
- **Elimination:** Metabolized by liver

SIDE EFFECTS: Hemolytic anemia in patients with G6-PD deficiency; its severity depends on drug dose and genetics of G6-PD deficiency. In African Americans, the reaction is usually mild, self-limited and asymptomatic; in patients of Mediterranean or certain Asian extractions, hemolysis may be severe. Hemolytic anemia may also occur with other forms of hemoglobinopathy. Warn patient of dark urine as sign and/or measure G6-PD level prior to use in susceptible individuals. Other hematologic side effects: Methemoglobinemia, leukopenia. GI: Nausea, vomiting, epigastric pain (reduced by administration with meals). Miscellaneous: Headache, disturbed visual accommodation, pruritus, hypertension, arrhythmias.

PREGNANCY: Category C

PROCRIT – see Erythropoietin (p. 214)

PYRAZINAMIDE (PZA)

TRADE NAME: Generic

FORM AND PRICE: 500 mg tab at $1.12 (usually 2 g/day at $4.48/day)

CLASS: Derivative of niacinamide

INDICATION AND REGIMEN: Tuberculosis, initial phase of three to four drug regimen, usually for 8 weeks (*MMWR* 1998;47[RR-20]; *MMWR* 2000;49:185). Treatment of latent tuberculosis: PZA + rifampin regimen (see rifampin p. 291). Note that the dose for PZA for treatment of latent infection is ≤20 mg/kg/day and not to exceed 2.0 g/day. For active TB, the dose is 20-25 mg/kg/day (2.0 g max). For intermittent therapy (DOT), the dose is 30-50 mg/kg 2 to 3 times/week (3.0-4.0 g max).

TREATMENT WITH *RIFATER* (tabs with 50 mg INH, 120 mg rifampin, and 300 mg PZA)

- <65 kg: 1 tab/10 kg/day
- >65 kg: 6 tabs/day

PHARMACOLOGY

- **Bioavailability:** Well absorbed; absorption is reduced about 25% in patients with advanced HIV infection (*Ann Intern Med* 1997;127:289).
- **T½:** 9 to 10 hours
- **CSF levels:** Equal to plasma levels
- **Elimination:** Hydrolyzed in liver; 4% to 14% of parent compound and 70% of metabolite excreted in urine.
- **Renal failure:** Usual dose unless creatinine clearance <10 mL/min – 12-20 mg/kg/day
- **Hepatic failure:** Contraindicated

SIDE EFFECTS: Hepatotoxicity in up to 15% who receive >3 g/day – transient hepatitis with increase in transaminases, jaundice, and a syndrome of fever, anorexia, and hepatomegaly; rarely, acute yellow atrophy. Monitor LFTs. Hyperuricemia is common, but gout is rare. Nongouty polyarthralgia in up to 40%; hyperuricemia usually responds to uricosuric agents. Use with caution in patients with history of gout. Rare – rash, fever, acne, dysuria, skin discoloration, urticaria, pruritus, GI intolerance, thrombocytopenia, sideroblastic anemia.

PREGNANCY: Category C. Not tested in animals or in humans. Conclusion is that risk of teratogenicity is unknown, so INH, rifampin, and EMB are preferred. PZA is advocated for pregnant women if resistant *M. tuberculosis* is suspected or established and is acceptable outside the United States per WHO guidelines.

PYRIMETHAMINE

TRADE NAME: *Daraprim* (GlaxoSmithKline) or generic

FORM AND PRICE: 25 mg tab at $0.55

PATIENT ASSISTANCE PROGRAM: 800-722-9294

CLASS: Aminopyrimidine-derivative antimalarial agent that is structurally related to trimethoprim

INDICATIONS AND DOSE REGIMENS: Toxoplasmosis

■ TABLE 6-36: **Toxoplasmosis Treatment**

	Acute Phase (3 to 6 weeks)	Maintenance
First line	Pyrimethamine 200 mg x 1 then 50-75 mg/d + leucovorin 10-20 mg/d + sulfadiazine 1-1.5 g qid	Pyrimethamine 25-50 mg/d + leucovorin 10-25 mg/d + sulfadiazine 0.5-1.0 g PO qid
Second line	Pyrimethamine + leucovorin (above doses) + clindamycin 600 mg PO or IV q 6-8h	Pyrimethamine + leucovorin (above doses) + clindamycin 300-450 mg PO q 6-8h
Third line	Pyrimethamine + leucovorin (above doses) + either ■ Atovaquone 1500 mg PO bid ■ Azithromycin 900-1200 mg/d ■ Clarithromycin 500 mg PO bid ■ Dapsone 100 mg PO/d ■ Minocycline 150-200 mg bid	Pyrimethamine + leucovorin + 2nd antimicrobial in same dose

- **Primary prophylaxis:** Pyrimethamine 50 mg PO/week + dapsone 50 mg PO/day + leucovorin 25 mg/week or pyrimethamine 75 mg/week + dapsone 200 mg/week and leucovorin 25 mg/week or atovaquone 1500 mg/day ± pyrimethamine 25 mg/day + leucovorin 10 mg/day.

PHARMACOLOGY

- **Bioavailability:** Well absorbed
- **T½:** 54 to 148 hours (average 111 hours)
- **Elimination:** Parent compound and metabolites excreted in urine
- **Dose modification in renal failure:** None

SIDE EFFECTS: Reversible marrow suppression due to depletion of folic acid stores with dose-related megaloblastic anemia, leukopenia, thrombocytopenia, and agranulocytosis; prevented or treated with folinic acid (leucovorin).

- **GI intolerance:** Improved by reducing dose or giving drug with meals
- **Neurologic:** Dose-related ataxia, tremors, or seizures
- **Hypersensitivity:** Most common with pyrimethamine plus sulfadoxine (*Fansidar*) and due to sulfonamide component of combination
- **Drug interactions:** Lorazepam – hepatotoxicity

PREGNANCY: Category C. Teratogenic in animals.

REBETOL – see Ribavirin (below)

RETROVIR – see Zidovudine (AZT, ZDV) (p. 327)

RHO (D) IMMUNE GLOBULIN

TRADE NAME: *WinRho* (Univax)

FORMS AND PRICES: Vials of 600 IU at $103 and 1500 IU at $324. Cost of IVIG (1000 mg/kg): $3,570 to $4,569 (*Med Letter* 1996;38:8). Cost of *Win Rho* (AWP) is $972/4500 units.

INDICATION AND DOSES: Idiopathic thrombocytopenic purpura (ITP) in patient who is Rh-positive. Advantages over IVIG: Short infusion time, modest cost reduction and, in some cases, availability. Usual dose: 50 μg/kg or 3500 IU (70 kg). With hemoglobin levels <10 g/dL, give 25-50 μg/kg to reduce the severity of anemia. A disadvantage is the slow onset of action.

- **Note:** Patients must have intact spleen and be Rho(D)-positive for a biologic effect with treatment for ITP.

REGIMEN: Initial dose – 50 μg/kg IV over 3 to 5 minutes. May repeat at 3 to 4 days and may increase dose up to 80 μg/kg. Most patients require maintenance doses of 25-60 μg/kg.

MECHANISM: This product was developed to provide anti-D globulin to prevent Rh-isoimmunization in Rh-negative pregnant women with an Rh-positive fetus. Injection of anti-D into Rh-positive patients with ITP coats the patient's D+ RBCs with antibodies; this spares splenic clearance of antibody-coated platelets (*Trans Med Rev* 1992;6:17).

CLINICAL TRIALS: The average increase in platelets, including in patients with HIV-associated ITP, is 50,000/mm^3 (*Am J Hematol* 1986;22:241; *Blood* 1991;77:1884). The response is somewhat delayed compared to IVIG. The effect lasts an average of 3 weeks.

SIDE EFFECTS: Hemolysis with decreases in hemoglobin of ≥2 g/dL in 5% to 10%. Monitor CBC. Fever and chills 1 to 2 hours after infusion (presumably due to hemolysis) in 10%; this can be avoided or reduced in severity with acetaminophen, *Benadryl*, or prednisone or by increasing infusion time to 15 to 20 minutes. Vial should not be shaken due to possible damage of protein or formation of aggregates.

PREGNANCY: Category C

RIBAVIRIN

TRADE NAME: *Rebetol* and *Rebetron* (combined *Rebetrol/Intron A*) (Schering-Plough)

FORMS AND PRICES: 200 mg caps at $9.83. Cost at 5/day x 6 months is $8,260. Ribavirin is also provided as a Therapy Pak (*Rebetron*) in combination with interferon (*Intron*); cost of 84 caps (6 caps/day) *Rebetron* + 6 vials *Intron* is $888.76 or 70 caps (5 caps/day) *Rebetron* + 6 vials *Intron* is $804.32. The relative AWP costs for a 70 kg patient treated 48 weeks are: Peginterferon alfa-2b + ribavirin – $28,608; interferon + ribavirin – $19,296.

NOTE: Use with caution when given with AZT, ddI, or d4T due to potentiation of mitochondrial toxicity. There has been an FDA warning for ddI + ribavirin based on 24 cases of pancreatitis and/or lactic acidosis (10/2/02). ddI + ribavirin should be avoided.

INDICATION (FDA labeling): Ribavirin in combination with interferon is recommended for treatment of chronic hepatitis C in patients with compensated liver disease who have not previously been treated, and in patients who have relapsed after interferon monotherapy.

REGIMEN: 400 mg PO bid or weight based dosing (preferred):

■ TABLE 6-37: **Ribavirin Regimen**

Weight	Ribavirin
<75 kg	2 x 200 mg caps AM 3 x 200 mg caps PM
>75 kg	3 x 200 mg caps bid

CLINICAL TRIALS: Several trials have tested the relative efficacy of HCV treatment using ribavirin + interferon vs interferon alone. The results show sustained viral suppression in up to 56% given the combination (*N Engl J Med* 2000;343:1677; *Gastroenterol* 1999; *Lancet* 2001;358: 958; *N Engl J Med* 2002;347:975). None of these large trials included HIV-HCV co-infected patients, but preliminary data show a sustained virologic response in 41% (*HIV Clin Trials* 2002;3:99).

PHARMACOLOGY

- **Oral bioavailability:** 64%, absorption increased with high-fat meal
- **T½:** 30 hours
- **Elimination:** Metabolized by phosphorylation and deribosylation; there are few or no cytochrome P450 enzyme-based drug interactions. Metabolites are excreted in the urine. The drug should not be used with severe renal failure.

SIDE EFFECTS: About 6% of patients receiving ribavirin/interferon discontinue therapy due to side effects. The main side effects are anemia, cough, and dyspepsia. Hemolytic anemia is noted in the first 1 to 2 weeks of treatment and usually stabilizes by week 4. In clinical trials, the mean decrease in hemoglobin was 3 g/dL, and 10% of patients had a hemoglobin <10 g/dL. Patients with a hemoglobin <10 g/dL or decrease in hemoglobin ≥2 g/dL *and* a history of cardiovascular disease should receive a modified regimen of ribavirin 600 mg/day + interferon 1.5 million units 3x/week. The drugs should be discontinued if the hemoglobulin decreases to ≤8.5 g/dL or if the hemoglobin persists at <12 g/dL in patients with a cardiovascular disease. Erythropoietin (40,000 units SQ every week) may be effective for anemia (*Am J Gastro* 2001;96:2802). Ribavirin is a nucleoside that may cause mitochondrial toxicity, especially when combined with NRTIs used in HIV therapy; 15 such cases with lactic acidosis have been reported (*Lancet* 2001;357:280). Other side effects ascribed to ribavirin include leukopenia, hyperbilirubinemia, increased uric acid, and dyspnea.

NOTE: See Interferon (p. 243) for side effects ascribed to that agent.

DRUG INTERACTION: Ribavirin probably interacts with thymidine-phosphorylated nucleoside analogs such as AZT and d4T resulting in *in vitro* antagonism (*Science* 1987;235:1376; *Antimicrob Agents Chemother* 1997;41:1231; *AIDS* 1998;14:1661); the significance of this interaction is unknown. In combination with ddI, there is potentiation of ddI toxicity due to inhibition of mitochondrial DNA polymerase gamma, resulting in pancreatitis and lactic acidosis (*Antimicrob Agents Chemother* 1987;31:1613; *Lancet* 2001;72:177). This combination should be avoided or used with caution.

PREGNANCY: Category X. Potent teratogen. Must be used with caution in women with childbearing potential and in their male sexual partners. Adequate birth control is mandatory.

RIFABUTIN

TRADE NAME: *Mycobutin* (Pharmacia)

FORM AND PRICE: 150 mg cap at $5.72

PATIENT ASSISTANCE PROGRAM: 800-242-7014

CLASS: Semisynthetic derivative of rifampin B that is derived from *Streptomyces mediterranei*

INDICATIONS AND DOSES

- ***M. avium* prophylaxis:** 300 mg PO qd. Efficacy established (*N Engl J Med* 1993;329:828); azithromycin or clarithromycin is usually preferred.
- ***M. avium* treatment:** Sometimes combined with clarithromycin or azithromycin and EMB using 300 mg/day, except in patients treated with PIs or NNRTIs where dose adjustment is recommended (see below).
- **Tuberculosis:** Preferred rifamycin for use in combination with most PIs or NNRTIs (*MMWR* 2000;49:185). Usual dose for TB treatment and prophylaxis: 300 mg/day, but dose must be adjusted for concurrent use with PIs and/or NNRTIs: See Table 6-38, p. 291.

ACTIVITY: Active against most strains of *M. avium* and rifampin-sensitive *M. tuberculosis*; cross-resistance between rifampin and rifabutin is common with *M. tuberculosis* and *M. avium*.

PHARMACOLOGY

- **Bioavailability:** 12% to 20%
- **T½:** 30 to 60 hours
- **Elimination:** Primarily renal and biliary excretion of metabolites
- **Dose modification in renal failure:** None

SIDE EFFECTS: Common: Brown-orange discoloration of secretions; urine (30%), tears, saliva, sweat, stool, and skin. Infrequent: Rash (4%), GI intolerance (3%), neutropenia (2%). Rare: Flu-like illness, hepatitis, hemolysis, headache, thrombocytopenia, myositis. Uveitis, which presents as red and painful eye, blurred vision, photophobia, or floaters, is dose-related, usually with doses >450 mg/day, or with standard dose (300 mg/day) plus concurrent use of drugs that increase rifabutin levels: Most PIs, clarithromycin, and fluconazole (*N Engl J Med* 1994;330:868). Treated with topical corticosteroids and mydriatics. These patients should be evaluated by an ophthalmologist.

DRUG INTERACTIONS: Rifabutin induces hepatic microsomal enzymes (cytochrome P450), although the effect is less pronounced than for rifampin. Concurrent treatment with rifabutin reduces the levels of APV (14% decrease), coumadin, barbiturates, benzodiazepines, ß-adrenergic blockers, chloramphenicol, clofibrate, oral contraceptives, corticosteroids, cyclosporine, diazepam, dapsone, digitalis, doxycycline, haloperidol, oral hypoglycemics, voriconazole, ketoconazole, methadone, phenytoin, quinidine, theophylline, trimethoprim, and verapamil. Drugs that inhibit cytochrome P450 and prolong the half-life of rifabutin: PIs and DLV, erythromycin, clarithromycin (56% increase), and azoles (fluconazole, itraconazole, and ketoconazole). With concurrent rifabutin and fluconazole, the levels of rifabutin are significantly increased, leading to possible rifabutin toxicity (uveitis, nausea, neutropenia) or increased efficacy (*Clin Infect Dis* 1996;23;685).

COMMENTS

- Rifampin and rifabutin are related drugs, but *in vitro* activity and clinical trials show that rifabutin is preferred for *M. avium*, and rifampin is preferred for *M. tuberculosis*.
- Clarithromycin plus EMB without rifabutin may be the preferred regimen for treatment of disseminated *M. avium* infection due to the clarithromycin–rifabutin interaction.
- Drug interactions are similar for rifabutin and rifampin, although rifabutin is a less potent inducing agent of hepatic microsomal enzymes.
- Uveitis requires immediate discontinuation of drug and ophthalmology consult.
- All PIs and NNRTIs require a dose adjustment when given with rifabutin except for NVP (see Table 6-38, p. 291).

■ TABLE 6-38: **Rifabutin Interactions and Dose Adjustments With Antiretroviral Drugs** (DHHS Guidelines for Use of Antiretroviral Agents in Adults and Adolescents, *MMWR* 2002;51[RR-7]:1)

Agent	AUC for ART Agent	AUC for Rifabutin	Comment
Nucleosides	NC	NC	Use standard doses†
APV	↓15%	↑193%	APV – standard; rifabutin – 150 mg/day or 300 mg 2x to 3x/week
DLV	↓80%	↑100%	Contraindicated
EFV*	NC	↓35%	EFV – standard; rifabutin – 450 mg/day or 600 mg 3x/week
IDV	↓32%	↑2x	IDV – 1000 mg q8h; rifabutin – 150 mg/day or 300 mg 2-3x/week
NVP*	↓16%	↓	NVP 200 mg bid; rifabutin 300 mg 2-3x/week
NFV	↓32%	↑2x	NFV – 1000 mg tid; rifabutin – 150 mg/day or 300 mg 2-3x/week
RTV	NC	↑4x	Rifabutin – 150 mg qod; RTV – standard
SQV (*Fortovase*)	↓40%	*	Not recommended
SQV + RTV*	SQV↓ RTV – NC	↑3 fold	SQV + RTV – standard rifabutin 150 mg 2x to 3x/week
LPV/r	NC	↑3 fold	LPV/r – standard rifabutin 150 mg qod

* Limited experience.

† Regimens for 2 to 3x/week should be given 3x/week in patients with a CD4 count <100 cells/mm³ due to risk of rifampin resistance (*Am J Respir Crit Care Med* 2001;164:1319).

NC = No change

PREGNANCY: Category C. High doses in rabbits caused skeletal abnormalities; no data in humans.

RIFAMATE – see Isoniazid (p. 245) or Rifampin (below) (*Ann Intern Med* 1995;122:951)

RIFAMPIN

TRADE NAME: *Rifadin* (Aventis) or generic; Combination with INH: *Rifamate* and *Rifater* (Aventis)

FORMS AND PRICES: Caps: 150 mg, 300 mg at $1.61. *Rifamate*: Caps with 150 mg INH + 300 mg rifampin. *Rifater*: Tabs with 50 mg INH + 120 mg rifampin + 300 mg pyrazinamide at $1.90. IV vials: 600 mg at $79.38

INDICATIONS AND DOSE: Tuberculosis (with INH, PZA, and SM or EMB)

- **Dose:** 10 mg/kg/day (600 mg/day max)
- **DOT:** 600 mg 2 to 3x/week (HIV infected patients with CD4 counts <100 cells/mm^3 should not receive DOT with rifampin dose <3x/week due to acquired rifamycin-resistance shown in trials of HIV-TB co-infected patients with CD4 counts <100 cells/mm^3 treated with rifapentine once weekly or rifabutin twice weekly, each in combination with INH (*Lancet* 1999;343:1843; *MMWR* 2002;51: 214).
- **Prophylaxis (alone or in combination with PZA or EMB):** 10 mg/kg/day (600 mg/day max)
- **Antiretrovirals and TB treatment:** Rifamycins should be included in any regimen for active TB. Options with HAART include:
  - Rifampin (standard dose) + EFV, RTV or RTV/SQV. With EFV, consider increasing EFV dose to 800 mg/day.
  - Rifabutin with IDV, APV, NFV, LPV/r, SQV, or any RTV-boosted regimen in which the RTV dose is ≤200 mg bid.
  - Consider delay in antiretroviral therapy.
- **Treatment of latent tuberculosis:** Rifampin (600 mg/day) + PZA (20 mg/kg/day with 2 g/day max) x 2 months was advocated as a preferred regimen for HIV infected patients with a positive PPD due to demonstrated efficacy comparable with the 12-month INH regimen and better compliance due to the abbreviated duration. In 2001, the CDC announced six hepatotoxic deaths with this regimen; none were known to have HIV Infection (*Am J Respir Crit Care Med* 2001;164:1319). This regimen is still advocated for HIV infected patients if completion of a 9-month INH course is unlikely. Recommendations are: 1) Prescribe only a 2 week supply of drugs at a time; 2) PZA dose is ≤20 mg/kg/day and not to exceed 2 g/day; 3) Assess clinically at 2, 4, 6, and 8 weeks; 4) Obtain LFTs at baseline, 2, 4, and 6 weeks; and 5) Stop treatment if ALT is >5x ULN in asymptomatic patients, with any elevation of ALT in symptomatic patients, or with any elevated bilirubin. Avoid rifampin/PZA if prior INH-associated hepatotoxicity or unreeling liver disease.
- ***Rifater* treatment**
  - <65 kg – 1 tab/10 kg
  - >65 kg – 6 tabs/day
- **Rifampin for:** *S. aureus* (with vancomycin, fluoroquinolones, or penicillinase-resistant penicillin): 300 mg PO bid

ACTIVE AGAINST: *M. tuberculosis, M. kansasii, S. aureus, H. influenzae, S. pneumoniae, Legionella*, and many anaerobes

PHARMACOLOGY

- **Bioavailability:** 90% to 95%, less with food. Absorption is reduced 30% in patients with advanced HIV infection; significance is unknown (*Ann Intern Med* 1997;127:289).
- **T½:** 1.5 to 5.0 hours, average – 2 hours
- **Elimination:** Excreted in urine (33%) and metabolized
- **Dose modification in renal failure:** None

SIDE EFFECTS

- **Common:** Orange-brown discoloration of urine, stool, tears (contact lens), sweat, skin.
- **Infrequent:** GI intolerance; hepatitis, usually cholestatic changes in first month of treatment (no increase in risk when given with INH); jaundice (usually reversible with dose reduction or continued use); hypersensitivity, especially pruritus ± rash (3%); flu-like illness with intermittent use – dyspnea, wheezing, purpura, leukopenia.
- **Rare:** Thrombocytopenia, leukopenia, hemolytic anemia, increased uric acid, and BUN. Frequency of side effects that require discontinuation of drug is 3%.

DRUG INTERACTIONS: Rifampin induces hepatic cytochrome P450 enzymes and should be avoided with all PIs and NNRTIs except RTV, RTV/SQV, and EFV. The following drugs inhibit cytochrome P450 enzymes and prolong the half-life of rifampin: IDV, RTV, LPV, clarithromycin, erythromycin, and azoles (fluconazole, itraconazole, and ketoconazole). EFV has no significant effect on rifampin levels, but rifampin reduces EFV levels by 20% to 26%; consider EFV 800 mg hs.

PREGNANCY: Category C. Dose-dependent congenital malformations in animals. Isolated cases of fetal abnormalities noted in patients, but frequency is unknown. Large retrospective studies have shown no risk of congenital abnormalities; case reports of neural tube defects and limb reduction (*Clin Infect Dis* 1995:21[suppl 1]:S24). May cause postnatal hemorrhage in mother and infant if given in last few weeks of pregnancy. Must use with caution.

RIFATER – see Isoniazid (p. 245) or Rifampin (above) (*Ann Intern Med* 1995;122:951)

RITONAVIR (RTV)

TRADE NAME: *Norvir* (Abbott Laboratories)

FORMS AND PRICES: 100 mg soft-gel capsules at $2.14/100 mg cap. Liquid formulation 600 mg/7.5 mL at $360/240 mL.

PATIENT ASSISTANCE PROGRAM: 800-659-9050

CLASS: PI

Dose: 600 mg bid when used as a single PI or 100-400 mg bid when used with another PI. Administration with food improves tolerability but is not required for absorption. Separate dosing with buffered ddl by ≥2 hours.

- **Recommended dose escalation regimen to improve GI tolerance:** Days 1 and 2: 300 mg bid; days 3 to 5: 400 mg bid; days 6 to 13: 500 mg bid; day 14 and thereafter: 600 mg bid
- **Dose regimen for RTV/SQV (hard-gel or soft-gel capsule):** Start SQV 400 mg bid and RTV 300 mg bid. Dose escalate RTV to 400 mg bid on day 3. Another approach that is popular is RTV 200 mg x 2 days, 300 mg x 3 days then 400 mg bid.

CLINICAL TRIALS: The activity of RTV has been extensively studied, alone initially, and more recently in combination with other PIs to exploit RTV inhibition of the P450 metabolic pathway, which increases AUC values of PIs ranging from 1.5x for NFV to >20x for SQV. Combinations with the RTV dose of ≥400 mg generally achieve therapeutic levels for RTV; when used in doses of 100-200 mg qd or bid, RTV levels are subtherapeutic, meaning RTV is used only for pharmacologic enhancement of the companion PI.

- **RTV:** RTV as a single PI in HAART appears to be about as effective as IDV (*AIDS* 2001;15:999).
- **RTV/SQV:** The combination of RTV/SQV (*Invirase* or *Fortovase*) has been used extensively for initial and salvage therapy. For initial therapy PI, the IRIS Study demonstrated that RTV/SQV/d4T was as effective as IDV plus two NRTIs (6th CROI, Chicago, Illinois, 1999, Abstract 630). RTV/SQV is one of the few non-NRTI-containing regimens with extensive experience and good virologic outcomes in treatment of naïve patients including patients with no additional drugs (dual combination). In M96-462, 120 of 141 patients (85%) treated with RTV/SQV had viral load <200 c/mL at 144 weeks, although 11% required intensification with NRTIs (7th CROI, San Francisco, California, 2000, Abstract 533). The Prometheus trial compared RTV/SQV (alone) with RTV/SQV/d4T as initial therapy in 208 patients with intensification using d4T at 12 weeks if the viral load was >500 c/mL. At 48 weeks, 63% and 68% had viral loads <500 c/mL without intensification, respectively (*AIDS* 2000;14:405). Retrospective, observational studies have shown EFV-based HAART to be superior to RTV/SQV (400/400 mg bid) (*AIDS* 2001;15:1679). More recent studies have examined regimens of SQV 1000 mg bid + RTV 100 mg bid; the results showed a superior pharmacokinetic profile for SQV compared with that achieved with the 400/400 mg bid regimen (*J Acquir Immune Defic Syndr* 2001;27:344). There has been a modest but encouraging experience with saquinavir 1600 mg +

RTV 100 mg once daily (*J Acquir Immune Defic Syndr* 2002;29:464). The use of RTV/SQV in salvage therapy has shown variable results. In a trial of RTV + SQV + two NRTIs in patients who failed NFV, 58% of participants had a viral load <500 c/mL at 60 weeks (6th CROI, Chicago, Illinois, 1999, Abstract 392). As expected, a relatively low viral load at the time of the switch predicted success. In ACTG 359, RTV/SQV/DLV successfully achieved viral suppression in only about one third of patients failing IDV based HAART (*J Infect Dis* 2000;182:1375).

- **RTV/IDV:** Pharmacokinetic studies demonstrate a highly favorable impact of RTV on IDV levels, permitting bid instead of q8h dosing (*Antivir Res* 2001;6:201). The main controversy concerns the dose: The 400/400 mg bid regimen has a good pharmacokinetic profile with lower IDV peak levels, which may reduce rates of nephrolithiasis, but the 400 mg dose of RTV is often poorly tolerated. The regimen of IDV 800 mg + RTV 100-200 mg, each bid, is better tolerated but results in higher peak levels of IDV and has been associated with a greater risk of nephrolithiasis (*HIV Clin Trials* 2000;1:13). An alternative strategy is to intensify with RTV in patients with virologic failure on IDV-containing regimens (7th CROI, San Francisco, California, 2000, Abstract 534). Once-daily regimens of IDV 800 mg/RTV 200 mg (*J Acquir Immune Defic Syndr* 2000;25:229) and IDV 1200 mg/RTV 200-400 mg (*J Acquir Immune Defic Syndr* 2000;25:236) have been studied in a small number of patients, but no definitive recommendations can be made.
- **RTV/NFV:** RTV has also been combined with NFV using regimens of RTV 400 mg bid + NFV 500-750 mg bid. Results of a small pilot trial demonstrate good antiviral activity but high rates of diarrhea (7th CROI, San Francisco, California, 2000, Abstract 393).
- **RTV/APV:** RTV increases APV AUC 2.5-fold and increases APV trough levels 10-fold (*Antimicrob Agents Chemother* 2002;46:746; *AIDS* 2001;15:1009). Dose regimens that have been studied include APV 600 mg bid/RTV 100 mg bid or APV 1200 mg qd/RTV 200 mg qd. The latter regimen is the only PI-based combination that is FDA approved for once-daily administration. When APV/RTV is used in combination with EFV, the recommended regimen is RTV 200 mg bid/APV 1200 mg bid/EFV 600 mg hs. This combination has been used as a popular salvage regimen (*HIV Clin Trials* 2002;3:125).
- **MaxCmin1:** The MaxCmin1 trial compared two boosted PI regimens, IDV/RTV (800/100 mg bid) and SQV/RTV (1000/100 mg bid), in naïve and experienced patients (XIV International AIDS Conference, Barcelona, July 2002, Abstract 1265). At 48 weeks, virologic suppression was similar in the two arms by as-treated analysis and intent-to-treat (ITT), switch-included analysis. However, by ITT switch=failure analysis, 68% of patients on SQV/RTV had viral loads <400 c/mL vs 53% on IDV/RTV. Treatment-related grade 3/4

adverse events were also significantly more common among IDV recipients, and lipid profiles were better in the SQV/RTV arm.

RESISTANCE: Phenotypic resistance correlates with primary mutations on the protease gene at codons 82 and 84 (*J Virol* 1995;69:701). Patients failing monotherapy have multiple mutations at codons 10, 20, 32, 33, 36, 46, 54, 71, 77, 82, 84, and 90 (*Nat Med* 1996;2:760; 7th CROI, San Francisco, California, February 2000, Abstract 565). The initial mutation was at codon 82, which was consistently seen and appeared necessary for phenotypic resistance (*Antimicrob Agents Chemother* 1998;42:2775). This was followed by mutations at codons 54, 71, and 36; mutations at codons 84 and 90 occurred late and less frequently.

PHARMACOLOGY

- **Bioavailability:** 60% to 80% (not well determined). Levels increased 15% when taken with meals. CNS penetration: No detectable levels in CSF.
- **T½:** 3 to 5 hours
- **Elimination:** Metabolized by cytochrome P450 CYP3A4>2D6. RTV is a potent inhibitor of cytochrome P450 CYP3A4.
- **Dose modification in renal or hepatic failure:** Use standard doses for renal failure. With hemodialysis, a small amount is dialyzed – dose post hemodialysis (*Nephron* 2001;87:186). There are no data for peritoneal dialysis, but it is probably not removed and should be dosed post dialysis. Consider empiric dose reduction in severe hepatic disease.

SIDE EFFECTS: The most frequently reported adverse events are GI intolerance (nausea, diarrhea, vomiting, anorexia, abdominal pain, taste perversion), circumoral and peripheral paresthesias, and asthenia. GI intolerance is often severe (*J Acquir Immune Defic Syndr* 2000;23:236) and improved by the graduated dose regimen and with continued administration for ≥1 month. Side effects are less severe with the reduced doses used in the dual PI combinations. Hepatotoxicity with elevated transaminase levels is more frequent and more severe with RTV than with other PIs; there does appear to be a modestly increased risk with hepatitis B or C co-infection (*JAMA* 2000;238:74; *J Acquir Immune Defic Syndr* 2000;23:236; *Clin Infect Dis* 2000;31:1234). This risk may be reduced with lower RTV doses used in dual-PI combinations. Laboratory changes include elevated triglycerides, cholestrol, transaminases, CPK, and uric acid.

- **Class adverse reactions:** Insulin-resistant hyperglycemia, fat accumulation, elevated triglycerides and cholesterol, and possible increased bleeding with hemophilia. The association between protease inhibitor therapy and osteonecrosis/avascular necrosis of the hips has not been determined. Hypercholesterolemia and triglyceridemia may be more frequent and severe with RTV compared with other PIs (*J Acquir Immune Defic Syndr* 2000;23:236; *J Acquir Immune Defic Syndr* 2000;23:261).

DRUG INTERACTIONS: RTV is a potent inhibitor of cytochrome P450 enzymes, including CYP3A4 and 2D6, and can produce large increases in the plasma concentrations of drugs that are metabolized by that mechanism.

- **Use with the following agents is contraindicated:** Amiodarone, astemizole, bepridil, cisapride, encainide, flecainide, lovastatin, midazolam, ergot alkaloids, pimozide, propafenone, quinidine, simvastatin, terfenadine, triazolam, and St. John's wort
- **Drugs that require dose modification**
  - Clarithromycin AUC increased 77% (*Clin Infect Dis* 1996;23:685); reduce clarithromycin dose for renal failure.
  - Methadone levels are decreased by 36%.
  - Desipramine levels are increased by 145%; decrease desipramine dose.
  - ddI, buffered form, reduces absorption of RTV and should be taken ≥2 hours apart or use ddI EC.
  - Ketoconazole levels are increased 3-fold; do not exceed 200 mg ketoconazole/day.
  - Rifampin reduces RTV levels 35%; limited data on combination use and concern for hepatotoxicity.
  - Rifabutin levels increased 4-fold; rifabutin dose of 150 mg qod or 150 mg 2 to 3 days/week with standard RTV dose.
  - Ethinyl estradiol levels decreased by 40%; use alternative or additional method of birth control.
  - Theophylline levels decreased by 47%; monitor theophylline levels.
  - Phenobarbital, phenytoin, and carbamazepine interaction anticipated; carbamazepine toxicity reported. Monitor anticonvulsant levels.
  - Sildenafil AUC increased 2- to 11-fold; do not use >25 mg/48 hours.
  - A potentially fatal reaction has been reported with MDMA ("Ecstasy") (*Arch Intern Med* 1999;159:2221).

■ TABLE 6-39: **RTV Interactions With Antiretroviral Drugs**

Drug	Effect	Recommendation
SQV	SQV – ↑20 fold RTV – no change	SQV 400 mg bid + RTV 400 mg bid (SQV as *Invirase* or *Fortovase*) or SQV 1000 mg + RTV 100 mg bid
NVP	RTV – ↓11% NVP – no change	Standard doses both drugs
NFV	NFV – 1.5x RTV – no change	RTV 400 mg bid + NFV 500-750 mg bid (limited data)
DLV	DLV – no change RTV – ↑70%	No data
IDV	IDV – ↑2 to 5x RTV – no change	IDV 400 mg bid + RTV 400 mg bid *or* IDV 800 mg + RTV 100 mg bid
EFV	EFV – ↑21% RTV – ↑18%	RTV 600 mg bid (500 mg for intolerance) + EFV 600 mg/day
APV	APV – ↑2.5x RTV – no change	APV 600 mg bid + RTV 100 mg bid *or* APV 1200 mg qd + RTV 200 mg qd. With EFV/APV/RTV use: RTV 200 mg bid + APV 1200 mg bid + EFV 600 mg hs

PREGNANCY: Category B. Negative rodent teratogenic assays; placental passage studies in rodents show newborn:maternal drug ratio of 1.15 at midterm and 0.15-0.64 at late term.

ROFERON – see Interferon (p. 243)

SAQUINAVIR (SQV)

TRADE NAME: *Invirase* (hard-gel capsule) and *Fortovase* (soft-gel capsule) (Roche)

FORMS AND PRICES: 200 mg cap (hard-gel, *Invirase*) at $2.50 and 200 mg cap (soft-gel, *Fortovase*) at $1.33. Cost/year (*Fortovase*) is $8,738; cost/year RTV + *Fortovase* 400/400 bid is $8,191.

PATIENT ASSISTANCE PROGRAM: 800-282-7780

CLASS: PI

PREPARATIONS AND DOSING: The soft-gel capsule of *Fortovase* was introduced in November 1997 as the preferred formulation due to improved bioavailability compared with the hard-gel capsule, which showed only 4% oral bioavailability. *Invirase* is now reemerging as the preferred SQV formulation due to favorable pharmacokinetics when combined with RTV and better GI tolerability compared with *Fortovase*. The difference in tolerability is attributed to the capsule used to stabilize the soft-gel form, which causes diarrhea.

- **Standard dose for *Fortovase*:** 1200 mg PO tid or with RTV: SQV/RTV 400/400 mg bid or 1000/100 mg bid. For once-daily dosing SQV/RTV 1600/100 mg qd.
- **Standard dose for *Invirase*:** Always with RTV: SQV/RTV 1000/100 mg bid or 400/400 mg bid. For once-daily dosing SQV/RTV 1600/100 mg qd.

CLINICAL TRIALS: Most trials have evaluated the *Invirase* formulation of SQV either alone or in combination with RTV. Trials with unboosted *Fortovase* show better bioavailability and better efficacy than with unboosted *Invirase*.

- **Combination treatment of RTV + SQV** showed a 2- to 3-log decrease in plasma HIV RNA levels that was sustained ≥52 weeks (package insert).
- **An open-label study (NV 15355)** compared *Invirase* and *Fortovase*, each in combination with two nucleosides in treatment-naïve patients with an average CD4 count of 429 cells/mm³. By intent-to-treat analysis, 57% of *Fortovase* recipients and 38% of *Invirase* recipients had viral loads <400 c/mL. At 48 weeks, 51% of *Fortovase* recipients had <50 c/mL. These results were sustained at 72 weeks. As expected, viral load <500 c/mL at 12 weeks or <50 c/mL at 24 weeks predicted a durable virologic response (6th CROI, Chicago, Illinois, February 1999, Abstract 165).
- **Combinations of SQV with RTV or NFV (plus NRTIs)** in treatment-naïve patients with CD4 cell counts >200 proved highly potent with plasma HIV RNA levels <500 c/mL in 65% to 80%. These combinations are also favored in patients with failed PI-containing regimens (5th CROI, Chicago, Illinois, February 1998, Abstracts 388, 394b, 396, 422, 423, 427, 510).
- **CHEESE** compared *Fortovase* vs IDV, each in combination with AZT/3TC in treatment-naïve patients (or AZT <12 mo) with viral load >10,000 c/mL and CD4 cell count <500. By intent-to-treat analysis, 80% in each group had <400 c/mL and 71% to 74% had <50 c/mL at 24 weeks. There was an unexplained, statistically significantly greater increase in the CD4 count among SQV recipients (mean increase 162 vs 85 cells/mm³) (*AIDS* 1999;13:F53). The 48 week data continued to show comparable results for viral load and CD4 response.
- **SPICE** included 157 PI-naïve patients randomized to *Fortovase* + two NRTIs, NFV + two NRTIs, *Fortovase* + NFV + two NRTIs, or *Fortovase* + NFV. At 48 weeks, 45% to 66% had <400 c/mL by as-treated analysis, and 35% to 51% had <50 c/mL by intent-to-treat analysis. Results were inferior in the regimen lacking NRTIs; the quadruple treatment regimen was well tolerated and possibly superior in patients with prior NRTI treatment or high baseline viral load. The dose used in the combination PI regimen was *Fortovase* 800 mg + NFV 750 mg tid. There is also evidence supporting twice-

daily dosing of this combination (1200/1250 mg bid) (*J Acquir Immune Defic Syndr* 2000;23:128).

- **ACTG 359** compared SQV/RTV (400/400 mg bid) with SQV/NFV (800/750 mg tid) in 277 patients who failed IDV. The responses were comparable (7th CROI, San Francisco, California, 2000, Abstract 235).
- **HIVNAT 001.3** is a "switch study" in which patients with viral load <50 c/mL after ≥2 years of treatment with AZT/3TC + *Fortovase* 1400 mg bid were switched to once-daily treatment with *Fortovase* 1600 mg/RTV 100 mg/2 NRTIs. At 24 weeks, 63/69 (93%) had viral loads <50/mL, SQV trough levels were therapeutic, and the regimen was well tolerated (*J Acquir Immune Defic Syndr* 2002;29:464).
- **MaxCmin1:** The MaxCmin1 trial compared two boosted PI regimens, IDV/RTV (800/100 mg bid) and SQV/RTV (1000/100 mg bid) in naïve and experienced patients (XIV International AIDS Conference, Barcelona, 2002, Abstract 1265). At 48 weeks, virologic suppression was similar in the two arms by as-treated analysis and intent-to-treat (ITT), switch-included analysis. However, by ITT switch=failure analysis, 68% of patients on SQV/RTV had viral loads <400 c/mL vs 53% on IDV/RTV. Treatment-related grade 3/4 adverse events were also significantly more common among IDV recipients, and lipid profiles were better in the SQV/RTV arm.
- **FOCUS:** The FOCUS trial was an open-label trial comparing once-daily SQV/RTV (1600/100 mg) vs EFV, both in combination with 2 nucleoside analogs (41st ICAAC, Chicago, 2001, Abstract I-670). The trial involved 161 treatment naïve patients. EFV was better tolerated: Eight patients discontinued therapy in the SQV/RTV arm vs one in the EFV arm. Nausea was seen in 22% vs 1%, and vomiting in 6% vs 0%. As a result, EFV was superior by intent-to-treat analyses, with 81% achieving viral loads <50 c/mL compared with 60% in the SQV/RTV arm (p=0.008). There was no difference in potency in either arm between patients with baseline viral loads <100,000 c/mL or those with >100,000 c/mL.
- **ATV/SQV:** Atazanavir (ATV) increases levels of other protease inhibitors through its inhibitory effect on the CYP 3A4 enzyme system. In BMS 009, patients experiencing virologic failure on HAART (HIV RNA 2000-100,000 c/mL) received ATV/SQV at a dose of 400/1200 mg qd (n=34) or 600/1200 mg qd (n=28) or RTV/SQV at a dose of 400/400 mg bid (n=23) (41st ICAAC, 2001, Chicago Abstract LB-16). Patients in each arm experienced a 1-1.5 log drop in viral load at 24 weeks, but those on the ATV-based regimens had more favorable lipid profiles.

RESISTANCE: Major resistance mutations are L90M (most common; 3-fold decrease in sensitivity) and G48V (less common and 30-fold decrease in sensitivity). Minor mutations conferring resistance are at codons 10, 54, 63, 71, 73, 77, 82, and 84. There is now evidence that patients with clinical resistance to SQV frequently have mutations associated with resistance to RTV and SQV, and clinical resistance to NFV has been demonstrated following SQV failure, despite the lack of the characteristic NFV resistance mutation at D30N.

PHARMACOLOGY

- **Bioavailability:** Absorption of hard-gel capsule is 4% with high-fat meal; absorption of the soft-gel capsule (*Fortovase*) is superior to *Invirase*, but percent absorption is not established. Food increases SQV levels with *Fortovase* 6-fold, so the drug should be taken within 2 hours of a large meal when not taken with RTV. *Invirase* and *Fortovase* absorption is not influenced by food when taken with RTV. CNS penetration is nil (CSF:serum ratio is 0.02).
- **T½:** 1 to 2 hours
- **Elimination:** Hepatic metabolism by cytochrome P450 isoenzyme CYP3A4; 96% biliary excretion; 1% urinary excretion
- **Storage:** *Invirase*: Room temperature. *Fortovase*: 30 days at room temperature; long-term storage in refrigerator
- **Dose modification in renal or hepatic failure:** Use standard dose for renal failure. The drug is not removed by hemodialysis (*Nephron* 2001;87:186) and is unlikely to be removed by peritoneal dialysis. Consider empiric dose reduction for hepatic failure.

SIDE EFFECTS: Gastrointestinal intolerance with nausea, abdominal pain, diarrhea in 5% to 15% (*Invirase*), 20% to 30% (*Fortovase*); headache, and hepatic toxicity; hypoglycemia in patients with type 2 diabetes (*Ann Intern Med* 1999;131:980). Class adverse effects include fat redistribution, increased levels of triglycerides and/or cholesterol, hyperglycemia with insulin resistance and type 2 diabetes, osteoporosis, and possible increased bleeding with hemophilia.

DRUG INTERACTIONS

- **Drugs that require dose modification with concurrent use:** Sildenafil AUC↑2x – use ≤25 mg/48 hours.
- **Drug interactions of uncertain significance:**
  - Dexamethasone decreases SQV levels.
  - Phenobarbital, phenytoin, and carbamazepine may decrease SQV levels substantially; monitor anticonvulsant levels.
  - Ketoconazole increases SQV levels 3x; standard dose.
  - Clarithromycin increases SQV levels 177% and SQV increases clarithromycin levels 45%; standard dose.
  - Oral contraceptives, no data.
  - Rifampin reduces SQV levels by 80% and is contraindicated; with combination SQV/RTV, use rifabutin 150 mg 3x/week.

- Methadone – with SQV (*Fortovase*). There is a 8% to 10% reduction in methadone levels; no dose adjustment.
- Other drugs that induce CYP3A4 (phenobarbital, phenytoin, NVP, dexamethasone, and carbamazepine) may decrease SQV levels; these combinations should be avoided if possible.
- Garlic supplements decrease SQV AUC, C_{max}, and C_{min} levels by about 50% (8th CROI, Chicago, Illinois, 2001, Abstract 743).
- Grapefruit juice increases SQV levels.

- **Drugs that are contraindicated for concurrent use:** Terfenadine, astemizole, cisapride, triazolam, midazolam, rifampin, rifabutin, ergot alkaloids, simvastatin, lovastatin, and St. John's wort

■ TABLE 6-40: **Combination Therapy With *Fortovase* Plus Second PI or an NNRTI**

Drug	AUC*	Regimen*
RTV	SQV ↑20x, RTV no change	SQV 400 mg bid + RTV 400 mg bid or SQV 1000 mg bid + RTV 100 mg bid or SQV 1600 mg qd + RTV 100 mg qd
IDV	IDV no change, SQV ↑4 to 7x	Insufficient data
APV	APV ↓32%, SQV ↓19%	SQV 800 mg tid + APV 800 mg tid (limited data)
EFV	EFV ↓62%, SQV ↓12%	Not recommended when SQV is a single PI
NVP	NVP no change, SQV ↓25%	Insufficient data
DLV	DLV no change, SQV ↑5x	*Fortovase* 800 mg tid + DLV standard; monitor ALT
NFV	NFV ↑20%, SQV ↑3 to 5x	*Fortovase* 800 mg tid or 1200 mg bid + NFV standard
LPV/r	SQV ↑3 to 5x, LPV no change	SQV 1000 mg bid + LPV/r 400/100 mg bid

* All data and recommended regimens are for the *Fortovase* formulation of SQV. The exception is SQV/RTV, which may be *Fortovase* (preferred) or *Invirase*.

PREGNANCY: Category B. Studies in rats showed no teratogenicity or embryotoxicity.

SEROSTIM – see Growth Hormone, Human (p. 235)

SOMATROPIN – see Growth Hormone, Human (p. 235)

SPORANOX – see Itraconazole (p. 247)

SOMNOTE – see Chloral Hydrate (p. 188)

STAVUDINE (d4T)

TRADE NAME: *Zerit* and *Zerit XR* (Bristol-Myers Squibb)

FORMS AND PRICES: Caps: 15 mg at $4.88, 20 mg at $5.06, 30 mg at $5.38, 40 mg at $5.48 ($4,003/year for 40 mg bid). Solution: 1 mg/mL at $61.26/200 mL. *Zerit XR* 37.5 mg, 50 mg, 75 mg, 100 mg extended release capsules.

PATIENT ASSISTANCE: 800-272-4878

INDICATIONS AND DOSES: d4T is relatively easy to administer (bid dosing) and generally well tolerated except in patients with peripheral neuropathy. AZT should not be combined with d4T due to pharmacologic antagonism (*J Infect Dis* 1996;173:355). The mechanism of pharmacologic antagonism is disputed. Coadministration with ddI leads to an increases risk of lactic acidosis, pancreatitis, and peripheral neuropathy.

- >60 kg – 40 mg PO bid or 100 mg PO qd
- <60 kg – 30 mg PO bid or 75 mg PO qd
- Dose reduction for peripheral neuropathy: Patients who develop peripheral neuropathy on d4T should discontinue d4T and switch to another agent. The package insert states that d4T can be reintroduced after complete resolution of symptoms at a reduced dose: 20 mg bid for patients ≥60 kg or 15 mg bid for patients <60 kg. However, treatment with an alternate agent is usually preferred because efficacy data for these lower doses are lacking.

CLINICAL TRIALS: There is extensive experience with d4T combined with 3TC and with ddI. Efficacy and short-term tolerability are good, but d4T appears to be associated with increased rates of lactic acidosis and peripheral neuropathy with long-term use, especially when combined with ddI. ACTG 384 showed that EFV/AZT/3TC had greater activity and less toxicity compared with EFV/ddI/d4T; the reduced antiviral effect was not noted when these two nucleoside combinations were combined with NFV (XIV International AIDS Conf, Barcelona, 7/02, Abstract LB20a).

RESISTANCE: *In vivo* d4T resistance is mediated primarily by thymidine analogue mutations (TAMs) (e.g., 41L, 67N, 70R, 210W, 215Y/F, 219Q/E), and d4T also selects for these mutations. As with AZT, the M184V mutation associated with 3TC resistance appears to increase susceptibility to d4T. Phenotypic resistance testing of patients in ACTG 306 who had received d4T for >6 months showed no phenotypic resistance despite virologic failure (7th CROI, San Francisco, California, 2000, Abstract 733). This reflected earlier phenotypic cutoffs that are now felt to have been too high. The multinucleoside resistance mutations (Q151M complex and the T69-insertion mutation) also result in resistance to d4T.

PHARMACOLOGY

- **Bioavailability:** 86% and not influenced by food or fasting
- **T½:** (serum) 1 hour. Intracellular T½: 3.5 hours
- **CNS penetration:** 30% to 40% (*J Acquir Immune Defic Syndr* 1998;17:235) (CSF: plasma ratio=0.16-0.97)
- **Elimination:** Renal – 50%
- **Dose modification in severe liver disease:** No guidelines; use standard dose with caution.

■ TABLE 6-41: **Dose Modification in Renal Failure**

CrCl	Body ≥60 kg	Weight <60 kg
>50 mL/min	40 mg bid or 100 mg qd	30 mg bid or 75 mg qd
26-50 mL/min	40 mg qd	30 mg qd
10-25 mL/min	20 mg qd	15 mg qd
Hemodialysis	20 mg qd post dialysis	15 mg qd post dialysis

SIDE EFFECTS

- **Mitochondrial toxicity:** d4T appears to be an important cause of side effects attributed to mitochondrial toxicity, including lactic acidosis with hepatic steatosis, peripheral neuropathy, and lipatrophy. In most studies of lactic acidosis, d4T is the most frequent NRTI (*Clin Infect Dis* 2001;33:1931; *Lancet* 2000;356:1423; *Ann Intern Med* 2000;133:192). A review of reported cases for 2000 to 2001 implicated d4T in 33 of 34 (*Clin Infect Dis* 2002;31:838). The frequency of pancreatitis, peripheral neuropathy, and lactic acidosis appears to be increased when d4T is combined with ddI. Milder, often subclinical elevations in lactate may occur more frequently.
- **Lactic acidosis and steatosis:** This is an infrequent form of mitochondrial toxicity, reported in 1 to 14/1000 patient-years of NRTI exposure (*AIDS* 2001;15:717), but it is important to recognize due to a potential for lethal outcome. Patients present with nausea, vomiting, abdominal pain, fatigue, dyspnea, and weight loss, usually after 1 to 20 months of exposure. Laboratory studies show elevated serum lactate (usually >5 mmol/L), sometimes combined with increased anion gap and elevated CPK, ALT, and LDH. CT scan or liver biopsy may show hepatic steatosis. NRTIs should be stopped when this diagnosis is considered. In mild cases, switching to NRTIs that are less toxic to mitochondria (e.g., ABC, 3TC, TDF) may be considered, provided the patient can be closely monitored. d4T/ddI should be avoided in pregnant women due to increased risk of lactic acidosis.
- **Peripheral neuropathy:** Frequency is 5% to 15% but as high as 24% in some early trials. The presumed cause is depletion of mitochondrial DNA (*N Engl J Med* 2002;346:811). Risk appears to be

substantially increased when d4T is combined with ddI or ddI and hydroxyurea (*AIDS* 2000;14:273). Onset is usually noted at 2 to 6 months after treatment is started and usually resolves if d4T is promptly stopped, although the recovery is generally slow. Peripheral neuropathy due to HIV infection or alternative nucleoside analog treatment (ddI, ddC) represents a relative contraindication to d4T. If it is necessary to resume d4T after resolution of neuropathy, recommended doses are 20 mg bid (≥60 kg) and 15 mg bid (<60 kg). However, the efficacy of these lower doses has not been systematically studied.

- **Motor weakness:** A syndrome of ascending motor weakness resembling Guillain-Barré syndrome has been described in a small number of patients treated with d4T. The weakness was accompanied by lactic acidosis and is presumed to be a result of mitochondrial toxicity.
- **Other clinical side effects:** Complaints are infrequent and include headache, GI intolerance with diarrhea, or esophageal ulcers.
- **Macrocytosis**, with MCV >100, which is inconsequential (*J Infect* 2000;40:160).

DRUG INTERACTIONS

- **Drugs that cause peripheral neuropathy** should be used with caution or avoided: ddC, ethionamide, EMB, INH, phenytoin, vincristine, glutethimide, gold, hydralazine, thalidomide, and long-term metronidazole. Can be coadministered with ddI, but risk of neuropathy higher.
- **Methadone** reduces the AUC of d4T by 24%, but this is not thought to be sufficiently severe to require d4T dose adjustment; d4T has no effect on methadone levels (*J Acquir Immune Defic Syndr* 2000;24:241).
- Use with caution when combined with ribavirin.

PREGNANCY: Category C. Rodent teratogenicity assay is negative; placental passage in rhesus monkeys showed a newborn:maternal drug ratio of 0.76. No studies in humans. d4T + ddI should not be given to pregnant women due to possible lactic acidosis and hepatic steatosis.

STOCRIN – see Efavirenz (p. 208)

SULFADIAZINE

TRADE NAME: Generic

FORMS: 500 mg tab at $1.22

CLASS: Synthetic derivatives of sulfanilamide that inhibit folic acid synthesis

INDICATIONS AND DOSES

- **Toxoplasmosis:** Initial treatment 1-1.5 g PO qid
- **Nocardia:** 1 g PO qid x ≥6 months
- **UTIs:** 500 mg-1 g PO qid x 3 to 14 days

PHARMACOLOGY

- **Bioavailability:** >70%
- **T½:** 7 to 17 hours
- **Elimination:** Hepatic acetylation and renal excretion of parent compound and metabolites
- **CNS penetration:** 40% to 80% of serum levels
- **Serum levels for systemic infections:** 100-150 μg/mL
- **Dose modifications in renal failure:** CrCl >50 mL/min – 0.5-1.5 g q4h-q6h; CrCl 10-50 mL/min – 0.5-1.5 g q8h-q12h (half dose); CrCl <10 mL/min – 0.5-1.5 g q12h-q24h (one-third dose)

SIDE EFFECTS: Hypersensitivity with rash, drug fever, serum-sickness, urticaria; crystalluria reduced with adequate urine volume (≥1,500 mL/day) and alkaline urine – use with care in renal failure; marrow suppression – anemia, thrombocytopenia, leukopenia, hemolytic anemia due to G6-PD deficiency.

DRUG INTERACTIONS: Decreased effect of cyclosporine, digoxin; increased effect of coumadin, oral hypoglycemics, methotrexate(?), and phenytoin. Use with caution with ribavirin.

PREGNANCY: Category C. Competes with bilirubin for albumin to cause kernicterus – avoid near term or in nursing mothers.

SULFAMETHOXAZOLE-TRIMETHOPRIM – see Trimethoprim-Sulfamethoxazole (p. 316)

SUSTIVA – see Efavirenz (p. 208)

3TC – see Lamivudine (p. 252)

TENOFOVIR DISOPROXIL FUMARATE (TDF)

TRADE NAME: *Viread* (Gilead Sciences)

FORM: 300 mg tab at $13.60; cost/year $4,964

PATIENT ASSISTANCE PROGRAM AND REIMBURSEMENT HOTLINE: 800-445-3235

CLASS: NRTI

DOSE: 300 mg qd with food. See Table 4-26 (p. 95) for dosing recommendations in renal insufficiency.

CLINICAL TRIALS

- **GS-97-901:** Dose-finding monotherapy study with 75, 150, and 300 mg qd x 28 days. Median decrease in viral load at 28 days with 300 mg dose was 1.2 log_{10}/mL.
- **GS-98-902:** Dose finding/toxicity study using 75, 150, and 300 mg added to antiretroviral regimen in 189 treatment-experienced patients with viral load 400-100,000 c/mL. At 48 weeks, the mean viral load decrease was 0.62 log_{10} c/mL among 54 patients receiving 300 mg/day.
- **GS-99-907:** Placebo-controlled trial in treated patients with viral load 400-10,000 c/mL given 300 mg tenofovir. At 24 weeks (n=552), the mean decrease in viral load was 0.61 log_{10} c/mL among tenofovir recipients compared with 0.03 log_{10} c/mL in placebo recipients.
- **GS-99-903** was a randomized, placebo-controlled trial comparing tenofovir DF vs d4T, each in combination with 3TC and EFV for treatment of ART-naïve patients (XIV International AIDS Conference, Barcelona, July 2002, Abstract LB17). In an intention-to-treat (missing data=failure) analysis after 48 weeks of follow-up, 82% of the patients in the tenofovir arm (n=299) had a viral load <50 c/mL, compared with 81% of the patients in the d4T arm (n=301)(p=NS). There were no differences in efficacy by baseline viral load. The drop-out rate was low, and rates of adverse events and drug discontinuation were similar in both arms, although fasting total and LDL cholesterol and triglycerides were significantly higher in d4T-treated patients (p<0.001), and there was a suggestion of increased peripheral neuropathy in the d4T arm as well (42nd ICAAC, San Diego, 2002, Abstract LB2).

RESISTANCE: Susceptibility is decreased in patients with three or more thymidine analog mutations (TAMs) that include 41L, 67N, 70R, 210W, 215Y/F, and 219Q/E. The 41L and 210W mutations are most important. Susceptibility is maintained with other TAM patterns and increased with M184V. There is substantial loss of susceptibility with K65R and T69 insertion, but it is maintained with Q151M complex (XIV International AIDS Conference, Barcelona, July 2002, Abstract 1390).

PHARMACOLOGY

- **Bioavailability:** 25% (fasting) to 40% (with food); improvement with food, especially high-fat meal
- **T½:** 12 to 18 hours; intracellular 10 to 50 hours
- **Elimination:** Renal

DRUG INTERACTION: ddI AUC is increased 40% to 60%, potentially causing increased rates of peripheral neuropathy and pancreatitis. Combination of TDF with lower doses of ddI (e.g., *Videx EC* 250 mg qd in patients >60 kg) should be used. Ganciclovir, valganciclovir, and cidofovir compete for active tubular secretion with increased levels of either tenofovir or the companion drug; monitor for toxicities. LPV increases levels of TDF 30% with co-administration.

SIDE EFFECTS

- **GI intolerance:** GI intolerance reported, but it is infrequent.
- **Other:** The incidence of laboratory and clinical adverse events has been similar to placebo in controlled clinical trials.

PREGNANCY: Category B. Studies in gravid monkeys showed a significant reduction in insulin-like growth factor (*J Acquir Immune Defic Syndr* 2002;29:207).

TESTOSTERONE

SOURCE

- Testosterone cypionate (various generic manufacturers)
- Testosterone enanthate (various generic manufacturers)
- Testosterone scrotal patch (*Testoderm* patch, Alza Pharmaceuticals)
- Testosterone non-scrotal patch (*Androderm*, Watson; and *Testoderm TTS* patch, Alza Pharmaceuticals)
- Testosterone gel (*AndroGel,* Unimed)

FORMS AND PRICES: Vials of 100 and 200 mg/mL at $12.71 to $20.65/10 mL vial or about $2/week

- *Testoderm* scrotal patch at $3.57/4 mg/24-hour patch or $3.57/6 mg/24-hour patch; $4.90/5 mg/24-hour *Testoderm TTS* (non-scrotal) patch.
- *Androderm* non-scrotal patch at $2.47/2.5 mg/24-hour patch.
- *AndroGel* 5 g packet at $5.98

INDICATIONS (for men only)

- **Hypogonadism:** Normal testosterone levels in adult men are 300-1,000 ng/dL at 8 AM, representing peak levels with circadian rhythm. Prior studies show subnormal testosterone levels in 45% of patients with AIDS and 27% of HIV infected patients without AIDS (*Am J Med* 1988;84:611; *AIDS* 1994;7:46; *J Clin Endocrinol* 1996;81:4108). Testing should be performed in the morning and should measure free (unbound) levels or unbound levels (normal: 34-194 pg/mL). Replacement therapy is recommended for men with low or low-normal levels. Restoration of normal testosterone levels can be achieved with testosterone enanthate 200 mg IM every 2 weeks, a 5 mg *Androderm* patch applied nightly, a 5 mg *Testoderm TTS* patch applied each morning, or 5 g of *AndroGel* per day. Therapeutic trials with testosterone treatment of hypogonadal men with HIV infection show substantial improvements in quality of life with increased libido, reduced fatigue, and reduced depression (*Arch Gen Psych* 2000;57:141). Benefit has also been shown in eugonadal HIV infected men receiving twice the physiological dose (200 mg every week), but long-term toxicity should be considered (*Ann Intern Med* 2000;133:348).

- **Wasting:** Testosterone is an anabolic steroid that may restore nitrogen balance and lean body mass in patients with wasting (*J Acquir Immune Defic Syndr* 1996;11:510; *J Acquir Immune Defic Syndr* 1997;16:254; *Ann Intern Med* 1998;129:18).
- **Fat redistribution:** Testosterone may reduce visceral fat and reduce cholesterol; however, studies are limited and risks include reduced HDL cholesterol, hepatotoxicity, and risk of prostatic cancer (*Clin Infect Dis* 2002;34:248).

REGIMEN

- **Intramuscular:** 200-400 mg IM every 2 weeks. The dose and dosing interval may need adjustment; many use 100-200 mg IM every week given by self administration to avoid low levels in the second week; many initiate therapy for wasting with 300-400 mg every 2 weeks, with taper to 200 mg when weight is restored, or combine with other anabolic steroids.
- **Transdermal systems:** Advantages are rapid absorption, controlled rate of delivery, avoidance of first-pass hepatic metabolism, avoidance of IM injections, and possibly less testicular shrinkage. Three delivery systems are available: Transscrotal and non-transscrotal patches and a topical gel. Transscrotal patches (*Testoderm*) are available in 10 and 15 mg sizes to deliver 4 and 6 mg testosterone. Serum testosterone levels peak at 3 to 8 hours. After 1 month, a morning testosterone level should be obtained. *Testoderm TTS* is a non-transscrotal patch with 5 mg testosterone. Another non-transscrotal patch (*Androderm*) consists of a liquid reservoir containing 12.2 g testosterone that delivers 2.5 mg of testosterone/day or a liquid reservoir containing 24.3 mg that delivers 5 mg testosterone daily. The usual dose is a system that delivers 5 mg/day. *AndroGel* is rubbed on to the skin starting with 5 mg qd and then titrating subsequent doses based on serum testosterone levels.

CONTROLLED SUBSTANCE: Schedule C-III

PHARMACOLOGY

- **Bioavailability:** Poor absorption and rapid metabolism with oral administration. The cypionate and enanthate esters are absorbed slowly from IM injection sites.
- **Elimination:** Hepatic metabolism to 17 ketosteroids that are excreted in urine.

SIDE EFFECTS: Androgenic effects – acne, flushing, gynecomastia, increased libido, priapism, and edema. Other side effects include aggravation of sleep apnea, salt retention, increased hematocrit, possible promotion of KS, and promotion of breast or prostate cancer. In women, there may be virilization with voice change, hirsutism, and clitoral enlargement. Androgens may cause cholestatic hepatitis. Patches are associated with local reactions, especially pruritus and occasionally blistering, erythema, and pain. Local reactions are more common with *Androderm* patches than with *Testoderm* or *Testoderm TTS* patches.

DRUG INTERACTIONS: May potentiate action of oral anticoagulants

PREGNANCY: Category X

THALIDOMIDE

TRADE NAME: *Thalomid* (Celgene)

FORM AND PRICE: 50 mg capsule at $7.50

AVAILABILITY: Thalidomide is FDA-approved for marketing through a restricted distribution program called "System for Thalidomide Education and Prescribing Safety" (STEPS). The STEPS Program is designed to eliminate the risk of birth defects by requiring registration of prescribing physicians, patients, and pharmacists, combined with informed consent, rigorous counseling, accountability, and a patient survey. Only physicians registered with STEPS may prescribe thalidomide. Call 888-423-5436 (option 1) to register and receive necessary forms. **Requirements for prescribing:** 1) Agreement to patient counseling as indicated in the consent form; 2) Patient consent form with one copy sent to Boston University; and 3) Completion of the physician monitoring survey. **Patients are registered if they:** 1) Agree to use two reliable methods of contraception; 2) Have pregnancy tests performed regularly (females); 3) Use latex condoms when having sex with women (males); and 4) Agree to participate in mandatory and confidential patient survey. **Pharmacies must register to dispense thalidomide by agreeing to:** 1) Collect and file informed consent forms; 2) Register patients by phone or fax; 3) Prescribe no more than a 28 day supply within 7 days of the prescription date; and 4) Verify patient registry with refills.

PATIENT ASSISTANCE: 888-423-5436 (option 2)

FDA LABELING: Approved for moderate to severe erythema nodosum leprosum

REGIMEN: Usual dose is 50-200 mg/day, most commonly 100 mg/day at hs to reduce sedative side effect. Often start at 100-200 mg/day and titrate down to 50 mg/day or give intermittent dosing (*J Infect Dis*

2001;183:343). Doses above 200-300 mg/day are poorly tolerated (*N Eng J Med* 1997;336:1487; *Clin Infect Dis* 1997;24:1223).

MECHANISM: Presumed mechanism for HIV-associated wasting is the reduction in TNF-alpha production (*J Exp Med* 1991;173:699). Thalidomide also has numerous other anti-inflammatory and immunomodulatory properties (*Int J Dermatol* 1974;13:20; *Proc Natl Acad Soc USA* 1993;90:5974; *Mol Med* 1995;1:384; *J Exp Med* 1993;177:1675; *J Acquir Immune Defic Syndr* 1997;13:1047).

CLINICAL TRIALS

- **Aphthous ulcers:** In a placebo-controlled trial using thalidomide (200 mg/day) in patients with oral aphthous ulcers, 16/29 (53%) in the thalidomide arm responded compared with 2/28 (7%) in the placebo group (*N Engl J Med* 1997;336:1489). ACTG 251 was a placebo-controlled trial involving 45 patients given thalidomide (200 mg/day x 4 weeks followed by 100 mg/day for responders and 400 mg/day for nonresponders for oral or esophageal ulcers). Among 23 recipients of thalidomide, 14 (61%) had a complete remission in 4 weeks, and 21 (91%) had a complete remission or partial response. In another ACTG trial for patients with aphthous ulcers of the esophagus, thalidomide (200 mg/day) was associated with a complete response at 4 weeks in 8 of 11 (73%) (*J Infect Dis* 1999;180:61). Ulcers usually heal in 7 to 28 days. The usual dose for aphthous ulcers is 100-200 mg/day, with increases up to 400-600 mg/day if unresponsive; after healing, discontinue or use maintenance dose of 50 mg/day (*J Am Acad Dermatol* 1993;28:271).
- **Wasting:** Two placebo-controlled trials and three open-label studies demonstrated that thalidomide (daily doses of 50-300 mg/day) for 2 to 12 weeks was associated with mean weight gains of 2.4% to 6.5%. Suggested initial dose is 100 mg PO qd with increases up to 200 mg/day (*AIDS* 1996;10:1501; *J Acquir Immune Defic Syndr* 1996; 11:247). The higher dose is often poorly tolerated due to sedation.
- **Chronic diarrhea due to microsporidia:** A trial in 18 HIV infected men with chronic diarrhea due to *E. bieneusi* that was unresponsive to albendazole were given thalidomide, 100 mg daily x 4 weeks. There was a complete response in 7 (38%) and a partial response in 3 (17%) (*Gastroenterology* 1997;112:1823).
- **Other possible uses in HIV infected patients:** Prurigo nodularis (200-400 mg/day), postherpetic neuralgia (100-300 mg/day), and AIDS-associated proctitis (300 mg/day) (*J Am Acad Dermatol* 1996;35:969)

PHARMACOLOGY (*Antimicrob Agents Chemother* 1997;41:2797)

- **Bioavailability:** Well absorbed
- **T½:** 6 to 8 hours. Peak levels with 200 mg dose are 1.7 μg/mL; levels >4 μg/mL are required to inhibit TNF-alpha (*Proc Natl Acad Soc USA*

1993;90:5974; *J Exp Med* 1993;177:1675; *J Am Acad Dermatol* 1996; 35:969). It is not known whether thalidomide is present in semen.

- **Elimination:** Nonrenal mechanisms, primarily nonenzymatic hydrolysis in plasma to multiple metabolites. There are no recommendations for dose changes in renal or hepatic failure.

SIDE EFFECTS

- **Teratogenic effects:** Major concern is in pregnant women due to high potential for birth defects, including absent or abnormal limbs; cleft lip; absent ears; heart, renal or genital abnormalities and other severe defects (*Nat Med* 1997;3:8). Maximum vulnerability is 35 to 50 days after the last menstrual period, when a single dose is sufficient to cause severe limb abnormalities in most patients (*J Am Acad Dermatol* 1996;35:969). It is *critical* that any woman of child-bearing potential not receive thalidomide unless great precautions are taken to prevent pregnancy (pills and barrier protection). Because thalidomide may be present in semen, condom use is recommended for men. Company records indicate that through January 2001, there were 26,968 patients treated, and there were no documented exposures during pregnancy. Several male exposures followed by conception were noted, but none resulted in birth defects.
- **Dose effect:** Teratogenic effects occur even with single dose. Neuropathy, rash, constipation, neutropenia, and sedation are common dose-related side effects found in up to 50% of AIDS patients and are more frequent with low CD4 cell counts (*Clin Infect Dis* 1997;24:1223; *J Infect Dis* 2002;185:1359).
- **Drowsiness:** Most common side effect is the sedation for which the drug was initially marketed. Administer at bedtime and reduce dose to minimize this side effect. There may be morning somnolence or "hangover."
- **Rash:** Usually pruritic, erythematous, and macular over trunk, back, and proximal extremities. TEN and Stevens-Johnson syndrome have been reported. Re-challenge following erythematous rash has resulted in severe reactions and should only be done with caution.
- **Neuropathy:** Dose-related paresthesias and/or pain of extremities, especially with high doses or prolonged use. This complication may or may not be reversible; it is not known whether the risk is increased by diabetes, alcoholism, or use of neurotoxic drugs including ddI, d4T, or ddC. Symptoms may start after the drug is discontinued. Neuropathy is a contraindication to the drug, and neurologic monitoring should be performed for all patients.
- **HIV:** Thalidomide may cause modest increase in plasma levels of HIV RNA (0.4 $\log_{10}$/mL) (*N Engl J Med* 1997:336:1487).
- **Neutropenia:** Discontinue thalidomide if ANC is <750/mm^3 without an alternative cause.

- **Constipation is common:** Use stool softener, hydration, milk of magnesia, etc.
- **Less common side effects** include dizziness, mood changes, bradycardia, tachycardia, bitter taste, headache, nausea, pruritus, dry mouth, dry skin, or hypotension.

DRUG INTERACTIONS: The greatest concern is in women of child-bearing potential who take concurrent medications that interfere with the effectiveness of contraceptives. Concurrent use of drugs that cause sedation or peripheral neuropathy may increase the frequency and severity of these side effects.

PREGNANCY: Category X (contraindicated)

TRAZODONE

TRADE NAME: *Desyrel* (Bristol-Myers Squibb) or generic

FORMS AND PRICES: Tabs: 50 mg at $0.40, 100 mg at $0.63, 150 mg at $1.41, 300 mg at $5.44

CLASS: Nontricyclic antidepressant (see Table 7-17, pp. 387-388)

INDICATIONS AND DOSE REGIMENS

- **Depression**, especially when associated with anxiety or insomnia: 400-600 mg/day in two doses. If insomnia or daytime sedation, give as single dose at hs. Increase dose 50 mg every 3 to 4 days up to maximum dose of 400 mg/day for outpatients and 600 mg/day for hospitalized patients.
- **Insomnia:** 25-150 mg qhs

PHARMACOLOGY

- **Bioavailability:** >90%, improved if taken with meals
- **T½:** 6 hours
- **Elimination:** Hepatic metabolism, then renal excretion

SIDE EFFECTS: Adverse effects are dose- and duration-related and are usually seen with doses >300 mg/day; may decrease with continued use, dose reduction, or schedule change.

- **Major side effects:** Sedation in 15% to 20%; orthostatic hypotension (5%); nervousness; fatigue; dizziness; nausea; vomiting; and anticholinergic effects (dry mouth, blurred vision, constipation, urinary retention). Rare – priapism (1/6000); agitation; cardiovascular; and anticholinergic side effects are less frequent and less severe than with tricyclics.

DRUG INTERACTIONS: Increased levels of phenytoin and digoxin; alcohol and other CNS depressants potentiate sedative side effects;

increased trazodone levels with fluoxetine; may potentiate effects of antihypertensive agents.

PREGNANCY: Category B

TRIAZOLAM

TRADE NAME: *Halcion* (Pharmacia)

FORMS AND PRICES: Tabs: 0.125 mg at $0.67, 0.25 mg at $0.70

CLASS: Benzodiazepine, controlled substance category IV (see p. 185)

INDICATIONS AND DOSE REGIMENS

- **Insomnia:** 0.125-0.5 mg (usually 0.25 mg) hs for 7 to 10 days
- **Note:** Current FDA guidelines state that triazolam should be prescribed for short-term use (7 to 10 days), the prescribed dose should not exceed a 1 month supply, and use for more than 2 to 3 weeks requires re-evaluation of patient.

PHARMACOLOGY

- **Bioavailability:** >90%
- **T½:** 1.5 to 5.0 hours
- **Elimination:** Metabolized by liver to inactive metabolites that are renally excreted.

SIDE EFFECTS: See Benzodiazepines, p. 185. Most common are drowsiness, incoordination, dizziness, and amnesia. Anecdotal reports of delirium, confusion, paranoia, and hallucinations.

INTERACTIONS: Contraindicated for concurrent use with all PIs, EFV, and DLV; "caution" with NVP.

PREGNANCY: Category X

TRICYCLIC ANTIDEPRESSANTS – see also Nortriptyline (p. 272)

Tricyclic antidepressants elevate mood, increase physical activity, improve appetite, improve sleep patterns, and reduce morbid preoccupations in most patients with major depression. The following principles apply:

INDICATIONS

- **Psychiatric indications:** Major depression – response rates are 60% to 70%. Low doses are commonly used for adjustment disorders including depression and anxiety.
- **Peripheral neuropathy:** Controlled trials have not shown benefit in AIDS-associated peripheral neuropathy, but clinical experience is

extensive and results in diabetic neuropathy are good. If used, choice of agents depends on time of symptoms (*JAMA* 1998;280:1590). Night pain: Amitriptyline (sedating) 25 mg hs; increase to a therapeutic serum level of 150-300 ng/mL. Day pain: Nortriptyline (less sedating and less of an anticholinergic effect) 25 mg hs; increasing to therapeutic serum level of 50-150 ng/mL.

DOSE: Initial treatment of depression is 4 to 8 weeks, which is required for therapeutic response. Much or all of the initial dose is given at hs, especially if insomnia is prominent or if sedation is a side effect. Common mistakes are use of an initial dose that is too high, resulting in excessive anticholinergic side effects or oversedation. The dose is increased every 3 to 4 days depending on tolerance and response. Treatment of major depression usually requires continuation for 4 to 5 months after response. Multiple recurrences may require long-term treatment.

SERUM LEVELS: Efficacy correlates with serum levels of nortriptylene. Therapeutic monitoring of drug levels allows dose titration.

PHARMACOLOGY: Well absorbed, extensively metabolized, long half-life, variable use of serum levels (see below).

SIDE EFFECTS: Anticholinergic effects (dry mouth, dizziness, blurred vision, constipation, tachycardia, urinary hesitancy, sedation), sexual dysfunction, orthostatic hypotension, weight gain

RELATIVE CONTRAINDICATIONS: Cardiac conduction block, prostatism, and narrow angle glaucoma. Less common side effects – mania, hypomania, allergic skin reactions, marrow suppression, seizures, tardive dyskinesia, tremor, speech blockage, anxiety, insomnia, Parkinsonism, hyponatremia; cardiac conduction disturbances and arrhythmias (most common serious side effects are with overdosage)

TRIMETHOPRIM

TRADE NAME: Generic

FORMS AND PRICES: Tabs: 100 mg at $0.17, 200 mg at $0.25

INDICATIONS AND DOSE REGIMENS

- **PCP** (with sulfamethoxazole as TMP-SMX or with dapsone): 5 mg/kg PO tid or qid (usually 300 mg tid or qid) x 21 days
- **UTIs:** 100 mg PO bid or 200 mg x 1/day x 3 to 14 days

PHARMACOLOGY

- **Bioavailability:** >90%
- **T½:** 9 to 11 hours
- **Excretion:** Renal

- **Dose modification with renal failure:** CrCl >50 mL/min – full dose; 10-50 mL/min – half dose

SIDE EFFECTS: Usually well tolerated; most common – pruritus and skin rash; GI intolerance; marrow suppression – anemia, neutropenia, thrombocytopenia; antifolate effects – prevent with leucovorin; reversible hyperkalemia in 20% to 50% of AIDS patients given high doses (*Ann Intern Med* 1993;119:291,296; *N Engl J Med* 1993;238:703).

DRUG INTERACTIONS: Increased activity of phenytoin (monitor levels) and procainamide; levels of both dapsone and trimethoprim are increased when given concurrently.

PREGNANCY: Category C. Teratogenic in rats with high doses; limited experience in patients shows no association with congenital abnormalities.

TRIMETHOPRIM-SULFAMETHOXAZOLE (TMP-SMX, cotrimoxazole)

TRADE NAME: *Bactrim* (Roche) or generic

■ TABLE 6-42: **TMP-SMX Forms and Prices**

	Single Strength 80/400 mg*	Double Strength 160/800 mg	IV Preparation TMP – 16 mg/mL SMX – 80 mg/mL
Generic	$0.14	$0.18	10 mL $2.68
Bactrim	$0.71	$1.18	10 mL $10.00

* 80 mg trimethoprim plus 400 mg sulfamethoxazole.

INDICATIONS AND DOSE REGIMENS

- **PCP prophylaxis:** 1 DS/day or 1 SS/day; alternative is 1 DS 3x/week. Discontinuation of PCP prophylaxis after HAART-associated immune reconstitution is safe and avoids significant toxicity (*Clin Infect Dis* 2001;33:1901; *MMWR* 2002;51[RR-8]:4).
- **Graduated initiation to reduce adverse effects** (ACTG 268) (*J Acquir Immune Defic Syndr* 2000;24:337)**:** Oral preparation (40 mg trimethoprim and 200 mg sulfamethoxazole/5mL) – 1 mL/day x 3 days, then 2 mL/day x 3 days, then 5 mL/day x 3 days, then 10 mL/day x 3 days, then 20 mL x 3 days, then 1 TMP-SMX DS tab/day
- **Desensitization:** See p. 318
- **PCP treatment:** 5 mg/kg (trimethoprim component) PO or IV q8h x 21 days, usually 5-6 DS/day
- **Toxoplasmosis prophylaxis:** 1 DS/day

- **Toxoplasmosis treatment** (third line): 5 mg/kg TMP PO or IV bid (*Eur J Clin Microbiol Infect Dis* 1992;11:125; *Antimicrob Agents Chemother* 1998;42:1346).
- ***Isospora:*** 1 DS PO bid or tid x 2 to 4 weeks; may need maintenance with 1-2 DS/day. IDSA recommendation: TMP-SMX 1 DS bid x 7 to 10 days, then 1 DS 3x/week or 1 *Fansidar* every week indefinitely.
- **Salmonellosis:** 1 DS PO bid x 5 to 7 days; treat >14 days if relapsing.
- ***Nocardia:*** 4-6 DS/day x ≥6 months
- **Urinary tract infections:** 1-2 DS/day x 3 to 14 days
- **Prophylaxis for cystitis:** ½ SS tab daily

ACTIVITY: TMP-SMX is effective in the treatment or prophylaxis of infections involving *P. carinii*, methicillin-sensitive *S. aureus*, *Legionella*, *Listeria*, and common urinary tract pathogens. Recent studies show increasing rates of mutations in the dihydropteroate synthase gene of *P. carinii* that are associated with increased resistance to sulfonamides and dapsone (*J Infect Dis* 1999;180:1969); the clinical significance is unclear, but it is generally thought to be unimportant because there is little correlation between resistance mutations and poor clinical outcome (*J Infect Dis* 2000;182:1192; *J Infect Dis* 2000;182:551; *JAMA* 2001;286:2450; *Lancet* 2001; 358:545). Current rates of resistance of *S. pneumoniae* to TMP-SMX are about 15% to 30% (*Antimicrob Agents Chemother* 2002;46:2651; *N Engl J Med* 2000;343:1917).

PHARMACOLOGY

- **Bioavailability:** >90% absorbed with oral administration (both drugs)
- **T½:** Trimethoprim, 8 to 15 hours; sulfamethoxazole 7 to 12 hours
- **Elimination:** Renal; T½ in renal failure increases to 24 hours for trimethoprim and 22 to 50 hours for sulfamethoxazole
- **Renal failure:** CrCl >50 mL/min – usual dose; 10-50 mL/min – half dose; <10 mL/min – manufacturer recommends avoidance, but ½-⅓ dose may be used

SIDE EFFECTS: Noted in 10% of patients without HIV infection and about 50% of patients with HIV. The gradual initiation of TMP-SMX noted above results in a 50% reduction in adverse reactions (*J Acquir Immune Defic Syndr* 2000;24:337), suggesting that it is not a true hypersensitivity reaction. The prevailing opinion is that these side effects are usually due to toxic metabolites ascribed to altered metabolism of TMP-SMX with HIV infection. The presumed benefit from gradual initiation or desensitization is to permit time for enzyme induction.

- **Most common:** Nausea, vomiting, pruritus, rash, fever, neutropenia, and increased transaminases. Many HIV infected patients may be treated despite side effects (GI intolerance and rash) if symptoms are not disabling; alternative with PCP prophylaxis is dose reduction usually after drug holiday (1 to 2 weeks) and/or "desensitization" (see below). The mechanism of most sulfonamide reactions is unclear, and cause of increased susceptibility with HIV is also unclear.
- **Rash:** Most common is erythematous, maculopapular, morbilliform, and/or pruritic rash, usually 7 to 14 days after treatment is started. Less common are erythema multiforme, epidermal necrolysis, exfoliative dermatitis, Stevens-Johnson syndrome, urticaria, and Schönlein-Henoch purpura.
- **GI intolerance** is common with nausea, vomiting, anorexia, and abdominal pain; rare side effects include *C. difficile* diarrhea/colitis and pancreatitis.
- **Hematologic side effects** include neutropenia, anemia, and/or thrombocytopenia. The rate of anemia is increased in patients with HIV infection and with folate depletion. Some respond to leucovorin (5-15 mg/day), but this is not routinely recommended.
- **Neurologic** toxicity may include tremor, ataxia, apathy, and ankle clonus that responds promptly to drug discontinuation.
- **Hepatitis** with cholestatic jaundice and hepatic necrosis has been described.
- **Hyperkalemia** in 20% to 50% of patients given trimethoprim in doses >15 mg/kg/day (*N Engl J Med* 1993;328:703)
- **Meningitis** (*Am J Med Sci* 1996;312:27)

PROTOCOL FOR ORAL "DESENSITIZATION" OR "DETOXIFICATION"

- **Rapid desensitization** (*Clin Infect Dis* 1995;20:849): Serial 10-fold dilutions of oral suspension (40 mg TMP, 200 mg SMX/5 mL) given hourly over 4 hours (see Table 6-43, below).
- **Note:** A prospective trial showed no difference in outcome with desensitization compared with rechallenge (*Biomed Pharmacother* 2000;54:45).

■ TABLE 6-43: **Rapid TMP-SMX Desensitization Schedule**

Time (hour)	Dose (TMP/SMX)	Dilution
0	0.004/0.02 mg	1:10,000 (5 mL)
1	0.04/0.2 mg	1:1,000 (5 mL)
2	0.4/2.0 mg	1:100 (5 mL)
3	4/20 mg	1:10 (5 mL)
4	40/200 mg	(5 mL)
5	160/800 mg	Tablet

- **8-day protocol:** Serial dilutions prepared by pharmacists using oral suspension (40 mg TMP, 200 mg SMX/5 mL). Medication is given 4 times daily for 7 days in doses of 1 cc, 2 cc, 4 cc, and 8 cc using the following dilutions.

■ TABLE 6-44: **8-Day TMP-SMX Desensitization Schedule**

Day	Dilution
1	1:1,000,000
2	1:100,000
3	1:10,000
4	1:1,000
5	1:100
6	1:10
7	1:1
8	Standard suspension – 1 mL 40 mg SMX – 8 mg TMP
≥9	1 DS tab/day

DRUG INTERACTIONS: Increased levels of oral anticoagulants, phenytoin, and procainamide. Risk of megaloblastic anemia with methotrexate.

PREGNANCY: Category C. Teratogenic in animals. No congenital abnormalities noted in 35 children born to women who received TMP-SMX in first trimester. Use with caution due to possible kernicterus, although no cases of kernicterus have been reported (*Clin Infect Dis* 1995;21[suppl 1]:S24).

TRIZIVIR – see also Zidovudine, p. 327; Lamivudine, p. 252; and Abacavir, p. 164 (GlaxoSmithKline)

FORMS AND PRICES: Film coated tab with AZT 300 mg + 3TC 150 mg + ABC 300 mg at $18.48 or $13,493/year ($234.50/week)

FINANCIAL ASSISTANCE: 800-722-9294

PRODUCT INFORMATION: 800-334-0089

DOSE: 1 PO bid with or without food

CLASS: Nucleoside analog

CLINICAL TRIALS

- **CNA 3003** compared AZT/3TC/ABC vs AZT/3TC in 173 treatment-naïve patients with CD4 cell counts >100/mm³. At 24 weeks, 70% of those in the three-drug arm had viral load <400 c/mL, and the mean CD4 cell count increase was 86/mm³. These results were sustained at 48 weeks, but subset analysis showed that only 33%

with a baseline viral load >100,000 c/mL had viral load <400 cells/mm³ (6th CROI, Chicago, Illinois, 1999, Abstract 16).

- **CNA 3005** compared AZT/3TC/ABC vs IDV/AZT/3TC in 562 treatment-naïve patients with CD4 cell counts >100/mm³. At 48 weeks, 51% in both groups had viral load <400 c/mL by intent-to-treat analysis; increases in CD4 cell counts were also comparable (40th ICAAC, Toronto, Canada, 1999, Abstract 505). Genotypic resistance tests in triple nucleoside failures showed wild-type virus or RT codon 184 mutations (7th CROI, San Francisco, California, 2000, Abstract 331).
- **TRIZAL** study (AZL 30002) compared 209 patients randomized to continue HAART or switch to AZT/3TC/ABC after achieving a viral load <50 c/mL on HAART. At 24 weeks, failure (viral load >400 c/mL) occurred in 20% who switched to the triple-nucleoside regimen compared with 17% who continued the original HAART regimen. Recipients of triple nucleosides had significant decreases in serum cholesterol and triglycerides (8th CROI, Chicago, Illinois, 2001, Abstract 316).
- **CNA 3014** compared the AZT/3TC (*Combivir*) plus either abacavir or indinavir in a randomized, multicenter open-label trial (1st IAS Conference, Buenos Aires, 2001, Abstract 63). A total of 342 patients were enrolled. By intent-to-treat analysis, 66% of ABC recipients had viral loads <400 c/mL compared to 50% of the IDV group ($p<0.002$). By as-treated analysis, success rates were 85% and 83%, respectively. When analysis was confined to patients with baseline viral loads >100,000 c/mL, proportions of ABC and IDV recipients with viral loads <400 c/mL were 60% and 51%, respectively, by intent-to-treat analysis, and 70% and 79% by as-treated analysis. Among patients with baseline viral loads >100,000 c/mL, viral load was <50 c/mL in 48% vs 46% by intent-to-treat analysis, and 59% vs 73% using an as-treated analysis. Adherence was significantly better among ABC recipients in this open-label trial.
- **Advantages**
  - Simplest regimen with regard to pill burden.
  - Appears to be associated with reduced hypertriglyceridemia, hyperglycemia, and fat accumulation compared with PI-containing regimens.
  - Reserves PI and NNRTI options.
  - Included as a "preferred regimen" for initial therapy in WHO guidelines and IAS-USA guidelines (*JAMA* 2002;288:222).
- **Disadvantages**
  - May be less potent than PI- or NNRTI-containing HAART regimens when baseline viral load >100,000 c/mL.
  - Hypersensitivity reactions (ABC) and tolerability issues (AZT).

■ TABLE 6-45: ***Trizivir* Summary**

	AZT	3TC	ABC
Absorption	60%	86%	80%
Elimination	Hepatic metabolism→ renal excretion	Metabolized	Metabolized→ renal excretion
T½ serum	1.1 hours	5 to 7 hours	1.5 hours
intracellular	3 hours	12 hours	3.3 hours
Drug interactions	Avoid d4T Marrow-suppressing drugs	None	None
Adverse reactions	■ GI intolerance ■ Anemia ■ Neutropenia ■ Asthenia	None	Hypersensitivity reaction; especially first 6 weeks; may be severe
Resistance	41L, 67N, 69ins, 70R, 151M, 210W, 215Y/F, 219Q/E	44D, 118I, T69ins, 151M, M184V	41L, 65R, 67N, 69ins, 70R, 74V, 115F, Q151M, 184V, 210W, 215Y/F, 219Q/E

PHARMACOLOGY, SIDE EFFECTS, DRUG INTERACTION AND RESISTANCE MUTATIONS: See individual agents: AZT, p. 327; 3TC, p. 252; ABC, p. 164.

PREGNANCY: Class C

VALACYCLOVIR – see Acyclovir, p. 168

VALGANCICLOVIR – see Ganciclovir, p. 229

VANCOMYCIN

TRADE NAME: *Vancocin* (Eli Lilly) or generic

FORMS AND PRICES

- **Parenteral:** 0.5 g vial at $12.61/500 mg
- **Oral:** Parvules 125 mg at $6.40 (10 day course at $256)
  500 mg vial for 4 oral doses at $5.76 ($5.76/day)

CLASS: Tricyclic glycopeptide antibiotic

INDICATIONS AND DOSES: Deep infections involving MRSA and *S. epidermidis*, infections involving other gram-positive bacteria in penicillin-allergic patients: 1 g IV q12h infused ≥1 hour (± rifampin or gentamicin). *C. difficile* colitis: 125 mg PO qid x 10 days. Usual dose: IV 1 g q12h; oral 125 mg qid (*C. difficile)*

ACTIVITY: Nearly all gram-positive bacteria, including all *S. aureus* are sensitive; 5% to 20% of hospital strains of *Enterococcus faecium* are resistant.

PHARMACOLOGY

- **Bioavailability:** Not absorbed with PO administration, but may accumulate in serum with inflamed gut plus renal failure.
- **T½:** 4 to 6 hours
- **Elimination:** Renal
- **Dose modification in renal failure:** CrCl >50 mL/min – 15 mg/kg IV q12h, CrCl 10-50 mL/min – 15 mg/kg qd-q3d; CrCl <10 mL/min – 15 mg/kg q 3 to 7 days.

SIDE EFFECTS

- **Red man syndrome:** Hypotension and flushing ± dyspnea, urticaria, pruritus, and/or wheezing ascribed to histamine release from mast cells, which is directly related to rate of infusion. This usually begins shortly after infusion starts and may require antihistamines, corticosteroids, or IV fluids; most patients benefit from dose reduction, prolongation of infusion, and/or pretreatment with antihistamine.
- **Ototoxicity and nephrotoxicity:** Infrequent and most likely with renal failure, high doses, long courses, and concurrent use of nephrotoxic or ototoxic drugs. Many authorities believe that current supplies of vancomycin are not nephrotoxic if used alone, but vancomycin appears to promote nephrotoxicity of other nephrotoxic drugs such as aminoglycosides. Relationship to serum levels is unclear and value of serum levels to monitor toxicity is unclear.
- **Thrombophlebitis** and pain at infusion site.
- **Hypersensitivity reactions** are rare; most reactions are the result of histamine release due to rapid infusion.

VIBRAMYCIN – see Doxycycline (p. 206)

VIDEX – see Didanosine (p. 202)

VIRACEPT – see Nelfinavir (p. 264)

VIRAMUNE – see Nevirapine (p. 267)

VITRASERT – see Ganciclovir (p. 229)

VITRAVENE – see Fomivirsen (p. 225)

VORICONAZOLE

TRADE NAME: *Vfend* (Pfizer)

FORMS AND PRICE: Tabs: 50 mg, 200 mg at $50; Vial for IV use: 200 mg at $127

CLASS: Triazole

REGIMENS

- **Oral:** 200 mg PO tid x 1 day (loading dose), then 200-300 mg PO bid
- **IV:** 6 mg/kg IV q12h x 2 doses (loading dose), then 3-4 mg/kg IV q12h
- **Hepatic failure:** Use half dose
- **Renal failure:** Use standard oral dose (Child-Pugh class A and B)

***IN VITRO* ACTIVITY:** Active against most *Candida* species, including fluconazole resistant strains. Active against >98% of *C. albicans, C. krusei, C. tropicalis,* and *C. parapsilosis* (*Antimicrob Agents Chemother* 2002;46:1032; *J Med Microbiol* 2002;51:479; *J Clin Microbiol* 2002;40:852). Very active against most *Aspergillus*; more active *in vitro* than itraconazole (*J Infect Chemother* 2000;6:101; *Clin Infect Dis* 2002;34:563; *Clin Micro* 2002;40:2648; *Antimicrob Agents Chemother* 2002;46:1032). Zygomycetes (mucor) are less susceptible (*Antimicrob Agents Chemother* 2002;46:2708; *Antimicrob Agents Chemother* 2002;46:1581; *Antimicrob Agents Chemother* 2002;46:1032). Activity against *Scedosporium apiospermum* (*Pseudoallescheria boydii*) is variable (*Antimicrob Agents Chemother* 2002;46:62). Most dermatophytes are sensitive (*Antimicrob Agents Chemother* 2001;45:2524). *C. neoformans* is usually highly susceptible with *in vitro* activity superior to both fluconazole and itraconazole (*Eur J Clin Microbiol* 2000;19:317; *Antimicrob Agents Chemother* 1999;43:1463; *Antimicrob Agents Chemother* 1999;43:169).

FDA APPROVAL: Voriconazole is approved for treatment of invasive aspergillosis and serious infections caused by *Scedosporium apiospermum* and *Fusarium* spp.

CLINICAL TRIAL: Major clinical trial compared voriconazole (6 mg/kg IV q12h x 2 doses, then 4 mg/kg IV q 12 x ≥7 days, then oral voriconazole 200 mg bid) with amphotericin B (1.0-1.5 mg/kg/day IV) in 277 patients with invasive *Aspergillus*. Voriconazole showed a significantly better response rate (53% vs 32%), better 12-week survival (71% vs 58%), and less toxicity (*N Engl J Med* 2002;347:408).

PHARMACOLOGY

- **Oral bioavailability:** 96%; AUC reduced by 24% when taken with high-fat meal

- **CNS penetration:** Preliminary data suggest that effective levels are achieved in CSF (*Br J Haematol* 1997:97:663).
- **Loading dose:** Day 1; without loading dose, the maintenance dose requires 6 days to reach steady state.
- **Metabolism:** Metabolized primarily by P450 CYP2C19 enzymes. >94% of metabolite is excreted in urine; metabolites have little or no antifungal activity; <2% parenteral formal is excreted in urine.
- **Hepatic failure:** AUC increases 2.3 fold – use 100 mg bid.
- **Levels:** Expect level ≥0.5 μg/mL.

DRUG INTERACTIONS: Based on induction or inhibition of P450 enzymes (*Antimicrob Agents Chemother* 2002;46:3091)

- **Contraindicated for concurrent use** (decrease voriconazole levels): Rifampin, rifabutin, carbamazepine, phenobarbital. (Voriconazole increases concurrent drug): Sirolimus, terfenadine, astemizole, cisapride, pimozide, quinidine, ergot derivatives
- **Alter dose**
    - Cyclosporine: Increase cyclosporine, use half dose cyclosporine and monitor levels.
    - Tacrolimus: Increase tacrolimus levels 2x; use ⅓ dose tacrolimus.
    - Warfarin: Increase prothrombin time, monitor.
    - Statins: Increase statin levels expected, reduce statin dose.
    - Benzodiazepines: Midazolam, triazolam + alprazolam increased levels expected, reduce benzodiazepine dose.
    - Calcium channel blocker: Felodipine level increase expected, may need dose decrease.
    - Sulfonylureas: Tolbutamide, glipizide + glyburide level increases expected, monitor blood glucose.
    - Vinca alkaloids: Vincristine + vinblastine levels increase expected, reduce dose to avoid neurotoxicity.
    - Phenytoin: Decrease voriconazole, double oral dose of voriconazole and monitor phenytoin levels.
    - Omeprazole: Levels double, reduce omeprazole to half dose.
- **Protease inhibitors:** IDV – no effect on either drug; other PIs – may increase levels of SQV, APV, and NFV, and these may increase voriconazole levels.
- **NNRTI:** Voriconazole levels may be increased by DLV or EFV and may be decreased by NVP or EFV, monitor.

SIDE EFFECTS

- **Visual effects** are most common; 30% in clinical trials; these include altered visual perception, color change, blurred vision, and/or photophobia. Changes are dose related, reversible and infrequently require discontinuing therapy, but patients should be warned.

- **Rash** in 6%, including rare cases of Stevens-Johnson syndrome, erythema multiforme and toxic epidermal necrolysis.
- **Hepatotoxicity:** Elevated transaminases in 13%, usually resolves with continued drug administration. Serious hepatic toxicity is rare, but supplier recommends monitoring liver enzymes.

PREGNANCY: Category D. Teratogenic in rodents and congenital anomalies in rabbits.

WINRHO –see Rho (D) immune globulin (p. 286)

XANAX – see Alprazolam (p. 172)

ZALCITABINE (ddC)

TRADE NAME: *Hivid* (Roche)

FORMS AND PRICES: Tabs: 0.375 mg at $2.18, 0.75 mg at $2.73 (cost per year is $2,989)

FINANCIAL ASSISTANCE: 800-282-7780

CLASS: Nucleoside analog

INDICATIONS: In ACTG 155, the addition of ddC after ≥6 months treatment with AZT provided no clear benefit based on clinical parameters – delayed progression and prolonged survival (*Ann Intern Med* 1994;122:24). ACTG 175 confirmed this finding but also demonstrated that ddC + AZT was superior to AZT monotherapy in AZT-naïve patients with CD4 cell counts of 200-500/mm^3 (*N Engl J Med* 1996;335:1081).

DOSE: 0.75 mg PO tid; food – no effect

RESISTANCE: Mutations on the RT gene that confer resistance are 69D/N/A, 74V, and 184V. The 74 and 184V mutations suppress AZT resistance. Resistance to ddC appears to be uncommon during combination treatment (*J Acquir Immune Defic Syndr* 1994;7:135; *J Infect Dis* 1996;173:1354). In Delta 1, there were no detectable mutations conferring ddC resistance after 112 weeks of treatment (*Lancet* 1996;348:283). Susceptibility to ddC is also decreased by thymidine analog mutations (TAMs).

PHARMACOLOGY

- **Bioavailability:** 70% to 88%
- **T½:** 1.2 hours

- **Intracellular T½:** 3 hours; CSF levels: 20% serum levels (CSF: plasma ratio=0.09-0.37)
- **Elimination:** Renal excretion – 70%
- **Dose adjustment in renal failure:** CrCl >50 mL/min – 0.75 mg PO tid; 10-50 mL/min – 0.75 mg PO bid; <10 mL/min – 0.75 mg PO qd. Dialysis – presumably 0.75 mg post dialysis.

SIDE EFFECTS

- **Neuropathy:** The major clinical toxicity is peripheral neuropathy, noted in 17% to 31% of patients in initial trials. It is more frequent than with ddI or d4T (*N Engl J Med* 1996;335:1099). Features are bilateral sensorimotor neuropathy with numbness and burning in distal extremities, usually after 2 to 6 months of therapy, followed by shooting or continuous pain. Symptoms usually resolve slowly if the drug is promptly discontinued; with continued use it may be irreversible and require narcotics. Frequency depends on dose and duration of ddC treatment. Pain requiring narcotics or progressive pain for ≥1 week represents a contraindication to future use; patients with less severe pain that resolves to mild intensity may be rechallenged with half dose.
- **Stomatitis and aphthous esophageal ulcers:** Seen in 2% to 4% (*Ann Intern Med* 1992;117:133) and usually resolve with continued ddC treatment.
- **Pancreatitis:** Noted in <1% of patients, but more frequently in those with a history of prior pancreatitis or elevated amylase levels at the time the treatment was started.
- **Rash** is common after 10 to 14 days of treatment; it is a red maculopapular rash over the trunk and extremities, and it usually resolves spontaneously.
- **Class adverse reactions:** NRTIs may cause lactic acidosis and steatosis. This drug appears to be associated with significant mitochondrial toxicity.

INTERACTIONS: Drugs that cause peripheral neuropathy should be used with caution or avoided: ddI, d4T, EMB, cisplatin, disulfiram, ethionamide, INH, phenytoin, vincristine, glutethimide, gold, hydralazine, and long-term metronidazole.

PREGNANCY: Category C. Teratogenic and embryolethal in doses >1000 x those used in patients; carcinogenicity studies – thymic lymphomas in rodents; placental passage in rhesus monkeys show newborn:maternal drug ratio of 0.3-0.5; no studies in humans.

ZERIT – see Stavudine (p. 303)

ZIAGEN – see Abacavir (p. 164)

ZIDOVUDINE (AZT, ZDV)

TRADE NAME: *Retrovir*, *Combivir* (AZT/3TC), *Trizivir* (AZT/3TC/ABC) (GlaxoSmithKline)

FORMS AND PRICES: 100 mg caps at $2.05, 300 mg tabs at $6.15 (cost per year is $4,490). IV vials: 10 mg/mL at $16.74 per 20 mL (200 mg). *Combivir* tabs with 3TC 150 mg + AZT 300 mg at $11.42. *Trizivir* tabs with 3TC 150 mg + ABC 300 mg + AZT 300 mg at $18.50.

PATIENT ASSISTANCE PROGRAM: 800-722-9294

CLASS: Nucleoside analog

DOSES: AZT 300 mg bid, 200 mg tid; food – no effect

- *Combivir*, 1 bid
- *Trizivir*, 1 bid
- IV AZT (ACTG 076 protocol-intrapartum) 2 mg/kg IV over 1 hour, then 1 mg/kg/hour until delivery

NOTE: Use with caution with ribavirin.

CLINICAL TRIALS: FDA-approved in 1987 based on a controlled clinical trial showing significant short-term benefit in preventing AIDS-defining opportunistic infections and death (*N Engl J Med* 1987;317:185). Early studies (ACTG 019, 076, 175, Concord, etc.) became sentinel reports. Despite 15 years of use, resistance in recently transmitted strains is only about 2% (*N Engl J Med* 2002;347:385). AZT is commonly paired with 3TC (*Combivir*), ddI, or ABC/3TC (*Trizivir*) as the nucleoside components of HAART regimens. Potency of these regimens is well established. ACTG 384 showed that AZT/3TC/EFV was superior to ddI/d4T/EFV, but this difference was not observed when nucleoside pairs were combined with NVP (XIV International AIDS Conference, Barcelona, July 2002, Abstract LB20a).

RESISTANCE: The thymidine analog mutations (TAMs) are 41L, 67N, 70R, 210W, 215Y/F, and 219Q/E. A total of 3 to 6 mutations result in a 100-fold decrease in sensitivity. About 5% to 10% of recipients of AZT + ddI develop the Q51M complex, and a larger number have the T69 insertion mutation, both of which confer high-level resistance to AZT, ddI, ddC, d4T, 3TC and ABC. The M184V mutation that confers high-level 3TC resistance delays or restores susceptibility to AZT unless there are multiple TAMs. Analysis of patients with early HIV infection indicates that 2% to 10% have genotypic mutations associated with reduced susceptibility to AZT (*N Engl J Med* 2002;347:385).

PHARMACOLOGY

- **Bioavailability:** 60%; high-fat meals may decrease absorption CSF levels: 60% serum levels (CSF:plasma ratio=0.3-1.35) (*Lancet* 1998;351:1547).
- **T½:** 1.1 hours; Renal failure: 1.4 hours
- **Intracellular T½:** 3 hours
- **Elimination:** Metabolized by liver to glucuronide (GAZT) that is renally excreted.
- **Dose modification in renal failure or hepatic failure:** Excreted in urine as active drug (14% to 18%) and GAZT metabolite (60% to 74%). In severe renal failure (CrCl <18 mL/min), AZT half-life is increased from 1.1 to 1.4 hours and GAZT half-life increased from 0.9 to 8.0 hours. Dosing recommendation: GFR >10 mL/min – 300 mg bid; GFR <10 mL/mm – 300 mg/day; hemodialysis and peritoneal dialysis – 300 mg/day. With severe liver disease, some authorities advocate 100 mg tid.

SIDE EFFECTS

- **Subjective:** GI intolerance, altered taste (dysgeusia), insomnia, myalgias, asthenia, malaise, and/or headaches are common and are dose related (*Ann Intern Med* 1993;118:913). Most patients can be managed with symptomatic treatment.
- **Marrow suppression:** Related to marrow reserve, dose and duration of treatment, and stage of disease. Anemia may occur within 4 to 6 weeks, and neutropenia is usually seen after 12 to 24 weeks. Marrow examination in patients with AZT-induced anemia may be normal or show reduced RBC precursors. Severe anemia should be managed by discontinuing AZT or giving erythropoietin concurrently (see pp. 360 and 214). With neutropenia, an ANC <750/mm^3 should be managed by discontinuing AZT or giving G-CSF concurrently (see p. 232).
- **Myopathy:** Rare dose-related complication possibly due to mitochondrial toxicity. Clinical features are leg and gluteal muscle weakness, elevated LDH and CPK, muscle biopsy showing ragged red fibers, and abnormal mitochondria (*N Engl J Med* 1990;322: 1098); response to discontinuation of AZT occurs within 2 to 4 weeks.
- **Macrocytosis:** Noted within 4 weeks of starting AZT in virtually all patients and serves as crude indicator of adherence.
- **Hepatitis** with reversible increases in transaminase levels, sometimes within 2 to 3 weeks of starting treatment.
- **Class adverse reaction:** Lactic acidosis, often with steatosis, is a complication ascribed to all nucleoside analogs but primarily to d4T and ddC, and to a lesser degree, ddl and AZT. This complication should be considered in patients with fatigue, abdominal pain,

nausea, vomiting, and dyspnea. Laboratory tests show elevated serum lactate, CPK, ALT and/or LDH, and reduced serum bicarbonate. Abdominal CT scan or liver biopsy may show steatosis. This is a life-threatening complication. Pregnant women and obese women appear to be at increased risk. NRTIs should be stopped or there should be a change to NRTIs that show low rates of mitochondrial toxicity.

- **Fingernail discoloration** with dark bluish discoloration at base of nail noted at 2 to 6 weeks.
- **Carcinogenicity:** Long-term treatment with high doses in mice caused vaginal neoplasms; relevance to humans is not known.

DRUG INTERACTIONS: Additive or synergistic against HIV with ddI, ddC, ABC, alpha interferon, and foscarnet *in vitro*; antagonism with ribavirin, ganciclovir, and d4T. AZT and d4T should not be given concurrently due to *in vitro* and *in vivo* evidence of antagonism. Clinical significance of interaction with ganciclovir and ribavirin is unknown. Methadone increases levels of AZT 30% to 40%; AZT has no effect on methadone levels (*J Acquir Immune Defic Syndr* 1998;18:435). Marrow suppression usually precludes concurrent use with ganciclovir. Other marrow-suppressing drugs should be used with caution: TMP-SMX, dapsone, pyrimethamine, flucytosine, interferon, adriamycin, vinblastine, sulfadiazine, vincristine, amphotericin B, and hydroxyurea. Probenecid increases levels of AZT, but concurrent use is complicated by a high incidence of rash reactions to probenecid.

PREGNANCY: Category C. Advocated for pregnant women beyond first trimester to prevent vertical transmission.

Positive in rodent teratogen assay at near lethal doses. Studies in humans show newborn:maternal ratio of 0.85. Prolonged high doses to pregnant rodents were complicated by the development of squamous epithelial vaginal tumors in 3% to 12% of female offspring (*Fund Appl Toxicol* 1996;32:148). The relevance of these studies to humans is questioned because the dose used in rodents was 10 to 12x higher and AZT in humans is largely metabolized, whereas unmetabolized AZT is excreted in urine of mice. A report from France found evidence of mitochondrial toxicity with neurologic consequences in 12 infants exposed to AZT *in utero* (*Lancet* 1999;354:1084). Subsequent reviews of ACTG 076 infants and several other cohorts with data on 20,000 infants exposed to AZT failed to show any neurologic, immunologic, oncologic, or cardiac complications (*N Engl J Med* 2000;343:759; *N Engl J Med* 2000;343:805; *AIDS* 1998;12:1805; *JAMA* 1999;281:151; *J Acquir Immune Defic Syndr* 1999;20:464). An expert NIH panel reviewed these data in January 1997 and concluded that the risk of perinatal transmission exceeded the hypothetical concerns of transplacental carcinogenesis. Nevertheless, they advised that pregnant women be warned of this risk.

Extensive study and experience have clearly documented the efficacy and safety of AZT for reducing perinatal transmission (*N Engl J Med* 1994;331:1173). This benefit is related to the reduction in maternal viral load (*N Engl J Med* 1996;335:1621) and to other factors that are less well understood. More recent studies show that rates of perinatal transmission are far lower with HAART than with AZT monotherapy (0% vs 8.8%) (*J Acquir Immune Defic Syndr* 2002;29:484). Current USPHS recommendations are for HAART if the maternal viral load is >1,000 c/mL or the CD4 count is <350/mm^3, and consideration of AZT monotherapy if the CD4 cell count is >350/mm^3 and the viral load is <1000 c/mL.

ZITHROMAX – see Azithromycin (p. 183)

ZOVIRAX – see Acyclovir (p. 168)

7 Systems Review
(Complications are listed alphabetically by organ system)

Cardiac Complications

Dilated Cardiomyopathy (*N Engl J Med* 1998;339:1153)

CAUSE: Unknown, but hypotheses include: 1) Mitochondrial toxicity from AZT (*Ann Intern Med 1992*;116:311), 2) HIV infection of myocardial cells (*N Engl J Med* 1998;339:1093), 3) L-carnitine deficiency (*AIDS* 1992;6:203), and 4) Selenium deficiency (*J Parenteral Ent Nutr* 1991;15:347).

FREQUENCY: 6% to 8% in longitudinal studies (*Eur Heart J* 1992;13:1452; *Clin Immunol Immunopath* 1993;68:234). This refers to symptomatic cardiomyopathy. Rates of left ventricular diastolic dysfunction with routine echo are much higher and correlate with stage of immunosuppression (*Heart* 1998;80:184).

SYMPTOMS: CHF, arrhythmias cyanosis, and/or syncope

DIAGNOSIS: Echocardiogram showing ejection fraction <50% normal ± arrhythmias on EKG, not otherwise explained.

TREATMENT (*Am J Cardiol* 1999;83:1A)

- **HAART**
- **ACE inhibitor:** Enalapril 2.5 mg bid; titrate up to 20 mg bid. Alternatives: Captopril 6.25 mg tid up to 50 mg tid or lisinopril 10 mg/day titrated up to 40 mg/day
- **Persistent symptoms:** Add diuretic – hydrochlorothiazide 25-50 mg/day, furosemide 10-40 mg/day (up to 240 mg bid) or spirolactone 25 mg/day (up to 50 mg bid)
- **Refractory:** Consider digoxin 0.125-0.25 mg/day
- **Others options:** Treat hypertension, treat hyperlipidemia, discontinue EtOH, d/c cocaine, d/c AZT, (?) supplemental carnitine, and/or selenium if deficient.

Pulmonary Hypertension

CAUSE: Unknown (*Ann NY Acad Sci* 2001;946:82)

FREQUENCY: Infrequent, does not correlate well with CD4 count. Histology is similar to primary pulmonary hypertension. The major current hypothesis is cytokine-related endothelial proliferation (*Am J Respir Crit Care Med* 2001;52:31).

SYMPTOMS: Major symptom is exertional dyspnea. Other symptoms are exertional chest pain, syncope, cough, hemoptysis, and fatigue.

DIAGNOSIS: X-ray shows enlarged pulmonary trunk or central pulmonary vessels (early), massive right ventricular and right atrial enlargement (late). Echo shows dilated right atrium and ventricle ± tricuspid insufficiency. Doppler echo shows pulmonary arterial systolic BP >30 mm Hg. The best test is cardiac catheterization to show increased pulmonary artery pressure, increased right atrial pressure, and normal pulmonary capillary pressure. Lung scan and pulmonary function tests are normal.

TREATMENT (usually progressive despite treatment)

- **Epoprostenol** (*Angiology* 2000;162:1846)
- **Diuretics**
- **Oral anticoagulant**
- **Sildenafil** 25 mg/day. Increase by 25 mg every 3 to 4 days up to 25 mg qid (*AIDS* 2001;15:1747; *AIDS* 2002;16:1568; *N Engl J Med* 2000;343:1342). Note drug interactions with antiretroviral agents.

Tricuspid Valve Endocarditis

CAUSE: *S. aureus* in 50% to 70%; streptococci in 20%

FREQUENCY: A longitudinal study of 2529 IDUs followed for 16,469 patient-years showed an endocarditis rate 4-fold higher with HIV infection (13.8/1000 patient-years vs 3.3/1000 patient-years) (*J Infect Dis* 2002;185:1761).

SYMPTOMS: Fever, dyspnea, weight loss

DIAGNOSIS: Duke criteria: Definite = 2 major, 1 major and 3 minor, or 5 minor. Possible = 1 major and 1 minor, or 3 minor.

- **Major:** 1) Positive blood culture for likely agent from ≥2 sticks or persistent bacteremia and 2) Endocardial involvement by echo or new murmur of valve regurgitation.
- **Minor:** 1) IDU or other predisposing cause; 2) Fever >38°C; 3) Vascular phenomena; 4) Immunologic phenomena; 5) bacteremia not meeting major criteria; and 6) Echo positive but not diagnostic (*Am J Med* 1994;96:200).

TREATMENT

- **Nafcillin** 12 gm IV/day x 4 weeks plus tobramycin 1 mg/kg q8h x 3 to 5 days (*Ann Intern Med* 1988;109:619; *Eur J Clin Microbiol Infect Dis* 1994;13:559). Note: The 2-week nafcillin/tobramycin course is advocated for uncomplicated *S. aureus* tricuspid valve endocarditis in IDUs but should not be used for patients with HIV infection.
- **Vancomycin** 1 gm IV q12h x 4 weeks plus tobramycin 1 mg/kg q8h x 3 to 5 days.

Dermatologic and Oral Complications

Aphthous Ulcers

CAUSE: Unknown

DIFFERENTIAL: HSV, CMV drug induced ulcers

CLASSIFICATION

- **Minor:** <1 cm diameter, usually self-limiting (usually heals in 10 to 14 days)
- **Major:** >1 cm, deep, prolonged, heals slowly, causes pain, and may prevent oral intake (*AIDS* 1992;6:963; *Oral Surg Oral Med Oral Path* 1996;81:141)

TREATMENT

- **Topical treatment 2 to 4x/day**
  - Lidocaine solution before meals
  - Triamcinolone hexacetonide in *Orabase*
  - Fluocinonide gel (*Lidex*) 0.05% ointment mixed 1:1 with *Orabase* or covered with *Orabase*
  - Amlexanox 5% oral paste (*J Oral Maxillofac Surg* 1993;51:243)
- **Oral and intralesional therapy (refractory cases)**
  - Prednisone 40 mg/day PO x 1 to 2 weeks then taper
  - Colchicine 1.5 mg/day (*J Am Acad Derm* 1994;31:459)
  - Dapsone 100 mg/day
  - Pentoxifylline (*Trental*) 400 mg PO tid with meals
  - Thalidomide 200 mg/day PO x 4 to 6 weeks ± maintenance with 200 mg 2x/week. Note: Thalidomide is "experimental" for aphthous ulcers. See p. 310 for purchase instructions. Thalidomide has strict requirements for use, but the experience is very favorable (*N Engl J Med* 1997;337:1086; *Clin Infect Dis* 1995;20:250; *J Infect Dis* 1999;180:61; *Arch Derm* 1990;126:923).

Bacillary Angiomatosis (*Arch Intern Med* 1994;154:524; *Dermatology* 2000;21:326)

CAUSE: *Bartonella henselae* and *quintana*. Both cause cutaneous lesions that do not differ in appearance, histopathologic findings, or treatment, although organ trophism differs.

PRESENTATION: Papular, nodular, pedunculated, and verrucous forms. Lesions usually start as red or purple papules that gradually expand to nodules or pedunculated masses. They appear vascular and may bleed extensively with trauma. There is usually one or several lesions, but there may be hundreds.

DIFFERENTIAL: Kaposi's sarcoma, cherry angioma, hemangioma, pyogenic granuloma, dermatofibroma.

DIAGNOSIS: Skin biopsy – lobular vascular proliferation with inflammation; Warthin Starry silver stain shows typical organisms as small black clusters. Serology is available (IFA and EIA), but utility in patients with AIDS is not established. IFA titers >1:256 usually indicates active infection.

TREATMENT (see p. 118)

- **Preferred regimen:** Erythromycin 500 mg PO qid x >3 months
- **Alternative:** Doxycycline 100 mg PO bid, azithromycin 0.5-1 g/day PO, or doxycycline + rifampin 300 mg IV or PO bid x >3 months

Candidiasis, Cutaneous (*Clin Infect Dis* 2000;30:652)

CAUSE: Superficial infection of skin/mucous membranes, usually by *C. albicans.*

PRESENTATION (SKIN): Moist, beefy red with scaling and satellite papules. Variations: Intertrigo, balanitis, glossitis, angular cheilitis, paronychia, nail dystrophies.

DIAGNOSIS: Usually clinical; KOH prep or fresh mount shows pseudohyphae.

TREATMENT

- **Topical:** Ketoconazole, miconazole, clotrimazole, econazole, or nystatin – all bid.

- **Systemic:** Ketoconazole (200-400 mg PO qd) or fluconazole (100-200 mg PO qd).

Candidiasis, Oropharygeal (thrush) (see p. 120)

PRESENTATION

- **White plaques** (pseudomembranous form) on inflamed base on buccal mucosa, gingiva palate, tongue, or oropharynx (most common).
- **Erythema without plaques** (atrophic form) with spotty or confluent red patches.
- **Angular cheilitis** ("perlèche") – painful fissure at the corner of the mouth.

PROVOCATIVE FACTORS: Antibiotics, radiation therapy, corticosteroids, dentures, immunosuppression.

SYMPTOMS: Taste loss, pain with eating and swallowing; often asymptomatic.

DIAGNOSIS: Usually clinical; KOH or gram stain of lesion shows budding yeast or pseudohyphae. Culture primarily for testing sensitivity.

TREATMENT: See p. 120

Cholangiopathy, AIDS (*Dig Dis* 1998;16:205)

CAUSE: Cryptosporidiosis is the most common identified microbial cause. Other causes: Microsporidia, CMV, and Cyclospora. About 20% to 40% are idiopathic.

FREQUENCY: Relatively rare and seen primarily in late stage AIDS

PRESENTATION: Right upper quadrant pain, LFTs show cholestasis. Late stage HIV with CD4 count <100 cells/mm^3

DIAGNOSIS: ERCP (preferred); ultrasound is 75% to 95% specific

TREATMENT: Based on cause. Treat pathogen when possible – CMV and Cyclospora. Usual treatment is mechanical and based on lesion.

- **Papillary stenosis:** ERCP with sphincterectomy for pain relief
- **Cholangiopathy without papillary stenosis:** Ursodeoxycholic acid 300 mg PO tid (*Am J Med* 1997;103:70). Experience limited.
- **Isolated bile duct structure:** Endoscopic stenting

Cryptococcosis (*Clin Infect Dis* 2000;30:652)

CAUSE: Disseminated cryptococcosis usually from a pulmonary portal of entry

PRESENTATION: Nodular, papular, follicular, or ulcerative skin lesions; may resemble molluscum. Usual locations are face, neck, scalp.

DIAGNOSIS: Serum cryptococcal antigen assay is usually positive. Skin biopsy – Gomori methenamine silver stain shows typical encapsulated, budding yeast, and positive culture. Perform LP in any patient with a positive culture for *C. neoformans.*

TREATMENT: If negative LP, fluconazole 400 mg/day PO x 8 weeks, then 200 mg/day. If positive LP, see pp. 122-123.

Dermatophytic Infections

DEFINITION: Fungal infection of skin, hair, and nails

CAUSE: *T. rubrum, T. mentagrophytes, M. canis, E. floccosum, T. tonsurans, T. verrucosum, T. soudanense* (*Candida* causes typical nail and skin lesions), *Malassezia furfur* causes tinea versicolor. (Note: *Candida* and *M. furfur* are not dermatophytes.)

PRESENTATION

- **T. pedis:** Pruritic, red lesions between toes ± interdigital fissures, extension to adjacent skin and nails, scaling is always present.
- **Onychomycosis:** Starts with discoloration, usually on distal nail at one side and spreads toward the other side and toward the cuticle, leaving heaped up keratinous debris.
- **T. corporis:** Circular erythematous scaling that spreads with central clearing (ringworm).
- **T. cruris:** Red scaly patch on inner thigh with sharply demarcated borders.

FORMS: Tinea corporis (ringworm), tinea cruris (jock itch), tinea pedis (athlete's foot), tinea unguium or onychomycosis (nail involvement), and tinea captis (ringworm of scalp)

DIAGNOSIS: Scrapings of skin lesion or discolored nail bed for KOH preparation. This may be supplemented with culture of scraping on Sabouraud's medium.

TREATMENT

- **Onychomycosis:** Topical therapy is usually not effective.
  - Preferred treatment: Terbinafine 250 mg/day x 8 weeks (fingernails) or 12 weeks (toenails). Terbinafine is also hepatotoxic and is expensive but has better long term results than itraconazole (*Brit J Dermatol* 1999;141[Suppl 56]:15).
  - Itraconazole "pulse therapy," 400 mg/day for 1 week/month x 2 months (fingernails) or x 3 months (toenails). Main concerns are hepatotoxicity, drug interactions, cardiotoxicity, and cost of treating a benign infection.
- **Tinea corporis, tinea cruris, tinea pedis:** Topical agent for 2 weeks (T. cruris) to 4 weeks (T. pedis):
  - Clotrimazole (*Lotrimin*)* 1% cream or lotion bid
  - Econazole (*Spectazole*) 1% cream qd or bid
  - Ketoconazole (*Nizoral*) 2% cream qd
  - Miconazole (*Monostat-Derm*)* 2% cream bid
  - Butenafine (*Mentax*) 1% cream
  - Terbinafine (*Lamisil*)* 1% cream or gel qd or bid
  - Tolnaftate (*Tinactin*)* 1% cream, gel, polder, solution, or aerosol bid

* Available over-the-counter.

- **Refractory, chronic, or extensive disease:** Griseofulvin 250-500 mg microsize bid; terbinafine 250 mg qd x 2 to 4 weeks; itraconazole 100-200 mg qd x 2 to 4 weeks.

Drug Eruptions

CAUSE: Most common are antibiotics, especially sulfonamides, beta-lactams, NNRTI, amprenavir

PRESENTATION: Most common – morbilliform, macular, and maculo-papular rash, usually pruritic ± low grade fever; usually within 2 weeks of new drug and days of re-exposure. Less common and more severe forms:

- Urticaria: Intensely pruritic, red and circumscribed
- Anaphylaxis: Laryngeal edema, nausea, vomiting ± shock
- "Hypersensitivity syndrome": Severe reaction with rash and fever ± hepatitis, arthralgias, lymphadenopathy, and hematologic changes with eosinophilia and atypical lymphocytes, usually at 2 to 6 weeks after drug is started (*N Engl J Med* 1994;331:1272). See abacavir (p. 164) and nevirapine (p. 267)

- Stevens-Johnson Syndrome: Fever, erosive stomatitis, disseminated dark red macules, ocular involvement; mortality – 5%
- Toxic epidermal necrolysis: Epidermal necrosis with scalded skin appearance ± mucous membrane involvement; mortality – 50% (*N Engl J Med* 1994;331:1272)
- Abacavir hypersensitivity: See p. 164
- NNRTI hypersensitivity: See p. 267

TREATMENT: Discontinue implicated agent (for TMP-SMX, see p. 318)

- Pruritic uncomplicated drug rashes – antihistamines, topical antipruritics, and topical corticosteroids
- Stevens-Johnson Syndrome and toxic epidermal necrolysis: Severe cases are managed as burns + support; corticosteroids are not indicated (*Cutis* 1996;57:223).

Folliculitis

CAUSE: Bacterial is most common, due to *Staphylococcus aureus, Pityrosporum ovale* (intrafollicular yeast), *Demodex folliculorum* (intrafollicular mite), eosinophilic inflammation without a detectable infectious agent in eosinophilic folliculitis

PRESENTATION: Follicular papules and pustules on face, trunk, and extremities; usually very pruritic causing excoriations; multiple exacerbations and spontaneous remissions; usually seen with CD4 counts <250 cells/mm^3 and >50 cells/mm^3.

DIAGNOSIS: Clinical presentation and biopsy – follicular inflammation ± follicular destruction and abscess formation. Special stains such as PASD and B+B may show infectious agent. Multiple eosinophils destroying the hair follicle wall and eosinophilic abscesses are seen in eosinophilic folliculitis. Culture of pustule may grow infectious agent if bacterial.

TREATMENT: Varies according to the etiologic agent involved.

- *S. aureus*: Topical erythromycin or clindamycin or systemic anti-staphylococcal antibiotic
- *P. ovale*: Topical or systemic antifungal agents
- *D. Folliculorum*: Permethrin cream or oral metronidazole
- Eosinophilic: Topical steroids, phototherapy with UVB and/or PUVA (*N Engl J Med* 1988;318:1183; *Arch Dermatol* 1995;131:360)
- General: Antihistamines (high dose, mixed classes together) for symptomatic relief

Gingivitis

CAUSE: Anaerobic bacteria

PHASES: Linear gingival erythema → necrotizing gingivitis → necrotizing periodontitis → necrotizing stomatitis

■ TABLE 7-1: **Phases of Gingivitis**

Lesion	Location	Clinical Features
Linear gingival erythema	Gingiva	Painless, bright red at gingival margin
Necrotizing gingivitis	Gingiva	Painful, red gingiva, and ulceration
Necrotizing periodontitis	Gingiva and bone	Painful, red gingiva, and loose teeth
Necrotizing stomatitis	Gingiva, bone, and soft tissue	Painful, red gingiva, and removable teeth

TREATMENT

- **Routine dental care:** Brush and floss ± topical antiseptics: *Listerine* swish x 30-60 seconds bid, *Peridex*, etc.
- **Dental consultation:** Curettage and debridement
- **Antibiotics** (necrotizing stomatitis): Metronidazole; alternatives – clindamycin and amoxicillin-clavulanate

Herpes Simplex (see p. 134)

Herpes Zoster (*N Engl J Med* 2002;347:340)

CAUSE: Varicella zoster virus (VZV). AIDS patients have high rate of VZV, zoster-associated complications, atypical disease, and refractory disease. HIV infected patients infrequently have post-herpetic neuralgia.

FORMS

- **Dermatomal:** See p. 135
- **Neurologic:** Complications include encephalitis, myelitis, aseptic meningitis, and stroke syndromes.
- **Zoster ophthalmicus:** Involves 1st division of trigeminal nerve with lesions on forehead, periorbital area, and nose; high rate of ocular complications and needs ophthalmologist.
- **Acute retinal necrosis:** May result in acute vision loss that can progress to involve other eye; needs IV acyclovir to protect vision (see p. 136).

- **Ramsey Hunt syndrome:** Polycranial neuropathy with facial paralysis, ear pain, and vesicles in auditory canal and auricle.

PRESENTATION: Prodrome of headache, photophobia, and malaise, but usually no fever; then tingling or pruritus at skin site, then painful maculopapular rash that evolves to vesicles, pustules, and scabs over 3 to 5 days with healing over 2 to 4 weeks.

DIAGNOSIS: Alcohol wiped lesion is unroofed by needle with vesicular fluid for stain and culture. Tzanck smear shows multinucleate giant cell diagnostic of HSV or VZV but is insensitive. A viral culture is definitive, but the virus is difficult to grow. DFA stain compared with culture is faster (2 hours vs 3 to 5 days), more sensitive, and less expensive.

TREATMENT (see p. 135)

- **Antiviral**
  - Valacyclovir 1 g tid x 7 days
  - Acyclovir 800 mg 5x/day x 7 to 10 days
  - Famciclovir 500 mg tid x 7 days
- **Corticosteroids** (controversial)
- **Acyclovir resistant:** Foscarnet 60 mg IV q12h or cidofovir 5 mg/kg qwk x 2
- **Postherpetic neuralgia**
  - Oxycodone 5 mg q6h
  - Nortriptyline 10-25 mg hs
  - Gabapentin 300 mg/day
  - Capsaicin topical 3 to 4x/day
  - Lidocaine patch ≤3/day

Kaposi's Sarcoma (KS) (see p. 363)

CAUSE: Human Herpesvirus Type 8 (HHV-8, KSHV)

PRESENTATION: Firm, purple to brown-black colored macules, patches, plaques, papules, nodules, or tumors; usually asymptomatic. Most common sites: Face, chest, genitals, oral mucosa, and feet; usually multiple; symmetric distribution. Visceral involvement and lymphatic obstruction are frequent.

DIFFERENTIAL: Pyogenic granuloma, hemangioma, hematoma, bacillary angiomatosis, B-cell lymphoma

DIAGNOSIS: Clinical presentation and biopsy confirmation

TREATMENT: Determined by symptoms, cosmetic concerns, and quality of life issues.

- **HAART:** Often induces resolution
- **Local:** 1) Surgical excision, 2) Intralesional vinblastine (0.1 mg/cm^2) (*Lancet* 1989;2:1100), 3) Intralesional 3% Na tetradecyl sulfate (*N Engl J Med* 1993;328:210), 4) Radiation (may cause severe mucositis), 5) Cryotherapy, and 6) Laser oblation.
- **Extensive and widespread:** Treat systemically; usually with liposomal doxorubicin or paclitaxel. See p. 364

Molluscum Contagiosum

CAUSE: A poxvirus

PRESENTATION: Flesh colored, pink, or whitish, dome-shaped papules with centra umbilication (dimpling). It can occur anywhere on the body, except palms and soles. Most common areas are the face (beard area), neck, and genitals. Lesions are usually less than 5 mm in diameter; occasionally lesions are greater than 1 cm (giant molluscum).

DIFFERENTIAL: Warts, folliculitis, cryptococcosis, and histoplasmosis

DIAGNOSIS: Clinical presentation; may be confirmed by KOH preparation, Tzanck smear, or biopsy that show intraepidermal molluscum bodies. EM shows a large brick-shaped virus resembling smallpox.

TREATMENT: An individual lesion may be treated with curettage, cryotherapy, electrocauterization (*Sex Trans Infect* 1999;75[suppl 1]:S80), chemical cauterization (trichloroacetic acid, cantharidin, podophyllin, 5-FU, tretinoin, silver nitrate, phenol), imiquimod, topical cidofovir. Lesions usually disappear in patients responding to HAART (*Eur J Dermatol* 1999;9:211).

Oral Hairy Leukoplakia (OHL) (*Clin Infect Dis* 1997;25:1392)

CAUSE: Intense replication of EBV

PRESENTATION: Unilateral or bilateral adherent white/gray patches on lingual lateral margins ± dorsal or ventral surface of tongue. Patches are irregular folds and projections.

DIFFERENTIAL: Candidiasis – OHL does not respond to azoles and cannot be scraped off, unlike *Candida*; Others – squamous cell carcinoma or traumatic leukoplakia.

DIAGNOSIS: Appearance; biopsy rarely necessary

IMPLICATIONS: Found almost exclusively with HIV, indicates low CD4 count, predicts AIDS, and responds to immune reconstitution with HAART.

TREATMENT (*Clin Infect Dis* 1997;25:1392): Rarely symptomatic and rarely treated, but occasional patients have pain or have concern about appearance. The options include:

- **HAART** (preferred)
- **Topical podophyllin**
- **Surgical excision**
- **Cryotherapy**
- **Anti-EBV treatment:** Acyclovir 800 mg PO 5x/day x 2 to 3 weeks, then 1.2-2 gm/day. Other effective antivirals include famciclovir, valacyclovir, foscarnet, ganciclovir, and valganciclovir. The problem with anti-EBV agents is that the lesions recur when treatment is discontinued.

Prurigo Nodularis

CAUSE: Unknown

FREQUENCY: Common usually with CD4 <200 cells/mm^3

PRESENTATION: Hyperpigmented, hyperkeratotic, often excoriated papules and nodules up to 1 cm; 90% are above nipple line. Major symptom is severe pruritus. Usually associated with other signs of chronic pruritus or excoriations, including lichen simplex chronicus, patches of hyperpigmentation, linear erosions, ulcerations, and scars.

DIFFERENTIAL: Other causes of pruritus: Dry skin, seborrhea, staph folliculitis, drug eruption

DIAGNOSIS: Clinical features; biopsy may be necessary

TREATMENT: Must interrupt vicious cycle: Pruritus → scratch trauma → lichenification → increased pruritus. Treat with high potency topical steroids under occlusive dressing. May benefit from oral antihistamines or phototherapy.

Salivary Gland Enlargement

CAUSE: May be lymphoid proliferation due to HIV (*Ann Intern Med* 1996;125:494)

PRESENTATION: Parotid swelling, cystic, unilateral or bilateral, non-tender, usually asymptomatic; may be painful, cosmetically disfiguring, or cause xerostomia (*Ear Nose Throat J* 1990;69:475).

DIFFERENTIAL: Must differentiate cystic vs solid lesion – CT scan (*Laryngoscope* 1998;98:772) and/or fine needle aspiration (FNA) for microbiology and cytology and decompression. May require biopsy.

TREATMENT

- FNA for decompression of fluid-filled parotid cysts
- **Xerostomia:** Sugarless chewing gum, artificial saliva, pilocarpine

Scabies (*MMWR* 2002;51[RR-6]:68)

CAUSE: *Sarcoptes scabiei* (mite)

PRESENTATION: Small red papules that are intensely pruritic, especially at night. Sometimes presentation is the "burrow," a 3-15 mm line which represents the superficial tunnel the female mite digs at 2 mm/day to lay eggs. Usual locations are the interdigital webs of the fingers, volar aspect of the wrist, periumbilical area, axilla, thighs, buttocks, genitalia, feet, and breasts. Scabies crostosus is a severe form seen in compromised hosts, including AIDS patients. There is uncontrolled spread to involve large areas, sometimes the total skin surface with scales and crusts that show thousands of mites.

DIAGNOSIS: The mite is 0.4 x 0.3 mm, 8 legged, and shaped like a turtle. It is visible to the naked eye but burrowing precludes detection. Scrape infected area, place on a slide with a coverslip, and examine under 10x magnification to demonstrate mites or eggs.

TREATMENT: All family members and close contacts must be treated at the same time.

- **Permethrin cream** (5%) (*Elimite*) applied to total body, neck down, and washed off at 8 to 14 hours. Re-treat at 1 to 2 weeks if symptomatic or if live mites are present, but this is usually unnecessary. A 30 g tube of *Elimite* is usually adequate for an adult.
- **Lindane** (1%) 1 oz lotion or 30 g cream applied as a thin layer to total body, neck down, and washed off at 8 hours is an alternative. Lindane is less expensive than *Elimite*, but there is rare resistance and more side effects.
- **Ivermectin** (*Stromectol*) 200 µg/kg PO repeated at 2 weeks (*N Engl J Med* 1995;333:26).
- Rash and pruritus may persist up to 2 weeks post treatment – warn patients.
- Bedding and clothing must be decontaminated; machine wash in hot water and machine dry with high heat, or dry clean.
- **Itching:** Hydroxyzine (*Atarax*) or diphenhydramine (*Benadryl*)

- **Scabies crustosus (crusted or "Norwegian" scabies):** Isolate immediately and use strict barrier precautions. Treat with ivermectin 200 µg/kg PO followed by a second dose 1 to 2 weeks later, plus permethrin topically until scales and crust have resolved.

Seborrheic Dermatitis

CAUSE: *Pityrosporum* yeast is the usual cause, but it may not play a central role in HIV-associated seborrhea (*J Am Acad Dermatol* 1992;27:37).

PRESENTATION: Erythematous plaques with greasy scales and indistinct margins on scalp, central face, post auricular area, trunk, and occasionally pubic area

DIFFERENTIAL: Psoriasis and tinea capis

DIAGNOSIS: Clinical features

TREATMENT

- **Topical steroid:** Mid-potency such as triamcinolone 0.1% or weaker (desonide 0.05%), hydrocortisone 2.5% for the face ± ketoconazole 2% cream applied twice per day for the duration of the flare only.
- **Shampoos:** Tar-based (*Z-tar, Pentrax, DHS tar, T-gel, Ionil T plus*), selenium sulfide (*Selsun, Exelderm*), or zinc pyrithione (*Head & Shoulders, Zincon, DHS zinc*) applied daily, or ketoconazole shampoo applied twice per week.

Gastrointestinal Complications

Anorexia, Nausea, Vomiting

MAJOR CAUSES: Medications (especially antiretrovirals, antibiotics, opiates, and NSAIDs), depression, intracranial pathology, GI disease, hypogonadism, pregnancy, lactic acidosis, acute gastroenteritis

EVALUATION: Drug holiday, lactic acid level, fasting testosterone level, GI evaluation (endoscopy, CT scan), intracranial evaluation (head CT scan or MRI)

TREATMENT: Treat underlying condition.

- **Anorexia**
  - *Megace* 400-800 mg qd. Weight gain is mostly fat. May decrease testosterone level; consider *Megace* + testosterone.
  - Dronabinol (*Marinol*) 2.5 mg PO bid; active ingredient of marijuana. Weight gain is mostly fat.

- **Nausea and vomiting**
  - *Compazine* 5-10 mg PO q6h-q8h; *Tigan* 250 mg PO q6h-q8h; *Dramamine* 50 mg PO q6h-q8h; *Ativan* 0.025-0.05 mg/kg IV or IM; haloperidol 1-5 mg bid PO or IM; dronabinol 2.5-5 mg PO bid; ondansetron (*Zofran*) 0.2 mg/kg IV or IM.
  - Note: Phenothiazines (*Compazine, Haldol, Tigan*, and *Reglan*) may cause dystonia. *Zofran* efficacy is established only for cancer chemotherapy and costs $16.64/4 mg.
  - PEG: May require percutaneous endoscopic gastrostomy (PEG) to deliver nutrition and meds, including HAART regimen.

Diarrhea, Acute

(Acute diarrhea defined as ≥3 loose or watery stools for 3 to 10 days)

DIAGNOSTIC EVALUATION

Medication-related

- Main antiretroviral agents: Nelfinavir, lopinavir/ritonavir, and saquinavir (*Fortovase)*
- Management (*Clin Infect Dis* 2000;30:908)
  - Loperamide 4 mg, then 2 mg every loose stool, up to 16/day
  - Calcium 500 mg bid; psyllium 1 tsp qd or 2 bars qd; oat bran 1500 mg bid
  - Pancreatic enzymes 1-2 tabs with meals

Pathogen detection (*Clin Infect Dis* 2001;32:331; *Arch Path Lab Med* 2001;125:1042)

- Blood culture: MAC, *Salmonella*
- Stool culture: *Salmonella, Shigella, C. jejuni, Vibrio, Yersinia, E. coli* 0157
- Stool assay for *C. difficile* toxin A and B
- O&P examination + AFB (*cryptosporidia, Cyclospora, Isospora*), trichrome or other stain for Microsporidia and antigen detection (*Giardia*)

Radiology

- Plain x-rays and contrast x-ray – usually not helpful
- CT scan – most helpful with CMV colitis and lymphoma

Endoscopy: Most useful for CMV, Kaposi's sarcoma, and lymphoma

CAMPYLOBACTER JEJUNI

FREQUENCY: 4% to 8% of HIV infected patients with acute diarrhea

CLINICAL FEATURES: Watery diarrhea or bloody flux, fever, fecal leukocytes variable; any CD4 count

DIAGNOSIS: Stool culture; most laboratories cannot detect *C. cinaedi, C. fennelli*, etc.

TREATMENT (*Clin Infect Dis* 2001;32:331): Erythromycin 500 mg PO qid x 5 days; fluoroquinolone resistance rates are >20%.

CLOSTRIDIUM DIFFICILE

FREQUENCY: 10% to 15% of HIV infected patients with acute diarrhea

CLINICAL FEATURES: Watery diarrhea, fecal WBCs variable; fever and leukocytosis common; prior antibacterial agents nearly always, especially clindamycin, ampicillin, and cephalosporins; any CD4 count

DIAGNOSIS

- Endoscopy: pseudomembranous colitis (PMC), colitis, or normal (this procedure is not usually indicated)
- Stool toxin assay: Tissue culture or EIA preferred
- CT scan: Colitis with thickened mucosa

TREATMENT (*N Engl J Med* 2002;346:334)

- Metronidazole 250 mg PO qid or 500 mg PO tid x 10 to 14 days (preferred)
- Vancomycin 125 mg PO qid x 10 to 14 days
- Antiperistaltic agents (*Lomotil* or *Loperamide*) are contraindicated.

RESPONSE: Fever usually resolves within 24 hours and diarrhea resolves in an average of 5 days. About 20% to 25% have relapses at 3 to 14 days after treatment stopped.

ENTERIC VIRUSES

FREQUENCY: 15% to 30% of HIV infected patients with acute diarrhea

CLINICAL FEATURES: Watery diarrhea, acute, but one-third become chronic; any CD4 cell count

DIAGNOSIS: Major agents: Adenovirus, astrovirus, picornavirus, calicivirus (*N Engl J Med* 1993;329:14); clinical laboratories cannot detect these viruses.

TREATMENT: Supportive treatment: *Lomotil* or *Loperamide*

ESCHERICHIA COLI

■ TABLE 7-2: ***E. coli* Strain and Treatment**

Agent	Clinical Presentation	Treatment
Enterotoxigenic (ETEC)	Traveler's diarrhea	■ *Cipro* 500 mg bid x 3 days ■ TMP-SMX DS bid x 3 days
Enterohemorrhagic 0157:H7 (EHEC)*	Bloody diarrhea	Antibiotics contraindicated
Enteroinvasive (EIEC)	Dysentery	■ *Cipro* 500 mg bid x 5 days ■ TMP-SMX DS bid x 5 days
Enteropathic (EPEC)	Watery diarrhea	Usually no antibiotic or *Cipro* 500 mg bid x 3 days

* Only *E. coli* that can be detected with stool analysis in most labs.

SALMONELLA

FREQUENCY: 5% to 15% of HIV infected patients with acute diarrhea

CLINICAL FEATURES: Watery diarrhea, fever, fecal WBCs variable; any CD4 count

DIAGNOSIS: Stool culture, blood culture

TREATMENT

- Ciprofloxacin 500 mg PO bid x ≥14 days
- TMP-SMX 1 to 2 DS PO bid x ≥14 days
- Third-generation cephalosporin or cefotaxime 4 to 8 g/day IV or ceftriaxone 2 g/day IV
- Treatment may need to be extended to ≥4 weeks
- AZT and TMP-SMX may prevent salmonellosis

SHIGELLA

FREQUENCY: 1% to 3% of HIV infected patients with acute diarrhea

CLINICAL FEATURES: Watery diarrhea or bloody flux, fever, fecal WBCs common; any CD4 count

DIAGNOSIS: Stool culture

TREATMENT (*Clin Infect Dis* 2001;32:331)

- Ciprofloxacin 500 mg PO bid x 3 days
- TMP-SMX 1 DS PO bid x 3 days

IDIOPATHIC

FREQUENCY: 25% to 40% of HIV infected patients with acute diarrhea

CLINICAL FEATURES: Variable noninfectious causes; rule out medications, dietary, irritable bowel syndrome; any CD4 cell count

DIAGNOSIS: Negative studies including culture, O&P examination, and *C. difficile* toxin assay

EMPIRIC TREATMENT, SEVERE ACUTE IDIOPATHIC DIARRHEA

- Ciprofloxacin 500 mg PO bid
- Ofloxacin 200-300 mg PO bid x 5 days ± metronidazole (*Arch Intern Med* 1990;150:541; *Ann Intern Med* 1992;117:202; *Clin Infect Dis* 2001;32:331).

Diarrhea, Chronic

(Advanced HIV infection and chronic diarrhea defined as >2 loose or watery stools/day for ≥30 days.)

CRYPTOSPORIDIA (see p. 126)

FREQUENCY: 10% to 30% of chronic diarrhea in AIDS patients

CLINICAL FEATURES: Enteritis; watery diarrhea; no fecal WBCs; fever variable; malabsorption; wasting; large stool volume with abdominal pain; remitting symptoms for months; CD4 cell count <150/mm^3 is associated with recurrent or chronic disease.

DIAGNOSIS: AFB smear of stool to show oocyst of 4-6 μm

TREATMENT (*Clin Infect Dis* 2001;32:331)

- Best results are with HAART.
- Paromomycin 1000 mg bid or 500 mg PO bid x 7 days; efficacy is marginal.
- Nitazoxanide 1000 mg/day (not FDA-approved)
- Azithromycin 600 mg/day + paromomycin (above doses) x ≥4 weeks
- Nutritional support plus *Lomotil*; may require parenteral hyperalimentation in severe cases.

RESPONSE: The most effective treatment is immune reconstitution; even small rises in CD4 count often succeed in controlling diarrhea.

CYCLOSPORA

FREQUENCY: <1% of chronic diarrhea in AIDS patients (not uniquely susceptible)

CLINICAL FEATURES: Enteritis; watery diarrhea; CD4 cell count <100/mm^3

DIAGNOSIS: Stool AFB smear: Resembles cryptosporidia

TREATMENT: TMP-SMX 1 DS bid x 3 days

CYTOMEGALOVIRUS

FREQUENCY: 15% to 40% of chronic diarrhea in AIDS patients

CLINICAL FEATURES: Colitis and/or enteritis; fecal WBC and/or blood; cramps; fever; watery diarrhea ± blood; may cause perforation; hemorrhage, toxic megacolon, ulceration; CD4 cell count <50/mm^3

DIAGNOSIS

- Biopsy to show intranuclear inclusion bodies, preferably with inflammation, vasculitis
- CT scan: segmental or pancolitis ± enteritis
- Cannot establish this diagnosis with CMV markers in blood or stool; need biopsy.

TREATMENT

- HAART
- Valganciclovir 900 mg PO bid x 3 weeks, then 900 mg qd
- Ganciclovir 5 mg/kg IV bid x 2 weeks, then valganciclovir 900 mg/day
- Foscarnet 40-60 mg/kg IV q8h 2 x weeks, then 90 mg/kg/day

RESPONSE: Results of antiviral treatment variable (*Ann Intern Med* 1990;112:505; *J Infect Dis* 1993;167:278); foscarnet and ganciclovir are equally effective or ineffective (*J Infect Dis* 1995;172:622).

ENTAMOEBA HISTOLYTICA

FREQUENCY: 1% to 3% of chronic diarrhea in AIDS patients

CLINICAL FEATURES: Colitis; bloody stools; cramps; no fecal WBCs (bloody stools); most are asymptomatic carriers; any CD4 cell count

DIAGNOSIS: Stool O&P examination. Must distinguish from non-pathogenic *E. dispar*.

TREATMENT: Metronidazole 500-750 mg PO or IV tid x 5 to 10 days, then iodoquinol 650 mg PO tid x 21 days or paromomycin 500 mg PO qid x 7 days

GIARDIA LAMBLIA

FREQUENCY: 1% to 3% of chronic diarrhea in AIDS patients (not uniquely susceptible)

CLINICAL FEATURES: Enteritis; watery diarrhea ± malabsorption, bloating; flatulence; any CD4 cell count

DIAGNOSIS: Antigen detection

TREATMENT: Metronidazole 250 mg PO tid x 10 days

ISOPORA BELLI (see p. 138)

FREQUENCY: 1% to 3% of chronic diarrhea in AIDS patients

CLINICAL FEATURES: Enteritis; watery diarrhea; no fecal WBCs; no fever; wasting; malabsorption; CD4 cell count <100/mm^3

DIAGNOSIS: AFB smear of stool; oocysts: 20 to 30 μm

TREATMENT: TMP-SMX 3-4 DS/day; Pyrimethamine 50-75 mg/day PO x 7 to 10 days

RESPONSE: Most respond promptly.

MICROSPORIDIA: *ENTEROCYTOZOON BIENEUSI* OR *ENTEROCYTOZOON (SEPTATA) INTESTINALIS* (see p. 140)

FREQUENCY: 15% to 30% of chronic diarrhea in AIDS patients

CLINICAL FEATURES: Enteritis, watery diarrhea, no fecal WBCs; fever uncommon; remitting disease over months; malabsorption; wasting; CD4 cell count <100/mm^3

DIAGNOSIS

- Special trichrome stain described (*N Engl J Med* 1992;326:161; *J Clin Microbiol* 993;31:3264)
- Alternative: Florescent stains with similar sensitivity (*J Clin Microbiol* 1995;33:805)

TREATMENT

- Albendazole 400-800 mg PO bid x ≥3 weeks; efficacy is established only for *Septata intestinalis*.

- Fumagillin 60 mg PO qd x 14 days for *E. bieneusi* (*N Engl J Med* 2002;346:1963); monitor for neutropenia and thrombocytopenia.

RESPONSE: Albendazole produces clinical response and pathogen clearance but only for *E. intestinalis*; fumagillin produces clinical response and microbial clearance for *E. bieneusi*, which causes 80% of cases of microsporidiosis, but some relapse and marrow suppression is common.

MYCOBACTERIUM AVIUM COMPLEX (MAC) (see p. 141)

FREQUENCY: 10% to 20% of chronic diarrhea in AIDS patients

CLINICAL FEATURES: Enteritis; watery diarrhea; no fecal WBCs; fever and wasting common; diffuse abdominal pain in late stage; CD4 cell count <50/mm^3.

DIAGNOSIS: Positive blood cultures for *M. avium* complex; biopsy may show changes typical of Whipple's disease, but with AFB; CT scan may be supportive: Hepatosplenomegaly, adenopathy, and thickened small bowel.

TREATMENT

- Clarithromycin 500 mg PO bid + EMB 15 mg/kg/day
- Azithromycin 600 mg/day + EMB 15 mg/kg/day ± rifabutin 300 mg/day

RESPONSE: Slow response over several weeks

IDIOPATHIC (PATHOGEN-NEGATIVE)

FREQUENCY: 20% to 30% of chronic diarrhea in AIDS patients who undergo a full diagnostic evaluation including endoscopy

CLINICAL FEATURES: Usually low-volume diarrhea that resolves spontaneously or is controlled with antimotility agents (*Gut* 1995;36:283). Typically not associated with significant weight loss and often resolves spontaneously.

DIAGNOSIS: Biopsy shows villus atrophy, crypt hyperplasia/no identifiable cause despite endoscopy with biopsy and EM for microsporidia (*Clin Infect Dis* 1992;15:726). These histologic changes are unlikely to explain diarrhea because they are seen in symptom-free persons with HIV (*Lancet* 1996;348:379). With pathogen-negative, persistent, large volume diarrhea, must rule out KS and lymphoma.

TREATMENT: Supportive care (frequent small feedings, bland food, avoid caffeine and lactose): *Lomotil* or *Loperamide*, nutritional support. Consider gluten-free diet.

Esophagitis

■ TABLE 7-3: **Esophageal Disease in Patients With HIV Infection**

	Candida	Cytomegalo-virus (CMV)	Herpes Simplex Virus	Aphthous Ulcers
Frequency as cause of symptoms	50% to 70%	10% to 20%	2% to 5%	10% to 20%
Clinical features				
Dysphagia	+++	+	+	+
Odynophagia	++	+++	+++	+++
Thrush	50% to 70%	<25%	<25%	<25%
Oral ulcers	Rare	Uncommon	Often	Uncommon
Pain	Diffuse	Focal	Focal	Focal
Fever	Infrequent	Often	Infrequent	Infrequent
Diagnosis				
Endoscopy	■ Usually treated empirically ■ Pseudo-membranous plaques; may involve entire esophagus	■ Biopsy required for treatment ■ Erythema and erosions/ulcers, single or multiple discrete lesions, often distal.	■ Biopsy required for treatment ■ Erythema and erosions/ulcers, usually small, coalescing, shallow	■ Similar in appearance and location to CMV ulcers
Micro-biology	■ Brush: Yeast and pseudo-mycelium on KOH prep or PAS ■ Culture with sensitivities may be useful with suspected resistance	■ Biopsy: Intra-cellular inclu-sions and/or positive culture. ■ Highest yield with histopath of biopsy and culture. Culture is often not recommended due to false positives.	■ Brush/biopsy: Intracytoplasmic inclusions + multinucleate giant cells, FA stain, and/or positive culture.	■ Negative studies for *Candida*, HSV, CMV, and other diagnoses.
Treatment				
Acute	■ Fluconazole 200 mg/day PO, up to 800 mg/day. ■ Refractory cases: Itraconazole 200 mg/day or voriconazole 200-300 mg PO or IV bid ■ Amphotericin 0.5-0.7 mg/kg/ day IV ■ Caspofungin 70 mg/day IV x 1 then 50 mg/day ■ Efficacy of fluconazole is 85% (*Ann Intern Med* 1993;118:825)	■ Ganciclovir 5 mg/kg IV bid x 2 to 3 weeks or valganciclovir 900 mg bid x 3 weeks, then 900 mg/day (when able to swallow). ■ Foscarnet 40-60 mg/kg q8h x 2 to 3 weeks. ■ Efficacy of antiviral treatment is 75%.	■ Acyclovir 200-800 mg PO 5x/day or 5 mg/kg IV q8h x 2 to 3 weeks or valacyclovir 1 gm PO tid (when able to swallow).	■ Prednisone 40 mg/day PO x 7 to 14 days, then taper 10 mg/week or more slowly. ■ Thalidomide 200 mg/day PO (*BJM* 1989;298: 432; *J Infect Dis* 1999;180:61). ■ Corticosteroids by intralesional injection.

■ TABLE 7-3: **Esophageal Disease in Patients With HIV Infection *(Continued)***

	Candida	Cytomegalovirus (CMV)	Herpes Simplex Virus (HSV)	Aphthous Ulcers
Maintenance	■ Fluconazole 100 mg/day PO (indicated with frequent or severe occurrences) ■ Lower dose or less frequent dosing may reduce resistance	■ Maintenance treatment is arbitrary. ■ May await relapse, then ganciclovir 5 mg/kg/day IV ■ Possible role for oral ganciclovir.	■ Maintenance treatment is arbitrary; acyclovir 200-400 mg PO 3 to 5x daily.	■ None

Notes:

1. One-third of AIDS patients develop esophageal symptoms (*Gut* 1989;30:1033). Esophageal ulcers are usually due to CMV (45%), or they are idiopathic/aphthous ulcers (40%); HSV accounts for only 5% (*Ann Intern Med* 1995;122:143).
2. Diagnostic studies may include barium swallow, but diagnostic yield is low (20% to 30%) compared with esophagoscopy; with endoscopy a diagnosis is established in about 70% to 95% (*Arch Intern Med* 1991;151:1567). Response to empiric treatment often precludes need for endoscopic diagnosis of fungal esophagitis.
3. Other diagnostic considerations: Drug-induced dysphagia (*Am J Med* 1988;88:512), including AZT (*Ann Intern Med* 1990;162:65) and ddC; infection, including *M. avium*, TB, cryptosporidia, *P. carinii*, primary HIV infection (acute retroviral syndrome), histoplasmosis, and tumor, including KS or lymphoma (*BMJ* 1988;296:92; *Gastrointest Endosc* 1986;32:96).
4. Esophageal brushing: Nonendoscopic method to establish the diagnosis of *Candida* esophagitis. Procedure is: pharyngeal anesthesia, 16 French nasogastric tube inserted to distal esophagus sheathed sterile brush extended through tube, brushing is done during withdrawal, brushings for cytopathy and fungal stain (*Arch Intern Med* 1991;151:1567; *Gastrointest Endosc* 1989;35:102). This procedure is inadequate to establish other diagnoses.
5. Fluconazole is the preferred treatment for *Candida* because of established efficacy, more predictable absorption, and fewer drug interactions compared with voriconazole, ketoconazole, and itraconazole.

EVALUATION

- Medication or food related
- Gastroesophageal reflux disease (heartburn ± regurgitation and dysphagia)
- Opportunistic infection or tumor
  - Common: *Candida* sp.
  - Less common: HSV, CMV, idiopathic (aphthous)
  - Rare: TB, *M. avium*, histoplasmosis, PCP, cryptosporidia, Kaposi's sarcoma, lymphoma

■ FIGURE 7-1: **Odynophagia in Patients With AIDS**

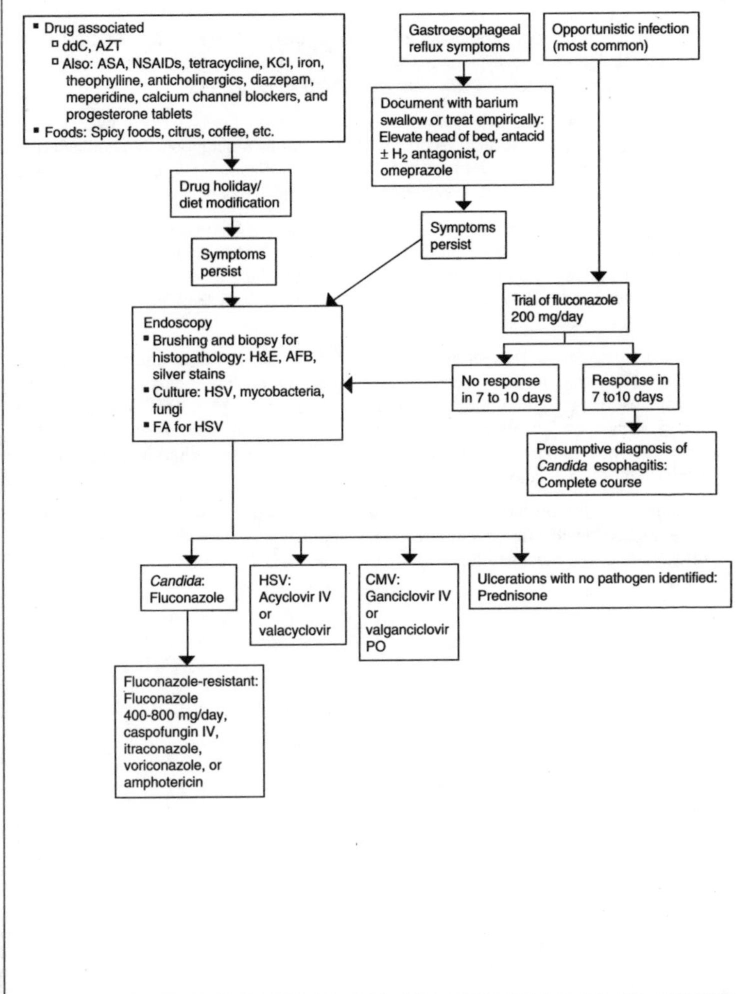

■ TABLE 7-4: **Hepatitis Forms**

Type	Seroprevalence* Transmission	Incubation Period	Diagnosis	Course
A	Fecal-oral; food ■ Gen. population: 40% to 50% immune ■ Acute hepatitis: 50%	15 to 50 days	■ Acute: IgM ■ Prior infection: Total HAV antibody	■ Fulminant and fatal in 0.6% ■ Self limited in >99% ■ No chronic form
B	Sex and blood ■ Gen. population: 3% to 14% ■ IDU: 60% to 80% ■ MSM: 35% to 80%	45 to 160 days	■ Acute: HBsAg + anti-HBc IgM ■ Chronic: HBsAg x 6 months + anti-HBc IgG ■ Vaccinated: HBsAb	■ Fulminant and fatal in 1.4% ■ Chronic hepatitis in 6%
C	Blood (primarily) ■ General population: 1.8% ■ IDU: 60% to 90% ■ Hemophilia: 60% to 90% ■ MSM: 2% to 8%	15 to 50 days	EIA Ab + HCV RNA	■ Chronic hepatitis in 85% ■ Cirrhosis in 10% to 15% in 20 years

* Seroprevalence for adults in the U.S.

HEPATITIS B TREATMENT

- **Indications**
  - HBsAg positive >6 months
  - Evidence of active viral replication (HBeAg + HBV DNA positive)
  - Active liver disease (elevated ALT + hepatitis on liver biopsy)

▪ Regimens

▪ TABLE 7-5: **Treatment of HBV**

Agent	Regimen	Comment
Interferon alfa	5 million units qd or 10 millions units 3x/week x 12 to 24 weeks	The response rate is lower than for non-HIV infected patients.
Pegylated interferon	90 or 180 mcg/week (*Hepatology* 2001;34:349A)	
Lamivudine	▪ 150 mg bid, duration indefinite ▪ 100 mg qd if anti-HIV activity not needed	At 12 months most have decreased ALT and loss of HBV DNA, but not HBe → anti-HBe seroconversion; YMDD mutations for lamivudine resistance in most patients.
Lamivudine + tenofovir	Lamivudine 300 mg/day + tenofovir 300 mg/day	No data
Adefovir ± lamivudine	Adefovir 10 mg/day ± lamivudine 300 mg/day	Adefovir is FDA-approved for HBV

HEPATITIS C TREATMENT

- Indications
  - HCV RNA >50 IU/mL
  - Liver biopsy with portal or bridging fibrosis and at least moderate inflammation and necrosis
  - No contraindications (see p. 276)
  - Stable HIV infection
- Regimens: Table 6-33, p. 277

▪ TABLE 7-6: **Treatment of HCV**

Genotype	Treatment
Genotype 1	Pegylated interferon + ribavirin x 48 weeks
Genotypes 2 and 3	Interferon or pegylated interferon, each with ribavirin x 24 weeks. Some experts would continue treatment for 48 weeks with HIV co-infection.

* Treatment should be stopped if HCV/RNA has not decreased ≥ 2 log_{10} IU/mL at 12 weeks (*N Engl J Med* 2002;347:975).

Pancreatitis (*Am J Med* 1999;107:78)

MAJOR CAUSES

- **Drugs**, especially ddI or ddI + d4T ± hydroxyurea. May be complication of lactic acidosis (NRTI-associated mitochondrial toxicity) or secondary to PI-associated hypertriglyceridemia with elevated triglyceride levels – usually >1000 mg/dL. Other drugs: d4T, 3TC (pediatrics), RTV, INH, rifampin, TMP-SMX, pentamidine, corticosteroids, sulfonamides, erythromycin, paromomycin.
- **Opportunistic infections:** CMV. Less common: MAC, TB, cryptosporidium, toxoplasmosis, cryptococcus
- **Conditions that cause pancreatitis in general population**, especially alcoholism. Less common: Gallstones, hypertriglyceridemia (avg level is 4500 mg/dL), post ERCP (3% to 5% of procedures), trauma

DIAGNOSIS

- **Amylase** >3x ULN [p-isoamylase is more specific but not usually measured (*Mayo Clin Proc* 1996;71:1138)]. Other causes hyperamylasemia – other intra-abdominal conditions, diseases of salivary gland, tumors (lung and ovary), renal failure; sensitivity: 85% to 100% (*Am J Gastroenterol* 1990;85:356).
- **Other tests**
    - Lipase: Compared with amylase shows same sensitivity but more specificity. Need for amylase plus lipase is arbitrary.
    - CT Scan: Best method to image (*Radiology* 1994;193:297). Used to: 1) Exclude other serious intra-abdominal conditions, 2) Stage pancreatitis, and 3) Detect complications.

TREATMENT: Supportive – IV fluids, pain control and NPO

Hematologic Complications

Anemia

■ TABLE 7-7: **Definition of Anemia**

		Men	Women
Normal	Hematocrit %	46.0 ± 4.0	40.0 ± 4.0
	Hemoglobin (g/dL)	15.7 ± 1.7	13.8 ± 1.5
	Reticulocytes	1.6 ± 0.5	1.4 ± 0.5
	Mean corpuscular Vol	88.0 ± 8.0	88.0 ± 8.0
Anemia	Hematocrit	<41%	<36%
	Hemoglobin (g/dL)	13.5	12.0

SYMPTOMS: Oxygen delivery becomes impaired with hemoglobin levels <8-9 g/dL and becomes impaired at rest with hemoglobin levels <5 g/dL (*JAMA* 1998;279:217). Symptoms of chronic anemia include exertional dyspnea, fatigue, and a hyperdynamic state (bounding pulses, palpitations, roaring in ears). Late complications include confusion, CHF, angina. Symptoms due to acute bleeding are those of hypovolemia with postural dizziness, lethargy, postural hypotension, and shock.

CAUSES

- **HIV:** HIV infection of marrow progenitor cells (*Clin Infect Dis* 2000;30:504). Incidence correlates with immune state: 12% with CD4 count <200 cells/mm^3, 37% with AIDS-defining OI (*Blood* 1998;91:301), and predicts death independently from CD4 count and viral load (*Semin Hematol Suppl* 4;6:18; *AIDS* 1999;13:943; *AIDS Rev* 2002;4:13).
    - Findings: Normocytic, normochromic, low reticulocyte count, low EPO level
    - Treatment: HAART. With immune reconstitution, prior reports show increases in Hgb of 1.0-2.0 gm/dL at 6 months (*J Acquir Immune Defic Syndr* 2001;28:221), but results are inconsistent (*Clin Infect Dis* 2000;30:504). Consider EPO (see Figure 7-2, p 360).
- **Marrow-infiltrating infection or tumor** (lymphoma, especially non-cleaved cell type, or Kaposi's sarcoma, rare) or infection (MAC, tuberculosis, CMV, histoplasmosis)
    - Findings: Normocytic, normochromic, low platelet count, evidence of etiologic mechanism
    - Treat underlying cause
- **Parvovirus B19:** Infects erythroid precursors; symptoms reflect marginal reserve (sickle cell disease, etc.) and inability to eradicate infection due to immune deficiency.
    - Findings: Normocytic, normochromic anemia, without reticulocytes, positive IgG and IgM serology for parvovirus, positive serum dot blot hybridization or PCR for parvovirus B19; the diagnosis is most likely with severe anemia, i.e., hematocrit <24%, no reticulocytes and CD4 count <100 cells/mm^3 (*J Infect Dis* 1997;176:269).
    - Treatment: IVIG 400 mg/kg/day x 5 days (*Ann Intern Med* 1990; 113:926)
- **Nutritional Deficiency:** Common in late stage HIV, including B12 deficiency in 20% of AIDS patients (*Eur J Haematol* 1987;38:141) and folate deficiency due to folic acid malabsorption (*J Intern Med* 1991;230:227).

- Findings: Megaloblastic anemia (MCV >100 not ascribed to AZT or d4T) ± hypersegmented polymorphonuclear cells, low reticulocyte count with serum B12 (cobalamin) level <125-200 pg/mL (*Semin Hematol* 1999;36:75) or a serum folate level <2-4 ng/mL (<2 ng/mL is more definitive). Note: A good hospital meal may normalize the folate level.
- Treatment: Folate deficiency – folic acid 1-5 mg/day x 1 to 4 months. B12 deficiency – cobalamin 1 g IM qd x 7 days, then every week x 4, then every month or 1-2 g PO qd (*Blood* 1998;92:1191).

- **Iron deficiency:** Usually indicates blood loss, especially from GI tract.
  - Findings: Most studies of iron indicate findings of anemia of chronic disease with decreased Fe (<60 ug/dL), low transferrin (<300 ug/dL), and normal or increased ferritin. Ferritin level <40 ng/mL suggests iron deficiency; <15 ng/mL is 99% sensitive for this diagnosis but only 50% specific (*J Gen Intern Med* 1992;7:145).
  - Treatment: Detect and treat source of loss + ferrous sulfate 300 mg tid between meals.
- **Drug-induced marrow suppression ± red cell aplasia:** Most common with AZT; less common with ganciclovir, amphotericin, ribavirin, pyrimethamine, interferon, TMP-SMX, phenytoin (also seen with HIV *per se*, parvovirus B19, and non-Hodgkin's lymphoma).
  - Findings: Normocytic, normochromic anemia (macrocytic with AZT or d4T), low or normal reticulocyte count.
  - Treatment: Discontinue implicated agent ± EPO (see algorithm, p. 360).
- **Drug-induced hemolytic anemia:** Most common with dapsone, primaquine, and ribavirin (Hemolytic anemia is also seen with TTP). The risk with dapsone and primaquine is dose related and most common with G6PD deficiency.
  - Findings: Reticulocytosis, increased LDH, increased indirect bilirubin, methemoglobinemia, and reduced haptoglobin. The combination of a haptoglobin <25 mg/dL + elevated LDH is 90% specific and 92% sensitive for hemolytic anemia (*JAMA* 980;243:1909). The peripheral smear may show spherocytes and fragmented RBCs. Note: Coombs test is commonly positive.
  - Treatment: Consists of oxygen, packed RBC transfusions and discontinuation of implicated drug. Severe cases in absence of G6-PD deficiency are treated with IV methylene blue (l mg/kg) (*J Acquir Immune Defic Syndr* 1996;12:477). Activated charcoal may be given to reduce dapsone levels (see p. 197).

■ FIGURE 7-2: **Guidelines for Use of Erythropoietin (EPO) in the Anemic HIV Patient**

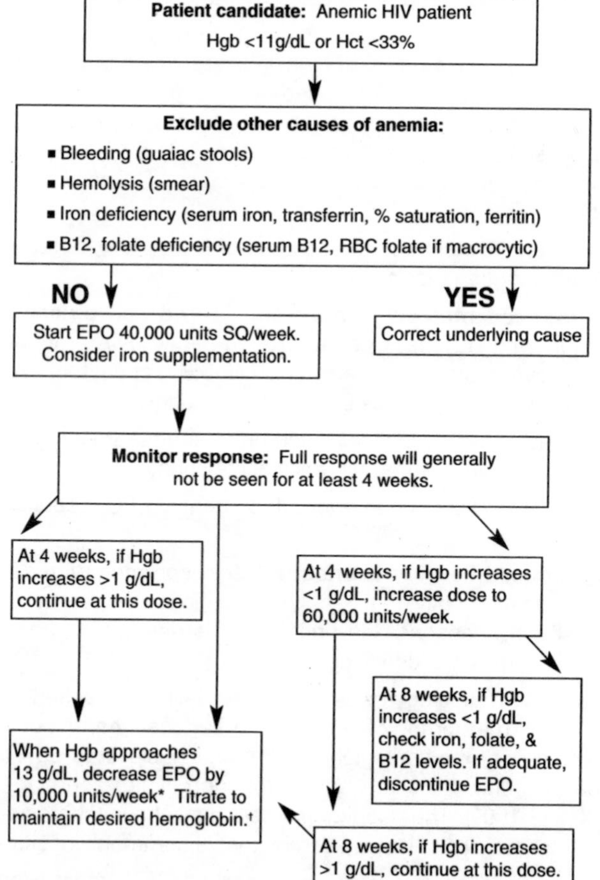
GOALS OF THERAPY:
■ Resolution of anemia: Hgb ≥12 g/dL or Hct ≥36%
■ Increased energy, activity, and overall quality of life for patients, prolonged survival
■ Reduced need for transfusions
Patient candidate: Anemic HIV patient
Hgb <11g/dL or Hct <33%
Exclude other causes of anemia:
■ Bleeding (guaiac stools)
■ Hemolysis (smear)
■ Iron deficiency (serum iron, transferrin, % saturation, ferritin)
■ B12, folate deficiency (serum B12, RBC folate if macrocytic)
NO
YES
Start EPO 40,000 units SQ/week. Consider iron supplementation.
Correct underlying cause
Monitor response: Full response will generally not be seen for at least 4 weeks.
At 4 weeks, if Hgb increases >1 g/dL, continue at this dose.
At 4 weeks, if Hgb increases <1 g/dL, increase dose to 60,000 units/week.
At 8 weeks, if Hgb increases <1 g/dL, check iron, folate, & B12 levels. If adequate, discontinue EPO.
When Hgb approaches 13 g/dL, decrease EPO by 10,000 units/week* Titrate to maintain desired hemoglobin.†
At 8 weeks, if Hgb increases >1 g/dL, continue at this dose.

* If Hgb >15 g/dL at any point, hold EPO and restart when Hgb <12 g/dL, using dose reduced by 10,000/week.

† During dose adjustment phase, hemoglobin should be monitored every 2 to 4 weeks. Allow at least 4 weeks to assess response to dose changes.

Algorithm by Joel E. Gallant M.D., M.P.H., Associate Professor of Medicine, Johns Hopkins University, School of Medicine, Baltimore, MD

Idiopathic Thrombocytopenia Purpura (ITP)

DEFINITION: Unexplained platelet count <100,000/mL

CAUSES

- **Most cases** are ascribed to HIV infection of multi-lineage hematopoietic progenitor cells in the marrow (*Clin Infect Dis* 2000;30:504; *N Engl J Med* 1992;327:1779).
- **Drug induced:** Review of 561 reports showed the best supporting data for a causal role for drugs were for heparin, quinidine, gold, and TMP-SMX (*Ann Intern Med* 1998;129:886). Others with "level 1 evidence" that are used in HIV infected patients: Rifampin, amphotericin, vancomycin, ethambutol, sulfisoxazole, and lithium.

TREATMENT (*Clin Infect Dis* 1995;21:415; *N Engl J Med* 1999;341:1239)

- **HAART:** Two reports showed that with viral suppression and CD4 count rebound, median platelet count increase was 18,000/mL and 45,000/mL at 3 months (*Clin Infect Dis* 2000;30:504; *N Engl J Med* 1999;341:1239).
- **Drug induced:** Median time to recovery with discontinuation of the implicated agent is 7 days (*Ann Intern Med* 1998;129:886).
- **Standard treatments of ITP** (prednisone, IVIG, splenectomy, etc.): Response rates are 40% to 90%; the main problem is durability (*Clin Infect Dis* 1995;21:415).

■ TABLE 7-8: **Treatment of ITP by Clinical Presentation**

Clinical Status	Treatment
Asymptomatic	■ HAART ■ Discontinue implicated drug and monitor response.
Persistent symptomatic or required for procedure	■ Above ■ Prednisone 30-60 mg/day with rapid taper to 5-10 mg/day. Risk of OI. Only 10% to 20% have sustained response. ■ IVIG 400 mg/kg days 1, 2 and 14, then every 2 to 4 weeks. Raises platelet count within 4 days; median peak response time is 3 weeks. Very expensive. ■ *WinRho* 25-50 µg/kg over 3 to 5 minutes, repeat day 3 to 4 prn, then at 3 to 4 week intervals as needed. Similar to IVIG but rapid infusion and less expensive. ■ Splenectomy – experience is variable: Some good (*Arch Surg* 1989;124:625), some bad (*Lancet* 1987;2:342).
Hemorrhage	Packed red cells/platelet transfusions plus prednisone 60-100 mg/day or IVIG 1 g/kg days l, 2, and 14.

Neutropenia

DEFINITION: Absolute neutrophil count <750/mm³ (Some use thresholds of 500/mm³ or 1000/mm³)

CAUSE: Usually due to HIV *per se* or to drugs.

SYMPTOMS: Reported risk of bacterial infections is variable, but the largest review shows an increase in hospitalization with an ANC <500/mm³ (*Arch Intern Med* 1997;157:1825). Other reviews show that few HIV infected patients have excessive neutropenia-associated infections (*Clin Infect Dis* 2001;32:469).

TREATMENT

- **HIV associated:** HAART – ANC increase with immune reconstitution is variable (*Clin Infect Dis* 2000;30:504; *J Acquir Immune Defic Syndr* 2001;28:221). Severe and persistent neutropenia may respond to G-CSF or GM-CSF.
- **Drug associated:** Most common causes are AZT, ganciclovir, or valganciclovir; other causes include d4T, ddI, foscarnet, ribavirin, flucytosine, amphotericin, sulfonamides, pyrimethamine, pentamidine, antineoplastic drugs, and interferon. Treatment is to discontinue the implicated drug and/or give G-CSF or GM-CSF.
- **G-CSF or GM-CSF:** Usually initial dose is 5 μg/kg/day with increases of 1 μg/kg/day at 5 to 7 day intervals to maintain ANC ≥1000-2000/mm³; usual maintenance dose is 300 μg 3 to 7x/week (*N Engl J Med* 1987;371:593). Monitor CBC during cytokine treatment 2x/week.

Thrombotic Thrombocytopenia Purpura

CAUSE: Platelet thrombi in selected organs

FREQUENCY: Unclear, may be early or late in course (*Ann Intern Med* 1988;109:194)

LAB DIAGNOSIS

- **Anemia**
- **Thrombocytopenia** (platelet count 5,000-120,000/mL)
- **Peripheral smear shows fragmented RBCs** (schistocytes, helmet cells) ± nucleated cells
- **Increased creatinine**
- **Evidence of hemolysis:** Increased reticulocytes, indirect bilirubin, and LDH
- **Normal coagulation parameters**

CLINICAL FEATURES: Fever, neurologic changes, renal failure – may be acute requiring dialysis

TREATMENT: The usual course is progressive with irreversible renal failure and death. Standard treatment is plasma exchange until platelet count is normal and LDH is normal (*N Engl J Med* 1991;325:393). An average of 7 to 16 exchanges are required to induce remission. With poor response, add prednisone 60 mg/day.

Malignancies

Kaposi's Sarcoma

CAUSE: HHV-8

FREQUENCY: Rate is 20,000-fold higher with HIV compared with general population and 300-fold higher than other immunosuppressed patients (*Lancet* 1990;335:123; *J Natl Cancer Inst* 2002;94:1204). The incidence is 10-20x higher in men and MSM; the rate has decreased in the HAART era (*JAMA* 2002;287:221).

PRESENTATION: Firm purple to brown-black macules, patches, nodules, papules that are usually asymptomatic – neither pruritic, nor painful, and usually on legs, face, oral cavity, and genitalia. Complications include lymphedema (especially legs, face, and genitalia) and visceral involvement (especially mouth, GI tract, and lungs).

DIFFERENTIAL: Bacillary angiomatosis (biopsy with silver stain to show organisms); hematoma, nevus, hemangioma, B-cell lymphoma, and pyogenic granuloma

■ TABLE 7-9: **Diagnosis of Kaposi's Sarcoma**

Site	Frequency*	Diagnosis
Skin	>95%	■ Appearance; biopsy if atypical
Oral	30%	■ Lesion – purple nodule usually on palate or gingiva; biopsy if atypical
GI	40%	■ Any level; screen – stool guaiac ■ Diagnosis: Endoscopy – hemorrhagic nodule (*Gastroenterology* 1985;89:102); biopsy often negative due to submucosal location
Lung	20% to 50%	■ X-ray variable – nodule(s), infiltrates, effusions, and/or mediastinal node ■ Diagnosis: Bronchoscopy shows cherry-red bronchial nodule (*Chest* 1995;105:1314)

* Frequency in HIV infected patients with Kaposi's sarcoma at any anatomical site.

PROGNOSIS: CD4 count plus tumor burden staging (ACTG – *J Clin Oncol* 1989;7:201). TIS: Extent of Tumor (T), Immune status (I), Severity of systemic illness (S). TIS predicts survival (*J Clin Oncol* 1997;15:385). Good prognosis – lesions confined to skin, CD4 count >150 cells/mm^3, no "B" symptoms.

TREATMENT

- **HAART:** Associated with lesion regression, decreased incidence, and prolonged survival (*J Clin Oncol* 2001;19:3848; *J Med Virol* 1999;57:140; *AIDS* 1997;11:261; *Mayo Clin Proc* 1998;73:439; *AIDS* 2000;14:987).
- **Antiviral therapy:** Foscarnet, cidofovir, and ganciclovir are active vs HHV-8 (*J Clin Invest* 1997;99:2082); long-term use of foscarnet or ganciclovir is associated with reduced incidence of Kaposi's sarcoma (*N Engl J Med* 1999;340:1063) but does not appear to cause tumor regression (J *Acquir Immune Defic Syndr* 1999;20:34).
- **Systemic vs local therapy:** Systemic treatment is preferred if extensive tumor burden (>25 skin lesions, visceral involvement with symptoms, extensive edema, "B" symptoms, or failure to respond to local treatment) (*Lancet* 1995;346:26).

■ TABLE 7-10: **Treatment of Kaposi's Sarcoma**

Local Treatment	Comment
Vinblastine	■ Inject 0.1 mL/0.5 cm^2 of solution with 0.2-0.3 mg/mL and repeat every 3 to 4 weeks as needed. ■ Most frequently used; lesions usually regress but don't disappear (*J Oral Maxillofac Surg* 1996;54:583).
Panretin gel	■ Topical 9-cis retinoic acid gel.
Liquid nitrogen	■ Usually restricted to small lesions.
Radiation	■ Usually low dose, 400 rads/week x 6 weeks; well tolerated on skin; mucositis common with oral lesions, usual indication is lesions that are too extensive for local treatment.
Cryosurgery	
Laser	
Systemic Treatment	**Comment**
Liposomal anthracyclines	■ Two FDA-approved formulations: Pegylated liposomal doxorubicin (*Doxil*) and liposomal daunorubicin (*DaunoXome*) – considered preferred over conventional chemotherapy for better response and reduced toxicity (*J Clin Oncol* 1998;16: 2445; *J Clin Oncol* 1998;16:683; *J Clin Oncol* 1996;14:2353). ■ Doses: *Doxil* – 20 mg/m^2 every 2 to 3 weeks; *DaunoXome* – 40 mg/m^2 every 2 weeks.
Paclitaxel (*Taxol*)	■ FDA-approved for Kaposi's sarcoma. Considered second line to anthracyclines due to greater toxicity (neutropenia and thrombocytopenia) (*J Clin Oncol* 1998;16:1112). ■ Lower doses (100 mg/m^2 every 2 weeks) appears to preserve efficacy with reduced toxicity (*Cancer* 2002;95:147).
Interferon alfa	■ Efficacy established especially with modest disease, but toxicity is great (*J Clin Oncol* 1998;16:1736). ■ Dose is 8,000 units SC/day.
Conventional chemotherapy	■ Commonly used combinations include adriamycin, bleomycin plus vincristine or vinblastine (ABV); bleomycin plus vinca alkaloids or vincristine/vinblastine (alone). ■ Newer treatments (paclitaxel and anthracyclines) are usually preferred.

RESPONSE: Kaposi's sarcoma cannot be cured; goals of therapy are to reduce symptoms and prevent progression. HAART is associated with reduced tumor burden. Antiviral drugs directed against HHV-8 have no established benefit.

- **Local therapy:** Local injections of vinblastine cause reduced lesion size but not elimination in most patients (*Cancer* 1993;71:1722).
- **Systemic therapy:** Liposomal anthracyclines usually show good results with few side effects. Paclitaxel is as effective but more toxic due to neutropenia and thrombocytopenia; side effects are dose related; lower doses appear as effective with less marrow suppression.

Non-Hodgkin's Lymphoma (NHL)

CAUSE: Immunosuppression (CD4 count <100 cells/mm^3) and EBV (50% to 80%)

FREQUENCY AND TYPE: NHL occurs 200- to 600-fold more frequently with HIV compared with the general population (*Int J Cancer* 1997;73:645). The rate is about 3% for patients with AIDS (*J Acquir Immune Defic Syndr* 2002;29:418). Most (70% to 90%) are high-grade diffuse large cell or Burkitt-like lymphomas (*Am J Med* 2001; *Brit J Haematol* 2001;112:863).

PRESENTATION: Compared with NHL in the general population, HIV infected patients have high rates of stage IV disease with "B" symptoms and sparse node involvement. Common sites of infection and forms of clinical presentation are fever of unknown origin, hepatic dysfunction, marrow involvement, lung disease (effusions, multinodular infiltrates, consolidation, mass lesions, or local or diffuse interstitial infiltrates, hilar adenopathy), GI involvement (any level – pain and weight loss), and CNS (aseptic meningitis, cranial nerve palsies, CNS mass lesions).

DIAGNOSIS: Screening tests include biopsy (usually required), but site depends on symptoms and results of CT scan to detect nodes and extranodal sites of involvement. Fine needle aspirate (FNA) of enlarged nodes is helpful if positive, but most are falsely negative, necessitating a biopsy. Bone marrow biopsy will often yield the diagnosis. With GI tract and hepatic involvement, the screening test is CT scan; endoscopy is not usually useful. Lung involvement usually shows an exudative pleural effusion; bronchoscopy is usually negative unless accompanied by lung biopsy, which has a diagnostic yield of about 60% (*Chest* 1996;110:729).

TREATMENT

- **Standard:** CHOP (cyclophosphamide, doxorubicin, adriamycin, vincristine, and prednisone). Intrathecal methotrexate or cytosine arabinoside may be given for CNS prophylaxis and should be given with meningeal involvement.
- **Alternatives to CHOP**
    - M-BACOD (methotrexate, bleomycin, doxorubicin, cyclophosphamide, vincristine, and dexamethasone + G-CSF) (*N Engl J Med* 1997;336:16)
    - EPOCH (etoposide, prednisone, vincristine, cyclophosphamide, and doxorubicin)

RESPONSE: Initial response rates are 50% to 60%, but the long-term prognosis is poor with median survival <1 year. The usual cause of death is progressive lymphoma or progressive HIV with OIs (*Semin Oncol* 1998;25:492). The prognosis is significantly better with HAART; one report showed an 84% 1 year survival with HAART + chemotherapy (*AIDS* 2001;15:1483).

Primary CNS Lymphoma (PCNSL) (see p. 373)

Primary Effusion Lymphoma

CAUSE: HHV-8 (*N Engl J Med* 1995;332:1186)

FREQUENCY: Rare – tumor registries crossed with AIDS registries show a frequency of 0.004% or 0.14% of non-Hodgkin's lymphoma in patients with AIDS (*J Acquir Immune Defic Syndr* 2002;29:418)

PRESENTATION: Serous effusions (pleural, peritoneal, pericardial, joint spaces) with no masses (*Hum Pathol* 1997;28:801)

DIAGNOSIS: Effusions are serous, contain high-grade malignant lymphocytes and HHV-8.

TREATMENT

- **HAART plus radiation ± CHOP** every 28 days
- **Alternatives:** Pegylated liposomal doxorubicin or liposomal daunorubicin

RESPONSE: This tumor usually does not extend beyond serosal surfaces, but prognosis is poor, with median survival of 2 to 3 months (*J Acquir Immune Defic Syndr* 1996;13:215). Most patients show response to therapy with decrease in effusion size. Failure to respond to two cycles of CHOP indicates additional cycles will fail, indicating a role for *DaunoXome* or *Doxil*.

Neurologic Complications

Acute Neuropathy and Lactic Acidosis Syndrome

CAUSE: Postulated to be mitochondrial toxicity attributed to deoxy NRTIs, primarily d4T (*N Engl J Med* 2002;346:811).

FREQUENCY: 25 cases reported to the FDA including 22 treated with d4T (9th CROI, Seattle, Washington, 2002, Abstract LB14).

CLINICAL FEATURES: Ascending paresis, areflexia, and cranial neuropathies; usually associated with prolonged dideoxynucleosides, especially d4T. Laboratory tests usually show elevated CPK and lactate levels.

DIAGNOSIS (ACTG, 2002)

- New onset limb weakness ± sensory involvement that is acute (1 to 2 weeks) or subacute (>2 weeks) involving legs or legs and arms
- Absence of alternative confounding illnesses: Myasthenia gravis, myelopathy, hypokalemia, stroke

TREATMENT: Discontinue d4T and/or other causative NRTIs

Cytomegalovirus Radiculitis

FREQUENCY: Uncommon (*Ann Neurol* 1994;35:53)

DIAGNOSIS: Advanced HIV with CD4 count <50 cells/mm^3, flaccid paralysis of legs, sacral pain, and sphincter dysfunction. CSF shows polymorphonuclear pleocytosis, elevated protein, and low glucose. CMV is detected in CNS by PCR in 50% to 60% (*Neurology* 1993;43:493). Many patients also have CMV retinitis.

TREATMENT: Standard treatment has been IV ganciclovir (*Neurology* 1993;43:493), but some patients develop this complication while receiving ganciclovir, and some presumably develop ganciclovir resistance, requiring alternative therapy with foscarnet. The role of valganciclovir for initial treatment is unclear. (See p. 131)

RESPONSE: Most patients achieve stabilization with IV ganciclovir but often worsen during the first 2 weeks (*Ann Neurol* 1994;35:53).

■ TABLE 7-11: **Differential Diagnosis of Lower Extremity Symptoms in Patients With HIV Infection**

Syndrome	Symptoms	Clinical Features	Ancillary Studies/ Treatment
Distal sensory neuropathy (DSN)	■ Pain and numbness in toes and feet; ankles, calves, and fingers involved in more advanced cases ■ CD4 cell count <200 cells/mm³, but can occur at higher CD4 level	■ Reduced pinprick/vibratory sensation ■ Reduced or absent ankle jerks ■ Contact allodynia (hypersensitivity) present most cases	■ Skin biopsy shows epidermal denervation ■ Electromyography/ nerve conduction velocities (EMG/NCV) show a predominantly axonal neuropathy ■ Quantitative sensory testing or thermal thresholds may be helpful
Antiretroviral toxic neuropathy (ATN)	■ Same as DSN (above), but symptoms occur after initiation of ddI, ddC, d4T. ■ Any CD4 cell count. ■ More common in older patients and patients with diabetes	■ Same as DSN (above)	■ EMG/NCVs show a predominantly axonal neuropathy ■ Discontinuation of presumed neuro-toxic medication if severe ■ Symptoms may worsen for a few weeks (coasting) before improving
Tarsal tunnel syndrome	■ Pain and numbness predominantly in anterior portion of soles of feet	■ Reduced sensation over soles of feet ■ Positive Tinel's sign at tarsal tunnel	■ Infiltration of local anesthetic in tarsal tunnel may provide symptomatic relief
Acute neuropathy and lactic acidosis syndrome	■ Ascending paresis with areflexia ± cranial nerve or sensory involvement ■ Usually associated with prolonged d4T use	■ Lactate and CPK levels usually ↑ ■ EMG/nerve conduction studies – axonal neuropathy and myopathy	■ Discontinue NRTIs, especially d4T
HIV-associated myopathy/AZT myopathy	■ Pain and aching in muscles, usually in thighs and shoulders. ■ Weakness with difficulty when rising from a chair or reaching above shoulders ■ Any CD4 cell count	■ Mild/moderate muscle tenderness ■ Weakness, predominantly in proximal muscles (i.e., deltoids, hip flexors) ■ Normal sensory exam/normal reflexes	■ CPK ↑ ■ EMG shows irritable myopathy ■ Discontinue AZT and follow CPK every 2 weeks. Symptoms/signs/ CPK should improve within 1 month

continued on next page

■ TABLE 7-11: **Differential Diagnosis of Lower Extremity Symptoms in Patients With HIV Infection *(Continued)***

Syndrome	Symptoms	Clinical Features	Ancillary Studies/ Treatment
Polyradiculitis	■ Rapidly evolving weakness and numbness in legs (both proximally and distally), with bowel/bladder incontinence ■ CD4 count >500 cells/mm³ or <50 cells/mm³	■ Diffuse weakness in legs ■ Diffuse sensory abnormalities in legs and buttocks ■ Reduced/absent reflexes at knees and ankles	■ EMG/NCV show multilevel nerve root involvement ■ Spinal fluid helpful in determining CMV or HSV as cause ■ Treat CMV polyradiculopathy with ganciclovir or foscarnet
Vacuolar myelopathy	■ Stiffness and weakness in legs with leg numbness. ■ Bowel/bladder incontinence in advanced cases ■ CD4 cell count <200 cells/mm³	■ Weakness and spasticity, mainly in hip, knee, and ankle flexors ■ Brisk knee jerks, upgoing toes ■ If sensory neuropathy coexists, then distal sensory loss and reduced/ absent jerks	■ Spinal fluid may show elevated protein 0-10 cells/mm³ ■ Exclude B-12 deficiency and HTLV-1 co-infection ■ Thoracic spinal imaging normal ■ No established therapy, but physical therapy or methionine (3 g bid) may be helpful (*Neurology* 1998;51:266)
Inflammatory demyelinating polyneuropathies	■ Predominantly weakness in arms and legs, with minor sensory symptoms. ■ CD4 count >500 cells/mm³ or <50 cells/mm³	■ Diffuse weakness including facial musculature, asymmetric in early cases, with diffuse absent reflexes ■ Minor sensory signs	■ EMG/NCVs show a demyelinating polyneuropathy ■ Spinal fluid shows a very high protein with mild to moderate lymphocytic pleocytosis, but all cultures are negative
Mononeuritis or *mono-neuritis* multiplex	■ Mix of motor and sensory defects ■ Asymmetric ■ Evolves over weeks ■ CD4 count is variable	■ EMG and nerve conduction – asymmetric and multifocal defects ■ R/O CMV (CSF or sural nerve biopsy) and HCV	■ CD4 count >200 cells/mm³ – possible steroids ■ CD4 counts <50 cells/mm³ and severe – treat for CMV

Cytomegalovirus Encephalitis

CAUSE: CMV + CD4 count <50 cells/mm^3

FREQUENCY: <0.5% of AIDS patients

PRESENTATION: Rapid progressive delirium, cranial nerve deficits, nystagmus, ataxia, headache with fever ± CMV retinitis

DIAGNOSIS: MRI shows periventricular confluent lesions with enhancement. CMV PCR in CSF shows sensitivity of >80% and specificity of 90%; cultures of CSF for CMV are usually negative.

TREATMENT: Ganciclovir, foscarnet, or both IV (see p. 131).

RESPONSE: Trial of foscarnet plus ganciclovir showed a median survival of 94 days compared with 42 days in historic controls (*AIDS* 2000;14:517).

Dementia (HIV-Associated Dementia or HAD)

CAUSE: Chronic encephalitis with progressive or static encephalopathy due to CNS HIV infection with prominent immune activation

INCIDENCE: 7% after AIDS in pre-HAART era; 2% to 3% more recently (*Neurology* 2001;56:257). Prevalence is increasing with longer survival.

PRESENTATION: Late stage HIV with CD4 count <200 cells/mm^3 and subcortical dementia. See Table 7-12 and 7-13. Early symptoms: Apathy, memory loss, cognitive slowing, depression, and withdrawal. Motor defects include gait instability and reduced hand coordination. Late stages show global loss of cognition, severe psychomotor retardation, and mutism. There may be seizures, which are usually easily controlled. The rate of progression is highly variable, but the average from first symptoms to death in the pre-HAART era was 6 months (*Medicine* 1987;66:407). Physical examination in early disease shows defective rapid eye movement, rapid limb movement, and generalized hyperreflexia. In late stages, there is tremor, clonus, and frontal release signs.

TESTING

■ TABLE 7-12: **HIV Dementia Scale (*AIDS Reader* 2002;12:29)**

Maximum Score	Test*
See below	Memory registration: 4 words given (hat, dog, green, peach) and have the patient repeat them.
6	Psychomotor speed: Record the time, in seconds, that it takes the patient to write the alphabet. Score: <21 sec = 6, 21.1-24 sec = 5, 24.1-27 sec = 4, 27.1-30 sec = 3, 30.1-33 sec = 2; 33.1-36 sec = 1, >36 = 0
4	Memory recall: Ask for the four words from above. For words not remembered give semantic clue, e.g. "animal" (dog), "color" (green), etc. 1 point for each correct answer.
2	Construction: Copy a cube and record time. Score: <25 sec = 2, 25-35 sec = 1, >35 = 0

* ≥7/12 is threshold for dementia but is non-specific requiring additional neurologic evaluation.

■ TABLE 7-13: **AIDS Dementia Complex Staging**

Stage 0	Normal
Stage 0.5	Subclinical: Minimal – equivocal symptoms; no work impairment.
Stage 1.0	Mild – minimal intellectual or motor impairment; able to do all but more demanding work or ADL.
Stage 2.0	Moderate – cannot work or perform demanding ADL; capable of self care.
Stage 3.0	Severe – major intellectual disability; unable to walk unassisted.
Stage 4.0	End stage – near vegetative stage; paraplegia or quadriplegia.

DIAGNOSIS: History, physical examination, and screening with HIV Dementia Scale as noted above. Formal testing includes: Trail Making B, Digital Symbol, Grooved Pegboard, and the HIV Dementia Scale. MRI shows cerebral atrophy (which can be present without symptoms), typically with rarefaction of white matter (*J Neurol Neurosurg Psych* 1997;62:346). CSF shows increased protein with 0-15 mononuclear cells; pleocytosis is absent in 65%. Main goal is to exclude alternative diagnosis because no test is specific for HAD.

TREATMENT: The HIV Dementia Scale (see Table 7-12) can be used to follow response to HAART. HAART has reduced the frequency of HAD, but there are sparce data to show efficacy of HAART for reversing established HAD (*J Neurovirol* 2002;8:136). It is also unclear if CNS penetration is important in the selection of agents. Antiretroviral agents with the best CNS penetration based on CSF levels are AZT, d4T, ABC, NVP, and IDV; levels are somewhat less for EFV, ddI, 3TC, and APV (*J Acquir Immune Defic Syndr* 1998;235:238; *AIDS* 1998;12:537). Adjunctive therapies to block immune activation are being tested in trials of NMbA receptor antagonists and antioxidants such as selegiline.

Inflammatory Demyelinating Polyneuropathy

CAUSE: Unclear; immunopathogenic mechanism with inflammation and breakdown of peripheral nerve myelin is suspected.

FREQUENCY: Uncommon

DIAGNOSIS: There are two forms: Acute demyelinating neuropathy (AIDP, Guillain-Barré Syndrome), that occurs early in the course of HIV, and a more chronic relapsing motor weakness, CIDP, that usually occurs in late-stage HIV. Both present with a progressive ascending paralysis with mild sensory involvement. CSF shows increased protein and mononuclear pleocytosis; EMG and nerve conduction studies are critical for diagnosis. Nerve biopsy may be needed and shows mononuclear, macrophage infiltrate, and internodal demyelination (*Ann Neurol* 1987;21:3240).

TREATMENT

- **AIDP**
  - Plasmapheresis: Five exchanges with maintenance as needed
  - Alternative is IVIG 0.4 g/kg/day x 5 days (monitor renal function)
- **CIDP:** Oral prednisone (1 mg/kg/day) or intermittent plasmapheresis or IVIG; each in continued until there is a therapeutic response.

RESPONSE: Treatment usually halts progression; CIDP may require prolonged courses (*Ann Neurol* 1987;21:3240).

Primary CNS Lymphoma (PCNSL)

CAUSE: Virtually all are EBV-associated (*Lancet* 1991;337:805).

FREQUENCY: 2% to 6% in pre-HAART era – 1000x higher than in the general population (*Lancet* 1991;338:969). Incidence reduced post HAART but not as much as other HIV complications (*J Acquir Immune Defic Syndr* 2000;25:451).

PRESENTATION: Focal or non-focal signs. Symptoms include confusion, headache, memory loss, aphasia, hemiparesis, and/or seizures without fever for <3 months. CD4 count is usually <50 cells/mm^3.

DIAGNOSIS: MRI shows single lesion or multiple lesions that are isodense or hypodense and usually homogeneous, but sometimes ring forms (*Am J Neuroradiol* 1997;18:563). With contrast, CT and MRI scans show enhancement that is usually irregular (due to rapid growth). These lesions usually involve the corpus callosum, periventricular area, or periependymal area; they are often >4 cm in diameter and usually show a mass effect (*Neurology* 1997;48:687). Major differential diagnosis is toxoplasmosis. Factors favoring CNS lymphoma are: 1) Typical neuro imaging results (above), 2) Negative *T. gondii* serology, 3) Failure to respond to empiric treatment of toxoplasmosis within 1 to 2 weeks, 4) Lack of fever, and 5) Thallium SPECT scan with early thallium uptake. CSF EBV DNA is >94% specific and 80% sensitive (*Clin Infect Dis* 2002;34:103; *J Natl Cancer Inst* 1998;90:364; *Lancet* 1992;342: 398). Stereotactic brain biopsy is definitive and usually reserved for patients who fail to respond to toxoplasmosis treatment (*AIDS* 1995;9:1243; *Clin Infect Dis* 2002;34:103). A review of five reports with 486 AIDS patients undergoing stereotactic brain biopsy showed a 4% morbidity rate (*Clin Infect Dis* 2002;34:103).

THERAPY

- **Standard:** Radiation plus corticosteroids (*J Neuro Sci* 1999;163:32)
- **Chemotherapy:** May be combined with radiation plus corticosteroids. Usually for patients with elevated CD4 counts. Preliminary results with methotrexate without radiation were promising (*AIDS* 1997;11:1725)

RESPONSE: Response rates to radiation treatment plus corticosteroids is 20% to 50%, but these results are temporary, and the average duration of life following the onset of symptoms was only about 4 months in the pre-HAART era (*Crit Rev Oncol* 1998;9:199; *Semin Oncol* 1998;25:492). Prolonged survival is possible with HAART response.

Progressive Multifocal Leukoencephalopathy (PML)

CAUSE: Activation of JC virus (which is ubiquitous) in patients who are immunodeficient.

FREQUENCY: 1% to 2% of AIDS patients (*J Infect Dis* 1999;180:261)

PRESENTATION: Cognitive impairment, visual field deficits, hemiparesis speech defects, incoordination with *no* fever. CD4 count is usually 35-100 cells/mm^3, but a subset of 7% to 25% have CD4 counts >200 cells/mm^3 (*Clin Infect Dis* 2002;34:103).

DIAGNOSIS

- MRI shows hypodense lesions of white matter without edema or enhancement.

- PCR for JCV in CSF with sensitivity of 80% and specificity of 95%.

TREATMENT: None with established merit. One report shows PML response to HAART with enhancing lesions on MRI (*AIDS* 1999;13:1426). There is conflicting evidence for cidofovir (*AIDS* 2002;16:1791; *J Neurovirol* 2001;7:364; *J Neurovirol* 2001;7:374).

PROGNOSIS: Median duration of survival is 1 to 6 months. Response to HAART is possible, but some patients have developed PML while receiving HAART (*Clin Infect Dis* 2002;34:103). The most important predictor of survival is baseline CD4 cell count.

Sensory Neuropathies

Distal sensory neuropathy (DSN) and antiretroviral toxic neuropathy (ATN)

CAUSE: HIV infection *per se*, usually with CD4 count <200 cells/mm^3 and/or dideoxy NRTIs (d-drugs) – ddI, d4T, and ddC; most common with ddI + d4T (*AIDS* 2000;14:273). DSN and ATN are indistinguishable by clinical features or biopsy.

FREQUENCY: 20% with advanced HIV over 1 year and 52% over 2 years (*Neurology* 2002;58:1764)

DIFFERENTIAL: Toxic neuropathies due to drugs (metronidazole, B6 overdose, dapsone, INH, vincristine), diabetes, entrapment neuropathies, B12 deficiency, alcoholism, uremia, inflammatory demyelinating polyneuropathy, and acute neuromuscular syndrome

DIAGNOSIS: Dysesthesia and contact hypersensitivity of feet with decreased or absent ankle reflexes. Invasive neurodiagnostic tests may be useful but are usually unnecessary. Skin biopsy shows epidermal denervation. Electromyography/nerve conduction studies show predominantly axonal neuropathy. Quantitative sensory tests or thermal tests show elevated thresholds. See Table 7-12, p. 372.

TREATMENT

- **ATN:** Avoid d4T, ddI, and ddC; acceptable alternative agents in this class are AZT, 3TC, ABC, and TDF.
- **DSN**: Possible response reported with HAART (*Lancet* 1998;352: 1906).
- **Symptomatic treatment**
    - Lamotrigine (*Lamictal*) 25 mg bid increasing to 300 mg/day over 6 weeks; one of the few treatments with confirmed benefit in clinical trials (*Neurology* 2000;54:2115).

- Tricyclics nortriptyline 10 mg hs increasingly by 10 mg q5d to maximum 75 mg hs or 10-20 mg PO tid; other tricyclics (amitriptyline, desipramine, or imipramine) are considered comparable. One trial failed to show response to tricyclics (*JAMA* 1998;280:1590).
- Ibuprofen 600-800 mg tid
- Gabapentin 300-1200 mg PO tid
- Capsaicin-containing ointments (*Zostrix,* etc.); often not well tolerated.
- *Lidocaine* 20% to 30% ointment (not very effective)
- Phenytoin 200-400 mg/day
- Severe pain: Methadone – up to 20 mg qid; *Fentanyl* patch 25-100 mcg/hour q72h or morphine
- Acupuncture failed in one reported trial (*JAMA* 1998;280;1590).
- Avoid tight footwear, limit walking, bridge at foot of the bed, use feet soaks.

RESPONSE: Sensory neuropathy due to NRTIs is usually reversible if the implicated agent is discontinued early, e.g. within 2 weeks of the onset of symptoms. If continued, the pain becomes irreversible and may be incapacitating. Response may require 12 weeks after discontinuing nucleosides (*Neurology* 1996;46:999). Treatment of sensory neuropathy, beyond discontinuing NRTIs, is symptomatic.

■ FIGURE 7-3: **Sensory Neuropathies in Patients With AIDS**

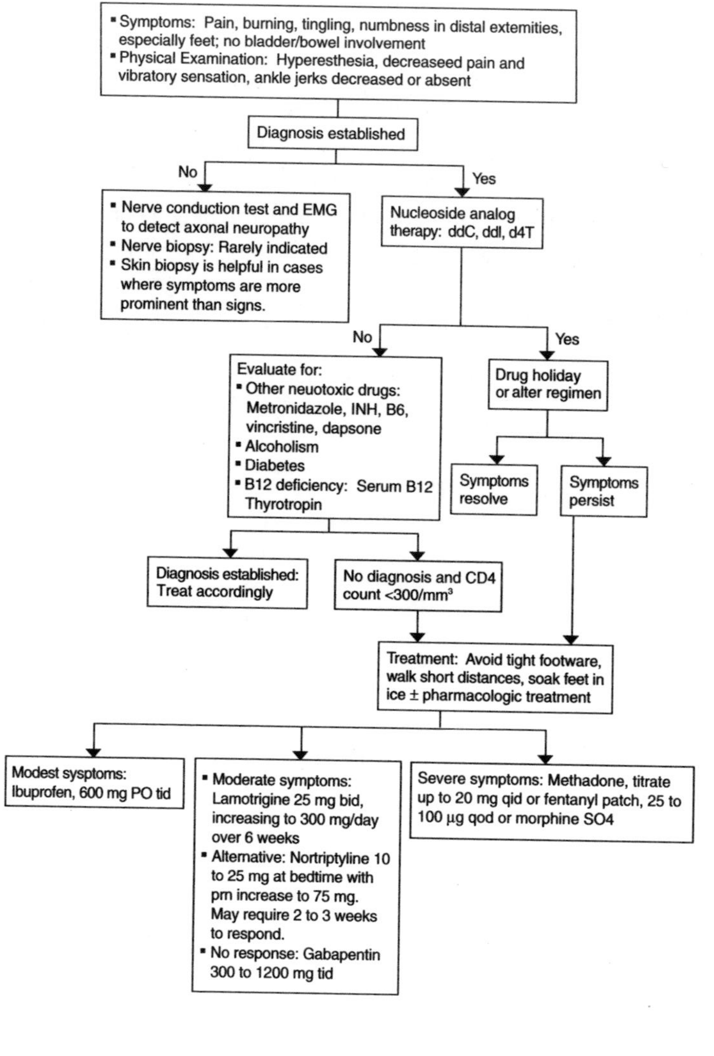

Toxoplasmosis

CAUSE: Latent *T. gondii* infection

FREQUENCY: 30% of AIDS patients with latent *T. gondii* infection (positive serology) and no prophylaxis

PRESENTATION: Subacute symptoms with headache, fever, behavior change, lethargy, focal neurologic finding; over 80% have CD4 <100 cells/mm^3.

DIAGNOSIS

- MRI shows ≥2 ring-enhancing lesions with edema. SPECT can facilitate distinction from lymphoma, but this is usually not necessary.
- *T. gondii* serology is positive in >95%.
- Response to therapy is characteristically prompt and impressive.
- PCR for *T. gondii* in CSF is 50% sensitive and 96% to 100% specific.

TREATMENT: See p. 156

RESPONSE: Treatment with pyrimethamine and sulfadiazine results in clinical improvement in 80% by 7 days and in 95% by 14 days. MRI response is noted within 2 weeks.

■ TABLE 7-14: **Central Nervous System Conditions in Patients With HIV Infection**

Agent/Condition Frequency (All AIDS Patients)	Clinical Features	CT Scan/MRI	Cerebrospinal Fluid (CSF)	Other Diagnostic Tests
Toxoplasmosis (2% to 4%) (see p. 156)	■ Fever, reduced alertness, headache, focal neurological deficits (80%), seizures (30%) ■ Evolution: <2 weeks ■ CD4 count <100 cells/mm³	■ Location: Basal ganglia, gray-white junction ■ Sites: Usually multiple ■ Enhancement: prominent; Usually ring lesions (1 to 2 cm) ■ Edema/mass effect: Usually not as great as lymphoma	■ Normal: 20% to 30% ■ Protein: 10 to 150/mg/dL ■ WBC: 0 to 40 (monos) ■ Experimental: Toxo ag (ELISA) or PCR	■ Toxoplasmosis serology (IgG) false-negative in <5% ■ Response to empiric therapy: >85%; most respond by day 7 (*N Engl J Med* 1993;329:995) ■ MRI: Repeat at 2 weeks ■ Definitive diagnosis: Brain biopsy
Primary CNS Lymphoma (2%) (see p. 373)	■ Afebrile, headache, focal neurological findings; mental status change (60%), personality or behavioral; seizures (15%) ■ Evolution: 2 to 8 weeks ■ CD4 count <100 cells/mm³	■ Location: Periventricular, anywhere, 2 to 6 cm ■ Sites: One or many ■ Enhancement: Prominent; usually solid, irregular ■ Edema/mass effect: Prominent	■ Normal: 30% to 50% ■ Protein: 10 to 150/mg/dL ■ WBC: 0 to 100 (monos) ■ EBV PCR in 50% ■ EBV DNA in CSF (*Lancet* 1992;342:398)	■ Suspect with negative toxo. IgG, single lesion, or failure to respond to empiric toxoplasmosis treatment (MRI and clinical evaluation at 2 weeks) ■ Thallium 201 SPECT scan (90% sensitive and specific)
Cryptococcal meningitis (8% to 10%) (see p. 123)	■ Fever, headache, alert (75%); less common are visual changes, stiff neck, cranial nerve deficits, seizures (10%); no focal neurologic deficits ■ Evolution: <2 weeks ■ CD4 count <100 cells/mm³	■ Usually normal or shows increased intracranial pressure ■ Enhancement: Negative or meningeal enhancement ■ Edema mass effect: Ventricular enlargement/ obstructive hydrocephalus	■ Protein: 30 to 150/mg/dL ■ WBC: 0 to 100 (monos) ■ Culture positive: 95% to 100% ■ India ink pos: 60% to 80% ■ Crypt Ag: >95% sensitive and specific	■ Cryptococcal antigen in serum – 95% ■ Definitive diagnosis: CSF antigen and/or positive culture

continued on next page

■ TABLE 7-14: **Central Nervous System Conditions in Patients With HIV Infection *(Continued)***

Agent/Condition Frequency (All AIDS Patients)	Clinical Features	CT Scan/MRI	Cerebrospinal Fluid (CSF)	Other Diagnostic Tests
CMV (>0.5%) (see p. 131)	■ Fever ±, delirium, lethargy, disorientation; headache; stiff neck, photophobia, cranial nerve deficits; no focal neurologic deficits ■ Evolution: <2 weeks ■ CD4 count <100 cells/mm³	■ Location: Periventricular, brainstem ■ Site: Confluent ■ Enhancement: Variable; prominent to none.	■ CSF may be normal ■ Protein: 100 to 1000/mg/dL ■ WBC: 10 to 1000 (polys)/mL ■ Glucose usually decreased ■ CMV PCR positive ■ CSF cultures usually negative for CMV	■ Definitive diagnosis: Brain biopsy with histopath and/or positive culture ■ Hyponatremia (reflects CMV adrenalitis) ■ Retinal exam for CMV retinitis
HIV Dementia (7%) (see p. 371)	■ Afebrile; triad of cognitive, motor, and behavioral dysfunction. ■ Early: Decreased memory, concentration, attention, coordination; ataxia ■ Late: Global dementia, paraplegia, mutism ■ Evolution: Weeks to months ■ CD4 count <200 cells/mm³	■ Location: Diffuse, deep white matter hyperintensities ■ Site: Diffuse, ill-defined ■ Enhancement: Negative ■ Atrophy: Prominent ■ No mass effect	■ Normal: 30% to 50% ■ Protein: Increased in 60% ■ WBC: Increased in 5% to 10% (monos) ■ Beta-2 microglobulin elevated (>3 mg/L)	■ Neuropsychological tests show subcortical dementia ■ HIV dementia scale for screening (see p. 372)
Neurosyphilis (0.5%) (see p. 158)	■ Asymptomatic meningeal: headache, fever, photophobia, meningismus ± seizures, focal findings, cranial nerve palsies ■ Tabes dorsalis: Sharp pains, paresthesias, decreased DTRs, loss of pupil response	■ Aseptic meningitis: May show meningeal enhancement ■ General paresis: Cortical atrophy, sometimes with infarcts ■ Meningovascular syphilis: Deep strokes	■ Protein: 45 to 200/mg/dL ■ WBC: 5 to 100 (monos) ■ VDRL positive: Sensitivity = 65%, specificity = 100% positive ■ Experimental: PCR for *T. pallidum*	■ Serum VDRL and FTA-ABS are clue in >90%; false-negative serum VDRL in 5% to 10% with tabes dorsalis or general paresis

■ TABLE 7-14: **Central Nervous System Conditions in Patients With HIV Infection *(Continued)***

Agent/Condition Frequency (All AIDS Patients)	Clinical Features	CT Scan/MRI	Cerebrospinal Fluid (CSF)	Other Diagnostic Tests
Neurosyphilis (0.5%) – *continued* (see p. 158)	■ General paresis: Memory loss, dementia, personality changes, loss of pupil response ■ Meningovascular: Strokes, myelitis ■ Ocular: Iritis, uveitis, optic neuritis ■ Any CD4 cell count			■ Definitive diagnosis: Positive CSF VDRL (found in 60% to 70%) ■ Note: Most common forms in HIV-infected persons are ocular, meningeal, and meningovascular.
PML (1% to 2%) (see p. 139)	■ No fever; no headache; impaired speech, vision, motor function, cranial nerves ■ Late: ↓ cognition ■ Evolution: Weeks to months ■ CD4 count <100 cells/mm³; some >200 cells/mm³	■ Location: White matter, subcortical, multifocal ■ Sites: Variable ■ Enhancement: Negative ■ No mass effect	■ Normal CSF ■ PCR for JC virus: 80%	■ Brain biopsy: Positive DFA stain for JC virus
Tuberculosis (0.5% to 1%) (see p. 145)	■ Fever, reduced alertness, headache, meningismus, focal deficits (20%) ■ CD4 count <350 cells/mm³	■ Intracerebral lesions in 50% to 70% (*N Engl J Med* 1992;326:668; *Am J Med* 1992;93:524)	■ Normal: 5% to 10% ■ Protein: Normal (40%) - 500/mL ■ WBC: 5 to 2000 (average is 60% to 70% monos) ■ Glucose: 4 to 0/mL ■ AFB smear positive: 20%	■ Chest x-ray: active TB in 50%; PPD positive: 20% to 30% ■ Definitive diagnosis: Positive culture CSF

Normal values: Protein: 15 to 45 mg/dL; traumatic tap: 1 mg/1000 RBCs; glucose: 40 to 80 mg % or CSF/blood glucose ratio >0.6; leukocyte counts: <5 mononuclear cells/mL, 5 to 10 is suspect, 1 PMN is suspect; bloody tap: 1 WBC/700 RBC; opening pressure: 80 to 200 mm H_2O.

CSF analysis in asymptomatic HIV infected persons shows 40% to 50% have elevated protein and/or pleocytosis (>5 mononuclear cell/mL); the frequency of pleocytosis decreases with progressive disease.

Ophthalmologic Complications

CMV Retinitis

CAUSE: CD4 count <50 cells/mm^3 + latent CMV infection (50% to 80% HIV infected patients have latent CMV)

FREQUENCY: 30% of patients with CD4 count <50 cells/mm^3

DIAGNOSIS: Symptoms include blurring, blind spots, flashing lights ("photopsia"), and loss of central vision; acute vision loss suggests retinal detachment. Ophthalmoscopy by experienced clinician shows characteristic fluffy white lesions and hemorrhages usually close to retinal vessels ("cottage cheese and catsup"). Tests for CMV (pp65Ag, blood DNA PCR, urine DNA PCR, NASBA early Ag, blood culture, urine culture, throat culture) are usually not necessary or useful (*J Clin Microbiol* 2000;38:563).

TREATMENT: Standard – HAART + intraocular ganciclovir release device + oral valganciclovir (*N Engl J Med* 2002;346:1119). See p. 128 and Table 7-15.

■ TABLE 7-15: **Treatments of CMV Retinitis**

Treatment	Regimen	Comment
Intraocular ganciclovir release device *(Vitrasert)*	Replace every 6 to 9 months	Advantages ■ Best record for time to relapse (average 216-226 days) ■ Avoids IVs ■ Can be done as an outpatient
		Disadvantage: Does not prevent CMV at other sites including other eye – must give oral valganciclovir or IV anti-CMV medication
Valganciclovir (oral)	900 mg bid x 3 weeks, then 900 mg qd	Advantages ■ Avoids IV ■ Levels are comparable with IV ganciclovir (*N Engl J Med* 2002;346:1119)
		Disadvantage: ADRs – marrow suppression and GI intolerance
Ganciclovir (IV)	5 mg/kg IV q12h x 14/21 days then 5 mg/kg qd	Advantage: Extensive experience and established efficacy
		Disadvantages ■ Time to relapse averages 47-104 days ■ ADRs – neutropenia, thrombocytopenia ■ Requires IV

■ TABLE 7-15: **Treatments of CMV Retinitis *(Continued)***

Treatment	Regimen	Comment
Foscarnet (IV)	90 mg/kg IV q12h x 14-21 days, then 90 mg/day	Advantages ■ Extensive experience and established efficacy ■ Active vs ganciclovir-resistant strains
		Disadvantages ■ ADRs – nephrotoxic (dose related), electrolyte changes with decreased Ca, Mg, K, PO4 ■ Requires infusion pump, long infusion time, saline hydration ■ Contraindicated with creatinine clearance <0.4 mL/min/kg
Cidofovir (IV)	3-5 mg/kg IV every week x 2 then 3-5 mg/kg IV every week + probenecid with each dose 2 g 3 hours before and 1 g 2 and 8 hours after	Advantage: Effective vs ganciclovir-resistant CMV
		Disadvantages ■ Requires co-administration of probenecid ■ ADRs – highly nephrotoxic, GI intolerance, anemia, neutropenia ■ Requires supervised IV administration ■ Contraindicated with creatinine >1.5 mg/mL
Fomivirsen	Intravitreal – 330 μg every 2 weeks x 2, then every month	Advantages ■ Avoids IVs ■ FDA-approved for salvage therapy
		Disadvantages ■ May cause ocular inflammation, increased ocular pressure, and/or vision loss (*Am J Ophthalmol* 2002;133:475) ■ Fails to prevent systemic CMV disease or protect other eye without concurrent systemic treatment
Intravitreal ganciclovir or foscarnet	■ Foscarnet 1.2-2.4 mg in 0.1 mL (*N Engl J Med* 1994;330:868) ■ Ganciclovir 2000 μg in 0.05-1.0 mL (*Brit J Ophthalmol* 1996;80:214)	Advantages ■ Avoids IVs ■ Easily done
		Disadvantages ■ Not FDA approved for intravitreal injection ■ Fails to prevent systemic disease or protect other eye

RESPONSE

- Vision loss prior to therapy typically is permanent.
- Effective therapy is usually accompanied by stabilization of vision in 80% to 90%. However, most patients relapse unless there is immune reconstitution.
- Time to relapse in absence of immune recovery depends on initial CMV treatment and averages from 40 to 220 days in various reports.

- Comparisons are difficult due to variable use of HAART, especially with *Vitrasert* + valganciclovir. The median time to relapse using standard treatment in the pre-HAART era using IV ganciclovir, foscarnet, or cidofovir was 50 to 120 days (*Ophthalmology* 1994;101:1250; *J Infect Dis* 1993;168:557; *N Engl J Med* 1995;333:615; *N Engl J Med* 1997;337:83). Early relapses (<3 months) following ganciclovir treatment are usually associated with ganciclovir-sensitive strains of CMV; late relapses usually involve ganciclovir-resistant strains.

COMPLICATIONS OF CMV AND ITS TREATMENT

- **Retinal detachment:** Traditionally repaired with vitrectomy and silicone oil treatment (*Arch Opthalmol* 1995;113;1401). With probable immune reconstitution, conventional retinal detachment surgery without silicone oil may be tried.
- **Cataract** (late complication of retinal detachment): Cataract surgery
- **Relapse:** Strategies vary and include
  - Reinduction of the currently used drug (IV ganciclovir or foscarnet 2x/day)
  - Switching to an alternative agent
  - Intravitreal injection of ganciclovir or foscarnet
  - Intravitreal injection of fomivirsen (FDA-approved for salvage therapy of CMV retinitis)
- **Immune recovery uveitis:** This is a complication of CMV retinitis treatment with immune reconstitution characterized by: 1) Quiescent CMV retinitis and 2) Visual loss with macular edema, epiretinal membrane formation of virtutis. Treatment may be effective using oral or periocular (*Am J Ophthalmol* 2000;130:49; *Retina* 2001;21:1).

Retinal Necrosis, Acute (see p. 136)

CAUSE: Usually ascribed to varicella-zoster virus and more common in AIDS patients with CD4 counts <50 cells/mm^3 (*Clin Infect Dis* 1998;26:34).

FREQUENCY: Rare

DIAGNOSIS: Visual changes noted weeks to months after zoster resolution with involvement of any dermatome (*N Engl J Med* 2002;347:340) or without cutaneous zoster. Funduscopic examination shows granular, yellowish non-hemorrhagic lesions which extend and coalesce.

TREATMENT: Acyclovir IV 10 mg/kg q8h

RESPONSE: Usually poor in AIDS patients with progression to blindness despite antiviral agents.

Zoster Ophthalmicus (see p. 135)

FREQUENCY: 0.6% AIDS patients (*AIDS* 2002;16:1045)

DIAGNOSIS: Herpes zoster on face in distribution of first branch of trigeminal nerve; usual diagnosis is made by appearance of lesion and can be confirmed by DFA stain of exudate (which is faster, less expensive, and more sensitive than culture).

TREATMENT

- Acyclovir 10 mg/kg q8h IV x 10 to 14 days followed by oral therapy with valacyclovir (1 g tid) until lesions healed
- Oral therapy from the start until lesions heal using valacyclovir 1000 mg tid or famciclovir 500 mg tid (*Brit J Ophthalmol* 2000;107:1507; *Antimicrob Agents Chemother* 1995;39:1546)

RESPONSE: Without therapy, about 50% result in vision loss (*Curr Eye Research* 1987;6:195). With antiviral therapy, the rate of ocular complications is reduced to 20% to 30% (*N Engl J Med* 2002; 347:340).

Psychiatric Complications

Bipolar Disorder (Manic Depression)

FREQUENCY: 9% of AIDS patients referred for psychiatric evaluation

DIAGNOSIS: Manic episodes and depressive episodes and mixed episodes. Differential includes familial bipolar disorder and AIDS mania (no family history, no episodes prior to late stage HIV, co-morbid cognitive impairment.

TREATMENT

- **AIDS Mania:** HAART
  - Haloperidol (*Haldol*) 2.5-10 mg bid
  - Fluphenazine (*Prolixin*) 2-10 mg bid
  - Risperidone (*Risperdal*) 1-4 mg bid
  - Olanzapine (*Zyprexa*) 10-40 mg hs

- One of the above ± lithium 300 mg bid titrated to level of 0.8-1.2 mEq/mL or valproic acid 20 mg/kg titrated to serum level of 75-100 ng/mL.
- **Adjunctive therapy:** Carbamazepine (*Tegretol*), gabapentin (*Neurontin*), lamotrigine (*Lamictal*)
- Care should be directed by a psychiatrist.

Delirium

DIAGNOSIS: Impaired consciousness, inability to focus or sustain interest, cognitive changes, global derangement of brain function, acute onset, altered consciousness, or disorganized thinking

TREATMENT: Correct underlying condition, which may be infection or medication related.

- **Agitation:** Neuroleptics such as haloperidol (*Haldol*) or risperidone
- **Agitation that puts others at risk:** Neuroleptics + low dose of lorazepam for sedation

Demoralization

FREQUENCY: 20% of AIDS patients referred for psychiatric evaluation

DIAGNOSIS: Exaggerated grief state, sad, hopelessness, often precipitated by life circumstances. Often mistaken for depression, but unlike depression, often can enjoy some facets of life, feels best in the mornings and does not respond to antidepressants.

TREATMENT: Psychotherapy

RESPONSE: Responds to psychotherapy and usually not to antidepressants

Grief (Normal state of low mood focused on loss)

Treatment is psychological rather than pharmacological (support groups, buddy systems).

Major Depression

FREQUENCY: 20% of AIDS patients referred for psychiatric evaluation (*JAMA* 2001;286:2849)

PRESENTATION: Depressed mood, loss of pleasure from activities (anhedonia), anorexia, morning insomnia or hypersomnia, difficulty concentrating, thoughts of suicide

DIFFERENTIAL: Dementia, delirium, demoralization, intoxications or withdrawal, neurologic diseases

TREATMENT: Antidepressants (Tables 7-16 and 7-17) starting with low doses and titrating slowly ("start low and go slow") with appropriate attention to side effects and serum levels.

■ TABLE 7-16: **Depression: Drug Selection**

Agent	Advantages	Disadvantages
SSRIs	■ Relatively safe and well tolerated ■ Compared with tricyclics: Fewer drug interactions and side effects ■ Safety with overdose	■ ADRs: Sexual dysfunction, substrate and inhibitor of P450 enzymes ■ Use with PI or NNRTI may increase level of SSRI
Tricyclics	■ Equally effective compared with SSRIs ■ Also useful for neuropathy insomnia and diarrhea	■ ADRs: Anticholinergic effects, dry mouth, blurred vision, orthostasis ■ Use with PI or NNRTI may increase tricyclic level ■ Refractory arrhythmia with overdose

RESPONSE: Response rates to antidepressants is 85%; cure rate >50% (*Psychosomatic* 1997;38:423).

■ TABLE 7-17: **Antidepressants**

Drug (Trade Name)	■ Start Dose ■ Therapeutic Dose	Serum Level*	Advantages	Interactions With HIV Medications
Nortriptyline (*Pamelor*)	■ 10 to 25 mg at bedtime ■ 50-150 mg at bedtime	70-125 ng/dL	Promotes sleep and weight gain; decreases diarrhea	Increases nortriptyline levels: Fluconazole, LPV/r, RTV
Desipramine (*Norpramin*)	■ 10 to 25 mg at bedtime ■ 50 to 200 mg at bedtime	>125 ng/dL	Promotes sleep and weight gain; decreases diarrhea	Increases desipramine levels: LPV/r, RTV
Imipramine (*Tofranil*)	■ 10 to 25 mg at bedtime ■ 100 to 300 mg at bedtime	>225 ng/dL	Promotes sleep and weight gain; decreases diarrhea	Increases imipramine levels: LPV/r, RTV
Amitriptyline (*Elavil*)	■ 10 to 25 mg at bedtime ■ 100 to 300 mg at bedtime	200 to 250 ng/dL	Promotes sleep and weight gain; decreases diarrhea	Increases amitriptyline levels: LPV/r, RTV
Clomipramine (*Anafranil*)	■ 25 mg at bedtime ■ 100 to 200 mg at bedtime	150 to 400 ng/dL	Promotes sleep and weight gain; decreases diarrhea	Increases clomipramine levels: LPV/r, RTV
Doxepin (*Sinequan*)	■ 10 to 25 mg at bedtime ■ 50 to 250 mg at bedtime	100 to 250 ng/dL	Promotes sleep and weight gain; decreases diarrhea	Increases doxepin levels: LPV/r, RTV

continued on next page

■ TABLE 7-17: **Antidepressants *(Continued)***

Drug (Trade Name)	■ Start Dose ■ Therapeutic Dose	Serum Level*	Advantages	Interactions With HIV Medications
Fluoxetine (*Prozac*)	■ 10 mg each morning ■ 20 mg at bedtime	Unclear	Activating	Increases HIV med levels: APV, DLV, EFV, IDV, LPV/r, NFV, RTV, SQV; decreases fluoxetine levels: NVP
Sertraline (*Zoloft*)	■ 25 to 50 mg each morning ■ 50 to 150 mg each morning	Unclear		Increases sertraline levels: LPV/r, RTV
Citalopram (*Celexa*)	■ 20 mg each morning ■ 20 to 60 mg each morning	Unclear		Increases citalopram levels: LPV/r, RTV
Paroxetine (*Paxil*)	■ 10 mg at bedtime ■ 20 to 40 mg at bedtime	Unclear	Somewhat sedating	Increases paroxetine levels: LPV/r, RTV
Fluvoxamine (*Luvox*)	■ 50 mg at bedtime ■ 150 to 250 mg at bedtime	Unclear	Somewhat sedating	Increases HIV med levels: APV, DLV, EFV, IDV, LPV/r, NFV, RTV, SQV; decreases fluvoxamine levels: NVP
Venlafaxine (*Effexor*)	■ 37.5 mg each morning ■ 75 to 300 mg each morning	Unclear		Increases venlafaxine levels: LPV/r, RTV
Mirtazapine (*Remeron*)	■ 7.5 to 15 mg at bedtime ■ 15 to 45 mg at bedtime	Unclear		Promotes sleep and weight gain
Nefazodone (*Serzone*)	■ 50 mg bid ■ 300 to 400 mg/day in divided doses	Unclear	Somewhat sedating	Increases HIV med levels: EFV, IDV
Trazodone (*Desyrel*)	■ 50 to 100 mg at bedtime ■ 50 to 150 mg at bedtime for sleep; 200-600 mg at bedtime for depression	Unclear	Promotes sleep	Increases trazodone levels: LPV/r, RTV
Bupropion (*Wellbutrin*)	■ 100 mg each morning ■ 150 to 400 mg/day in divided doses	Unclear	Activating; no sexual side effects	Increases bupropion levels (unclear if clinically significant): RTV, EFV, NFV

* Correlation of serum level and therapeutic efficacy has been established with nortriptyline.

Reprinted and modified with permission from: Angelino AF, Treisman GJ. Management of psychiatric illness in HIV infected patients (*Clin Infect Dis* 2001;33:847).

Obsessive Compulsive Disorder

DIAGNOSIS: Recurrent obsessions (preoccupying thoughts that the patient finds irrational and tries to resist) and/or compulsions (actions driven by obsessions to reduce anxiety)

TREATMENT: Refer to psychiatrist or a mental health specialist.

Panic Attacks

DIAGNOSIS: Recurring anxiety attacks with fear plus somatic symptoms of excitation lasting <1 hour

TREATMENT: SSRI and refer to a psychiatrist

Sleep Disturbance

Medications with FDA approval for insomnia have potential for reinforcement and habituation. Evaluate patient for cause (major depression, mania, substance use disorder, demoralization) and refer for appropriate treatment. Insomnia temporally related to a specific stress (pre-op, grief etc.) may be treated with sedatives or hypnotics up to 1 week or with trazodone 25-150 mg hs for up to 4 weeks.

Substance Use Disorders

DIAGNOSIS: Use of substances despite clear evidence of negative consequences. Dependence: Persistent use or seeking use, withdrawal, tolerance, and physical dependence.

■ TABLE 7-18: **Detoxification**

Agent	Treatment
Sedative/hypnotic EtOH, benzodiazepines, and barbiturates	■ Long acting benzodiazepines (chlordiazepoxide – *Librium*, diazepam – *Valium*)
Alprazolam (*Xanax*)	■ Substitute clonazepam and taper
Cocaine	■ Suicidal symptoms common; may need brief hospitalization
Opioids	■ Clonidine for autonomic instability. Buprenorphine or methadone tapers; dicyclomine for GI distress

Pulmonary Complications

Pneumonia (PCP)

PRESENTATION: Cough, dyspnea, and fever ± sputum production

CAUSE: The single major prospective study of pulmonary complications of HIV was discontinued in the pre-HAART era – 1995 (*Am J Respir Crit Care Med* 1997;155:72). Data from 3 years (1992-1995) showed 521 infections: PCP – 232 (45%), pyogenic bacteria – 220 (42%), tuberculosis – 25 (5%), CMV – 19 (4%), *Aspergillus* – 12 (2%), and cryptococcosis – 7 (1%). Critical factors in evaluating the HIV infected patient with suspected pneumonia are

- **HIV stage** based on CD4 count (see Table 7-19, p. 391)
- **Tempo:** Pyogenic infections and influenza evolve rapidly with acute symptoms; most other causes evolve more slowly. PCP shows a slow tempo in HIV infected patients with an average duration of 3 weeks prior to presentation.
- **X-ray changes:** A negative chest x-ray generally excludes pneumonia, except 10% to 20% with PCP have a false negative x-ray (*J Acquir Immune Defic Syndr* 1994;7:39); infiltrates can be shown in these cases with thin-section CT scan (*Am J Radiol* 1997;169:967). Rare false-negative x-rays can be seen with tuberculosis, MOTT, and cryptococcosis (see Table 7-20, p. 392).
- **Injection drug use:** Associated with high rates of pneumococcal pneumonia, *S. aureus* endocarditis with septic pulmonary emboli, tuberculosis, and aspiration pneumonia.
- **Prophylaxis:** TMP-SMX (see Figure 7-5, p. 402) effectively reduces incidence of PCP, pyogenic pneumonia including *S. pneumoniae, Legionella, H. influenzae,* and *S. aureus*. Influenza vaccine appears to prevent influenza, which is associated with substantial morbidity and mortality in HIV infected patients (*Arch Intern Med* 2001;161:441). Pneumovax does not appear to be protective (*BMJ* 2002;325:292). INH or PZA/rifampin regimens substantially reduce the risk of TB.
- **Atypical:** Pneumonia due to *M. pneumoniae, C. pneumoniae,* and *Legionella* appears to be relatively uncommon in patients with HIV infection (*Eur J Clin Microbiol Infect Dis* 1997;16:720; *N Engl J Med* 1997;337:682; *N Engl J Med* 1995;333:845; *Am J Resp Crit Care Med* 1995;152:1309; *Clin Infect Dis* 1996;23:107; *Am J Resp Crit Care Med* 2000;162:2063).

DIAGNOSTIC SPECIMENS (see Figure 7-4, p. 400 and Table 7-21, p. 393)

- **Expectorated sputum:** Controversial, due in part to poor technique in collecting, transporting, and processing specimens.

- **Expectorated sputum for *M. tuberculosis*:** The yield with three specimens is 50% to 60% for AFB stain; the yield is somewhat higher with PCR at 75% to 85% (*Am J Respir Crit Care Med* 2001;164:2020).
- **Induced sputum:** Recommended as an alternative to expectorated sputum for detection of AFB in patients who cannot produce an expectorated sample and as an alternative to bronchoscopy for detection of PCP. Sensitivity for detection of TB by AFB smear is about the same as it is for expectorated sputum. For PCP, the sensitivity is 60% to 95% in published reports (*JAMA* 2001;286:2450), but it may be much lower in centers that don't publish their results.
- **Bronchoscopy:** The yield for PCP is 95% or about the same as it is for open-lung biopsy (*JAMA* 2001;286:2450). For *M. tuberculosis*, bronchoscopy shows a yield that is similar to that for expectorated sputum. For other bacteria, bronchoscopy is no better than expectorated sputum unless it is done by quantitative culture.

■ TABLE 7-19: **Etiology Correlated With CD4 Count**

CD4 count >200 cells/mm^3	*S. pneumoniae, M. tuberculosis, S. aureus* (IDU), Influenza
CD4 count 50-200 cells/mm^3	Above + *P. carinii*, cryptococcosis, histoplasmosis, coccidioidomycosis, *Nocardia, M. kansasii*, Kaposi's sarcoma
CD4 count <50 cells/mm^3	Above + *P. aeruginosa, Aspergillus*, MAC, CMV

■ TABLE 7-20: **Correlation of Chest X-ray Changes and Etiology of Pneumonia**

Change	Common	Uncommon
Consolidation	Pyogenic bacteria, Kaposi's sarcoma, cryptococcosis	*Nocardia, M. tuberculosis, M. kansasii, Legionella, B. bronchiseptica*
Reticulonodular infiltrates	*P. carinii, M. tuberculosis,* histoplasmosis, coccidioidomycosis	Kaposi's sarcoma, toxoplasmosis, CMV, leishmania, lymphoid interstital pneumonitis
Nodules	*M. tuberculosis,* cryptococcosis	Kaposi's sarcoma, *Nocardia*
Cavity	*M. tuberculosis, S. aureus* (IDU), *Nocardia, P. aeruginosa,* cryptococcosis, coccidioidomycosis, histoplasmosis, aspergillosis, anaerobes	*M. kansasii,* MAC, *Legionella, P. carinii,* lymphoma, *Klebsiella, Rhodococcus equi*
Hilar nodes	*M. tuberculosis,* histoplasmosis, coccidioidomycosis, lymphoma, Kaposi's sarcoma	*M. kansasii,* MAC
Pleural effusion	Pyogenic bacteria, Kaposi's sarcoma, *M. tuberculosis* (congestive heart failure, hypoalbuminemia)	Cryptococcosis, MAC, histoplasmosis, coccidioidomycosis, aspergillosis, anaerobes, *Nocardia,* lymphoma, toxoplasmosis, primary effusion lymphoma

■ TABLE 7-21: **Pulmonary Infection: Differential Diagnosis**

Agent	Course*	Frequency, Setting	Typical Findings	Diagnosis†	Treatment
Bacteria					
Gram-negative bacilli	Acute, purulent sputum	Uncommon, except with nosocomial infection or neutropenia. *Pseudomonas aeruginosa* is relatively common in late-stage disease, cavitary disease, or chronic antibiotic exposure (median CD4 50 cells/mm^3)	Lobar or bronchopneumonia	Sputum GS and culture (sensitivity is >80%, but specificity is poor)	■ Need *in vitro* susceptibility tests ■ Long-term ciprofloxacin usually results in relapse and resistance to *P. aeruginosa.*
Haemophilus influenzae	Acute, purulent sputum	Incidence is 100-fold higher than in healthy controls; most infections are caused by unencapsulated strains	Bronchopneumonia	Sputum GS and culture (sensitivity of culture is 50%; prior antibiotics usually preclude growth)	■ Oral: Amox-CA, azithromycin, TMP-SMX, fluoroquinolone, cephalosporin; ■ Intravenous: Cefotaxime, ceftriaxone
Legionella	Acute mucopurulent sputum	Uncommon. HIV-associated risk is debated.	Bronchopneumonia; sometimes multiple infiltrates in noncontiguous segments	Sputum culture; urinary antigen (*Legionella pneumophila* serogroup 1)	Fluoroquinolone, macrolide, doxycycline
Nocardia	Chronic or asymptomatic; sputum production	Uncommon; frequency higher with chronic corticosteroid use (median CD4 count 50 cells/mm^3)	Nodule or cavity	Sputum or fiberoptic bronchoscopy (FOB); GS, modified acid-fast bacillus (AFB) stain and culture; should alert lab if suspected (?)	Sulfonamide/TMP-SMX
Staphylococcus aureus	Acute, subacute, or chronic, purulent sputum	Uncommon, except with injected drug use and tricuspid valve endocarditis with septic emboli	Bronchopneumonia, cavitary disease, septic emboli with cavities ± effusion	Blood sputum GS and culture (sputum culture is sensitive, but specificity is poor). Blood cultures are nearly always positive with endocarditis.	■ MSSA: Nafcillin/oxacillin, cefuroxime, TMP-SMX, clindamycin ■ MRSA: Vancomycin

■ TABLE 7-21: **Pulmonary Infection: Differential Diagnosis** ***(Continued)***

Agent	Course*	Frequency, Setting	Typical Findings	Diagnosis†	Treatment
Bacteria *(Continued)*					
Streptococcus pneumoniae	Acute, purulent sputum ± pleurisy	Common, all stages HIV infection; incidence is 100-fold higher than in healthy controls; recurrence rate at 6 months is 6% to 24%; higher with low CD4 counts and with smoking	Lobar or bronchopneumonia ± pleural effusion	Blood cultures often positive, sputum gram stain (GS), Quellung, culture (sensitivity of culture is 50%; prior antibiotics usually preclude growth)	■ Oral: Amoxicillin, macrolide, cefdinir, cefprozil, cefpodoxime, fluoroquinolone; ■ Intravenous: Cefotaxime, ceftriaxone, fluoroquinolone
Fungi					
Aspergillus	Acute or subacute	Up to 4% of AIDS patients; usually advanced HIV infection (median CD4 count 30 cells/mm^3); about 50% have severe neutropenia (ANC <500/mm^3) ± chronic steroids; disseminated disease is uncommon	Focal infiltrate; cavity – often pleural-based, diffuse infiltrates or reticulonodular infiltrates	Sputum stain and culture; false-positive and false-negative cultures common. Best tests: Tissue pathology or sputum smear and typical CT and clinical features	Amphotericin B or itraconazole or caspofungin
Candida	Chronic or subacute	Common isolate, rare cause of pulmonary disease (median CD4 count 50 cells/mm^3)	Bronchitis; rare cause of pneumonia (some say it does not exist)	Recovery in sputum or FOB specimen is meaningless (up to 30% of all expectorated sputum and FOB cultures in unselected patients yield *Candida* sp.); must have histologic evidence of invasion on biopsy	Fluconazole or amphotericin B

Agent	Course*	Frequency, Setting	Typical Findings	Diagnosis†	Treatment
Fungi *(Continued)*					
Coccidioides immitis‡	Chronic or subacute	Up to 10% of AIDS patients in endemic area; usually advanced HIV infection (median CD4 count 50 cells/mm^3); disseminated disease in 20% to 40%	Diffuse nodular infiltrates, focal infiltrate, cavity; hilar adenopathy (*Clin Infect Dis* 1996;23:563)	Sputum, induced sputum, or FOB stain and culture; KOH of expectorated sputum is rarely positive; PAP stain or silver stain of BAL positive in 40%; culture of BAL usually positive; serology (CF) positive in 70%; skin test positive in <10%; blood cultures positive in 10%	Fluconazole, itraconazole, or amphotericin B
Cryptococcus	Chronic, subacute, or symptomatic	Up to 8% to 10% in AIDS patients; late-stage HIV infection (median CD4 count 50 cells/mm^3); 80% have cryptococcal meningitis	Nodule, cavity, diffuse or nodular infiltrates	Sputum, induced sputum, or FOB stain and culture; serum cryptococcal antigen usually positive; CSF analysis indicated if antigen or organism found at any site	Fluconazole without CNS involvement amphotericin B
Histoplasma capsulatum‡	Chronic or subacute	Up to 15% of AIDS patients in endemic area; usually advanced HIV infection with disseminated histoplasmosis (median CD4 count 50 cells/mm^3); common features: Fever, weight loss, hepatosplenomegaly, lymphadenopathy	Diffuse nodular infiltrates, nodule, focal infiltrate, cavity, hilar adenopathy (*N Engl J Med* 1986;314:83; *Medicine* 1990;69:361)	Best test for diagnosis and follow-up of treatment is serum and urine polysaccharide antigen assay, with yield of 85% (blood) and 97% (urine). Available only through J. Wheat (Indianapolis, IN) 800-HISTO-DG for $70/assay; serology positive in 50% to 70%; yield with culture of sputum – 80%, marrow – 80%; blood cultures positive in 60% to 85%	Itraconazole or amphotericin B

■ TABLE 7-21: **Pulmonary Infection: Differential Diagnosis** ***(Continued)***

Agent	Course*	Frequency, Setting	Typical Findings	Diagnosis†	Treatment
Fungi ***(Continued)***					
Pneumocystis carinii	Acute or subacute; nonproductive cough; dyspnea	Very common in late stages of HIV infection (CD4 <200 cells/mm³) (median CD4, without prophylaxis, 100 cells/mm³; with prophylaxis 20 cells/mm³; >95% have CD4 <200 cells/mm³); infrequent in patients compliant with TMP-SMX prophylaxis; main predictor of prophylaxis failure is late-stage disease with very low CD4 count (*JAMA* 1995;273:1197)	Fnterstitial infiltrates with characteristic ground glass appearance; negative x-ray in early stages, about 15% to 20%; atypical findings in 20%; atypical findings: Upper lobe infiltrates, focal infiltrates, nodules, cavitary disease, or mediastinal lymphadenopathy	Cytology of induced sputum (mean yield of 60% in proven cases) and bronchoalveolar lavage (BAL) (mean yield of 95%); yield is lower in patients receiving aerosolized pentamidine; yield depends on technical expertise, which is highly variable	■ TMP-SMX or pentamidine dapsone/trimethoprim clindamycin/primaquine atovaquone trimetrexate ■ pO_2 <70 or A-a gradient >35 mm: Prednisone
Mycobacteria					
Mycobacterium avium complex (MAC)	Chronic or asymptomatic	Moderate for disseminated disease but uncommon for pulmonary disease; late stage HIV (median CD4 20 cells/mm³)	Variable	■ Sputum, FOB, or induced sputum AFB stain and culture; must distinguish from MTB (DNA probe or radiometric culture technique); MAC may colonize airways without causing pulmonary disease; requires 1 to 2 weeks for growth in Bactec system ■ Most positive AFB smears are TB and not MAC	■ Clarithromycin + ethambutol ■ Azithromycin + ethambutol ± rifabutin
Mycobacterium kansasii	Chronic or asymptomatic	Uncommon: Late-stage HIV (median CD4 50 cells/mm³)	Cavitary disease, nodule, cyst, infiltrate, or normal chest x-ray	Sputum, induced sputum, or FOB, AFB stain and culture	INH, ethambutol + rifampin ± clarithromycin or ciprofloxacin

Agent	Course*	Frequency, Setting	Typical Findings	Diagnosis†	Treatment
Mycobacteria *(Continued)*					
Mycobacterium tuberculosis (tuberculosis, miliary tuberculosis, MTB)‡	Chronic, subacute, or asymptomatic; usually has productive cough ± hemoptysis	Frequency is 5% (170-fold increase) in all AIDS patients, higher in some cities, including New York, NY, Newark, NJ, and Miami, FL; with injected drug use; and in African-American patients (median CD4 count 200 to 300 cells/mm^3)	Variable: Focal infiltrates, reticulonodular, cavitary disease, hilar adenopathy, lower and middle lobe involvement common, pleural effusion; early-stage HIV infection-upper lobe cavitary; late-stage HIV-pneumonitis mid or lower lobes or miliary pattern with minimal granuloma formation. Extrapulmonary TB is common – especially in meningitis, adenopathy	■ Sputum AFB stain and culture, if no sputum production, induced sputum, or FOB; requires 1 to 4 weeks for growth in Bactec system with rapid ID by Gen Probe; requires 3 to 8 weeks for growth on conventional media; sensitivity of sputum AFB smear = 50% ■ Most positive AFB smears indicate *M. tuberculosis* (not MAC) ■ Drug sensitivity tests should be performed on all isolates. Requires reporting to health department.	See pp. 145-148
Viruses					
Cytomegalovirus (CMV)	Subacute or chronic	Common isolate, rare cause of pulmonary disease; advanced HIV infection (median CD4 count 20 cells/mm^3)	Interstitial infiltrates	Yield with FOB is 20% to 50%, culture requires more than 1 week; shell culture 1 to 2 days; diagnosis of CMV pneumonitis (disease) requires CMV seen on cytopath or biopsy, progressive disease, and no alternative pathogen	Ganciclovir, foscarnet or cidofovir

■ TABLE 7-21: **Pulmonary Infection: Differential Diagnosis** ***(Continued)***

Agent	Course*	Frequency, Setting	Typical Findings	Diagnosis†	Treatment
Virsuses *(Continued)*					
Herpes simplex virus (HSV), varicella zoster (VZV), respiratory syncitial virus (RSV), parainfluenza	Acute	Rare causes of pneumonia	Diffuse or nodular pneumonia, bronchopneumonia	■ Culture of sputum or FOB commonly yields HSV as a contaminant from upper airways ■ RSV is rare in adults but has increased frequency in immunosuppressed host, is easily detected with DFA stain of respiratory secretions, and is possibly treatable with aerosolized ribavirin	HSV, VZV: Acyclovir RSV: Ribavirin (?)
Influenza	Acute, purulent sputum	■ Influenza is common; influenza pneumonia is rare ■ Any stage of HIV infection. ■ Frequency and course minimally different from patients without HIV infection	Bronchopneumonia, interstitial infiltrates	■ Culture of throat, nasopharyngeal aspirates, washing, and serology; most rely on epidemiology in community and typical symptoms. ■ Bacterial super-infection is common with *S. pneumoniae, S. aureus* and *H. influenza*	Amantadine/ramantadine neuramidase inhibitors: Oseltamivir or zanamivir
Miscellaneous					
Aspiration pneumonia	Acute or subacute	Accounts for 5% to 10% of pneumonia cases	Infiltrates in dependent pulmonary segment + cough and fever ± cavitation/empyema	It is not possible to verify anaerobic bacterial pneumonia; putrid drainage is diagnostic	■ Clindamycin ■ Beta-lactam + Beta-lactamase inhibitor
Enigmatic	Acute or subacute	Accounts for most acute pneumonias	Most are presumably due to *S. pneumoniae* or *P. carinii;* distinguish based on CD4 count, tempo and radiographic changes	Antibiotic treatment precludes recovery of *S. pneumoniae* or *H. influenzae*; it does not reduce yield of *P. carinii*	TMP-SMX/cephalosporin or fluoroquinolone

Agent	Course*	Frequency, Setting	Typical Findings	Diagnosis†	Treatment
Miscellaneous *(Continued)*					
Kaposi's sarcoma (KS)	Asymptomatic or chronic progressive cough and dyspnea	Moderately common in patients with cutaneous KS and advanced HIV disease	Interstitial, alveolar, or nodular infiltrates, hilar adenopathy (25%), scan usually negative, pleural effusions (40%); gallium	■ FOB often shows discolored endobronchial nodule(s); yield of histopathology from transbronchial or transthoracic biopsy is only 20% to 30%. Pulmonary infiltrate on x-ray with negative gallium scan is highly suggestive ■ Suspect with enigmatic pulmonary infiltrates, chronic course, cutaneous lesions, and/or bloody pleural effusion	■ Liposomal daunorubicin or doxorubicin ■ Taxol ■ Adriamycin, bleomycin/ vincristin, or vinblastin
Lymphocytic interstitial pneumonia (LIP)	Chronic or subacute	Uncommon in adults (median CD4 count 200 to 400 cells/mm³)	Diffuse reticulonodular infiltrates, resembles PCP on chest x-ray; CD4 count is higher and LDH is lower; course is subacute and resembles PCP	Requires tissue for histopathology; yield with FOB biopsy is 30% to 50%; open lung biopsy often required	Prednisone (?)
Lymphoma	Chronic or asymptomatic	Uncommon, but may be presenting site	Interstitial, alveolar, or nodular infiltrates; cavity, hilar adenopathy, pleural effusions	Requires tissue for histopathology; yield with FOB biopsy is poor; open lung biopsy often required	CHOP BACOD + G-CSF

* Course: Acute = symptoms evolve over days; subacute = symptoms evolve over 2-6 weeks; chronic = symptoms evolve over >4 weeks.

† Diagnosis: Expectorated sputum for bacterial culture should have cytologic screening to show predominance of PMN, GS, and Quellung (if GS suggests *S. pneumoniae*). Induced sputum often is reserved for patients with nonproductive cough and suspected PCP or *M. tuberculosis*. Culture for conventional bacteria gives results similar to expectorated sputum (*J Clin Microbiol* 1994;32:131). FOB assumes BAL ± touch preps, bronchial washings, bronchial brush, or transbronchial biopsy; the usual specimen for PCP is BAL. Detection of fungi requires stains (KOH and/or Gomori methenamine silver stain) and culture (Sabouraud's media); *Candida* sp. grow on conventional bacterial media. Detection of viruses requires cytopathology for inclusions (herpes viruses, CMV, HSV, VZV); FA for HSV and influenza; cultures are for herpes viruses and with special request for influenza virus.

‡ Detection of these organisms in respiratory secretions is essentially diagnostic of disease; other organisms may be contaminants colonizing mucosal surfaces or commensals.

■ FIGURE 7-4: **Cough, Fever, Dyspnea**

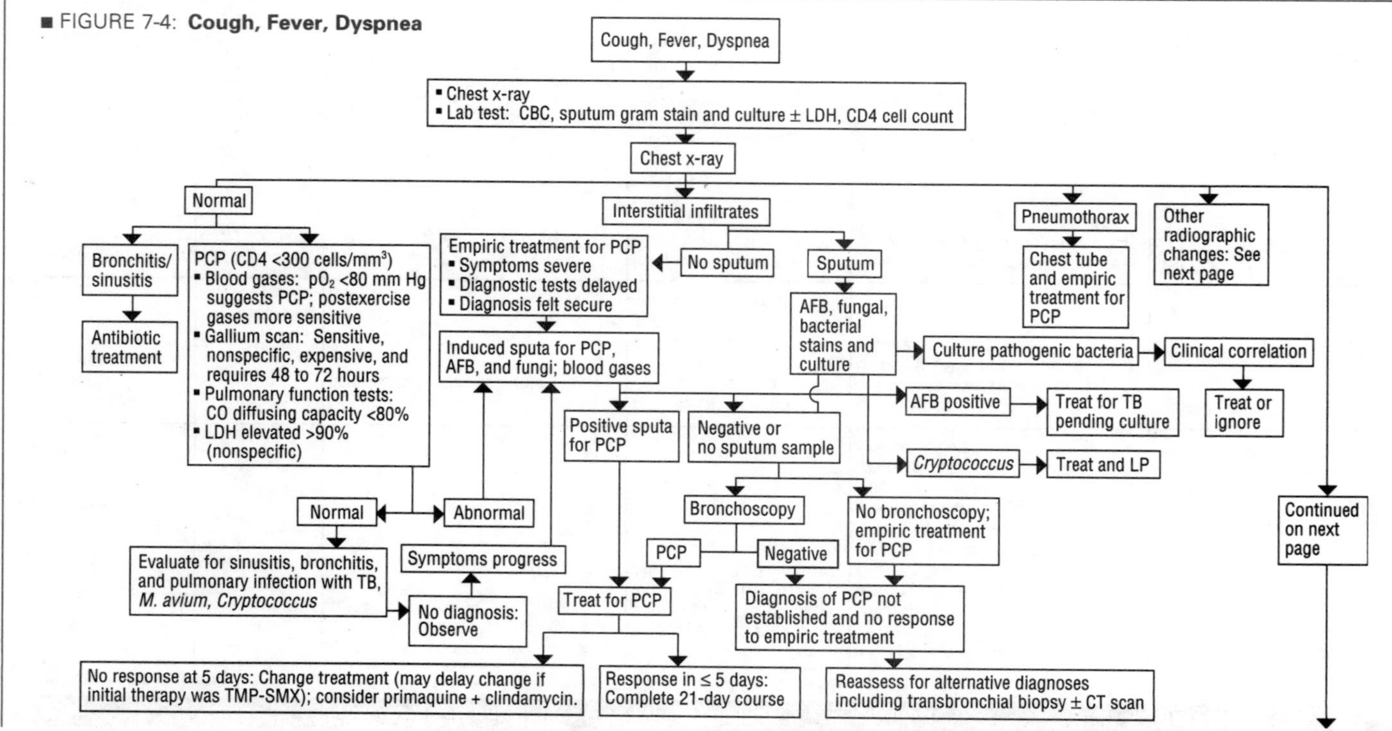

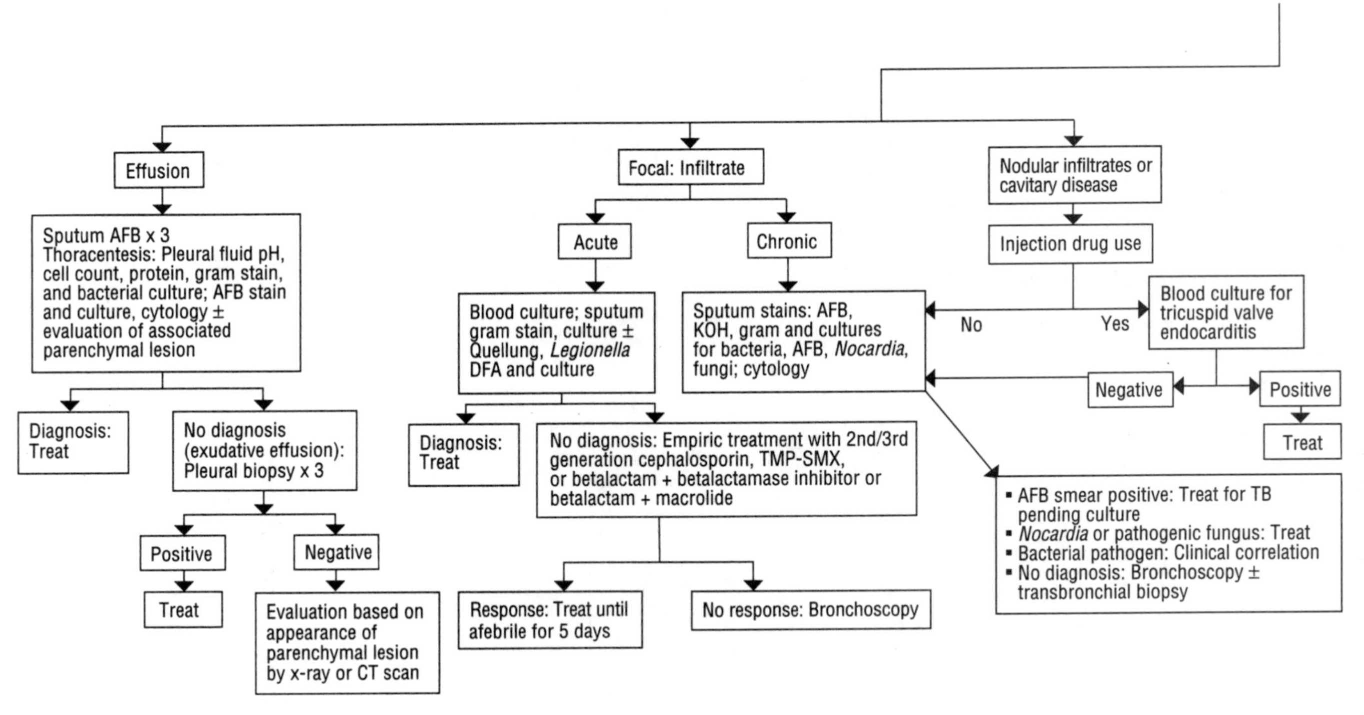
Effusion
Sputum AFB x 3
Thoracentesis: Pleural fluid pH, cell count, protein, gram stain, and bacterial culture; AFB stain and culture, cytology ± evaluation of associated parenchymal lesion
Diagnosis: Treat
No diagnosis (exudative effusion): Pleural biopsy x 3
Positive
Treat
Negative
Evaluation based on appearance of parenchymal lesion by x-ray or CT scan
Focal: Infiltrate
Acute
Blood culture; sputum gram stain, culture ± Quellung, *Legionella* DFA and culture
Diagnosis: Treat
No diagnosis: Empiric treatment with 2nd/3rd generation cephalosporin, TMP-SMX, or betalactam + betalactamase inhibitor or betalactam + macrolide
Response: Treat until afebrile for 5 days
No response: Bronchoscopy
Chronic
Sputum stains: AFB, KOH, gram and cultures for bacteria, AFB, *Nocardia*, fungi; cytology
Nodular infiltrates or cavitary disease
Injection drug use
No
Yes
Blood culture for tricuspid valve endocarditis
Negative
Positive
Treat
▪ AFB smear positive: Treat for TB pending culture
▪ *Nocardia* or pathogenic fungus: Treat
▪ Bacterial pathogen: Clinical correlation
▪ No diagnosis: Bronchoscopy ± transbronchial biopsy

■ FIGURE 7-5: **PCP Prophylaxis**

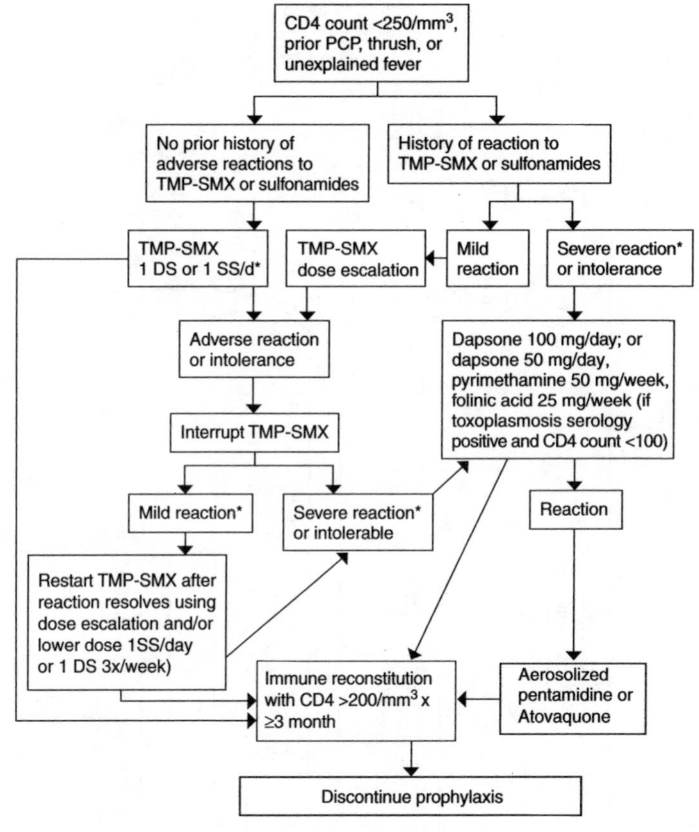

* **Severe:** Urticaria, angioedema, Stevens-Johnson reaction, or fever. **Intolerance:** GI symptoms, rash/pruritis. **Mild:** Tolerable with aggressive supportive care and/or dose reduction.

Renal Complications

Hepatitis C Co-Infection (see *J Am Soc Nephrol* 1999;10:1566)

CAUSE: Mixed cryoglobulinemia

SYMPTOMS: Palpable purpura, decreased complement, and renal disease

DIAGNOSIS

- **Evidence of HCV** (Positive EIA + HCV RNA)
- **Renal disease** with hematuria and proteuria often in nephrotic range ± renal insufficiency
- **Low complement**
- **Renal biopsy** with evidence of HCV-related immune complexes
- **Circulating cryoglobulins** ± skin biopsy of purpuric lesion

TREATMENT: Pegylated interferon + ribavirin is preferred (see p. 276), but ribavirin is not recommended with creatinine clearance <50 mL/min due to increased risk of toxicity (e.g. hemolytic anemia).

Heroin Nephropathy (HAN)

CAUSE: Unknown, possibly glomerular epithelial cell injury from toxin contaminant (*Am J Kidney Dis* 1995;25:689)

FREQUENCY: Unknown, but decreasing with increasing purity of street heroin. Frequency is increased in African Americans accounting for 94% of renal failure cases in one series of 98 patients (*JAMA* 1983;250:2935).

DIFFERENTIAL: Main differential is HIVAN. HAN shows: 1) Hypertension. 2) Small kidneys by echo. 3) Less rapid progression to end-stage renal disease (20 to 40 months vs 1 to 4 months). 4) Less proteinuria. 5) Differences on renal biopsy.

HIV-Associated Neuropathy (HIVAN)

CAUSE: Unknown, possibly due to HIV infection of glomerular endothelial and mesangial cells (*N Engl J Med* 2001;344:1979)

FREQUENCY: 2% to 10% of HIV infected patients. Rates are higher in African American males; may occur with high CD4 counts.

DIAGNOSIS: Role of renal biopsy is controversial, but some have alternative treatable diagnoses (*Kidney Int* 1995;48:311). If done, findings include characteristic microcytic dilation of tubules plus focal and segmental glomerulosclerosis. Course is characterized by rapid progression of nephrosis and no hypertension.

CLINICAL AND LABORATORY FEATURES: Proteinuria >1 g/day + hypoalbuminemia and rapid progressive renal failure to end stage renal disease in 1 to 4 months (*Kidney Int* 1995;48:311). Echo shows enlarged or normal sized kidneys, which distinguishes this from many other causes of renal failure.

TREATMENT

- **HAART:** Preliminary data based on biopsy results suggest benefit from HAART (*Lancet* 1998;352:783).
- **Dialysis** (*Am J Kidney Dis* 1997;29:549)
- **Corticosteroids** (60 mg/day x 2 to 11 weeks, then taper over 2 to 26 weeks) shows variable results (*Am J Med* 1994;97:145; *Kidney Int* 2000;58:1253).
- **ACE Inhibitors** (Captopril 6.25-25 mg PO tid) show variable results (*Am J Kidney Dis* 1996;28:202).

Nephrotoxic Drugs

Amphotericin, aminoglycoside, cidofovir, foscarnet, pentamidine, IV acyclovir, TMP-SMX, indinavir (see below), sulfonamides (crystal induced)

INDINAVIR: Renal calculi ± nephropathy (*Ann Intern Med* 1997;127:119)

- **Cause:** Crystallization of indinavir
- **Prevention:** Should be taken without food, but with water ≥150 mL within 3 hours post dose and ≥1500 mL/day.
- **Dose dependent:** Especially with ritonavir in 800/100 mg bid regimen.
- **Diagnosis:** Urine shows indinavir sulfate crystals – rectangular plates of various sizes with needle-shaped crystals and pyuria (*Clin Nephrol* 2000;54:261; *N Engl J Med* 1997;336:139).
- **Symptoms:** Review of urinalysis from 140 IDV recipients showed 20% had crystalluria; 3% of these had renal colic and most of the rest had frequency plus dysuria and/or flank pain (*Ann Intern Med* 1997127:119).
- **Treatment**
  - Remove stones by ureteroscopy or by passage.
  - Discontinue IDV in symptomatic patients (discontinue all antiretroviral drugs or substitutes).
  - May resume IDV (usually at a modified dose) and increase fluid consumption, especially post dose.

Thrombotic Thrombocytopenic Purpura: See p. 362

Abbreviations

Drug Abbreviations

3TC	Lamivudine	IDV	Indinavir
5-FC	Flucytosine	INH	Isoniazid
ABC	Abacavir	LPV/r	Lopinavir/Ritonavir
APV	Amprenavir	NFV	Nelfinavir
AZT	Zidovudine	NVP	Nevirapine
d4T	Stavudine	PZA	Pyrazinamide
ddC	Zalcitabine	RIF	Rifampin
ddI	Didanosine	RTV	Ritonavir
DLV	Delavirdine	SM	Streptomycin
EFV	Efavirenz	SMX	Sulfamethoxazole
EMB	Ethambutol	SQV	Saquinavir
EPO	Erythropoietin	TDF	Tenofovir disoproxil fumarate
G-CSF	Filgrastim	TMP	Trimethoprim
HU	Hydroxyurea	TMP-SMX	Trimethoprim-sulfamethoxazole

Drug Administration Abbreviations

bid	Twice a day	m^2	Meters squared
caps	Capsules	max	Maximum
cc	Cubic centimeter	mcg	Microgram
cm	Centimeter	mEq	Milliequivalent
cm^2	Centimeters squared	mg	Milligram
d/c	Discontinue	mil	Million
dL	Deciliter	min	Minimum
DS	Double strength	mL	Milliliter
dx	Diagnosis	mm	Millimeter
g	Gram	mM	Millimole
H_20	Water	mo	Month
Hg	Mercury	MU	Million units
hr	Hour	N	Normal (solution) or total sample size
hs	Hours of sleep	ng	Nanogram
IM	Intramuscular	OTC	Over-the-counter
IU	International unit	PO	By mouth
IV	Intravenous	PSI	Pounds per square inch
kg	Kilogram	pt-yrs	Patient-years
L	Liter	q	Every
m	Meter		

Drug Administration Abbreviations *(Continued)*

qd	Every day	VD	Volume of distribution
qhs	At bedtime	vol	Volume
qid	Four times a day	wk	Week
qod	Every other day	wgt	Weight
SQ	Subcutaneously	x	Times
sol'n	Solution	XL	Extended release
SS	Single strength	yr	Year
supp	Supply	μg	Microgram
tabs	Tablets	μL	Microliter
tid	Three times per day	μM	Micrometer
tiw	Three times per week	μmol	Micromole
U	Unit		

General Abbreviations

ACTG	AIDS Clinical Trial Group (U.S.)
ADL	Activities of daily living
ADR	Adverse drug reaction
AETC	AIDS Education Training Center (U.S.)
AFB	Acid-fast bacillus
AHCPR	Agency for Health Care Policy and Research (U.S.)
Al	Aluminum
ALT	Alanine aminotransferase
ANC	Absolute neutrophil count
anti-HAV	Hepatitis A antibody
anti-HBc	Hepatitis B core antibody
anti-HBs	Hepatitis B surface antibody
anti-HCV	Hepatitis C antibody
ART	Antiretroviral therapy
ASCUS	Atypical sqamous cells of undetermined significance
AST	Aspartate aminotransferase
AWP	Average wholesale price
BUN	Blood urea nitrogen
Ca	Calcium
CBC	Complete blood count
CDC	Centers for Disease Control and Prevention (U.S.)
CF	Complement fixation
CMV	Cytomegalovirus
CNS	Central nervous system
CPK	Creatine phosphokinase
CrCl	Creatine clearance
CROI	Conference on Retroviruses and Opportunistic Infections
C-section	Cesarean section
CSF	Cerebrospinal fluid
CT	Computerized tomography
CTL	Cytotoxic T lymphocyte
DEXA	Dual energy x-ray absorptiometry
DFA	Direct fluorescent antibody
DHHS	Department of Health and Human Services (U.S.)
DOT	Directly observed therapy
EBV	Epstein-Barr virus
EDTA	Ethylenediamine tetraacetic acid
EIA	Enzyme immunosorbent assay
EM	Electron microscopy
ERCP	Endoscopic retrograde cholangio-pancreatography
ETOH	Alcohol
FOB	Fiberoptic bronchoscopy
FDA	Food and Drug Administration (U.S.)
G6-PD	Glucose-6-phosphate dehydrogenase
GFR	Glomerular filtration rate
GI	Gastrointestinal
HAART	Highly active antiretroviral therapy
HAD	HIV-associated dementia
HAV	Hepatitis A virus
$HBeAg^-$	Hepatitis B early antigen
HBIG	Hepatitis B immune globulin
HBV	Hepatitis B virus

General Abbreviations *(Continued)*

HCFA Health Care Financing Administration (U.S.)
HCV Hepatitis C virus
HCW Health care worker
HDL High density lipoprotein
Hgb Hemoglobin
HPV Human papillomavirus
HSIL High-grade squamous intraepithelial lesion
HSV Herpes simplex virus
HSV-1 Herpes simplex virus 1
HSV-2 Herpes simplex virus 2
HTLV-1 Human T-cell leukemia virus 1
HTLV-2 Human T-cell leukemia virus 2
IAS International AIDS Society
IAS-USA International AIDS Society-U.S.A.
ICAAC Interscience Conference on Antimicrobial Agents and Chemotherapy
ICL Idiopathic CD4 lymphocytopenia
IDSA Infectious Diseases Society of America
IG Immune globulin
IgE Immunoglobulin E
IgG Immunoglobulin G
IgM Immunoglobulin M
IL-2 Interleukin 2
IM Intramuscular
IOM Institute of Medicine
ITP Idiopathic thrombocytopenic purpura
ITT Intent-to-treat (analysis)
IVIG Intravenous immune globulin
JCV JC virus
KOH Potassium hydroxide
KS Kaposi's sarcoma
LDH Lactate dehydrogenase
LDL Low-density lipoprotein
LFT Liver function test
LP Lumber puncture
LSIL Low-grade squamous intraepithelial lesion
LVEF Left ventricular ejection fraction
MAC *Mycobacterium avium* complex
MACS Multicenter AIDS Cohort Study
MAO Monoamine oxidase
MCV Mean corpuscular volume
Mg Magnesium
MSM Men who have sex with men
MSSA Methicillin sensitive *Staph aureus*
NASBA Nucleic acid sequence-based amplification
NCEP National Cholesterol Education Program (U.S.)
NCI National Cancer Institute (U.S.)
NIAID National Institute of Allergy and Infectious Diseases (U.S.)
NIH National Institute of Health (U.S.)
NNRTI Non-nucleoside reverse transcriptase inhibitor
NRTI Nucleoside reverse transcriptase inhibitor
NS Not significant
NSAID Nonsteroidal anti-inflammatory drug
OHL Oral hairy leukoplakia
OI Opportunistic infection
OP Opening pressure
PAP smear Papanicolaou smear
PBMC Peripheral blood mononuclear cells
PCP *Pneumocystis carinii* pneumonia
PCR Polymerase chain reaction
PEP Postexposure prophylaxis
PGL Persistent generalized lymphadenopathy
PHS Public Health Service (U.S.)
PID Pelvic inflammatory disease
PI Protease inhibitor
PML Progressive multifocal leukoencephalopathy
PMN Polymorphonuclear leukocyte
PPD Purified protein derivative of tuberculin
Pr Protease
PUVA Psoralen ultraviolet A-range
RBC Red blood cells
rHU EPO Recombinant human erythropoietin
RIBA Recombinant Immunoblot assay

General Abbreviations *(Continued)*

RPR	Rapid plasma regain
RT	Reverse transcriptase
RT-PCR	Reverse transcriptase polymerase chain reaction
SIL	Squamous intraepithelial lesion
SSRI	Selective serotonin reuptake inhibitors
STD	Sexually transmitted disease
STEPS	Systems for Thalidomide Education and Prescribing Safety
STI	Structured treatment interruption
TAM	Thymidine analog mutation
TB	Tuberculosis
TEN	Toxic epidermal necrolysis
THC	Tetrahydrocannabinol
TLC	Total lymphocyte count
TNF-alpha	Tumor necrosis factor-alpha
TSH	Thyroid stimulating hormone
TST	Tuberculin skin test
ULN	Upper limit of normal
USPHS	Public Health Service (U.S.)
UTI	Urinary tract infection
UVB	Ultraviolet B
VRDL	Venereal disease research laboratory
vs	Versus
VZIG	Varicella zoster immune globulin
VZV	Varicella zoster virus
WBC	White blood count
WB	Western blot
WHO	World Health Organization

Index

Page numbers followed by "f" indicate figures; those followed by "t" indicate tables.

Medical Management of HIV Infection: Index

N

O

P

T

U

V

Enfuvirtide (T-20)

TRADE NAME (MANUFACTURER): *Fuzeon* (Roche-Trimeris)

FORMULATION: Enfuvirtide is packaged in a 30-day kit containing: 60 (90 mg) single-use vials of enfuvirtide, 60 vials of sterile water for injection, 60 reconstitution syringes (3 cc), 60 administration syringes (1 cc), and alcohol wipes. Enfuvirtide kit can be stored at room temperature. However, once enfuvirtide powder has been reconstituted, it must be refrigerated and used within 24 hours.

COST: Approximately $20,000/year

MECHANISM OF ACTION: Enfuvirtide binds to HR1 site in the gp41 subunit of the viral envelope glycoprotein and prevents conformational change required for viral fusion and entry into cells.

DRUG RESISTANCE AND CROSS-RESISTANCE: A 21-fold (range: <1-422-fold) decrease in susceptibility to enfuvirtide has been correlated with genotypic changes in gp41 amino acids 36-45 (36, 38, 40, 42, 43, and 45) (P<0.0001) [Greenberg, et al. 10th CROI 2003, Abstract 141]. *In vitro*, clinical isolates resistant to NRTI, NNRTI, or PIs retained susceptibility to enfuvirtide.

PHARMACOKINETIC

- **Absorption:** Well absorbed from subcutaneous (SC) site with an absolute bioavailability of 84.3% (+/- 15.5%). Following 90 mg SC, the mean C_{max} was 5.0 +/-1.7 mcg/mL, C_{min} was 3.3 +/-1.6 mcg/mL, and AUC was 48.7 +/- 19.1 mcg/mL • hr.
- **Distribution:** Vd=5.5 +/- 1.1 L
- **Protein binding:** 92%
- **Metabolism:** The exact pathway of enfuvirtide metabolism is unknown. *In vitro*, enfuvirtide undergoes a non-NADPH dependent hydrolysis.
- **T ½:** 3.8 +/- 0.6 h

USUAL ADULT DOSE: 90 mg (1 mL) SC q12h into upper arm, anterior thigh or abdomen with each injection given at a site different from the preceding injection site (prior to administration, reconstitute with 1.1 mL of sterile water for infection giving a volume of 1.2 mL).

PEDIATRIC DOSE: Pediatric patients 6-16 years of age: 2 mg/kg (max 90 mg) SC q12h.

DOSING WITH HEPATIC INSUFFICIENCY: No data

DOSING WITH RENAL INSUFFICIENCY: Estimated CrCl >35 mL/min: 90 mg SC q12h; CrCl <35 mL/min: No data, usual dose likely.

DRUG INTERACTIONS: None. *In vitro*, enfuvirtide did not inhibit or induce the metabolism of CYP3A4, CYP2D6, CYP1A2, CYP2C19 or CYP2E1 substrates. Does not interact with SQV/r, RTV, or rifampin [Boyd, et al. 10th CROI 2003, Abstract 541].

